PLANT COMMUNITIES
OF THE
SCOTTISH HIGHLANDS

A study of Scottish mountain, moorland
and forest vegetation
by
DONALD N. McVEAN, B.Sc., Ph.D.
AND DEREK A. RATCLIFFE, B.Sc., Ph.D.

MONOGRAPHS
OF THE NATURE CONSERVANCY
NUMBER ONE

LONDON
HER MAJESTY'S STATIONERY OFFICE
1962

© *Crown copyright* 1962

Published by
HER MAJESTY'S STATIONERY OFFICE

To be purchased from
York House, Kingsway, London w.c.2
423 Oxford Street, London w.1
13A Castle Street, Edinburgh 2
109 St. Mary Street, Cardiff
39 King Street, Manchester 2
50 Fairfax Street, Bristol 1
35 Smallbrook, Ringway, Birmingham 5
80 Chichester Street, Belfast 1
or through any bookseller

Price £3 17s. 6d. net

Printed in England by
William Clowes and Sons, Limited, London and Beccles

MONOGRAPHS OF THE NATURE CONSERVANCY
NUMBER ONE

PLANT COMMUNITIES OF THE SCOTTISH HIGHLANDS

AUTHORS' PREFACE

THIS phytosociological study of the Scottish Highlands has its origin in the pioneer work of Professor Duncan Poore in 1952 in the Breadalbane district of Perthshire. The Breadalbane work was the first attempt to record Scottish mountain vegetation in terms familiar to Continental ecologists and it established standardised descriptions of vegetation types for that district. It was however clear that this one district could not be regarded as representative of the whole of the Highlands. Although the region contains the largest area of natural and semi-natural vegetation in Great Britain, the previous total of descriptive plant ecological studies covered no more than a fraction of the area.

It was therefore natural to extend this vegetation survey to the rest of the Highlands, using the same descriptive methods. Sponsored by the Nature Conservancy, these wider investigations were begun by Poore and McVean and findings of the first two years (1954–1956) were reported by them in 1957. From 1956 onwards the present writers continued the survey until it seemed clear that the areas covered were an adequate sample of the whole of the Highlands. The work reported here has taken full account of the earlier studies mentioned above, and so covers the areas with which they dealt. Many floristic lists from these published papers have been incorporated in this monograph, generally re-arranged and with occasional slight changes in classification and nomenclature.

The debt we owe to Professor Poore, whose field methods and concepts we have followed closely and whose data we have borrowed freely, will be apparent throughout this book. We are no less grateful to Miss M. C. Gray, who has carried out all the soil analyses, thereby contributing in large measure to the factual core of the work. Distribution maps and line drawings have kindly been prepared for us by Mrs. E. L. Bradshaw, and we are indebted to Mr. B. H. Grimes for his assistance with figures and illustrations, and to Mr. V. T. H. Parry for help with the bibliography and production of the work. Professor W. H. Pearsall and Dr. J. D. Ovington have made helpful comment on the manuscript and Mr. F. H. W. Green gave us the benefit of his views on the climate chapter. Mr. T. T. Elkington has kindly allowed us to reproduce some of his floristic lists for birchwoods, and we wish to acknowledge the permission given by the Meteorological Office and Controller of H.M. Stationery Office to reproduce a figure from the *Meteorological Magazine*. Mr. J. Grant Roger has given us much useful information and advice, especially on flora, and we should like to thank the many other people who have at some time helped us with discussion, information or practical assistance. Our thanks are due besides to the many landowners throughout the Highlands who have granted us access to their lands and expressed an interest in our work.

Finally, we should like to express our gratitude to Professor Rolf Nordhagen of Oslo University and Dr. Eilif Dahl of the Agricultural College of Norway for inspiring us with the Scandinavian approach to vegetation and for their stimulating companionship in the field.

D. N. McVean

D. A. Ratcliffe

Edinburgh

February, 1960

CONTENTS

	page
AUTHORS' PREFACE	V
INTRODUCTION	I
CHAPTER I. PHYTOSOCIOLOGICAL METHODS AND TERMINOLOGY	5
CHAPTER 2. FOREST AND SCRUB	10
Pine Forest	11
Pinetum Hylocomieto-Vaccinetum	11
Pinetum Vaccineto-Callunetum	13
Structure and dynamics of pine forest	14
Birch and Oak Forest	15
Betuletum Oxaleto-Vaccinetum	15
Betula-herb *nodum*	16
Moss communities of birch and oak forest	18
Structure and dynamics of birch and oak forest	19
Ashwood	20
Fraxinus-Brachypodium sylvaticum *nodum*	20
Mixed Deciduous Woodland	21
Other Kinds of Woodland	23
Sub-alpine Scrub	25
Juniperus-Thelypteris *nodum*	25
Salix lapponum-Luzula sylvatica *nodum*	26
CHAPTER 3. DWARF SHRUB HEATH	28
Callunetum vulgaris	28
Arctostaphyleto-Callunetum	30
Vaccineto-Callunetum	31
Juniperetum nanae	33
Arctoeto-Callunetum	34
Cladineto-Callunetum	35
Rhacomitreto-Callunetum	38
Vaccinetum chionophilum	39
Vaccineto-Empetretum	41

page

Cladineto-Vaccinetum   43
Festuceto-Vaccinetum   45
Rhacomitreto-Empetretum   46
Dryas octopetala *noda*   47

CHAPTER 4.   GRASS HEATHS   51
  Anthropogenic Grass Heaths   52
    Species-poor Agrosto-Festucetum   52
    Alchemilleto-Agrosto-Festucetum   53
    Species-rich Agrosto-Festucetum   54
    Saxifrageto-Agrosto-Festucetum   54
    Relationships between the four Agrosto-Festuceta .   .   57
    Thalictrum-Ctenidium provisional *nodum*   .   .   57
    Nardetum sub-alpinum   58
    Juncetum squarrosi sub-alpinum   59
    Deschampsietum caespitosae alpinum .   .   .   61
    Luzula sylvatica Grassland *nodum*   64
    Molinia Grasslands   64
    Relationships between forest, anthropogenic grassland
      and dwarf shrub heath   65
  Montane Grass Heaths   67
    Low-alpine Nardus *noda*   67
      Nardus-Pleurozium *nodum*   67
      Nardus-Trichophorum *nodum*   68
      Nardus-Rhacomitrium provisional *nodum*   .   .   68
    Nardetum medio-alpinum   69
    Polytricheto-Caricetum bigelowii   72
    Dicraneto-Caricetum bigelowii   73
    Cladineto-Juncetum trifidi   75
    Juncus trifidus-Festuca ovina *nodum*   .   .   .   77

CHAPTER 5.   HERB AND FERN MEADOWS .   .   .   80
    Tall Herb *nodum*   80
    Cryptogrammeto-Athyrietum chionophilum   .   .   82
    Dwarf Herb *nodum*   84
    Alchemilla-Sibbaldia *nodum*   85
    Saxifragetum aizoidis   87
    Cliff Vegetation   88

CHAPTER 6.   MOSS HEATHS   89
    Cariceto-Rhacomitretum lanuginosi   .   .   .   89
    Polygoneto-Rhacomitretum lanuginosi .   .   .   92
    Deschampsieto-Rhytidiadelphetum   94
  Late Snow-Bed Heaths   96
    Polytricheto-Dicranetum starkei   96
    Rhacomitreto-Dicranetum starkei   96
    Gymnomitreto-Salicetum herbaceae   .   .   .   97

CONTENTS ix

page

CHAPTER 7. OMBROGENOUS MIRES OR BOGS 101
Trichophoreto-Eriophoretum typicum 101
Calluneto-Eriophoretum 103
Empetreto-Eriophoretum 106
Trichophoreto-Callunetum 106
Molinieto-Callunetum 108
Degeneration of ombrogenous bogs 109

CHAPTER 8. SOLIGENOUS MIRES 111
Oligotrophic Mires 112
Trichophoreto-Eriophoretum caricetosum . . . 112
Molinia-Myrica *nodum* 112
Sphagneto-Juncetum effusi 113
Sphagneto-Caricetum sub-alpinum 114
Sphagneto-Caricetum alpinum 115
Carex aquatilis-rariflora *nodum* 115
Mesotrophic to Eutrophic Mires 117
Juncus acutiflorus-Acrocladium cuspidatum *nodum* . 117
Hypno-Caricetum alpinum 118
Carex rostrata-Sphagnum warnstorfianum *nodum* . 119
Carex panicea-Campylium stellatum *nodum* . 120
Carex rostrata-brown moss provisional *nodum* . 122
Schoenus nigricans provisional *nodum* . . . 124
Caricetum saxatilis 125
Topogenous fens and their relationship to mires . 126
Complexes of bog, mire and fen 127

CHAPTER 9. SPRINGS AND FLUSHES 130
Philonoto-Saxifragetum stellaris 130
Pohlietum glacialis 131
Anthelia-Deschampsia caespitosa provisional *nodum* . 132
Narthecium-Sphagnum provisional *nodum* . . 132
Cratoneuron commutatum-Saxifraga aizoides *nodum* . 133
Cariceto-Saxifragetum aizoidis 133

CHAPTER 10. CLASSIFICATION 137
A comparison with Scandinavian vegetation . . . 142

CHAPTER 11. CLIMATE AND VEGETATION 144
Temperature and humidity 144
Local climatic variations 153
Snow cover 155
Solifluction 159

CHAPTER 12. SOILS 161
Pedogenic tendencies and soil types 161
Chemical factors 164
Plant indicators of soil 169

CHAPTER 13. PLANT GEOGRAPHICAL FACTORS . . . 173

x CONTENTS

page

BIBLIOGRAPHY 178

FLORISTIC ANALYSES 181

VEGETATION DISTRIBUTION MAPS 357

VEGETATION CHARTS 393

SOIL ANALYSES, PLANT INDICATORS AND LIST OF VEGETATION

    TYPES 409

PLATES . . . . *following page* 430

INDEX 431

PLATES

Following page 430

---

1 Pinetum Hylocomieto-Vaccinetum
2 Pine Forest
3 Birchwood-pinewood transition
4 Juniper-rich birchwood
5 Betuletum Oxaleto-Vaccinetum
6 Sub-alpine Scrub
7 *Juniperus-Thelypteris* nodum
8 Arctostaphyleto-Callunetum
9 Juniperetum nanae
10 Arctoeto-Callunetum
11 Transition from Rhacomitreto-Callunetum to Cariceto-Rhacomitretum
12 *Dryas octopetala-Salix reticulata* nodum
13 Alchemilleto-Agrosto-Festucetum
14 Deschampsietum caespitosae alpinum
15 *Juncus trifidus-Festuca ovina* community on windswept erosion surface
16 Solifluction terraces and associated vegetation patterns
17 Tall Herb Nodum
18–19 Tall herb and fern communities
20 Soil hummocks in *Rhacomitrium* heath
21 Late snow-beds and associated vegetation
22 Rhacomitreto-Dicranetum starkei
23 Gymnomitreto-Salicetum herbaceae
24 Western blanket-bog with associated communities
25 Lichen-rich Calluneto-Eriophoretum
26 Complex of calcareous flush and mire vegetation

MAPS AND FIGURES

MAPS

		page
1	Study areas of the Vegetation Survey	359
2	Map showing geographical subdivision of the Highlands and position of the chief hills and massifs which have been studied in some detail	360
3	The main tendencies of woodland distribution	361
4	Juniper scrub	362
5	Tall herb nodum and willow scrub	363
6	Heather moors	364
7	Vaccineto-Callunetum	365
8	Mixed dwarf shrub heaths	366
9	Dwarf *Calluna* heaths	367
10	*Vaccinium* heaths	368
11	Cladineto-Vaccinetum	369
12	Festuceto-Vaccinetum	370
13	Rhacomitreto-Empetretum	371
14	*Dryas* heaths	372
15	Mesotrophic grasslands and mires	373
16	Deschampsietum caespitosae alpinum	374
17	Chionophilous *Nardus* noda	375
18	*Carex bigelowii* heaths	376
19	*Juncus trifidus* heaths	377
20	Cryptogrammeto-Athyrietum chionophilum	378
21	Dwarf herb nodum	379
22	Snow-bed springs and dwarf herb vegetation	380
23	Saxifragetum aizoidis and mixed saxifrage facies	381
24	*Rhacomitrium* heaths	382
25	Deschampsieto-Rhytidiadelphetum	383
26	Snow-bed moss heaths	384
27	Bogs and mires	385
28	Calluneto-Eriophoretum	386
29	Empetreto-Eriophoretum	387
30	Calcareous flushes	388
31	Montane mires	389
32	Caricetum saxatilis	390
33	Bryophyte dominated communities	391
34	Lichen-rich dwarf shrub heaths and bogs	392
A	Scottish woodlands: present distribution of oak, pine and birchwood	*endpocket*
B	Scottish woodlands: reconstructed distribution of oak, pine and birchwood during the present climatic period	*endpocket*

TEXT FIGURES   *page*

1 Typical pinewood podsol profile 12
2 Typical leached brown earth profile 17
3 Relationships between oligotrophic communities on Leacann Bhreac, Ben Wyvis, East Ross 36
4 Relationships between communities of moderately late snow-beds at about 2500 ft. in the East-central Highlands 40
5 Snow-bed vegetation in the Cairngorms at about 2400 ft. 40
6 Relationships between eutrophic and oligotrophic dwarf shrub heath . . . 49
7 Irrigation effects amongst oligotrophic vegetation 53
8 Limestone vegetation surrounded by oligotrophic heather moor 56
9 Relationships between anthropogenic grasslands 56
10 Snow-bed vegetation in the Cairngorms at about 2700 ft. 70
11 Snow-bed vegetation in the Cairngorms at 3400 ft. 70
12 Snow-bed vegetation in the Cairngorms at about 3800–4000 ft. 76
13 Vegetation pattern on elongated stone-nets 78
14 Snow-bed vegetation in the Cairngorms at about 3500–4000 ft. 83
15 Transition from Cariceto-Rhacomitretum to Cladineto-Callunetum . . . 90
16 Vegetation pattern on stone polygon system 93
17 Snow-bed vegetation. Coire Mhoir of Ben Wyvis at 3000–3300 ft. . . . 95
18 Snow-bed vegetation in the Cairngorms at 3800–4000 ft. 98
19 Restriction of Calluneto-Eriophoretum to dolomite in quartzite areas . . . 105
20 Deforested moraine vegetation in the Western and Eastern Highlands . . . 107
21 Montane communities of a hollow in the Glas Maol plateau, Angus, at 3200 ft. . 116
22 Calcareous mire basin on Tulach Hill, Blair Atholl, Perthshire 122
23 Mire system on Ben Vrackie, Perthshire, at 2100 ft. 123
24 Complex of calcareous flushes and oligotrophic hummocks 135
25 Mean annual number of wet days (0·04 in.) 1947–1956 146
26 The altitudinal descent of vegetation types towards the north-west of the Highlands 149
27 Dwarf shrub heaths almost at sea-level, Bettyhill Links, Sutherland . . . 151
28 Distribution of snow cover in relation to altitude 154
29 Snow-cover in relation to selected types of vegetation 157
30 Calcicolous vegetation 167
31 Vegetation types of the Ben Lui-Ben Heasgarnich district 396
32 Vegetation types of the Clova-Caenlochan district 398
33 Vegetation types of the Cairngorms 400
34 Vegetation types of the Kintail-Glen Affric district 402
35 Vegetation types of the Ben Wyvis area 404
36 Vegetation types of the Ben More Assynt-Foinaven district 406

INTRODUCTION

MANY regional studies of Scottish mountain vegetation have been made, as in central Perthshire (Smith, R., 1900), Caithness (Crampton, 1911), east Sutherland (Crampton and Macgregor, 1913), Ben Lui (Patton, 1922), the Cairngorms (Watt and Jones, 1948; Metcalfe, 1950; Burges, 1951; Ingram, 1958) and Breadalbane (Poore, 1955b). Tansley (1949) summarised those published prior to 1939. References to the Scottish mountains have also been made in ecological works of wider scope such as that of Pearsall (1950), while Poore and McVean (1957) reviewed the general features and compared some of our native plant associations with those of Scandinavia. None of these accounts claims, however, to deal with more than limited parts of the Highlands.

Our aim in this fuller survey has been to describe semi-quantitatively the different types of terrestrial vegetation of the Highlands and to relate these as far as possible to the ecological picture. The further objects of the survey are to provide a basis for work related to conservation and land utilisation, and to define ecological problems. Only natural and semi-natural vegetation has been examined and coastal habitats such as sand-dunes, machair and salt marsh have been ignored. The study has been made in the part of Scotland to the north of the Highland line but excludes those eastern districts which are largely agricultural. The areas covered are indicated in Map 1 and we believe that most of the important vegetation types have been seen in each of the 10 km. grid squares marked as surveyed. Although sizeable gaps remain, especially in the Hebrides and the Southern Highlands, and neither the Orkneys nor Shetland have been examined, the recorded climate, geology and land use of these areas suggest that their vegetation is similar to that of adjacent districts which we have studied.

For the purposes of this survey, the Highlands have been sub-divided into separate geographical regions, longitudinally into Eastern and Western, and latitudinally into Northern, Central and Southern (Map 2). These divisions may be considered individually or in combination, e.g. Northern or North-western. Because the area involved is small, no South-eastern region has been recognised, and eastern Breadalbane (which might be separated thus) has been regarded as part of the East-central region. When one of these regions is expressly indicated, the cardinal points are given capital initials. This geographical sub-division is also a climatic one and the main climatic features of each region are discussed in Chapter 11. Map 2 also shows the position of the chief mountain massifs which we have examined during the survey.

A vegetation monograph can be arranged in three ways—ecologically, or according to the main habitat types and altitudinal zonation; systematically, or according to an hierarchical classification of the units distinguished; and physiognomically, or according to the life-form of the dominant species. The first system has much to commend it and it has formed the basis of the arrangement adopted by most British authors. If used in conjunction with a strictly phytosociological treatment, however, difficulties arise that are not encountered in a wider ecological approach and it becomes difficult to avoid a certain amount of repetition. The second system has found great favour on the Continent and is the obvious one to use where the approach to vegetation is primarily a taxonomic one. Nevertheless we feel that it will be unfamiliar to the majority of readers and that any taxonomic arrangement had best be relegated to a single chapter rather than diffused throughout the work. We have therefore employed mainly the third system since an arrangement according to life-form has been shown by many authors, notably Professor Rolf Nordhagen, to be compatible with the phytosociological approach.

This arrangement is similar to one based on altitudinal zonation, giving the sequence —forest, scrub (tall shrub), dwarf shrub heath, grass heath, tall herb and fern 'meadow', and moss heath. In both these systems some difficulty is encountered with bogs, flushes and springs, which vary a good deal in their dominant life-form and are to some extent azonal: for these a grouping according to habitat is thus more or less inevitable. When any of the broad vegetation classes contains types with contrasting edaphic requirements, those associated with acidic, base-poor soils are dealt with first.

We have adopted a standard treatment for each vegetation type in order to allow a ready comparison of the various features. The full analyses of floristic composition are given in the tables (4–64), and only the main floristic features of each type are outlined in the text. The range of variation shown by the type and the criteria which distinguish it from other related types are indicated. The geographical distribution, range of habitat, size of stands and spatial relationships to other communities are then given, together with a discussion of any relevant ecological features. Soil analyses are given in Tables 65–68. Lastly we have made a comparison with types of vegetation elsewhere in the British Isles and on the Continent. In doing this we have been limited by a combined personal experience which extends to the Southern Uplands, the Cheviots, the Lakeland Fells, the Pennines, North Wales, southern and central Norway and Iceland.

Following the main account of vegetation we have dealt, in separate chapters, with other topics which this study has raised. It has been possible to assign most of our types of vegetation to an appropriate place in the hierarchical classification devised by Continental phytosociologists, and the degree of similarity between the vegetation of the Highlands and that of Scandinavia is discussed. The relationships between various climatic factors and vegetation are considered qualitatively, as far as the standard meteorological data permit, and a climatic grouping of types is made. In the chapter on edaphic factors, vegetation is grouped according to both soil type and chemical factors, the second being a quantitative arrangement based on numerous soil analyses. A supplementary account of plant indicators of soil is likewise based on the analytical data. The effects of land management on vegetation are not dealt with in a single account, but are discussed in suitable places throughout the text. Finally, there are some reflections on the geographical distribution of plant species, particularly those comprising the montane flora of the Highlands.

A selection of vegetation types and habitats is illustrated by photographs, and we have tried to demonstrate a number of ecological features by means of diagrams and sketches. Dot distribution maps (for explanation see p. 357) have been used to show the geographical range of many types of vegetation, but maps of those types which occur in nearly every study area are mostly omitted, as their distribution is largely given by Map

1. Since the monograph does not otherwise discuss the range of vegetation to be found within a particular area, charts (Figs. 31–36) have been produced showing all the described vegetation types of a representative area for each main region of the Highlands.

Botanical nomenclature is according to the following authorities:

Vascular plants—Clapham, Tutin and Warburg (1952).

Mosses—Richards and Wallace (1950).

Liverworts—MacVicar (1926). (The tables had been arranged accordingly before the 'Annotated List of British Hepatics' (Jones, 1958) appeared.)

Lichens—Watson (1953).

The spelling of place-names follows that of the Ordnance Survey (Popular Edition, One-inch, 1947).

Chapter 1

PHYTOSOCIOLOGICAL METHODS
AND TERMINOLOGY

OUR procedure in the field and methods of arranging the data collected do not differ appreciably from those of Poore (1955a) and Dahl (1956), to whom the reader is referred for further details. Poore has given a full discussion of both theoretical and practical problems involved in phytosociological studies, and we do not intend to deal with these any more than is necessary to clarify the following outline of concepts and methods.

As the work progressed it became increasingly apparent that variation in Highland vegetation is virtually continuous. A gradual spatial change is common and even where there are fairly sharp discontinuities locally, it is usually possible to find a complete series of intermediates to link any two related types, if a wider area is examined. The essential problem was therefore to select vegetational 'reference points' sufficient in kind and number to represent adequately the total range of variation. The concept of reference points in a field of more or less continuous variation has been expressed by Poore (1955a) in the term NODUM, an abstract vegetation unit of any category, and we have adopted this term here.

There has thus been no attempt at a complete description of the total range of vegetation within our prescribed field, but we hope that our noda are an adequate sample of the whole. In other words there is a good chance that even if a randomly picked community does not fit well into any one of these described vegetation units, then it could readily be assigned to an intermediate position between two units.

The practical difficulty largely turns on the spacing of the reference points—whether to take a larger number close together or a smaller number farther apart. We have tended to the first course in heterogeneous and floristically-rich vegetation, where change in space is often rapid, and to the second in more homogeneous, floristically-poor vegetation where change is more gradual. The choice of reference points has obviously been influenced by the districts which were studied first.

Having established noda we have naturally tried to avoid analysing communities which are 'mixtures' in terms of these. It is quite likely that another observer working independently would sometimes choose for his reference points various 'mixtures' which we have expressly avoided, but on the other hand our personal experience is that independent observers are more likely to decide upon the same units. We admit at once that mixed vegetation may sometimes cover a larger area, and may accordingly be more important economically, than the actual noda we have distinguished. It is, for instance, particularly extensive on ground which has been greatly disturbed by human activity; the anthropogenic grasslands and shrub heaths and the bogs and mires contain some especially heterogeneous complexes of vegetation. Some may judge that our reference points are at times too widely spaced, and certain of the undescribed intermediate types might, with further study, justifiably be defined as separate noda. Moreover, some types of vegetation such as lowland fen, lake and maritime communities are not mentioned simply because we have judged them to be beyond the scope of this survey.

In the field, the first essential is the recognition and selection of uniform, homogeneous areas of vegetation (STANDS) on which a square plot slightly larger than the estimated minimal area (see Poore, 1955a, p. 265) is then marked out. A standard plot size of 4 sq. m. has been adopted but 1, 2 and 16 sq. m. plots are also used when appropriate. Some fragmentary rock-ledge and spring communities, for instance, seldom give homogeneous stands as large as 4 sq. m.; while for tall shrub vegetation the minimal area tends to be larger.

Species occurring in the plot are then listed and their cover and abundance estimated by eye on the ten-point Domin scale:

1. One or two individuals
2. Sparsely distributed
3. Frequent but low cover ($< 1/20$)
4. Cover $1/20–1/5$
5. Cover $1/5–1/4$
6. Cover $1/4–1/3$
7. Cover $1/3–1/2$
8. Cover $1/2–3/4$
9. Cover $3/4–9/10$
10. Cover complete or almost so.

Cover is taken here to mean the projection on the soil of all living parts of the plants. When more than one layer is present, each is estimated separately. Species occurring in the stand immediately surrounding the plot, but not in the plot itself ($+$), are then added to the list and various habitat factors noted. The mature trees of woodland vegetation are not normally included in the analysis, the dominant being taken for granted as a constant, but seedlings are always noted. Finally a soil pit is dug close to the sample plot and the separate horizons described and measured. Soil samples are taken from the top 9 in. (22·5 cm.) or from the combined A horizons if their depth is less than this. The various horizons of the profile are sampled separately if this seems advisable. Photographs are then taken and sketches made of as many vegetational features as possible, particularly those which throw some light on the ecology of the individual noda. Floristic lists and other data are later copied from the field notebook on to index cards which are the same as those of the Botanical Society of the British Isles Distribution Map Scheme (Walters, 1954) with an additional leaf for non-vascular plants and miscellaneous notes.

Some parts of the Scottish Highlands are surprisingly inaccessible and, short of bivouacking in the rare periods of fine weather, the student of mountain vegetation finds that much of his day is spent in walking. Too often he arrives at the study area to find that low cloud, wind and rain allow only a short period of efficient note taking, and these conditions may be repeated day after day throughout a working season which extends only from late May to early October.

Against such a background we have found the above field methods to be practicable and reasonably sound. The procedure may be carried out within fifteen minutes in fair weather and on species-poor vegetation; in floristically-rich communities an hour or more may be spent upon it. In either situation it is more expeditious than the involved statistical examination advocated by some authors on largely theoretical grounds. As Dahl (1956) has pointed out, this method of analysis of the individual stands is not a statistical method in the mathematical sense but merely a method for the standardised description of vegetation to permit qualitative comparison of the results.

In any one locality analyses are made of stands which are judged to belong to different plant communities and these then become the reference points. In many cases, our experience of previously described vegetation types from Britain and elsewhere has greatly influenced this initial choice. Communities which are extensive or which occur frequently from place to place naturally suggest themselves as reference points. As much as possible of the range of variation in vegetation within the study area is sampled in this way until the ground has been well covered. In moving to a fresh study area it is usually found that a proportion of the same vegetation types is encountered again, together with others recognisable as modifications of previous types, and some completely new ones: all these are listed. The actual field assessment of similarity depends on the observer's memory for vegetational physiognomy as determined by dominance and constancy of certain species.

When a number of areas has been worked there are some groups of lists which clearly belong to the same vegetation types, and if at least nine of each group are available these can be put together in a floristic table as a nodum. Many lists, however, fall less readily into distinct groups, and these have to be arranged by the 'process of progressive approximation' described by Poore (1955a), comparing similarities and rejecting those which upset the consistency of a group. In a complex of vegetation where there is much variation from place to place, the units may not become defined until the data have been thus treated. Inevitably, therefore, a minority of lists prove to be intermediate between two noda and have to be omitted from the tables.

We have used as many as possible of our species lists in the floristic tables illustrating this monograph in order to bring out the full range in composition of the units and to emphasise the connections between them. To do this we have often had to make some sacrifice in the homogeneity and integration of the units themselves, but we have tried to make a compromise between a neat classification which covers only a small proportion of the possible vegetation types and an undigested mass of data so comprehensive as to be bewildering. Out of 1100 lists in our card index some 5 per cent remain unclassified but most of these can be compared closely (often as intermediates) with one or more of the units that have been distinguished. A high proportion of Poore's Breadalbane lists (Poore, 1955b and unpublished) has also been incorporated in the system.

Where noda have shown sufficient indication of homogeneity and organisation they have been raised to the status of an ASSOCIATION. In making this distinction we have depended upon the test of homogeneity given by the ratio between the numbers of species in the two highest constancy (presence or frequency) classes. If it proved possible with little rejection and selection of lists to obtain a floristic table with a greater number of species in class V (present in 81 to 100 per cent of the lists—constants in the strict sense) than in class IV (61 to 80 per cent) the unit was given association rank (this status was also usually given when the numbers were equal). If this proved impossible even after rigorous selection, or if there were an insufficient number of lists to choose from, the unit was described as a *nodum*. Where less than seven lists are available the *noda* have been regarded as provisional. In order to avoid confusion, the word nodum is italicised when referring to a described vegetation type which does not merit the rank of an association. When used otherwise it indicates any abstract vegetation unit without qualification and is then a more convenient synonym of 'vegetation type' or 'community' (in the abstract and not the particular sense). To summarise, two concepts of vegetation are involved. First there is 'real' vegetation, i.e. particular stands (for which we have preferred to use the term community) while secondly there is an abstract definition (nodum) based on the common features of a number of these stands. The abstract units are further sub-divided according to degree of homogeneity.

The use of the constancy test for homogeneity is only valid when lists have been made from equal areas throughout. While we have often departed from the standard plot size of 4 sq. m., species occurring outside the plot (+) were generally recorded from the immediate surroundings (about 100 sq. m.) only, so that the lack of uniformity in size has been reduced.

About three-quarters of the vegetation units described in this work have been named as associations. We have usually found that noda founded on lists from a single district are more homogeneous than if the lists are drawn from a much wider area. It would therefore have been possible to increase the above proportion by concentrating on the production of local associations, but at this stage we have tried to obtain lists from a wide part of the Highlands in creating a nodum.

The homogeneity of a described vegetation unit obviously depends partly on the degree of selection used, both in the initial choice of stands for analysis and in the choice of lists in compiling the floristic table. With more careful selection at both stages during future study it might well be possible to give association status to all our noda. A good measure of homogeneity in an abstract vegetation unit is desirable because it simplifies the tasks of characterising vegetation in terms of consistent features (constancy and dominance) and of subsequent recognition by the same or other observers. We see no point, however, in forcing our units to conform to a prescribed standard of uniformity merely for its own sake, since there are real as well as artificial variations in homogeneity of vegetation, related mainly to instability or spatial variation of habitat; to chance as it affects plant dispersal and ecesis; and to modes of vegetative spread in some plants. In general, too, floristic heterogeneity of vegetation tends to increase with number of constituent species. We believe that because the degree of selection has been kept within reasonable and similar bounds throughout, the defined units give a fair reflection of natural uniformity or diversity in the floristic composition of vegetation.

Where there is an obvious discontinuity in the floristic variation within a vegetation unit (i.e. several species appearing or disappearing from the lists together) but one hardly great enough to warrant the recognition of separate units, the distinctive groups of lists have been described as separate FACIES. In a few cases, facies have been distinguished when the difference is merely a change in dominance of one or two species, or in presence and absence of a few noteworthy species. Sometimes facies have been formed by subdivision of an association, and may separately fulfil the requirements of association rank. In other instances facies are represented by an extra group of lists additional to the association itself, and the term is applied also to sub-divisions of or additions to a unit of *nodum* rank.

Some of the variation at certain vegetational reference points has been shown by the recognition of facies, but we have avoided applying this designation to communities which were obviously midway between two noda. Certain vegetation units at present regarded as facies are represented by a very few lists and might with further study be found to warrant association rank.

By applying mathematical methods of measuring the degree of similarity between floristic lists (see Poore, 1955b and Dahl, 1956) it would eventually be possible to provide numerical criteria for the classification of vegetation, giving an even spacing of reference points and defining the limits of the units themselves, the associations, *noda* and facies. This would involve the rejection of many lists and the collection of many more. Altogether it would be a lengthy process and for the present we believe that the methods outlined, subjective though they may be, have served our purpose.

Associations and *noda* have been named according to their most prominent species or genera (dominants or constants) and characteristic species (in the sense of Braun-Blanquet (1932)) have not been used for this purpose. The conventional *-etum* suffix has been used for associations, with the addition of non-floristic qualifications where desirable. Alternative names have generally been provided to meet possible objections to Latin terminology, but some of these are more cumbersome and we have found it more convenient and precise to emphasise the Latin name throughout. Wherever possible we have retained association names already in existence on the Continent (e.g. Polytricheto-Caricetum bigelowii) but we have sometimes wished to alter the emphasis even when the two associations are almost identical (e.g. Cariceto-Rhacomitretum lanuginosi in place of the Norwegian Rhacomitreto-Caricetum bigelowii). When facies have been distinguished *within* an association they have been named by the addition of the suffix *-osum* to their most prominent species or group of species, e.g. Cladineto-Vaccinetum empetrosum. Names for other facies have been given in anglicised form.

The constants of an association are termed the *association element*. Both constants and dominants together are found to be the most useful means of characterising a nodum (cf. Poore, 1955a) and are emphasised throughout. Tables 1 and 2 show the distribution of constants (C) and dominants which are also constant (D) throughout the noda.

Characteristic species are divided by Braun-Blanquet (1932) into *exclusive* species which are completely or almost completely confined to one community, *selective* species which are found most frequently in one community but occur sparsely in others and *preferential* species which occur more or less abundantly in several communities but which reach their optimum development in one particular community. We have used these terms mainly with reference to the tables only and not as an expression of our total field experience. Thus a species may be described as exclusive to a certain association, although we are aware that it also occurs in certain fragmentary or mixed stands of other communities which have not been analysed. *Differential* species are non-characteristic species which can nevertheless be used in distinguishing between two closely related noda. Table 3 lists characteristic species, native to the Highlands, of the higher units of vegetation classification, the orders and alliances, distinguished by continental phytosociologists (see Chapter 10).

Chapter 2

FOREST AND SCRUB

THE destruction of the original forest cover of Scotland has been taking place since Neolithic times and is now virtually complete while the advent of re-afforestation programmes, both private and national, is tending increasingly to obscure the last evidence of the native forest pattern.

The first folding map (A) shows the present distribution, or the distribution until comparatively recently, of oak (*Quercus petraea* and *Q. robur*), pine (*Pinus sylvestris*) and birch (*Betula pubescens* and *B. verrucosa*) wood on the scale of ten miles to the inch. The second folding map (B) is an attempted reconstruction of the distribution of these woodland types during the present climatic period but prior to the onset of large-scale human forest clearance. It is based on the available evidence from present distribution of woodland types and tree species, known ecological requirements of these, pollen analysis, sub-fossil remains in peat and recorded history.

While native pine can generally be distinguished with some confidence from self-seeded introductions the status of oakwoods is more confused. As a working system all apparently unplanted woods of oak have been marked, and, although many of these may well be the remains, or the descendants, of planted woods, it is fairly safe to assume that the planting was carried out on the site of native oak forest where the soil and situation would obviously be most favourable.

Where extensive planting of pine has been carried out on areas that were until recently under natural pine forest the former extent of the forest cannot now be accurately determined, and this state of affairs has been indicated by striping the map.

The resulting pattern indicates that native Scottish forest forms, or rather formed, a western phase of the European temperate deciduous forest–coniferous forest–boreal deciduous forest transition, but there is no evidence from present tree distribution that the pine extended farther to the north than oak within historical times. Tansley (1949) remarks that in ascending the hillsides one evidently passed from oakwood to pine and birch which were therefore zoned above the oak both altitudinally and latitudinally. Traces of pine above oak can, in fact, still be seen in many places, the most convincing of all being at Ardlair on the north side of Loch Maree. The zonation is always traceable to edaphic factors rather than to any climatic effect with increasing altitude, the oak occupying the richer alluvial and colluvial soils in the glens and concavities of the slope with pine above on the crags and coarser rock fragments where peat and raw humus formation have taken place. Where free-draining siliceous sands and gravels extend over the low ground in the north-east or where there has been some drying out of deep peat deposits, pine reaches almost to the sea. On the other hand where the underlying rocks or their glacial derivatives consist of calcareous and easily weathered material the pine zone appears to be missing and oak passes directly to remnants of an upper mixed deciduous zone of *Betula pubescens*, *Sorbus aucuparia*, *Corylus avellana*, *Prunus padus* and *Juniperus communis*. The evidence for this is rather scanty since woodland and scrub have been all but eliminated on these upper base-rich slopes which are now valuable hill grazing. Much the same phenomenon takes place latitudinally also and certain Sutherland birchwoods are found to have an oakwood flora of *Allium ursinum*, *Mercurialis perennis*, *Melandrium dioicum* and other tall herbs. Evidence of the natural occurrence of birch above pine is even harder to find than that of pine above oak. It does occur in many places as a result of pine felling and birch re-colonisation but it is just as likely to be found the wrong way round as at Rhidorroch Lodge in Ross-shire (Darling, 1947). A natural pine-above-birch zonation may occur where steep slopes with brown soil flatten out to a peat-covered plateau above. This is found in Amat Forest, west of Bonar Bridge, where the altitude is a little too great to allow the growth of oak on the brown forest soil. The occurrence of birchwood above pine in Crannach Wood, Perthshire, may be a genuine survival of the original zonation. On the other hand, the highest natural forest limits now remaining in Britain are in the pinewoods of the Cairngorms, with pine passing directly into a tall shrub zone dominated by juniper.

The lack of relict pine in extreme western and south-western areas, combined with the restricted development of the associated heather moor, make it appear probable that the gradual restriction of the pine belt there, even on acid rocks, is a natural one. At the present day oak soon gives way to an upper birch zone on the sides of many western sea lochs.

In the south and east of the country the latitudinal transition from oak to pine and birch is first seen on north-facing slopes. In the west and north the replacement takes place readily on the more favourable exposures also. The occurrence of pine on north-facing slopes, with oak on the opposite side of the glen or loch, can still be seen at Loch Maree, Loch Arkaig and Loch Rannoch and in Glen Moriston, a segregation which is primarily geological and only secondarily climatic since the more lime-rich rocks usually seem to occur on the south-facing slopes.

Another feature of present woodland distribution which appears to be almost entirely natural is the passage of oakwood to hazel scrub as one goes westward on the exposed Tertiary basalt country of Skye, Mull and Morvern. An upper fringe of hazel to oak is rare but can be seen at 700 ft. near Strontian in Argyll. Seral hazel scrub, where oak has been extracted, is more common and can be seen on the Lorne plateau east of Oban.

We may summarise by saying that while a simple climatic zonation of forest types is not found in the Highlands some climatic control is discernible, particularly in latitudinal distribution (Map 3 and folding maps).

PINE FOREST
Pinetum Hylocomieto-Vaccinetum
(Pinewood *Vaccinium*-moss association)
(Table 4)

Two well-defined pinewood associations can be recognised in Scotland. The first of these, Pinetum Hylocomieto-Vaccinetum is characteristic of moderately dense pinewood throughout the Central and Northern Highlands and is frequently developed in pine plantations also. The association element consists, besides *Pinus sylvestris* itself, of the four species *Calluna vulgaris*, *Vaccinium myrtillus*, *V. vitis-idaea* and *Hylocomium splendens*. The forest floor may be dominated by *Vaccinium myrtillus*, *V. vitis-idaea*, *Hylocomium splendens* or *Rhytidiadelphus triquetrus*, but *Deschampsia flexuosa* and *Ptilium crista-castrensis* occasionally attain co-dominance with the dwarf shrubs and other mosses. Tall shrubs are almost completely absent although an occasional moribund juniper bush may be found. *Betula pubescens* and *Sorbus aucuparia* may form a small proportion of the tree canopy and their seedlings are frequent in the field and ground layers. *Goodyera repens* (constancy class II) is exclusive to the association, although it may sometimes be found also on the tussocks in Pinetum Vaccineto-Callunetum.

The total number of species is not high; the fourteen stands in Table 4 give 45 species in all, the numbers ranging from 11 to 18 and with an average of 14 species per stand.

Two facies of the association can be recognised—the myrtillosum in which *Vaccinium* species are dominant (Plate 1), and the triquetrosum dominated by *Hylocomium splendens* or *Rhytidiadelphus triquetrus*. The two facies generally occur together, the myrtillosum under a tree canopy of average density and the triquetrosum where the canopy is particularly close or where it has been close in the recent past. The triquetrosum may persist for many years after the shade which gave rise to it has been lightened, and the quantity of *Vaccinium* remaining determines whether a transition to the myrtillosum will take place or whether the more rapidly colonising *Calluna* will assume dominance of the dwarf shrub layer.

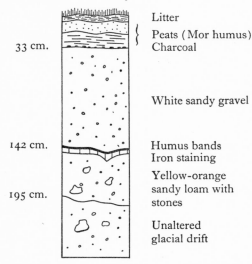

Fig. 1. Typical pinewood podsol profile

The association is found from sea level to over 1500 ft. (475 m.) occupying extensive areas of forest and plantation in the east of Scotland but forming only localised patches in the west. Where felled pine has been replaced by natural birch there may be a gradual change to either the Betuletum Oxaleto-Vaccinetum or Betula-herb *nodum* or to Pinetum Vaccineto-Callunetum. The change to Pinetum Vaccineto-Callunetum may also take place where the pine has been thinned out in the absence of grazing animals.

Soils are invariably well-drained sands and gravels with raw humus and a well-developed podsol profile (Fig. 1).

The association can be equated with the Pineto-Vaccinetum myrtilli of Braun-Blanquet, Sissingh and Vlieger (1939, p. 61). The following list was made on 4 sq. m. of pinewood floor in the Norwegian research forest of Hirkjølen and shows close affinities with the lists of Table 4:

Vaccinium myrtillus	.	.	.	7
V. vitis-idaea	.	.	.	5
Empetrum hermaphroditum		.	6
Betula odorata (seedlings)	.	.	3
Juniperus communis	.	.	.	3

Melampyrum pratense	.	.	3
Pleurozium schreberi		.	8
Campylopus flexuosus	.	.	6

Labels on Fig. 1 (from top): Litter; Peats (Mor humus); Charcoal; White sandy gravel; Humus bands; Iron staining; Yellow-orange sandy loam with stones; Unaltered glacial drift. Depths marked: 33 cm., 142 cm., 195 cm.

					Cladonia sylvatica	.	.	.	4
Sorbus aucuparia	.	.	.	+	C. rangiferina	.	.	.	3
Calluna vulgaris	.	.	.	+	C. deformis	.	.	.	3
					C. squamosa	.	.	.	2
Trientalis europaea	.	.	.	+	C. pyxidata	.	.	.	1
Luzula sylvatica	.	.	.	1					
Deschampsia flexuosa	.	.	.	4	Nephromium arcticum	.	.	.	+

Pinetum Vaccineto-Callunetum
(Pinewood *Vaccinium-Calluna* association)
(Table 5)

The second association, Pinetum Vaccineto-Callunetum is characteristic of the more open pine forest, pine-birch mixtures and even pure birchwood where this has recently colonised former pine ground. It differs from the first association in being dominated by a mixture of tall, leggy heather and *Vaccinium myrtillus* with deep *Sphagnum* tussocks and a wide range of other mosses and hepatics. The forest floor is almost always thrown into hummocks due to the presence of undecayed tree stumps and boulders. A greater variety of species may also enter the tree canopy and *Ilex aquifolium* is a feature of the West Highland woods. Juniper is the characteristic tall shrub and it may be abundant in certain areas of the Central and Eastern Highlands (Plate 2).

The association element consists of eight species: *Pinus sylvestris, Calluna vulgaris, Vaccinium myrtillus, V. vitis-idaea, Deschampsia flexuosa, Hylocomium splendens, Plagiothecium undulatum* and *Ptilium crista-castrensis*. *Calluna, Vaccinium myrtillus, Hylocomium splendens, Ptilium crista-castrensis* and *Sphagna* of the Acutifolia group may all dominate their respective layers. *Ptilium crista-castrensis* is selective for the order Vaccinio-Piceetalia to which the association belongs but there are no other characteristic species.

The nine lists of Table 5 muster 60 species with a range of 15 to 29 species per stand and an average of 22.

Separate facies have not been distinguished but the addition of further lists should make it possible to separate a *Sphagnum*-dominated variant for the high rainfall areas of west Scotland.

Floristically the association can be distinguished from the Pinetum Hylocomieto-Vaccinetum by the presence of *Aulacomnium palustre, Calypogeia trichomanis* and several other species of hepatic. The occurrence of this association is co-extensive with that of native pine forest and it is generally absent from the denser shade of planted forests. Pinetum Vaccineto-Callunetum is found from sea level to almost 1000 ft. (305 m.) in the west and from about 900 to 2000 ft. in the Eastern Highlands where it tends to replace the previous association with increasing altitude. Sites are again well drained but most stands occur on damp, north-facing slopes (Plate 3). The light intensity at ground level is greater than for the Pinetum Hylocomieto-Vaccinetum (daylight factor of 1/3 to 1/5 as against 1/6).

The association also occurs, and can persist indefinitely without a tree canopy, as a result of tree felling especially on north-facing slopes which are normally too moist to be converted to ordinary heather moor by rotational burning. It is the only woodland association occurring independently of trees and its relationships with Callunetum vulgaris are discussed on p. 31.

Soils are again podsolic with accumulation of raw humus and the A_2 horizon may attain a thickness of over 1 m.

The closest Continental equivalents of the Pinetum Vaccineto-Callunetum appear to lie among the spruce forest associations of Central Europe such as the Mastigobryeto-Piceetum (Braun-Blanquet, Sissingh and Vlieger (1939), p. 32).

Other types of vegetation such as *Molinia* grassland may be found in open pinewood, apart from various communities of natural clearings and boggy hollows, but these are usually the result of human interference and cannot be described as forest vegetation.

Structure and Dynamics of Pine Forest

As a former of climax forest, pine would be expected to give rise to natural stands of mixed-age composition and to follow the classic cycle of regeneration to maturity in the gaps left by the death of parent trees. There is no evidence at the present day that this ever took place in Scottish pine forests whereas everything points to a mosaic of segregated age classes as the normal structure of the forest. Three main arrangements are now found:

1. Quasi-even-aged stands of 80–150 years of age. Different crown forms and the occurrence of both dominant and suppressed trees may give the appearance of age diversity. Vegetation may belong to either of the two associations described above depending on canopy density but the Pinetum Hylocomieto-Vaccinetum is the more common (Plate 1). Pine seedlings in their first and second year are not uncommon but regeneration is seldom found, due principally to the depth of the undecomposed moss and litter layer and to its liability to rapid drying out in spring. Sapling pines from Pinetum Hylocomieto-Vaccinetum at Curr Wood, Dulnain Bridge, proved to be five to eight years old although only 10 cm. high. Advance growth of this age is exceptional in Scottish pine forests and is found only in the drier eastern districts. A proportion of the Curr Wood saplings could probably commence active growth on the felling of the parent trees as happens in Continental forests.

These stands appear to be the result of sudden mass regeneration following a forest or moor fire (p. 15).

2. A two-generation composition in which pioneer trees of 150–200 years of age are embedded in a matrix of straight stemmed 80–100-year-old progeny.

The vegetation is a mixture of both pinewood associations and much of it may be in the intermediate stage of development. Regeneration is absent from the older stands which have closed their canopy but may still be taking place locally as in parts of the Coille na Glas Leitire (Beinn Eighe Nature Reserve) and by Loch Garten (Abernethy Forest). This structure offers the best hope of development to an intimate mixture of age classes if fire and browsing animals are withheld. A small area of some twenty acres at the north-west corner of Loch Garten exhibits many of the features of young mixed-age pine forest (Plate 2). A certain amount of advance growth is taking place in both the Pinetum Hylocomieto-Vaccinetum and Pinetum Vaccineto-Callunetum which in this locality have a considerable shrub layer of juniper, birch and rowan and many mild-humus species such as *Viola riviniana* and *Oxalis acetosella* in the field layer. Group regeneration of the pines can be found at all stages showing the formation of dense thickets in the neighbourhood of the parent trees, the self-thinning of these thickets and the eventual death of the parent. Active regeneration is also taking place on enclosed and neighbouring areas of heather which have not been recently burned. The heather is consequently of mixed age and offers opportunities for pine colonisation not given by old stands of uniform age.

3. Pine heaths in which the trees are in varying density and generally 150–200 years of age, with spreading pioneer crowns.

The vegetation belongs to the Pinetum Vaccineto-Callunetum or to non-woodland Callunetum vulgaris (p. 28) if there has been heather burning through open stands. The lack of regeneration here is due to the combination of slow seedling growth in the deep moss and long dwarf shrubs with damage caused by browsing deer during the winter and early spring. Seedlings and saplings can be found in the pine heath but they are invariably topped by deer again and again and seldom exceed 15 cm. in height. In the absence of browsing animals it is probable that the small numbers of trees that become established would just be sufficient to maintain open forest.

The extent to which our pine forests have been dependent upon forest and heath fires for their perpetuation can never be known. Tamm (1950) points out that in Scandinavia edaphic conditions under old pine become unsuitable for regeneration, the mor becoming biologically inactive. Fire generally restores activity and enables regeneration to take place. Handley (1954) considers that this biological stagnation may be a result of Man's activities through the segregation and encouragement of mor-forming species. He suggests that really natural communities consisted of mixtures of the mull and mor formers and that coniferous forest should have at least some intermixture of deciduous trees and mull-forming herbs.

All areas of dense natural pine regeneration in Scotland result from the seeding of heather moor at the correct stage following fire. The young trees, after a slow start, grow up vigorously along with the heather and by the time they overtop it are able to tolerate a certain amount of deer damage. The heather eventually becomes killed out by shading and a pine stand of the first type described above is the result. If the amount of seed available is not sufficient to give a close thicket of young trees, open pine heath develops. Unfortunately the fire which encouraged the sudden outburst of regeneration may also produce conditions which make it more difficult for the next generation to perpetuate itself. Good regeneration occurs locally in the pinewoods of Deeside and Speyside, but in many places it is poor or absent.

A comprehensive account of the native Scottish pinewoods has recently been given by Steven and Carlisle (1959).

BIRCH AND OAK FOREST

The vegetation of most Highland birchwoods can be assigned to one or other of two noda which grade into one another to some extent but which cover too wide a range to form separate facies of the one association.

Betuletum Oxaleto-Vaccinetum
(*Vaccinium*-rich birchwood)
(Table 6, lists 1–11)

The eleven lists of the Betuletum Oxaleto-Vaccinetum have ten constants besides *Betula pubescens: Sorbus aucuparia, Blechnum spicant, Vaccinium myrtillus, Deschampsia flexuosa, Galium hercynicum, Oxalis acetosella, Potentilla erecta, Hylocomium splendens, Pleurozium schreberi* and *Thuidium tamariscinum*. The forest floor can be dominated by *Vaccinium myrtillus, Luzula sylvatica, Hylocomium splendens* or *Thuidium tamariscinum*; and *Blechnum spicant, Pteridium aquilinum, Vaccinium vitis-idaea, Agrostis tenuis, Anthoxanthum odoratum, Rhytidiadelphus loreus* and *Ptilium crista-castrensis* may almost attain co-dominance.

A tall shrub layer is usually absent but *Juniperus communis* is occasionally dominant (Plates 4–5) and *Corylus avellana* and *Lonicera periclymenum* may be abundant, the last species being exclusive to the nodum. Oak (*Quercus* spp.) can replace birch as the dominant tree to about 900 ft. (275 m.) in the Southern and East-central Highlands and 500 ft. in the West, with little or no change in the associated field-layer but most of the Highland oakwoods may be referred to the following nodum (Table 6). *Sorbus aucuparia* is a common constituent of the tree layer and may be co-dominant or even dominant in places (Anderson, 1950, McVean, 1958).

Numbers of species per stand range from 18 to 39 with an average of 28, and thus tend to be higher than in either the Pinetum Hylocomieto-Vaccinetum or Pinetum Vaccineto-Callunetum. The association may also be distinguished from these closely related associations by the presence of many species such as *Corylus avellana, Lonicera periclymenum, Rubus idaeus, Endymion non-scriptus, Luzula sylvatica, Viola riviniana* and *Thuidium tamariscinum*, and by the absence of *Goodyera repens*.

Betula-herb *nodum*
(Herb-rich birchwood)
(Table 6, lists 12–20)

The nine lists of the Betula-herb *nodum* have the following constants: *Betula pubescens, Blechnum spicant, Anthoxanthum odoratum, Galium hercynicum, Oxalis acetosella, Potentilla erecta, Viola riviniana* and *Hylocomium splendens*. The dominants of the *nodum* are *Thelypteris oreopteris, Agrostis tenuis, Anthoxanthum odoratum, Hylocomium splendens* and *Thuidium tamariscinum*. Grasses are often the most prominent plants but the *nodum* includes communities (e.g. Table 6, lists 12 and 13) in which basiphilous herbs are abundant. It is likely that further study would justify the separation of these two types into distinct noda. Tall shrubs are even less common than in the preceding nodum but this is entirely due to the more intense grazing and browsing by wild and domestic animals to which this type of vegetation is subjected throughout the year. Numbers of species range from 24 to 48 with an average of 33.

The *nodum* is common to birchwoods and to the poorer stands of oak which typically make up Highland oakwoods. It is distinguished from the Betuletum Oxaleto-Vaccinetum by the virtual absence of *Vaccinium* spp. and by the appearance of, or increase in, *Holcus lanatus, Endymion, Anemone nemorosa, Conopodium majus, Lysimachia nemorum, Primula vulgaris, Ranunculus ficaria, R. repens, Viola riviniana, Mnium hornum, M. undulatum, Thuidium tamariscinum* and *Plagiochila asplenioides*. The most herb-rich stands are similar to the ground layer of mixed deciduous woodland (p. 21). There are no species exclusive to the nodum but a few, such as *Anemone nemorosa* and *Conopodium majus* are selective for it.

The birchwood noda are found throughout the Highlands from sea level to almost 2000 ft. (610 m.). Above the tree line, or sometimes well below it, the vegetation of siliceous rock ledges or corrie slopes dominated by *Vaccinium myrtillus* and/or *Luzula sylvatica* can be regarded as a treeless facies of Betuletum Oxaleto-Vaccinetum (lists 21–26, Table 6). On the other hand the vegetation of dense stands of *Pteridium aquilinum* or *Thelypteris oreopteris* in dwarf shrub or grass heaths belongs to the Betula-herb *nodum*, the shade of the ferns acting in much the same way as a tree canopy (lists 27–30, Table 6). Nordhagen's *Vaccinium myrtillus*-rich birchwood (Nordhagen 1927, p. 112) resembles the Betuletum Oxaleto-Vaccinetum in many ways, particularly list 6 (Table 6) which contains a greater number of northern and montane species than the other stands (Plate 4). There is less resemblance between his grass and herb-rich birchwoods (op. cit. p. 126) and the Betula-herb *nodum* although the *Agrostis tenuis-Deschampsia flexuosa* rich birchwood (op. cit. p. 138) resembles certain of our high-lying woods, on or below calcareous rocks, in which *Cirsium heterophyllum*, *Trollius europaeus* and *Polygonum viviparum* occur in the grazed grassy vegetation of the woodland floor. Ungrazed tall herb communities of this type are rare in birchwoods of the Highlands, but fragments occur locally and are similar to those near High Force in Teesdale (cf. Pigott, 1956).

Affinity can also be found of the Betuletum Oxaleto-Vaccinetum with the Betuleto-Vaccinietum lapponicum (Braun-Blanquet, Sissingh and Vlieger, 1939, p. 57) while both noda, particularly the Betula-herb *nodum*, tend to transgress the borders of the whole order Vaccinio-Piceetalia and show some of the characteristic species of the Quercetalia roboris.

Soils of these two noda are not so markedly podolised as those of the Pinetum Hylocomieto-Vaccinetum and Pinetum Vaccineto-Callunetum and the 'truncated podsol' or leached brown earth is typical (Fig. 2). The Betuletum Oxaleto-Vaccinetum tends to occur on black, mildly acid humus of good crumb structure lying directly on block scree or on a shallow A₂ horizon. The Betula-herb *nodum*, on the other hand, tends to occupy a brown mineral soil with mull humus while the B horizon of both is a deep reddish-brown sandy and stony loam. Stands rich in basiphilous herbs usually occur on periodically irrigated fertile brown loams, with pH and lime status greater than soils of the grass-dominated examples.

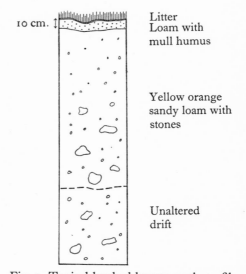

10 cm.

Litter
Loam with
mull humus

Yellow orange
sandy loam with
stones

Unaltered
drift

Fig. 2. Typical leached brown earth profile

Several localities are known where the change from one of the pinewood associations to one of the birchwood noda has apparently been brought about by a single generation of birches following the removal of the pines. All have soil parent materials of intermediate base status so that the balance between mull and mor formation has been a delicate one. The most convincing demonstration can be seen in Rothiemurchus between Tullochgrue and Achnagoichan where the two humus and vegetation types are separated only by a stone wall. On the Tullochgrue side of the wall there are

24 species including *Anemone nemorosa, Trientalis europaea, Conopodium majus* and *Pyrola media*; on the Achnagoichan side only 16 species. The soil profiles are compared below.

AoL .	.	0·5 cm. birch leaves, etc.	1·0 cm. pine needles, etc.	
AoF .	.	0·5 ,, dark brown rooty mull	2·0 ,, moist black, rooty mor	
A₁ .	.	13·0 ,, brown sandy loam with schist pebbles	2·0 ,, black mor	
A₂ .	.		1–5 ,, white sand	
B₁ .	.	22·0 ,, bright red-brown sandy loam with schist pebbles	1·0 ,, indurated coffee-coloured sand	
B₂ .	.		36·0 ,, light red-brown sandy loam	
C .	.	Grey-brown sandy drift with pebbles of schist and granite.		

On siliceous parent material such as granitic and quartzitic glacial drift the growth of birch fails to convert mor to mull so that felled pinewood which has been recolonised by birch retains a type of vegetation which can be compared with one or other of the pinewood associations. Sheep-grazed birchwoods tend to develop a grass- and moss-dominated floor.

Moss Communities of Birch and Oak Forest

Many mountain woods have a floor consisting largely of rocks too large to allow the development of a continuous soil layer. The individual boulders remain distinct although overgrown by vegetation in which bryophytes are the chief component. In many western birch and oakwoods the bryophyte growth on these block screes is luxuriant, forming a discontinuous, hummocky carpet over hundreds of square metres or even several hectares. The degree of cover depends chiefly on the size of the blocks and the steepness of their sides.

Richards (1938) has shown that in the Killarney oakwoods it is possible to recognise distinct bryophyte communities on both rocks and trees, and similar types have been found in the Western Highlands. These bryophyte micro-communities depend chiefly on gravity and differences in their maturity are to be regarded as the effects of an environmental gradient and not as the results of a varying rate of succession. There may be minor successional and perhaps cyclical changes involving the growth of bryophytes on bare rock but, on the whole, these individual communities are permanently arrested stages of development. The most immature phases are on steep or moist rocks where soil does not accumulate and the various species remain in intimate contact with the rock surface.

There are more mature types in which the cover of bryophytes is dense and complete, with the formation of a loose humus layer but containing few or no vascular plants. This is distinguished from a still later phase in which hypnaceous mosses are dominant, but grasses and herbs are abundant, giving an approach to the birch and oakwood field communities already described, and passing into these where there is a well developed layer of soil on less rocky ground.

These bryophyte communities are similar for both oak and birchwoods, but in pinewoods there is more *Sphagnum* and except where the blocks are large the vegetation can generally be assigned to one or other of the pinewood associations.

The open rock assemblages of bryophytes are often best described by a simple list with frequency estimates but the closed micro-communities are more uniform and may be analysed in the normal way using a small sample plot. The lists given for Stack Wood in Sutherland (Table 7) are fairly representative of acidic rocks in birch or oakwoods in similar situations throughout the Western Highlands. *Bazzania trilobata* is a frequent member of such communities but was not found in Stack Wood, while more local species include *Adelanthus decipiens* and *Lepidozia pinnata*. Eastern woodland moss communities of this type differ mainly in the scarcity of oceanic species.

The trees in western deciduous woods often carry a luxuriant growth of bryophytes, including many species of the rocky floor, and large foliose lichens (especially *Lobaria* and *Sticta* spp.). Detailed descriptions of these have not been made.

Structure and Dynamics of Birch and Oak Forest

In birchwoods the absence of seedlings and saplings is invariably attributed to sheep grazing and this is difficult to confirm or disprove since sheep and other grazing animals have access to practically all our birchwoods. There is some evidence, however, that domestic stock are not always to blame, at least directly. The commonest birchwood structure is a virtually even-aged stand with seedlings of one or two years of age but no further regeneration. The stands may be found at all stages from dense brushwood thickets to aged, open and moribund woodland. A rarer type contains trees of two generations, the mother trees, which are usually of spreading pioneer form, embedded in a 'matrix' of younger growth. In the more recently formed examples of this second structure it is at once apparent that saplings avoid the immediate vicinity of the parent trees, each of which is thus surrounded by a clear area some 15 m. in diameter. As the wood matures and natural thinning takes place this clear area becomes less obvious.

Since birch saplings can often be found in the dense shade cast by the canopy of other species it is clear that some other effect such as root competition is in operation as well as reduction in light intensity. If this is generally true then birchwood in which trees are spaced at less than about 30–40 ft. apart cannot be expected to regenerate even in the absence of grazing. Birch regeneration seldom takes place within birchwood even when the canopy has opened out through the death of the older trees. On the rare occasions when it does the vegetation is usually found to be ericaceous rather than grassy.

Over most of the country the birch is not a former of climax woodland and the species (pine and oak) that once followed in the succession are either not present or are not able, for other reasons, to take their rightful place. We can speculate that the edaphic or vegetational conditions following one birch crop are usually unsuitable for the establishment of a second crop though why this should be so is a matter for further investigation. The familiar mosaic pattern of birch regeneration thus emerges. Being a prolific seeder with good powers of dispersal, birch regenerates more freely than any other of the native trees, and extensive areas of colonising birchwood on open moor or grassland may be seen in many places, especially on Deeside.

Yapp (1953) would extend his concept of non-continuous tree cover in upland Britain to include the pine and oak. He considers the grassy floor and lack of internal regeneration of so many woods to be natural and not due to grazing as hitherto supposed. The occurrence of external regeneration he regards as evidence that woodland is merely a cyclo-climax in which tree cover comes and goes. While this may be true for the pioneer species, forced into a new role by Man's activities, it is doubtful if it can be applied to

3

the climax shade bearers as well. McVean (1958) has demonstrated that birch regeneration is missing from island woods that are free from sheep while it occurs freely on adjacent unwooded islands. On the other hand the regeneration of *Sorbus aucuparia* benefits from the absence of sheep and may take place within the birchwoods to give rise to a low scrub which is kept trimmed back by the red deer which are able to swim out to the islands.

Even-aged and two-generation stands are again commonly found in oakwoods with the entire wood sometimes consisting of coppice shoot trees. These coppice trees are generally thin, crooked and badly grown so that they give little idea of the full development of which the oak would be capable on any particular site. The oakwoods differ from those of pine and birch already described, in that a few seedlings and saplings can usually be found on the floor of even fairly dense stands. Most of the young plants will be found to lack their leading shoot after the first season's growth and further development is obviously prevented by browsing animals. Seedlings are often most abundant in heathwoods with abundant *Vaccinium* (Betuletum Oxaleto-Vaccinetum) where grazing is not so close and where more light penetrates the tree canopy. In the absence of any semi-natural hill oakwoods which are fenced against the grazing animal it is impossible to say how this potential regeneration would develop. Enclosed woodlands are often found in the policies of the larger estates but the planting of exotics and the presence of the ubiquitous *Rhododendron* almost always gives a highly unnatural appearance to the vegetation. Even where the oaks themselves survive, the accompanying shrub layer of hazel, holly, thorns, bird cherry, etc., has generally been eliminated so that truly natural conditions for regeneration are absent.

ASHWOOD

Pure ashwood is a rarity in the Scottish Highlands and has not previously been described. We have been unable to find more than three stands but the four analyses give the basis for a distinct nodum.

Fraxinus-Brachypodium sylvaticum *nodum*
(*Brachypodium*-rich ashwood)
(Table 8, lists 1–4)

This *Fraxinus-Brachypodium sylvaticum* provisional *nodum*, has six herb constants: *Agrostis tenuis*, *Brachypodium sylvaticum*, *Dactylis glomerata*, *Filipendula ulmaria*, *Lysimachia nemorum* and *Viola riviniana*. The tree canopy may be dominated by either *Fraxinus excelsior* or *Betula pubescens* and the woodland floor by *Endymion non-scriptus*, *Circaea intermedia*, *Cirsium heterophyllum*, *Primula vulgaris* or *Brachypodium sylvaticum*. The number of species present ranges from 26 to 45 with an average of 36.

All the stands listed in Table 8 occur on the Durness dolomite of north-west Scotland and the soil is a deep red loam resting directly on bedrock.

The status of the *nodum* is uncertain in view of the limited material available for study but the ground vegetation of many *Corylus avellana* scrubs on the north coast of Sutherland (influenced by shell sand) (list 5) and on the Tertiary basalt of Ardnamurchan, Morvern and the Inner Hebrides (Spence, unpubl.) appears to belong to it. A final decision must await the examination of the richer oak and ash-oak woods surviving in the Lowlands.

The best example (structurally) of Scottish ashwood occurs at the head of Loch Kishorn. It is entirely free of birch and oak and the most abundant shrubs are hazel and hawthorn. The ash trees cover an area of about 30 acres (12 ha.) and grow mostly rooted in the crevices of scattered blocks of limestone pavement. Between the pavements the soil is deep and carries a smooth, heavily grazed turf with patches of invading bracken. Typical calcicolous species are few and restricted to the outcrops and crevices of the limestone. Most of the trees are old and badly cankered. Scattered ash trees and hazel scrub are found over most of the limestone outcrop to an altitude of about 500 ft. but in only one other locality nearby do the trees become dense enough to constitute woodland. This is a mixed birch and ashwood occupying a steep south-facing slope of red limestone soil below limestone crags. The instability and steepness of the slope has limited sheep and deer grazing and a floristically-rich *Brachypodium* community has been able to develop.

Tokavaig wood in the Sleat peninsula of Skye is larger (over 100 acres) and the limestone pavement is only feebly developed. The ash trees are generally larger than those at Kishorn and without canker. They are also more widely scattered and the space between them is occupied by *Corylus* scrub and birches with abundant *Prunus padus* and *Crataegus monogyna*. Oak is again absent from the limestone itself but is common in the adjacent birchwood which lies on quartzite. The Coille Gaireallach in Strath Suardal shows the retrogression of the ashwood carried one stage further and now consists almost entirely of birch. The wood occurs partly on glacial drift overlying the Durness limestone where ash trees are absent, and partly on limestone pavement similar to that at Kishorn where only scattered ash trees and a few hazel clumps remain but where the composition of the woodland floor bears a strong resemblance to that of Tokavaig wood. There can be little doubt that the abundance of the birches is a result of the selective removal of ash. No ashwood is found on the limestone north of Kishorn and nothing but planted trees occur north of Inchnadamph. South of this area the only extensive limestone pavement in Scotland occurs on the island of Lismore, where scattered ash trees are abundant but there is no woodland. It is quite likely, therefore, that ashwood constitutes the climax vegetation on shallow limestone soil and pavements south of Sutherland. Since such a habitat has always been restricted ashwood can never have been widespread but this extension of what must have been a significant element in the forest cover of northern England at one time is of considerable interest.

MIXED DECIDUOUS WOODLAND

Locally in the Southern and Central Highlands there are patches of a mixed deciduous woodland in which *Quercus spp.*, *Betula spp.*, *Fraxinus excelsior* and *Ulmus glabra* share dominance, and *Corylus avellana*, *Sorbus aucuparia* and *Prunus padus* form an understorey. The Keltneyburn Wood in Perthshire is a good example, with a distinctive *Mercurialis perennis-Allium ursinum* field-layer which has been described by Poore (unpubl.). Most of the undisturbed stands of mixed deciduous wood in our area are small and confined to the steep sides of stream gorges or precipitous hillsides. Due partly to topographic irregularity, the field-layer usually tends to be heterogeneous and the above community is represented along with several others, including a type similar to the *Fraxinus-Brachypodium nodum*. We have not analysed these in detail and include here simple floristic lists from a western and an eastern example of this kind of woodland (Table A). These are the gorge wood at 400 ft. (122 m.) on Resipol Burn, Sunart, Argyll (A), and the hanging wood at 600–1000 ft. (183–305 m.) on Craig Fonvuick, Killie-crankie, Perthshire (B). The trees and shrubs are the same for both (as named above), but *Ilex aquifolium* is present in the Resipol wood.

These mixed woods with their rich field communities are confined to calcareous rocks, and the soils are fertile brown loams with variable amounts of mull-humus. In floristics they represent a type intermediate between oak and birchwoods on acidic rocks and ashwood on true limestone but they may be closer to the original mixed oakwoods of the country than the even-aged stands of oak described above. Very similar oak-ash-elm woods are widespread in North Wales and Northern England and some account of these is given by Tansley (1949).

Table A. Mixed Deciduous Woodland

	A	B		A	B
Hedera helix	+	−	Chrysosplenium oppositifolium	+	−
Helianthemum chamaecistus	−	+	Circaea lutetiana	+	+
Rubus idaeus	−	+	Cirsium heterophyllum	−	+
			C. palustre	+	+
Athyrium filix-femina	+	+	Conopodium majus	+	+
Dryopteris austriaca	+	+	Crepis paludosa	+	+
D. filix-mas	+	+	Digitalis purpurea	+	−
Polypodium vulgare	+	+	Epilobium montanum	+	+
Polystichum lobatum	+	−	Filipendula ulmaria	+	+
Thelypteris dryopteris	+	−	Fragaria vesca	−	+
T. oreopteris	+	−	Geranium lucidum	−	+
T. phegopteris	+	+	G. robertianum	+	+
			Geum rivale	+	+
Agrostis canina	−	+	G. urbanum	−	+
Anthoxanthum odoratum	+	+	Hypericum hirsutum	−	+
Arrhenatherum elatius	−	+	H. pulchrum	+	+
Brachypodium sylvaticum	+	+	Mercurialis perennis	+	+
Deschampsia caespitosa	+	+	Oxalis acetosella	+	+
Festuca rubra	+	+	Potentilla erecta	+	+
Melica uniflora	−	+	P. sterilis	−	+
Poa nemoralis	−	+	Primula vulgaris	+	−
			Prunella vulgaris	+	+
Carex remota	+	−	Ranunculus acris	+	+
C. sylvatica	+	−	Rumex acetosa	−	+
Luzula pilosa	−	+	Sanicula europaea	+	−
L. sylvatica	+	+	Scrophularia nodosa	−	+
			Senecio jacobaea	+	+
Anemone nemorosa	+	+	Succisa pratensis	+	+
Angelica sylvestris	+	−	Taraxacum officinalis agg.	+	+
Asperula odorata	+	−	Teucrium scorodonia	−	+

Valeriana officinalis . . . + +	E. praelongum . . . . + +
Veronica chamaedrys . . . + +	E. striatum . . . . + +
V. officinalis . . . . — +	Hylocomium brevirostre . . + —
Vicia sepium . . . . — +	H. splendens . . . . + +
Viola riviniana . . . . + +	H. umbratum . . . . + —
	Mnium undulatum . . . + +
Brachythecium rutabulum . . — +	Rhytidiadelphus loreus . . + —
Cratoneuron commutatum . . + +	R. squarrosus . . . . + +
Ctenidium molluscum . . + —	R. triquetrus . . . . + +
Dicranum majus . . . + +	Thamnium alopecurum . . + —
D. scoparium . . . + +	
Eurhynchium myosuroides . . + +	Plagiochila asplenioides . . — +
E. myurum . . . . — +	Lophocolea bidentata . . . + +

OTHER KINDS OF WOODLAND

On Eilan Mor of Loch Sionascaig, Inverpolly Forest, there are several acres of pure rowan wood surrounded by an intermixture of birch and rowan, and such a feature is not uncommon throughout the birchwoods of the west Highlands. There are a few reasons for thinking that rowan wood may have been much more widespread at one time both as pure and as mixed stands. It may, indeed, have replaced oak to some extent both altitudinally and to the west on the more base-rich soils. At the present day it exceeds the birch in altitudinal limit and is not much more exacting in its soil requirements. Rowan regeneration is potentially more widespread than that of birch in that more seedlings become established, but these seedlings are heavily grazed by sheep and deer on account of their palatability. On ungrazed islands, and in other situations protected from stock, such as coniferous plantations, the rowan may form a complete understorey of young trees. The holly behaves in much the same way in western districts and there is no doubt that but for the presence of grazing animals it would be a more prominent constituent of our western woodlands as it is in the south-west of Ireland. McVean (1958b) has described a small island in the Fionn Loch of Wester Ross which carries a small fragment of pure holly wood.

As a naturally growing species the yew has virtually disappeared in Scotland but the distribution of place names involving the yew tree indicates a former extensive distribution in the South-west Highlands. In the days of the long bow the fact that certain districts of Scotland were famed for the quality of their yew seems to indicate that the species may have attained local concentrations amounting to small areas of pure woodland such as still exist in Killarney. In 1814 300 yews on Inch Lonaig in Loch Lomond were cut down (Lowe, 1897).

McVean (1956) has published three floristic lists for alderwood in Scotland but there has been no attempt at a phytosociological treatment. In unpublished work Poore distinguishes a *Lysimachia nemorum-Crepis paludosa nodum* of alder and *Salix* swamps which is obviously present in at least two of McVean's lists. In the absence of further studies it is perhaps worth reproducing McVean's table (Table B) of floristic variation in relation to soil water and base content.

Many of the remarks on the cyclo-climactic nature of birchwoods apply to alder also. Even-aged stands are the rule and the two-generation structure is rare. Regeneration is at its optimum on moist soils with short and open herbaceous vegetation.

Particular interest attaches to the occurrence of moribund open alderwood at altitudes of 1000–1500 ft. (305–457 m.) at Loch Treig, Inverness-shire, and Loch Coire, Sutherland. The alder does not set good seed above 900–1000 ft. (275–305 m.) at the present day so that these woodlands are doomed irrespective of any changes in land management which might allow the growth of seedlings.

Table B. Effect of soil water and base content on the subordinate species of alder communities (from McVean, 1956)

INCREASING WATER

→

	1	2	3
a	Ilex aquifolium Betula pubescens Sorbus aucuparia Agrostis spp. Anthoxanthum odoratum Galium hercynicum Dryopteris spp. Pteridium aquilinum	Betula pubescens Molinia caerulea Sphagnum spp. Carex binervis Juncus spp. Luzula multiflora Dryopteris spp. Cirsium palustre	Salix aurita Myrica gale Molinia caerulea Narthecium ossifragum Eriophorum angustifolium Sphagnum spp. Pinguicula vulgaris Potamogeton polygonifolius
b	Fraxinus excelsior Corylus avellana Prunus spinosa Oxalis acetosella Prunella vulgaris Agrostis stolonifera Poa trivialis Deschampsia caespitosa Luzula sylvatica	Fraxinus excelsior Quercus spp. Crepis paludosa Chrysosplenium oppositifolium Myosotis scorpioides Lysimachia nemorum Athyrium filix-femina Dryopteris spp. Carex remota	Salix spp. Ligustrum vulgare Hydrocotyle vulgaris Caltha palustris Filipendula ulmaria Mentha aquatica Epilobium hirsutum Galium palustre
c	Sambucus nigra Hedera helix Urtica dioica Galium aparine Ajuga reptans Bryonia dioica Glechoma hederacea (bare ground)	Betula pubescens Salix atrocinerea Viburnum opulus Calamagrostis lanceolata Eupatorium cannabinum Phragmites communis Thelypteris palustris Solanum dulcamara Carex acutiformis Lysimachia vulgaris	Salix atrocinerea Carex acutiformis Eupatorium cannabinum Filipendula ulmaria Phragmites communis Solanum dulcamara Thelypteris palustris Peucedanum palustre

INCREASING BASES (↓)

Most of the Scottish alderwoods lie within the range of 1, 2, 3 (a and b)

SUB-ALPINE SCRUB

The transition from forest to the birch, juniper and willow scrub of the Sub-alpine zone has been discussed by Poore and McVean (1957) who point out that the scrub birch belt which often follows above the pine and spruce forest of Scandinavia is fragmentary in Scotland, and the picture still further confused by the replacement of pine and oak by secondary birchwoods at lower altitudes.

Juniperus-Thelypteris *nodum*
(Fern-rich juniper scrub)
(Table 9)

The Cairngorm juniper scrub at 2000 ft. (610 m.) first mentioned by Watt and Jones (1948) and again commented upon by Poore and McVean (1957), remains the best example of Sub-alpine scrub in this country (Plate 6). It can now be referred to the provisional *Juniperus-Thelypteris nodum*. It is inadvisable to distinguish constant species when only four lists are available for discussion, but the *nodum* is dominated by *Juniperus communis*, *Vaccinium myrtillus*, *V. vitis-idaea*, ferns and woodland mosses (Plate 7).

The altitudes given in Table 5 show that the stands occur below the potential forest limit and, in fact, similar lists can be made from tall and dense juniper thickets in pine-wood clearings. The affinities of the *nodum* with the pinewood associations and the birch noda are obvious and it is not at all easy to justify the separation of these lists on purely floristic grounds at the present stage. The distribution of the *nodum* is shown in Map 4 and though fairly widespread in the East-central Highlands the stands are mostly small.

A similar juniper scrub is widespread in the Norwegian mountains but this may have *Betula nana* as co-dominant, a feature which is missing in Scotland. Nordhagen (1928, p. 50) names it the *Vaccinium myrtillus*-rich *Juniperus nana* scrub in Sylene and in Rondane the corresponding association is the Hylocomieto-Betuletum nana juniperetosum (Dahl, 1956, p. 151).

The soil below juniper scrub is not strongly podsolised and the juniper humus is friable and mildly acid. A brisk release of nitrate in the humus can be inferred from the frequent presence of *Urtica dioica* and other nitrophilous species. Patches of this scrub are of common occurrence in damp hollows and north-facing slopes of high-level heather moors in the East-central Highlands, where the contrast between the floristics and humus type of the scrub and the fire climax Callunetum is particularly instructive.

There is a tendency in the north of Scotland for a scrub of *Salix aurita* and *S. atrocinerea* to develop in damp *Calluna* and grass heaths between successive burnings. Whether this is a purely secondary development or whether it represents a formerly widespread type of community above the forest limit is not certain but in any case the stands are mostly too fragmentary to be analysed in the usual way. The most extensive development of this low-level willow scrub occurs at 700 ft. (213 m.) on the moors near Edderton in East Ross and the following species list was compiled in a dense thicket of *Salix capraea* 2–3 m. high and measuring 20 × 30 m. in area.

Sorbus aucuparia	Lysimachia nemorum
Prunus padus	Rumex acetosella
	Prunella vulgaris
Blechnum spicant	Filipendula ulmaria

Dryopteris spinulosa	Stellaria graminea
D. borreri	Potentilla erecta
Thelypteris oreopteris	Trientalis europaea
	Ranunculus acris
Deschampsia flexuosa	Oxalis acetosella
Holcus lanatus	Viola riviniana
Juncus effusus	
Luzula campestris	Thuidium tamariscinum
	Mnium undulatum
Cardamine hirsuta	Polytrichum commune
Cirsium palustre	Sphagnum recurvum
Galium hercynicum	
Epilobium montanum	

Spence (1960) has described patches of willow scrub (*Salix aurita* and *S. atrocinerea*) from islands in lochs of Shetland and South Uist, where they are associated with other low shrub growth (*Rubus fruticosus* agg., *Rosa* spp., *Lonicera periclymenum*) and tall herb communities.

Salix lapponum-Luzula sylvatica *nodum*

(Montane willow scrub)
(Table 10)

Map 5 shows that the *Salix lapponum-Luzula sylvatica nodum* is widely distributed in the Northern and Central Highlands but has a rather eastern bias. Most of the stands are fragmentary and confined to ungrazed crag ledges and only in the Clova region of Angus do they exceed a few square metres in area.

The constants of the eleven lists in Table 10 are: *Salix lapponum, Vaccinium myrtillus, Deschampsia caespitosa, Luzula sylvatica, Rumex acetosa, Hylocomium splendens, Rhytidiadelphus loreus* and *Thuidium tamariscinum*. The scrub may be dominated by *Salix lanata, S. lapponum, S. myrsinites, S. arbuscula, Luzula sylvatica, Hylocomium splendens* and *Rhytidiadelphus loreus*. In addition *Salix phylicifolia, Alchemilla glabra, Angelica sylvestris, Geum rivale, Saussurea alpina* and *Thuidium tamariscinum* may almost attain co-dominance. *Salix lanata* (constancy class I) is exclusive to the *nodum*.

There are 119 species listed in the table while species numbers per stand range from 29 to 43 with an average of 38.

The *nodum* has obvious affinities with the *Vaccinium* and *Luzula*-dominated lists 17–22 of Table 6 as well as with the Tall Herb *nodum* (p. 80). The factors determining whether particular ledges shall be dominated by tall herbs or willow, apart from the obvious historical ones of willow distribution, are not clear. The *Salix myrsinites* scrub of Inchnadamph described by Poore and McVean (1957) cannot be included in this *nodum* and this lends support to the theory of its secondary origin.

On some of the Breadalbane hills, notably Ben Lui and Meall nan Tarmachan, *Salix arbuscula* is the predominant willow of basic cliff ledges, often to the exclusion of *S. lapponum*.

Soils are wet and stony with much silt accumulation, or peaty muds with silt particles right to the surface, indicating irrigation* and instability. The altitudinal range of the

---

* We have used this term for the continual lateral movement of free drainage water through soils.

stands is from 2200 to 3000 ft. (671–914 m.) and exposure to north and east seems to be usual. No information is available about the winter snow cover on these ledges and banks, and while it must often be considerable, having regard to altitude and aspect, it cannot be particularly reliable. Exposure to winter frosts may indeed be a factor of importance localising the occurrence of the tall willows compared with that of the deciduous tall herbs.

In Norway the Rumiceto-Salicetum lapponae of Rondane (Dahl, 1956) closely resembles this *nodum*; there are 38 species in common and two of these are constants. The *Salix lapponum* scrubs described by Nordhagen from the Sylene and Sikilsdalen areas of Norway are much richer in tall herbs or in species of moist ground, and are rather to be compared with the Tall Herb *nodum* (p. 80) and *Carex rostrata-Sphagnum warnstorfianum nodum* (p. 119).

Vegetation of this type was probably once extensive on damp base-rich soils at higher levels, within the geographical range of these montane willows. Many of the mesotrophic mires and damp grasslands are likely to have carried a willow shrub layer, and there were probably transitions to the lower level communities of *Salix aurita* and *S. atrocinerea*.

Chapter 3

DWARF SHRUB HEATH

In Continental climates the dwarf shrub is the characteristic life form of the Low-alpine zone. In an oceanic and deforested country such as Scotland this is not quite true but, nevertheless, completely natural dwarf shrub vegetation is characteristic of an altitudinal belt from 1200 ft. (366 m.) to 2800 ft. (854 m.) in the north of Scotland and from 2300 ft. (702 m.) to 3600 ft. (1098 m.) in the Cairngorms. This belt has been referred to the combined Low- and Middle-alpine zone by Poore and McVean (1957) and its vegetation falls into two main classes. The first has *Calluna vulgaris* as its characteristic shrub, and the second, which on average occupies the higher part of this altitudinal zone, is dominated by *Vaccinium* spp. and/or *Empetrum hermaphroditum*. We shall begin, however, by considering an anthropogenic heath which has been derived mainly from forest, especially pine forest, except at altitudes above the natural tree limit.

Callunetum vulgaris

(Dry heather moor)

(Table 11)

The purple heather moors of Scotland are renowned the world over but in recent times it has become accepted that they are almost completely artificial. Analyses from all parts of the country, including those of the successional stages following burning, are best placed under the one association Callunetum vulgaris, or heather moor in the strict sense.

The constants of the association, apart from *Calluna* itself, are the mosses *Dicranum scoparium*, *Hylocomium splendens*, *Hypnum cupressiforme* and *Pleurozium schreberi*. *Calluna vulgaris* is always overwhelmingly dominant in the shrub layer of the mature community but *Erica cinerea* and *Vaccinium vitis-idaea* may attain local co-dominance after a fire (cf. Gimingham, 1949). In the ground layer *Hylocomium splendens*, *Hypnum cupressiforme*, *Pleurozium schreberi* and *Cladonia impexa* may be the dominant species. There are no species characteristic of the association.

The number of species per stand is generally low (12–23 with an average of 17) and 76 species in all have been recorded from the seventeen lists in the table. It is interesting to compare these figures with the corresponding ones from the Vaccineto-Calluneta from which Callunetum vulgaris often appears to have been derived.

The seral stages to mature Callunetum have not been described as separate facies but the Arctostaphyleto-Callunetum which is described on pages 30, 31 can be regarded either as a facies of Callunetum vulgaris or as a full association. The second course has been adopted as a matter of convenience.

Floristically, Callunetum vulgaris is distinguished from all other Calluneta by the overwhelming dominance of *Calluna*, the virtual absence of *Empetrum* spp. and the constancy and abundance of *Dicranum scoparium* and *Hypnum cupressiforme*, combined with low amounts of *Rhacomitrium lanuginosum* and *Sphagnum* spp. In a few widely separated parts of the Highlands small areas of a herb-rich *Calluna* heath have been found. These are clearly related to Callunetum vulgaris but from the abundance of herbs and grasses, the five lists have been put in a separate table (Table 11a). This type shows floristic similarity to the species-rich Agrosto-Festucetum and relationships between the two are discussed on p. 66. It is always associated with a calcareous parent rock, and the soils are brown loams with a much higher base-status than those of Callunetum vulgaris. The stands on Rhum are closely related to the short *Calluna*-grass heaths which are widespread in the Western Highlands and Islands on coastal lands affected by blown sand and salt spray.

The distribution of Callunetum vulgaris in the Highlands is shown in Map 6. East of the line AB heather moor is widespread on all suitable habitats and may be the most prominent vegetation type over wide areas. Nearly all the good grouse moors have a corresponding distribution for this is their most important vegetation type. To the west of the line the association can still be found but has a restricted distribution mainly of small stands of a few square metres to a few hectares on well-drained sites facing south or west. It is largely replaced in the west by Vaccineto-Callunetum, Trichophoreto-Callunetum or Molinieto-Callunetum.

In altitude the association ranges from near sea level to nearly 2500 ft. (763 m.) but the majority of heather moors lie between 500 and 1500 ft. (153–457 m.) on free-draining morainic country of moderate gradients. In the Eastern Highlands it may occupy slopes of any aspect.

The soil is typically an iron-humus podsol but other podsol varieties are common and the A_2 horizon is often missing or completely masked at the base of the raw humus. Exceptionally, the raw humus or peat may rest directly on rock debris as in the Vaccineto-Callunetum.

A wide literature exists on the phytosociology and ecology of Calluneta but it cannot be reviewed here. The Callunetum vulgaris now described forms part of the Callunetum of many British authors (W. G. Smith in Tansley, 1949, p. 751; Watt and Jones, 1948; Metcalfe, 1950; Nicholson and Robertson, 1958, p. 260) but this also includes our Trichophoreto-Callunetum, Molinieto-Callunetum and Arctostaphyleto-Callunetum as well as the various dwarf Calluneta to be described. The best comparison of all is with the *Calluna-Pleurozium nodum* of Poore (unpublished) on which the Callunetum vulgaris is based. Callunetum on thin peat of well-drained slopes throughout the uplands of England and Wales is probably identical with the present association (Ratcliffe, 1959), but the local type with *Ulex gallii* does not occur in the Highlands.

Beijerinck (1940) quotes lists of Calluneta of various authors from Southern Norway, Jutland, Netherlands, North-western Germany, West and Central Alps, Southern France and Spain. The *Calluna* heaths of the Netherlands and North-western Germany, assigned by Tüxen (1937) to the order Calluneto-Ulicetalia, are very close floristically and physiognomically to the Scottish heaths which often contain indicator species of that order such as *Genista anglica*, *Antennaria dioica* and *Sieglingia decumbens* (but see p. 138). The same resemblance can be detected in the Swedish heaths described by Damann (1957) which are characterised by the presence of *Vaccinium vitis-idaea*,

Hylocomium splendens and *Dicranum undulatum*. Most of them are classified by him under various facies or variants of Hylocomieto-Callunetum which he has also recorded locally in Eastern Jutland among the Calluneto-Genistetum heaths prevailing there.

Arctostaphyleto-Callunetum

(*Arctostaphylos*-rich heather moor)
(Table 12)

As mentioned previously Arctostaphyleto-Callunetum is close enough to pure heather moor to be regarded as a mere facies of it.

The constants are *Arctostaphylos uva-ursi, Calluna vulgaris, Erica cinerea, Vaccinium vitis-idaea, Deschampsia flexuosa, Lathyrus montanus, Pyrola media* and *Hypnum cupressiforme*. Either *Calluna* or *Arctostaphylos* may dominate among the dwarf shrubs and *Hylocomium splendens* and *Pleurozium schreberi* may occasionally rise to dominance in the ground layer. *Pyrola media* (constancy class V) is exclusive to the association and *Genista anglica* (constancy class III) and *Lathyrus montanus* (constancy class V) are weakly preferential for it.

Species numbers are higher than in Callunetum vulgaris with a total record of 63 for eight lists and a range from 16–29 species per stand (average 23).

Floristically the association is distinguished from pure heather moor by the presence of *Lathyrus montanus, Lotus corniculatus, Pyrola media* and *Viola riviniana* apart from the co-dominance of *Arctostaphylos* (Plate 8). There are some extensive species-poor stands of *Calluna* and *Arctostaphylos* which would be difficult to assign to either association but the extremes of the series are quite distinct and have a different soil profile (see below). Again, *Arctostaphylos* is often abundant in Callunetum vulgaris on rocky ground in many districts beyond the range of the present association.

The distribution of Arctostaphyleto-Callunetum is shown in Map 6 and it can be seen that occurrences are nearly all in the East-central Highlands with the headquarters in Speyside. All occur within the area of abundant Callunetum vulgaris to the east of the line AB (Map 6).

Soils exhibit a wide range of profile development from the typical iron-humus podsol of heather moor to brown loams resembling those of the Betula-herb *nodum* (p. 17). The characteristic profile lies between these extremes and can be illustrated by the following example from Glen Banchor, Inverness-shire:

0–2·5 cm.	.	. fibrous, moder-like *Calluna* humus
2·5–15 cm.	.	. sandy loam, light brown above, becoming yellow-brown below.

The parent material could not be examined here but brown loams of pH ca. 4·8 are generally associated with an intermixture of soft lime-rich material in the glacial till (see also p. 29).

The ecological factors at work differentiating the association from Callunetum vulgaris are not certain but clearly the separation depends on the inability of heather to oust seral *Arctostaphylos* following moor-burning under certain conditions. In the region where the association occurs, burning often seems to favour *Arctostaphylos*, whereas in many western districts it appears to have the reverse effect. In the same way *Erica cinerea* may remain dominant or co-dominant with *Calluna* on free-draining sunny slopes whereas it is generally replaced by *Calluna* some years after the fire on normal sites (Gimingham, 1949). The same applies locally to *Vaccinium vitis-idaea*. Apart from the probable climatic effect, Arctostaphyleto-Callunetum tends on the whole to be associated with rather better soils than most pure stands of heather. It is, however, probably almost entirely anthropogenic, and reverts locally to birch or pinewood.

The two types of heather moor just described give way to blanket bog (Trichophoreto-Callunetum and Calluneto-Eriophoretum) where drainage is poor and deep peat accumulates. At higher levels burning encourages an early transition to Trichophoreto-Callunetum or, in the absence of fire, there may be a gradual passage to Cladineto-Callunetum as exposure increases. Where heather moor remains unburned it may develop into a Vaccineto-Callunetum resembling that of pine and birchwoods, from which most of it would originally be derived, and where dense pine colonisation of the moor is taking place there is a direct development to Pinetum Hylocomieto-Vaccinetum as the heather is shaded out. Arctostaphyleto-Callunetum on the richer soils shows the same floristic and successional relationships with the Betula-herb *nodum* as Callunetum vulgaris does with Pinetum Hylocomieto-Vaccinetum. In the Cairngorms Arctostaphyleto-Callunetum may pass to Cladineto-Callunetum arctostaphyletosum through an intermediate type of vegetation at about 2200 ft. (671 m.).

Vaccineto-Callunetum

(Damp heather moor)

(Table 13)

The next vegetation type to be considered, the Vaccineto-Callunetum, or damp heather moor, lies almost entirely within the forest and Sub-alpine zones and has probably been partly derived from woodland and scrub.

There are 12 species in the association element: *Calluna vulgaris, Empetrum hermaphroditum, Vaccinium myrtillus, Deschampsia flexuosa, Dicranum scoparium, Hylocomium splendens, Plagiothecium undulatum, Pleurozium schreberi, Rhytidiadelphus loreus, Sphagnum nemoreum, Anastrepta orcadensis* and *Cladonia uncialis*. The only shrub dominant is *Calluna* although *Empetrum hermaphroditum* and *Vaccinium myrtillus* may almost attain co-dominance; the moss layer may be dominated by *Sphagnum nemoreum, Hylocomium splendens* or *Rhytidiadelphus loreus. Dicranodontium uncinatum* and *Bazzania pearsoni* are exclusive to the association and a number of other oceanic hepatics are strongly preferential for it: *Anastrophyllum donianum, Herberta hutchinsiae, Jamesoniella carringtonii, Mastigophora woodsii, Scapania nimbosa* and *S. ornithopodioides*.

A division has been made into two well-marked facies—hepaticosum (lists 1–11) and suecicosum (lists 12–19). Eighty-five species have been listed from the nineteen stands analysed in Table 13. The number of species per stand ranges from 21 to 42 with an overall average of 33 and facies averages of 37 and 29 in the hepaticosum and suecicosum respectively. The hepaticosum is distinguished by a quite remarkable assemblage of oceanic liverworts, many of which are constant and occur only in this facies, and the suecicosum by the constancy of *Rubus chamaemorus* and *Chamaepericlymenum suecicum*, and the abundance of *Eriophorum vaginatum*, all of which are absent or rare in the hepaticosum. The large leafy liverworts which characterise the hepaticosum facies are widely distributed in the Western Highlands but reach their greatest abundance in the

North-western districts where this facies is well developed. In this region, Vaccineto-Empetretum, Juniperetum nanae and occasionally *Vaccinium-Luzula* communities may be equally rich in these hepatics. Some species, such as *Anastrophyllum donianum* and *Scapania nimbosa* find their optimum at higher levels and most of them occur plentifully in rather different, heterogeneous vegetation, especially on rock ledges, but only in the dwarf shrub communities have they all been consistently found within a space of 4 sq. m. Most of these species extend as far east as the Cairngorms but they appear to depend on late snow cover there.

Floristically the association is distinguished from the closely related Pinetum Vaccineto-Callunetum (p. 13) by the presence of species such as *Vaccinium uliginosum, Chamaepericlymenum suecicum, Carex bigelowii, Polytrichum alpinum* and the oceanic liverworts. The distinction might not be clear in a well-forested country but deforestation has generally separated the two associations altitudinally. There is unlikely to be any confusion with other dwarf shrub heaths but further distinctions will be mentioned later under the appropriate noda.

The hepaticosum is confined to the higher hill ranges of the west, mainly in Ross-shire and Sutherland, and has most precise habitat requirements, occurring between 1000 ft. and 2000 ft. (305–610 m.) on steep north to east facing slopes, especially in sheltered corries (Map 7). Since the whole region is extremely wet, these situations must experience an unusually high atmospheric humidity throughout the year. While the lack of suitable topography accounts partly for the localisation of this facies, it has evidently been greatly reduced in extent by moor-burning and grazing. Even where the heather has regenerated well after fire, the liverworts have seldom reappeared in abundance, and in many places there has been a general destruction of the shrub layer essential to the full development of the liverwort carpet. A small stand of hepatic-rich *Calluna*-juniper heath occurs on gentle slopes of an unburned island in Loch an Eoin, Beinn Damph Forest, whereas comparable situations on the shores and adjacent hillsides are covered with open Trichophoreto-Callunetum containing *Pleurozia* as the only notable liverwort. Within the region of maximum humidity the hepaticosum thus probably once had a wider distribution than our records show, extending at least as far south as Glencoe, where fragments still occur on large cliff ledges, and may well have favoured a wider range of situation and aspect. The suecicosum is widely distributed in the Highlands and, though more favoured by the wetter climate of the west, it extends well to the east (Map 7). There is, for example, an extensive stand on Ben Rinnes in Aberdeenshire. The altitudinal range is from 1000 ft. to 2600 ft. (305–793 m.) and this facies is restricted to steep north to east facing slopes in the Eastern Highlands but sometimes occurs on other aspects in the far west. It is again sensitive to fire and has been eradicated or greatly modified in many places. The frequent restriction of the whole association to north to east aspects may be exaggerated, as these damp and shaded slopes are less easily burned than dry ones.

Either facies of the association passes laterally into burned Callunetum vulgaris or Trichophoreto-Callunetum and where the angle of slope decreases downhill there is a gradual, or sometimes fairly abrupt, transition to Calluneto-Eriophoretum. In hollows or on steeper banks where snow accumulates in winter the association gives way to Vaccineto-Empetretum or Vaccinetum chionophilum (pp. 39–43).

The soil is a well-humified liverwort or *Sphagnum-Calluna* peat of varying depth directly overlying coarse block scree with occasional pockets of leached mineral soil (A_2)

between the peat and the stones. The peat is decidedly deeper and wetter under the suecicosum facies.

Both facies are oceanic but the hepaticosum is the most outstanding of our vegetation types in this respect, and nothing comparable seems to have been described from elsewhere, though it may well occur in the west of Ireland. It is an interesting analogy that a few bryophytes of similar western distribution are endemic to the British Isles, e.g. *Leptodontium recurvifolium* and *Campylopus shawii*.

Juniperetum nanae
(Dwarf juniper scrub)
(Table 14)

Juniperetum nanae represents a transitional type between Sub-alpine scrub and Low-alpine dwarf shrub heath. Although extreme prostrate forms of the dwarf juniper (*Juniperus communis* ssp. *nana*) are found throughout the Highlands this association is confined to the western seaboard of the Northern Highlands (Map 4) where it probably represents the remnants of a former widespread distribution on the Cambrian quartzite and Torridonian sandstone. Additional information has become available about the Juniperetum nanae since it was first described as the *Juniperus-Arctostaphylos* sociation by Poore and McVean (1957, p. 419).

The association element consists of the eight species *Arctostaphylos uva-ursi, Calluna vulgaris, Juniperus nana, Deschampsia flexuosa, Hypnum cupressiforme, Rhacomitrium lanuginosum, Trichophorum caespitosum* and *Cladonia uncialis*. An undescribed species of *Herberta* (recorded as *Herberta adunca* by Poore and McVean) is exclusive to the association and to the stands on the Beinn Eighe Nature Reserve.

In Table 14, 67 species are recorded from the ten lists, numbers ranging from 17 to 31 species per plot and with an average of 24.

Two facies of the association have been recognised although inadequate data are available, particularly of the second, to say what their true status may be. The hepaticosum (lists 1–7) is distinguished by the abundance of mosses and liverworts and has the additional constants *Pleurozia purpurea* and *Cladonia impexa* (Plate 9). In the lichenosum (lists 8–10) the prominence of liverworts and lichens is reversed and *Pleurozia, Herberta* spp. and *Cladonia impexa* are absent.

The association is found from just over 1000 ft. (305 m.) to just under 2000 ft. (610 m.) on level or gently sloping quartzite moraine; occasionally on more steeply sloping scree. The hepaticosum is found only on exposures from north to east and the lichenosum on the drier south-western slopes. The stands occur as numerous patches with the areas of complete vegetation cover developed around one or a few juniper plants and having a total area of only a few square metres. Between these patches there is bare quartzite rubble with a sparse growth of *Molinia, Trichophorum, Calluna*, etc. This vegetation mosaic covers many hectares on Beinn Eighe in Ross-shire and Foinaven in Sutherland.

The soil is a ranker (Kubiena, 1953, p. 163) consisting of a few inches of juniper and bryophyte humus directly overlying the quartzite rubble or separated from it by a thin A_2 horizon.

The prostrate juniper scrub is blown clear of snow in the winter (chionophobous) and in hollows and badly drained situations it is replaced by Callunetum with much

Trichophorum or by a thin growth of *Narthecium*, *Trichophorum* and *Molinia*. Vegetation intermediate between this association and Arctoeto-Callunetum is found at its upper limit wherever finer morainic material occurs and the cover of vegetation then becomes continuous.

Braun-Blanquet et al. (1939) provisionally assign the *Juniperus nana-Arctostaphylos uva-ursi* vegetation described by Praeger from Mayo and Galway to their Juniperion nanae alliance and it is clear that the Irish and Scottish juniper heaths represent an oceanic development of the Continental Junipereto-Arctostaphyletum.

McVean (1957) has described a juniper covered island lying at 1150 ft. (351 m.) in West Ross which provides evidence of a former gradual transition from juniper-rich pine and birch forest (still to be seen on the islands of Loch Maree in Ross-shire and Loch Syre in Sutherland) to Low-alpine juniper heath. Patches of shrub heath dominated by small junipers intermediate in growth form between the sub-species *nana* and *communis* occur in a few scattered places from the corries of the Cairngorms to the exposed coast at Bettyhill. In floristics they perhaps lie nearer to Juniperetum nanae than to the *Juniperus-Thelypteris nodum*. The taxonomy of the juniper forms in these communities is obscure.

All juniper scrub, but especially the present type, is exceedingly sensitive to burning and in some places has evidently been destroyed by a single fire. Juniperetum nanae is mostly restricted to unburned ground and many degraded examples occur on fire-swept hillsides. In the Lewisian country of North-west Sutherland most of the islands in the numerous lochs have at least some *Juniperus nana*, but this species is absent or scarce on the surrounding burned moorlands. It is likely, therefore, that the association or related communities were once widespread on a variety of acidic parent rocks (see also Spence, 1960).

Durno and McVean (1959) trace the history of these Sub-alpine and Low-alpine juniper communities back to Sub-atlantic times on the Beinn Eighe massif and conclude that as relics of a former widespread vegetation type they are as worthy of conservation as the nearby fragments of pine forest.

Arctoeto-Callunetum
(Species-rich dwarf shrub heath)
(Table 15)

The closely related association, Arctoeto-Callunetum has also been previously described (*Arctous-Loiseleuria nodum* of Poore and McVean, 1957). Further lists are now available and a more complete picture of its distribution has been obtained.

Thirteen constants form the association element: *Calluna vulgaris*, *Arctous alpina*, *Empetrum hermaphroditum*, *Loiseleuria procumbens*, *Lycopodium selago*, *Rhacomitrium lanuginosum*, *Cetraria aculeata*, *C. islandica*, *Cladonia sylvatica*, *C. uncialis*, *Platysma glaucum*, *Ochrolechia frigida* and *Sphaerophorus globosus*. *Platysma lacunosum* (constancy class III) is exclusive to the association and *Calluna* is the sole dominant (Plate 10).

The association can be distinguished floristically from the Juniperetum nanae (lichenosum facies) by the reduced importance of juniper and the constancy of *Empetrum*, *Arctous*, *Platysma glaucum* and *Ochrolechia frigida* (see also Cladineto-Callunetum, p. 35).

Seventy species are listed for the association in Table 15 and numbers per plot vary from 20 to 31 with an average of 26.

The association is confined to the Highlands north of the Great Glen and attains its finest development on the hills lying between Applecross and the Cromarty Firth (Map 8). Apart from an extensive outlying stand at 900–1200 ft. (275–366 m.) on Whiten Head, Sutherland, the altitudinal range is from 1700 ft. (519 m.) to 2400 ft. (732 m.). Within this comparatively narrow zone it is confined to windswept crests and ridges of fine morainic material usually of Cambrian quartzite, Torridonian sandstone or Moine schist. The ground is level or gently sloping and may be exposed in any direction.

The soil varies from a typical ranker, in which dark brown or black sandy humus passes directly to morainic debris, to podsolic types with well-developed B horizons. The surface humus is moder-like and well mixed with sandy and silty mineral particles (pH 4·5–5·0).

Stands vary considerably in size from fragments of only a few square metres to uniform areas of the order of 3–5 hectares. A sharp transition occurs to the *Nardus-Rhacomitrium* and *Nardus-Trichophorum noda* where snow accumulates in winter and where there is seasonal waterlogging, and also the Calluneto-Eriophoretum (p. 103 and fig. 3, p. 36) where permanent wetness leads to peat formation. On the other hand the transition to Rhacomitreto-Callunetum (p. 38) and Cladineto-Callunetum (see below) is generally a more gradual one and not associated with any obvious environmental discontinuity.

Table 15 also presents two fragments (lists 12, 13) of closely related vegetation from 3300 ft. (1007 m.) in the Cairngorms. They are mentioned here because they are the only examples encountered in this country of chionophobous dwarf shrub-lichen heaths dominated by *Empetrum* and *Loiseleuria* and lacking *Calluna vulgaris*. McVean (1955) lists closely similar vegetation from east Iceland at an altitude of 650 ft. (198 m.).

Many similar dwarf shrub/lichen communities, mostly lacking or with little *Calluna*, have been described from Scandinavia:

1. Compact *Calluna* association locally occurring in Sylene (Nordhagen 1927, p. 238) which has 27 species in common with the Arctoeto-Callunetum.
2. *Cetraria nivalis-Alectoria ochroleuca*-rich *Loiseleuria* association of Sylene (p. 203) with 28 species in common.
3. Alectorieto-Arctostaphyletum uvae-ursi of Rondane (Dahl, 1956, p. 100) with 25 species in common.
4. Cetrarietum nivalis typicum (a lichen heath) from Rondane (p. 91) with 27 species in common.

Cladineto-Callunetum

(Lichen-rich dwarf *Calluna* heath)

(Table 16)

The Cladineto-Callunetum now to be described has a wider distribution than Arctoeto-Callunetum and occurs in both the Central and Northern Highlands (Map 9). It includes the dwarf *Calluna* mat or mountain Callunetum of many British authors, such as Metcalfe (1950), and the *Calluna*-lichen heaths of Poore and McVean (1957).

The association element consists of *Calluna vulgaris*, *Empetrum hermaphroditum*,

Cetraria aculeata, C. islandica, Cladonia sylvatica and *C. uncialis.* Either *Calluna vulgaris* or *Cladonia sylvatica* may be dominant. There are no species exclusive to the association but *Alectoria ochroleuca* (constancy class I) and *Cetraria nivalis* (constancy class II) are preferential for it although they also occur in the Arctoeto-Callunetum and Rhacomitreto-Empetretum (p. 46).

Only 61 species have been recorded for the association and numbers per plot are low, ranging from 9 to 26 with an average of 19.

Three facies have been distinguished: typicum (lists 1–10) which is dominated by *Calluna* alone or with *Empetrum hermaphroditum* or *Cladonia sylvatica* co-dominant; arctostaphyletosum (lists 11–13) in which *Arctostaphylos uva-ursi* replaces *Empetrum*; and sylvaticosum (lists 14–18) a true lichen heath with dominant *Cladonia sylvatica* (*C. rangiferina* occasionally co-dominant). Lists 10 and 14 are intermediate between typicum and sylvaticosum.

Floristically the association is distinguished from Arctoeto-Callunetum by the

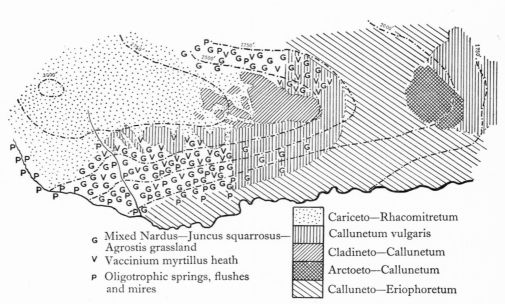

G	Mixed Nardus—Juncus squarrosus—Agrostis grassland
V	Vaccinium myrtillus heath
P	Oligotrophic springs, flushes and mires

Cariceto—Rhacomitretum
Callunetum vulgaris
Cladineto—Callunetum
Arctoeto—Callunetum
Calluneto—Eriophoretum

Fig. 3. Relationships between oligotrophic communities on Leacann Bhreac, Ben Wyvis, East Ross

smaller variety of dwarf shrubs (particularly the scarcity of *Loiseleuria* and absence of *Arctous*), the reduction in the number of herbs and the partial replacement of lichens such as *Platysma glaucum* and *P. lacunosum* by *Cetraria nivalis* and *Alectoria ochroleuca.*

The association occupies the same topographic position as the Arctoeto-Callunetum (Fig. 3) but has a wider altitudinal range from 2200 ft. (671 m.) to 3200 ft. (976 m.) and on hills where both occur, the present association thus tends to replace the other above 2400 ft. (732 m.). Where the two types are contiguous the greater average depth of the shrub mat shows that the exposure is often less severe on ground occupied by Cladineto-Callunetum.

Soils exhibit much the same range of profile formation as the Arctoeto-Callunetum but the surface humus is a mor rather than moder and may be deeper and unmixed with mineral particles (pH 4·3–4·4). Podsolisation is more pronounced to give either a podsol ranker (Kubiena, 1953, pl. 175) with distinct grey A_2 horizon or a podsol of raw humus with bleached mineral grains overlying a B horizon of reddish-brown, often mottled and humus-stained, sandy gravel.

The distribution centre of the association lies in the East-central Highlands where large areas of ground on exposed ridges and summits may be occupied by one or other of the facies (Map 9). The arctostaphyletosum is confined to the granite tract of the central Cairngorms where it often replaces Trichophoreto-Callunetum (p. 106) as peat thins out uphill and the exposed crests of the ridges are reached. The sylvaticosum has a slightly wider distribution in the same area and although not confined to granite is a markedly eastern type in the Highlands as a whole. It occupies more sheltered sites and slight hollows on the ridges so that it enjoys an intermittent light snow-cover in winter. On the westward spurs of the Cairngorms these *Calluna*-lichen heaths are seen to occupy an intermediate position between erosion surface or Cladineto-Callunetum typicum and the *Nardus-Trichophorum nodum* in slight nivation hollows.

In the Highlands north of the Great Glen the Cladineto-Callunetum has a more eastern position than the Arctoeto-Callunetum, which is widely distributed and overlaps with both this association and the Rhacomitreto-Callunetum (Maps 8–9). In the districts where both associations occur either may occupy the larger area and intermediate vegetation is found. The transition from the one association to the other is always gradual.

Metcalfe (1950) divides his mountain Callunetum into a *Calluna-Arctostaphylos* community which is the equivalent of our arctostaphyletosum facies and a *Calluna-Loiseleuria* community, the equivalent of our typicum.

Good Cladineto-Callunetum seems to be confined to the Highlands, but on the ranges of White Coomb and Dollar Law in the Southern Uplands there are stands with a rather low cover of lichens, and fragments occur on Skiddaw in Lakeland. Dwarf *Calluna* heaths hardly occur in England or Wales, evidently having been eradicated on these southern hills by moor-burning and sheep grazing.

The closest relationship that can be found in the Continental literature is with the *Calluna* and *Empetrum* rich birchwoods of the Sylene National Park in Norway (Nordhagen, 1927, p. 107). If we ignore the birch trees which are usually in open and park-like stands there are three constants and 22 species in all common to our Table 16 and Nordhagen's table (pp. 108–109). Nordhagen's (loc. cit. p. 218) *Cladonia sylvatica-rangiferina*-rich *Calluna* association has 24 species and three constants in common with the Cladineto-Callunetum, and the large homogeneous stand of a *Betula nana*-rich *Cetraria nivalis-Cladonia sylvatica* association also described from Sylene (p. 198) makes another interesting comparison. In the last association *Betula nana* appears to replace *Calluna vulgaris* of the Scottish association (see p. 105 and Dahl, 1956, p. 246). It is significant that Sylene lies in a relatively oceanic area of Norway whereas the normal Norwegian lichen heath of continental areas such as Rondane is dominated by *Cladonia alpestris*, a Scottish lichen which we have not yet succeeded in finding, and *Alectoria ochroleuca*. In Rondane *Cladonia mitis* (a lichen of the *C. sylvatica* complex) forms a narrow zone in Polytricheto-Caricetum bigelowii callunetosum, between Cladonietum alpestris of exposed ground and Cetrarietum delisei which is protected by a winter cover of ice and snow. Knaben (1950) records that in the district of Middle Sogn in western Norway lichen-dominated communities are absent, but that dense patches of chionophobous brown and yellow lichens are found on the tops of the easternmost ridges with localised patches on the rising tops of crags and crests further west. The puzzling, disjunct distribution of lichen heath in Scotland is typical of a vegetation type, or a species, on the edge of its range. Poore and McVean (1957, p. 427) are of the opinion that its potential habitat at the junction of the Low-alpine and Middle-alpine zones is occupied by *Rhacomitrium* heath and *Juncus trifidus* communities in our oceanic climate.

Rhacomitreto-Callunetum

(*Rhacomitrium*-rich dwarf *Calluna* heath)
(Table 17)

The Rhacomitreto-Callunetum is a wind-clipped heather mat in which *Rhacomitrium lanuginosum* replaces the lichens of the Cladineto-Callunetum. The association element is somewhat similar: *Calluna vulgaris, Empetrum hermaphroditum, Hypnum cupressiforme, Rhacomitrium lanuginosum, Cladonia sylvatica, C. uncialis* and *Sphaerophorus globosus. Calluna* and *Rhacomitrium* are the two dominants while *Empetrum hermaphroditum, Cladonia uncialis* and *C. sylvatica* may approach co-dominance. There are no exclusive species and none selective or preferential for the association alone.

Seventy-three species are recorded in the thirteen lists of the association with numbers per stand ranging from 19 to 34 (average 23).

An unsatisfactory division can be made into an empetrosum facies corresponding to the Cladineto-Callunetum and an arctostaphyletosum in which *Arctostaphylos uva-ursi* and *Arctous alpina* replace *Empetrum hermaphroditum* to a large extent and which corresponds to the Arctoeto-Callunetum. The facies have not been distinguished in the distribution map (Map 9) but the arctostaphyletosum is confined to the Northern Highlands while the empetrosum covers the entire range of the association. List 13 (Table 17) comes very close to Arctoeto-Callunetum although it is without *Arctostaphylos* or *Arctous* and list 1 is intermediate to Cladineto-Callunetum.

Floristically the association is distinguished from Cladineto-Callunetum and Arctoeto-Callunetum principally by the abundance of *Rhacomitrium lanuginosum* and *Hypnum cupressiforme* and occasionally by a wide variety of oceanic hepatics (lists 5, 6). The lichens *Alectoria ochroleuca* and *Cetraria nivalis* are absent.

The association is markedly western in both the Northern and Central Highlands, and is not found to the east of a line from Ben Clibreck and Ben Wyvis to Ben Alder. Its distribution is therefore complementary to that of the eastern Cladineto-Callunetum (Map 9).

Rhacomitreto-Callunetum has a wider altitudinal range and a lower limit than the other two dwarf Calluneta (1000–2500 ft. or 305–763 m.) but occupies the same range of exposed habitats. It appears to be differentiated from Arctoeto-Callunetum by less extreme exposure, and so tends to replace this association on windswept moraines and shoulders at lower levels. The association nevertheless owes its existence to frequent exposure to gale force winds even at the comparatively low altitude of 1000 ft. (305 m.). It may form extensive stands passing uphill to *Rhacomitrium* heath (Plate 11) and below to various heath and bog communities such as Trichophoreto-Callunetum (p. 106)and Trichophoreto-Eriophoretum (p. 101). With increasing snow cover and associated drainage impedance it often shows a sharp transition to the *Nardus-Trichophorum nodum* (p. 68) or to patches of *Trichophorum, Nardus* and *Juncus squarrosus* on deeper peat.

Soils too are similar to those of the other dwarf Calluneta, ranging from rankers to podsols and grey-brown podsolic types but there is a tendency for less mineral matter to be incorporated in the humus. Raw *Calluna* and *Rhacomitrium* humus may directly overlie large rock fragments, a feature not found in either Cladineto-Callunetum or Arctoeto-Callunetum (cf. Rhacomitreto-Empetrum p. 46). The pH of the surface soil again lies around 4·5.

Rhacomitrium-rich *Calluna-Arctostaphylos* vegetation occurs below the limit of dwarf Callunetum in the North-west Highlands and two lists (14, 15) have been added to Table 17 for comparison with Rhacomitreto-Callunetum. They also exhibit some resemblance to the Arctostaphyleto-Callunetum described on p. 30 and may be an oceanic development of this type.

Corresponding associations have not been described from Iceland, the Faeroes or the Continent.

Vaccinetum chionophilum

(*Vaccinium* snow-bed)

(Table 18)

All the noda described so far occur on ground which is blown clear of snow in winter (chionophobous) or, at least, any accumulating snow soon melts and there is no reduction in the length of the growing season. By contrast the next association, the Vaccinetum chionophilum, owes its existence to the accumulation and persistence of winter snow fall.

There are 8 species in the association element: *Vaccinium myrtillus, Empetrum hermaphroditum, Blechnum spicant, Deschampsia flexuosa, Galium hercynicum, Nardus stricta, Pleurozium schreberi* and *Hylocomium splendens*. The dominants are *Vaccinium myrtillus, V. uliginosum* and *Pleurozium schreberi* while *Dicranum scoparium, Hylocomium splendens* and *Rhytidiadelphus loreus* may come close to co-dominance in the moss mat. *Chamaepericlymenum suecicum* (constancy class III) is selective for this association as well as for the Vaccineto-Callunetum suecicosum (class IV).

There are 85 species listed in the thirteen stands analysed in Table 18, 15–31 species per stand and an average number of 25.

Separate facies have not been distinguished here but the collection of further data should make possible the separation of the *Sphagnum*-rich stands of wetter places from those with a layer of hypnaceous mosses. The association is distinguished floristically from the other dwarf shrub heaths described so far by the near absence of *Calluna*. Apart from the next association and biotically produced *Vaccinium* heaths, the closest relationship seems to be with the Betuletum Oxaleto-Vaccinetum and the *Luzula-Vaccinium* lists of Table 6 (see also Dahl, 1956, p. 132).

Distribution of the Vaccinetum chionophilum is shown in Map 10 to be predominantly Central and Eastern. Except on Ben Wyvis there are only fragmentary stands north of the Great Glen. The altitudinal range of the community is even more restricted, from 1800 ft. to 2500 ft. (549–763 m.) on moderate to steep slopes generally with a northern or eastern aspect.

Stands are not generally extensive and vary in size from a few square metres to one or two hectares. There may be a central patch of the *Nardus-Pleurozium nodum* (p. 67) where snow lies longer, or the *Vaccinium* may give way to the *Nardus-Trichophorum nodum* (p. 68) below, where there is an intermittent flow of melt water (Fig. 4). There may be an intermediate zone of Vaccineto-Empetretum (p. 41) between the Vaccinetum and the surrounding vegetation but the transition may be direct to Callunetum or to Calluneto-Eriophoretum (Fig. 5). In many places stands of Vaccinetum chionophilum appear to have extended, and to be extending still, due to the burning and grazing of

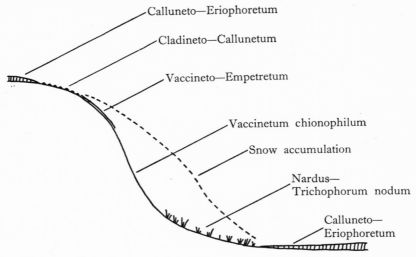

Fig. 4. Relationships between communities of moderately late snow-beds at about 2500 ft. in the East-central Highlands

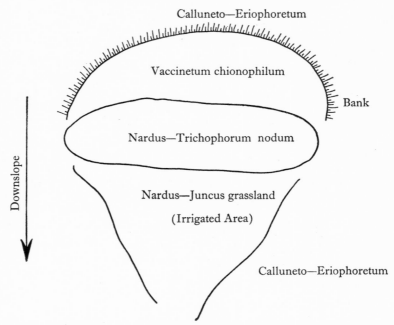

Fig. 5. Snow-bed vegetation in the Cairngorms at about 2400 ft.

surrounding Callunetum. The anthropogenic *Vaccinium* heath lacks many of the chionophilous indicators such as *Blechnum*, *Oxalis* and *Chamaepericlymenum* but it is difficult to tell where the transition lies. Trampled and fouled patches in the *Vaccinium* beds sometimes show where groups of sheep have survived below the winter snow and we suspect that a tendency for *Agrostis-Festuca* grassland to develop in these situations may be due primarily to this. Another unclassified *Vaccinium* heath which may also be anthropogenic in origin, like those of the Welsh and English mountains and Southern Uplands, occurs mainly in the south-east of the Highlands and occupies substantial areas of ground between 2000 and 2500 ft. (locally below 2000 ft.) on the calcareous schists between Glen Shee and Glen Tilt. There is a sharp boundary between the *Vaccinium* heath and Callunetum on the adjacent quartzite although both communities have a raw humus soil, and the change-over may be connected with the higher grazing pressure which the better rocks sustain. The *Vaccinium* heath passes over to *Agrostis-Festuca* and *Nardus* grassland below, and where lateral streams form ridges in the slope, tongues of *Vaccinium* heath descend into the grassland on the summits of the ridges.

Vaccineto-Empetretum
(*Vaccinium-Empetrum* heath)
(Table 19)

The range of communities now distinguished as Vaccineto-Empetretum was included with Vaccinetum chionophilum in the *Vaccinium-Chamaepericlymenum nodum* by Poore and McVean (1957, p. 430). Sixteen lists are presented in Table 19, the constants being *Empetrum hermaphroditum*, *Vaccinium myrtillus*, *Hylocomium splendens*, *Pleurozium schreberi*, *Rhytidiadelphus loreus*, *Ptilidium ciliare* and *Cladonia sylvatica*. There are five other species in constancy class IV and the vegetation may be dominated by *Empetrum*, *Vaccinium myrtillus*, *V. uliginosum*, *Hylocomium splendens* and *Pleurozium schreberi*. *Phyllodoce caerulea* is exclusive to the association but so far it has been recorded only from the one mountain in Atholl.

The number of species recorded is exactly the same as for the Vaccinetum chionophilum but the range is from 10 to 29 with an average of 20. Separate facies have not been distinguished.

The association is distinguished floristically from Vaccinetum chionophilum by the abundance of *Empetrum* and parallel reduction of *Vaccinium* spp., the reduced amount of *Blechnum* and *Chamaepericlymenum* and the increase in *Carex bigelowii*, *Rhacomitrium lanuginosum* and the variety and abundance of hepatics and lichens. From Vaccineto-Callunetum it is distinguished by the virtual absence of *Calluna*, the dominance of *Empetrum* and the increase of *C. bigelowii*. *Listera cordata* is a good differential species, absent in the Vaccineto-Empetretum and of constancy class III in Vaccineto-Callunetum.

The distribution of the association is more widespread in the Central and Northern Highlands than that of Vaccinetum chionophilum (Map 10), but the habitats occupied are similar. The altitudinal range is greater, from 2000 ft. (610 m.) in the Northern Highlands to 3000 ft. (914 m.) in the Central Highlands, on less steep slopes with a greater variety of aspect. Stands of many hectares in area are found in association with large shallow snow-beds in the Central Highlands and smaller stands measurable in square metres occur around Vaccinetum chionophilum in nivation hollows as indicated above. In the North-west Highlands the average size of the stands is much smaller, the association is less dependent on snow cover and is found at lower altitudes where it is usually *Sphagnum* and hepatic-rich. A local facies in the north-west is as rich in hepatics as the best examples of Vaccineto-Callunetum hepaticosum and differs from it mainly in the absence of *Calluna*. It is clearly an altitudinal extension of the Callunetum and is likewise confined to overgrown block screes on north to east-facing corrie slopes (Table 19, lists 1 and 19).

Two lists (17 and 18) of an *Empetrum hermaphroditum*-hypnaceous moss heath have been added to Table 19 for comparison with the Vaccineto-Empetretum. This is a relatively rare vegetation type whose affinities lie also with Rhacomitreto-Empetretum (p. 46). It is northern in distribution and is found as patches in the *Rhacomitrium* heath of summit ridges where the change of moss dominance coincides with the edge of the *Empetrum* mat (see p. 47), or in specially sheltered hollows of Rhacomitreto-Empetretum on boulder slopes.

In the Western Highlands, this association and the last are often replaced by a type in which *Vaccinium* and *Empetrum* share dominance with *Nardus* and *Rhacomitrium* (see p. 70 and Table 19, lists 20 and 21). These mixed communities are often extensive on the higher hills above 2000 ft. and in situations with moderate snow-lie: their approximate distribution is shown in Map 10.

The soils of this and the last association are similar and consist either of deep, wet, raw humus (up to 50 cm.) resting directly on stony detritus and boulders or well developed podsols which may shows signs of mottling in the B. horizons. The humus may contain mineral particles almost to the surface but is usually purely organic in composition. Thin raw humus over stones is found only in the Vaccineto-Empetretum and one profile (M56071, Table 12) consisted of a moss mat and thin skin of peat (5 cm.) over a deep undifferentiated mudstone soil. The soils of the Vaccinetum chionophilum tend to be drier and with more typical podsols, as in the following example (M56123, Table 18):

0–7·5 cm.	. .	undecomposed moss
7·5–15 cm.	. .	black silty peat
15–16·5 cm.	. .	compact grey silt
16·5–29 cm.	. .	reddish-yellow compact silty clay with stones.

Only one of these two associations has already been described from Scotland. Both the typical and mossy facies of the Empetreto-Vaccinetum of Burges (1951) seem to belong to our Vaccineto-Empetretum although the more lichen-rich stands from high levels might be more appropriately referred to the Cladineto-Vaccinetum empetrosum (p. 43). Part of the Highland Vaccinieta described by R. Smith in Tansley (1949) might be Vaccinetum chionophilum. To the south of the Highlands, Vaccinetum chionophilum has been found only in rather small patches on the highest hills in the central part of the Southern Uplands. This district would appear to be the southern British limit for the occurrence of snow-influenced vegetation. Communities agreeing with Vaccineto-Empetretum are more widespread, occurring locally in the Southern Uplands, Lakeland and Snowdonia, but they usually merge imperceptibly into biotically derived *Vaccinium* heaths, and in places are indistinguishable.

Many similar communities have been described from Scandinavia. Dahl (1956, p. 117) says that his Phyllodoco-Vaccinetum myrtilli (Myrtilletum) is one of the most characteristic communities of Rondane (central Norway) and covers appreciable areas. It compares most closely with the drier, lichen-rich lists of the Vaccinetum chionophilum. On the other hand Nordhagen (1943, p. 133) lists an oceanic *Vaccinium myrtillus* heath with *Chamaepericlymenum* and *Hylocomium* from Myrdal in western Norway which has 24 species and four constants in common with the Vaccinetum chionophilum and 21 species and three constants in common with the Vaccineto-Empetretum. There is also a close resemblance between the Vaccinetum chionophilum and the *Vaccinium myrtillus*-rich birchwoods of Sylene (Nordhagen, 1927, p. 112), particularly the *Chamaepericly-menum* variant.

Cladineto-Vaccinetum

(Lichen-rich *Vaccinium* heath)
(Table 20)

Another *Vaccinium myrtillus* association of somewhat similar distribution to the Vaccinetum chionophilum is the Cladineto-Vaccinetum.

In this case the association element consists of the 11 species *Vaccinium myrtillus*, *Empetrum hermaphroditum*, *Deschampsia flexuosa*, *Carex bigelowii*, *Rhacomitrium lanuginosum*, *Cetraria islandica*, *Cladonia gracilis*, *C. rangiferina*, *C. sylvatica*, *C. uncialis*, and *Ochrolechia frigida*. *V. myrtillus*, *E. hermaphroditum*, *C. rangiferina*, and *C. sylvatica* may each attain dominance or co-dominance. There are no characteristic species and the species list is a short one, with 52 recorded from the 23 lists, a range of 12–25 species per list and an average of 19.

Three facies have been distinguished: typicum (lists 11–16) which is lichen-rich but not lichen-dominated, sylvaticosum (lists 1–10) which is dominated by the lichens *Cladonia sylvatica* and *C. rangiferina*, and empetrosum (lists 17–23) which is lichen-rich but dominated by *Empetrum hermaphroditum*.

The association as a whole is distinguished from Vaccineto-Empetretum by the prominence of *Cladonia* spp. combined with scarcity of the hypnaceous mosses. Some lichen-rich lists of Vaccineto-Empetretum come very close to the empetrosum facies of Cladineto-Vaccinetum (e.g. list 8, Table 19) but these always have considerable quantities of *Pleurozium schreberi* or *Rhytidiadelphus loreus* in addition. The floristic differences from Festuceto-Vaccinetum are described under that association on p. 45. Lists 12 and 15 of Table 20 show features intermediate between the present association and the Dicraneto-Caricetum bigelowii (p. 73) but this difficulty is only encountered in the Clova area.

The distribution of the three facies is shown in Map 11 and it can be seen that while all are East-central the typicum has a more western spread than the other two. The typicum and sylvaticosum facies range from 2300 ft. (702 m.) to 3150 ft. (960 m.) on level to moderately sloping ground of any aspect on the tops of spurs and ridges while most of the stands of the empetrosum are rather higher, all but two lying above 3000 ft. and one reaching a height of 3700 ft. (1129 m.).

The stands of this association are seldom large although the typicum occupies an area of many hectares on the south-west facing slopes of Meall Odhar (Loch Lochy) between 2500 and 2800 ft., and again in Clova and on the White Mounth at about 3000 ft. It is more usual to find a mosaic of Cladineto-Vaccinetum with Cladineto-Callunetum or Dicraneto-Caricetum bigelowii, the individual patches ranging from a few square metres to hundreds of square metres in size. Patches of *Pleurozium*-rich Vaccineto-Empetretum often occur within it. We do not have measurements or direct observations of the regime of snow-cover characteristic of the association but this can sometimes be guessed from its field relationships. In the area between Beinn a' Ghlo and the Cairnwell, and in the Cairngorms, the community can be seen forming a zone between chionophilous *Nardus* communities and Cladineto-Callunetum, which is the expected position if it is to be regarded as an upward extension of Vaccinetum chiono-philum and Vaccineto-Empetretum. At other times snow-lie would appear to be identical with that of Cladineto-Callunetum particularly where the lichenosum facies of both associations are involved. Uphill, or on more exposed ground, the association passes to *Rhacomitrium* heath.

The lichenosum facies of Cladineto-Vaccinetum is a true lichen heath and in it the dominance of lichens over dwarf shrubs is generally more complete than in the other lichen heath, Cladineto-Callunetum lichenosum. *Vaccinium* spp. and *Empetrum herma-phroditum* are seldom vigorous even in the typicum, and *Deschampsia flexuosa* and *Carex bigelowii* are physiognomically as prominent.

The empetrosum on the other hand forms a dense springy shrub and lichen mat up to 10 cm. deep, often in the sheltered angle of a soli fluction lobeor among large boulders. It was at first regarded as a lichen-rich facies of Vaccineto-Empetretum but has since been found to have greater floristic affinities with Cladineto-Vaccinetum, into which it passes abruptly through loss of *Empetrum*.

The soils are podsolic, occasionally with a distinct A_2 horizon but more often having a combined A horizon of black or grey sandy peat. The following profile (R57280) is typical:

0–2·5 cm.	.	.	black humus
2·5–4 cm.	.	.	dark grey, sandy, micaceous loam
4–16 cm.	.	.	dark brown sandy, micaceous loam.

The pH of the A horizon varies from 3·7 to 4·3.

The cladinosum and empetrosum facies of the association are confined to the Highlands, but patchy and rather grassy stands corresponding to Cladineto-Vaccinetum typicum have been observed on the Dollar Law range in the Southern Uplands and on Skiddaw in Lakeland. A similar type of vegetation occurs on the northern part of the Cross Fell range in the Pennines but is distinguished by patchy dominance of lichens and by an unusual abundance of *Cetraria islandica*.

The *Cladonia sylvatica*-rich *Vaccinium myrtillus* association of Sylene (Nordhagen 1927, p. 224) has 27 species in common with the Cladineto-Vaccinetum and seven of these are constants. There is thus a close floristic resemblance between the two although *Vaccinium* is more vigorous in the Norwegian association. The Norwegian soil profiles are also similar with a better development of the A_2 and surface humus (pH 4·1–4·2). They have a reliable winter snow cover melting comparatively late in the season. The empetrosum facies compares better with Nordhagen's *C. sylvatica*-rich *Empetrum* association (loc. cit. p. 210) which is also floristically close to his *Empetrum*-rich birch-woods (loc. cit. pp. 102, 107). The Norwegian *Empetrum* heaths have a thinner winter snow-cover than the *Vaccinium* heaths and melt out sooner in spring but the snow cover is fairly reliable. Knaben (1950, pp. 69–71) describes similar *Empetrum*-lichen heaths from Middle Sogn and ascribes their brown and withered appearance on crag tops in 1942 to a deficiency of snow in the previous winter.

In general the continental *Vaccinium* heath of Norway combines the floristics of the present association with the physiognomy and snow regime of our Vaccinetum chiono-philum.

Festuceto-Vaccinetum

(*Alchemilla*-rich *Festuca-Vaccinium* heath)

(Table 21)

Poore (1955b, p. 639) has already described a lichen-rich *Vaccinium-Festuca* association from Ben Lawers and Carn Mairg which forms the basis of our next association, the Festuceto-Vaccinetum.

There are eleven constants: *Vaccinium myrtillus, V. vitis-idaea, Festuca ovina, Carex bigelowii, Alchemilla alpina, Galium hercynicum, Pleurozium schreberi, Rhacomitrium lanuginosum, Ptilidium ciliare, Cladonia sylvatica* and *C. uncialis*. There is a wide variety of possible dominants: the most common being *Vaccinium myrtillus, Festuca ovina, Alchemilla alpina, Pleurozium schreberi, Rhacomitrium lanuginosum* and *Cladonia sylvatica* with *Carex bigelowii* and *Nardus stricta* attaining co-dominance in one or two lists. There are no characteristic species.

The association is floristically richer than the closely related Cladineto-Vaccinetum and 82 species have been recorded in the 24 stands in Table 21 with numbers ranging from 16–33 per stand (average of 25).

Two facies have been distinguished—cladinosum which is rich in lichens and rather poor in herbs and mosses, and rhacomitrosum which may be dominated by *Rhacomitrium lanuginosum* or hypnaceous mosses, especially *Pleurozium schreberi*, and which is richer in herbs and grasses and poorer in lichens than the first. Other differences in constancy will be noted in the table. A further division of the cladinosum could be made according to whether the dominant vascular species is *Vaccinium myrtillus* or *Alchemilla alpina*.

The association as a whole is distinguished from the Cladineto-Vaccinetum by the presence of *Alchemilla alpina* and the abundance of grasses, especially *Festuca ovina*. *Vaccinium myrtillus* is more abundant and vigorous, lichens are generally less important, and mosses, especially *Pleurozium schreberi* and *Rhacomitrium lanuginosum* play a more important role. From Vaccineto-Empetretum the association is distinguished by the scarcity of *Empetrum*, the absence of species of moist habitats such as *Sphagna* and *Oxalis*, and the abundance of grasses and *Alchemilla alpina*.

The distribution of the two facies of the association is shown in Map 12 and it can be seen that in the Central and South-west Highlands the occurrences of the cladinosum facies closely follow the line of the Dalradian limestones. This is in accordance with the observation that where limestone or calcareous schist is in juxtaposition with quartzite the Festuceto-Vaccinetum cladinosum is found on the calcareous rock, replacing Vaccineto-Empetretum or Cladineto-Vaccinetum on the siliceous rock. A particularly sharp transition of this kind can be seen on the summit ridge of Carn a'Chlarsaich to the south-west of the Cairnwell. Festuceto-Vaccinetum is completely replaced by the other Vaccineta on the Cairngorm granite.

The rhacomitrosum facies has a more western distribution and, apart from a few fragments of the cladinosum, is the only facies represented to the north of the Great Glen. It is not obviously associated with calcareous rocks and often occurs extensively on the higher Torridon sandstone hills.

In altitude the association ranges from 2400 ft. (732 m.) to 3500 ft. (1068 m.) but the cladinosum facies has not been recorded from over 2900 ft. (885 m.). In aspect too the cladinosum appears to be more restricted to moderately steep southern to eastern slopes while the rhacomitrosum is largely indifferent. Dominance of hypnaceous mosses is usually associated with some degree of shade or shelter and a north to east aspect, suggesting prolonged snow-cover as a controlling influence. In many places both facies of the association may be quite natural but some stands, especially those below 3000 ft. may have been derived from other vegetation types by burning and grazing. These examples at lower levels are very similar to the mixed *Vaccinium*-grass heaths common and obviously biotically derived in Southern Scotland, Northern England and Wales, so that their frequent restriction to good soils could be due partly to selective exploitation (see p. 66).

Stands may be quite extensive, especially on the Breadalbane hills, but there is often a lack of homogeneity and transitions to *Rhacomitrium* heath, *Alchemilla*-rich grasslands, *Vaccinium-Empetrum* heaths and Dicraneto-Caricetum bigelowii (p. 73) are frequent.

Soils are typically brownish-black peaty loams 10–30 cm. deep, micaceous or with a high silt and sand content. Podsolisation is well masked in the A horizons but occasional reddish-brown colorations below this indicate that some leaching has taken place. Recorded pH of surface soil varies from 3·8 to 4·8.

Poore (1955b, p. 641) has already pointed out that this association corresponds in part to the Arctic-alpine grassland of W. G. Smith (Tansley, 1949) but his comparison with the *Empetrum-Vaccinium* zone of the Cairngorms is now unnecessary. The Cladineto-Vaccinetum corresponds more closely to Nordhagen's *Cladonia sylvatica*-rich *Vaccinium myrtillus* association (p. 44) than does the present association which, as Poore points out, compares better with Nordhagen's *Alchemilla alpina*-rich *Vaccinium myrtillus* heath. The Festuceto-Vaccinetum also has a certain amount in common with the *Festuca ovina-Cladonia sylvatica* sociation of Sikilsdalen (Nordhagen, 1943, p. 193), particularly in physiognomy.

Rhacomitreto-Empetretum

(*Rhacomitrium-Empetrum* heath)

(Table 22)

The last of the acidophilous dwarf shrub noda to be considered here, the Rhacomitreto-Empetretum is a rather unsatisfactory one since it lacks sharp delimitations from *Rhacomitrium* heath and is floristically similar. The association might well be considered a facies of Cariceto-Rhacomitretum lanuginosi were it not that well developed stands have certain consistent differences from the moss heath (p. 89).

There are 8 species in the association element: *Empetrum hermaphroditum, Vaccinium myrtillus, Carex bigelowii, Rhacomitrium lanuginosum, Cetraria islandica, Cladonia gracilis, C. sylvatica* and *C. uncialis. Empetrum hermaphroditum, Rhacomitrium lanuginosum* and *Juncus trifidus* are the possible dominants. There are no characteristic species.

Only 71 species have been recorded from the eleven stands of Table 22, numbers per stand ranging from 17 to 35 with an average of 23.

Separate facies have not been distinguished since the lists with *Juncus trifidus* have no other differences in common. Floristically the association is distinguished from *Vaccinium-Empetrum* heath and from Cladineto-Vaccinetum empetrosum by the dominance of *Rhacomitrium* coupled with low values for lichens and hypnaceous mosses. Lists 17 and 18 of Table 19 have been repeated here as lists 12, 13 (Table 22) to show how the various communities are floristically linked. While it has already been noted (p. 42) that a change in moss dominance may take place at the edge of the *Empetrum* mat the very existence of the present association shows that this is not necessarily so.

The association is constant and widespread throughout the Highlands from 2200 ft. (671 m.) to 3600 ft. (1098 m.) but it has its distribution centre in the North-west, where it may occupy substantial areas (Map 13). There are two main habitats:

1. On steep block scree, bedrock or summit block detritus with undeveloped soil
   and
2. On level or gently sloping ridges and summits where it generally occurs below
   true *Rhacomitrium* heath and sometimes in mosaic with it.

It may also occur at lower levels in the north-west on rock ledges or among isolated boulder fields where north exposures may give a wide variety of oceanic liverworts. Aspect appears to be unimportant to distribution.

Rhacomitreto-Empetretum may pass abruptly to *Rhacomitrium* heath especially where a litter of boulders or angular detritus gives way to smooth ground. Slight hollows may contain the *Empetrum*-hypnaceous moss community, although this is generally found only in association with Cariceto-Rhacomitretum, and where the topography encourages larger amounts of snow accumulation *Nardus* communities take over. There is frequently a gradual transition to Vaccineto-Empetretum downslope as shelter and moisture encourage *Vaccinium* and hypnaceous mosses at the expense of the *Rhacomitrium*.

The soils are rankers with damp and greasy raw humus resting directly on angular fragments of siliceous rocks or they are shallow, well-developed podsols. Buried humus horizons are sometimes encountered. The following is a typical profile:

M55046

0–5 cm.	. .	undecomposed *Rhacomitrium*
5–7 cm.	. .	black, greasy peat
7–14 cm.	. .	white sand with peaty patches
>14 cm.	. .	sandy colluvial debris of Torridon sandstone slightly ferruginous above.

This association has been developed from the *Empetrum hermaphroditum* facies of the *Rhacomitrium-Carex nodum* of Poore and McVean (1957). No comparable vegetation has been described from Norway but Steindorsson (1951) lists several sociations containing *E. hermaphroditum* under the Icelandic *Rhacomitrium* heath. Wace and Holdgate (1958, p. 610) describe heaths of *Empetrum rubrum* and *R. lanuginosum* from 3000–5000 ft. (914–1524 m.) on Tristan da Cunha.

Dryas octopetala *noda*

(*Dryas* heaths)
(Table 23)

Calcicolous dwarf shrub heath is rare and fragmentary in Scotland but since Poore and McVean (1957) listed a number of *Dryas* heaths from shell sand and coastal limestone in Sutherland further localities have been examined and a greater wealth of data is available for discussion. All are essentially heaths of *Dryas octopetala* and the floristic lists have been presented together in Table 23.

The fragments of three overlapping noda can now be distinguished:

    i. *Dryas-Salix reticulata* (lists 1–6)
    ii. *Dryas-Carex rupestris* (lists 7–12)
    iii. *Dryas-Carex flacca* (lists 13–18)

but each is too sparsely represented to warrant any discussion of separate constants and characteristic species. *Rhytidium rugosum* is, however, exclusive to the *Dryas* heaths as a whole. The 20 lists contain 215 species in all with an extremely wide range of species per stand (16–65, average 38). The *Dryas-Salix reticulata* stands are the most consistently species-rich.

The cliff ledge fragments of *Dryas* communities are the most difficult to classify. Those in Caenlochan Glen, for instance, show affinities with all three noda in that *Carex rupestris*, *C. flacca* or *Salix reticulata* may be closely associated with *Dryas*: yet from their floristic similarity there would be good grounds for uniting all these particular fragments under a single nodum. In part the difficulty is due to the smallness and heterogeneity of the stands. Even where the ledges are large, dominance of *Dryas* is usually patchy, so that the shrub tends to occur in mosaic with herbaceous species, and where the ground is broken there is typically an admixture of chomophytic or rupestral species. Other patches of *Dryas* heath have been found which did not fit well into any of the three noda and these have been indicated as an unclassified type in Map 14.

Map 14 shows that the three provisional noda have rather different distribution patterns, the first being confined to the edges, ledges and inclined faces of mountain cliffs from 2300 ft. (702 m.) to 3000 ft. (914 m.) mainly in the Breadalbane and Clova districts but with an outlier on Seana Bhraigh in Ross-shire (Plate 12); the second having its well developed stands confined to outcrops of the Durness dolomite from near sea level on the north coast to 1700 ft. (519 m.) in the foothills of Ben More Assynt and the third occurring mainly on coastal shell sand but also on coastal limestone and on calcareous rocks in a few inland stations. Stands of the first nodum are measurable in square metres but the other two (lists 7, 11, 12, 13, 14, 15) often occur over areas of one or two hectares.

List 11 is rather different from all the others and could be described as a *Dryas-Empetrum hermaphroditum* heath, a type which is also found in Iceland (Steindorsson, 1951). It forms a level sward above a rotten and eroding sugar limestone outcrop and passes quickly into a rich *Vaccinium-Empetrum* grass heath away from the outcrop (Fig. 6).

On unprotected sites *Dryas* heath generally gives way to herb-rich grassland or to dwarf herb vegetation, the dwarf shrubs being quickly eliminated by the intense grazing pressure that such fertile sites endure. List 6 of Table 23 and list 3 of Table 40 are from the same locality and show this process at work.

On suitable soils *Dryas* heaths are likely to have covered wider areas before the advent of sheep-farming, but the limited distribution of the species even in ungrazed places suggests that they have never been extensive in the Highlands during the recent past. *Dryas* in Britain appears to need highly calcareous substrata and it has a predilection for dry or at least well-drained sites; the combination of these conditions occurs

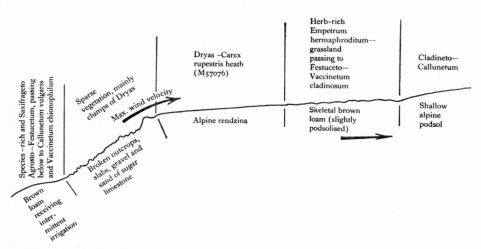

Fig. 6. Relationships between eutrophic and oligotrophic dwarf shrub heath. The Cairnwell, Perthshire, at 2750 ft.

The vegetational gradient accompanies declining calcium status of the soil away from the eroding limestone edge, due partly to reduction in the amount of wind-blown limestone sand. The sequence suggests that *Dryas* heath is the counterpart of dwarf *Calluna* heath on strongly exposed, well drained ground where the soil is calcareous.

only locally. Although *Dryas* heaths may have been widespread in parts of the British Isles during the Late-glacial Period (Godwin, 1956) there is no evidence yet to show that they were ever present on non-calcareous mountains of the Highlands. Even within their probable Highland headquarters, the dwarf shrub zone of calcareous areas, the gradual leaching of soils under a wet climate is likely to have caused a considerable restriction of suitable habitats within the Post-glacial Period. The same probably applies to *Salix reticulata*, *Carex rupestris* and other strongly calcicolous montane species of dry soils.

Soils are rendzina-like (cf. Brown Rendzina of Kubiena, 1953, p. 188) or moist loams owing their high calcium content to irrigation from calcareous rock close at hand. The dry limestone or dolomite soils are usually bright red loams whose pedology has not yet been investigated. Number M57076 is one of the few stands examined under which there was a distinct profile development:

Alpine Rendzina

0–8 cm.	.	.	dark brownish-black sandy loam
8–14 cm.	.	.	light brown sandy loam
14–24 cm.	.	.	dark brown sandy loam
24–34 cm.	.	.	reddish-brown, sandy loam
			white sandy, disintegrating sugar limestone.

The pH of the surface soil was 7·5. Other pH values determined for the noda range from 6·8 to 7·8.

The *Dryas-Salix reticulata* provisional *nodum* belongs without question to the species-rich *Dryas* association of Nordhagen (1927, p. 242). Besides the two dwarf shrubs they have a number of species in common including *Astragalus alpinus*, *Bartsia alpina*, *Carex rupestris*, *C. atrata*, *C. capillaris* and *Solorina saccata*. Table 23 has 48 species in common with Nordhagen's table (loc. cit. p. 243). The range of intermediates from the *Dryas-Salix reticulata nodum* to the *Dryas-Carex flacca nodum* establishes the claim made by Poore and McVean (1957) that the coastal *Dryas* heaths of Scotland belong to the alliance Kobresio-Dryadion. The last *nodum* seems to be similar to the extensive *Dryas* heaths of the Burren district in western Ireland (Praeger, 1909).

Also referable to the Kobresio-Dryadion is a fairly extensive *Arctostaphylos*-grass heath recorded from the Blair Atholl limestone at Edintian, Perthshire (Fig. 8, p. 56). The heath occupies the level tops of limestone ridges at 1300 ft. (397 m.) where the soil consists of 10 cm. of brown calcareous loam (pH 7·9) over sugar limestone debris. Between the ridges various types of Calluneta grow on deeper leached soil and a sample from below a nearby stand of Arctostaphyleto-Callunetum gave a pH of 4·9.

List from 4 m²

Arctostaphylos uva-ursi	7	Dicranum scoparium	2
Helianthemum chamaecistus	2	Ditrichum flexicaule	1
Thymus drucei	3	Hypnum cupressiforme	2
Vaccinium vitis-idaea	+	Rhacomitrium lanuginosum	1
		Rhytidium rugosum	3
Agrostis canina	1	Tortella tortuosa	1
Briza media	3		
Festuca ovina	4	Cladonia impexa	1
Helictotrichon pratense	3		
Koeleria gracilis	2		
Carex flacca	2		
Anthyllis vulneraria	+		
Campanula rotundifolia	2		
Galium verum	2		
Linum catharticum	1		
Plantago lanceolata	1		
Senecio jacobaea	+		
Taraxacum officinalis agg.	1		

This is exposed ground but it is likely that scrub growth during the Post-glacial Climatic Optimum eliminated *Dryas* and other montane species, which subsequently failed to recolonise the site. It seems probable that *Arctostaphylos* is a life-form replacement of *Dryas* here, and the situation should be compared with the survival of *Dryas* heath at 1700 ft. (519 m.) on Cronkley Fell in Yorkshire (cf. Pigott, 1956). The Cronkley fragment of *Dryas* heath on sugar limestone is strikingly similar in general appearance and habitat to that on the Cairnwell. Praeger (1909) records *Arctostaphylos* communities along with *Dryas* heaths on the coastal limestones of County Clare in Western Ireland, but in Scotland *Arctostaphylos* is normally a plant of non-calcareous substrata.

Chapter 4

GRASS HEATHS

In mountain country with vegetation unmodified by man, grass heaths belong mainly to a zone lying above the dwarf shrub heaths, the Middle-alpine zone of Du Rietz and Nordhagen. Grass heaths extend to the limit of vascular plant growth and are replaced beyond this by open communities of bryophytes and lichens. In Scotland grass heaths and grasslands are found at all levels from the Forest zone to the highest summits but apart from maritime swards all those lying below about 2500 ft. (763 m.) are evidently anthropogenic in origin.

The term grass heath is here used in the wide sense to include vegetation dominated by sedges and rushes as well as by the Gramineae.

The anthropogenic grasslands and their relationships to forest and dwarf shrub heaths will be considered first. Within the Forest and Sub-alpine zones some grasslands are recognisable as derivatives of the original woodland and scrub layers but with the herbs suppressed by grazing in favour of the grasses. Human activities have also produced other types of grassland which show little or no affinity with any known field layer.

Economically the grasslands are probably the most important of the main groups of Highland vegetation at the present day.

The whole complex shows two main directions of variation. First there is a series which reflects differences in soil moisture and secondly, at each level of soil moisture, floristic richness varies according to the base status of the soil. Within the complex, dry soils are occupied by *Agrostis-Festuca* grasslands, wetter soils by *Nardus stricta* grasslands and the wettest soils by *Juncus squarrosus* communities. Each of these groups has species-rich and species-poor types on base-rich and base-deficient soils respectively.

The *Agrostis-Festuca* grasslands have been most closely studied and from the many analyses it has been possible to separate four distinct types each with the status of an association. The *Nardus* and *Juncus squarrosus* grass heaths have received less attention and, although the separation into species-rich and species-poor groups is clear, these can at present rank only as facies.

The *Deschampsia caespitosa* grasslands do not fit easily into the above scheme as they are evidently influenced by late snow-lie and are not wholly anthropogenic in origin but, again, a sub-division into species-poor and species-rich facies of the one association can be made.

These relationships are summarised in Fig. 9, p. 56

ANTHROPOGENIC GRASS HEATHS

Species-poor Agrosto-Festucetum

(*Agrostis-Festuca* acidic grassland)

(Table 24)

The species-poor Agrosto-Festucetum has the constants *Agrostis canina, A. tenuis, Anthoxanthum odoratum, Festuca ovina* agg., *Galium hercynicum, Potentilla erecta, Viola riviniana, Rhytidiadelphus squarrosus* and *Hylocomium splendens*. The four grasses usually share dominance but *A. tenuis* tends to have the highest cover. Other abundant species include *Nardus stricta, Carex pilulifera, Luzula campestris, L. multiflora, Pleurozium schreberi* and *Thuidium tamariscinum*.

The vegetation usually consists of a close-cropped sward less than 10 cm. high but it grows much taller if grazing is light. Some stands are particularly rich in hypnaceous mosses and there are usually numerous dwarfed shoots of *Vaccinium myrtillus*, but despite certain other floristic similarities they differ ecologically from stands of Festuceto-Vaccinetum, which are usually richer in lichens (p. 45).

This is a widespread type of grassland in the Highlands but is found most extensively in the relatively dry south and east. In the Western and Northern Highlands suitable soils occur mainly on well-drained alluvial flats beside the larger streams or on steep slopes receiving intermittent irrigation with water of low base-status. These stands rarely exceed a few hundred sq. m. in any one place, but in the south the association often covers many hectares of the steeper hillsides.

The altitudinal range is from 100 to 2700 ft. (30–824 m.) and so the association belongs chiefly to the potential forest zone. Patches of a similar grassland often occur up to and above 3000 ft. (914 m.), where they are mixed with high altitude noda and less obviously owe their origin to biotic influences.

The soils are dry, base-deficient, brown podsolic loams with moder humus. There is often a shallow raw humus layer and where the slope is gentle there may be a further differentiation into A_2 and B horizons. More usually the slope is too steep for this and the soils remain skeletal and show a characteristic orange-brown colour similar to podsolic B horizons ('truncated podsol' of Robinson, 1949). Podsolisation is less apparent on the periodically irrigated sites where the rate of leaching is evidently balanced by that of enrichment. The association occurs on a wide variety of rocks but has not been seen on the very poorest such as quartzite.

Many accounts of the species-poor Agrosto-Festucetum appear in the British literature, for this is one of the most important pasture types of rough grazings in the Southern Uplands, Northern England and Wales. Although essentially the same as the Highland association the equivalent communities of the southern hills tend to be richer in *Festuca* than *Agrostis* spp. and this probably represents the effect of a longer grazing history.

As soils become wetter with decreasing slope there is usually a change to Nardetum sub-alpinum (p. 58) but in the north and west the association generally passes on non-irrigated or more stable ground to some form of *Calluna* heath or even blanket bog.

Alchemilleto-Agrosto-Festucetum
(*Alchemilla*-rich *Agrostis-Festuca* grassland)
(Table 25)

The next grassland association, Alchemilleto-Agrosto-Festucetum has the same constants as species-poor Agrosto-Festucetum except that *Agrostis canina* and *Potentilla
erecta* are exchanged for *Alchemilla alpina*, *Thymus drucei* and *Pleurozium schreberi*. It
differs most markedly in floristic richness with an average of 34 species per stand instead
of 25. *Festuca ovina* tends to have a higher cover than *Agrostis tenuis* but *Alchemilla
alpina* is usually the most abundant plant and thereby gives the vegetation its distinctive
appearance. *Thymus drucei* also has a moderate cover and species indicative of better
base-status such as *Selaginella selaginoides*, *Campanula rotundifolia*, *Ranunculus acris* and
Thalictrum alpinum are typically present. The grasses again form a short sward in which
a few badly developed shoots of *Vaccinium myrtillus* sometimes occur (Plate 13).

Lists 15–19 are stands of a *Rhacomitrium*-rich facies which is floristically poorer than
Alchemilleto-Agrosto-Festucetum but probably closer to it than to species-poor Agrosto-
Festucetum in view of the abundant *Alchemilla alpina*. It also has affinities to the rhacomi-
trosum facies of Festuceto-Vaccinetum.

The lists of Alchemilleto-Agrosto-Festucetum are from widely separated parts of the
Highlands but the association has its headquarters on the calcareous mica-schist mountains between Breadalbane and Clova. The *Vaccinium-Alchemilla* grassland *nodum*
which Poore (unpublished) recognised provisionally on Ben Lawers agrees closely with
our own association and we have incorporated one of Poore's lists in Table 25. On these
calcareous schists, where even the unirrigated, steeper slopes have fairly base-rich soils,
the *Alchemilla* grassland is often extensive and stands of a hectare or more occur on the
upper slopes of Ben Lawers and its neighbours. Elsewhere it occurs mainly in small
patches on well-drained sites receiving intermittent irrigation from moderately calcareous
rocks. In Drumochter it forms a distinct but narrow zone on the alluvial banks of the
stream draining Coire Chuirn (Fig. 7).

The association occurs from 1100 ft. (336 m.) to 3300 ft. (1007 m.) on slopes of up
to 45 degrees and shows no preference for aspect. The soils are rather shallow, brown

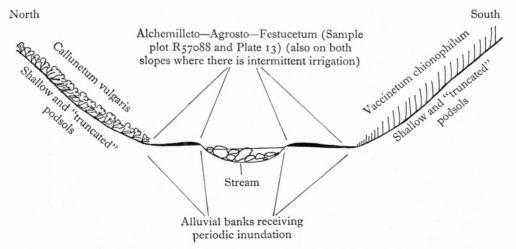

Fig. 7. Irrigation effects amongst oligotrophic vegetation. Coire Chuirn, Drumochter, at 2000 ft.

to dark brown silty loams, loose textured and stony, and they are developed on alluvium, colluvium or scree. Humus tends towards mull rather than moder and although the humus content of the upper 10–15 cm. is variable there is never any tendency for raw humus accumulation. Incipient podsolisation has been detected in one or two profiles, but calcium status is usually moderate and pH values range from 5·3 to 6·0.

The *Rhacomitrium*-rich facies is widespread in the Western Highlands on similar soils but occurs mainly above 2500 ft. (763 m.) and in rather small patches except on steep upper slopes of Torridon sandstone mountains.

At low levels Alchemilleto-Agrosto-Festucetum may occur as patches within almost any of the dwarf shrub heaths or acidic grasslands of dry to moderately wet podsolic soils. Above 2500 ft. (763 m.) it is usually associated with one of the Vaccineta on poorer soils and passes into the Dwarf Herb *nodum* on ground where enrichment by intermittent irrigation is stronger. The sub-montane stands clearly have an anthropogenic origin and Poore believes that even the highest-lying examples on Ben Lawers may have been derived from other dwarf shrub or herb-rich communities by grazing.

As Poore points out this association corresponds largely to the Arctic-alpine grassland of W. G. Smith in Tansley (1949). Sizeable patches of an identical *Alchemilla* grassland occur locally on similar soils in the Lake District but nowhere else in Britain. In Lakeland this vegetation is evidently stable under a heavy grazing regime and so does not seem to be related serally to other *Agrostis-Festuca* grasslands.

Species-rich Agrosto-Festucetum
(*Agrostis-Festuca* basic grassland)
(Table 26, lists 1–16)

Saxifrageto-Agrosto-Festucetum
(*Saxifraga aizoides*-rich *Agrostis-Festuca* grassland)
(Table 26, lists 17–28)

The last two associations of the *Agrostis-Festuca* group are best treated together. They are species-rich Agrosto-Festucetum and Saxifrageto-Agrosto-Festucetum. These two are less distinct from each other than they are from Alchemilleto-Agrosto-Festucetum and could be regarded as a single nodum. Together they form a completely inter-grading series but, as it is possible to select two groups with different constants and with some differential species, we have recognised these as separate associations. Only a few of the many lists have had to be discarded in order to do this.

The constants common to both associations are *Festuca ovina* agg., *Prunella vulgaris*, *Ranunculus acris* and *Thymus drucei*. Those belonging only to species-rich Agrosto-Festucetum are *Agrostis tenuis*, *Anthoxanthum odoratum*, *Festuca rubra*, *Hylocomium splendens* and *Rhytidiadelphus squarrosus* and those peculiar to Saxifrageto-Agrosto-Festucetum are *Selaginella selaginoides*, *Agrostis canina*, *Carex panicea*, *C. pulicaris*, *Linum catharticum*, *Polygonum viviparum*, *Saxifraga aizoides*, *Viola riviniana* and *Ctenidium molluscum*. Most of the species which are constants for only one association also occur abundantly (class III–IV) in the other, but *Selaginella*, *Carex panicea* and *Saxifraga aizoides* are good differential constants for the second.

Agrostis spp. and *Festuca ovina* agg. again have the consistently highest cover but there are more species of sedge and other grasses than in the first two Agrosto-Festuceta and the vegetation is characterised by a profusion of basiphilous herbs and bryophytes. Both associations appear as a close grazed sward less than 10 cm. high but some of the herbs are dwarfed forms of species which are tall and robust when ungrazed, e.g. *Alchemilla glabra, A. vestita, Rumex acetosa* and *Trollius europaeus.* Both are extremely rich floristically with species totals of 179 and 153 and averages of 43 and 44 per stand respectively. *Helianthemum chamaecistus* and *Carex caryophyllea* are the only characteristic species in either and most of the other species have a wide distribution in other noda.

The two associations may be regarded as low-level equivalents of the Dwarf Herb *nodum.* The main difference is that montane species, especially *Silene acaulis*, are fewer and grasses have a higher cover in the two grasslands.

Species-rich Agrosto-Festucetum is just as widely distributed in the Highlands as the species-poor association (Map 15) but its stands are seldom as extensive. Its distribution is almost co-extensive with that of calcareous rock and so is represented quite well by Fig. 30., p. 167. This is a sub-montane grassland occurring between 300 ft. and 2300 ft. (91–702 m.) on ground which varies from level to steeply sloping and on all aspects it occupies sites which are enriched by intermittent irrigation from calcareous rocks or steep slopes where the parent material is so calcareous that a high calcium status is maintained merely by soil instability. It therefore occurs most extensively on hills where such rocks predominate but even here individual stands rarely exceed one hectare. In most places it is evidently the biotic derivative of herb-rich communities of former woodland and scrub, but some extensive stands on limestone at Durness have been derived from *Dryas* heath. Soils are rather similar to those of the previous association, being mostly light to dark brown silty loams with mull humus and a good crumb structure and containing earthworms and sometimes moles. Although the upper few centimetres may be dark and humus-rich there is no raw humus formation and signs of podsolisation are rarely present. The parent material is either a glacial drift or colluvium and the soils are shallow and rather stony. The pH of the surface soil ranges from 5·3 to 7·2.

Like the last association the species-rich Agrosto-Festucetum may occur amongst any of the sub-montane associations of fairly well-drained ground. It is a widespread and economically important type outside the Highlands under comparable edaphic conditions, and is frequently mentioned in the literature but under a variety of names. The dry limestone grasslands of Northern England are essentially the same with slight floristic differences such as local abundance of *Sesleria caerulea* and *Minuartia verna.* Tansley (1949) gives floristic lists of such grasslands for various localities with different basic rocks. In the Teesdale area the rich *Agrostis-Festuca* grasslands contain notable montane species such as *Myosotis alpestris* and *Gentiana verna* (Pigott, 1956) but in the Highlands, species of this rarity occur mainly in the Dwarf Herb *nodum* or on the rock ledges at higher altitudes.

Saxifrageto-Agrosto-Festucetum has a more restricted distribution than the species-rich type and has been noted mainly on the calcareous schists between Breadalbane and Clova. It occurs over the same range of altitude as species-rich Agrosto-Festucetum and shows a similar indifference to angle of slope and aspect. Stands are small, however, and rarely exceed 10 sq. m. The only habitat difference between the two appears to be that sites of the present association receive more continuous irrigation than those of the other (Fig. 8). Soils therefore tend to be wetter than those of the previous association as indicated by the greater abundance of hydrophilous species, especially *Saxifraga aizoides*.

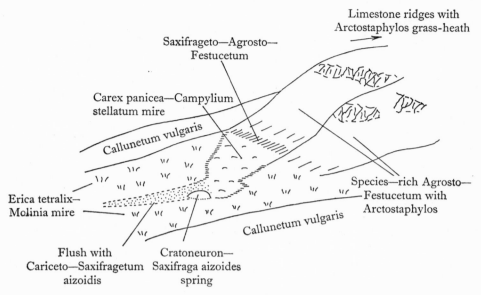

Fig. 8. Limestone vegetation surrounded by oligotrophic heather moor. Tulach Hill, Blair Atholl, Perthshire, at 1200 ft.

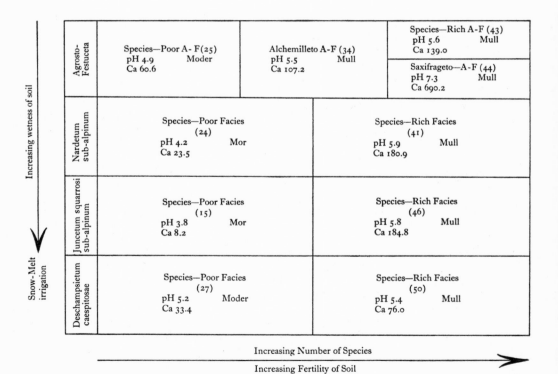

Fig. 9. Relationships between Anthropogenic Grasslands. Average numbers of species per stand are given in brackets. Humus type is indicated and lime status given as mg./100 gm. soil

The soils are similar in field appearance but tend to be slightly darker in colour and richer in the clay fraction. Definite humus horizons are unusual, signs of podsolisation are absent and all profiles show mull humus and a good crumb structure. Earthworms are usually present. The local distribution and close connection with strongly calcareous rock, combined with the field appearance and laboratory analyses, show that these soils are more calcium-rich than those of the previous association. The pH range is slightly higher, from 6·5–7·0.

This association nearly always occurs along with species-rich Agrosto-Festucetum but the reverse frequently does not apply. Quite often it passes into the *Carex panicea-Campylium stellatum nodum* (p. 120) as irrigation becomes more continuous, and the two communities are closely related floristically. There is also a close relationship, spatially and floristically, to the Saxifragetum aizoidis (p. 87) of calcareous rock faces.

Comparable types of grassland occur as fragments on calcareous soils in Lakeland and they may exist on limestone in the Pennines, but *Saxifraga aizoides* is local in that region. Otherwise this association is evidently confined to the Highlands.

Relationships between the four Agrosto-Festuceta

There is no doubt that species-poor Agrosto-Festucetum is differentiated from the other three by a lower soil base status (Fig. 9). Heddle and Ogg (1936) have shown convincingly that species-poor grassland can be converted to rich grassland merely by diverting the natural flow of stream water to irrigate fresh ground. Incidence of irrigation alone can thus produce the change but most markedly where the drainage is from base-rich rocks.

The factors separating the remaining three Agrostis-Festuca grasslands are less certain. The *Alchemilla* grassland occurs on soils with a slightly lower range of soil fertility than the other two and is absent from the most calcareous sites. Some stands, however, are assignable to this association largely because of the high cover of *A. alpina*. This species evidently competes successfully with many smaller herbs and mosses so that its abundance tends to be correlated with a reduced amount of certain other species. If this is so then the factors which govern the distribution and abundance of *A. alpina* also determine whether the resulting grassland is the Alchemilleto or species-rich type in habitats suitable for both.

Enough has been said already to suggest that the species-rich and Saxifrageto-Agrosto-Festucetum are differentiated from each other by a varying soil moisture controlled by irrigation. This difference is accompanied by slight variations in base status, the wetter soils usually being the more base-rich.

Thalictrum-Ctenidium provisional *nodum*

(Table 27)

Another closely related vegetation type, the *Thalictrum-Ctenidium nodum* may be mentioned here. This was originally selected for the abundance of *Thalictrum alpinum* and other species of wet calcareous soils but it became apparent later that there was a close similarity to irrigated *Agrostis-Festuca* grasslands, particularly Saxifrageto-Agrosto-Festucetum. Although only six lists are available, and the *nodum* is provisional, four of the five constants and most of the other species occur in the *S. aizoides* grassland.

Thalictrum alpinum is usually the most abundant species and has a higher cover than in any of the grasslands, where it does not exceed constancy class II.

The *nodum* does not show any particular pattern of geographical distribution and is found in widely separated parts of the Highlands. There seems to be no preference for aspect or angle of slope and the altitudinal range is wide, from 1200 ft. to 2750 ft. (366–839 m.). Stands rarely exceed a few square metres in size and are confined to sites where a flow of base-rich water is present in all but long spells of dry weather. In consequence the soils tend to be much more humus-rich and wet than those of the irrigated grasslands but they are otherwise similar.

Stands of the *Thalictrum-Ctenidium nodum* are particularly characteristic of steep slopes below outcrops of the Durness dolomite in the North-west Highlands. On the Meall a'Ghuibhais outlier of Beinn Eighe hundreds of square metres of such vegetation are found at 1500 ft. (457 m.) on 20–30 cm. of black humus (pH 7·1–7·4) overlying dolomitic colluvium. The humus appears to have been originally laid down as acid *Eriophorum* peat and subsequently converted to a friable 'fen' peat by percolating water from the dolomite. The slope is now quite dry except in the wettest weather and the sward is kept closely cropped by red deer.

Thalictrum-Ctenidium patches usually occur among complexes of calcareous spring vegetation and wet grassland and so they may have spatial connections with a number of different noda.

Nardetum sub-alpinum

(Sub-alpine *Nardus* grassland)
(Tables 28 and 29)

Nardetum sub-alpinum has been divided into a species-poor facies (Table 28, lists 1–14) and a species-rich facies (Table 29, lists 1–8). The separation of the facies in two tables has been made to allow immediate comparison with the corresponding facies of the closely related *Juncetum squarrosi*.

The species-poor Nardetum sub-alpinum is similar in floristic composition to species-poor Agrosto-Festucetum except that *Nardus* replaces the other two grasses as dominant. Besides *Nardus* itself the constants are *Agrostis tenuis*, *Anthoxanthum odoratum*, *Festuca ovina* agg., *Carex pilulifera*, *Galium hercynicum*, *Potentilla erecta*, *Hylocomium splendens*, and *Rhytidiadelphus squarrosus*. The average number of species per stand is 24.

The association as a whole is distinguished from the non-anthropogenic and chiono-philous Nardeta (p. 67) by the scarcity of *Carex bigelowii*, *Trichophorum caespitosum*, *Rhacomitrium lanuginosum*, *Cetraria islandica* and *Cladonia uncialis* and other more montane and chionophilous species. List 12 (Table 28) is from an intermediate stand.

The distinctive species-rich facies (Table 29, lists 1–8) has an average of 43 species per stand and differs also in having *Agrostis canina*, *Carex echinata*, *C. panicea*, *C. pulicaris*, *Juncus squarrosus*, *Luzula multiflora* and *Ranunculus acris* as additional constants. Apart from a greater abundance of rather hydrophilous species such as sedges it can be separated from the other facies at a glance by the large number of mildly calci-colous herbs. Bryophyte species are numerous but have a low total cover due to the supremacy of vascular plants.

Although widespread and often extensive in the Central Highlands, the species-poor Nardetum sub-alpinum is encountered less frequently, and then in smaller stands, in the North and North-west. It occurs mainly on hills which have carried considerable sheep stocks for a long time. The altitudinal range is from 1000 ft. to 2300 ft. (305–702 m.) and above this level it merges with the chionophilous Nardeta. Slopes are usually moderate (5–25 degrees) and there is no bias with regard to aspect. On some hillsides in the south and east there are extensive stands covering many hectares but the areas are often dissected into many smaller patches.

The poor *Nardus* grassland occurs on a variety of parent rocks and sometimes over-lies base-rich substrata. In the Eastern Highlands many slopes covered mainly with Callunetum vulgaris carry Nardetum wherever the ground is irrigated, and here the differentiating factor would seem to be edaphic rather than biotic. Soils are invariably lime-deficient, however, and some form of podsol is usual, often with gleying in the B horizon. There is a raw humus layer of variable depth but the vegetation may root into the upper layers of the mineral soil. The following is a typical soil profile:

R57260

0–8 cm.	. .	dark brown, highly humified peat, blackish at the surface and silty at the base
8–18 cm.	. .	fawn-brown, compact, silty and micaceous loam
18–25 cm.	. .	deep brown loam as above but with slight ferruginous mottle.

The profile becomes stony below 13 cm.

There is some variation in the soils encountered and stands occur on base-deficient, undifferentiated stream alluvium, definite gley podsols and on redistributed peat below eroding blanket bogs (cf. Smith, 1918). All show a similar range of base deficiency and acidity with pH varying from 4·2 to 4·7.

Species-rich Nardetum sub-alpinum has not been seen outside the Central Highlands where it is local and confined to calcareous mountains (Map 15). The habitats occupied by this facies are exactly comparable with those of the species-poor type in topography and altitude, and differ only in soil conditions. It is the counterpart of the poor facies on rather wet slopes where the drainage water comes from extensive areas of calcareous rocks, as on the flanks of the Ben Lawers range where stands cover a total area of many hectares.

The stands are wetter than before and the soils contrast with those just described in being non-podsolised silty grey-brown loams with no raw humus horizon and the higher pH range of 5·1–6·2. Gleying varies in intensity and may be pronounced on the wetter sites.

Both facies are found along with other grasslands and Juncetum squarrosi, Calluneto-Eriophoretum and many of the mire noda. Their ecological relationships to other anthropogenic grasslands are shown in Fig. 9, p. 56.

The species-poor Nardetum sub-alpinum is identical with the *Nardus* grasslands which are widespread and extensive in the Southern Uplands, Lakeland, the Pennines and North Wales. Tansley (1949) has given a detailed account of these southern grass-lands. Scandinavian counterparts are considered along with the chionophilous Nardeta on p. 71.

Juncetum squarrosi sub-alpinum
(Sub-alpine Juncus squarrosus 'grassland')
(Tables 28 and 29)

Juncetum squarrosi sub-alpinum has also been divided into a species-poor (Table 28, lists 15–24) and a species-rich (Table 29, lists 9–11) facies which correspond closely with those of Nardetum sub-alpinum. The species-poor lists can stand as an association by themselves with the constants *Agrostis canina, Anthoxanthum odoratum, Deschampsia flexuosa, Festuca ovina* agg., *Nardus stricta, Juncus squarrosus, Galium hercynicum, Pleurozium schreberi* and *Rhytidiadelphus squarrosus. Juncus squarrosus* is the sole dominant and, perhaps because of its competitive powers, the association is poorer in species than the corresponding Nardetum and has an average of only 15 species per stand. Lists 21–23 of Table 28 are intermediate between Nardetum and Juncetum but typical Juncetum squarrosi is quite distinctive in the constancy of the dominant, *Agrostis canina* and *Deschampsia flexuosa* and in the scarcity of *Agrostis tenuis, Carex pilulifera, C. binervis, Potentilla erecta, Viola riviniana* and *Hylocomium splendens.*

The species-rich facies shows even greater similarity to species-rich Nardetum and when the two are placed together, as in Table 29, they fulfil the requirements of association status. Although only three lists are available it is evident that the constants (see p. 58) are common to both rich facies. There is again an abundance of the same hydrophilous species, herbs and mosses, and the three stands average 46 species. Species-rich Juncetum squarrosi comes close floristically to Hypno-Caricetum alpinum but is distinguished by the dominance of *J. squarrosus* instead of *Carices* and by the lower values of moss cover.

Another closely related type of vegetation, *Juncus squarrosus* bog, has not been studied closely and as no more than four stands (Table 28, lists 25–28) have been analysed it can be regarded only as a facies of species-poor Juncetum squarrosi. The facies differs from the typical association in the reduced abundance of grasses and the increase in bog plants such as *Trichophorum* and *Sphagna*. Yet another facies in which short *Calluna vulgaris* is co-dominant with *Juncus squarrosus* is rare and has not been studied at all.

Juncetum squarrosi usually occurs with Nardetum sub-alpinum but does not extend so far east. It is most abundant in the Central Highlands whereas most examples of *J. squarrosus* bog have been found in the West and North-west. The altitudinal range is from 1500 to 2600 ft. (457–793 m.) and the usual situation is on gentle inclines of up to 15 degrees. Individual stands may extend to one hectare but are often much smaller: the total area on some hills is, however, considerable.

The species-poor facies shows an indifference to the underlying rock and the soils are either gley podsols or shallow blanket peats. The ground is wet throughout the year, although moisture content varies according to season, and the bog facies usually occurs in places where a water-table is present in the peat horizon. The peats are always well-humified, base-deficient and acidic (pH 3·3–4·1).

The species-rich facies is usually found with species-rich Nardetum but, as well as being confined to the calcareous hills of the Central Highlands, it is more western in its distribution (Map 15). The three lists are from Breadalbane where the facies is widespread on slopes which receive drainage from the calcareous mica-schists. It is differentiated from the corresponding facies of Nardetum merely by the greater degree of soil waterlogging and usually occurs on slopes of less than 15 degrees at the same altitude as species-poor Juncetum squarrosi.

The soils are peaty gleys which are distinctly less acidic (pH 5·5–6·0) and more base-rich than those of the species-poor facies. The humus horizon is more distinct than in herb-rich Nardetum but is of mull type.

Though much more local at high levels than the Low-alpine Nardeta (p. 67)

Juncetum squarrosi occurs in many comparable situations and may then be a chiono-philous type of vegetation. These high-lying stands do not differ markedly in floristics from the Sub-alpine examples and they may depend on impeded drainage rather than late snow-cover *per se*, since they usually occupy situations where these two factors are inseparable. Many stands of species-poor Juncetum squarrosi occur on ground where there are signs of lateral water-movement, and they grade into Sphagneto-Caricetum sub-alpinum: a facies of this association is dominated by *Juncus squarrosus* instead of sedges. In such places Juncetum squarrosi would seem to be naturally differentiated from dwarf shrub heath by soil conditions. Extensive complexes of mixed *Juncus squarrosus*, *Nardus stricta*, other grassland and oligotrophic mire communities occur on wet slopes on the north-west side of Ben Wyvis and at the head of Glen Fiadh (Affric). These are not obviously of biotic origin, and the irrigation on which they more probably depend may in turn be influenced by the moderately long snow-cover on the slopes.

Juncetum squarrosi sub-alpinum is associated with the same Sub-alpine vegetation complex as Nardetum sub-alpinum. It passes less often into dry *Agrostis-Festuca* grassland and more frequently into Calluneto-Eriophoretum or Sphagneto-Caricetum sub-alpinum.

Species-poor Juncetum squarrosi and its bog facies are the same as the *J. squarrosus* communities which occur extensively in Snowdonia, Lakeland and the Cross Fell area and which are described by Pearsall (1950) and Ratcliffe (1959). The species-rich facies occurs in the Moffat Hills but is otherwise evidently confined to the Highlands.

Deschampsietum caespitosae alpinum

(Alpine *Deschampsia caespitosa* grassland)
(Table 30)

The remaining grassland association, Deschampsietum caespitosae alpinum shows some floristic divergence from the previous types. The constants are *Deschampsia caespitosa*, *D. flexuosa*, *Agrostis canina*, *A. tenuis*, *Anthoxanthum odoratum*, *Galium hercynicum*, *Alchemilla alpina*, *Rumex acetosa*, *Hylocomium splendens*, *Polytrichum alpinum*, *Rhytidia-delphus loreus* and *R. squarrosus*. *Deschampsia caespitosa* is the usual dominant but in most stands the other constant grasses together have a moderate cover. We have again made a sub-division into species-poor and species-rich facies. The first has an average of 27 species per stand compared with an average of 50 for the second, which has a larger number of herbs and bryophytes including the additional constants *Ranunculus acris* and *Viola riviniana*. *Phleum commutatum* is selective for the association but there are no other characteristic species.

The abundance of *Deschampsia caespitosa* serves to distinguish this from the pre-ceding grassland associations. There is more chance of confusion with Deschampsieto-Rhytidiadelphetum (p. 94) with which the present association intergrades. Lists 1 and 8 (Table 30), for instance, are from intermediate stands and could also be placed under the moss heath association. The chief criterion used to separate the two is domi-nance of grasses as against dominance of the hypnaceous mosses—not a completely satisfactory position.

The species-poor facies is distributed over the whole of the Highlands and is parti-cularly common and extensive in the west (Map 16). It occurs between 1600 ft. and 3000 ft. (488–914 m.) and is therefore more montane than the completely anthropogenic grasslands. The association occurs mainly on steep slopes (30–40 degrees) facing between north and east and the typical situation is on the sides of a deep corrie, often below cliffs (Plate 14). Stands may cover many hectares on western hills.

This facies occurs on a wide range of parent rocks but the soils are more uniform and are inclined to be podsolic. The following is a typical soil profile:

R57081

0–3 cm.	. .	blackish sandy mor humus
3–9 cm.	. .	dark brown sandy loam
9–28 cm.	. .	medium brown sandy loam with faint mottle, loose textured and stony, passing into colluvium.

A separation into well-defined A and B horizons has not been seen and the bleaching of the surface mineral grains is masked by the incorporated humus. The skeletal soils more normal to such steep slopes are sometimes found, but there is usually a little surface humus accumulation.

Snow cover is moderate so that there is an increase in effective precipitation without the solifluction movements associated with strong exposure or really late snow-lie. This probably accounts for the podsolic soil profiles. Snow melt water must play an important part in the drainage regime of such sites and when the snow has gone the slopes remain damp throughout the rest of the year. Although the drainage is rapid there is usually a great deal of water seepage, especially from below rock faces. Deschampsietum caespitosae thus appears to depend largely on late snow-lie but its predominantly western distribution also suggests a connection with wetness of climate. The association is not found in the Cairngorms and this could mean that it requires soils which are neither too base-deficient nor too porous. The controlling factors are clearly complex and, as yet, far from fully understood.

The species-rich facies resembles the other in all requirements except that of soil base-status. It is therefore more localised than the species-poor Deschampsietum but occurs in comparable situations on calcareous rocks throughout the Highlands. The stands tend to be smaller and their size depends on the area of ground receiving calcareous drainage water.

The soils are non-podsolic, dark brown silty loams, loose textured and nearly always stony, with some mull humus concentration in the surface layers. Chemical analysis shows a higher calcium content than for soils of the species-poor facies.

Here and there we have encountered *Deschampsia caespitosa* grasslands which could not be assigned to the present association. These are mostly distinguished by the overwhelming dominance of *Deschampsia* and, consequently, by floristic poverty. Most of the occurrences are either in the deep corries of the Cairngorms around perennial springs of icy water, or on high plateaux such as those of Ben Alder, Creag Meagaidh and Aonach Beag of the Nevis range. One of these (Table 30, list 17) has closer affinities with Polytricheto-Caricetum bigelowii.

Deschampsietum caespitosae alpinum has been placed with the anthropogenic grasslands but it evidently depends less on human influence than do the other members of the group.

In most places the species-poor facies is not obviously derived from a different type of vegetation by grazing. If, however, comparison is made between corrie slopes bearing poor *Deschampsia caespitosa* grassland and large ungrazed cliff ledges above, where other conditions appear comparable, it is usually found that the ledge communities show a greater abundance and luxuriance of *Vaccinium myrtillus*, *Luzula sylvatica*, *Rumex acetosa*, *Ranunculus acris* and ferns. Such communities (Table 31, list 6) are remarkably close to the *Vaccinium-Luzula* group, of birchwood affinities (p. 17). It may be, however, that snow-cover and irrigation are not the same on corrie slopes and cliff ledges and that the dominance of *Deschampsia caespitosa* is quite natural.

On Beinn Bhan, Applecross, part of a corrie slope about 300 m. × 50 m. in size is protected from grazing by cliffs above and below, and its vegetation gives a striking contrast to that of the grazed slopes at the foot of the cliffs (Plates 18 and 19). This 'ledge' is sufficiently large to show duplication of all other conditions of the slopes below, so that differences in its vegetation are attributable mainly to absence of grazing. Except where irrigation from moderately basic beds of the Torridon sandstone gives richer soils and a lush growth of tall herbs, the vegetation consists either of luxuriant fern-beds or dense *Vaccinium-Luzula* communities. The soil is generally shallow, often consisting of a thin layer of fern humus over blocks, but the cover of vegetation is continuous. By contrast, the grazed slopes below the cliffs are largely composed of unstable scree, with a patchy development of species-poor Deschampsietum caespitosae alpinum. Here, it would seem that where grazing has not reduced the original fern or *Vaccinium-Luzula* vegetation to bare scree, there has been change to the *Deschampsia* grassland. This is, however, a markedly oceanic district, and it is perhaps unjustifiable to imply that this interpretation applies widely in the Highlands, suggestive though it may be. Fern beds of this type were perhaps always confined to the extreme west, and Deschampsietum caespitosae may be a more natural type where snow-cover is more prolonged.

On the other hand there is little doubt that the species-rich facies is often the biotically produced equivalent of the Tall Herb *nodum* and owes its existence to grazing by sheep and deer. The two communities are nearly always found in the same corrie and with no apparent difference in habitat except that the tall herb stands are confined to ungrazed cliff ledges and the grassland covers the grazed slopes adjoining (Plates 14 and 17). Many tall herbs survive in the grassland but they are dwarfed and *Deschampsia caespitosa* has clearly increased at their expense for it is considerably less abundant on the ledges.

Both facies pass into other vegetation as drainage and snow-cover alter. Wherever block screes occur on the same corrie slopes they usually carry *Vaccineto-Empetretum* and, in the North-west Highlands, this is usually the hepatic-rich facies. The porous block scree has the effect of buffering its vegetation against the irrigation which affects the rest of the slope and this again suggests that the *Deschampsia* grassland depends particularly on irrigation. A change to dwarf shrub heath also occurs where there are other checks to irrigation. As snow cover increases on the upper slopes the grassland gives way to chionophilous moss heath (Deschampsieto-Rhytidiadelphetum) in the west or to stands of Dicraneto-Caricetum bigelowii in the Central Highlands. The species-rich facies passes into species-rich Juncetum squarrosi or Nardetum as the ground becomes wetter on decreasing slopes. The factors governing the transition from species-rich Deschampsietum to the Dwarf Herb *nodum* are not clear, but the amount of irrigation and snow-cover and the extent to which calcium enrichment takes place may all be involved.

The *Deschampsia caespitosa* grasslands described above appear to be confined to the

Highlands. They are quite different from the sub-montane and definitely anthropogenic vegetation dominated by this species in Northern England, Southern Scotland and some southern parts of the Highlands.

Deschampsia caespitosa meadows are local in Fennoscandia but the Deschampsietum caespitosae alpicolum of Nordhagen (1943, p. 33), including the *D. caespitosa-Geranium sylvaticum* Association and the Sub-alpine *D. caespitosa* meadow of Sylene (Nordhagen 1927, pp. 344, 348) has much in common, both floristically and in its ecological relationships, with the Scottish association.

Luzula sylvatica Grassland *nodum*
(Table 31)

We have included with the anthropogenic grassland a group of communities which could equally be considered with the *Luzula-Vaccinium* vegetation described on p. 17. The stands have dominance of *Luzula sylvatica* and an abundance of grasses in common and so have been described as a provisional *Luzula sylvatica* grassland *nodum*.

There are six constants in our seven lists, *Agrostis tenuis*, *Deschampsia flexuosa*, *Luzula sylvatica*, *Rumex acetosa*, *Rhytidiadelphus loreus* and *R. squarrosus*. In two of the stands listed *Vaccinium myrtillus* is co-dominant with *Luzula* but these are distinguished from the *Vaccinium-Luzula* type by the absence of predominantly woodland species such as *Thelypteris dryopteris* and *Oxalis acetosella*.

The *nodum* has a distinctly western and oceanic distribution and is particularly characteristic of hilltops about 1500 ft. (457 m.) high along the Atlantic seaboard. We do not yet know if the small, discrete patches of *Luzula sylvatica* which are frequently found in *Agrostis-Festuca* and *Nardus* grassland throughout Scotland can be said to belong here. Larger stands in the Moffat and Ettrick Hills certainly appear to show some affinity.

Stands vary in size from a few square metres to several hectares and the largest area of this vegetation that we have seen lies on Ben Loyal in Sutherland where it occupies most of the corrie slopes and may experience considerable winter snow-cover in places. Spence (1960) has described similar stands of *Luzula sylvatica* mixed with fragmentary willow, tall herb and fern communities on islands in Shetland lochs, and on rock ledges in South Uist. His evidence shows that they are replaced by some form of *Calluna vulgaris* heath on the surrounding burned and grazed moorlands.

Most of the soils examined were deep layers (up to 60 cm.) of moist or distinctly wet reddish-brown to black raw humus with a good fibrous or friable structure. One of the St. Kilda peats smelled like marsh mud and showed blue-black mottling towards the base.

Molinia Grasslands

Grasslands dominated by *Molinia caerulea* occur widely in the Western Highlands but are only locally extensive. They have not been studied in detail because their floristic composition is covered adequately by the tables for closely related noda, e.g. Molinieto-Callunetum, *Molinia-Myrica nodum*, from which many stands appear to have been derived by loss of the co-dominant species. Examples occur in which *Molinia* is completely dominant, often in large distinct tussocks and these are usually associated with periodic flooding and sedimentation, as along the edge of sluggish streams on boggy ground. Locally there are herb-rich types of *Molinia* grassland on damp basic soils at low levels and these have some affinity with *Juncus acutiflorus* mires. Finally, there are *Sphagnum*-rich *Molinia* communities which are related to the oligotrophic mires or even to Trichophoreto-Eriophoretum.

Relationships between Forest, Anthropogenic Grassland and Dwarf Shrub Heath

At present most of the remaining oak and birchwoods have field layers which are modified by grazing and show great similarity to either *Agrostis-Festuca* grassland or sub-montane *Vaccinium* heaths. Disappearance of the trees would probably lead directly to the formation of these communities. In the same way it is easy to visualise the conversion of pine forest into *Calluna* or *Vaccinium* heath (p. 31). This poses a problem, for in many parts of the Highlands *Calluna* heaths seem also to have been derived from oak and birchwoods. Moreover, we have to explain why in some places *Calluna* heath, *Vaccinium* heath and acidic grassland occur together on ground where soil, topography and climate suggest that the vegetation should be uniform.

There is abundant evidence to show that on the hills of the Southern Uplands, England and Wales sub-montane Callunetum has been and is still being replaced by *Vaccinium* heath, *Agrostis-Festuca* grassland and Nardetum as a result of repeated heather burning combined with intensive sheep grazing. *Vaccinium* heath can act as an intermediate stage and has often been converted to one or other of the acidic grasslands. This evidence has been considered in detail by Ratcliffe (1959) for North Wales and we believe that it is sufficient to say here that exactly the same kind of evidence may be found in many parts of the Highlands which have long been managed for sheep. The correspondence is closest in the south-east of the Highlands where in climate and vegetation the similarity to the more southerly regions is greatest.

The juxtaposition of the two dwarf shrub heaths with each other and with the grassland is therefore to be explained as the result of an uneven biotic pressure. In other words, where there are mosaics of these vegetation types, grazing and/or burning have been more intensive in some places than in others. On such ground it is usually evident that the grasslands are still spreading at the expense of the shrub heaths.

It is, however, sometimes difficult to tell whether a particular area of acidic grassland has been produced secondarily from shrub heath after woodland or directly from the woodland itself. Grazing was generally lighter during the main period of forest clearance so that replacement of woodland by *Calluna* or *Vaccinium* heath was probably usual in earlier times and the grasslands followed later. In recent years the formation of grassland has probably been direct more often than not.

Similar tendencies are present in the Western Highlands although rather different vegetation is involved. In the wet climate of the west *Calluna* normally has to compete with moisture-tolerant species and burning thus places it at a greater disadvantage. The prevailing Molinieto-Callunetum and Trichophoreto-Callunetum which so largely replaced forest in this region readily lose their *Calluna* when burning is carried out and especially where winter grazing is fairly heavy. Complete dominance of *Juncus squarrosus* at lower levels would also seem to be biotically determined and has probably involved at least some decline in the abundance of *Calluna*.

The vegetation types mentioned so far are those of the most acid soils. On base-rich soils mixed herb and grass communities would remain after woodland clearance but would be readily converted to grassland when grazed by domestic stock.

Although Callunetum is not usually regarded as an association of the better soils we have found several stands which are rich in basiphilous herbs. Two analyses of these herb-rich Calluneta from Slioch and Beinn Enaiglair in Ross-shire and three from Rhum are given in Table 11a, and similar communities have been observed elsewhere only in Glen Clova, Glen Shee, Glen Lyon and Glen Girnaig (Perthshire) and on Ben Vrackie. They are rare probably because sites with base-rich soils are grazed selectively by wild and domestic animals alike and are therefore the first places to undergo modification. Some of the stands of herb-rich *Calluna* heath in Glen Lyon are still being replaced by herb-rich *Agrostis-Festuca* grassland as a result of burning combined with grazing, and it is now impossible to tell how widespread they have been in the past.

The grasslands of base-rich soils are particularly valuable as pasturage for sheep and deer and there is usually a good correlation between their extent and the number and quality of the grazing stock in any particular area. Variations in land use according to productivity have often accentuated any edaphically controlled difference in the original vegetation and may have produced differences where none existed before. This has happened when hills with mixtures of base-rich and base-deficient rocks have been more heavily stocked with sheep than adjacent ground composed solely of acidic rocks. The vegetation of both rocks in the first area then shows greater modification than that of the second. For a good example of this effect we may compare Caenlochan Glen with some of its neighbours. Caenlochan, with its mixture of calcareous and acidic rocks, has much acidic grassland but no Callunetum (except on cliffs) even on the poorest soils, whereas Callunetum predominates on similar poor soils in adjoining glens.

On the other hand, because they are grazed selectively, sites with base-rich soils often show modifications under a local rate of stocking too low to affect dwarf shrub heaths on base-deficient soils.

The ratio of dwarf shrub heath to grassland on hill grazings has been discussed from the agricultural point of view by Crompton (1958).

The change from dwarf shrub heath to *Agrostis-Festuca* grassland has been accompanied in many places by the spread of bracken (*Pteridium aquilinum*). While this is partly a woodland relic it easily invades both species-rich and species-poor Agrosto-Festucetum and produces communities which, although they have been described along with the birchwoods, may also be regarded as facies of the grasslands. Growth and spread of bracken is also encouraged by heather burning and stands of bracken sometimes replace Callunetum directly.

On the whole, the Highlands have been exploited less intensively than the other British uplands—certainly not for so long. The smaller proportion of anthropogenic grassland and low-level screes in the Highlands are the chief indication of this difference. During the last hundred years a large part of the Highlands has been managed as deer-forest or grouse moor and anthropogenic grasslands are poorly represented or absent in these areas. This is due partly to the wide extent of siliceous rocks on which a sufficient level of stocking cannot be maintained to produce changes other than to Molinietum and Trichophoretum.

For an illustration of this last point and as a contrast to the changes which have been induced on relatively poor rocks in places such as Caenlochan, the situation at the head of the River Oykell under Ben More Assynt may be mentioned. The east side of the valley is composed largely of basic Lewisian rocks and the level of stocking has been heavy enough to produce a complex of acidic and basic grasslands, and ericaceous vegetation has been largely eradicated. The Breabag ridge to the west is quartzite, and has evidently received a share of the heavy grazing and moor-burning which the rather high productivity of the eastern ridge encouraged. The effect has been to cause considerable degradation of soil and vegetation on the quartzite, with substantial peat erosion and the formation of worthless mixtures of *Trichophorum*, *Molinia* and *Calluna* communities of a heterogeneous type. The east side of the glen is now green but the west has remained 'black' and is much impoverished.

MONTANE GRASS HEATHS

The 'natural' montane grass heaths of the Highlands will now be considered, beginning with those that lie at the lowest levels. *Nardus stricta* communities which are obviously influenced by snow-lie more than by grazing animals begin to appear around 2000 ft. (610 m.), generally in association with chionophilous Vaccineta, and they extend to the summits of the hills at over 4000 ft. (1220 m.).

Low-alpine *Nardus noda*
(*Nardus* snow-beds)
(Table 32)

The three Low-alpine *Nardus noda* have been placed together in Table 32. The hitherto undescribed *Nardus-Trichophorum nodum* has been well represented by lists 1–8 but only a few sample lists of the others have been given to illustrate the range in floristics.

Nardus-Pleurozium *nodum*
(Table 32, lists 12–16)

The *Nardus-Pleurozium nodum* is based on the high-altitude *Nardus stricta* sociation of Poore (1955) but its status as an association has been lost on the addition of lists from outside the Breadalbane district in which it was originally compiled. Only five stands are presented in the table, two of these being from Poore's original table. Two other stands have been analysed but have not been included here.

The constants of the lists shown are *Nardus stricta*, *Galium hercynicum*, *Pleurozium schreberi*, *Rhytidiadelphus loreus* and *Ptilidium ciliare*. This is similar to Poore's list but with *R. loreus* and *Ptilidium* in place of *Rhytidiadelphus squarrosus* and *Carex bigelowii*. *Nardus stricta* is the sole dominant. Numbers of species per stand range from 12–33 with an average of 20.

The *Nardus-Pleurozium nodum* is distinguished from the other chionophilous *Nardus noda* by the abundance of the hypnaceous mosses (*Rhytidiadelphus squarrosus* and *Hylocomium splendens* in addition to the two constants *Pleurozium schreberi* and *R. loreus*) and the small amounts of dwarf shrubs and lichens.

The distribution of the *nodum* is shown in Map 17 and it can be seen that it is the most widespread of the group. Although Poore (1956) records it as occurring indifferently on sericite and quartz-schist or quartzite there does seem to be an overall tendency for

6

it to avoid the wholly siliceous rocks and especially sites liable to more than seasonal irrigation. It is entirely absent from the Cairngorm granite.

Nardus-Trichophorum *nodum*
(Table 32, lists 1–8)

The next most widespread type is the *Nardus-Trichophorum nodum* which has the following constants: *Empetrum hermaphroditum*, *Vaccinium myrtillus*, *Nardus stricta*, *Trichophorum caespitosum*, *Rhacomitrium lanuginosum*, *Cetraria islandica* and *Cladonia uncialis*. Again *Nardus* is the usual dominant but *Trichophorum*, *Loiseleuria procumbens* and *Rhacomitrium lanuginosum* may be co-dominant. The lists shown have 13 to 31 species with an average of 23.

This *nodum* is characterised by the abundance of dwarf shrubs and *Trichophorum caespitosum* and the partial or complete replacement of hypnaceous mosses by *Rhacomitrium lanuginosum*. It is also the most lichen-rich vegetation of the group. Lists 9–11 (Table 32) are closely related and show the rise to dominance of *Trichophorum* on the wettest sites where deep peat is able to form, a feature noted by Poore and McVean (1957) in their brief survey of *Nardus* snow-beds. Gjaerevoll (1956) also comments upon the existence of *Trichophorum* 'fen' below *Nardus*-dominated snow-beds in the oceanic regions of Scandinavia.

Map 17 shows that the distribution of the *nodum* is predominantly western with an important subsidiary centre in the Cairngorms. The stands are well irrigated by both rainwater and melt water and may occupy many hectares on the sides and bottoms of large corries or on high watersheds.

Nardus-Rhacomitrium provisional *nodum*
(Table 32, lists 17–19)

Three lists of the *Nardus-Rhacomitrium nodum* are given in the table and five other lists have been made in the North-west Highlands. To a certain extent this vegetation is intermediate between the *Nardus-Trichophorum nodum* and Cariceto-Rhacomitretum (*Rhacomitrium* heath) so that its status as a nodum must be regarded as provisional.

Constants of the eight lists are *Vaccinium myrtillus*, *Nardus stricta*, *Carex bigelowii*, *Rhacomitrium lanuginosum*, *Cetraria islandica* and *Cladonia uncialis*. Either *Nardus stricta* or *R. lanuginosum* may be dominant.

The typical stand has co-dominant *Nardus* and *Rhacomitrium* with a little *Vaccinium myrtillus* and *Empetrum hermaphroditum* but no other dwarf shrubs. *Trichophorum* if present is in small amounts; the mosses and lichens are those of *Rhacomitrium* heath but there may be a number of oceanic liverworts such as *Anastrepta orcadensis*. Species numbers per stand are low, from 7–25 with an average of 19.

Apart from one record from the Loch Laggan area, vegetation of this type has been seen only in the North-west Highlands (Map 17), where it often occupies sites equivalent in snow-cover and drainage to those of the *Nardus-Pleurozium nodum*, although some stands are on more exposed ground. On the level or gently sloping ground of high watersheds it often forms mosaics with *Rhacomitrium* heath. In several places such as the outliers of Ben More Assynt the *Nardus-Pleurozium nodum* has been found as a patch in the centre of a *Nardus-Rhacomitrium* hollow, i.e. where snow-lie is presumably longest. Even the more exposed stands tend to collect snow among the dead grass leaves so that effective precipitation and protection from wind and frost are greater than on the adjacent *Rhacomitrium* heath.

Both the *Nardus*-moss *noda* may be found as a strip along either side of drystone dykes built across *Rhacomitrium* heath to mark estate boundaries. A visit to these localities in winter reveals that the *Nardus* strips coincide with the main snow accumulations on the heath. The dykes are generally 50–90 years old so that the change in vegetation must have taken place within that period.

Nardetum medio-alpinum

(Alpine *Nardus* grassland)
(Table 33)

Although the foregoing *Nardus noda* exhibit a wide range of altitude (2000–3600 ft., 610–1098 m.) the stands are found mainly within the Low-alpine zone and represent a downward extension of grass heaths into the zone of dwarf shrubs due to prolonged snow-cover in winter and spring. The next type to be described, the Nardetum medio-alpinum, is confined to a narrow zone from 3500 ft. (1068 m.) to 4000 ft. (1220 m.) and has been given the status of an association although represented by only six lists.

The association element consists of *Nardus stricta, Carex bigelowii, Dicranum fuscescens, Cetraria hiascens, C. islandica, Cladonia bellidiflora, C. delessertii* and *C. sylvatica. Nardus stricta* is always completely dominant and only *Dicranum fuscescens* and *D. scoparium* ever attain dominance among the cryptogams. The chionophilous lichens *Cetraria hiascens* and *Cladonia delessertii* are strongly selective for this association. Species numbers per stand (15–19) are low due to the thick growth of the dominant.

Nardetum medio-alpinum is confined to the Cairngorm massif (Map 17), where it is associated with the extensive complexes of late snow vegetation on the 4000 ft. (1220 m.) plateaux of Braeriach, Cairngorm and Ben MacDhui with outliers on Beinn Bhrotain and Ben a'Bhuird.

The soils of all the chionophilous *Nardus noda* are podsolic (Alpine sod Podsol of Kubiena, 1953, p. 266) and similar to those described by Poore (1955b) except that the A_2 horizon is generally less distinct than he describes. The Nardetum medio-alpinum shows least peat accumulation and the following soil profile is typical:

0–7·5 cm.	.	humose sandy gravel. pH 5·0
7·5–11·5 cm.	.	grey, non-humose sandy gravel
11·5–24 cm.	.	dark reddish-brown gravel
>24 cm.	.	boulders.

The other *noda* may have up to 15 cm. peat resting directly on rock detritus or forming the A_1 horizon of a podsol profile. Sand grains may be present all the way to the surface and the peat sometimes shows signs of having been redistributed. Mottling is common in the A and B horizons and buried A_1 and A_2 horizons are sometimes encountered. Under the *Trichophorum*-dominated vegetation of lists 9–11 (Table 32) the peat varied from 20 to 60 cm. in depth. The pH of the surface peat varies from 4·4 to 5·4.

The occurrence of *Nardus* vegetation in the centre or at the bottom of a *Vaccinium* or *Vaccinium-Empetrum* snow-bed has already been mentioned (p. 70, Fig. 10). The transition may be gradual or abrupt according to the gradient in the controlling habitat factor. Fig. 10 illustrates the situation already described on p. 39 in which the transition from windswept erosion surface to sheltered *Nardus* hollow takes place within a few metres.

At higher altitudes the *Nardus noda* give way to moss heath, rather than to dwarf shrub heath, with decrease in snow-lie and these transitions will be described later. In the Cairngorms a vertical distance of only 300 ft. to 500 ft. (91–153 m.) sometimes separates the highest stand of the *Nardus-Trichophorum nodum* from the lowest stand of the Nardetum medio-alpinum, the two communities being separated by moss heaths of semi-permanent snow-beds. Where snow-lie is of intermediate duration there are sometimes communities transitional between Vaccineto-Empetretum and the three Low-alpine *Nardus noda*, particularly the *Nardus-Trichophorum nodum*. These mixed shrub and grass heaths occur mainly in the Cairngorms and the Western Highlands (Map 10) and they are extensive on some hills in the North-west where the pure noda are poorly

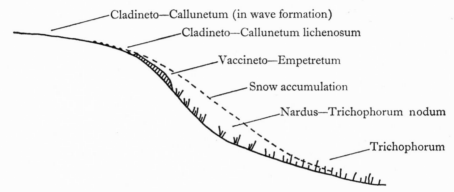

Fig. 10. Snow-bed vegetation in the Cairngorms at about 2700 ft.

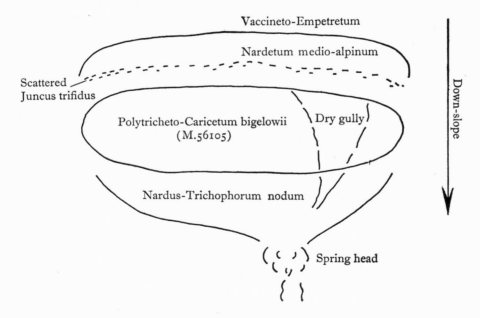

Fig. 11. Snow-bed vegetation in the Cairngorms at 3400 ft.

represented. We have not tried to define such intermediates in terms of a separate nodum, but give two analyses (Table 19, lists 20 and 21) for comparison with the related noda. List 20 is fairly typical, although in some stands *Rhacomitrium lanuginosum* is more abundant than hypnaceous mosses. List 21 from Ben Hope is about equally rich in liverworts, mosses and lichens and the stand passed below into liverwort and *Rhaco-mitrium*-rich Vaccineto-Empetretum on shaded north slopes. With increasing exposure there are usually transitions to *Rhacomitrium* heath of one kind or another.

Mice and voles often congregate on *Nardus* beds below the winter snow and the heaps of chopped grass and droppings are found after the spring thaw. In Norway lemmings behave in the same way in snow-bed vegetation (Nordhagen, 1927, p. 361–2).

Comparisons between the chionophilous *Nardus* communities of British authors have already been made by Poore (1955b) and Poore and McVean (1957). These can now be summarised as follows.

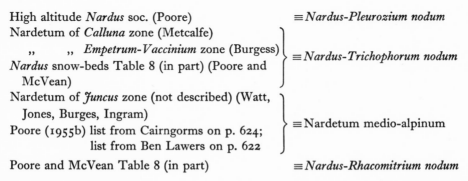

High altitude *Nardus* soc. (Poore)   ≡ *Nardus-Pleurozium nodum*
Nardetum of *Calluna* zone (Metcalfe)
   „   „   *Empetrum-Vaccinium* zone (Burgess) } ≡ *Nardus-Trichophorum nodum*
Nardus snow-beds Table 8 (in part) (Poore and McVean)
Nardetum of *Juncus* zone (not described) (Watt, Jones, Burges, Ingram)
Poore (1955b) list from Cairngorms on p. 624; } ≡ Nardetum medio-alpinum
     list from Ben Lawers on p. 622
Poore and McVean Table 8 (in part)   ≡ *Nardus-Rhacomitrium nodum*

Comparisons with published continental lists have also been made by Poore (1955) but since further information is now available from both Scotland and Norway there is need for revision.

There is no continental equivalent of the *Nardus-Rhacomitrium nodum*. The *Nardus-Trichophorum nodum* has little in common with Norwegian Nardeta except the dominance of *Nardus* and the closest floristic equivalents must be sought among the associations of the Phyllodoco-Vaccinion myrtilli rather than the Nardeto-Caricion bigelowii (cf. Phyllodoco-Juncetum trifidi of Dahl, 1956, p. 123 and its equivalents in other areas). In habitat and physiognomy if not in floristics, it bears some resemblance to the Cetrarietum delisei loiseleurietosum of Rondane (loc. cit. p. 144).

Poore (1955b) compares his high-altitude *Nardus* sociation with the Alpine *Nardus* association of Sylene (Nordhagen, 1927, p. 317), which is the equivalent of the Nardetum chionophilum of Rondane (Dahl, 1956, p. 166) but the Nardetum medio-alpinum now described seems to be closer to these in its lack of hypnaceous mosses and presence of more chionophilous species. It is much less species-rich, however. The high-altitude *Nardus* and the *Nardus-Pleurozium noda* resemble the Sub-alpine *Nardus* association of Sylene (Nordhagen, 1927, p. 321) in the abundance of hypnaceous mosses, floristic poverty and snow regime. The Nardetum sub-alpinum (p. 58) on the other hand is not influenced by snow-lie and lacks many mountain species, but is otherwise also similar to the Sylene association.

The closest correspondence of all is found between our Nardetum medio-alpinum and several of the lists in the Alpine *Nardus stricta* sociation of Gjaerevoll (1956, Table 8).

The two tables have 20 species in common and Gjaerevoll's species-impoverished lists, especially I and V from Torne Lappmark and Vågå, are particularly like the Cairngorm lists.

The two following associations can be either moss heaths or grass heaths according to whether mosses or grasses are dominant.

Polytricheto-Caricetum bigelowii
(*Polytrichum alpinum-Carex bigelowii* snow-beds)
(Table 34)

The first of these, the Polytricheto-Caricetum bigelowii incorporates the *Polytrichum alpinum nodum* of Poore (unpublished) as a distinct local facies. There are only two constants, after which the association has been named. Either of the two constants may be dominant and *Anthoxanthum odoratum*, *Cherleria sedoides* and *Rhytidiadelphus loreus* may approach co-dominance in the Ben Lawers facies (rhytidiadelphetosum). *Cetraria hiascens* (constancy class II) is selective for the typicum facies of Polytricheto-Caricetum bigelowii as well as for the Nardetum medio-alpinum (p. 69). Eighty-one species have been recorded and numbers per stand are low, with averages of 23 and 15 for the rhytidiadelphetosum and typicum respectively.

The typicum facies is distinguished by dominance of *Carex bigelowii* and abundance of lichens while the rhytidiadelphetosum (local Ben Lawers facies) has a greater variety of grasses and other herbs, with dominance of *Polytrichum alpinum* and scarcity of *C. bigelowii* (see p. 95).

The association is confined to the Central Highlands and forms a band stretching from Ben Nevis in the west to Clova in the east with a southern outlier on Ben Lawers (Map 18). The altitude of the stands ranges from 2000 ft. (610 m.) in Clova and on Ben Lawers to over 4000 ft. (1220 m.) in the Cairngorms and Nevis areas. The ground is generally level or gently sloping and there is a preponderance of northern and eastern exposures as with most communities of late snow-lie. The stands are neither extensive nor particularly homogeneous except on Lochnagar and they are usually found in mosaic with Nardeta, Dicraneto-Caricetum bigelowii (p. 73) and chionophilous moss heaths around the margins of large snow-fields. The ecology of the association is not clear and while many stands are obviously associated with the drainage channels of melt water and wet hollows others occupy well-drained and un-irrigated sites or even raised soil patches on erosion surfaces. There is reason to believe that many dry stands are relict from a fairly recent regime of locally impeded drainage.

Stands of Polytricheto-Caricetum bigelowii in the Cairngorms may not melt out until the month of June when winter snow-fall has been heavy.

Soils are podsolic and gleying of all horizons is frequent although downwash of fine sand and silt may mask the tendency to leaching. The following soil profile is typical:

(M56127)

0–6 cm.	. .	rooty black peat with fine sand
6–9·5 cm.	. .	grey sandy gravel
9·5–23 cm.	. .	compact rotten gravel mottled red and dark brown
>23 cm.	. .	tough compact sandy clay, light orange brown in colour.

In the Cairngorms wet, sandy peat overlying mottled gravel gives way to a deeper peat with less sand under the neighbouring *Nardus* vegetation. On Ben Lawers the more base and clay-rich soils show less sign of podsolisation and this is reflected in the greater floristic variety of the rhytidiadelphetosum. The pH of the surface soil varies from 4·4 to 4·7, considerably less than the values given by Poore (1955b).

Some relationships with other noda are shown in Fig. 11.

Communities referable to this association often occur on steep slopes in shallow corries which hold snow until late, as below the plateau of Glas Maol, where they have a high cover of *Polytrichum alpinum* and *Salix herbacea*. List 17 (Table 34) is dominated by *Deschampsia caespitosa* but is included here because of the obvious floristic affinity and because the stand graded into more typical Polytricheto-Caricetum bigelowii. The stand was extensive (several hectares) and quite different from other high level *D. caespitosa* grasslands (p. 62).

The Polytricheto-Caricetum bigelowii of Rondane (Dahl, 1955b, p. 162) is similar to our association in many ways. They have 35 species and the two constants in common and occupy closely similar habitats. The Rondane association is seasonally wet and may be covered by ice in winter although snow-cover is variable. Where there is little snow-cover the ground is thrown into hummocks by frost action; this has been observed in the Scottish association only on the 3500 ft. (1068 m.) plateaux of Lochnagar, Ben Alder and Glas Maol. The Rondane soils also have well developed podsol profiles and the pH of the surface humus or sandy humus has a mean value of 4·4.

Gjaerevoll (1956, p. 67) also lists several stands of his Caricetum bigelowii-lachenalii in which *Carex bigelowii* and *Polytrichum alpinum* are the most prominent species. The stands are from Torne Lappmark and Beiarn and the habitat is similar to that of Poly-tricheto-Caricetum bigelowii in Rondane and Scotland. On the other hand the rhytidia-delphetosum has more in common with the *Deschampsia flexuosa-Polytrichum alpinum* sociation of Torne Lappmark and the Borgefjell Mts. (loc. cit. pp. 42–44) in the domi-nance of *Polytrichum*, the higher constancy of *Salix herbacea* and the greater abundance of grasses and forbs.

Many Scandinavian authors regard vegetation of this kind as the Middle-alpine equivalent of Low-alpine *Sphagnum* mires (Dahl, 1956, p. 289).

Dicraneto-Caricetum bigelowii

(*Dicranum fuscescens-Carex bigelowii* heath)
(Table 35)

The second mixed moss and grass heath, the Dicraneto-Caricetum bigelowii, has been based on the *Dicranum fuscescens-Carex bigelowii* sociation of Breadalbane (Poore, 1955b).

Five species form the association element: *Carex bigelowii*, *Dicranum fuscescens*, *Polytrichum alpinum*, *Rhacomitrium lanuginosum* and *Cladonia bellidiflora*. Either *C. bigelowii* or *D. fuscescens* may be dominant and the lichen *Cladonia alpicola* (constancy class I) is exclusive to the association. Only 49 species have been recorded from the stands and there are 8–24 species per stand with an average of 13·5, one of the lowest counts from any nodum.

The distribution of the association (Map 18) is similar to that of the previous one but there are two fragmentary outliers in the Northern Highlands on Ben Wyvis and the Glen Cannich Sgurr na Lapaich. The altitudinal range is from 2600 ft. (793 m.) to 3800 ft. (1159 m.) on level or gently sloping terrain of north-west to south-east aspect. The tendency for the association to be missing from the areas of 'poor' rocks is surprising since none of the species involved can be described as calcicolous. There may be a connection with the mechanical composition of the soil and the freedom of drainage but the situation requires further study.

Outside Breadalbane we have not experienced the difficulty described by Poore (1955b) of drawing the line between this *nodum* and *Rhacomitrium* heath although intermediates are encountered here and there. With the exception of list 8 (Table 35) which has been copied from Poore's Table 4, the intermediates have been omitted. *Carex bigelowii* attains greater dominance in this association than in any stands of the *Rhacomitrium* heath and this is a useful distinguishing feature when both mosses are present in abundance. Otherwise there is little to distinguish the two associations floristically.

Actual records of the snow regime for the Dicraneto-Caricetum bigelowii are scanty but in its topographical position in hollows of the *Rhacomitrium* heath or on sheltered slopes above late snow-beds it corresponds to the Deschampsieto-Rhytidiadelphetum (p. 94) which is known to be chionophilous and weakly hygrophilous. Its close association with the *Nardus-Pleurozium nodum* in vegetation mosaics signifies a similar snow-cover for both. It forms both sharp and gradual transitions to Vaccineto-Empetretum, Festuceto-Vaccinetum and Polytricheto-Caricetum bigelowii, and mixed vegetation types with the last three associations are common in the Clova-Caenlochan area, where the Dicraneto-Caricetum bigelowii forms some of its most extensive stands of many hectares on the 3000 ft. (914 m.) plateaux.

As Poore has pointed out, the soils are invariably podsolic with considerable humus accumulation. Gleying of the B horizon is commonly present. One stand on the summit of Glas Maol was found to have only a few centimetres of black, wet, slightly humified moss humus over large boulders but the following soil profile is more typical:

R57192

0–16 cm.	. .	black humified peat, slightly sandy at base
16–17·5 cm. .	.	greyish-fawn sand
17·5–28 cm. .	.	dark brown sandy loam mottled with rust brown.

Adjacent *Nardus* patches have been observed to have deeper peat accumulation, a thinner A_2 horizon and more intensive mottling. The pH of the surface soil varies from 3·6 to 4·4.

Records of comparable Scandinavian vegetation are few. Gjaerevoll (1949, p. 69) describes a *Carex bigelowii* sociation with *Dicranum fuscescens* dominant, from the Oviksfjällen Mts. of Central Sweden, and Dahl (1956, p. 134) describes a *Deschampsia flexuosa-Dicranum fuscescens* association rich in *C. bigelowii* from Rondane, but otherwise one must look among the lists of Nardetum, Caricetum bigelowii-lachenalii and Anthoxantho-Deschampsietum flexuosae (*Lycopodium alpinum* sociation) for vegetation with abundant *C. bigelowii* and *D. fuscescens*.

Cladineto-Juncetum trifidi

(Lichen-rich *Juncus trifidus* heath)

(Table 36)

In Scotland as elsewhere throughout its range the rush *Juncus trifidus* exhibits a wide ecological amplitude. It has already been described as abundant in some stands of the Rhacomitreto-Empetretum and a *J. trifidus-Rhacomitrium* heath will be described later, but in the two following noda it plays its most important phytosociological role. The first of these, the Cladineto-Juncetum trifidi, is decidedly chionophilous.

The association element consists of *Carex bigelowii*, *Juncus trifidus*, *Cetraria islandica*, *Cladonia bellidiflora*, *C. sylvatica*, *C. uncialis*, *C. gracilis* and *C. pyxidata*. *Juncus trifidus* is the only dominant but several species of *Cladonia* and *Rhacomitrium lanuginosum* may almost reach co-dominance. There are no specially characteristic species and species numbers are low (48 for the eight lists of Table 36, ranging from 15 to 25 with an average of 19).

Map 19 shows that the Cladineto-Juncetum trifidi is confined to a small area of the East-central Highlands centred upon the granite mass of the Cairngorms, where it is confined to level or gently sloping summit plateaux above 3000 ft. (914 m.). Stands are developed as a network on loose erosion surfaces, with an increasing amount of cover as the shallow basins with Nardetum medio-alpinum are approached. It is difficult to select a sample plot of more than 4 sq. m. which excludes bare granite gravel or the hepatic crust of a different association.

The relationships of the *Juncus trifidus* communities of the high Cairngorm plateaux to exposure and snow-cover can be summed up as follows:

(i) Moderately exposed site which does not form a collecting ground for snow . . *Rhacomitrium* heath with *J. trifidus* (p. 89).

(ii) Moderately exposed site with intermittent cover of up to 50 cm. powder snow throughout winter . . . . . . Cladineto-Juncetum trifidi containing chionophilous lichens and a little *R. lanuginosum*

(iii) Severely exposed site where snow can never lie and *Rhacomitrium* cannot form a carpet *J. trifidus* tussocks with a few chionophobous lichens and a little *R. lanuginosum* (probably the equivalent of the *Juncus trifidus-Festuca ovina* nodum)

There is a gradual transition from the one habitat to the next so that it is difficult to say where the Cladineto-Juncetum ends and the isolated *Juncus* tussock ground begins. The edge of the *Rhacomitrium* heath is usually well defined. On aerial photographs communities (ii) and (iii) show up as a dark reticulum or stipple against the pale background of loose erosion surface while the *Rhacomitrium* heaths, Nardeta and late snow communities form areas of uniform colour.

Outside the Cairngorms the association has only been seen in fragmentary form on the Dalradian quartzite of An Socach, south of Braemar and on part of the Clova plateau.

Most of the soils examined were uniform mixtures of humus and sandy gravel with a surface crust (Alpine Rawmark of Kubiena) but stand M56116a was developed on a podsol profile:

0–8 cm.	.	undecomposed roots and lichen
8–12 cm.	.	black peaty sand pH 4·3
12–27 cm.	.	grey sand
>27 cm.	.	dark brown stony sandy gravel.

The *Juncus trifidus* communities of the Cairngorms have been described by Ingram (1958, pp. 707–737), but he considers all vegetation of which *J. trifidus* is the most prominent vascular constituent to be the one association: hence his conclusion that the minimal area of the 'Juncetum trifidi scoticum' must have a size of many square metres.

Some of the larger complexes of chionophilous vegetation in the Cairngorms provide a compendium of information on the snow-cover of *Juncus trifidus* and its communities. This can be shown diagrammatically as in Fig. 12. *J. trifidus* is largely excluded from the Nardetum but its tolerance of snow-cover extends to the outer zone of the moss communities of the snow-bed centre.

The Juncetum trifidi nudum of Rondane (Dahl, 1956, p. 165) has a total list of 41 species (mean per list 18), 20 species and three constants in common with our Cladineto-Juncetum. In the more oceanic region of Sylene the *Cetraria crispa-Cladonia sylvatica-Juncus trifidus* association (Nordhagen, 1927, p. 289) has a list of 49 species of which

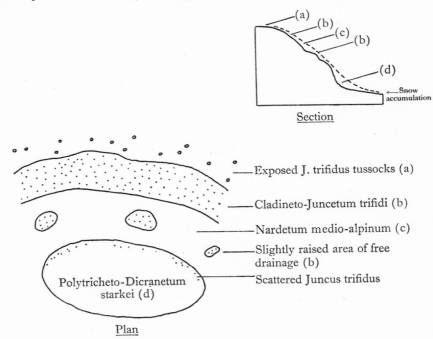

Fig. 12. Snow-bed vegetation in the Cairngorms at about 3800–4000 ft.

26 species, including six constants, are in common with our association. When comparable associations are matched there seems to be little justification for Ingram's contention that the Scottish Juncetum trifidi reveals a pronounced paucity in species compared with similar European communities, at least so far as Scandinavia is concerned.

The Norwegian Junceta are found between 1100 m. and 1400 m. and they experience a reliable but only moderately deep winter snow-cover which disappears before that on the *Deschampsia-Anthoxanthum* and *Nardus* communities. They remain moister in summer than the Cladineto-Juncetum and occur on deeper soils with humus accumulation, but no podsolisation, generally over boulders.

Juncus trifidus-Festuca ovina *nodum*
(Table 37)

The second of the *Juncus trifidus* noda, the *Juncus trifidus-Festuca ovina nodum*, is markedly chionophobous and occupies some of the most exposed ground of the Scottish mountains.

The constant species are *Salix herbacea, Juncus trifidus, Deschampsia flexuosa, Festuca ovina, Alchemilla alpina* and *Rhacomitrium lanuginosum,* and there are 12 other species in constancy class IV. It is rather misleading to speak of dominants in such open vegetation but the six constants reach the highest cover-abundance values and certain species such as *Cherleria sedoides, Thymus drucei* and *Stereocaulon vesuvianum* are prominent in certain sites. *Solorina crocea* (constancy class II) is highly selective for this *nodum* as well as for the Gymnomitreto-Salicetum herbaceae (p. 97). Two recent additions to the vascular flora of Scotland, *Diapensia lapponica* and *Artemisia norvegica,* have their stations in this type of vegetation. There are 78 species in the table and numbers of species per stand range from 18 to 34 with an average of 25.5.

The distribution of the *nodum* is shown in Map 19 and it can be seen that apart from one or two small stands or variants it is confined to the North-west Highlands. Since this is a community of windswept erosion surface the map has been zoned according to the mean number of days with gale force winds experienced at climatological station levels (*Climatological Atlas of the British Isles,* 1952). Records of the *nodum* are practically confined to the windiest region of the mainland, and it can safely be assumed that winds at higher levels will be proportionately stronger than at the points of observation.

Vegetation of this type is found from just under 2000 ft. (610 m.) to 3700 ft. (1129 m.) on exposed ridges and cols (Plate 15). Lists 13 and 14 (Table 37) from Ben Lawers are intermediate in composition between this *nodum* and the Gymnomitreto-Salicetum herbaceae and lack several constants of both. Transitional stands are also frequent in the North-west Highlands. This merging of the two types in certain places is almost certainly due to the similar effects of extreme exposure and late snow-lie in encouraging species which are sensitive to competition from less hardy plants. The ground is level, or with a moderate slope of any aspect, and consists of typical wind-eroded, stone-littered ground with small and large rock fragments firmly set in a matrix of finer particles as though rolled in (Plates 15 and 16). Vegetation cover is almost non-existent on some sites and there are all stages up to closed *Rhacomitrium* heath. In the stands analysed, cover varies from 20 per cent to 60 per cent of the total area.

Soils are often surprisingly deep and fertile in appearance below the surface armour of stone (Alpine Hamada Rawmark of Kubiena, 1953, p. 150). Ferreira (unpublished thesis) records more than 60 cm. of friable, light brown micaceous soil pH 4·3–4·8 under the stones of the Ben Hope summit plateau in North-west Sutherland and remarks that this soil apparently lacks grains of felspar and quartz. We have not encountered soils deeper than 25 cm. in our own investigations and these have given pH values of 4·7–4·9. There may be an ill-defined and crusted layer of humus accumulation at the surface while the loam immediately below is reddish or orange brown and becomes brighter in colour with depth. These soils often appear to be truncated types which formed beneath a rather different vegetation, probably closed *Rhacomitrium* heath.

Solifluction phenomena are common on this exposed ground. The level and homogeneous pavement often passes to terracing as the slope increases, with a distinctive vegetation pattern resulting from alternation of *Rhacomitrium* heath and the present *nodum*, as the exposure changes repeatedly (Plate 16). Stone polygons and stripes can sometimes be distinguished and flat slabs may be tilted on end to give the so-called gravestones. Figure 13 shows a vegetation pattern on the summit of Beinn Dearg, Inverlael with the present *nodum* occupying the centres of polygons.

There may be abrupt or gradual transitions from stands of the *Juncus trifidus-Festuca ovina nodum* to either rich or poor *Rhacomitrium* heath. The extent of erosion surface with this vegetation may be increasing at the present day after an earlier period of stability, or the situation may be as summed up by Poore and McVean (1957) that, 'where the summit soils are deep and sandy, as on the Torridonian formation of the north-west, there often appears to be a cyclical alternation between *Rhacomitrium* heath and erosion pavement according to the vagaries of the wind in producing local erosion

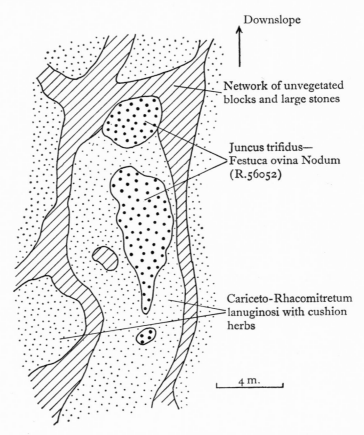

Downslope

Network of unvegetated
blocks and large stones

Juncus trifidus—
Festuca ovina Nodum
(R.56052)

Cariceto-Rhacomitretum
lanuginosi with cushion
herbs

4 m.

Fig. 13. Vegetation pattern on elongated stone-nets. Beinn
Dearg, Loch Broom, West Ross at 3300 ft.

or deposition'. Whichever explanation is true, there certainly appears to have been a great deal of recent erosion and in places, as on Ben Hope, small islands with eroded sides remain as evidence of once extensive *Rhacomitrium* heaths on the denuded ground. The wind-blown soil often builds up to the leeward and these recently formed deposits may themselves be cut away (Plate 15). On the ridge of Sgurr na Lapaich, Cannich, the eroding edge of the wind-blown soil exceeds a depth of one metre in places.

The corresponding nodum in the East-central Highlands is the exposed variant of the Gymnomitreto-Salicetum herbaceae, and on the loose gravelly soils of the Cairngorm plateaux it appears to be a community of isolated *Juncus trifidus* tussocks (p. 75).

Similar erosion surfaces or 'fell-field' have been described under various names from the Faeroes by Ostenfeld (1908), from Iceland by Hansen (1930) and from Shetland by Spence (1957).

Chapter 5

HERB AND FERN MEADOWS

In Scandinavia forb and fern-dominated vegetation is described from Sub-alpine birch woods and willow scrub and from areas of deep snow-lie in the Low-alpine zone. In Scotland we have fragmentary examples of all these communities, some of which have already been mentioned in previous chapters, but the ones to be described here are those that can conveniently be grouped under the term 'meadow' (Orders Lactucion alpinae and Ranunculeto-Oxyrion, pp. 139, 140).

For various reasons, both biotic and climatic, natural herb meadows are rare in the Scottish Highlands, and grazing by wild and domestic animals is everywhere responsible for the restriction of such vegetation to precipitous or otherwise protected ground. Poore recognised the existence in Breadalbane of a Tall Herb *nodum* (unpublished) on inaccessible rock ledges and one of his three lists has been included in Table 38. His *Sibbaldia nodum* (Poore, 1955b), a heavily grazed herb mat on calcium-rich soils, is the only published example of this kind of vegetation.

Tall Herb *nodum*
(Table 38)

The Tall Herb *nodum* provides the best introduction to the group. There are six constants: *Deschampsia caespitosa*, *Luzula sylvatica*, *Angelica sylvestris*, *Geum rivale*, *Sedum rosea* and *Hylocomium splendens* and a wide variety of possible dominants, notably *Geranium sylvaticum*, *Chamaenerion angustifolium*, *Heracleum sphondylium*, *Geum rivale*, *Sedum rosea*, *Succisa pratensis*, *Trollius europaeus*, *Luzula sylvatica*, *Alchemilla vulgaris* agg., *Angelica sylvestris*, *Cirsium heterophyllum*, *Cicerbita alpina*, *Hylocomium splendens*, *Thuidium tamariscinum*. *Heracleum sphondylium* and *Leptodontium recurvifolium* are exclusive to the *nodum* and *Rubus saxatilis*, *Angelica sylvestris*, *Geranium sylvaticum*, *Saussurea alpina*, *Sedum rosea* and *Trollius europaeus* are selective or preferential. *Leptodontium recurvifolium* is an extremely oceanic moss and only appears in stands from the North-west Highlands. A total of 225 species is recorded, with an average of 47 for each stand.

It has not been possible to divide this rather broad vegetation unit into local associations. There are, however, distinct Central and North-west Highland facies due to differences of geographical plant distribution; for example, *Heracleum sphondylium* and *Geranium sylvaticum* are confined to stands south of the Great Glen. A series from oligotrophic to eutrophic can also be made out, evidently corresponding to the calcium content of the bedrock or the irrigation water, but the vegetation at the acid end of the series, dominated by *Vaccinium myrtillus* and *Luzula sylvatica*, has been transferred to Table 6 (lists 21–26) for comparison with Betuletum Oxaleto-Vaccinetum.

We believe that the apparent lack of uniformity within the *nodum* may be due to the restricted size of the habitats available and hence of the stands themselves. Small and isolated ledges have come to be dominated by one species at the expense of floristic variety, and it is often difficult to list a standard sized plot without including marginal fragments of chomophytic vegetation.

Nevertheless, the Tall Herb *nodum* is a widespread one (Map 5) and is found where-ever the mountains above the forest limit offer a sufficient number and extent of cal-careous crags and broken ground to provide protection from grazing animals (Plates 17 and 19). Tall herb communities may be developed at altitudes well below the actual or potential forest limit (see also Sub-alpine willow scrub, p. 26), and they occur in the rare ungrazed patches of woodland and scrub on fertile soils, especially on islands in lochs (McVean, 1958, Spence, 1960). The total altitudinal range is from under 1000 ft. (305 m.) to 2800 ft. (854 m.). Good examples can be seen on Meall Cumhan of Ben Nevis, Ben Lui, the Ben Lawers range, Seana Bhraigh, Beinn Bhan (Applecross), and at the head of Caenlochan.

The size of the stands varies from a few square metres to several hundred square metres, the larger ones (more suitable for floristic analyses) tending to be on steep or precipitous slopes in inaccessible or hazardous situations. Soils vary considerably in depth and moisture content but all are fertile brown loams of moderate acidity (pH 4·8–5·4) and the rate of nitrification is obviously high. Fertility results either from the con-tinual enrichment by fragments of soft and calcareous rocks or from intermittent irrigation with drainage water from soft or hard calcareous rocks. Where the enrichment fails dominance of *Vaccinium myrtillus* and *Luzula sylvatica* or ferns is established as explained above. This is strikingly shown on the great ungrazed 'ledge' of Beinn Bhan (see p. 63) where irrigation lines are marked by strips of luxuriant tall herb vegetation in an otherwise continuous cover of the other oligotrophic communities.

Tall herb ledges are also to be found in Lakeland and in North Wales. Pigott (1956) describes mowing meadows with related vegetation from Upper Teesdale and similar examples, usually undisturbed patches on banks and in corners of upland hay meadows, occur quite widely in northern England. Poore (unpublished) notes the same affinities in the riverbank vegetation of the Tay.

Individual lists which would fit into one or other of several Scandinavian associations can be selected from Table 38. Our *nodum* is therefore best regarded as an unorganised or fragmentary Lactucion (p. 140). The species after which this alliance has been named, *Cicerbita (Lactuca) alpina*, is a rare species in Scotland but a stand in which it is prominent has been included in Table 38 (list 14).

In the Rondane district of central Norway tall herb vegetation has a distribution which recalls the situation in Scotland since it is restricted to steep slopes in areas of better rock. Dahl (1956, p. 192 et seq.) distinguishes two associations in this area, the Geranietum sylvatici alpicolum, which he compares with the *Deschampsia flexuosa* variant of Nordhagen's association of the same name, and the Chamaenerietum angusti-folii nudum. The soils of the tall herb meadows are similar in Scotland and Norway (Nordhagen, 1943, pp. 339, 360).

We have no direct records of the snow-cover experienced by the Scottish tall herb ledges but circumstantial evidence indicates a fairly thick accumulation in most winters, melting out early in spring. On the other hand, we believe that in all but the most oceanic parts of the Highlands communities of *Athyrium alpestre* and *Cryptogramma crispa* are completely dependent on the protection that a snow-cover provides against winter frost and records show the early accumulation of a considerable depth of snow reaching its maximum in March and melting out quickly thereafter.

Cryptogrammeto-Athyrietum chionophilum
(*Cryptogramma-Athyrium* snow-bed)
(Table 39)

These fern-dominated snow beds have just sufficient integration to be described as an association, the Cryptogrammeto-Athyrietum chionophilum. There are eleven constants: *Athyrium alpestre, Cryptogramma crispa, Deschampsia flexuosa, D. caespitosa, Alchemilla alpina, Galium hercynicum, Hypnum callichroum, Polytrichum alpinum, Rhytidiadelphus loreus, Lophozia floerkii* and *Cladonia bellidiflora*. The field layer may be dominated by either *Athyrium* or *Cryptogramma* but *Rhytidiadelphus loreus* is the only bryophyte dominating the ground layer. Apart from isolated occurrences in moss-dominated snow-beds *Cryptogramma crispa* is exclusive to this association. Low-level screes in which *Cryptogramma* may also be abundant (cf. Leach, 1930) do not come within the scope of this survey since they are not found in the Highlands to the same extent as in England, Wales and the Southern Uplands. This may be due in part to the greater scarcity of suitable habitats. *Cryptogramma* is abundant from 100 m. upwards on the screes of Applecross but this is a markedly oceanic district of the Highlands.

Floristically the association cannot well be confused with any other but its limits are occasionally ill-defined. *Thelypteris oreopteris* stands such as list 27, Table 6, and tall herb communities (list 14, Table 38) may contain a little *Athyrium alpestre*, and *Cryptogramma*-dominated beds sometimes pass gradually to the Polytricheto-Dicranetum starkei of later snow-lie (p. 96). Again, the extensive fern-beds on the Beinn Bhan 'ledge' (p. 63) are mostly dominated by *Athyrium alpestre* (Plate 18), with several other species of fern, but snow-cover is probably not unduly prolonged here, and the community appears to represent an oligotrophic and oceanic equivalent of the Tall Herb *nodum*. The evidence (p. 63) suggests that it is sensitive to grazing and so is rare even in the west.

The association is mainly western in distribution but is well represented in the Cairngorms (Map 20). The stands are found on stabilised block scree, as small patches among large tumbled boulders (Fig. 14) or on ledges between 2700 ft. (824 m.) and 3600 ft. (1098 m.) and they vary in size from one or two to several hundred square metres. These larger stands are not usually continuous nor particularly homogeneous but there is seldom any difficulty in obtaining a plot of 4 sq. m. for analysis. Soils may consist of almost pure humus up to 14 cm. deep resting on boulders or be composed of humus, sand and silt intermixtures over smaller rock fragments. The pH of pure *Athyrium* humus (M56135) was found to be 4·1.

We have an insufficient representation of the association in the Highlands to attempt a floristic separation of the *Athyrium* from the *Cryptogramma*-dominated stands. Gjaerevoll (1956) follows Nordhagen (1943) in dividing the Scandinavian chionophilous fern communities into two separate associations, the Athyrietum alpestris and the

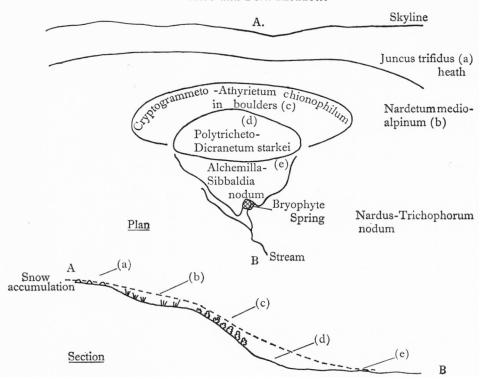

Fig. 14. Snow-bed vegetation in the Cairngorms at about 3500–4000 ft.

Cryptogrammetum crispi. The Athyrietum alpestris is represented in all parts of Scandinavia but forms a greater proportion of the vegetation in western Norway, while the second association is confined to the west. A further subdivision is sometimes made within the Athyrietum according to whether tall herbs or species of later snow-lie such as *Salix herbacea* and *Sibbaldia procumbens* accompany the fern. The Cryptogrammetum is floristically closer to the second group.

Our association, which also exhibits the tall herb and late snow elements, has 22 species in common with the Athyrietum alpestris of Gjaerevoll (1956, Table 17) and 25 species in common with his Cryptogrammetum (loc. cit. Table 18). Snow regime and soils also appear to be similar. Nordhagen (1927) describes a distinct podsol profile from Athyrietum in Sylene.

Knaben (1950, p. 49) emphasises the importance of ferns in the vegetation of mid-west Norway both in Sub-alpine woods and scrub and in the Low-alpine snow-beds. She finds that 'the development of fern meadows (*Athyrium* spp. *Dryopteris* spp. *Thelypteris* spp. etc.) depends on precipitation and moisture' and that 'they concentrate in the districts with the highest precipitation' within her study area of the Middle Sogn. In Scotland, fern-dominated vegetation is widespread at low levels, indicating the generally oceanic nature of the climate, but even here it is often best developed in the west, especially those types associated with woodlands. *Pteridium aquilinum* communities occur most extensively in those districts with a long history of sheep-grazing but are scarce when soils are predominantly peaty. Bracken does not usually extend far above 1500 ft. (457 m.) indicating an intolerance to cold or exposure. A comparable type dominated by *Thelypteris oreopteris* is locally extensive, reaching well to the east. All these

7

fern communities have close affinities to other noda, such as the Betula-herb *nodum* (p. 16) and are not described separately.

Dwarf Herb *nodum*
(Table 40)

While the meadow communities dealt with so far have a relatively luxuriant growth the remainder contrast with them in dwarfness of stature, the herbs forming a dense, low sward. We have called the first of these the Dwarf Herb *nodum* since so many species of herbs are present.

The nine constants are *Selaginella selaginoides, Agrostis tenuis, Deschampsia caespitosa, Festuca ovina* agg., *Alchemilla alpina, Sibbaldia procumbens, Silene acaulis, Thymus drucei* and *Polytrichum alpinum*. This is a rich type of vegetation floristically with 191 species in all and an average of 39 species per stand. *Silene acaulis* is the most frequent dominant and forms a discontinuous carpet in which its associates are rooted. Grasses and small herbs are usually abundant and together they may sometimes replace *Silene* entirely. *Cherleria sedoides* is often plentiful and may replace *Silene* as the carpet-former (list 6). Bryophytes are numerous but, apart from *Rhacomitrium lanuginosum* and *R. canescens*, usually have a low cover. *Sagina saginoides* and *Myosotis alpestris* are exclusive and *Cerastium alpinum* is selective or preferential for the *nodum*. Montane species in general are particularly well represented and some are rarities otherwise confined to rock ledges (cf. Poore, 1955b).

The Dwarf Herb *nodum* is similar to many stands of Polygoneto-Rhacomitretum lanuginosi and differs mainly in the lesser abundance of *Rhacomitrium* and the greater variety of other mosses. It is also closely related to *Deschampsieto-Rhytidiadelphetum triquetrosum* but this has a higher cover of hypnaceous mosses. Another dwarf herb community which often occurs in close proximity to the present one in Breadalbane is distinguished by the dominance of *Alchemilla vulgaris* agg. This could probably rank as a distinct nodum but only one stand has been listed and it has been included (list 21) in Table 40 for comparison.

The *nodum* has a widespread western distribution (Map 21) but is confined to calcareous rocks throughout its range. Although present on all the rich mica-schist hills of Breadalbane it is represented by only one or two small patches on the equally calcareous rocks of Caenlochan and Clova. In the Ben Alder and Ben Nevis massifs there are fine examples on Dalradian limestone while all occurrences north of the Great Glen are on lime-bearing rocks of the Moine and Lewisian series. In some of the northerly localities the associated rock appears to be less calcareous than is usual in the south.

The *nodum* is distinctly montane with an altitudinal range of 2300 ft. to 3900 ft. (702–1190 m.) and does not occur on calcareous rocks at lower levels, e.g. in the Glen Tilt area. Stands may be sited almost anywhere on stable ground regardless of aspect and slope provided that there is good drainage accompanied by intermittent irrigation. Steep ground below cliffs is the usual situation but stands often occur on gently inclined summit slopes: snow-cover is fairly prolonged in these places and the *nodum* may be somewhat chionophilous.

The soils are fertile brown loams of high base-status pH 4·8–5·8 with or without some surface accumulation of mull humus and commonly containing earthworms.

Some sites are enriched by the downwash of mineral particles or by the gravitational addition of material from disintegrating rock and unstable banks.

Stands vary in size from a few square metres to several hundred square metres. The largest ones occur on hills where there are extensive areas of highly calcareous rock, as on the upper south-east slopes of Ben Lawers. On some Breadalbane hills the total area occupied by the *nodum* amounts to many hectares.

Snow-cover is moderate on most sites but its significance in the distribution of the *nodum* has not been studied. Some other factor would appear to cause the western bias in distribution and it may be that the greater rainfall of the west leads to more frequent irrigation than in the drier east. Calcareous rocks are much scarcer in the east so that a lack of suitable soils seems to be partly responsible.

The Dwarf Herb *nodum* is the high level equivalent of the sub-montane species-rich and Saxifrageto-Agrosto-Festuceta; edaphic conditions show close similarity and there is a good deal of floristic overlap. Like the two grassland associations the *nodum* may have been produced by heavy grazing in some places. A few stands contain tall herbs which have been dwarfed by grazing so that there are affinities with the Tall Herb *nodum* also. Where there is a little *Dryas* in the turf and this species is plentiful on adjacent cliff faces the Dwarf Herb *nodum* may be a biotic derivative of *Dryas* heath.

In spite of what has just been said the *Silene acaulis* carpets give an impression of 'naturalness' in many places, especially on the high tops, and many seem to be climatically controlled. Moreover, the *nodum* shows great similarity to certain rock face communities in which banks of *Silene* are conspicuous and in which there is a mixed growth of small herbs and mosses.

On the steep north to east slopes the Dwarf Herb *nodum* often passes into Deschampsietum caespitosae alpinum, evidently in response to a change in irrigation and snow-cover. On the gentler inclines of high watersheds and summits it often merges imperceptibly into Polygoneto-Rhacomitretum or Deschampsieto-Rhytidiadelphetum triquetrosum. Where stands occur among poorer *Rhacomitrium* heath they usually mark the site of an intermittent spring.

The dwarf herb community dominated by species of the *Alchemilla vulgaris* aggregate is a more local type and usually occupies more strongly irrigated sites alongside those of the present *nodum*. The relationships between the two have been discussed by Poore (1955b).

The Dwarf Herb *nodum* corresponds to the *Sibbaldia procumbens nodum* which Poore (loc. cit.) described from Breadalbane and Table 40 includes seven of his lists. Although it certainly reaches its optimum development in Breadalbane the *nodum* has proved to be more widespread northwards but it appears, nevertheless, to be confined to the Highlands in Britain.

Poore (loc. cit.) gives detailed reasons for equating his *Sibbaldia nodum* with the moss-rich *Potentilla crantzii-Polygonum viviparum* sociation described by Nordhagen (1927) for Sylene and he traces connections with Norwegian species-rich *Dryas* heath also.

Alchemilla-Sibbaldia *nodum*

(Table 41, lists 1–12)

The constants of this *nodum* are *Agrostis tenuis*, *Deschampsia caespitosa*, *Alchemilla alpina* and *Sibbaldia procumbens*. *Alchemilla* and *Sibbaldia* are the usual dominants but grasses may be abundant and moss cover, mainly of *Rhacomitrium* spp., is high. There are no characteristic species.

The *Alchemilla-Sibbaldia nodum* differs from the Dwarf Herb *nodum* in its lack of *Silene acaulis* and many other species of herbs and mosses. The average number of species per stand is lower (22). Closely related *Alchemilla alpina*-dominated vegetation (Table 41, lists 13–15) is distinguished by an abundance of *Potentilla erecta* instead of *Sibbaldia* and a still more restricted list of species. Intermediates do occur. Some stands of Rhacomitreto-Dicranetum starkei contain abundant *Sibbaldia* but they differ from the present *nodum* in the greater abundance of chionophilous species and the higher cover of mosses.

The geographical distribution is rather similar to that of the last *nodum* but it is more widespread in the east probably because its dependence on snow-cover rather than soil base-status gives it an important niche in the Cairngorms (Map 22). The stands are usually situated in hollows and corries which hold snow readily, and a north to east aspect is particularly favoured. The position of a moderately late snow cornice around the steep rim of a corrie is sometimes marked by an interrupted band of *Alchemilla-Sibbaldia* patches. The *nodum* also occurs far below in the corries or on the summit slopes above so that the altitudinal range varies from 2100 ft. (641 m.) to 3500 ft. (1068 m.). Individual stands seldom exceed 100 sq. m. in area and are usually much less.

Like the Dwarf Herb *nodum*, the *Alchemilla-Sibbaldia nodum* depends on inter-mittent irrigation, but more particularly on irrigation by melt water or permanent springs issuing from late snow-beds (Fig. 14). The first nodum often passes into the second as snow-lie increases and the relationship between the two is well shown on Eididh nan Clach Geala, near Loch Broom. At 2400 ft. (732 m.) on this hill an enclosed basin amongst moraines acts as a temporary reservoir during wet weather and also holds a moderately late snow-bed. The sides of the basin show a clear vegetational zonation, passing from Rhacomitreto-Callunetum on the moraines through an upper Dwarf Herb zone to an *Alchemilla-Sibbaldia* zone, and finally to a central *Carex saxatilis* com-munity on the stony floor. This corresponds to a gradient of increasing snow-lie and irrigation from the rim towards the centre of the hollow.

This type of vegetation occurs on all but the poorest rocks and so is more widespread than the Dwarf Herb *nodum*: nevertheless, it is best developed on areas of calcareous rock. The soils tend to show incipient podsolisation, sometimes with mottling of the B horizon. There is usually a surface humus layer but profiles vary greatly, some being shallow peats (up to 24 cm.) with mineral soil below passing quickly to rock brash, whereas others are silty or sandy loams with only a few cm. of humus at the surface. The pH of the surface soil is 4·8–5·4.

The *Alchemilla-Sibbaldia nodum* usually occurs amongst other late snow communities and may be irrigated by melt water from sites with chionophilous Nardeta or the moss-dominated associations of the latest snow-beds (Fig. 14). Rhacomitreto-Dicranetum starkei is often in close proximity but appears to be differentiated from the *Alchemilla-Sibbaldia* patches by a longer snow-cover.

The *Alchemilla-Potentilla* communities belong chiefly to the Western Highlands but although they also depend on intermittent irrigation this does not come so often from melting snow. Stands may occupy sites exactly equivalent to those of the *Alchemilla-Sibbaldia nodum* but more often they are found below intermittent springs or solifluction lobes. The widespread occurrence of this vegetation on non-calcareous rocks such as

Torridon sandstone and Moine granulite suggests that low soil calcium-status as well as a shorter snow-cover is responsible for its separation from the *Alchemilla-Sibbaldia nodum*. In some areas *Sibbaldia* grows most abundantly on soils which have a rather higher calcium-status than those formed from the poorest rocks, although it appears to be quite indifferent to base-status when snow-cover is prolonged.

Typical *Alchemilla-Sibbaldia* vegetation is confined to the Highlands but in the Lake District there are equivalents of the *Alchemilla-Potentilla* communities of the Western Highlands. In floristics and habitat the *nodum* can be compared with the Alchemilletum alpinae of Rondane (Dahl, 1956, p. 184) and either the Sibbaldietum procumbentis or the *Alchemilla alpina* sociation of the Anthoxantho-Deschampsietum flexuosae (Gjaerevoll, 1957, pp. 177, 53). The first two Norwegian associations occur in sites resembling that of the irrigated stands of the *Alchemilla-Sibbaldia nodum* while the third is closer in habitat to the snow cornice stands mentioned above.

Saxifragetum aizoidis

(*Saxifraga aizoides* banks)
(Table 42)

The association element of the Saxifragetum aizoidis consists of the twelve species *Selaginella selaginoides, Deschampsia caespitosa, Festuca ovina* agg., *F. rubra, Alchemilla glabra, Parnassia palustris, Pinguicula vulgaris, Polygonum viviparum, Ranunculus acris, Saxifraga aizoides, S. oppositifolia* and *Ctenidium molluscum*. The nine lists of Table 42 have a total of 142 species with a stand average of 47·5. *Saxifraga aizoides* is the usual dominant but *S. oppositifolia* may occasionally be co-dominant as in list 9. *Cystopteris montana* is exclusive to the association. In a closely related type of vegetation *Saxifraga aizoides* more frequently shares dominance with *S. oppositifolia*, as well as with *S. hypnoides* and hypnaceous mosses, and there are fewer hydrophilous species (Table 42, lists 10–13). Saxifrageto-Agrosto-Festucetum differs in the dominance of grasses and low cover values for *S. aizoides*; it occurs at lower altitudes as a rule.

This association is confined to cliff faces, steep banks at the base of cliffs, or other steep rocky ground; the angle of slope lies between 25 degrees and 70 degrees. It has been found only on calcareous mountains and mainly on those lying between Breadalbane and Clova (Map 23). Ferreira (unpublished thesis) has described the same type of vegetation on Ben Hope, Ben Lui and elsewhere and believes that it is a more reliable indicator of highly calcareous rocks than any other community. Our own observations support his view.

A copious seepage of water down the rock face is as essential as the high lime content of the rock. The association occurs most often on north-facing cliffs since these tend to be the wettest but it has been found on sites of all aspects. The altitudinal range is from 1850 ft. to 2600 ft. (564–793 m.). The necessary habitat conditions occur over limited areas only, so that the biggest continuous stands are not usually more than 20 sq. m. Where Saxifragetum aizoidis occurs on steep banks there is usually a moderate depth (up to 30 cm.) of wet, silty soil containing variable amounts of humus. Some sites show a definite accumulation of mull humus. On cliff faces the vegetation may overlie the rock surface almost directly with hardly any soil between.

The mixed saxifrage communities also occur on steep earthy banks at the base of calcareous cliffs but they are drier than typical Saxifragetum aizoidis and tend to be found at higher elevations. Sometimes these stands appear to be intermediate between the present association and the Dwarf Herb *nodum*. Both types of vegetation show transitions to various open rock-face communities and on the cliffs of Ben Lui Saxifragetum aizoidis passes into *Dryas* ledge communities as the flow of water fails. There are other transitions to the Tall Herb *nodum* on more stable ledges and to heavily grazed Saxifrageto-Agrosto-Festucetum on the slopes below.

Fragments of a similar *Saxifraga aizoides* community occur on a few calcareous crags in Lakeland but the association otherwise seems to be confined to the Highlands.

The equivalent Norwegian associations are not found on such steep ground and they experience a deep winter snow-cover. They are the species-rich *Saxifraga* association of Sylene (Nordhagen, 1927, p. 352) and the Oppositifolietum (Gjaerevoll, 1956, p. 303) which is dominated by *S. oppositifolia* rather than *S. aizoides*.

Cliff Vegetation

Calcareous mountain cliffs, especially those at high levels, support a wealth of herbaceous vegetation which is best considered with the mountain meadows. The cliff communities include many montane species which are sensitive to grazing and competition; some of our rarities are more or less confined to steep rocks, or at least grow most successfully there. To many botanists this heterogeneous cliff vegetation is the most interesting of all but to the phytosociologist it is easily the most baffling. The larger, stable ledges usually bear tall herb communities and are amenable to the normal method of analysis but the open and patchy vegetation consisting of small herbs, sedges, grasses and bryophytes is very difficult to describe. It is possible to recognise small vegetation units which occur repeatedly but these vary enormously in size and floristic composition because of the fundamental instability of the habitat and its complexity of variation. A straightforward list of species with frequency estimates is perhaps the most efficient way of describing a complex of cliff vegetation although the Domin scale can sometimes be used on the bryophyte and lichen communities of steep or vertical rock faces.

We have therefore analysed only those cliff communities which provided stands of at least the normal minimal area of 2 × 2 m. and these belong to the *Salix lapponum-Luzula sylvatica nodum*, the Tall Herb *nodum*, *Dryas noda* and Saxifragetum aizoidis. In floristics these noda, together with the Dwarf Herb *nodum* and Cariceto-Saxifragetum aizoidis cover much of the range of variation shown by the other calcareous cliff vegetation which we have not studied. They contain many of the rare montane species of such habitats (in this country) but lack completely rupestral species, especially bryophytes.

All the cliff ledge noda were once widespread in other habitats and so none of them is truly chomophytic. Description of the micro-communities naturally confined to open rocks is best reserved for detailed studies of individual rupestral species.

Chapter 6

MOSS HEATHS

Moss-dominated vegetation is characteristic of oceanic climates throughout the World and is well represented in Scotland in the Low and Mid-alpine zones above 2000 ft. (610 m.). The accompanying vascular plants may be either grasses or dwarf shrubs according to the altitude and the length of snow lie.

Heaths dominated by the moss *Rhacomitrium lanuginosum* are one of the most prominent features of Scottish mountain vegetation and there are numerous references in literature from R. Smith (1900) to Poore and McVean (1957). *Rhacomitrium* heath represents the chionophobous end of the moss heath series, and in this chapter we intend to consider also the substantially smaller areas of bryophyte-dominated vegetation of late snow beds or 'schneetälchen' which are found in oceanic and continental climates alike.

Cariceto-Rhacomitretum lanuginosi

(*Rhacomitrium* heath)
(Table 43)

First we should like to revise the arrangement of the *Rhacomitrium-Carex bigelowii nodum* of Poore and McVean (1957) by assigning most of their facies to separate noda and returning to the typical species-impoverished heath of Poore (1955b) which we shall regard as of association rank.

For our present illustration of the *Cariceto-Rhacomitretum lanuginosi* we have chosen eleven lists from the forty available in our records from widely separated parts of the Highlands (including three of Poore's Breadalbane lists) to show the full range in floristics encountered. There are six constants: *Vaccinium myrtillus*, *Deschampsia flexuosa*, *Carex bigelowii*, *Galium hercynicum*, *Rhacomitrium lanuginosum* and *Cladonia uncialis*. *Rhacomitrium* is always the physiognomic dominant (Plate 20) but *Carex bigelowii* and *Deschampsia flexuosa* may attain co-dominance locally. There are no characteristic species.

The species list is almost as restricted as that of the Dicraneto-Caricetum bigelowii with 60 species from eleven stands and numbers per stand varying from 10–23 (average of 16).

A facies rich in *Juncus trifidus* (lists 7, 8) differs from Rhacomitreto-Empetretum containing *J. trifidus* only in the absence of *Empetrum hermaphroditum* itself but in practice it is exceptional to encounter intermediate stands. This facies has been seen forming a zone between the *Juncus trifidus-Festuca ovina nodum* of erosion surfaces and the *Nardus-Rhacomitrium nodum* on both Beinn Eighe and Ben More Assynt. It is widespread and good examples occur in the East-central Highlands, as on Lochnagar and nearby hills. Another facies differs only in having an abundance and even co-dominance of cushion herbs, which may be *Silene acaulis*, *Cherleria sedoides* or *Armeria maritima* or all three together (Table 44, lists 12–14).

The typical association has been recorded from most of the grid squares surveyed (Map 24) and was found to be most extensive on Creag Meagaidh, the Drumochter hills and Ben Wyvis. On the last hill it occupies square kilometres of summit ridge and plateaux and along the main ridge stretches in a continuous carpet for over 5 miles (8 km.). The cushion-herb facies is also extensive on high ground in the West-central and North-west Highlands, particularly in Fannich Forest, the Beinn Dearg group, Ben More Assynt and the Reay Forest.

The association descends to a little under 2000 ft. (610 m.) and extends to the highest summits at 3800 ft. (1159 m.) in the west and north-west. In the Central Highlands the *Rhacomitrium* heaths are not found much below 3000 ft. (914 m.) and the highest extensive stand that we have seen lies at 3900 ft. (1190 m.) in the Ben Nevis range, although fragments extend to over 4000 ft. (1220 m.) in the Cairngorms wherever there is a little shelter from the prevailing winds. On the east side of the Cairngorms the lower limit lies 200–800 ft. (61–244 m.) higher than on the exposed western spurs.

The ground is level or gently sloping as a rule and there is no restriction to any particular aspect. Steeper ground is usually terraced and an eroded form of *Rhacomitrium* heath, richer in species, passes to *Juncus trifidus-Festuca ovina* stands on the terrace flats (Plates 15 and 16).

On fairly level ground the transition to the *Juncus trifidus-Festuca ovina nodum* is often abrupt, along an erosion edge, showing that this kind of vegetation has, in some places at least, been developed by the erosion of closed *Rhacomitrium* heath. Where dwarf shrub or grass heaths pass over to Cariceto-Rhacomitretum the transition generally takes place through a mosaic ecotone. This is finely illustrated on parts of Ben Wyvis and in the Dalnaspidal Forest where the situation can be represented diagrammatically as in Fig. 15. Gradual transitions take place to the herb-rich facies and then to Polygoneto-Rhacomitretum (p. 92) on some hills in the Western Highlands. Increasing

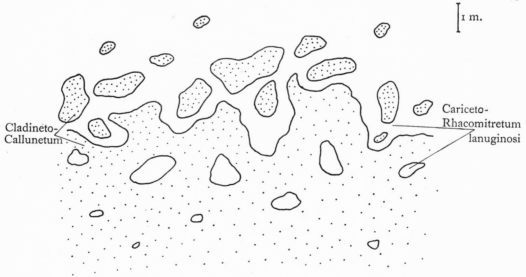

1 m.

Cladineto-
Callunetum

Cariceto-
Rhacomitretum
lanuginosi

Fig. 15. Transition from Cariceto-Rhacomitretum to Cladineto-Callunetum. Ben Wyvis at 2500 ft.

depth of snow accumulation and/or increasing wetness of soil lead to replacement of *Rhacomitrium* heath by the *Nardus noda*, Dicraneto-Caricetum bigelowii, Deschamps-ieto-Rhytidiadelphetum, *Trichophorum* or *Juncus squarrosus* bogs and Empetreto-Eriophoretum.

An interesting variant has been recorded from just under 4000 ft. (1220 m.) on the summit of Aonach Mor near Ben Nevis. Over an area of some tens of square metres *Rhacomitrium lanuginosum* is replaced by *R. canescens* apparently because of the frequent additions of wind-blown sand from a neighbouring erosion surface. This is a frequent occurrence on a smaller scale around the margins of 'blow-outs' in *Rhacomitrium* heath, and both *Alchemilla alpina* and *Festuca ovina* are other frequent species of these places although they may be scarce or lacking in the surrounding heath. The soil profiles at the Aonach Mor site confirm that fresh sand is continually being added:

R. canescens heath		*R. lanuginosum* heath	
0–9 cm.	brown, coarse sandy humus	0–3 cm.	black, greasy humus
9–10 cm.	light brown sand, no humus	3–5 cm.	light grey sand
10–15 cm.	brown sandy humus	5–>15 cm.	reddish brown sandy grit.
15–19·5 cm.	light grey sand		
19·5–>25 cm.	coffee-coloured humous sand.		

R. canescens is often the dominant species in Icelandic moss heaths (McVean, 1955, p. 333) and in the moss mat of Jan Mayen (Warren Wilson, 1958, p. 407, 1952, p. 249).

Since moss heath is a characteristic oceanic formation and lichen heath an equally characteristic continental one, any juxtaposition of these vegetation types is of considerable interest. On the ridge of Carn Ban Mor, a western spur of the Cairngorms, Cladineto-Callunetum sylvaticosum passes to Cariceto-Rhacomitretum at 3000 ft. (914 m.). Little difference in habitat can be detected for the lichen heath patches in the moss heath, but the moss patches in the lichen heath invariably occupy damp hollows, sometimes with distinct water seepage. The constituents of the two associations do not mingle. Fifteen miles to the south-east true lichen heath can be seen occupying sheltered hollows in the *Rhacomitrium* heath of Carn nan Sac, a curious reversal of the situation in Norway described below. The summit ridge of Carn a'Gheoidh and Carn nan Sac in the Cairnwell hills is also remarkable for the extent of a lichen-rich *Rhacomitrium* heath which has also been seen in small patches elsewhere. *Calluna vulgaris* and *Empetrum hermaphroditum* are missing from these hybrid heaths which are thus closer to the present association than to true lichen heath.

In continental Norway *Rhacomitrium* heath has been found occupying small depressions, or localities with slightly impeded drainage, and apparently depending upon some supply of soil water (Nordhagen, 1943, p. 205, and Dahl, 1956, p. 101).

Soils are either shallow rankers or there is an incipient to well developed podsol. The most floristically poor heaths are frequently found on a few cm. of undecomposed moss and black moss humus over siliceous rock debris. The wet moss peat may also rest directly on stony brown loams over better rock. These soils have an appearance of fertility which is not borne out by chemical analyses and in floristics the vegetation is often no richer than on obviously poor soils. The quantities of *Silene acaulis*, *Cherleria sedoides* and *Armeria maritima* in the poor heaths increase with distance north and west quite irrespective of the base status of the soil parent material (Map 24 and Table 44, lists 12–14). Two more typical profiles are given below:

M57032   R56032

cf. Northern Nanopodsol of Kubiena

0–2 cm.	.	black, greasy humus
2–8 cm.	.	white sand
8–11 cm.	.	black, humous sand
11–23 cm.	.	red-brown, sandy gravel
>23 cm.	.	fresh granite gravel.

0–2 cm.	.	greasy, greyish-black humus
2–9 cm.	.	grey-brown sandy loam
9–12 cm.	.	dark chocolate brown sandy loam
12–22 cm.	.	reddish-brown sandy loam
22 cm.	.	rock debris.

Gleyed and mottled profiles have never been observed. Surface pH is from 4·2 to 4·8.

The identity of *Rhacomitrium* heaths in Britain, Scandinavia, Iceland and the Faeroes has been sufficiently established by previous authors and we do not propose an extensive review. The Rhacomitreto-Caricetum bigelowii of Rondane (Dahl, 1956, Table 18) has 20 species and two constants in common with our Table 43. In general the Icelandic and Scandinavian heaths have a eutrophic element only found in our Polygoneto-Rhacomitretum (see below).

Polygoneto-Rhacomitretum lanuginosi

(Species-rich *Rhacomitrium* heath)

(Table 44)

The *Polygoneto-Rhacomitretum lanuginosi* has an association element consisting of *Carex bigelowii, Alchemilla alpina, Armeria maritima, Polygonum viviparum, Silene acaulis, Thymus drucei, Polytrichum alpinum, Rhacomitrium lanuginosum, Rhytidiadelphus loreus, Cetraria islandica, Cladonia uncialis* and *Sphaerophorus globosus. Deschampsia flexuosa, Cherleria sedoides, Salix herbacea* and *Silene acaulis* may reach co-dominance with *Rhacomitrium. Plagiothecium striatellum, Aulacomnium turgidum* and *Hypnum hamulosum* are strongly selective for the association. The rare foliose lichen *Nephromium arcticum* has been recorded only from this association but it does not appear in the Table. Species numbers per stand range from 29 to 48, with an average of 35 and the total record from eleven lists is 93.

The Polygoneto-Rhacomitretum is distinguished floristically from the Cariceto-Rhacomitretum by the presence of *Polygonum viviparum, Thymus drucei* and *Aulacomnium turgidum* as well as by the occurrence of a wide variety of species of lower constancy. Other species such as *Sphaerophorus globosus* are more constantly present in the one than in the other and the whole position has been summarised in Table 44. The principal distinction from the Dwarf Herb *nodum* is the dominance of *Rhacomitrium lanuginosum* instead of hypnaceous mosses but intermediates can be found in places where there is a gradual increase in intermittent irrigation on the rich moss heath. The species-rich *Agrostis-Festuca* grasslands are separated by the dominance of grasses as compared with mosses.

The distribution of the present association is shown in Map 24 along with that of the poor heath; it is a distinctly western and northern type with outliers in west Perthshire and tends to follow the general increase of *Silene acaulis, Cherleria sedoides* and *Armeria maritima* in moss heath towards the north-west. The restriction of the association to outcrops of Cambrian dolomite pointed out by Poore and McVean (1957) cannot now be maintained since rich heath has been recorded from a wide variety of base-rich rocks in the Northern Highlands and from the calcareous schists of Perthshire.

The contrast between poor heath on quartzite and rich heath on dolomite or dolomitic mudstone on Beinn Eighe, Foinaven and elsewhere remains a striking one, however.

The altitudinal range is more restricted than that of the Cariceto-Rhacomitretum, from 2500 ft. (763 m.) to 3500 ft. (1068 m.), although the terrain on which the two heaths are developed is similar. The ground is often steeper, stonier and more wind-eroded than that of *Rhacomitrium* heath in the Eastern Highlands and the stands of species-rich heath are less extensive and homogeneous. Nevertheless they can vary from patches of a few square metres to areas of many hectares where situations and soils allow.

The soil profile may be almost completely undifferentiated, as on the dolomitic mudstones, or may show signs of distinct podsolisation with or without trace of gleying in the B horizon.

R57046	R56045
(on dolomitic mudstone)	(on Moine gneiss)

0–7 cm.	. brown, friable loam pH 5·9	0–2 cm.	. black, friable humus
7–38 cm.	. dark brown, loose loam.	2–7 cm.	. grey-brown, sandy loam
		7–10 cm.	. black-brown, stony humus pan
		10–38 cm.	. dark brown, sandy loam, with iron mottle
		> 38 cm.	. gneiss debris.

The pH values of the surface soil vary from 4·6 to 5·9 so that there is little overlap with pH values from the Cariceto-Rhacomitretum. Apart from richness of parent rock, nutrient-status appears to be maintained by intermittent irrigation (to a lesser extent than in the Dwarf Herb *nodum*) or the stirring of the soil by frost movement. Solifluction cannot be active everywhere in view of the more or less continuous carpet of vegetation

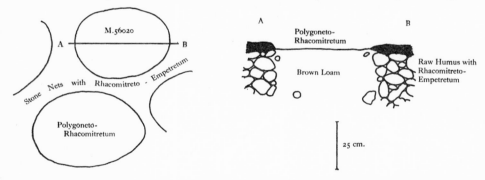

Fig. 16. Vegetation pattern on stone polygon system. Sgurr na Feartaig, West Ross, at 2600 ft.

but on some of the mudstone outcrops periodic soil flows take place and are gradually recolonised. The pH of one mudstone soil flow was found to be 7·1 in contrast to the surface of R57046 above. At 2600 ft. (793 m.) on Sgurr na Feartaig in west Ross-shire rich *Rhacomitrium* heath occurs in a mosaic with Rhacomitreto-Empetretum on irregular polygon soils as shown in Fig. 16. Otherwise, transitions are generally to the species-poor heath or to erosion surface with the *Juncus trifidus-Festuca ovina nodum*.

The Polygoneto-Rhacomitretum lanuginosi was first described as the *Polygonum viviparum-Salix herbacea* facies of the *Rhacomitrium-Carex bigelowii nodum* (Poore and

McVean, 1957) and its relationship to hypnaceous moss heath (now Deschampsieto-Rhytidiadelphetum) on Beinn Eighe illustrated.

While the Icelandic and Faeroese *Rhacomitrium* heaths bear a closer resemblance to this association than to the Cariceto-Rhacomitretum, those of Norway are insufficiently described for us to decide if they cover as wide a range of floristics as the two Scottish heaths. The Hygro-Festucetum ovinae of Rondane (Dahl, 1956) is quite close to our Polygoneto-Rhacomitretum floristically (they have 45 spp. in common) and in its relationships to snow-lie and soil enrichment, but *Rhacomitrium lanuginosum* is only sparsely present in it. None of the other *Festuca ovina* associations of Norway have this close correspondence except perhaps the moss-rich *F. ovina* association of Nordhagen (1927).

Deschampsieto-Rhytidiadelphetum
(*Rhytidiadelphus* snow-bed)
(Table 45)

Continuing our description of the moss heaths in the direction of increasing snow-lie we come to a community dominated by hypnaceous mosses.

The association element consists of the six species *Agrostis tenuis, Deschampsia caespitosa, Carex bigelowii, Galium hercynicum, Polytrichum alpinum* and *Rhytidiadelphus loreus.* The physiognomic dominants are all mosses: *Rhytidiadelphus loreus, R. squarrosus, R. triquetrus* and *Pleurozium schreberi* but *D. caespitosa* and *C. bigelowii* may sometimes attain co-dominance with them. There are no characteristic species.

A total of 107 species is recorded from 20 stands and numbers range from 13–47 per stand with an overall average of 24.

Two facies have been recognised, a species-poor typicum (13–30 species, average 21) and a species-rich triquetrosum (20–47 species, average 32). Although there is some overlap in species numbers many good differentials such as *Rhytidiadelphus triquetrus, Silene acaulis* and *Ranunculus acris* separate the two facies (cf. separation of Polygoneto-Rhacomitretum from Cariceto-Rhacomitretum in the corresponding *Rhacomitrium* heaths).

The Deschampsieto-Rhytidiadelphetum is distinguished floristically from *Rhacomitrium* heaths by the change in moss dominance and from the more closely related Deschampsietum caespitosae alpinum by the substitution of moss for grass dominance (see p. 61).

The distribution of the association (both facies) is distinctly western with only fragmentary stands developed east of Creag Meagaidh and Ben Heasgarnich in the Central Highlands (Map 25). With the exception of an extensive area of the triquetrosum facies in Coire Heasgarnich it is a local vegetation type south of the Great Glen and it can be regarded as the Northern Highland equivalent of Dicraneto-Caricetum bigelowii so far as snow-lie is concerned.

Stands may be only a few square metres in area where they occur in the damper hollows of *Rhacomitrium* heath or they may extend over many hectares as a zone surrounding late snow-bed vegetation. Fig. 17 illustrates the zonation on Ben Wyvis where the Deschampsieto-Rhytidiadelphetum typicum is well represented.

The transition from *Rhacomitrium* to hypnaceous moss heath may be gradual or abrupt (Fig. 17) according to change in slope of ground with attendant change in snow

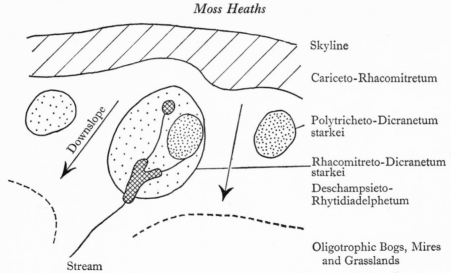

Skyline

Cariceto-Rhacomitretum

Polytricheto-Dicranetum
starkei

Rhacomitreto-Dicranetum
starkei
Deschampsieto-
Rhytidiadelphetum

Oligotrophic Bogs, Mires
and Grasslands

Downslope

Stream

Fig. 17. Snow-bed vegetation. Coire Mhoir of Ben Wyvis at 3000–3300 ft.

regime and moisture content. On some summits, such as that of Fionn Bheinn near Achnasheen, extensive soil hummock systems show a mosaic pattern of these two associations with *Rhacomitrium* heath occupying the exposed hummock tops and *Rhytidiadelphus* heath the sheltered hollows in between. The association ranges altitudinally from 2300 ft. (702 m.) in the far north to a maximum of 3500 ft. (1068 m.) in the Central Highlands. Slopes are generally moderate to steep with a northerly or easterly aspect. The relationships with Polytricheto-Caricetum bigelowii, the *Nardus-Trichophorum* and the *Nardus-Pleurozium noda* are not clear; the hypnaceous moss heath may occasionally be found as a zone around one of the others, separating them from chionophobous vegetation. On Ben Lawers a vegetation type intermediate in some respects between the present association and Polytricheto-Caricetum bigelowii is quite widespread. (This has already been mentioned as the rhytidiadelphetosum facies of *Polytrichum-C. bigelowii* heath) (p. 72, Table 34, lists 1–5).

In the tract from Ben Wyvis to Ben Alder where Deschampsieto-Rhytidiadelphetum and Dicraneto-Caricetum bigelowii overlap they are not found in juxtaposition and the factors determining their separation have not been investigated. In large corries the hypnaceous moss heaths pass gradually to *Deschampsia caespitosa* grassland with decrease in altitude and the transition is never abrupt.

Soils are well developed podsols with strongly gleyed B horizons (mostly under typicum) or deep sandy loams with little profile development except for traces of mottling below (mostly under triquetrosum). The typicum has also been seen occupying deep redistributed peat on Sgurr a'Ghlas Leathaid, Ross-shire. The pH of the surface soil various from 4·1–4·9 (typicum) and from 4·5–5·4 (triquetrosum).

The association was first described as the *Rhytidiadelphus-Deschampsia caespitosa nodum* and hypnoid moss facies of the *Rhacomitrium-C. bigelowii nodum* (Poore and McVean, 1957, p. 429). *Hylocomium splendens* may be an important constituent, or even dominant, in Icelandic moss heaths (McVean, 1955, p. 333) but *Rhytidiadelphus* spp. seem to be absent. The corresponding vegetation in Scandinavia appears to be the Ranunculetum acris acidophilum of Gjaerevoll (1956), a series of hydrophilous low herb meadows poor in calciphile species. There are 29 species common to our list and the

Ranunculus acris-Anthoxanthum odoratum sociation (op. cit. Table 20), which also has three constants (*R. acris*, *Polygonum viviparum* and *Sibbaldia procumbens*) in common with our triquetrosum facies.

LATE SNOW-BED HEATHS

The moss-dominated communities of late snow areas or 'schneetälchen' have proved rather troublesome to classify floristically. To some extent the situation resembles that of the tall herb ledge vegetation where we find a complex that can only be referred to an entire Continental alliance. In this instance, however, a greater quantity of data was available and by rejecting many analyses that appeared to have been made in hybrid stands it proved possible to recognise three separate noda. This procedure was vindicated when later field work made it possible to raise these noda to the status of associations which were found to have distinct habitat preferences and different geographical distributions.

Polytricheto-Dicranetum starkei

(*Polytrichum norvegicum-Dicranum starkei* snow-bed)
(Table 46)

The first of these, the Polytricheto-Dicranetum starkei, has six constants, *Deschampsia caespitosa*, *Saxifraga stellaris*, *Dicranum starkei*, *Oligotrichum hercynicum*, *Polytrichum alpinum* and *P. norvegicum*. *Dicranum starkei* is the usual dominant but other species such as *D. falcatum*, *Pohlia ludwigii*, *Lophozia floerkii* and *Gymnomitrium concinnatum* may replace it or be co-dominant. Some stands are rich in *Salix herbacea*. *Dicranum falcatum* (constancy class I) is exclusive to the association.

Species numbers per stand range from 12 to 26 with an average of 19 and there are 64 species recorded from the ten lists. In making these lists areas with some variety of vascular plants and cryptogams were chosen. Where snow lies particularly late *Dicranum starkei* may form an almost pure carpet (cf. *Gymnomitrium varians* lists in Table 48).

This is the most widely distributed of the late snow-bed group and is found in all the principal high mountain areas of the Highlands (Map 26). Only fragmentary stands occur north of Beinn Dearg in West Ross.

Rhacomitreto-Dicranetum starkei

(*Rhacomitrium-Dicranum starkei* snow-bed)
(Table 47)

The Rhacomitreto-Dicranetum starkei has a closely similar association element, *Carex bigelowii* and *Gnaphalium supinum* replacing *Saxifraga stellaris* and *Polytrichum alpinum* among the constants of the previous association. No single species stands out as the principal dominant and *Gnaphalium supinum*, *Sibbaldia procumbens*, *Dicranum starkei*, *Rhacomitrium canescens*, *R. fasciculare* and *R. heterostichum* can each be dominant or co-dominant from time to time (Plate 22).

The species list is longer than that of the Polytricheto-Dicranetum starkei; there are

71 species on record from nine lists and numbers range from 14 to 30 with an average of 22.

This association has not been found so far to the south as the previous one but within the Central and Northern Highlands it is the more widely distributed of the two (Map 26).

Gymnomitreto-Salicetum herbaceae
(*Gymnomitrium-Salix herbacea* snow-bed)
(Table 48)

The third 'schneetälchen' association, the Gymnomitreto-Salicetum herbaceae, should strictly have been considered with the dwarf shrub heaths and not with the moss heaths, but it is more convenient to deal with it here for the sake of floristic and other comparisons.

There are seven constants: *Salix herbacea, Conostomum tetragonum, Dicranum starkei, Oligotrichum hercynicum, Rhacomitrium lanuginosum, Alicularia scalaris* and *Gymnomitrium concinnatum*. The usual dominants are *Salix herbacea* and/or *Gymnomitrium concinnatum* (Plate 23) while *D. starkei* and *Rhacomitrium fasciculare* may occasionally become co-dominant. A number of species, all in constancy class I, are exclusive to the association: *Ochrolechia gemminipara, Gymnomitrium varians, Luzula arcuata, Gymnomitrium alpinum* (class II), *Diplophyllum taxifolium* and *Lecidea alpestris. Solorina crocea* appears only in this association and in the *Juncus trifidus-Festuca ovina nodum.* Lists 10 and 11 (Table 48) were made on exposed ground, not in snow-beds (see below) and lists 12–14 represent a facies in which *G. varians* replaces *G. concinnatum* and becomes completely dominant (cf. *D. starkei*). We have used four of Poore's Breadalbane lists in the table. Species numbers and averages are almost exactly the same as in the Rhacomitreto-Dicranetum starkei.

This association is not found north of the Achnashellach Forest in Ross-shire, being apparently replaced by the *Juncus trifidus-Festuca ovina nodum* (see p. 77), but it has a more general distribution than the other two associations in the South-west Highlands (Map 26).

All three late snow-bed associations have a similar altitudinal range from just under 3000 ft. to 4000 ft. (914–1220 m.). The Gymnomitreto-Salicetum herbaceae is largely indifferent to aspect and occupies gentle to moderate slopes while the other two are confined to moderate or steep slopes mostly of northerly and easterly aspect. Vegetation cover is more often incomplete in the Gymnomitreto-Salicetum herbaceae.

The edaphic situation is confusing and only general tendencies can be indicated here. The profile under Polytricheto-Dicranetum starkei generally shows incipient podsolisation with marked surface humus accumulation and sometimes traces of mottle in the B horizon. Buried humus horizons are quite common. Under the Rhacomitreto-Dicranetum starkei mottling and the occurrence of buried horizons are more frequent and there is less accumulation of surface humus. The Gymnomitreto-Salicetum herbaceae has undifferentiated soils or incipient podsols without banding or mottling.

Other observations are mostly in keeping with the soil evidence although there are a few anomalies. The Polytricheto-Dicranetum starkei favours situations that are relatively stable and not liable to solifluction or the downwash of sand and gravel (Figs. 17 and 18 and Plate 21), while the Rhacomitreto-Dicranetum starkei is generally to be found

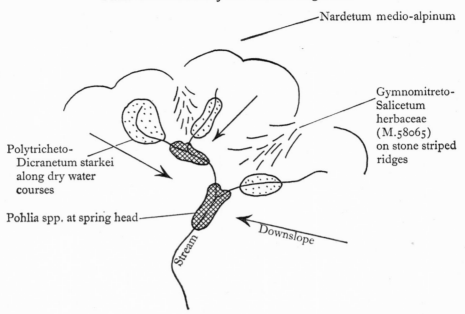

Fig. 18. Snow-bed vegetation in the Cairngorms at 3800–4000 ft.

where there is intermittent irrigation by melt water and rainwater and where downwash may completely bury the vegetation from time to time. The surface of the Gymnomitreto-Salicetum herbaceae indicates a continually high water content with considerable amorphous solifluction taking place whether the association is occupying exposed ground or areas of deep snow accumulation.

The following profiles can be taken as typical:

Gymnomitreto-Salicetum
R57164

0–2·5 cm. .	grey-black, humous sand with surface crust
2·5–15 cm. .	brown, sandy, gravelly loam.

Polytricheto-Dicranetum
M56128

0–2·5 cm.	. black, greasy humus
2·5–17 cm.	. coarse, brown sand
17–20 cm.	. light brown sand
20–>40 cm.	. dark brown, silty sand with reddish, gritty streaks.

Rhacomitreto-Dicranetum
M56121

0–8·5 cm.	. black, humous sandy gravel
8·5–19 cm. .	grey, black and brown banded and mottled sandy gravel
>19 cm.	. flesh coloured, gravelly clay with large stones.

As a generalisation the three associations can be arranged in order of increasing depth and length of snow-lie thus: Gymnomitreto-Salicetum, Rhacomitreto-Dicranetum, Polytricheto-Dicranetum, but we have never encountered a simple, complete zonation of this kind around a late snow-bed. They may be found together in a large snow-bed each occupying the appropriate habitat as described above or they may occur in an intimate mosaic with little apparent relation to topography. Much of our snow-bed vegetation consists of hybrid stands difficult to classify and this can only be ascribed to the variability of the climate acting directly and through the soil.

Apart from the general climatic shift which seems to be causing a withdrawal of snow-bed vegetation everywhere (Nordhagen—personal communication—describes a Salicetum herbaceae which has become grown over with birch scrub in the last thirty years) pronounced deviations from the mean depth and length of snow-lie are continually taking place in the Scottish mountains. Individual plants may be killed by frost at a time when they would normally experience a deep snow-cover and others may be damaged by an unusually prolonged snow-lie in spring (Poore, 1955b, p. 634). The volume of melt water produced at any time of the year from our larger snow-fields, combined with frequent heavy rain storms, disrupts the feeble vegetation cover of these areas and causes much erosion and deposition. This is particularly well seen on the Cairngorm plateaux and many writers of general and popular articles have described the substantial deposition of sand and gravel that may take place even on top of the snow-beds at such times. Another factor of importance to all our snow-influenced moss heaths is the deposition of wind-blown plant and mineral debris. This may be found arranged in wind rows over the ground when the snow has disappeared or it may completely bury the vegetation over an area of many square metres so that the mechanical influence must be considerable apart from any nutritional effect of the top dressing (cf. Warren Wilson, 1958).

There have been no further publications on the vegetation of Scottish snow-beds since Poore (1955b) reviewed the existing literature. We agree with him that Smith's (1912) Anthelietum 'occupies stony localities irrigated by melt water rather than snow beds *per se*'. *Anthelia* spp. are frequent constituents of both the Polytricheto and Rhaco-mitreto-Dicranetum associations but they cannot be regarded as 'pioneers' nor can Anthelietum be regarded as standing in successional relationship to Polytrichetum and Salicetum as Tansley (1949) maintained.

In Poore's own Table 5 (op. cit. p. 630) lists 1–5 seem to correspond to our Gymno-mitreto-Salicetum, lists 6, 7 to the Polytricheto-Dicranetum starkei, and lists 8–11 to the Rhacomitreto-Dicranetum, but his soil data for these lists are not what would have been expected. Here as in other situations we find we must regard the Ben Lawers area as being somewhat anomalous and difficult to reconcile with the rest of the Highlands.

There is a wealth of Scandinavian material to compare with the scanty Scottish data and we shall discuss only the most closely related associations that we can find in the literature.

The Dicranetum starkei of Rondane (Dahl, 1956, p. 169) has 9 species and two constants in common with our Polytricheto-Dicranetum starkei. It occurs in moist depressions in snow-beds of the Low-alpine zone and is characteristic of relatively stable ground. The *Kiaeria (Dicranum) starkei* sociation of Polytrichetum norvegici (Gjaere-voll, 1956, p. 224) is similar and has 15 species and two constants in common with our association. Gjaerevoll describes it as occurring in places not subject to irrigation and sedimentation and remarks that it is more abundant in the west of Norway.

The *Rhacomitrium fasciculare* sociation of the Weberetum commutatae acidophilum occurs in Torne Lappmark and the Sognefjell mountains (Gjaerevoll, 1956, p. 246). It is almost devoid of phanerogams but has 9 species and one constant in common with the Rhacomitreto-Dicranetum starkei. An even better comparison can be made between the *Gnaphalium supinum-Dicranum starkei* sociation of the Salicetum herbaceae (op. cit. p. 129) and the Rhacomitreto-Dicranetum, which have 22 species and three constants in common.

8

While the *Rhacomitrium fasciculare* sociation occurs on stony ground subject to periodic melt-water irrigation (a rather specialised habitat) the *Gnaphalium supinum* sociation occupies steep and well drained slopes in the snow-fields where it receives seasonal irrigation and sedimentation but dries out quickly in summer.

The Lophozieto-Salicetum herbaceae of Rondane (Dahl, 1956, p. 168) has 36 species and two constants in common with the Gymnomitreto-Salicetum herbaceae. It occupies wet slopes subject to considerable movement due to amorphous solifluction and the soil is a sandy humus in which buried humus horizons are frequent. Dahl regards it as a continental type of snow-bed vegetation. His Luzuleto-Cesietum (op. cit. p. 169) has more in common with our lists of the Gymnomitreto-Salicetum from exposed ground. There are 18 species and one constant common to both lists. The Luzuleto-Cesietum is a high-alpine association and the ground may sometimes be without winter snow-cover. It is characteristic of the unstable fine soil in the centre of stone polygons.

The *Salix herbacea-Anthelia juratzkana-Gymnomitrium varians* sociation of the *Salicetum herbaceae* and the *Anthelia juratzkana-Gymnomitrium varians* sociation of the Anthelietum juratzkanae of Gjaerevoll (1956, pp. 116 and 229) are also related to our Gymnomitreto-Salicetum and particularly to the *G. varians* facies. Gjaerevoll makes a fundamental distinction between snow-bed communities with some vascular plant cover and those with none (p. 96), but we find, with Dahl, that this cannot be maintained in our area since vascular plants appear to drop out gradually with increasing duration of snow-cover.

Deschampsia flexuosa may be the dominant vascular plant locally in some of the large Cairngorm snow-fields but the stands are too fragmentary for analysis. This appears to be the only Scottish representation of a series of *D. flexuosa* sociations of Norwegian late snow-beds on acid soils.

Chapter 7

OMBROGENOUS MIRES OR BOGS

PEAT lands in the Highlands are mostly ombrogenous or soligenous and although there are topogenous bogs locally on the low ground little attention has been paid to these. Throughout this work we have used 'bog' as the shortened term for all ombrogenous mires or blanket bogs and 'mire' for the soligenous types. We have reluctantly decided to use 'mire' in this restricted sense since the Scandinavian use of 'fen' for mountain soligenous mires is not appropriate in Britain, where it is traditionally used for lowland topogenous mires only, and something shorter than 'flush bog' or 'valley bog' is preferable.

Both floristic and ecological criteria (summarised below) have been used to separate mires from bogs.

The topography of mires clearly indicates water movement and the soils show signs of this in gleyed mineral horizons, the incorporation of mineral matter in the peat, and a relatively high base-status. The vegetation contains species known to be particularly associated with lateral water movement or with moderate to high base-status and pH.

Bogs show the reverse trends, indicating stagnation of drainage and lack of dependence of the vegetation on base status of mineral soils in the vicinity. Since mires thus depend on a more complex and variable set of soil conditions they include a greater variety of vegetation than the bogs.

Base-status and acidity of bog peats are fairly uniform and edaphic variations are related mainly to the height of the water-table. The first point is shown by the predominance of *Sphagna* in the moss layer of all bog communities and the second by the variations in the cover of the moss layer in proportion to that of the vascular plants. The abundance of strongly hydrophilous species and the growth habit of others also reflect the degree of wetness of the ground.

Blanket bogs are one of the most characteristic features of Highland vegetation and include some of the most uniform and extensive of all our noda.

Trichophoreto-Eriophoretum typicum

(Western blanket bog)

(Table 49, lists 1–12)

Trichophoreto-Eriophoretum typicum has the following constants: *Calluna vulgaris, Erica tetralix, Myrica gale, Eriophorum vaginatum, E. angustifolium, Molinia caerulea, Trichophorum caespitosum, Narthecium ossifragum, Drosera rotundifolia, Sphagnum papillosum, S. rubellum* and *Hypnum cupressiforme*. The *Sphagna*, mainly *S. papillosum, S. rubellum* and *S. magellanicum*, are the only plants ever to attain true dominance although the vascular species are always abundant and form the more conspicuous part of the vegetation when seen from a distance. *Carex pauciflora*, *Drosera anglica*, *Pleurozia purpurea* and *Sphagnum imbricatum* are selective for the association although the last appears in only one list. *Myrica* is not always present and may be missing from the association over large areas as it is on the island of Rhum.

The lists in the table cover a wide range of variation, from a *Sphagnum*-dominated facies to types in which vascular plants predominate, according to differences in water-table. On the wettest level ground the association forms the major hummock element in a pool and hummock complex where *Sphagna* often have a complete cover. On such bog surfaces continuity of this main vegetation type is broken by complex systems of pools which are mostly grown with aquatic vascular plants (*Menyanthes trifoliata*, *Eriophorum angustifolium*, *Carex limosa*) and *Sphagna* (*S. auriculatum*, *S. cuspidatum*, *S. papillosum*) (for a detailed account see Pearsall, 1956, and Ratcliffe and Walker, 1958). On Rannoch Moor, its only remaining Scottish station, *Scheuchzeria palustris* inhabitats these wet depressions amongst areas of Trichophoreto-Eriophoretum.

Trichophoreto-Eriophoretum typicum is one of the most widespread vegetation types in the Western Highlands on ground below 1500 ft. (457 m.) and on slopes of less than 10 degrees. It covers large areas wherever badly drained ground is extensive at low levels, as on the floors and gently inclined sides of broad valleys (Plate 24), but especially on the large plains which form the 'flowe' country of Sutherland. The association is less well represented in the rugged mountain country of West Inverness and Argyll where the topography is generally unsuitable, but it covers much of the great Moor of Rannoch on the Perthshire-Argyll march.

Pool and hummock bog consisting essentially of Trichophoreto-Eriophoretum typicum occurs locally from Sutherland to Argyll and in Galloway in south-west Scotland. A series of fine examples alongside Loch Shiel in Sunart would perhaps best be described as raised bogs from their appearance but have not been examined strati-graphically.

The association is present in many extreme coastal areas of the west, even down to sea level, but nowhere reaches the east coast. Map 27 shows that it extends farther east in the Northern than in the Central Highlands. To the south of the Great Glen the easternmost outposts are around the Laggan side of the Monadhliath and at the head of the Atholl Glen Garry. In these places it occurs only at the relatively high levels of 1000–1500 ft. (305–457 m.). At the southern end of its range the association becomes even more markedly western.

The peats of this bog type vary greatly in depth, composition and humification. *Grenz* horizons and recurrence surfaces have not been studied but, in general, wherever *Sphagnum* cover is high, or has been until recently, as on deep level bogs, the underlying peat tends to be 'fresh' and composed largely of this moss. Shallower peats on sloping ground often show abundant remains of *Eriophorum* spp., *Trichophorum* and Ericaceae and vary from fibrous to completely amorphous in structure. All these peats are base deficient and acid (pH 3·6–3·8), but acidity tends to be highest in the driest and most humified types (cf. Pearsall, 1938).

The Irish Blanket Bog of Tansley (1949) which is very extensive in that country, especially in the west, differs only in the constancy of *Schoenus nigricans*. Elsewhere in Britain our *nodum* is found widely in S.W. Scotland and locally in Lakeland and North Wales.

Calluneto-Eriophoretum
(Pennine blanket-bog)
(Table 50)

The second main bog association, Calluneto-Eriophoretum, differs considerably from the last in its floristics. The constants are *Calluna vulgaris*, *Empetrum hermaphroditum*, *Vaccinium myrtillus*, *Eriophorum vaginatum*, *Rubus chamaemorus*, *Hylocomium splendens*, *Pleurozium schreberi* and *Sphagnum nemoreum*. *Calluna* and *Eriophorum vaginatum* are usually co-dominant but the cover of *Sphagnum*, especially *S. nemoreum* and *S. rubellum*, is high on the wetter ground. Locally there are patches of a facies dominated by other *Sphagna* such as *S. papillosum* and *S. magellanicum*.

Oxycoccus microcarpus is exclusive to the association and *Betula nana* and *Sphagnum fuscum* are highly selective. *Rubus chamaemorus* can be described as preferential since it is perhaps the most distinctive species, occurring more constantly and abundantly than in any other vegetation (Plate 25). Calluneto-Eriophoretum is floristically poor with an average of only 21 species in the stands listed.

Besides the *Sphagnum* type two other facies have been recognised which may occur together and intergrade. The first (lists 14–21), described by Poore and McVean (1957) as *Betula nana* bog, is rich in dwarf shrubs, especially *B. nana* and *Arctous alpina*, and has a moderate *Sphagnum* cover which often includes *S. fuscum*. The second facies (lists 11–13) is distinguished by a high cover of lichens of the *Cladonia sylvatica* group (Plate 25). Stands rich in *Rhacomitrium lanuginosum* occur locally at high levels but have not been analysed. They are often associated with peat erosion and are seldom as extensive as the undisturbed communities of this type which occur in Shetland.

Betula nana is much more local and eastern than *Arctous alpina* but occurs also, although more sparingly, in Trichophoreto-Callunetum and both facies of Trichophoreto-Eriophoretum. The possibility of soligenous influence in *B. nana* bogs mentioned by Poore and McVean (op. cit.) can now be discounted.

This association differs from Trichophoreto-Eriophoretum typicum in showing a greater quantity of shrubs, hypnaceous mosses and lichens and a reduced abundance of *Erica tetralix*, *Molinia caerulea*, *Eriophorum angustifolium*, *Narthecium ossifragum*, *Trichophorum caespitosum*, *Drosera rotundifolia* and, as a rule, *Sphagna*. The smaller cover value of *Sphagna* suggests that water-tables generally tend to be lower in Calluneto-Eriophoretum. *Rubus chamaemorus* is a montane species and does not occur in Trichophoreto-Eriophoretum whereas *Myrica gale*, a species of low levels, is constant in that association and completely absent from the present one. This agrees with the observation that although the two associations overlap a good deal in geographical distribution (Maps 27 and 28) they show altitudinal separation within the zone of overlap.

Whereas *Calluna-Eriophorum* bogs are widespread in the east on wet moors from nearly sea-level upwards, in the west they occur mainly above 1000 ft. (305 m.). An upper limit is reached at about 3000 ft. (914 m.) in the Central Highlands and 2500 ft. (763 m.) in the Northern Highlands.

The association is most extensive in the Eastern Highlands where it is favoured by the prevalence of plateaux and broad watersheds. Over many square kilometres of ground in the Monadhliath, the Forest of Atholl and the Angus hills this type of vegetation prevails. By contrast the steep and rocky terrain so typical of the Western Highlands is unsuitable for its development although there are patches wherever topography allows. Both the dwarf shrub and lichen-rich facies occur mainly in the Eastern Highlands but have two unexpected outposts on the north coast of Sutherland on the moorlands which stretch back from the cliffs of Whiten Head and Cape Wrath. On Whiten Head the lichen-rich bog occupies the drier, more exposed places and passes into the shrub-rich facies (with *Arctous alpina* and *Arctostaphylos uva-ursi* but not *Betula nana*) on wetter, more sheltered ground. Another interesting stand of shrub-rich bog with *Arctostaphylos* and *Pyrola media* occurs not far inland on the south-east side of Ben Loyal. Lichen-rich bog is finely developed on the Ladder Hills and near Cawdor (Plate 25). The facies are generally less extensive than the type and both appear to have contracted in area as a result of moor burning. The *Sphagnum*-dominated facies occurs on badly drained plateaux, as on the Monadhliath and above Glen Clova.

Calluneto-Eriophoretum occupies level or gently sloping ground, commonly with 2–3 metres of well humified peat but sometimes with a far greater depth. The present-day dominants are conspicuous in the identifiable plant remains from this peat but a search in several places has failed to reveal macroscopic remains of *Arctous alpina* or *Betula nana* even where these species are present in the vegetation. Wood, fruits, catkin-scales and even leaves of *Betula pubescens* and *B. verrucosa* are sometimes abundant at the base of the section and the wood of pine and dwarf juniper is encountered here and there (Durno and McVean, 1959). There is thus evidence that the present association has been in uninterrupted possession of the ground in many places from Atlantic times. Below the rooting depth of the vegetation the peats are strongly reducing and yellow-brown in colour, quickly oxidising to black on exposure to air. Where the water-table is high and the vegetation rich in *Sphagna*, several metres of 'fresh peat' may be formed. The peat of these bogs (humified or unhumified) is invariably acidic and base-deficient and, as Pearsall (1938) has shown, acidity tends to rise when the deposits dry out as a result of erosion and 'hagging'.

At low levels Calluneto-Eriophoretum grades into Vaccineto-Callunetum on steeper but still damp north to east facing slopes and into Callunetum vulgaris on dry hillsides. In sheep country there are transitions to the wetter types of sub-montane acidic grassland including Juncetum squarrosi. At higher altitudes the association passes into Cladineto-Callunetum or, in the north, Arctoeto-Callunetum, as exposure becomes severe (Fig. 3, p. 36). This particular transition often shows one of the most abrupt vegetational discontinuities to be found anywhere in the Highlands, involving a steep gradient in soil moisture over a distance of one or two metres as blanket bog peat gives way to a well drained podsol. The edge of the bog towards the heath is often visibly convex.

Trichophoreto-Eriophoretum of the low-level bogs is often completely separated from the higher-level Calluneto-Eriophoretum simply because the ground at intermediate altitudes is too steep for the development of deep peat. Where the topography is suitable within the zone of geographical overlap the two associations grade imperceptibly into one another. The transition is marked by the occurrence of intermediate communities usually at about 1200–1500 ft. (366–457 m.). Intermediate types of vegetation also occur widely at lower levels towards the eastern limit of the Trichophoreto-Eriophoretum. They are, for instance, extensive in East Sutherland on the moorlands around Ben Griam More at 750–1500 ft. (229–457 m.).

Calluneto-Eriophoretum corresponds to the Pennine Eriophoretum vaginati (Tansley,

1949) which has locally lost *Calluna* as a result of repeated burning and grazing (Pearsall, 1941). Typical Calluneto-Eriophoretum is, however, still widespread in parts of the Pennines. The same association is locally extensive in North Wales, Lakeland, the Cheviots and the Southern Uplands, and shows great uniformity throughout its entire range. The *Sphagnum*-rich facies of the Highlands corresponds to the extensive Sphagneta of Stainmore (Pearsall, 1941), Alston Moor and the Butterburn–North Tyne Moors. Small patches of the lichen-rich facies have been noted on Dollar Law in Peebleshire and amongst the eroded blanket bogs of Knock Fell in the Northern Pennines.

Poore and McVean (1957) have made a detailed comparison between the shrub and lichen-rich facies of *Calluna-Eriophorum* bog and corresponding associations within Nordhagen's Oxycocco-Empetrion hermaphroditi alliance. The similarities between the Scottish and Norwegian associations are close.

Dahl (1956, p. 246) states that 'the occurrence of *Betula nana* and *Calluna vulgaris* (in ombrogenous mires) is clearly complementary and only some analyses published by Nordhagen and Paasio show any appreciable blending of the two species'. By contrast, in Scotland *Betula nana* usually grows with *Calluna*, and although its distribution has an eastern bias, it cannot be regarded as a markedly continental species. As Poore and McVean (1957) have suggested, a separate ecotype may occur in the Highlands.

Dahl (1956) also notes that his *Betula nana-Sphagnum fuscum* community is associated with the presence of 'better' rocks among the Rondane sparagmites, a peculiar situation since *S. fuscum* is one of the least demanding of the *Sphagna*. In the Northwest Highlands we have often found that the Calluneto-Eriophoretum on deep peat is present on the Cambrian quartzite only where small outcrops of dolomitic mudstones and grits also occur. The vegetation pattern sketched below (Fig. 19) occurs repeatedly and suggests that the quartzite itself is too poor to allow peat formation through luxuriant (albeit oligotrophic) plant growth (but see p. 110).

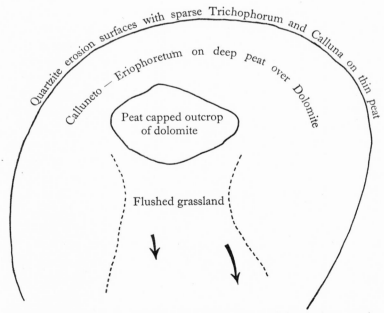

Fig. 19. Restriction of Calluneto-Eriophoretum to dolomite in quartzite areas. Beinn Eighe, West Ross, at 1700 ft.

Empetreto-Eriophoretum

(High-level blanket bog)

(Table 51)

In the closely related association, Empetreto-Eriophoretum, *Empetrum hermaphroditum* replaces *Calluna vulgaris* as the co-dominant of *Eriophorum vaginatum*. This association also differs from the previous one in the greater abundance of *Vaccinium* spp. and the greater constancy of lichens. Apart from gaining *Carex bigelowii* and *Cladonia sylvatica* and losing *Calluna* and *Hylocomium splendens* the constants are the same as those of Calluneto-Eriophoretum. The *Empetrum* bogs tend to be richer in species with an average of 25 compared with 21 for *Calluna* bogs. Various *Sphagna* or *Cladonia* spp. may again be dominant locally but separate facies have not been distinguished.

The association may be regarded as a high-level counterpart of Calluneto-Eriophoretum since it has not been found below 2500 ft. (763 m.). It is extensive on some of the elevated table-lands of the Cairngorm and Lochnagar massifs but is less frequent elsewhere and does not occur north of Seana Bhraigh in Ross-shire (Map 29). It is absent from Sutherland because there is no suitable ground at the necessary altitude (i.e. above the limits of *Calluna*).

Ecological relationships are much the same as for Calluneto-Eriophoretum but water-tables are seldom high over extensive areas above 2500 ft. (763 m.) and deep peats are rare.

Empetreto-Eriophoretum is found with a variety of other high level associations such as Vaccineto-Empetretum on well-drained ground, chionophilous Nardeta where snow-cover is prolonged and *Rhacomitrium* heath on exposed tops and ridges. It does not occur south of the Highlands but has clear affinities with Norwegian associations such as the Chamaemoreto-Sphagnetum acutifolii of Rondane (Dahl, 1956, p. 241). In his Rondane survey Dahl gives a useful list of references to descriptions of Scandinavian ombrogenous mires.

Trichophoreto-Callunetum

(*Trichophorum-Calluna* bog)

(Table 52, lists 1–12)

There remain two associations of shallow ombrogenous peats and these can be regarded either as blanket bogs or as wet grass-shrub heaths. The first, Trichophoreto-Callunetum, is distinguished largely by constancy and dominance of *Trichophorum caespitosum* subsp. *germanicum* and *Calluna vulgaris* and has only two other constants, *Erica tetralix* and *Cladonia uncialis*. Floristically it is a poor association with stands averaging only 17 species. There are three facies, one *Sphagnum*-rich (lists 10 and 11), another rich in peat-encrusting lichens, e.g. *Cladonia coccifera* (lists 1–3), and a third dominated by lichens of the *Cladonia sylvatica* group (list 12). There are also locally extensive stands with little or no *Calluna* but these represent a fire-climax in which heather has been destroyed by burning (list 22).

The geographical range of Trichophoreto-Callunetum completely covers that of Trichophoreto-Eriophoretum typicum but extends much farther east, and in the Cairngorms it is the predominant bog vegetation between 1500 ft. and 2500 ft. (457–763 m.).

On the whole it is most extensive in the Western Highlands on moderate slopes which are too well drained to support deep blanket bog (Plate 24). In the mountainous country of the West-central Highlands it thus tends to replace Trichophoreto-Eriophoretum typicum as the principal type of blanket bog. Some indication of the humidity of this region may be gathered from the observation that on north-facing hillsides in Glen Shiel this association occurs on slopes of at least 30 degrees. In the west it is mainly submontane, occurring from sea level to 2000 ft. (610 m.) but it has a higher range in the Cairngorms, from 1000 ft. to 3000 ft. (405–914 m.).

Nevertheless, the association is extensive on moorlands in some of the driest parts of the Highlands, such as the district between Inverness and Grantown-on-Spey. Here it tends to occupy the wettest ground and there are 'flowes' covered with the *Sphagnum*-rich facies. Occurring in these dry districts mainly below 1500 ft. (457 m.) Trichophor-eto-Callunetum often replaces Calluneto-Eriophoretum, which is then found at rather higher levels. On the other hand, in some areas the two associations occur together on the same stretch of moor, and at levels well below 1000 ft. (305 m.). Their ecological relationships are obscure, but some parts of the Western Highlands give the impression that moor-burning has favoured *Trichophorum caespitosum* at the expense of *Eriophorum vaginatum*.

The drier, crustaceous lichen facies is characteristic of deforested morainic country throughout the entire range of the association but on some moors it may have been derived by burning from a more natural *Trichophorum-Calluna* vegetation above the forest limit. The *Cladonia sylvatica*-rich facies occurs in a few parts of the East-central Highlands. The *Sphagnum*-rich facies certainly appears to exist as an original bog type and is found locally on ground apparently unaffected by recent fires or drainage.

Fig. 20 shows how the relationship of Trichophoreto-Callunetum to topography varies according to the wetness of the climate. The association occurs on peat which is from several cms. to over one metre deep and usually well humified except where *Sphagna*

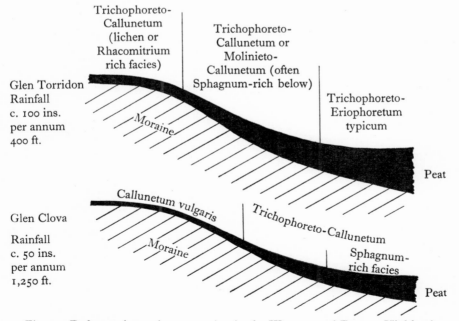

Fig. 20. Deforested moraine vegetation in the Western and Eastern Highlands

have a high cover. Peat acidity is usually high (3·4–4·6) and base-status low. Where the peat is shallow the remainder of the profile is a typical podsol but under deeper deposits the glacial till sometimes appears to be undifferentiated.

Besides being commonly associated with Trichophoreto-Eriophoretum typicum on low ground (Plate 24), in the west Trichophoreto-Callunetum often forms an altitudinal zone separating the two other blanket bog associations. Some stands are floristically as well as spatially intermediate between the two Eriophoreta. The association passes into Trichophoreto-Eriophoretum caricetosum (p. 112) where water movement in the peat becomes rapid and into the *Molinia-Myrica nodum* where irrigation involves the periodic deposition of silt. On dry ground, especially where there is a southern exposure, it changes to Callunetum vulgaris. The close relationships with Molinieto-Callunetum are discussed under that association.

Molinieto-Callunetum
(*Molinia-Calluna* bog)
(Table 52, lists 13–21)

This is floristically similar to the last association and the two could be regarded as facies of the one unit. There are five constants: *Calluna vulgaris, Erica tetralix, Molinia caerulea, Potentilla erecta* and *Hypnum cupressiforme. Molinia* is co-dominant with *Calluna* in place of *Trichophorum* and mosses rather than lichens tend to be abundant. The stands have an average of 18 species and are composed largely of plants which occur in a wider variety of dwarf shrub heaths and bogs. The only facies is one in which *Calluna* is sparse or absent, once again the result of repeated moor burning.

The geographical distribution of Molinieto-Callunetum is similar to that of the last association although in the East-central Highlands it has few stations outside the Cairngorms. It has rather lower altitudinal limits which vary from about 1500 ft. (457 m.) in the west to slightly more than 2000 ft. (610 m.) in the east. In the Western Highlands it covers many square kilometres of the gently sloping lower hillsides. The pure *Molinia* grassland facies is also widespread in the extreme west although hardly as extensive as it is in Galloway.

Molinieto-Callunetum often occurs in places which, from their topography, suggest that it is not a true ombrogenous bog but one associated with a moderate rate of water movement through the peat. It frequently occupies slight hollows or flats where Trichophoreto-Callunetum covers the surface convexities (Plate 24). Large areas lie on valley floors and where steep slopes flatten out. All these places appear likely to collect a large volume of surface and sub-surface water which rapidly drains away.

The soils themselves suggest movement rather than stagnation of drainage water. Typical profiles show about 50 cm. of dark brown peat, sometimes pseudofibrous in the upper half, but becoming increasingly humified and amorphous towards the basal drifts. The bottom few centimetres are frequently a mixture of sand, silt and humus, which could mean that once-strong irrigation influence still has some effect although movement of solid particles has ceased. The peats are again acidic (3·6–4·5) and base-deficient so that the influence of water movement is probably on aeration rather than nutrient content of the soil. This is again indicated by the indifference of the association to type of rock for it occurs on Cambrian quartzite, Torridon sandstone, various members of the Moine and Lewisian series, and on ultra-basic igneous complexes.

The association often grades into *Molinia-Myrica* mire where the soligenous influence becomes more definite (Plate 24). Without careful study of the peats it is often difficult to decide whether some of the pure stands of *Molinia* grassland have been derived from this *nodum* or from Molinieto-Callunetum. Some localised *Molinia* grasslands which belong chiefly to the Western Highlands contain other grasses, sedges and herbs. From their frequent occurrence on fairly base-rich soils and their relationships to *Juncus acutiflorus-J. articulatus* and *Schoenus nigricans* communities, these evidently have closer affinities to mires than to bogs (see p. 64).

The close relationships between Trichophoreto-Callunetum and Molinieto-Callunetum should already be apparent and sometimes it seems clear that the two are separated by subtle differences in drainage. They intergrade a great deal in most places and on the island of Rhum there is evidence that in mixed stands with roughly equal amounts of *Molinia* and *Trichophorum*, cessation of burning leads to the formation of Molinieto-Callunetum and the deer sedge is largely suppressed.

As ground water becomes really stagnant the Molinieto-Callunetum passes into Trichophoreto-Eriophoretum typicum but where the ground becomes drier it grades into lichen-rich Trichophoreto-Callunetum or Callunetum vulgaris.

'*Calluna* heaths with *Molinia*' are described by Tveitnes (1945) for the Masfjord area of western Norway and by Knaben (1950) for Mid Sogn.

Degeneration of Ombrogenous Bogs

In all parts of the Highlands there are examples of peat erosion, usually involving dissection of the bog by a characteristic ramifying system of 'haggs' (gullies). Less often there is sheet erosion in which the peat surface is bared more extensively and wastage takes place by the repeated removal of the top layer. Sometimes the two types of erosion are combined.

The process of bog degeneration is equally widespread on hills elsewhere in Britain and has been a subject of great interest and frequent comment for some time. In an account of blanket bogs in many parts of the British Isles Osvald (1949) pays a good deal of attention to erosion and gives detailed descriptions of the process in its various forms.

The chief agents of peat erosion are undoubtedly wind and water but the factors which caused the onset of this degeneration are far less obvious. Some ecologists believe that human activity of one kind or another was largely responsible for initiating bog erosion. Others contend that the process is mainly climatically controlled and represents a natural end-point to bog growth. It may well be that both sets of factors have been responsible but in the Highlands we have found plenty of evidence to support the first view. Deforestation and moor burning have been universal in the region and we have encountered many certain instances of the erosion of shallow peat and mineral soils as a result of these activities.

The degradation of thin peat is well shown on the deforested morainic country of the Western Highlands. Moor burning on such ground is almost inevitably followed by a breakdown of the continuous cover of Trichophoreto-Callunetum. *Trichophorum caespitosum* becomes more tussocky in its growth, leaving bare or lichen-crusted patches between the tufts. Later stages involve the complete breakdown of the peat to give a sparsely vegetated mixture of greasy, black humus, stones and gravel. The frequent development of a surface lichen or algal crust renders the peat impermeable and increases the run-off.

This degraded vegetation and irreparably damaged habitat has not only replaced forest but has obviously encroached on large areas of natural dwarf-shrub heath such as Juniperetum nanae and Cladineto-Callunetum. It is possible that the association of deep peat with mudstone outcrops in the middle of quartzite pavement and moraine in North-west Scotland may be at least partly an erosion phenomenon and not entirely due to the differential accumulation of peat on the two rocks.

Bogs bearing Trichophoreto-Eriophoretum typicum often show fire degeneration more by changes in floristic composition than by active peat wastage since they tend to occupy situations where marginal erosion does not readily take place. Such changes involve a decrease in *Sphagnum* cover, increased tussock formation in the vascular plants, and often the development of large mounds of *Rhacomitrium lanuginosum* on the drying bog. The spread of *Rhacomitrium* is most marked in the North-west Highlands where sheets of the moss often envelop the drier ground as well. Around the south-east end of Loch Meadie in Sutherland at only 500 ft. (153 m.) above sea-level a continuous carpet of *Rhacomitrium* occupies at least one square kilometre of moorland leaving only a sparse scattering of *Calluna vulgaris* and *Trichophorum caespitosum* except in those places that have escaped the full effects of the fires.

During a dry spring and summer it is possible to burn even the wettest *Sphagnum-*dominated bog and this surface disturbance combined with marginal interference probably explains the degeneration of many pool and hummock complexes. Although some examples, such as the Strathy Bog described by Pearsall (1956), have escaped serious interference, the majority have been burned and show every stage of drying and wastage. The pools of the drying bogs are mostly bare of vegetation and rounded, with steep, scoured sides, and they look rather like salt-marsh pans. There seems often to have been an appreciable drop in water-table and later stages of the degeneration show pools becoming confluent, drying out and finally leading to a disruption of the entire bog surface by irregular systems of haggs.

Hagging is generally more prevalent on the high-level blanket bogs with Calluneto- or Empetreto-Eriophoretum. This is probably because their position on watersheds and spurs, passing on the downslope edges into steeper and better drained ground, makes them especially susceptible to marginal erosion. Only in a few places such as the north end of Ben Clibreck and Ben Hutig in Sutherland are there extensive areas of Calluneto-Eriophoretum which show little sign of hagging. It is significant that these show equally little sign of burning and have large stands of the fire-sensitive shrub-rich facies. In bogs of this type, drying out may again be accompanied by an increase in *Rhacomitrium lanuginosum* although seldom to the same extent as in Trichophoreto-Eriophoretum.

Empetreto-Eriophoretum cannot have been affected by deforestation since it lies well above the tree limit but it too is often badly eroded. Extensive areas of the high-level Eriophoreta occur on the undulating plateaux between Glen Clova and Caenlochan and between Glen Muick and Mount Keen but they have suffered severely from hagging and show a great deal of the underlying glacial till. Once erosion has begun at the higher levels the process may be accelerated by the severity of the climate.

The peat from the wasting bogs is washed down over the slopes below and the site of its deposition is marked by a vigorous growth of *Nardus* and other Gramineae of acidic grassland. Sometimes, particularly in the west, bog communities regenerate in the haggs but these communities are usually related to the soligenous Sphagneto-Cariceta or to oligotrophic flushes and springs.

Chapter 8

SOLIGENOUS MIRES

MIRE communities have been grouped broadly according to the nutrient (especially calcium) content of their soils and waters, which in turn gives a sub-division according to the nutritional requirements of the vegetation. Types placed in the oligotrophic group are composed largely of calcifuge or indifferent species whereas those regarded as mesotrophic or eutrophic have a predominance of basiphilous species. As with the ombrogenous bogs certain mire noda are associated with low or high altitude and others evidently depend on regional differences in oceanicity. Further differentiation results from varying aeration according to the degree of waterlogging, which in turn depends on such factors as topography and porosity of the substratum.

Soligenous mires occur wherever topography concentrates the flow of drainage water whether on ordinary slopes, in hollows and channels, on valley floors or beside springs and rills (Plate 26). The most extensive occurrences of mire naturally tend to be on the lower hillsides and valley flats since these receive much of the drainage water from higher parts of the catchment area. Some small basin bogs could perhaps be regarded as topogenous but have been included here because their vegetation shows such close affinities with that of soligenous mires in the strict sense. The open water and swamp communities of topogenous hydroseres belong mainly to the lowlands and have not been studied although they intergrade with certain types of mire.

Because the rate of decomposition of humus depends on base-status as well as on aeration the mesotrophic and eutrophic mires tend to have less peaty soils than oligotrophic types of comparable wetness. This may be shown either as a greater degree of humification or as a lower humus content. Mineral soils are typically strongly gleyed. Conditions in most oligotrophic mires favour the growth of *Sphagna*, which tend to form a peat on top of the mineral soil, whereas in some meso- and eutrophic types the prevailing vegetation does not form peat actively so that the humus often remains mixed with the mineral layer. In the most waterlogged situations, however, there is a development of base-rich peat beneath meso- and eutrophic mire vegetation. When the flow of water is very strong not only is humus decomposition rapid but mineral particles are transported as well. This condition gives rise to silty muds of variable humus content and is associated more with open flushes and springs than with closed mire vegetation.

Mires tend to be less affected by human disturbance than bogs since they are usually more difficult to burn and it is more difficult to alter their water regime. Many types are, however, modified in that their original scrub growth has been lost. Alders and willows are certain to have formed part of many sub-montane mires in earlier times and, since their clearance, grazing by sheep and deer has ruled out the possibility of recolonisation.

OLIGOTROPHIC MIRES

Trichophoreto-Eriophoretum caricetosum
(*Trichophorum-Carex* mire)
(Table 49, lists 13–21)

Trichophoreto-Eriophoretum caricetosum is the mire association of closest affinity to blanket bog. Table 49 shows this and the Trichophoreto-Eriophoretum typicum as facies of the one association but they may also be regarded as separate associations. Constants common to the two facies are *Calluna vulgaris*, *Erica tetralix*, *Molinia caerulea*, *Eriophorum angustifolium*, *Narthecium ossifragum* and *Drosera rotundifolia* while those which distinguish the caricetosum are *Carex echinata*, *C. panicea* and *Potentilla erecta*. Other contrasting features, further indicating the soligenous influence in the carice-tosum, are the frequent presence of *Selaginella selaginoides*, *Nardus stricta*, *Carex nigra*, *Juncus kochii*, *Succisa pratensis*, *Aulacomnium palustre*, and *Sphagnum recurvum* together with the reduced amount of species such as *Eriophorum vaginatum*. An average of 28 species compared with 23 shows that the caricetosum is richer floristically than the typicum facies. *Erica tetralix* rather than *Calluna* is the most abundant shrub but sedges and *Molinia* may have a high cover and *Sphagna* usually dominate the moss layer. A related mire of eastern districts is dominated by *Erica tetralix*, *Molinia* and *Tricho-phorum*, but *Sphagna* are less plentiful and basiphilous species such as *Carex pulicaris*, *Juncus articulatus* and *Ranunculus acris* are usually present.

The caricetosum occurs over the entire range of the Trichophoreto-Eriophoretum typicum but it extends farther east and reaches higher levels—up to 2000 ft. (610 m.). There is a difference in habitat, and in the west the present facies usually occupies areas of water seepage in the predominant typicum or occurs independently on wet ground where drainage is too rapid to support the other facies. In the east, where it occurs beyond the limits of the other, the caricetosum seems to be even more closely associated with the influence of irrigation. The related eastern type with basiphilous species occurs on fairly base-rich soils, and is often transitional between calcareous flushes or mires and oligotrophic bogs, shrub heaths and grasslands.

The soils are usually shallow, well humified peats overlying a strongly gleyed mineral substratum. From the nature of the habitat, stands are seldom continuous over areas of more than a few hundred square metres and are commonly much smaller but their total area is sometimes considerable. The pH range of 4·0–4·4 (peat) and 4·3–4·8 (water) is slightly higher than that of the typicum facies.

There are frequent transitions to Trichophoreto-Callunetum and to the following *nodum*.

Molinia-Myrica *nodum*
(Table 53)

The *Molinia-Myrica nodum* is another sub-montane mire closely associated with Trichophoreto-Eriophoretum typicum although fairly distinct floristically. *Molinia caerulea* and *Myrica gale* are both constant and dominant and *Potentilla erecta* is the only other constant species. The dominants are so luxuriant that most other species have a low cover and the *nodum* is rather poor floristically. *Molinia* often shows the dense, tussocky habit which Jefferies (1915) attributed to a copious supply of well aerated drainage water but which may be affected by other factors such as light intensity and grazing. The *nodum* has a number of species typical of irrigated mineral soils and *Sphagna* are not usually abundant.

The *Molinia-Myrica nodum* occurs at all levels below about 1200 ft. (366 m.) and like the previous one has a geographical range which covers that of the Trichophoreto-Eriophoretum typicum and extends farther to the south and east (Map 27). It is, however, rather localised and occurs most frequently in the Western Highlands. The typical situation is on periodically flooded flats alongside streams which drain the peat communities of lower slopes and valley floors (Plate 26). It occurs also where there is strong irrigation on steeper slopes or amongst low-level blanket bogs. Stands are sometimes extensive in the aggregate and may reach a hectare or more in size individually. The peats are usually shallow (50–80 cm.) and well humified although sometimes appearing fibrous in the upper part (pseudo-fibrous—Fraser, 1933) and often show intercalated layers of silt as a result of periodic sedimentation. pH varies widely according to the amount of irrigation and silting and samples give the range 3·8–6·1.

Towards the southern and eastern distribution limits of this type of mire Trichophoreto-Eriophoretum typicum has disappeared but the caricetosum facies still occurs and is often associated with the *Molinia-Myrica nodum*. These two mires intergrade locally in all regions.

In the East-central Highlands *Myrica* tends to replace *Molinia* as the dominant and, moreover, it appears to become more exacting in soil requirements, growing on ground strongly irrigated with mineral-rich water. For instance, in Glen Lyon *Molinia-Myrica* mires grade into vegetation in which *Myrica* is completely dominant, forming a dense shrub growth; the drainage water comes from calcareous substrata and the soil is a saturated humus-rich silt rather than a peat. The *nodum* here tends to pass into drier grasslands and shrub heaths as the flush effect fades instead of into blanket bog as in the west. There are close relationships with *Juncus acutiflorus* mires which are discussed under that *nodum* (p. 117). List 5 of Table 53 shows some affinity with *Schoenus nigricans* mires.

In life form *Myrica gale* is the counterpart of the willows which would naturally form a shrub layer in many other types of mire but which have largely been eradicated by human influence (p. 111). The stand from which list 9 of Table 53 was drawn still contains thickets of *Salix aurita*. *Myrica* suffers far less from grazing and can withstand a great deal of burning but its growth rarely exceeds 60 cm. in these mires in contrast to the potential height of 2 m. commonly reached in completely undisturbed places.

Some nearly pure Molinieta of alluvial ground in the sheep country of the west may once have contained *Myrica* in greater quantity. Beyond the Highlands the *nodum* occurs in Galloway and locally in Lakeland and North Wales.

Sphagneto-Juncetum effusi
(*Juncus effusus-Sphagnum* mire)
(Table 54)

The Sphagneto-Juncetum effusi is a distinctive type of mire with *Juncus effusus*, *Sphagnum recurvum*, *Carex nigra*, *Galium hercynicum*, *Potentilla erecta*, *Polytrichum commune* and *Sphagnum palustre* as constants. *Juncus effusus* is the physiognomic dominant but has a lower cover than the moss layer, in which *Polytrichum commune* and the two *Sphagna* are inter-changeable dominants. The *nodum* is floristically poor with *J. effusus* itself as the only selective species. *Sphagna* typical of ground with moving water, such as *S. girgensohnii*, *S. russowii* and *S. squarrosum*, are usually present.

This mire is widespread although not always extensive, but it is most characteristic of the Eastern Highlands and becomes rather local in the west. It may be identified with *Juncus effusus* mires common in North Wales (Ratcliffe, 1959), Lakeland, the Pennines, Cheviots and Southern Uplands. The *nodum* is essentially sub-montane, occurring mainly below 2000 ft. (610 m.) and on gentle slopes (usually under 10 degrees) in stands varying in size from a few square metres to one or two hectares. The water-table varies seasonally in the drier sites but is permanently high in the wetter places. These drainage differences are shown by the abundance of *Polytrichum* over gley podsols compared with dominance of *Sphagna* on deep peaty gleys. The pH range is from 4·4–5·0 for water samples.

As irrigation decreases the *nodum* usually passes into oligotrophic communities of either dry or wet ground such as the various acidic grasslands, *Vaccinium* and *Calluna* heaths or Calluneto-Eriophoretum.

Sphagneto-Caricetum sub-alpinum

(Sub-alpine *Sphagnum-Carex* mire)
(Table 55, lists 1–9)

Closely related to the Sphagneto-Juncetum effusi is the Sphagneto-Caricetum sub-alpinum which has the constants *Carex echinata*, *C. nigra*, *Eriophorum angustifolium*, *Potentilla erecta* and *Sphagnum recurvum*. The first two species are co-dominant in their own layer but once again mosses have a greater cover. Several species of *Sphagnum* are usually present and dominance may be reached by *S. recurvum*, *S. palustre*, *S. papillosum*, *S. subsecundum* or *S. auriculatum*. Closely allied communities show replacement of the sedges by *Juncus squarrosus*, but with the same composition of the *Sphagnum* layer, and these are evidently transitional between the present association and Juncetum squarrosi sub-alpinum.

This mire is also widely distributed and occurs in most mountain groups of the Highlands as well as in the mountains of England and Wales. The altitude ranges from 300 ft. (91 m.) to 2400 ft. (732 m.) and the angle of slope from 0 to 20 degrees. It thus replaces the Sphagneto-Juncetum to some extent at higher levels but the two commonly show some altitudinal overlap and the reason for their ecological separation is not clear. The Sphagneto-Caricetum sub-alpinum often occupies more definite hollows and channels so that its stands tend to be smaller (usually less than 200 sq. m.). This slight habitat difference suggests that rate of water flow and aeration are the differentiating factors especially as there seem to be no significant variations in base-status between the two soils. Values of pH for water samples are similar to those of the previous *nodum*, with a range of 4·5–5·7.

Like the *Juncus effusus* mire this type usually occupies strongly irrigated sites on ground where oligotrophic grassland, dwarf shrub heath or blanket bog predominate. Locally there are transitions to Trichophoreto-Eriophoretum caricetosum.

Sphagneto-Caricetum alpinum

(Alpine *Sphagnum-Carex* mire)

(Table 55, lists 10–20)

Above 2000 ft. (610 m.) Sphagneto-Caricetum sub-alpinum is replaced by a high level counterpart with sufficiently different floristics to warrant the rank of a separate association—Sphagneto-Caricetum alpinum. *Carex echinata* and *Eriophorum angusti-folium* remain constant with *Nardus stricta*, *Viola palustris*, *Polytrichum commune*, *Sphagnum papillosum* and *S. russowii* in addition. *Carex echinata* is the most abundant sedge although it sometimes shares dominance with *C. nigra* and once again the *Sphagnum* carpet may be composed of several species equally or one species in particular.

The influence of high altitude is shown less distinctively in these prominent features of the vegetation than in the presence of *Carex curta* and montane species such as *Carex bigelowii*, *Saxifraga stellaris* and *Sphagnum lindbergii*. The last species is exclusive to this and the following *nodum* but is local, chiefly in the Eastern Highlands, and its strong representation in the table is due to deliberate selection of stands in which it was present. *Sphagnum lindbergii* is an important member of many Scandinavian mire communities and another abundant Scandinavian species, *S. riparium*, grows in its few Scottish stations either in Sphagneto-Caricetum alpinum or in closely related communities of oligotrophic springs.

This association often occurs alongside high-lying springs and rills and may pass into various communities on the drier ground. More usually it is associated with high level blanket bogs, mainly Empetreto-Eriophoretum or variants produced by erosion, and occupies either haggs or the original drainage channels and hollows. Individual stands are generally less than 100 sq. m. in area.

Snow and ice cover is often high in these situations and it is noteworthy that list 12 of Table 55, dominated by *Eriophorum angustifolium* and containing *Carex saxatilis*, is very similar to a fen community with the same dominants described by Knaben (1950) for late snow areas of western Norway.

Sphagnum swamps with *Eriophorum angustifolium* as physiognomic dominant occur frequently but mainly as part of a topogenous hydrosere with open water remaining and they have not been studied in detail.

Carex aquatilis-rariflora *nodum*

(Table 55, lists 21–29)

In parts of the East-central Highlands, notably on the broad watersheds around Caen-lochan and Clova, there are small areas of a related mire, the *Carex aquatilis-rariflora nodum*. The *nodum* has no constants, partly because of the limited choice of stands, and has been named from its most characteristic species. Dominance is often shared by the montane form of *Carex aquatilis* and *C. curta* but some lists show a high cover of *C. bigelowii*, *C. nigra*, or *C. rariflora*. The *Sphagnum* carpet has a range of variation similar to that of Sphagneto-Caricetum alpinum both in actual species and in their relative abundance.

The restricted distribution of the *Carex aquatilis-rariflora nodum* probably

9

depends on the phytogeographical factors which have governed the distribution of these two local species. The *nodum* occupies similar situations to the Sphagneto-Caricetum alpinum and the two are frequently in close proximity. The factors differentiating them are obscure but the *Carex aquatilis* mires often appear to be on deeper peat and they occupy situations where waterlogging is probably more stagnant (Fig. 21).

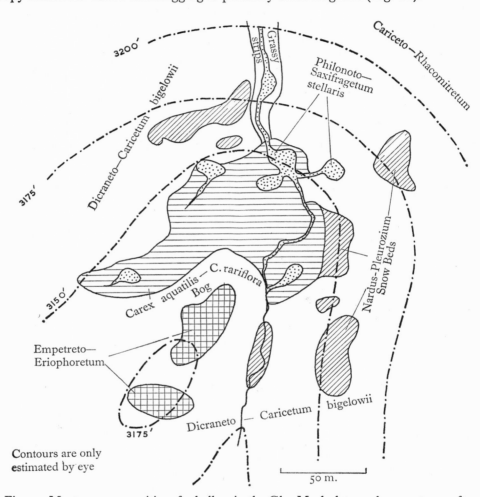

Fig. 21. Montane communities of a hollow in the Glas Maol plateau, Angus, at 3200 ft.

The two montane mires have an upper limit at about 3500 ft. (1068 m.) partly because suitable ground is scarce above this height and perhaps also since *Sphagnum* growth is discouraged climatically at the highest levels. Both types show transitions to associated blanket bogs; a widespread intermediate has many of the distinctive mire species, with more *Eriophorum vaginatum*, and is dominated by *Sphagnum papillosum*. In the high corries of the Cairngorms there are patches of a related community with few species other than *Deschampsia caespitosa* and *Sphagnum papillosum* but often containing *Carex lachenalii*, an eastern montane and chionophilous species which occurs occasionally in other oligotrophic mires (cf. list 22, Table 55) and in late snow-beds. There is another local oligotrophic mire dominated by *Carex rostrata*, but from its floristic composition assignable to either of the Sphagneto-Cariceta according to altitude. An example is given in list 8 of Table 54, showing its affinity to Sphagneto-Juncetum also, the *Carex* replacing *Juncus effusus*. The *Carex rostrata-Sphagnum* mire occurs mainly to the south of the Great Glen and is more widespread on hills in the north of England. It occurs mostly in small basins or waterlogged hollows and flats and extends from low levels to 3350 ft. (1022 m.) on the saddle of Creag Meagaidh.

Mesotrophic to Eutrophic Mires

The range of topographic and climatic habitats occupied by this group is similar to that of the oligotrophic mires. In comparing the two series it is thus often possible to match pairs of noda which seem to be differentiated solely by the base-content of the drainage water. In general the vegetation of the meso- and eutrophic mires usually has a much greater abundance of grasses and herbs and in the moss layer the sub-class Bryales tends to replace the *Sphagna* of the oligotrophic mires.

Juncus acutiflorus-Acrocladium cuspidatum *nodum*
(Table 56)

The *Juncus acutiflorus-Acrocladium cuspidatum nodum* is regarded as the mesotrophic equivalent of the Sphagneto-Juncetum effusi. *J. acutiflorus* is constant and dominant and *Epilobium palustre, Potentilla erecta, Acrocladium cuspidatum* and *Rhytidiadelphus squarrosus* are also constant. The flora is rich with 87 species recorded from only six lists and an average of 33 per stand but it is unusual for any one species to have a high cover apart from the dominant. *Achillea ptarmica, Cirsium palustre, Epilobium palustre* and *Juncus acutiflorus* itself are selective for the *nodum*. Stands may cover up to two or more hectares but are usually considerably smaller.

Although this *nodum* occurs in exactly the same situations as the *Juncus effusus* mire it is more localised and is restricted to the Southern and East-central Highlands at altitudes mainly below 1200 ft. (366 m.) (Map 27). It would thus seem to favour the more continental parts of the country but is perhaps better regarded as a southern type since the same vegetation occurs more widely in the Southern Uplands, Lakeland and North Wales (Ratcliffe, 1959). This compares with the distribution of *Juncus acutiflorus* on the Continent for the species occurs in Denmark but not in any other part of Scandinavia (Hulten, 1950).

The water-table is typically high and there is a 'fen' peat overlying a gleyed mineral horizon. The drainage water usually comes from ground with fairly base-rich rocks and soils, and samples showed pH values of 5·7–6·4 while for the peats the figures were 5·2–5·5. *J. acutiflorus* itself grows successfully on soils with a wide range of base-status and overlaps considerably with *J. effusus* in oligotrophic mires. List 9 of Table 54, for example, is a community which has all the features of typical Sphagneto-Juncetum effusi except that the dominant is *J. acutiflorus*. The dominant in this case is thus unsatisfactory in characterising the *nodum* ecologically and the herb and moss layers give a much better indication of soil conditions. *J. acutiflorus* tends to occur most frequently in oligotrophic mires in the west.

All gradations between *J. acutiflorus* and *J. effusus* mire may occur on the same ground but the typical communities are quite distinct floristically and ecologically. At the geographical limit of the *Juncus acutiflorus-Acrocladium cuspidatum nodum*, which tends to follow a south-west to north-east line there are interesting relationships with the *Molinia-Myrica nodum* which has a complementary northern and western distribution. There is a broad zone of overlap across which *Myrica gale* appears in increasing abundance in the *J. acutiflorus nodum*, finally replacing the rush. Within this zone some localities have only the mixed communities but others have pure stands of one or both noda in addition (see Map 27).

At low levels in the Western Highlands and especially in coastal districts there are mires similar in physiognomy and floristic composition to the *Juncus acutiflorus-Acrocladium cuspidatum nodum*, but with either *Juncus articulatus* or a presumed hybrid between this species and *J. acutiflorus* as the dominant rush. There is again an abundance of grasses, sedges and herbs and *Parnassia palustris* is often a distinctive member of such communities. These *J. articulatus* mires occur on base-rich peats, often within the limits of enclosed marginal or improved ground, and are usually associated with good pastures. There are many examples on Rhum where they often contain *Schoenus nigricans*, and elsewhere there are affinities to lowland fen communities, as indicated by the presence of plants such as *Mentha aquatica* and *Senecio aquaticus*.

Hypno-Caricetum alpinum

(*Carex*-brown moss mire)

(Table 29, lists 12–23)

The mesotrophic equivalent of the Sphagneto-Cariceta is the Hypno-Caricetum alpinum. Whereas two separate associations, sub-alpinum and alpinum, were recognised in the oligotrophic series no such altitudinal separation has been made here since too few stands were examined. Most of those listed lie at moderate elevations and contain montane species so that the term *alpinum* has been preferred. List 21 is the only example from low levels.

The association element contains no less than fourteen constants—*Selaginella selaginoides, Festuca ovina* agg., *Nardus stricta, Carex nigra, C. panicea, C. pulicaris, Eriophorum angustifolium, Leontodon autumnalis, Polygonum viviparum, Thalictrum alpinum, Acrocladium cuspidatum, Hylocomium splendens, Philonotis fontana* and *Rhytidiadelphus squarrosus*. There are 9 other species in constancy class IV and a total of 139 species has been recorded for the association, with the high average of 42 species per stand. *Carex nigra* is the only vascular plant ever to reach dominance, although *C. echinata, C. pulicaris* and various grasses sometimes have a moderate cover. The distinctive character of Hypno-Caricetum alpinum is shown not by the sedges but by the number of basiphilous herbs and mosses. The cover of these indicator plants is usually high but no single species is especially prominent. Most of them are distributed through a number of mesotrophic to eutrophic communities but *Camptothecium nitens* and *Cinclidium stygium* are exclusive to this association and to one or two related mires. The floristic contrast between the Hypno-Caricetum alpinum and its oligotrophic counterparts is best appreciated by a comparison of the complete Tables 29 and 55. The association is related to the *Carex panicea-Campylium stellatum nodum* but differs in the greater luxuriance of the sedge layer and greater humus content of the soil, and floristically in the constancy of *Nardus stricta, Carex nigra, Polygonum viviparum, Thalictrum alpinum, Acrocladium cuspidatum* and *Philonotis fontana*.

The association occurs most frequently in the two districts of Breadalbane and

Caenlochan-Clova where calcareous rocks are extensive at moderate to high elevations (Map 15). It has been found mainly between 1700 and 3200 ft. (519–976 m.) and in situation and size of stands there is great similarity to Sphagneto-Caricetum sub-alpinum. There are few occurrences on high watersheds, evidently because the drainage water there is seldom sufficiently enriched, and the usual sites are where steep and often rocky slopes begin to flatten out (Plate 26 and Fig. 23, p. 123).

The soils are mostly well-humified peats over strongly gleyed horizons. Some sites, especially beside rills, show an intimate mixture of silt and humus throughout the profile, again with pronounced gleying. They show a pH range of 5·3–5·6.

Hypno-Caricetum alpinum often passes into herb-rich Nardetum sub-alpinum or Juncetum squarrosi sub-alpinum on slightly drier, although still well-irrigated ground. From their floristic similarity these three associations have been grouped together in Table 29, but the present association is obviously richer in hydrophilous species than the other two.

A similar type of vegetation occurs patchily on basic soils in the Moffat and Tweedsmuir Hills of the Southern Uplands.

Carex rostrata-Sphagnum warnstorfianum *nodum*

(Table 57)

A related mire, the *Carex rostrata-Sphagnum warnstorfianum nodum* corresponds to the oligotrophic *Carex rostrata-Sphagnum recurvum* mire. *Carex rostrata* is the physiognomic dominant but *Sphagna* usually have a complete cover. Besides the sedge, *Selaginella selaginoides*, *Festuca ovina* agg., *Viola palustris*, *Aulacomnium palustre*, *Mnium pseudopunctatum*, *Hylocomium splendens*, *Sphagnum teres* and *S. warnstorfianum* are constant. The two *Sphagna* and *S. subsecundum* (*sens. strict.*) are preferential for the *nodum*, while *S. contortum* is exclusive to it. *Camptothecium nitens* is exclusive to this and the previous nodum, and neither *Aulacomnium palustre* nor *Mnium pseudopunctatum* reach constancy in any other type of vegetation. A variety of sedges and herbs is usually present and the table shows a total of 110 species with an average of 36 per list.

Within the geographical range of the *nodum* there occurs a facies differing only in the absence of *Carex rostrata*, which is replaced as dominant by other sedges such as *C. nigra* or even *Juncus squarrosus* or *J. acutiflorus*.

The *Carex rostrata-Sphagnum warnstorfianum* mire is confined to the Central Highlands where it is extremely local and occurs exclusively on hills with strongly calcareous rocks (Map 31). The known examples lie between 1400 ft. and 2700 ft. (427-824 m.) and the largest stand yet found covers about half a hectare. The *nodum* is rare evidently because the necessary stagnation of ground water is associated with acidic peat formation even on calcareous hills. Sites which are suitable topographically (i.e. waterlogged basins and flats) are usually occupied by oligotrophic mires.

The higher and more stagnant water-table also differentiates the *nodum* from the Hypno-Caricetum alpinum.

Although *Sphagnum*-dominated the *nodum* is distinctly mesotrophic and always has at least a few indicators of better base-status such as *Selaginella selaginoides*, *Carex demissa*, *Thalictrum alpinum*, *Camptothecium nitens* and *Drepanocladus revolvens*. Moreover, the predominant *Sphagna* are those associated with relatively nutrient-rich waters such as *S. warnstorfianum*, *S. teres*, *S. squarrosum*, *S. subsecundum* (*sens. strict.*) and

S. contortum. There is a close relationship with lowland 'poor fens' containing *Carex rostrata*, *C. lasiocarpa*, *Potentilla palustris*, *Menyanthes trifoliata* and the above *Sphagna*. The underlying peat is usually fairly deep (more than 1 m.) and also resembles that of some lowland fens. pH values of water samples range from 5·8–6·0 and those of peats from 5·5–5·7.

This vegetation type seems to be undescribed for Britain but is closely related to important mire (i.e. fen) communities of Scandinavia such as the *Salix lapponum-Carex inflata (rostrata)-Sphagnum warnstorfii* sociation of Nordhagen (1943) and the Aulacomnieto-Sphagnetum warnstorfiani of Dahl (1956). These Norwegian associations differ mainly in their greater abundance of montane plants, especially willows. The Scottish community, which frequently contains seedlings of *Salix aurita*, is evidently less montane, although *Salix myrsinites* grows on cliff ledges only about 150 ft. (46 m.) above one stand on Ben Vrackie (Fig. 23, p. 123). Small patches of the *nodum* occur in a complex of *Carex rostrata* mires on Matterdale Common in Lakeland and there are fragments in the Moffat Hills.

The *nodum* sometimes grades into Hypno-Caricetum alpinum or it may occur independently. Where irrigation disappears altogether it usually changes into Calluneto-Eriophoretum or into grassland if the ground is well drained. Occasionally it passes into swamp and open water *Carex rostrata* stands of definite hydroseres, and in a wet hollow on Ben Vrackie it occurs in mosaic with the *Carex rostrata*-brown moss *nodum* (see p. 123).

Carex panicea-Campylium stellatum *nodum*
(Table 58, lists 1–18)

A eutrophic mire which has no real equivalent in the oligotrophic series is the *Carex panicea-Campylium stellatum nodum*. Besides the two definitive species there are only three other constants—*Selaginella selaginoides*, *Juncus articulatus* and *Pinguicula vulgaris* —but there are ten species in constancy class IV.

The vegetation is essentially a close-grazed sedge sward with plentiful forbs and grasses and a variable cover of somewhat hydrophilous mosses. *Carex demissa*, *C. dioica*, *C. echinata*, *C. flacca*, *C. nigra*, *C. panicea* and *C. pulicaris* commonly form a mixed growth but any one of them may be dominant locally. *Eleocharis pauciflora* is usually present and may itself attain dominance at times. *Eriophorum angustifolium* and *Juncus kochii* usually add to the sward and basiphilous herbs, notably *Leontodon autumnalis*, are always present. The noteworthy mosses are *Campylium stellatum*, *Cratoneuron commutatum*, *Drepanocladus revolvens* var. *intermedius*, *Ctenidium molluscum*, *Fissidens adianthoides*, *Bryum pseudotriquetrum* and *Scorpidium scorpioides*. Total moss cover is not usually high but any of the pleurocarpous species may be dominant locally.

The *nodum* numbers 129 species with an average of 31 per stand. *Isolepis setacea* is exclusive to it, while *Equisetum variegatum*, *Briza media*, *Eriophorum latifolium*, *Juncus alpinus*, *Tofieldia pusilla*, *Mnium seligeri* and *Philonotis calcarea* are selective.

The *nodum* fails to qualify as an association largely because of the interchange of species in the sedge and moss layers. For instance, *Carex demissa* and *C. hostiana* are sometimes mutually exclusive and *Cratoneuron commutatum* and *Drepanocladus revolvens* var. *intermedius* may replace each other. While further study might allow sub-division according to consistent combinations of these species we prefer to regard this meanwhile as a single rather variable unit. There is considerable overlap with the *Carex demissa-*

Carex panicea nodum described by Poore (1955b) for Breadalbane. Poore's *nodum* may be considered as a local high-level facies of the present one with *Scorpidium scorpioides* and the montane moss *Acrocladium trifarium* exchanged for *Selaginella selaginoides* and *Campylium stellatum* as constants. The greater abundance of *Saxifraga aizoides* and the consistently more open vegetation would, however, suggest that the Breadalbane *nodum* lies closer to our Cariceto-Saxifragetum aizoidis than to the *Carex panicea-Campylium stellatum nodum*. The present *nodum* is floristically similar to Saxifrageto-Agrosto-Festucetum, but differs in the predominance of sedges and other hydrophilous species, as compared with that of grasses: *Ctenidium molluscum* instead of *Campylium stellatum* is the most abundant moss in the grassland. Relationships to Hypno-Caricetum alpinum are discussed on p. 118: list 18 of Table 58 is intermediate between these two noda.

This type of mire vegetation is confined to strongly calcareous rocks and so occurs most frequently in the hills between Breadalbane and Clova (Map 30). It is well represented on Dalradian limestone around Blair Atholl. There are also occurrences in wet places on coastal lands affected by blown shell sand as at Bettyhill on the north coast of Sutherland, where *Primula scotica* is a distinctive feature of the stands.

The altitudinal range of 100 ft. to 2400 ft. (30–732 m.), excluding list 18, makes this a sub-montane community and as this range also corresponds to the former forest zone it is clearly biotically maintained. The *nodum* usually occurs as a strip of variable width adjoining a rill or an open calcareous flush with Cariceto-Saxifragetum aizoidis and corresponds to a zone of less intense irrigation (Plate 26 and Fig. 24, p. 135). The sedge sward may, however, occur without the associated open habitat when drainage is suitable. Individual stands range from a few square metres to about 500 sq. m. in area but are usually small.

The soils are silty muds of variable humus content and are normally saturated with water, but the ground is much firmer to the tread than that of the previous mires. The pH ranges from 5·9 to 6·3 and the calcium content is high.

Where *Carex panicea-Campylium stellatum* mires pass into drier ground there is usually a change to species-rich Agrosto-Festucetum or Saxifrageto-Agrosto-Festucetum (Fig. 8, p. 56). Where the transition is to more waterlogged but still calcareous ground either Hypno-Caricetum alpinum (Plate 26) or the *Carex rostrata*-brown moss *nodum* may replace it depending on the degree of stagnation. List 18 is from an isolated stand which comes close to Hypno-Caricetum alpinum but is dominated by *Cratoneuron commutatum*.

Sometimes the *nodum* passes into wet ground with base-poor soils and the change is then to more oligotrophic mire characterised by an abundance of *Erica tetralix* (Fig. 22). This vegetation may sometimes be assigned to Trichophoreto-Eriophoretum caricetosum and it is noteworthy that in the Western Highlands the same community often occurs alongside open calcareous flushes instead of the *Carex panicea-Campylium stellatum nodum*.

The present *nodum* corresponds closely to wet calcareous pastures described by Pigott (1956) for Upper Teesdale and there containing *Primula farinosa* and *Gentiana verna* besides some of the rarer plants of the Scottish mire. Related communities occur elsewhere on limestone in Northern England and on basic rocks in Lakeland and the Southern Uplands. In these regions there are other meso- to eutrophic mire communities which show affinities to both the *Carex panicea-Campylium stellatum nodum* and Hypno-Caricetum alpinum. They occupy comparable situations and have a similar flora to the

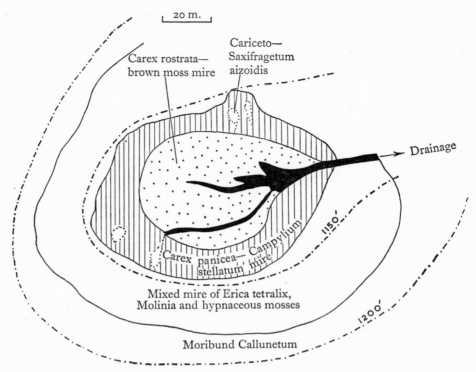

Fig. 22. Calcareous mire basin on Tulach Hill, Blair Atholl, Perthshire

two Highland mires, but typically show a complete cover of brown mosses and reduced abundance of sedges and other vascular plants. Pigott (1956) has described an Upper Teesdale example and in this area, though not in the Highlands, *Saxifraga hirculus* is a characteristic species of such mires.

Carex rostrata-brown moss provisional *nodum*
(Table 58, lists 19–22)

The *Carex rostrata*-brown moss *nodum* mentioned above is extremely local and although only four lists are available their similarity makes us feel justified in regarding it as a provisional *nodum*. *Carex rostrata* is the physiognomic dominant and while Carices of the previous *nodum* occur, sometimes plentifully, the sedge growth tends to be rather open and the moss layer is conspicuous. There is usually a complete spongy cover of pleurocarpous 'brown mosses' with *Campylium stellatum*, *Cratoneuron commutatum*, *Drepanocladus revolvens* var. *intermedius* and *Scorpidium scorpioides* as interchangeable dominants. Herbs are few and have a low cover value.

The few known localities are on limestone and other highly calcareous rocks in the East-central Highlands with an outlier on the shell sand at Bettyhill in Sutherland. Altitude varies between 100 ft. and 2600 ft. (30–793 m.). Scarcity of such vegetation appears to be due to the infrequent essential combination of lime-rich ground water and stagnant drainage of hollows and basins. The stands do not exceed a few hundred square metres in size but are usually homogeneous.

Soils are mesotrophic or eutrophic 'fen' peats usually with little or no mineral matter and are fairly deep. They correspond to the *Hypnum* peat moor of Kubiena

(1953, p. 101). Water samples show a pH range of 6·5–6·8 and peats of 5·5–5·8. *Carex rostrata* is clearly another physiognomic dominant which is indifferent to base-status (cf. *Juncus acutiflorus*) since it occurs in this role in oligotrophic, mesotrophic and eutrophic mires.

The *Carex rostrata*-brown moss *nodum* may pass into *C. rostrata-Sphagnum warnstorfianum* mire as on Ben Vrackie, Perthshire (Fig. 23) evidently in response to a lowering of the water nutrient content.

Lowland fen hydroseres consisting largely of swamp communities dominated by sedges, *Menyanthes trifoliata* and *Sphagna* often show patches of vegetation similar to the present *nodum*.

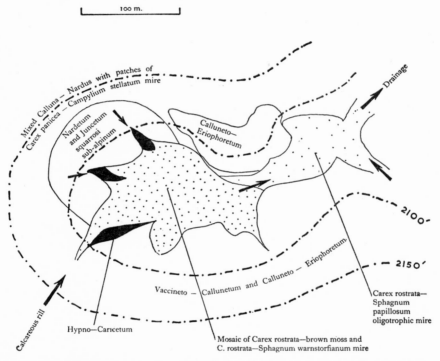

Fig. 23. Mire system on Ben Vrackie, Perthshire, at 2100 ft. The calcareous flush effect gradually disappears towards the right-hand side of the mire system

Similar calcareous fen vegetation occurs more extensively at Sunbiggin Tarn, Westmorland, as described by Holdgate (1955a). Dahl (1956) describes a Scorpidieto-Caricetum limosae for topogenous mires in Rondane and this is evidently similar to our *nodum*. An even greater resemblance to Dahl's association, however, is shown by a series of pools in blanket bog near Laxford Bridge in Sutherland, evidently marking the emergence of mineral-rich drainage water in otherwise oligotrophic peat. The following list with frequency estimates refers to several of these rather uniform pools:

Schoenus nigricans	. . . a	Eriophorum angustifolium	. .	va
Juncus kochii	. . . a	Carex dioica	. . .	f
Carex limosa	. . . f	Drosera anglica	. . .	f
Menyanthes trifoliata	. . o	Utricularia vulgaris	. .	a
Potamogeton polygonifolius	. a	Acrocladium trifarium	.	f
Scorpidium scorpioides	. ld	Chara sp.	. . .	f

This would seem to be an oceanic counterpart of the Rondane association.

The bog pools with *Scorpidium* and *Schoenus* provide a link with the next mire to be described.

Schoenus nigricans provisional *nodum*

(Table 64, lists 26–29)

Although only four lists are available at present other examples have been seen and the uniformity of all the stands is noteworthy. The vegetation is dominated by dense tussocks of *Schoenus nigricans* and most of the associates have a low cover value. *Eriophorum angustifolium* and *Campylium stellatum* are the only other species present in all four analyses and with an average of only 19 species per stand the *nodum* is floristically poor compared with most eutrophic mires. Although the sites are wet the vegetation is normally so dense that the ground is firm to the tread and, in contrast to many other mires, the moss layer is poorly developed.

Schoenus nigricans mires have been found only in the Western Highlands and even here they are rare since a highly calcareous substratum is evidently essential (Map 27). The known examples occupy waterlogged hollows receiving drainage from limestone, shell sand or ultra-basic igneous rocks. All occur at low levels (below 600 ft. (183 m.)) and close to the sea (Fig. 27, p. 151). The soils are calcareous peats or marls with a high pH (8·0 in one sample).

Despite its lower altitudinal range the *Schoenus* mire seems to be the western counterpart of the *Carex rostrata*-brown moss *nodum* of calcareous waterlogged hollows in the Central Highlands. Both types meet at Bettyhill in Sutherland where they occur in badly drained places which come within the range of blown shell sand.

The present *nodum* may pass into *Carex panicea-Campylium stellatum* mire or species-rich *Agrostis-Festuca* grassland as the drainage improves or into the low-level facies of Cariceto-Saxifragetum aizoidis where the flow of water becomes rapid. Sometimes it appears as part of a complex of mire and fen vegetation where enriched drainage water emerges on moors otherwise covered with Trichophoreto-Eriophoretum typicum. The *nodum* is then associated with *Carex lasiocarpa* and *C. rostrata* communities of open water (see p. 126).

The Schoenetum nigricantis which Tansley (1949) describes as extensive on the blanket bogs of western Ireland would seem to be a more mixed vegetation than the Scottish *nodum*. The Irish Schoenetum is probably similar to Trichophoreto-Eriophoretum typicum with abundant *Schoenus*, a mixture which also occurs frequently in the Western Highlands. In Scotland the presence of *Schoenus* in blanket bogs would seem usually, if not always, to indicate an irrigation effect in the peat. This is suggested largely by the distribution of the plant. When sparse it is evenly scattered as separate shoots throughout the vegetation but with increasing abundance it tends to be more and more confined as a tussocky growth to distinct seepage areas and lines on the bogs. *Schoenus* grows most abundantly and luxuriantly in hollows, channels and flushes where enrichment by irrigation is undoubtedly strong but it appears to be less strictly calcicole in the Western Highlands than in lowland England. The connection with irrigation is evidently a real one quite apart from the possibility that sea spray is another essential factor determining the occurrence of *Schoenus* in Scottish blanket bogs (cf. Tansley, op. cit.). Even in the Western Highlands the species still grows most abundantly on calcareous soils and its presence in a variety of communities on the island of Rhum may well reflect the widespread occurrence in drift of material from the basic and ultra-basic igneous rocks rather than the influence of sea spray. It is nevertheless true that on the west coast of Scotland *Schoenus* sometimes grows abundantly close to the sea and even in brackish habitats, so that it may have a preference for both saline and calcareous conditions.

The *Schoenus nigricans* communities described by Holdgate (1955b) for limestone ground near Orton in Westmorland seem to be similar to our *nodum*. Small patches of a comparable *Schoenus* vegetation have been noted on basic soils in Galloway and the *nodum* itself may prove to be more widely distributed than our present information suggests.

Caricetum saxatilis

(*Carex saxatilis* mire)
(Table 59)

The montane equivalent of the *Carex panicea-Campylium stellatum nodum* is the Caricetum saxatilis first described by Poore (1955b) from Breadalbane. The association described here is substantially the same as Poore's but analyses have been added from other districts. The association element consists of *Carex saxatilis, Drepanocladus revolvens, Hylocomium splendens, Aneura pinguis* and *Scapania undulata* but, as a result of expanding the table, *Eriophorum angustifolium* is no longer constant. *Carex saxatilis* is the usual dominant although *C. demissa, C. dioica, C. echinata* and *C. nigra* may be abundant and *Drepanocladus revolvens* often has a high cover in the moss layer. Certain montane species are exclusive to this association and to the high-level facies of the Cariceto-Saxifragetum aizoidis, under which they are discussed (p. 134).

Like its low-level counterpart this association belongs to strongly calcareous rocks and so it is restricted to hills where these outcrop at high levels. It shows the characteristic distribution of many calcicolous montane communities (Map 32) with its headquarters along the whole Breadalbane tract from Ben Lui to Ben Lawers and with only scattered outposts to the north, mainly in the Western Highlands (cf. the Dwarf Herb *nodum*, Map 21).

In Breadalbane it is found only on the Ben Lawers schist and, apart from two localities on Dalradian Limestone, the more northerly stands are on calcareous rocks of the Moine or Lewisian series.

The association is much more local than *Carex saxatilis* itself, even on calcareous soils, and it is absent from Caenlochan where the sedge is present. *C. saxatilis* is more widely distributed because it can grow on quite base-poor rocks and often occurs amongst *Anthelia* spp. and even *Sphagnum papillosum* communities on acidic mountains. Like *Carex rostrata*, it tolerates a wide range of soil base-status, although it is most frequently dominant on calcareous soils, and the eutrophic tendency of Caricetum saxatilis is shown better by the subordinate species. Moreover, although Caricetum saxatilis is the most calcicolous mire of the montane zone, some of its most abundant species are not calcicole, and the soils tend to be less calcareous than those of some low-level eutrophic mires.

Caricetum saxatilis typically borders rills or open Cariceto-Saxifragetum aizoidis flushes at altitudes between 2500 ft. (763 m.) and 3200 ft. (976 m.) (cf. Plate 26). Individual stands rarely exceed 50 sq. m. in size but on suitable ground the total extent of the association may be considerable.

The soils are wet humus-rich muds similar to those of the *Carex panicea-Campylium stellatum nodum* and vary from almost pure peat to silts with little humus, with pH values from 4·6–5·7.

Poore (op. cit.) regards prolonged snow-cover as an important controlling factor for this association, which is certainly most extensive in high corries where the snow lies late. He notes the close similarity of the *Acrocladium sarmentosum*-rich *Carex saxatilis* sociation and the *Carex saxatilis-Drepanocladus intermedius* sociation of Nordhagen (1927, 1943).

Caricetum saxatilis may be regarded as the mesotrophic to eutrophic counterpart of the oligotrophic Sphagneto-Caricetum alpinum and it sometimes passes into this association or to related *Sphagnum papillosum* communities on poor soils. More often, as irrigation disappears, there is a change to *Deschampsia caespitosa*, *Juncus squarrosus* or *Nardus stricta* grasslands or, with intermittent irrigation, to the Dwarf Herb *nodum*.

Topogenous Fens and their Relationship to Mires

Fens occur locally in the Highlands, usually below 1,000 ft. (305 m.) where there are permanently waterlogged hollows or valley bottoms. They are often developed around the margins of lakes of all sizes, wherever conditions favour the accumulation of organic debris. All these situations owe their high water-table largely to the topography. The surface of a fen is usually level and although there may be some water movement, the total depth of peat and water is usually much greater than in mires. Furthermore, whereas the water-table in mires usually lies below the surface (except in the wettest weather), fens normally contain at least some open water or swamp communities and their vegetation tends to be dominated by hydrophytes. The vegetation of many soligenous mires resembles and intergrades with that of true fens, and some fens are composed largely of communities referable to certain mire noda but with a number of additional aquatic species.

Many fens lie within the limits of enclosed land but others form part of vegetation complexes which we have studied in some detail. In particular, one type of oligotrophic fen is widespread throughout the Highlands although its occurrences are usually scattered and seldom extensive. The very large fen system between Kingussie and Loch Insh would seem, however, to be mainly of this type. No analyses have been made and no separate communities recognised in these 'poor fens', but the following list includes species which are nearly always present. Other less distinctive species of the surrounding drier ground are usually present but have not been named. Species marked with an asterisk may be locally dominant or co-dominant.

Agrostis stolonifera	E. palustre
Caltha palustris	Erica tetralix
Carex curta	Eriophorum angustifolium*
C. echinata*	Galium palustre
C. lasiocarpa*	Juncus effusus
C. limosa*	J. kochii
C. nigra*	Menyanthes trifoliata*
C. rostrata*	Myrica gale
Eleocharis multicaulis	Narthecium ossifragum
Epilobium palustre	Pedicularis palustris
Equisetum fluviatile	Phragmites communis*

Potamogeton polygonifolius
Potentilla palustris*
Ranunculus flammula
Sparganium minimum agg.
Succisa pratensis
Utricularia intermedia
U. minor
U. vulgaris agg.
Viola palustris

Acrocladium cuspidatum
A. stramineum
Aulacomnium palustre
Drepanocladus fluitans

Rhytidiadelphus squarrosus
Sphagnum cuspidatum
S. palustre*
S. papillosum*
S. recurvum*
S. russowii
S. squarrosum*
S. subsecundum
    var. auriculatum*
    var. inundatum*

Lophocolea bidentata
Pellia epiphylla

Other species are locally present, such as *Nymphaea occidentalis, Nuphar pumila* (both in open water) and *Oxycoccus palustris.*

Many fens of this type have patches of vegetation usually associated with meso-trophic or even eutrophic conditions, evidently in response to local enrichment of the water. These richer communities are most often dominated by the 'brown mosses' *Scorpidium scorpioides, Campylium stellatum, Drepanocladus revolvens, Cratoneuron commutatum* and *Acrocladium giganteum*; or by *Sphagna* such as *S. teres, S. warnstorfianum, S. contortum* and *S. subsecundum.* The associated vascular plants are at least mildly basiphilous, such as *Carex pulicaris, C. dioica, C. demissa, C. paniculata* (rather rare), *Eleocharis pauciflora, Triglochin palustre* and *Cardamine pratensis.* In the west these richer fen communities commonly include *Schoenus nigricans* and more rarely *Cladium mariscus.*

Within the range which the rather limited flora allows, this fen vegetation shows a good deal of heterogeneity, and while there may be consistent combinations of species assignable to separate communities, these often vary greatly within the one site. The lack of uniformity is probably due to the relatively rapid change and sharp environmental gradients which often characterise this kind of habitat. Hydroseral development may give a zonation from the centre to the edge of the fen or else a mosaic of different stages with no definite pattern. The species marked with an asterisk tend to form the most conspicuous element of the vegetation, and any one of them may attain dominance locally. If a name for this class of vegetation is desired, *Carex lasiocarpa-Menyanthes* fen would perhaps be the most suitable choice. It is probable, though, that careful study of good examples would allow the definition of noda within this broad category. Patches with obvious similarity to one or other of the sub-montane mire noda are usually to be found, and their recognition would give a basis for the selection of new reference points.

Complexes of Bog, Mire and Fen

Here and there we have encountered systems of peat-forming vegetation best considered as single topographic units, but composed of a mixture of bog, mire and fen communities. Sometimes the separate components are well-defined and occupy distinctive parts of the habitat complex, but more often they blend gradually and their spatial relationships lack any clear pattern. As there is no obvious topographic separation in the second case, a sub-division is best made first according to difference in floristics and the controlling water-regime. The vegetation types recognised can then be assigned to bog, mire or fen according to floristic affinities.

Contrasting areas will be described briefly for illustration of the point.

Abernethy Forest, Inverness-shire

An interesting series of peat communities occupies a system of glacial drift hollows and channels in the pine-woods to the west of Loch Garten. Marked differences in movement and base-content of the water in these situations give a range of vegetation varying from strongly oligotrophic to mesotrophic. The complex would seem to be strikingly similar to some of those described and illustrated by Sjörs (1948) in Sweden.

Where there is stagnant waterlogging and a low base-status, the vegetation is similar to the *Sphagnum*-dominated facies of Calluneto-Eriophoretum, but contains an abundance of *Erica tetralix*, *Carex pauciflora* and *Narthecium ossifragum* instead of *Vaccinium myrtillus* and *Rubus chamaemorus*. Some species such as *Calluna vulgaris*, *Eriophorum vaginatum* and *Narthecium* tend to be clumped or tussocky, and in places the bog surface has developed systems of pools and hummocks similar to those often found on Trichophoreto-Eriophoretum 'flowes'. These bogs are quite thickly colonised by pine, but the seedlings rarely grow more than a few feet high and either die or remain 'in check' due to the high water-table. Growth is increasingly successful towards the drier edges, and in places there is a natural transition to the mature pinewood, with gradual increase in stature and abundance of the trees.

While this oligotrophic vegetation is clearly related to that of many blanket bogs, there are equally strong affinities to lowland raised bogs, especially when the topogenous origin is considered. There is no regular arrangement of marginal 'laggs' but there are frequent transitions in various parts of the mire system to soligenous communities either in separate patches or as narrow 'soaks' (Sjörs, 1948). The soligenous influence is shown first by the increased abundance of *Erica tetralix* and *Narthecium*, followed by the appearance of sedges, which gradually increase to dominance. *Carex rostrata*, *C. lasiocarpa*, *C. nigra*, *C. echinata* are the predominant species and associated with them are many other plants typical of soligenous mires in the Highlands. Some stands are referable to Sphagneto-Caricetum sub-alpinum (list 8, Table 55) but others pass into 'poor fen' *Carex* communities of open water, with *Equisetum* spp., *Potentilla palustris*, *Menyanthes trifoliata*, *Utricularia intermedia* and *Potamogeton polygonifolius*. One enclosed hollow has a central open-water *Carex rostrata* swamp surrounded by a broad marginal zone of *Sphagnum recurvum* and *Eriophorum angustifolium*.

In a few places, mineral-charged water emerges amongst the mixed mire communities, giving a patchy occurrence of the *Carex rostrata*-brown moss *nodum*, often with a hummock and hollow surface structure. The change from the oligotrophic *Sphagnum*-rich *Calluna-Eriophorum* bog to soligenous mire, and occasionally to the mesotrophic brown-moss carpet, occurs repeatedly and often rapidly. In addition the *Sphagnum* pools of the oligotrophic bog show all stages in breakdown to bare peaty flats, so that the hydrology of the mire system must be extremely complex.

Rannoch Moor, Argyll-Perthshire

The contrasting treelessness of this large blanket bog area is not a natural condition, for the numerous morainic mounds and ridges which break the level surface of the Moor are certain to have carried pinewood before the advent of Man. The wetter parts of the area are covered with Trichophoreto-Eriophoretum typicum, passing on better-drained but still moist ground to Trichophoreto-Callunetum and Molinieto-Callunetum. The wetter bogs are often drained by soaks, and where slight slopes or hollows occur there are bigger patches of soligenous mire. Sometimes these seepage areas discharge into small peaty tarns (dubh-lochans) with hydroseral swamps around their edges.

The soligenous sites are commonly marked by an abundance of *Carex rostrata*, *C. nigra* and *C. lasiocarpa*, which attain dominance where the flow of water is strongest. There are often peaty pools or runnels with a moving current and containing species such as *Carex limosa*, *Juncus kochii*, *Utricularia vulgaris* agg., *U. intermedia* and *U. minor*.

The extent of marginal swamp and fen vegetation around the lochan edges varies greatly, but typically there are open water communities dominated by the above Carices, with abundant *Menyanthes trifoliata*, *Eriophorum angustifolium* and sometimes *Nymphaea* cf. *occidentalis*, *Nuphar pumila*, *Potentilla palustris* and *Phragmites communis*. The *Carex* swamp usually passes into a shore-ward zone of spongy *Sphagnum* flats which show affinities to Sphagneto-Caricetum sub-alpinum. The predominant *Sphagna* are *S. papillosum*, *S. recurvum*, *S. auriculatum*, *S. magellanicum* and *S. cuspidatum* and the moss-carpet is often hummocky. Associated vascular plants consist of a mixture of species from the open water swamps and the surrounding blanket bogs, but a few are characteristic of this habitat—*Carex echinata*, *C. curta*, *C. paupercula* (rare), *Oxycoccus palustris* and *Viola palustris*.

It is not clear whether this zonation represents an actual succession for, although there is often a suggestion of hydroseral development, this may be largely illusory. The fen communities of Rannoch Moor are better defined topographically than those of Abernethy Forest, but their spatial connection with blanket bog is close.

A similar development of mire and fen vegetation in areas of low-level blanket bog occurs frequently in the Western Highlands. In the north-west, *Schoenus nigricans* communities are often well represented in the soligenous sites, and may pass into mixtures of bog and fen vegetation on pool and hummock ground. A list from such fen pools is given on p. 123.

These bog, mire and fen complexes illustrate the close relationships which can exist between vegetation types normally found separately, and emphasise the lack of clear distinction between these classical sub-divisions of peat-forming vegetation.

Chapter 9

SPRINGS AND FLUSHES

WE have used the term flush for strongly irrigated sites, closely related to mires, where the flow of water is sufficient to prevent the development of closed vegetation. Flushes appear as patches of bare soil, gravel and stones with a sparse and patchy plant growth where water seeps diffusely over the surface or is confined to rills (Plate 26). The superficial appearance is the same whatever the base content of the mud and water and there are numerous transitions to closed mire communities with increasing stability of the substratum.

The flushes are often fed from spring-heads which are typically bryophyte-dominated and appear as large spongy mats with a flat or convex surface. Sometimes, however, especially among blanket bogs, the open flush suddenly emerges from quite a different soil-vegetation complex and the source of the fresh water is less concentrated.

The size of the flush varies from a few square metres to hundreds of square metres although the larger examples are usually mixed with patches of other communities and form intimate mosaics. The spring-head moss patch is generally not more than a few square metres in area but much larger examples occur locally, especially in late snow-beds.

Philonoto-Saxifragetum stellaris
(Oligotrophic bryophyte springs)
(Table 60, lists 1–23)

The oligotrophic springs and flushes are treated as a single complex, the *Philonoto-Saxifragetum stellaris*, although a distinctive high level association dominated by *Pohlia glacialis* is considered separately. Not only are there numerous transitions between the closed spring and open flush communities but several species act as interchangeable dominants and the variations in their proportions show little sign of correlation with habitat differences. *Philonotis fontana*, *Deschampsia caespitosa* and *Saxifraga stellaris* are the only constants of the association and of these only *Philonotis* is found as a dominant. Other species appearing as dominants are *Dicranella squarrosa*, *Drepanocladus exannulatus*, *Acrocladium sarmentosum*, *Sphagnum subsecundum* var. *auriculatum*, *Scapania undulata* and *Scapania uliginosa*. Most of these usually occur in the one stand, either in roughly equal abundance and forming a growth mosaic or else with one or two predominating. *Splachnum vasculosum* is exclusive to the association and *Montia lamprosperma*, *Stellaria alsine* and *Aplozia cordifolia* are highly selective for it, while *Agrostis stolonifera*, *Caltha palustris* var. *minor*, *Chrysosplenium oppositifolium* and *Epilobium anagallidifolium* are also characteristic.

Separate facies have not been recognised, although a sub-division could be made according to the different dominants. The type dominated by *Sphagnum auriculatum* is the most common and may be the only representative of the association on acidic mountains. Although unsupported by chemical analyses our observations suggest that a slightly lower range of soil base-status may differentiate it from the more species-rich *Aplozia cordifolia*, *Philonotis* and *Dicranella* types. At high levels the Philonoto-Saxifragetum stellaris differs only in the addition of montane species such as *Deschampsia alpina*, *Veronica humifusa* and, very locally, *Alopecurus alpinus*.

This is one of the most widespread types of vegetation in Scotland, occurring with much the same range of variation in nearly all the main hill groups. Although not much in evidence below 1500 ft. (457 m.) the association is common at the higher levels wherever the rock has a low calcium content.

Oligotrophic springs and flushes may emerge amongst or disappear into a wide variety of communities. There are frequent transitions to one or other of the Sphagneto-Cariceta as the water flow decreases, and more sudden changes to dry grassland, dwarf shrub heath or shallow blanket bogs are quite usual (Fig. 21, p. 116). Montane examples occur among *Rhacomitrium* heaths but they are more frequent in association with *Pohlia glacialis* springs and *Anthelia* flushes of late snow-beds.

The association is closely comparable to the Philonoto-Saxifragetum stellaris of Nordhagen (1943, p. 429) and Dahl (1956, p. 206), both in floristics and habitat but its wider range of variation appears to include Dahl's Scapanietum uliginosi as well. Identical spring vegetation is common on the higher hills of Southern Scotland, Northern England and Wales.

Pohlietum glacialis

(*Pohlia glacialis* springs)

(Table 60, lists 24–31)

This is a spring-head association completely dominated by *Pohlia albicans* var. *glacialis*. The soft spongy carpets of this moss have a bright apple-green colour which makes the vegetation conspicuous at some distance so that its entire distribution may be recorded quite easily. *Deschampsia caespitosa* is the only other constant but *Saxifraga stellaris*, *Cerastium cerastoides* and *Epilobium anagallidifolium* are often present. *Pohlia glacialis* and *Marchantia polymorpha* var. *alpestris* are exclusive to the association.

Pohlia glacialis springs are restricted to the neighbourhood of the longest lasting snow-beds and so occur mainly in the Central Highlands (Map 22) above 2800 ft. (854 m.). The water temperature is consistently less than 4° C but not all cold springs have the Pohlietum. Stands vary in size from one sq. m. to 200 sq. m. Carn Eige in Glen Affric carries the largest continuous stand that we have seen but more extensive discontinuous examples have been encountered in the Cairngorm corries. Although dominance of *Pohlia glacialis* is so localised the species occurs in small quantities over a wider range of altitude and area.

The soils of Pohlietum glacialis and Philonoto-Saxifragetum are humus-rich and often fluid muds with variable amounts of mineral matter.

With distance from the spring-head and thus with decreasing snow-lie the *Pohlia* carpet passes into *Philonotis-Saxifraga stellaris* flushes provided that the water flow remains substantial. A transitional community is given in list 27 of Table 60. Above the

10

Pohlia springs there are sudden transitions to dry ground with Polytricheto-Dicranetum starkei and Rhacomitreto-Dicranetum starkei.

Dahl (1956) has already remarked upon the strong similarity between the Scottish Pohlietum glacialis, his Mniobryo-Epilobietum hornemanni of Rondane and other Norwegian *Pohlia glacialis* associations. The associations are identical in physiognomy for they have the same dominant and most of the subordinate species in common. *Epilobium anagallidifolium* is replaced in the Norwegian association by the closely related *E. hornemanni*.

Anthelia-Deschampsia caespitosa provisional *nodum*
(Table 61)

This is another bryophyte flush of distinctive appearance for it consists of a firm springy mat of either *Anthelia julacea* or *A. juratzkana* with subordinate species present only in low abundance. The two *Anthelia* species do not appear to occur together in the one stand. Since only four lists are given the *nodum* must be regarded as provisional although it has been seen in many additional localities. Besides *Anthelia* spp. only *Deschampsia caespitosa* and *Scapania dentata* show any signs of constancy and only 28 species in all have been recorded in the four lists.

Anthelia communities belong to areas of late snow-lie above 2800 ft. (854 m.) but are more widespread than Pohlietum glacialis with occurrences on most of the higher hills of the Central Highlands. They are best developed on the gently sloping floors of corries or smaller hollows on the summit slopes and plateaux. Although situated on permanently wet ground they evidently experience a slower rate of water movement than the Philonoto-Saxifragetum stellaris, with which they form intimate mixtures. During part of the year irrigation comes largely from snow melt water.

Stands may individually cover 100 sq. m. and the total area is large in some extensive complexes of late snow vegetation. The soils are again humus-rich muds of varying depth and content of silt and sand.

The Scottish *nodum* can be compared with the *Anthelia-Cesia*-rich *Carex rufina*, *Luzula arcuata* or *Ranunculus glacialis* associations of Nordhagen (1927, pp. 309–314) or with a wide variety of *Anthelia* sociations described by Gjaerevoll (1956) under different associations and alliances.

In high-lying corries where snow lies late there are many minor bryophyte-dominated spring and flush communities which have not been studied, including types transitional between those just described and the moss-heaths of the latest snow-beds. They occur especially along the broken foot of cliffs and in earthy gullies, and some are best regarded as rupestral communities. Their flora includes a number of rare mosses and liverworts which appear to depend on a prolonged snow-cover.

Narthecium-Sphagnum provisional *nodum*
(Table 62)

The last of the oligotrophic flushes so far distinguished is the provisional *Narthecium-Sphagnum nodum. Narthecium ossifragum* is usually dominant and *Sphagnum tenellum* or *S. compactum* may have a high cover. *Lycopodium selago, Nardus stricta* and *Trichophorum caespitosum* also appear in all three lists, which have a total of only 24 species.

The *nodum* is widely distributed but local on highly acidic rocks such as the Cairngorm granite and its occurrences do not follow any particular geographical pattern. It occurs mostly above 2000 ft. (610 m.) in channel-like depressions or small seepage areas, although one of the largest stands encountered lies at only 1100 ft. (336 m.) at the north end of Loch Tanna in the island of Arran. Although they may be numerous, homogeneous patches are usually small and do not cover more than a few square metres each. Irrigation is by slow-moving water charged with peat acids and may be intermittent. The soils are dark brown, shallow mixtures of sand and peat with a firm consistency.

Narthecium-Sphagnum flushes are most commonly associated with shallow peat communities at high levels such as various Nardeta, Trichophoreto-Callunetum, Empetreto-Eriophoretum or Sphagneto-Caricetum alpinum.

Cratoneuron commutatum-Saxifraga aizoides *nodum*
(Table 63)

This *nodum* appears as large patches of the moss *Cratoneuron commutatum*, often forming a mound or bank and carrying a sparse growth of grasses, sedges and other herbs. *Cratoneuron commutatum*, *Festuca rubra* and *Saxifraga aizoides* are the constants and *Philonotis fontana* and *Cardamine pratensis* fall into constancy class IV.

The *nodum* occurs only where the spring water is strongly charged with calcium carbonate (Table 68) and so has its principal stations on the Dalradian limestones and calcareous mica-schists between Breadalbane and Clova with outliers on the Durness dolomite and Moine schist of the north-west. It has a wide altitudinal range from 1000 ft. to 3000 ft. (305–914 m.) but is absent from the highest ground where soils are mostly leached and the drainage water poor in calcium, even when the underlying rock is calcareous. Dominance of *Cratoneuron* seldom extends over an area of more than a few square metres and stands are often fragmentary (less than one square metre). Incipient tufa formation may take place at the base of the moss cushion but the underlying soil is usually a silty mud rich in humus.

The *Cratoneuron* spring may give rise to a sharply defined rill or extend into open Cariceto-Saxifragetum aizoidis flanked by *Carex panicea-Campylium stellatum* mire at low altitudes and Caricetum saxatilis at higher levels (Fig. 8, p. 56). *Cratoneuron* banks sometimes abut markedly oligotrophic communities such as *Calluna* and *Vaccinium* heaths, thereby showing a sharp soil discontinuity.

The Cratoneureto-Saxifragetum aizoidis described by Nordhagen (1943) from Sikilsdalen and by Dahl (1956) from Rondane is similar to our *nodum*. Although agreeing in habitat it tends to be more montane and in Rondane the dominant moss is *Cratoneuron decipiens*, a species which is rare in Scotland and found in calcareous flushes mainly at high altitudes in Breadalbane and Clova. *Cratoneuron* springs occur locally in Southern Scotland, Northern England and Wales, but only in Lakeland and Upper Teesdale do they contain *Saxifraga aizoides*.

Cariceto-Saxifragetum aizoidis
(*Carex-Saxifraga aizoides* flush)
(Table 64)

The flush vegetation associated with these springs forms a separate association, the

Cariceto-Saxifragetum aizoidis. The plant cover among the bare mud and stones may be less than 50 per cent but there are eight constants: *Festuca ovina* agg., *Carex demissa*, *C. panicea*, *Juncus triglumis*, *Pinguicula vulgaris*, *Saxifraga aizoides*, *Thalictrum alpinum* and *Blindia acuta*. *Blindia acuta* and brown mosses such as *Drepanocladus revolvens* are the only species ever to reach dominance.

This is a floristically rich association with 133 species recorded from 18 lists and an average of 30 species per stand. *Equisetum hyemale* and *Acrocladium trifarium* are exclusive to it and *Equisetum variegatum* occurs only in this association and in the *Carex panicea-Campylium stellatum nodum*. There are in addition a number of other characteristic species, mostly montane plants, which find a refuge in these open calcareous habitats. They include the constant *Juncus triglumis* and less frequent species such as *Tofieldia pusilla* and *Juncus alpinus*. Although absent from or poorly represented in our lists the mosses *Amblyodon dealbatus*, *Meesia uliginosa* and *Catoscopium nigritum* belong mainly to this habitat and *Orthothecium rufescens* grows otherwise only in rock face communities.

At high levels the Cariceto-Saxifragetum aizoidis becomes modified as lowland species disappear and montane plants show an increase in cover and abundance. At over 2500 ft. (763 m.) in Breadalbane certain rare and exacting montane species appear and allow us to distinguish a high-level facies of the association (e.g. list 11). *Carex atrofusca*, *C. microglochin*, *Kobresia simpliciuscula*, *Juncus biglumis* and *J. castaneus* grow mainly here or in the closely related Caricetum saxatilis.

A more distinctive low-level facies (Table 64, lists 19–25) shows the replacement of montane species by others such as *Schoenus nigricans*, *Drosera anglica*, *Pinguicula lusitanica*, *Eriophorum latifolium* and *Carex hostiana*. *Scorpidium scorpioides* and *Campylium stellatum* are constant in this type.

Although the *Cratoneuron commutatum* springs seldom occur without the Cariceto-Saxifragetum aizoidis the reverse does not hold and the flush association has a much wider distribution (Map 30). It occurs wherever there are calcareous rocks, with its finest development on the Dalradian tract between Ben Lui and Glen Clova, and in many localities in the Western Highlands on less calcareous rocks of the Moine and Lewisian series. The low-level facies, which is found mainly in the Western Highlands, ranges from near sea level on ground influenced by blown shell sand at Bettyhill, Sutherland, to about 1200 ft. (366 m.); above this level it is replaced by the typical Cariceto-Saxifragetum. The montane facies occurs chiefly in Breadalbane between 2500 ft. (763 m.) and 3000 ft. (914 m.).

Moss cover is evidently related to permanence and rate of flow of the surface water and the humus content of the soil varies accordingly. Vegetation cover and especially that of *Saxifraga aizoides* nevertheless tends to be higher in stands on limestone than in those on less highly calcareous rocks (Plate 26). Some sites have peaty muds while others have little but silt, sand and gravel. All the muds have a high pH (5·6–7·0) and are usually calcareous, sometimes strongly so. The surface of the flush is commonly littered with partially embedded stones and gravel. The open flushes of this type have a water-scoured appearance and often give the impression that they have formed or enlarged by cutting back into more stable soils and vegetation. This impression may be largely illusory but slight marginal erosion does sometimes take place and on Tulach Hill near Killiecrankie, Meall nan Tarmachan and Ben Heasgarnich we have noticed calcareous flush communities developing on the mineral soil of recently formed peat haggs.

The flushes emerge amongst a wide variety of other vegetation, from oligotrophic to eutrophic. In the Central Highlands they are often separated from communities of un-irrigated soils by an intervening zone of mire. The typical association is often bordered here by the *Carex panicea-Campylium stellatum nodum* (Plate 26 and Fig. 24), and the high-level facies by Caricetum saxatilis. It is less usual to find that the low-level facies of the Western Highlands is bordered by *Schoenus nigricans* mire (p. 124). One of the most extensive occurrences of this association yet found is on limestone drift of the lower slopes of Morrone above Braemar. Together with rich grassland and mire communities it occupies clearings within and adjoining the interesting herb-rich birch and juniper wood (Plate 4).

Poore (1955b) has described and illustrated the close juxtaposition between these eutrophic flushes and communities which are decidedly oligotrophic. This is a widespread phenomenon, especially in the Western Highlands where the flushes often appear as sharply defined patches amongst Trichophoreto-Eriophoretum caricetosum, Trichophoreto-Callunetum or other acidic peat vegetation. The mire or bog is then usually separated from the flush by a fairly steep bank marking a sudden change from shallow peat to irrigated mud. The flush quite commonly contains hummocks and mounds with peat-forming vegetation similar to that of the adjoining bog. There is a striking example near Killiecrankie in Perthshire where the two contrasting communities form an extensive network, with

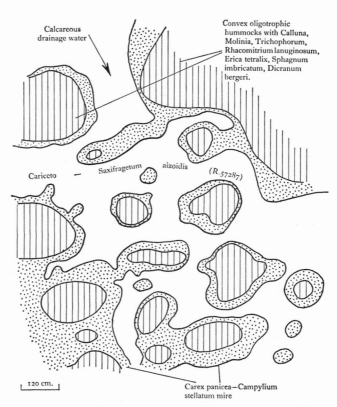

Fig. 24. Complex of calcareous flushes and oligotrophic hummocks. Ardtulichan, Killiecrankie, Perthshire, at 1000 ft.

peat vegetation dissected by a system of calcareous flushes (see Fig. 24 and another example in Plate 26). Some of the hummocks have notable species of undisturbed blanket bog such as *Sphagnum imbricatum* and *Dicranum bergeri*. Both these species are adversely affected by fire and artificial drainage and the *Dicranum* has a markedly relict distribution. Their presence thus indicates that the flush and hummock complex is a well-established one and that the flushes have insulated the hummocks from fires which would otherwise have destroyed these mosses.

The most intriguing feature of such systems is the apparent separation of contrasting soil conditions within so short a lateral and vertical distance. The peat hummocks and confining banks are often fringed at their bases with growths of calcicolous mosses but within a few centimetres there is a change to vegetation composed of presumed calcifuge species. At Killiecrankie, the surface of the drift forming the open flushes is slightly depressed in relation to that beneath the larger oligotrophic mounds, but the bases of the mounds are still strongly affected by the calcareous drainage water. The surface drift and overlying peat of these hummocks have a much higher pH (6·5–7·3) and calcium status than soils of similar bog vegetation elsewhere. Lower hummocks are more obviously influenced by the water of the open flushes, for they have fairly rich soils throughout and their vegetation is referable to *Carex panicea-Campylium stellatum* mire.

A small pool and hummock bog on Tulach Hill, Blair Atholl shows analogous features. The hummocks are composed of oligotrophic bog vegetation referable to Calluneto-Eriophoretum with abundant *Sphagnum papillosum*, *S. nemoreum* and *S. fuscum* while the hollows are occupied by patches of the *Carex rostrata*-brown moss *nodum* or by open water with *Hippuris vulgaris*, *Utricularia vulgaris*, *U. intermedia* and *Chara* spp. Again, the persistence and growth of calcifuge vegetation is feasible once the hummocks have risen above the influence of the calcareous water but it is difficult to explain the origin of the hummocks on a eutrophic site.

Both the *Carex hostiana-C. demissa nodum* and the *Carex demissa-C. panicea nodum* described by Poore (1955b) for Breadalbane could be placed in the present association. The first *nodum* corresponds mainly to the low-level facies and the second contains several lists which clearly belong to the typical association; one of these has been incorporated as list 18 of Table 64. The distinction between Poore's two noda seems too slender to be maintained throughout the Highlands although it may be useful within the district he studied.

Poore compares the two Breadalbane noda with Norwegian vegetation described by Nordhagen. There is some similarity to the *Drepanocladus intermedius-Campylium stellatum*-rich *Carex panicea* and *C. flava* sociations of Sylene and the *C. flava-Campylium stellatum-Drepanocladus intermedius* sociation of Sikilsdalen but these belong to closed mire vegetation and therefore correspond more closely with the Scottish *Carex panicea-Campylium stellatum* and *Carex rostrata*-brown moss *noda*.

In Britain similar flushes have been described by Pigott (1956) for the sugar limestone of Upper Teesdale in the Northern Pennines and they occur locally in Lakeland, North Wales and the Southern Uplands as well, though *Saxifraga aizoides* does not grow in the last two regions.

Chapter 10

CLASSIFICATION

In our comparison of Scottish and Norwegian vegetation types we have found it just as simple to refer our noda to existing alliances and orders as to embark upon an hierarchical classification of our own. It can perhaps be regarded as a vindication of the existing system that this has proved to be so. Moreover such a procedure has brought out many points of interest that are not immediately apparent in making the straightforward comparison of association with association that we have carried out in the descriptive chapters. We have not based any of our comparisons on the lengthy calculation of indices of floristic similarity (Poore, 1955b, Dahl, 1956 p. 64) but simply on the inspection of species and constants present and by noting the habitats normally occupied. The Scottish noda have then been placed in the alliances and orders to which their nearest Continental equivalents have been assigned unless there is some good reason for not doing so. We are prepared for others to disagree with our procedure and its results and hope that this will lead to a further advance in the phytosociological approach to British vegetation.

In view of the intermingling of xeromorphic, hydrophilous, chionophilous, chionophobous, calcicole and calcifuge species that takes place in Scottish vegetation, allied to the fact that much of this vegetation is anthropogenic, we have been surprised at the number of species characteristic of particular associations, and of entire alliances and orders, that we have been able to distinguish (summarised for the higher units of classification in Table 3). This has been achieved partly by separating the facies of one association and assigning them to different positions in the system. On the Continent the equivalents of our species-poor and species-rich facies would generally form separate associations in different alliances or orders, but apart from one or two examples such as the *Rhacomitrium* heaths, we have not followed this procedure.

A tentative classification of the Scottish noda follows.

Vaccinio-Piceetalia (Braun-Blanquet, Sissingh and Vlieger, 1939)

Vaccinio-Piceion

> Pinetum Vaccineto-Callunetum
> Pinetum Hylocomieto-Vaccinetum
> Juniperus-Thelypteris *nodum*
> Betuletum Oxaleto-Vaccinetum
>
> Arctostaphyleto-Callunetum
> Callunetum vulgaris
> Vaccineto-Callunetum hepaticosum

Juniperion nanae

Juniperetum nanae

This order comprises the spruce and pine forests and related vegetation of Europe and Northern Asia.

Dahl (1956) places his juniper scrub equivalent of the *Juniperus-Thelypteris nodum* in the alliance Nardeto-Caricion bigelowii of the order Deschampsieto-Myrtilletalia but the Scottish *nodum* seems best in the sub-alliance Phyllodoco-Vaccinion of Vaccinio-Piceion. The heath Calluneta have been placed in the Vaccinio-Piceion rather than the Oxycocco-Empetrion hermaphroditi because of the absence of bog indicators and the floristic affinities with the forest associations from which they have been derived. This has resulted in a separation of the hepaticosum facies of Vaccineto-Callunetum from the suecicosum which does possess indicators of the Oxycocco-Empetrion, a situation which is repeated again and again in the following pages.

On present evidence it is impossible to decide the systematic position of our remaining woodland noda, the *Betula*-herb *nodum* and the *Fraxinus-Brachypodium nodum*; affinities can be seen with several of Braun-Blanquet's orders such as the Quercetalia roboris and the Fagetalia sylvaticae.

Caricetalia curvulae (Braun-Blanquet, Nordhagen, emend. Krajina, 1933)

Loiseleurieto-Arctostaphylion (Nordhagen) Arctostaphyleto-Cetrarion nivalis (Dahl)

Cladineto-Callunetum
Rhacomitreto-Callunetum
Arctoeto-Callunetum
Rhacomitreto-Empetretum
(Cladineto-Vaccinetum)
Festuceto-Vaccinetum
Juncus trifidus-Festuca ovina *nodum*
Cariceto-Rhacomitretum lanuginosi
(Nardus-Rhacomitrium *nodum*)

Nardetum sub-alpinum
Juncetum squarrosi sub-alpinum
Alchemilleto-Agrosto-Festucetum
(Saxifrageto-Agrosto-Festucetum)
Species-rich Agrosto-Festucetum
Species-poor Agrosto-Festucetum

We have followed Krajina and Dahl in uniting all chionophobous and oligotrophic mountain heaths in the order Caricetalia curvulae, and Dahl in uniting grass and dwarf shrub heaths in the one alliance within this order. The noda within brackets can also be considered under the Deschampsieto-Myrtilletalia as they possess characteristics which cut across the limits of the two orders. The Agrosto-Festuceta are virtually unclassifiable since they are almost entirely anthropogenic and range from oligotrophic to eutrophic. They may belong to the Nardeto-Agrostion tenuis (Nordhagen, 1943) of the Arrhena-theretalia elatioris (Braun-Blanquet).

Deschampsieto-Myrtilletalia (Dahl, 1956)

Phyllodoco-Vaccinion myrtilli (Nordhagen)

    Vaccinetum chionophilum
    Vaccineto-Empetretum
    Nardus-Trichophorum *nodum*
    (Cladineto-Vaccinetum)

Deschampsieto-Anthoxanthion (Du Rietz, Gjaerevoll)

    Deschampsieto-Rhytidiadelphetum typicum
    Deschampsietum caespitosae alpinum
    Nardus-Pleurozium *nodum*
    (Nardus-Rhacomitrium *nodum*)

Nardeto-Caricion bigelowii (Nordhagen)

    Nardetum medio-alpinum
    Polytricheto-Caricetum bigelowii
    Cladineto-Juncetum trifidi
    Dicraneto-Caricetum bigelowii

This order includes all chionophilous or seasonally wet oligotrophic vegetation of soils not liable to solifluction.

The chionophilous *Nardus* noda have been distributed amongst all three alliances of the order Deschampsieto-Myrtilletalia according to the affinities shown by the accompanying species.

Salicetalia herbaceae (Braun-Blanquet, Nordhagen, emend. Dahl)

Communities of late snow-lie on soils liable to solifluction or those with a restricted growing season due to irrigation with melt water.

Cassiopeto-Salicion herbaceae (Nordhagen)   *Herbaceon* (Gjaerevoll)
                                                Polytrichion   ,,

    Polytricheto-Dicranetum starkei
    Rhacomitreto-Dicranetum starkei
    Gymnomitreto-Salicetum herbaceae
    Anthelia-Deschampsia caespitosa *nodum*

Ranunculeto-Oxyrion digynae (Nordhagen, emend. Dahl)

Ranunculo-Anthoxanthion (Gjaerevoll)

    Deschampsieto-Rhytidiadelphetum triquetrosum
    Deschampsietum caespitosae alpinum
    Dwarf Herb *nodum*
    Alchemilla-Sibbaldia *nodum*
    Saxifragetum aizoidis
    Thalictrum-Ctenidium provisional *nodum*
    (Saxifrageto-Agrosto-Festucetum)

Gjaerevoll (1956) distinguishes an alliance Polytrichion norvegici (late snow-bed communities without field layer) from the alliance Herbaceon (corresponding communities with field layer) but for reasons given on page 100 we cannot recognise this distinction. We agree with Dahl (1956) in placing the Dwarf Herb *nodum* (*Sibbaldia nodum* of Poore) in the Ranunculeto-Oxyrion digynae rather than the Potentilleto-Polygonion vivipari of the order Elyno-Seslerietalia (Poore, 1955b, p. 639), but the distinction is a fine one.

Elyno-Seslerietalia

Chionophobous and calcicolous grass and dwarf shrub heaths of mountain regions.

Kobresio-Dryadion

> Dryas octopetala *noda*
> Arctostaphylos grass heath

Potentilleto-Polygonion vivipari

> Polygoneto-Rhacomitretum lanuginosi

The Polygoneto-Rhacomitretum can either be placed here or in Caricetalia curvulae according to the importance placed on the various indicators of acidic and lime-rich soil occurring in it.

Adenostyletalia (Braun-Blanquet)
Aconitetalia (Nordhagen)

This order comprises tall herb and broad leaved grass meadows of the Low-alpine and Sub-alpine zones. Willow and birch scrub with tall herb components and fern meadows are included.

Lactucion alpinae

> Cryptogrammeto-Athyrietum chionophilum
> Tall Herb *nodum*
> Salix lapponum-Luzula sylvatica *nodum*
> (Species-rich Deschampsietum caespitosae alpinum)

The Cryptogrammeto-Athyrietum chionophilum and part at least of the *Salix lapponum-Luzula sylvatica nodum* should be placed in the sub-alliance Dryoptero-Calamagrostidion purpureae of Nordhagen which includes the relatively oligotrophic communities of the alliance. We have followed Dahl (1956) in placing the first of these noda here rather than in the Salicetalia herbaceae as Nordhagen and Gjaerevoll have done, although, as we point out on p. 83, the *Cryptogramma* end of the series has more affinity with the late snow-beds.

Oxycocco-Ledetalia palustris (Nordhagen)

Oxycocco-Empetrion hermaphroditi (Nordhagen)

Mire communities dominated by hummock-building *Sphagna* and ericaceous shrubs. In Scotland all ombrogenous bogs.

Vaccineto-Callunetum suecicosum
Calluneto-Eriophoretum
Empetreto-Eriophoretum
Trichophoreto-Eriophoretum typicum
Trichophoreto-Callunetum

There is clearly scope for the formation of at least one further alliance among these noda.

Scheuchzerietalia palustris

These are oligotrophic mires and all are soligenous in Scotland.

Leuco-Scheuchzerion (Nordhagen)

Sphagneto-Caricetum sub-alpinum
Sphagneto-Caricetum alpinum
Carex aquatilis-rariflora *nodum*
Sphagneto-Juncetum effusi
Narthecium-Sphagnum *nodum*

Caricetalia fuscae (Nordhagen)

Mesotrophic to eutrophic soligenous mires

Caricion canescentis-fuscae (Nordhagen)

Carex rostrata-Sphagnum warnstorfianum *nodum*
Hypno-Caricetum alpinum
Juncus acutiflorus-Acrocladium cuspidatum *nodum*

Caricion bicoloris-atrofuscae (*Caricion atrofuscae-saxatilis*) (Nordhagen)

Caricetum saxatilis
Carex panicea-Campylium stellatum *nodum*
Carex rostrata-brown moss *nodum*
Cariceto-Saxifragetum aizoidis

Schoenion ferruginei

Schoenus nigricans *nodum*
Cariceto-Saxifragetum aizoidis (Low-level facies)

Montio-Cardaminetalia (Braun-Blanquet, Nordhagen)

Vegetation of spring water of more or less even temperature

Mniobryo-Epilobion hornemanni (Nordhagen)

Philonoto-Saxifragetum stellaris
Pohlietum glacialis

Cratoneureto-Saxifragion aizoidis (Nordhagen)

Cratoneuron commutatum-Saxifraga aizoides *nodum*

Noda of Uncertain Position

Molinieto-Callunetum
Molinia-Myrica *nodum*
Luzula sylvatica Grassland *nodum*

A comparison with Scandinavian Vegetation

The closeness of the comparisons that can be drawn between these Scottish noda and their Scandinavian counterparts emphasises that Scottish mountain vegetation is best regarded as an oceanic extension of that of north-west Europe. Floristic comparisons, sometimes in detail, have been made throughout the foregoing chapters but a few general conclusions may be drawn here (for a more detailed account see Poore and McVean, 1957).

There is a fundamental similarity in flora and climate in Scotland and Norway which results in much the same altitudinal zonation and physiognomy of the vegetation in the two countries. Differences can be referred mainly to the following features of the Scottish environment:

1. Greater oceanicity including exposure to Atlantic gales.
2. A higher range of summer and winter temperatures.
3. More intensive land use with grazing by domestic animals throughout the year.

1. Wind shaping of trees and damage to mountain plants by high winds and blizzards are relatively more frequent in Scotland. Altitudinal tree limits thus tend to lie lower in the Highlands, especially in the west, where tree growth is evidently limited by wind rather than by low temperatures. This would explain why, compared with Scandinavia, the upper limits of forest in Scotland are depressed more than those of other life-form zones, thereby increasing the altitudinal range of the dwarf shrub heaths. Only a narrow region of the south-west coast of Norway gives Kotilainen indices of oceanicity (see p. 144) as great as those for the whole of the Scottish Highlands. This is in accord with the fact that we have found it simpler to fit noda with a 'continental' distribution in Scotland (see Chapter 10) into the Scandinavian hierarchy and that even these have their closest analogues in the vegetation of the most western districts of Norway. It is also shown by the importance in vegetation throughout Scotland of species such as *Juncus squarrosus*, *Galium hercynicum*, *Luzula sylvatica*, *Narthecium ossifragum* and *Thelypteris oreopteris*, all of which are confined to the most oceanic parts of Scandinavia. Scottish vegetation types which show least resemblance to anything in Scandinavia, including noda peculiar to Scotland (e.g. Vaccineto-Callunetum hepaticosum), are those with an extreme oceanic distribution. Communities dominated by bryophytes, especially *Rhacomitrium lanuginosum* are a notable feature of Scottish vegetation, but true lichen heath, an equally characteristic Scandinavian type, hardly occurs outside the most continental parts of the Highlands. The intensively studied continental districts of Norway have many vegetation types which are not represented in this country.

The higher rainfall and atmospheric humidity of Scotland have also resulted in a greater prevalence of peaty, leached soils (and therefore of markedly oligotrophic noda) in spite of the fact that the metamorphic rocks of the Highlands belong to the same petrological complex as those of the Norwegian mountains. Blanket-bog is a much more characteristic formation of Scotland and, conversely, there are few eutrophic, topogenous mountain mires, for stagnation of drainage is usually accompanied by oligotrophic peat formation in the Highlands.

2. The effects of the higher temperature range cannot always be separated from the general effects of oceanicity, and climatic warmth may be expressed in various ways, such as in length of growing season, and reliability and duration of snow-cover. These factors together with the edaphic differences mentioned above are responsible for the greater prominence of montane plants in Scandinavian vegetation although it should be emphasised that stands of comparable noda in Scotland and Norway have total floristic lists of much the same length; the Norwegian types are correspondingly poorer in oceanic and southern species. The far richer montane flora of Scandinavia is a reflection of a more optimal climate for this group of plants as a whole, but apart from this direct effect other factors are involved, such as greater extent of suitable refuges during the Post-glacial Period. The unreliability of snow-cover in Scotland particularly affects communities of intermediate depth and length of snow-lie such as the Low-alpine Nardeta and these have been the most troublesome of the chionophilous noda to classify according to the continental system.

3. Despite the paucity of natural forest and scrub remaining in Scotland there is still quite strong similarity between the noda that we have recognised within the remaining fragments and the more extensive Norwegian forest vegetation. On the other hand Scotland has the greater relative area of anthropogenic grassland and dwarf shrub heath, much of which lacks a Scandinavian counterpart.

The strong similarity between Scottish and Norwegian spring and flush communities is due not only to the lack of grazing in such habitats but also to the fact that the main controlling factor, wetness of the ground, is topographically determined and largely independent of climatic differences.

Chapter 11

CLIMATE AND VEGETATION

Temperature and Humidity

THE Climatological Atlas of the British Isles (1952) shows that there are considerable differences in climate on a regional scale within the Highlands. These differences become most apparent when widely separated hills are compared and they are not usually revealed within a single massif, where climatic variations are purely local and related mainly to altitude and aspect.

The geographical distribution of many noda follows these regional differences in climate so closely that it seems justifiable to infer a causal relationship—even though confirmatory evidence on the climatic requirements and tolerances of individual species is seldom available. In Britain as a whole much of the evidence for climatic control of species and vegetation distribution rests on inference of this kind.

Noda which have distributions corresponding to the main regional climatic gradients are listed below, pp. 145–153 (see also Table 74). Their apparent dependence on these climatic trends will be appreciated best if the particular maps of distribution are compared with those of climate (Fig. 25, p. 146, and *Climatological Atlas*, 1952). Brockmann-Jerosch (1913) pointed out that standard meteorological data often show little correlation (or even a misleading correlation) with the distribution of vegetation types and plant species, especially when a single datum such as mean, maximum or minimum temperature is tested as the possible controlling factor. His insistence on the significance of 'climatic character' as a whole rather than of any single readily measurable climatic factor is, however, really an indication of the complexity of the problem, and careful analysis should ultimately lead to the definition of controlling conditions for particular vegetation types and species. For the present we have tried to trace only qualitative correlations between climate and vegetation and have not attempted to define quantitatively the conditions which control the distribution of the noda.

There are several climatic trends within the Highlands and those involving humidity and temperature are most familiar. Gradients of the separate factors are largely parallel and in passing from east to west there is an increase in precipitation (both in amount and uniformity of distribution), atmospheric humidity and wind speeds, and a decrease in insolation, radiation and temperature range. Many ecologists prefer to consider the interaction of these separate factors, as expressed in the concept of 'oceanicity', in tracing broad correlations between climate and vegetation. Various indices of oceanicity are used to unite these factors. Greig-Smith (1950) has applied Amann's formula in calculating values for localities over the whole of the British Isles and Poore and McVean (1957) have used Kotilainen's index in doing the same for the Highlands.

Poore and McVean discuss this subject and show that although Scotland is generally oceanic compared with Norway there are large differences in oceanicity within the Highlands. The Eastern, and especially the East-central, Highlands are relatively continental whereas the Western Highlands are markedly oceanic. The area of maximum oceanicity is probably a fairly narrow strip lying parallel to the western mainland coast but about ten to twenty-five miles inland.

Many noda have a distribution which is either distinctly eastern or western and so within the Highlands we may recognise one group of continental and another of oceanic vegetation types (see Table 74 and the appropriate distribution maps). Some distinctive general trends in vegetation also accompany the trends in oceanicity. One is the greater importance of low-level ombrogenous bog communities in the Western Highlands where, on similar topography, there is a much greater tendency for peat formation than in the Eastern Highlands. Another is the increasing number and extent of bryophyte-dominated communities (excluding those of the latest snow-beds) towards the west (Map 33). The actual composition of the bryophyte flora of a district is also closely related to the degree of oceanicity; many species which need high atmospheric humidity become abundant in the Western Highlands. The corresponding increase in the development of lichen-rich and lichen-dominated vegetation in the opposite direction reflects the change towards continentality (Map 34).

The replacement of the eastern Cladineto-Callunetum by Rhacomitreto-Callunetum in the west (Map 9) is a good example of a particular oceanic trend in vegetation. The abundance of *Rhacomitrium lanuginosum* at all levels is a conspicuous feature of the Western Highlands and, with the exception of Cariceto-Rhacomitretum lanuginosi, all extensive occurrences of noda with a high cover of this moss are in the west. The other markedly oceanic noda are Trichophoreto-Eriophoretum typicum, *Schoenus* mire and the low-level facies of Cariceto-Saxifragetum aizoidis, the *Juncus trifidus-Festuca ovina nodum* and, most of all, Vaccineto-Callunetum hepaticosum. Those with a decidedly continental distribution are Vaccinetum chionophilum, Cladineto-Vaccinetum, Poly-tricheto-Caricetum bigelowii, Dicraneto-Caricetum bigelowii and Arctostaphyleto-Callunetum.

After the extreme groups there are other noda which are mainly, but less exclusively, western (e.g. Molinieto-Callunetum, Pinetum Vaccineto-Callunetum) or eastern (e.g. Callunetum vulgaris, Pinetum Hylocomieto-Vaccinetum). These appear to be less exacting than the others in their climatic requirements. Some noda evidently have an eastern or western bias for reasons other than degree of oceanicity. For instance, in the Northern Highlands most of the high hills are concentrated in the western half so that communities which need high ground are perforce confined to the west. Similarly, Cladineto-Juncetum trifidi and Nardetum medio-alpinum are probably confined to the Cairngorms because the necessary combination of high altitude and certain soil factors occurs nowhere else in the Highlands. It so happens that extensive plateaux occur mainly in the east and sharp peaks mainly in the west and that the highest hills of the Eastern Highlands are mainly granite and have no topographic counterpart in the west. The rather eastern distribution of Empetreto-Eriophoretum, Calluneto-Eriophoretum and Sphagneto-Caricetum alpinum could be principally an expression of this topographic difference.

Although the various factors concerned in the east to west gradient of oceanicity interact and so cannot be considered in complete isolation it would seem necessary to separate their individual effects as far as possible if these crude correlations are to be refined. The evidence suggests, for instance, that rainfall and atmospheric humidity are the primary agents controlling most of the above vegetational trends. The maps of total rainfall, rainfall distribution (number of rain days or wet days) and precipitation/evaporation (N/S) ratio show a much closer correlation with the distribution of most of these vegetation types than do the maps of the other factors. There is, for example, a particularly striking parallelism between the map of number of rain days and the distribution of Trichophoreto-Eriophoretum typicum and, by interpolation, the critical number of

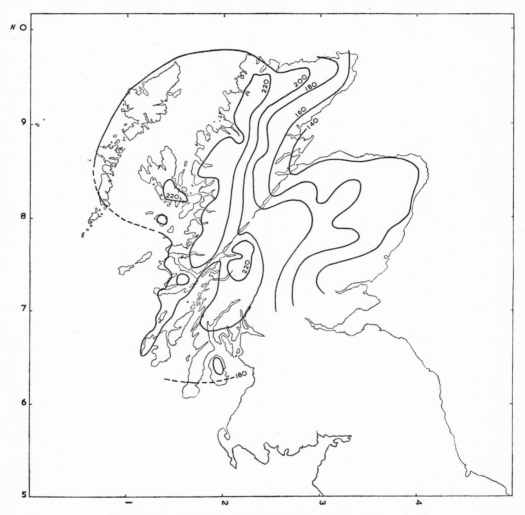

Fig. 25. Mean annual number of wet days (0·04″) 1947–1956

This map has been compiled from data published in *British Rainfall* (1947–1956). A 'wet-day' is defined as a period of 24 hours during which 0·04 in. or more of rain is recorded. Most of the recording stations in the west are at low levels (below 300 ft—91 m.) but a few in the east are at elevations up to 1000 ft. (305 m.). The number of wet-days tends to increase with altitude and proximity to high mountains. The map will thus tend to show minimum values for particular localities and these will be increased on the high ground.

Using this index of humidity there are revealed certain notable climatic features which have vegetational parallels. The wettest part of the Highlands is the belt of high mountains lying parallel to the west coast and stretching from Mull and Ben Cruachan to Foinaven and Ben Hope. A fairly wet climate extends far east in both Caithness and Inverness-shire, giving two pronounced bulges to the isolines. The North-east Region is thus generally wetter than the East-central, but the Grampians around Dalwhinnie and even the Cairngorms have quite a humid climate.

rain days appears to be 235–240 for the development of this association (or alternatively 175–180 wet days).

Ecologists have long experienced difficulty in expressing wetness of climate most suitably for biological phenomena supposed to be controlled by this factor. Tansley (1949) has pointed out that in the British Isles a map of the mean number of rain days shows a closer correspondence with the geographical distribution of blanket bog than a map of total rainfall. This certainly applies to the particular blanket bog cited above. Potential evapotranspiration is perhaps the best way of unifying all the separate influences which determine climatic wetness in relation to vegetation but maps are not available yet. Measurements of potential evapotranspiration are, however, being made at a chain of stations established by the Nature Conservancy on Nature Reserves in various parts of Britain, and a discussion of the available data (Green, 1959) indicates that this technique will be valuable to studies of the relationships between climate and vegetation. For the present we have found that a map of mean annual number of 'wet days' (a day with at least 0·04 in. of rain) gives the best correlation with the distribution of vegetation types which show a pronounced east–west bias (see Fig. 25).

It is perhaps impossible to express temperature in any one way which is meaningful for all ecological phenomena controlled by this factor. Brockmann-Jerosch (1913) has shown that while the limits of tree growth in the northern hemisphere may be said to depend on warmth of climate, there is a far better correlation with annual temperature range than with average annual temperature. In the Highlands, summer maxima, winter minima, annual average, annual range, or accumulated values for certain periods may each give the best index of temperature according to the particular vegetational phenomenon with which a correlation is sought. Species which appear to be particularly sensitive to frost or cold, mainly certain ferns and bryophytes, are mostly restricted to the Western Highlands and especially the extreme coastal areas where equable temperatures prevail. The greater temperature range of the continental east gives winters which are evidently too cold for these plants. Many such thermophilous species are confined to specialised habitats and do not appear in the noda described. The distribution of Cryptogrammeto-Athyrietum chionophilum nevertheless seems to bear out this point. Both dominant ferns are frost sensitive and it is almost certainly for this reason that they occur mainly in late snow-bed communities in the Highlands. The association has a rather western distribution and is confined in the east to those places where snow-cover is sufficiently reliable to give protection from frost every year (see pp. 155–158).

It may well be that other oceanic noda depend on equable temperatures rather than on wetness of climate; the distribution of *Schoenus nigricans* in North-west Europe (Hulten, 1950) suggests that this could be true of Scottish *Schoenus* communities. Many oceanic species, especially those with a southern distribution (see p. 148), evidently need an equable *and* humid climate.

While the main gradient of oceanicity is from east to west, the thermostabilising influence of the sea everywhere produces smaller, local gradients and associated vegetational trends as the coast is approached, even in the east.

There is another important climatic gradient, the decrease in warmth from south to north (*Climatological Atlas*, pp. 34–36), which cuts across the gradient of oceanicity and has to be considered separately. A climatic map based on an index of oceanicity thus gives good correlations with ecological phenomena only when places of similar latitude are compared. The map given by Greig-Smith (1950), for instance, shows that the index of oceanicity for the Isle of Wight is almost the same as that for the east coast of Sutherland and Caithness.

The gradual fall in temperature (measured as daily mean, maximum or range) towards the north of the Highlands is paralleled by the increasing development of communities rich in calcifuge or indifferent montane species and by the disappearance of those distinguished by the presence of thermophilous 'southern' species. The distribution of Arctoeto-Callunetum, Juniperetum nanae and *Rhacomitrium* heath containing *Silene acaulis*, *Cherleria sedoides* and *Armeria maritima* (Map 24) illustrates the first trend while that of the *Juncus acutiflorus* mires (Map 27) exemplifies the second. The first three noda belong to the group that has a distribution centre in the Northern Highlands and the last to the corresponding group which occurs mainly in the south. The increasing importance of montane vegetation northwards in Britain is even more marked if the Welsh mountains are taken as the southern starting point.

Some vegetation types which depend directly or indirectly on low temperatures do not show the same trend. This is especially true of noda which are associated with the longest lasting snow-beds. Their headquarters are in the Central Highlands, particularly the Cairngorms, which in terms of minimum temperatures is the coldest part of the Highlands. During winter the gradient of falling temperature runs mainly from west to east.

Most calcicolous communities have to be disregarded in the present context; their distribution has a southern bias due to the fortuitous concentration of calcareous mountains in the south (Table 74 and Fig. 30, p. 167). Low-level *Dryas* heaths seem to bear out the point, nevertheless. It is possible, too, that while the greater abundance of some montane species such as *Arctous alpina* and *Betula nana* in the Northern Highlands matches the lower temperatures of this region, the responsible factors might be those governing the past migration of these species, rather than any present condition.

The effect of the temperature gradient on vegetation is most noticeable within the oceanic western half of the Highlands. It is shown well by the cryptogamic flora of shady glens and rocks on or close to the west coast (p. 152). A number of species whose world distribution is in warm oceanic and even sub-tropical regions are confined to low levels in the South-west Highlands and most of them are not known north of Mull and Sunart. These include the Macaronesian-Tropical liverworts (Greig-Smith, 1950) *Jubula hutchinsiae*, *Adelanthus decipiens*, *Acrobolbus wilsoni*, *Radula carringtoni*, *Marchesinia mackaii* and *Cololejeunea minutissima*, the filmy ferns *Trichomanes speciosum* and *Hymenophyllum tunbrigense*, *Dryopteris aemula* and the lichen *Sticta damaecornis*.* These species and several other Macaronesian-Tropical bryophytes unknown in Scotland are much more abundant in the extreme south-west of Ireland which has a warmer climate than any part of the Highlands.

Conversely, although the notable liverworts of the Vaccineto-Callunetum hepaticosum occur plentifully in the South-west Highlands they reach their greatest abundance north of Moidart and, except as fragments, the association itself has not been found south of Strathcarron in West Ross (Map 7). These liverworts are all somewhat montane species both in Scotland and elsewhere, and are evidently adapted to a cool oceanic climate. Accordingly, although some occur in the west of Ireland, the Western Highlands are evidently their headquarters in the British Isles.

Since oceanicity indices suggest uniformity of climate within the humid coastal belt

* This information on distribution is mostly drawn from published records.

where these differences in the cryptogamic element of the vegetation occur, there is justification for regarding the north-south temperature gradient separately. Temperature clearly exerts a direct effect on vegetation, apart from its influence on humidity. This is even more apparent in a comparison of the North-west Highlands with South-west Ireland, which shows still larger differences in the vegetation of comparable habitats although indices of oceanicity in the two regions are similar, i.e. the climatic difference is in temperature much more than in humidity.

Some south to north vegetational trends are also apparent in an east to west direction and the resultant is thus orientated towards the North-west Highlands. These are best

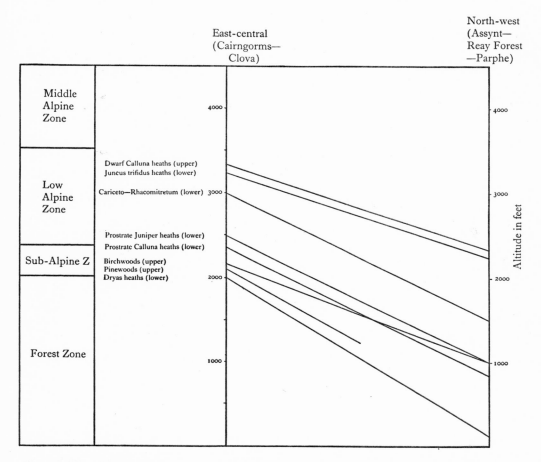

Fig. 26. The altitudinal descent of vegetation types towards the north-west of the Highlands. Upper or lower limits are indicated in brackets

Pronounced regional changes in the altitudinal limits of noda are mentioned under the particular types, and some indication is also given in the regional vegetation charts (Figs. 31–36). Even on the same hill the altitudinal limits of any vegetation type may vary greatly according to differences in exposure, so that only general trends can be indicated. Again, the sudden increase in exposure as the actual coast is reached gives a further sharp descent in altitudinal limits compared with hills only a few miles inland, so that the characteristic zonation on the hills of the area representing the North-west Highlands does not indicate the minimum limits which are attained in the region.

Only a few noda which show their natural upper and/or lower limits can be considered in tracing the altitudinal descent of vegetation. Cariceto-Rhacomitretum gives quite a good datum in all parts of the Highlands, although *Rhacomitrium lanuginosum* itself shows a great altitudinal expansion in the north-west and communities dominated by this moss occur almost at sea-level. On the whole, life-form zones or broad vegetation classes such as dwarf *Calluna* heath illustrate this trend better than individual noda. The levels shown in the diagram are intended to be only approximate and are based merely on general observations and impressions.

regarded as the results of the combined influence of the gradients of falling temperatures and increasing oceanicity. The above-mentioned distribution of Vaccineto-Callunetum hepaticosum and the cushion-herb facies of Cariceto-Rhacomitretum illustrate this point, and the altitudinal descent of certain noda and species in a north-westerly direction is another good example. Before discussing this last trend it is necessary to consider the altitudinal zonation of vegetation in Scotland, a topic which Poore and McVean have dealt with in detail.

The generalised altitudinal zonation of vegetation for the Highlands may be summarised as follows in the direction of increasing altitude:

trees→tall shrubs→dwarf shrubs→grasses and cryptogams.

This vegetational sequence reflects a gradient of increasing severity of climate which occurs on any mountain and involves decreasing temperature and increasing cloud cover, humidity and wind exposure. The altitudinal gradient is similar to the general climatic change from the south-east towards the north-west of the Highlands although there is less correspondence in the trends of minimum temperature, precipitation and snow-cover, as has been indicated above. With increasing distance north-west, climate becomes progressively more severe at equivalent altitudes or, alternatively, a given set of climatic conditions occurs at increasingly low levels. This phenomenon is matched by a downward shift in the altitudinal limits of the various vegetation zones, including those of agricultural land.

Such effects are shown clearly by several noda which have well-defined and climatically determined upper and/or lower limits such as the dwarf *Calluna* and *Rhacomitrium* heaths (Fig. 26 and Plate 11). Woodland seldom shows its natural upper limit but the same trend is evident. Spence (1960) has traced the gradual fall in the upper limits of Sub-alpine scrub in passing from the Central Highlands to the Outer Hebrides and Shetland, where this life-form is the nearest approach to woodland under present conditions. On the most exposed coasts of the North-west Mainland, the Outer Isles,

Table C. Montane vascular plants showing descent of lower limits in a north-westerly direction

Agropyron donianum (2000–250)
Arctous alpina (2000–500)
Betula nana (1500–400)
Carex bigelowii (1500–500)
C. capillaris (800–S.L.)
C. rupestris (1500–S.L.)
C. edmonstonii (1800–S.L.)*
Draba rupestris (3000–1700)
Dryas octopetala (1500–S.L.)
Empetrum hermaphroditum (1000–S.L.)
Epilobium anagallidifolium (1250–500)
Juniperus nana (1500–S.L.)
Juncus triglumis (1000–200)
J. trifidus (2000–1000)
Loiseleuria procumbens (2000–1000)

Luzula spicata (2000–1000)
L. arcuata (3000–2500)
Oxyria digyna (1000–S.L.)
Polystichum lonchitis (1300–200)
Salix herbacea (1500–300)
S. myrsinites (1000–200)
Saussurea alpina (1400–S.L.)
Saxifraga oppositifolia (800–S.L.)
S. nivalis (2000–1100)
S. rivularis (3000–2500)
Sedum rosea (1000–S.L.)
Silene acaulis (1200–S.L.)
Thalictrum alpinum (950–S.L.)
Tofieldia pusilla (1000–150)

* Some botanists believe that the plant at sea level on Unst, Shetland, is taxonomically distinct from the usual form of the mainland.

The figures represent the lowest altitudes (in feet) at which there occurs at least one good colony of each species. The first figure is for the East-central Highlands (from Ben Lawers to the Cairngorms and Lochnagar) and the second for the North-west Highlands, particularly the coastal areas. These levels, which are only intended to be approximate, have been based on our own field experience supplemented by the extensive series of records given by Wilson (1955). Only species with a widespread distribution can be used to illustrate the trend and while many more probably show the same tendency, we have omitted those for which there is insufficient information at present.

Orkney and Shetland the forest and tall shrub zone vanishes altogether and the climax vegetation virtually at sea level is dwarf shrub heath (Fig. 27). The altitudinal descent of montane plants towards the north-west is well-known and although not all species reach sea level most of them occur at lower levels than in the south and east of their Highland range (Table C).

The *Juncus trifidus-Festuca ovina nodum* has a markedly north-western distribution and even within this region the erosion surfaces carrying this type of vegetation occur at increasingly low levels towards the far north-west. The high wind-speeds which are part of the oceanic climate alone account satisfactorily for these trends, but in nearly all other cases it is difficult to isolate the particular factors which control the altitudinal descent of vegetation types and individual species. Severity of exposure to wind and lack of summer warmth are probably the main factors limiting growth and reproduction of trees and shrubs at high levels in the Highlands and thus determine the limits of the main vegetation zones. Similarly the replacement of oak and pine forest by birchwood in Sutherland is an expression of increasing exposure as much as falling temperatures. Spence (1960) has correlated the fall in upper limits of Sub-alpine scrub towards the north and north-west with decrease in duration of growing season at a given altitude, on the assumption that a mean temperature of 50° F (10° C) for at least one month is a minimum requirement for tree growth. Using this index, Spence showed that the

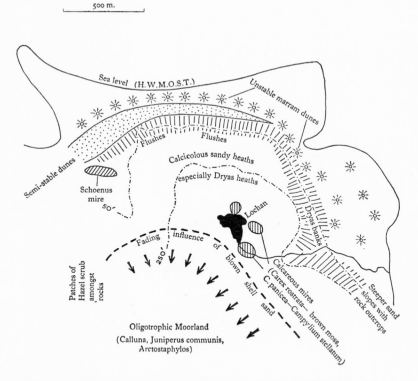

Fig. 27. Dwarf shrub heaths almost at sea level, Bettyhill Links, Sutherland. With increasing altitude and distance from the sea, enrichment by blown shell-sand gradually disappears, and the eutrophic dwarf shrub heaths (*Dryas, Arctostaphylos, Empetrum hermaphroditum* and *Salix repens*) give way to *Calluna*-juniper communities

theoretical upper limits for tall shrub vegetation agree well with the observed upper limits in the Central Highlands, but that with increase in oceanicity northwards and westwards allowance has to be made for the extra inhibition which increasing wind exposure places upon tree growth.

Brockmann-Jerosch (1913) showed that tree growth takes place at much lower mean temperatures in a continental than in an oceanic climate, indicating that lack of summer warmth is a far more important limiting factor than winter cold. This author pointed out that the polar tree limit is displaced northwards by at least 12 degrees of latitude in continental Arctic regions (or alternatively that the continental climate displaces the tree limit from an average annual temperature of about $+6°$ C to one of $-11°$ C) and that in passing from the oceanic margins to the continental centre of the Alps the altitudinal tree limit is raised by about 800 m.

For some warmth-demanding species, the extremes of winter cold may well be a critical factor in both geographical and altitudinal distribution. This could be true of the group of oceanic bryophytes and ferns which have their headquarters in South-west Ireland (see p. 148). Though most of these ascend to moderate elevations in that district, their upper limits descend with distance north and in their northernmost British stations, in Argyll and West Inverness-shire, they are confined both to coastal districts and to levels close to that of the sea. This geographical distribution is paralleled by the January and February mean minimum temperature isotherm of $35°$ F ($1·7°$ C) as far as eastern limits are concerned. It agrees less well with the northern limits, suggesting that some other aspect of winter temperature, such as accumulated values below a certain level, may be the determining condition.

The geographical and altitudinal distribution of many montane plants suggests that their lower limits result from intolerance to a warm climate. Dahl (1951) has shown that in Fennoscandia the lower distribution limits of many Arctic-alpines are closely correlated with the isotherms of maximum summer temperature (see also p. 176). Maximum summer temperatures in the Highlands fall towards the north-west and with proximity to the sea and this trend would account more satisfactorily than any other for the gradual drop in the lower limits of montane plants in the same directions. Dahl calculated that the critical temperature varied from $22°$ C to $29°$ C for different species in Fennoscandia but was reluctant to claim more than a correlation, pointing out that maximum summer temperature itself might not be directly responsible as a controlling factor. Accumulated temperatures above a certain level might be a limiting factor for some species, and for both montane and southern species growth-period curves may be more significant than extremes of temperature.

It is also evident that many montane plants are absent from the low ground not because of temperature intolerance but because they cannot withstand the intensity of competition from tall shrubs and trees. When the limits of these more robust life forms are depressed by severity of wind exposure the montane species are enabled to descend to lower levels accordingly. The occurrence of *Dryas* heath nearly at sea level in Sutherland is due not only to favourable temperatures but also to the lack of tree cover.

The conditions given by increasing oceanicity would thus alone be sufficient to account for altitudinal descent of vegetation, but when the latitudinal fall in temperature is superimposed the effect becomes more marked.

Another tendency which becomes increasingly pronounced towards the north-west is the apparent change in soil requirements of some species which instead of being calcicole become indifferent to soil calcium status. Perhaps the best examples are the cushion-herbs of *Rhacomitrium* heath. In its southernmost British localities in North Wales and Lakeland *Silene acaulis* is a strict calcicole but from the Cairngorms towards the North-west Highlands it becomes increasingly abundant on the poorest rocks and soils of high summits. Similarly, *Armeria maritima* (the montane form) and *Cherleria sedoides* appear to be somewhat calcicole in the southern part of their range but in the North-west Highlands they occur with *Silene acaulis* in the greatest profusion on mountain tops composed of poor rocks including quartzite. *Rhacomitrium* heath with these cushion-herbs is most extensive in the North-west Highlands and the closely related Polygoneto-Rhacomitretum also has its headquarters in this region. Polygoneto-Rhacomitretum and the Dwarf Herb *nodum* both appear to need less calcium towards the north-west; they are confined to calcareous mica-schists at their southern limits but occur on rather poorer rocks of the Moine series in the north-west.

Some fen and mire plants of the low ground show a similar tendency. In the Western and especially the North-west Highlands *Schoenus nigricans, Cladium mariscus, Utricularia vulgaris, Campylium stellatum* and *Scorpidium scorpioides* may be found in habitats where calcium status is evidently much lower than in the calcareous fens, mires and flushes which they usually inhabit in the south and east. Cariceto-Saxifragetum aizoidis is likewise less strictly associated with strongly calcareous substrata than in the southern part of its range.

These changes in soil requirements have not been studied and beyond the general correlation already made there can be no more than a presumption that the climatic changes produce physiological adjustments in some species, or that genotypic variation has produced locally adapted races. It may be, however, that these climatic changes work indirectly, through their influence on soils. Pearsall (1956) has shown that bog waters in the extreme North-west Highlands have a much higher ion content than those from comparable types of vegetation in the north of England. His data are consistent with the idea of greater influence of wind-driven salt spray in the stormy north-west corner of Scotland, itself largely a measure of increasing oceanicity. While these chemical differences seem to have little effect on most plants, it may be that they allow some normally calcicolous species to grow in calcium deficient soils.

By contrast some plants such as *Dryas octopetala* and *Saxifraga oppositifolia* appear to remain strongly calcicole throughout their entire Scottish range.

Local Climatic Variations

Local differences in climate are superimposed on the main regional trends. Altitude has already been discussed and accounts for most of the climatic variation within a single massif. Rainfall does not show a simple relationship to altitude although it tends to increase with height on any one mountain slope. The area of high precipitation usually extends some distance to the leeward of the highest ground to affect low ground as well and may be followed by a rain shadow. The rainfall gradient is sometimes sufficiently steep to produce differences in humidity between the west and east sides of a single large massif.

Aspect affects insolation and wind exposure directly and evaporation and transpiration rates indirectly. North to east slopes thus tend to be wetter in both atmosphere and soil than those facing south to west and the differences are often illustrated strikingly by the vegetation. Communities of steep north and east slopes tend to contain a greater abundance of bryophytes and shade or moisture-loving vascular plants than do those of other aspects. Vaccineto-Callunetum hepaticosum appears to be confined to such situations and especially where they lie within sheltered corries. By contrast, a few species, such as the moss *Rhytidium rugosum*, have a decided restriction to dry, sun-exposed situations.

Wind exposure also depends on topography on both a large and small scale. Steep slopes, especially those to leeward, are usually less windswept than plateaux and flat-

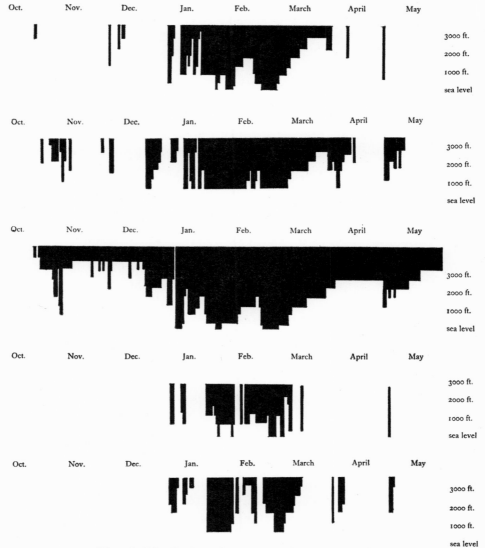

Fig. 28. Distribution of snow-cover in relation to altitude

Snow-cover is estimated from meteorological stations in the low country adjoining each massif. At station level a day with snow lying is defined as a day on which more than half the ground representative of the station is covered with snow at the morning observation hour. Extent of snow-influenced vegetation: Top. Cuillins: not examined but probably less extensive than in 2, due to unsuitable topography. 2. Glen Lyon: moderately chionophilous types well represented, but little of latest snow-bed types. 3. Ben Nevis: extensive with many types, including those of latest snow-beds, 4. Paps of Jura: none. 5. Snowdonia: none.
Adapted from Fig. 2, Snow survey of Great Britain 1953-54, Met. Mag. Lond., 83.

topped spurs at the same altitude. Sometimes it appears that a high summit may give shelter to a lower one in its lee and this may be the reason for the occurrence of *Rhaco-mitrium* heath at nearly 4000 ft. (1220 m.) on Aonach Mor mentioned on p. 91. Shelter effects may be discerned wherever the ground is irregular, as on a terraced slope or, on the micro-climatic scale, wherever rocks project a few inches above the ground surface on exposed tops. All these variations are reflected to some extent in the vegetation and they have been dealt with adequately in local studies such as those made by the Cambridge botanists on the Cairngorms.

Topography and altitude also have a profound influence on local snow-cover.

Snow-cover

The importance of unequal snow-cover in determining the vegetation pattern of mountain areas has been emphasised by Scandinavian and Central European writers from Vestergren (1902) to Dahl (1956). In Britain this has been a neglected aspect of plant ecology and the only comparative studies involving direct measurement of depth and duration of snow-lie on different vegetation types are those of Poore and McVean (1957) and McVean (1958a).

Snow-lie acts upon vegetation in several different ways: redistribution of precipitation; shortening of the growing season both by prolonged snow-cover and by spring irrigation with melt water; protection from frost; and the deposition of wind-blown mineral and plant debris accumulated on snow-beds. While the general vegetation pattern is determined by the 'normal' snow regime, deviations from the mean may leave their mark either in the form of frost damage to particular species or their death through unusually prolonged snow-cover (see p. 99).

Prolonged snow-cover results in the formation and persistence of open communities in which certain plants intolerant of competition from more vigorous species can find a niche. But extreme exposure, often attended by solifluction movements in the soil, also produces these effects so that the same plant species, such as *Salix herbacea, Gnaphalium supinum, Luzula arcuata* and *Solorina crocea*, take advantage of both situations. With a few exceptions, such as *Cerastium cerastoides* and *Saxifraga rivularis*, individual species of vascular plants cannot therefore be regarded as good indicators of winter snow accumulation in the Highlands, although whole communities are a more reliable guide. Certain bryophytes are, nevertheless, quite faithful indicators, seldom if ever being found outside late snow-beds, e.g. *Polytrichum norvegicum, Andreaea nivalis, Dicranum glaciale, Moerckia blyttii, Pleuroclada albescens* and *Gymnomitrium varians*. Others such as *Dicranum starkei, D. falcatum, Rhacomitrium heterostichum* and *R. aquaticum* grow on soil, as distinct from rock, only when snow-cover is prolonged.

When the whole of upland Britain is considered, the effect of the south to north gradient of falling temperatures on vegetation is well illustrated by chionophilous types. Although Snowdon reaches 3560 ft. (1086 m.) snow-cover on the mountains of North Wales is too ephemeral or unreliable to have any effect on vegetation. Snow-cover is distinctly longer on the Lakeland fells and even more so on the Northern Pennines, but here again its effects are indistinguishable from those of impeded drainage, and there are no definite snow-bed communities. In the Southern Uplands of Scotland the 2700 ft. (824 m.) hills around Moffat and Tweedsmuir have a still longer snow-cover and show small areas of Vaccinetum chionophilum and the *Nardus-Pleurozium nodum*. Reference to the *Climatological Atlas* shows that this corresponds to an average of

Table D. Noda associated with prolonged snow-cover

INCREASING LENGTH OF SNOW-LIE

Dwarf Herb nodum	Deschampsietum caespitosae alpinum	Anthelia-Deschampsia nodum	Pohlietum glacialis
Caricetum saxatilis	Nardus-Trichophorum nodum	Nardetum medio-alpinum	Cryptogrammeto-Athyrietum
Vaccineto-Empetretum	Nardus-Pleurozium nodum	Polytricheto-Caricetum bigelowii	Gymnomitreto-Salicetum herbaceae
Vaccinetum chionophilum	Vaccinium-Nardus provisional nodum	Dicraneto-Caricetum bigelowii	Rhacomitreto-Dicranetum starkei
Cladineto-Vaccinetum	Alchemilla-Sibbaldia nodum	Deschampsieto-Rhytidiadelphetum	Polytricheto-Dicranetum starkei
Nardus-Rhacomitrium nodum	Cladineto-Juncetum trifidi		

As snow-cover regimes for most of these noda are still imperfectly known they can at present only be arranged in groups in general order of increasing snow-lie. The Dwarf Herb *nodum* and Caricetum saxatilis are included, although it is uncertain whether they are truly chionophilous types of vegetation. Although placed in the same group, Vaccineto-Empetretum usually has a shorter snow-cover than Vaccinetum chionophilum. No one massif contains examples of all these noda.

somewhere between 50 and 100 mornings with snow lying. Within the Highlands, snow-influenced vegetation is still rather poorly represented in the extreme south, but soon increases to the north, and though reaching a maximum development on the 3500–4000 ft. (1068–1220 m.) peaks of the Central Highlands, is well represented on all but the most oceanic of the high hills from Breadalbane northwards. Fig. 28 shows the general regime of snow-lie for one year in a number of districts with and without chionophilous vegetation.

A list of chionophilous noda is given in Table D and some indication of the snow regime of each will be found in the appropriate parts of the text.

In an attempt to express earlier observational data numerically monthly readings of the depth of winter snow were taken on a series of wooden posts on Ben Lawers in 1954–1955. In the following year activities were transferred to the Cairngorm Nature Reserve where two wardens were already taking part in the Snow Survey of Great Britain. The Cairngorm observations have continued inter-mittently ever since.

Fig. 29 presents one typical record for each of the associations studied so far. The records as a whole emphasise the unreliability of snow-cover in any winter and from year to year. Readings for the months of November, December and May are particularly variable and weekly readings at those times would give a truer picture. This variability means, amongst other things, that the boundaries of stands of chionophilous vegetation are less sharply defined and the vegetation itself contains fewer frost-sensitive species than in conti-nental regions. The redistribution of precipitation brought about by snow drifting is not affected by alternating accumulation and ablation throughout the winter, so that vegetational features attributable to this are common to oceanic as well as continental snow-beds, and continual wetness is especially characteristic of most Scottish chiono-philous vegetation.

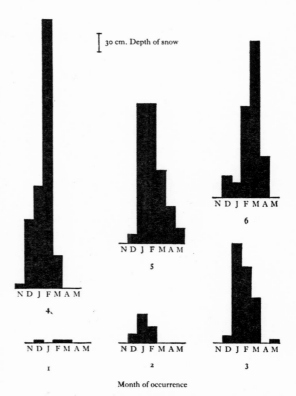

Fig. 29. Snow-cover in relation to selected types of vegetation. 1. Cariceto-Rhacomitretum. 2. Cladineto-Callunetum. 3. *Nardus-Trichophorum nodum*. 4. Crypto Grammeto-Athyrietum. 5. Gymnomitreto-Salicetum Herbaceae. 6. Caricetum Saxatilis

Only the longest lasting snow-fields of high levels give a really reliable snow-cover throughout the Scottish winter. Wherever the snow-beds lie they owe their existence not only to the altitude but also to the area of the gathering ground above them from which the snow can drift. Thus, other things being equal, a narrow 4000 ft. (1220 m.) ridge with holding ground for the snow 1000 ft. (305 m.) below will produce less late snow vegetation than a 3500 ft. (1068 m.) plateau with shallow corries at 3000 ft. (914 m.) (Plate 21). A north to east aspect also favours the retention of late snow by reducing the rate of melting. Partly because of their suitable topography and partly because they lie in that part of Scotland which is coldest in winter, the Cairngorms have the most extensive area of really late snow-bed vegetation in the Highlands.

In the oceanic winter climate of the Scottish mountains, with high precipitation and gale force winds, snow is packed into the corries to a considerable depth and wind-blown debris accumulates along with it. The abrasive action of ice crystals and sand grains is a factor of importance to the vegetation of the exposed ground above 2000 ft. (610 m.) and must be held partly responsible for the low plant cover of the *Juncus trifidus-Festuca ovina nodum* and its Central Highland equivalents. The rapidity with which paint, and the surface of the wood itself, abrades from observation poles in the Cairngorms is some indication of the purely mechanical effect of the blizzards.

The Cryptogrammeto-Athyrietum chionophilum is the best example in this country of a plant community completely dependent on the protection that snow gives against winter frost. In most years slight frost outside the period of snow protection in late spring or early autumn changes the bright green of the fern beds to shades of brown and bronze overnight. *Calluna vulgaris* is a species intolerant of prolonged snow-cover and while Callunetum vulgaris is often covered for short periods it is rare to find more than a thin coating of snow on Cladineto-Callunetum. Since it is also sensitive to severe winter frost, in cold climates *Calluna* must obviously exist somewhere between the two extremes of shelter and exposure and oceanic conditions provide its best chance of attaining dominance in the vegetation.

Vaccinetum chionophilum and Vaccineto-Empetretum owe their existence not to the shelter afforded by snow-cover from frost but simply to the fact that their dominant species tolerate a long snow-cover better than *Calluna*. Records are available for fragmentary stands of the Vaccineto-Empetretum only, but numerous observations confirm that the two associations take their place as shown in the accompanying sequence of increasing snow-cover (Table D).

Nardus stricta takes over when the growing season becomes too short for *Vaccinium myrtillus* and also where periodic inundation by melt water takes place. Some chionophilous noda, such as the three *Nardus*-dominated types and Deschampsietum caespitosae, usually occupy sites where topography causes both impeded drainage and prolonged snow-cover. Snow-cover may therefore be important to these vegetation types chiefly through its effect on soil moisture, tending to enhance irrigation and drainage impedance. Dependence on moisture rather than on other effects of late snow-lie would explain the predominantly western distribution of the *Nardus-Trichophorum* and *Nardus-Rhacomitrium noda* and Deschampsietum caespitosae. It is interesting that the separation of vegetation into oceanic and continental types mentioned earlier in the chapter can be extended to some noda of moderate snow-cover, notably Vaccinetum chionophilum and Deschampsieto-Rhytidiadelphetum, while those of really late snow-lie cannot be differentiated in this way.

The snow-cover regime of other chionophilous noda such as Nardetum medio-alpinum and Cladineto-Juncetum trifidi must remain conjectural until a sufficient number of records can be accumulated. In trying to identify controlling conditions for other montane noda such as the Dwarf Herb *nodum* and Caricetum saxatilis, it is difficult to separate the influence of prolonged snow-cover *per se* from other effects of high altitude.

Solifluction

Solifluction is the slow downhill movement of soil and fine rock debris that takes place in areas with arctic or montane climates. It appears to be associated with the alternate freezing and thawing of soil water and may be manifest in a number of different ways.

Soil instability resulting from active solifluction has an important effect on vegetation both mechanically and chemically. Many plants are unable to grow where the root systems are constantly subjected to the stresses of soil movement while others benefit from the stirring up of the soil which tends to counteract the removal of plant nutrients by leaching.

Although solifluction phenomena in the Scottish mountains have received less attention than they deserve they are not of the same importance to vegetation as in lands farther north. In general, an increase in the amount of active solifluction in the Highlands can be made out towards the north and west, while the signs of former activity (fossil solifluction) are widespread. Both active and fossil features affect vegetation through microclimatic differences in moisture, snow-lie and exposure.

Scandinavian authors (see Dahl, 1956) have recognised two main types of solifluction, 'amorphous' and 'structured'.

Amorphous solifluction takes place in localities with deep and prolonged snow-cover and is not associated with any pronounced separation of the soil constituents although lobing of the surface may be common. Movement seems to take place mainly in the spring when melt water from snow saturates the surface soil and causes it to flow over the deeper, still frozen, horizons. These localities may be recognised by the presence of buried humus layers or by an absence of profile development and on the surface by the presence of a puckered and broken crust of small, foliose hepatics with few or no vascular plants. This is a local type in Scotland and is found principally in association with the largest snow-fields of the Cairngorms such as that on the east side of Ben MacDhui. The effects are frequently obscured by the erosion and deposition caused by abundant rain and melt water.

Structured solifluction phenomena are found on exposed ground which is unprotected from winter frost and the extent to which they are developed may depend on the number of times per annum that soil temperature crosses freezing point. Soil polygons, stone nets, stone stripes, hillside terraces and soil hummocks and ridges can all be considered as belonging to this category, and are widespread in the Highlands, especially at over 2500 ft. (763 m.). While most of those with large dimensions owe their formation to a former more arctic climate in Scotland, many with a smaller pattern-size are still partially active and have some influence on vegetation.

Spots of active solifluction (ostioles) can be seen as low as 1000 ft. (305 m.) in the heather moors of the Cairngorms area. These result from the removal of vegetation and thin surface peat by moor burning which allows winter frost to act upon the mineral soil. The flesh colour of the 'erupting' B horizon renders these spots conspicuous. Both ostioles and small terraces occur on clayey soils of the *Dryas* heaths at Knockan at a similar altitude.

Hillside terraces are probably the most widespread of the structured phenomena in the Scottish Highlands (Plates 15 and 16) and particularly good examples of a medium size can be seen on Ben Rinnes in Banffshire, Am Faochagach and the Fannichs in Ross-shire, Ben More Assynt and Ben Clibreck in Sutherland and on Toll Creagach north of Glen Affric. The bank of many of these terraces is still actively curling over to envelop the surface humus and vegetation especially where soils have a high content of clay (cf. Warren Wilson, 1952). Terraces on the dolomitic mudstone outcrops at 3000 ft. (914 m.) on Beinn Eighe have at times become so charged with water when thaw and heavy rain coincided that they burst and formed mud flows which swept into the corrie below carrying boulders along and ripping up the turf. The terrace flats often bear small-scale stone nets and stripes. The large-scale irregular boulder terraces described by Watt and Jones (1948) from the Cairngorms appear to be related to the more regular and active large terraces of periglacial conditions in Arctic regions.

Stone nets may be completely inactive and covered with *Rhacomitrium* heath or they may still possess active centres with an hepatic crust or patch of the *Juncus trifidus-Festuca ovina nodum*. Upended slabs of rock ('gravestones') are often abundant on these active areas, as on Carn nan Gobhar north of Glen Affric. Soil hummocks may still be in process of formation on damp sites where they are occupied by the Polytricheto-Caricetum bigelowii (p. 73) but they are perhaps purely relict structures where covered with *Rhacomitrium* or hypnaceous moss heath. These features belong to high plateaux, ridges and spurs with fairly level ground and a continuous vegetation cover. Where the ground begins to slope the hummocks first elongate and then become confluent to form parallel ridges running down the incline. Both hummocks and ridges are sometimes well developed on deep, sandy soils which have been built up by the wind to the leeward of high-lying erosion surfaces. The differences in conditions between the crests of the hummocks or ridges and the intervening hollows have given rise to some elegant vegetation patterns. Soil hummocks and ridges occur in all the main regions of the Highlands and particularly good examples may be seen on the hills surrounding the Pass of Drumochter and on Ben Wyvis (Plate 20).

Exposed stands of Gymnomitreto-Salicetum herbaceae (hepatic crust) are found only on the less porous (clay-rich) mountain soils, matching the occurrence of structured solifluction on these soils rather than on porous granitic soils, such as those of the Cairngorm plateau. On the mica-schist summit of Aonach Beag, east of Ben Nevis, solifluction soils with hepatic crust are abundant but the neighbouring granite ridge of Aonach Mor is covered with stable soil bearing *Rhacomitrium* heath at the same level.

Chapter 12

SOILS

In purely phytosociological works the soils of the various units of classification may be completely ignored while in detailed ecological studies the influence of soil structure and chemical composition upon the vegetation may form the crux of the entire investigation. In this study, with its accent upon vegetation description, we can give only an outline account of the associated soils but have provided some data for certain edaphic factors which seem to be of paramount importance to vegetation in the Highlands.

Methods of sampling have been described briefly in Chapter 1, while the account of each nodum gives some idea of the range of soil type and often, too, the range of pH and parent rock. Sometimes typical profiles have been described, but as this does not profess to be a detailed pedological survey, profile descriptions are omitted from the soil analytical data (Tables 65–67) and only soil types are mentioned.

Pedogenic Tendencies and Soil Types

In an area such as the Highlands with a wide diversity of pedogenic factors a considerable range of soil types is only to be expected, but certain tendencies in soil development are predominant. Over the whole of the Highlands there is a preponderance of acidic rocks such as granite, quartzite, sandstone and the non-calcareous schists and gneisses. These give rise to soils with a low content of available plant nutrients and soils with fertility of agricultural standards are extremely localised. Base-saturated soils are associated chiefly with limestones and dolomites, calcareous mica schists of the Dalradian and Moine series, calcareous basalt and serpentine. Even rocks which are mainly non-calcareous, such as the Torridon and Old Red Sandstones, contain calcareous bands which give richer soils locally. Hard, siliceous rocks such as granite and quartzite tend to give shallow, coarse-textured and porous soils whereas the impermeable soils of high clay content are especially associated with soft, argillaceous and calcareous rocks.

Under the cool, wet climate of the Highlands podsolisation is one of the foremost pedogenic tendencies and, in combination with the extensive occurrence of acidic rocks, is responsible for the prevalence of base-poor soils. The associated tendency for raw humus development is therefore widespread but becomes increasingly apparent towards the west coast along the gradient of increasing climatic wetness (see Fig. 20, p. 107). There are also variations in surface humus development within a single mountain group according to aspect and to sharp changes in annual rainfall, e.g. from 50–100 in. or more.

Intensity of leaching would also be expected to follow regional variations in climatic wetness within the Highlands, thereby accompanying the trends of increasing peat development, but we have found no clear evidence to support this idea. Our limited analytical studies have not shown that, other things being equal, there is a greater extent of base-impoverished soils or a lower base-status of soils in comparable situations, in the west than in the east. Impressions gained from field observation suggest that this may well be true when the driest eastern hills are compared with the wettest western ones. Such an effect would be expected to appear in soils which in the east have a base-status just above or below the threshold for podsolisation. The eastern distribution of Arcto-staphyleto-Callunetum might be due to the fact that the slightly podsolised brown soils of its particular situation are too strongly leached (as well as more peaty) in the west. A great difficulty in this problem is that 'other things', notably parent material, are so seldom equal when widely separated parts of the Highlands are compared.

Nor have we found obvious indications of varying soil base-status according to marked rainfall differences within a single massif (e.g. 50–150 in. (127–380 cm.) as in some western areas). Such a relationship is the more difficult to trace because rainfall differences within a single massif depend largely on altitude, and other factors connected with changing altitude may have an obscuring effect.

However likely they may be in theory, these questions must remain open and need a detailed, statistically acceptable treatment.

Base-rich soils are maintained largely by irrigation with water which is strongly charged with ions removed from the rock and other soil by leaching, or by mechanical instability due to gravity or frost movements. On any one parent rock most differences in soil base-status are due to a varying incidence of such processes of enrichment. Even on base-rich rocks leaching usually produces base-poor soils unless this opposite tendency is at work. Base-rich rocks always support more extensive areas of fertile soil than acidic rocks since leaching is less effective in causing impoverishment and at the same time gives a greater re-distribution of bases on irrigated ground. In this context it is suggested that although leaching may be more rapid under the heavy rainfall of the west there is a corresponding increase in the amount of enrichment by irrigation. In general, on sloping ground, the composition of the rock and soil through which drainage water has percolated is at least as important as that of the actual soil parent material at any particular site.

Pearsall (1950) has pointed out that the uppermost altitudinal zone of any mountain is inevitably leached and that the zone of enrichment (by flushing) lies at a lower level. This is particularly noticeable on the Breadalbane range for even where the calcareous Lawers schist forms the hill-tops the summit soils are leached and acidic although they may be more base-rich than comparable soils developed from acidic parent material. This would explain why the soils of Caricetum saxatalis and the Dwarf Herb *nodum* are more acidic and less base-rich on the average than those of their lower level counterparts, the *Carex panicea-Campylium stellatum nodum* and the two rich Agrosto-Festuceta.

While some montane calcicolous noda, such as the Dwarf Herb *nodum*, may be more chionophilous than present evidence suggests, it is noteworthy that base-rich soils are rarely, if ever, found in the latest snow-beds of the Highlands. All the extreme snow-bed communities are oligotrophic, even when the parent rock is calcareous, and the same is true of most of the other chionophilous noda, except for the triquetrosum facies of Deschampsieto-Rhytidiadelphetum, which is associated with base-rich soils and a fairly prolonged snow-cover. Late snow-lie evidently favours leaching except when it is accompanied by strong irrigation from rich substrata.

Calcareous rocks such as limestone may be overlain by acidic peat when the slope is gentle, but on rock faces and in the skeletal soils of steep ground or flushes the high base content of the parent material is revealed. Mull humus is usually associated with high base content of the parent rock or with enrichment by irrigation but moder humus may occur in soils derived from base-deficient rocks provided that conditions favour biological activity. Base-rich peats are found only in soligenous and topogenous mires since they depend for their formation on a good supply of mineral ions in the drainage water.

The prevailing soil types of the Highlands may be grouped as acidic peats, podsols, brown earths and gleys. This indicates the pedogenic uniformity of climate, and differentiation within the group is largely due to topography and parent material. Altitudinal variation is encountered chiefly in the well-drained podsolic soils and brown earths, and the peats and gleys show considerable uniformity at different elevations. The climatic modification of soil at high altitudes gives a number of types which are more or less confined to the Highlands in Britain and some of these have not been described previously in this country. Whenever possible we have tried to relate Highland soils to the comprehensive scheme of Kubiena (1953) but this has not always been easy. The soils of the Scottish mountains clearly offer ample scope for a survey by experienced pedologists.

Perhaps the most widespread soil type within the survey area is that variously known as deep peat, hill peat or blanket peat. It is found in association with Calluneto-Eriophoretum, Empetreto-Eriophoretum, Trichophoreto-Eriophoretum and Trichophoreto-Callunetum. Redistributed and truncated peats are occupied by Nardetum and Juncetum squarrosi sub-alpinum as well as by a variety of mixed vegetation types.

Next in order of abundance are the many varieties of podsolic soils within the Forest and Sub-alpine zones (Fig. 1, p. 12). These are encountered with Pinetum Hylocomieto-Vaccinetum, Pinetum Vaccineto-Callunetum, Betuletum Oxaleto-Vaccinetum, Callunetum vulgaris, Vaccineto-Callunetum, Trichophoreto-Callunetum, Molinieto-Callunetum and Nardetum sub-alpinum.

The shallow alpine and nano-podsols are found in the Low and Middle-alpine zones with vegetation belonging to Cladineto-Callunetum, Rhacomitreto-Callunetum, Cladineto-Vaccinetum, Cariceto-Rhacomitretum lanuginosi, Vaccinetum chionophilum, Vaccineto-Empetretum, Deschampsieto-Rhytidiadelphetum typicum and the *Nardus-Rhacomitrium nodum*.

Brown soils showing various degrees of podsolisation (Fig. 2, p. 17) are encountered with Arctostaphyleto-Callunetum, the *Betula*-herb *nodum*, *Fraxinus-Brachypodium nodum*, the *Dryas noda*, herb-rich Callunetum, Festuceto-Vaccinetum, Deschampsieto-Rhytidiadelphetum triquetrosum, the *Agrosto-Festuceta*, species-rich Deschampsietum caespitosae alpinum, Saxifragetum aizoidis, the Dwarf Herb *nodum* and the Tall Herb *nodum*.

Red calcareous loams of rendzina affinity are confined to outcrops of the Durness dolomite in the North-west Highlands and to isolated fragments of limestones of other formations. They may bear one of the *Dryas noda* or patches of the *Fraxinus-Brachypodium nodum* but have generally been extensively utilised and the vegetation is now mostly unclassified grassland with fragments of secondary birch and hazel scrub. More typical rendzinas have been recorded in association with *Arctostaphylos*-grass heath near Blair Atholl and *Dryas* heath in the Cairnwell hills (pp. 49–50).

Alpine rankers are typical of Vaccineto-Callunetum, Vaccineto-Empetretum, Juniperetum nanae, Cryptogrammeto-Athyrietum chionophilum, Arctoeto-Callunetum.

12

Cladineto-Callunetum and Rhacomitreto-Empetretum as well as occurring frequently with many of the noda mentioned under alpine podsols above.

Skeletal and solifluction soils are most frequent in association with certain of the species-poor Agrosto-Festuceta (mainly skeletal), the *Juncus trifidus-Festuca ovina nodum*, Cariceto-Rhacomitretum, Polygoneto-Rhacomitretum, Cladineto-Juncetum trifidi, Polytricheto-Dicranetum starkei, Rhacomitreto-Dicranetum starkei and Gymnomitreto-Salicetum herbaceae.

Alpine sod podsols are found with the Low-alpine *Nardus noda*, Nardetum medioalpinum, Deschampsietum caespitosae alpinum, the *Alchemilla-Sibbaldia nodum*, Dicraneto-Caricetum bigelowii and Polytricheto-Caricetum bigelowii.

Basin peats and peaty gleys of varying base-status are characteristic of the *Juncus acutiflorus-Acrocladium cuspidatum nodum*, Hypno-Caricetum alpinum, *Carex rostrata-Sphagnum warnstorfianum nodum*, Sphagneto-Juncetum effusi and the two Sphagneto-Cariceta.

Gleying of the lower soil horizons is also common within Nardetum and Juncetum squarrosi subalpinum, Polytricheto-Caricetum bigelowii, Deschampsieto-Rhytidiadelphetum and Trichophoreto-Eriophoretum caricetosum.

True 'fen' peats and marls are rare and confined to the *Schoenus nigricans nodum* and *Carex rostrata*-brown moss *nodum* and to some stands of the *Juncus acutiflorus-Acrocladium cuspidatum nodum* and *Carex panicea-Campylium stellatum nodum*.

In the foregoing lists noda have been assigned to their most characteristic soil type. It has been found, however, that a few noda occur on a fairly wide range of soils and that most others show some variation in the field appearance of their soils. Even where laboratory analyses suggest that closely related noda such as the Agrosto-Festuceta are differentiated largely by soil factors a good deal of overlap is found in their range of profile development.

Chemical Factors

Measurements of pH, exchangeable calcium, potassium and sodium, and soluble phosphate (P_2O_5) have been made on soil samples in the laboratory. Magnesium and nitrogen have not been studied. At least one sample for most of the important noda has been analysed in this way. We have, however, concentrated on obtaining data for vegetation types whose soils have hitherto been neglected, and have paid less attention to those (e.g. Callunetum vulgaris) for which there is a wealth of published information. In the case of certain bogs, mires, flushes and springs we have preferred to use water samples rather than peats for analysis: completely unhumified peat has proved an unsatisfactory medium for the application of normal techniques.

Usually only one sample was taken from each vegetation plot, at a depth of 1–9 in. (2·5–23 cm.): in many alpine soils the sample had perforce to be taken from a shallower layer, often of only 0–3 in. (0–7·6 cm.). The layer sampled was that held to be most important to the bulk of the vegetation growing on the site. One sample thus often deliberately overlapped two or more distinct horizons, but sometimes, in profiles with marked differentiation, samples were collected from two or three separate horizons, and the analyses then revealed or confirmed tendencies such as podsolisation. For recording in the soil tables, however, different samples from the same profile (at depths of up to 9 in.) have been averaged to give one set of data. Our purpose is not to characterise soils in terms of chemical stratification but to give a comparative measure, from one site to another, of certain factors likely to be significant to the vegetation. In effect, we have tried, by using these indices, to arrange soils and their associated noda according to a scale of fertility.

The soil samples were air dried and broken up before passing through a 2 mm. sieve to remove stones and larger root fragments. After subsequent oven-drying at 100–110°C each was ignited at about 600° C in a muffle furnace. Loss on ignition is taken as the approximate equivalent of humus content. No correction has been applied for additional loss of weight from the clay fraction or from free calcium carbonate. Soils containing free calcium carbonate are extremely localised in the Highlands and only occur in association with a few noda on highly calcareous rocks.

It is essential to obtain a measure of humus content, as most peats give relatively high values for the various available ions, due to their enormous contraction on drying, i.e. a large volume gives a small dry weight. Allowance has to be made accordingly in drawing comparisons with the analyses of soils containing little organic matter. Because of the field sampling method, loss on ignition figures do not give a true indication of the amount of surface humus when only a shallow layer is present. They do, nevertheless, give a comparative measure of the 'peatiness' of the soil in the upper 9 in.

pH was determined on a 1:2·5 suspension of soil in distilled water, using an E.I.L. glass electrode potentiometer. When it was not possible to transport the fresh samples to the laboratory quickly, pH determinations were carried out on the air-dried soil. Measurements made on a number of samples when fresh and after drying showed pH variations within 0·3 of a unit for soils with a low humus content. The values for peats mostly refer to fresh samples, although here again drying does not always cause an appreciable change in pH.

The exchangeable ions were extracted by leaching with 0·5 N acetic acid, the soil and acid being shaken together for two hours. Sodium and potassium in the extract were determined by flame photometry, using an E.E.L. meter.

Calcium was determined by E.D.T.A. titration using murexide as indicator. The same method was used for determination of calcium in water samples. Soluble phosphate was measured colorimetrically by Spekker absorptiometer, using the molybdenum blue method, with stannous chloride as reducing agent.

Results of the analyses are shown in Tables 65–68. Coverage of the various noda is far from uniform and this makes any comparison of the results, and a decision on the significance of differences in the figures, more difficult. Nevertheless it is evident that only pH and exchangeable calcium show any indication of correlation with floristic groupings.

The pH values remain reasonably constant within each nodum (i.e. the range of variation usually lies within one pH unit) although there is considerable overlap between noda in the range of the values. This is precisely the situation revealed by other phytosociologists such as Poore (1955b), Dahl (1956) and Gjaerevoll (1956) who have relied solely upon a large number of pH determinations for chemical characterisation of soils. We do not have a sufficient number of pH readings to draw curves for each nodum in the way that Gjaerevoll (loc. cit.) has done but a comparison, for example, of the six values of the Dicraneto-Caricetum bigelowii with the six values of the Tall Herb *nodum* indicates a significant difference between the two groups.

The values for exchangeable calcium do not give quite such a simple pattern but, nevertheless, certain noda such as the Tall Herb *nodum* and Caricetum saxatilis are characterised by generally high calcium levels, with occasional anomalously low values, while others such as Dicraneto-Caricetum bigelowii are consistently low. There is a general correspondence between calcium status and pH in the soils of many noda but a few noteworthy discrepancies occur. Some soils with a low pH and an acidic parent material have relatively large amounts of calcium, and sometimes this condition is reversed. For example, M57073 (Vaccinetum chionophilum) has pH 3·8 and 48·9 mg. Ca/100 gm. while M56087 (Polytricheto-Dicranetum) has pH 5·4 and 2·0 mg. Ca/100 gm. No measurements of exchange capacity have been made, but it is probable that soils with low pH and high calcium content have a high exchange capacity, and vice versa. Again, in peats the volume/weight distortion produced on drying tends to increase calcium values in relation to those of pH, since the latter are measured when the material is moist. Bog, mire and spring waters show more consistent relationships between these two factors, and the pH values of water samples are generally higher than those of the peats from the same sites (Table 68).

On the other hand, no such pattern can be distinguished for soluble phosphate or exchangeable sodium and potassium and it is evident that these can vary widely without an appreciable effect on the floristic composition of the vegetation. Nevertheless, many of the mountain soils and the vegetation they carry may differ considerably in nutrient value for grazing animals as a result of differences in amounts of elements other than calcium. Even differences in calcium status which are too small to affect the vegetation may give significant variations in productivity for grazing animals.

Some of the above results, such as the high calcium status of the *Dryas* and Tall Herb soils, were only to be expected; others are more surprising and it is interesting to note how certain species such as *Juniperus nana* and *Athyrium alpestre*, although growing upon siliceous and acidic soil parent material, have apparently been able to build up a layer of humus relatively rich in exchangeable mineral ions and soluble phosphate. In view of the restriction of Festuceto-Vaccinetum to calcareous schists and its rapid replacement by Vaccineto-Empetretum and Cladineto-Vaccinetum where siliceous rocks outcrop, the similarity in base status of its soils to those of the other two associations is rather strange. The explanation given on p. 66 may apply, namely, that selective exploitation induced by areas of rich rock has led to modification of vegetation even on poor soils in the same areas. A greater difference was also expected between the soils of the Cariceto-Rhacomitretum lanuginosi and Polygoneto-Rhacomitretum.

In his examination of the distribution of the Scottish mountain plants in relation to geology and soil Ferreira (1959) found that calcium status was the most significant soil factor and that the presence of most species which are generally regarded as basiphilous was invariably associated with the occurrence of free calcium carbonate in the parent material or irrigating water. He pointed out that the pH of non-calcareous basalt soils might vary from 6·0 to 6·6, but that the soils lacked the calcicolous flora present on adjacent calcareous basalts. Ferreira showed too that the floristically rich calcareous schists of Ben Lawers yield soils that are generally poor in available mineral elements apart from calcium, which is present in large amounts.

Our experience in the field, supported by soil analyses, leads us to agree with Ferreira and we would extend his emphasis of the importance of calcium status to Highland mountain vegetation in general.

Ferreira showed that some basiphilous species grow equally well when magnesium replaces calcium as the predominant cation. Spence (1957) has also drawn attention to the distinctive flora of serpentine outcrops in Shetland but there would seem to be very few species which are associated with a high concentration of available magnesium alone.

Ferreira pointed out that the available calcium status of the soil depends greatly on the speed with which calcium is released from the parent rock. Calcium becomes avail-

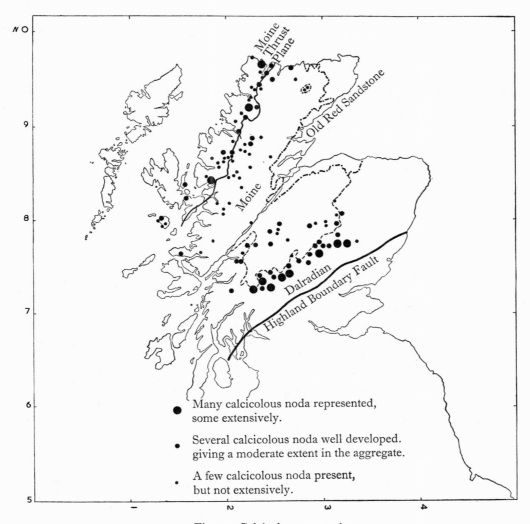

Fig. 30. Calcicolous vegetation

This map shows the distribution of calcicolous (mesotrophic and eutrophic) vegetation in the areas surveyed, the extent of each occurrence being indicated by the size of dot. Each dot is placed over the centre of the occurrence and not according to the 10 km. squares of the National Grid. Since even on the most calcareous hills there is seldom a large and continuous area of calcicolous vegetation, a conventional symbol is the most suitable method of representation. The soil of these vegetation types are base-saturated, with calcium as the predominant cation, and are mostly derived from parent rocks containing free calcium carbonate.

able most rapidly when present as calcium carbonate and he reserves the term 'calcareous' for such rocks. We too have found that hard calcium-bearing but non-calcareous rocks carry much the same range of vegetation as acidic rocks devoid of calcium minerals except where percolating water emerges at the surface. However rich in calcium silicates the non-calcareous rocks may be, the concentration of calcium ions in the drainage water or soil is never comparable with that from calcite-bearing rocks. The high rate of leaching under the Highland climate is probably responsible for the great importance of readily available calcium in the parent rock.

Ferreira has further shown that soils derived from soft non-calcareous rocks are no richer in available calcium than those formed from hard non-calcareous rocks although there may be pronounced differences in soil profile and physical properties.

The close correspondence between the distribution of certain noda and that of calcareous rocks has been indicated in the particular accounts. In place of an orthodox geological map we have shown the distribution (Fig. 30) of all the main occurrences of calcicolous (i.e. mesotrophic and eutrophic) vegetation encountered during the survey, for this virtually represents a map of the occurrences of calcareous rock. It has the advantage of showing which exposures of calcareous rock are particularly important to the vegetation: some areas of limestone, for instance, are largely overlain by drift and peat, and so exert little influence on the vegetation. Again, in some places the influence of calcareous parent material is shown in drift lying well away from the occurrences of the actual bed-rock.

Repeated mention has been made of the most extensive and important stretch of calcareous rocks within our study area—that lying in a south-west to north-east direction between East Argyll and the Aberdeenshire-Angus border. These rocks of the Dalradian series consist mainly of limestones and calcareous mica-schists and the line of their outcrop includes many of the botanically famous hills and glens of Scotland, notably the Breadalbane range from Ben Lui to Ben Lawers, Ben Vrackie and Glen Loch, Caenlochan and Glen Callater. At the north-east end there is another important outcrop of calcareous rocks of a different complex in Glen Doll and Corrie Fee (Fiadh), Clova.

Many other massifs have patches of calcareous rocks but these are seldom extensive and give only local occurrences of calcicolous vegetation. Much of the Moine series, such as the pelitic gneisses of Ben Wyvis, is micaceous but non-calcareous and gives rise to mountain soils with an illusory appearance of fertility. In the Western Highlands a few of the higher Moine and Lewisian hills have good exposures of calcareous rock but the main occurrences are at low levels following the line of the Moine Thrust Plane (Fig. 30). Most important is the Durness dolomite with its associated mudstones and grits. Much of this limestone is drift and peat covered but it outcrops extensively at Kishorn, Knockan, Inchnadamph and Durness. There are local occurrences of limestone and calcareous igneous rocks in the Inner Hebrides and on the west coast of the mainland and local areas of blown shell sand on the Sutherland coast (see Fig. 27, p. 151) and in the Outer Hebrides.

Because of the concentration of calcareous rocks in the south of the Highlands most calcicolous noda show a corresponding bias in distribution (Table 74 and Fig. 30). This tendency rather obscures the relationships of certain of these vegetation types to other factors such as climate, but on the other hand the distribution of certain noda seems to be limited only by that of calcareous rock (Table 74).

The chemical composition of the parent material seems to have little influence on vegetation within the range of acidic rocks but Juniperetum nanae and Cladineto-Juncetum trifidi are confined to quartzite and granite respectively, although this is perhaps fortuitous.

In describing soils and vegetation it has been useful to adopt the terms oligotrophic, mesotrophic and eutrophic to indicate relative levels of soil fertility. Since these levels seem to be related more closely to available calcium status than to any other soil factor (including pH) they may be defined accordingly for the purposes of the present study.

Fertility level	Exchangeable Ca (mg./100 gm.)
Oligotrophic	< 30
Mesotrophic	30–300
Eutrophic	> 300

Subject to the discrepancies mentioned above, these levels correspond approximately, in order of increasing calcium, to pH ranges of: less than 5·0; 5·0–6·0; and over 6·0.

Differences in available calcium status of the soil therefore produce one of the main 'directions of variation' in Highland vegetation comparable in importance to wetness of soil, snow-cover, wind exposure and temperature. Noda may be arranged in the broad groups from oligotrophic to eutrophic which illustrate this differentiation, but within each group it is likely that other soil factors not yet studied (e.g. nitrogen content and aeration) may cause separation of vegetation types. This simple arrangement of soils according to calcium status is completely empirical, and merely a first step in examining edaphic differentiation of Highland vegetation.

In conclusion, our data emphasise the very local distribution of fertile soils in the Highlands. Although many mesotrophic and eutrophic noda have been distinguished, most of these cover an insignificant area compared with widespread vegetation types which have soils (whether these are peats, podsols or brown mineral soils) of extremely low exchangeable base and phosphate content. For our soil samples, pH ranges from 3·1 to 8·0, exchangeable sodium from 0·5 to 90·5 mg./100 gm., potassium from 0·8 to 73·8 mg./100 gm. and calcium from 1·1 to 1116 mg./100 gm. (the highest values for calcium being on Dalradian limestone and mica-schist). Calcium values exceeding 500 mg./100 gm. are exceptional. Soluble phosphate lies between 0·04 and 31·94 mg./100 gm.

Such figures, but especially those for the predominant vegetation types, should be borne in mind by those who would still regard the Highlands as undeveloped terrain capable of exploitation whether for sheep, cattle or timber. Albrecht (1957) has pointed out that areas with these soil characteristics are suited only to carbohydrate (primarily cellulose and lignin) production and not the production of plant and animal protein. The removal of calcium and phosphorus in animal carcasses from the unenclosed soils of the Highlands over the last few hundred years, in combination with deforestation and burning and under the limitations of climate and parent rock, must bear the responsibility for such advanced chemical degradation. Even the timber croppers of the future must consider whether they can sustain production without resorting to fertilisation on an agricultural scale.

Plant Indicators of Soil

Most ecologists are familiar with the indications of soil fertility which are given by the presence of certain species with a restricted range of tolerance of pH and base status. The soil analyses carried out as part of the present study allow us to attempt a quantitative definition of the range which many species show for requirements of soil pH and exchangeable calcium. Many species have too wide an amplitude of soil requirements to be used in this way and we have already drawn attention to the point that certain species show a decided change in edaphic needs in different parts of Scotland, some being calcicole in the south and east of their range and indifferent to lime status in the north and west. Not only montane species (e.g. *Silene acaulis* and *Cherleria sedoides*) but widespread lowland plants such as *Helianthemum chamaecistus* show these tendencies.

Again, we have found that some species which are often regarded as indicators of acidic, base-poor soils in Britain are not reliable in this respect within the Highlands. This is particularly true of the Ericaceae. A great deal has been written about the calcifuge habit of *Calluna vulgaris*, and it has been suggested (cf. Webb, 1947) that when this plant occurs on calcareous rocks it is rooted in layers or pockets of raw humus. *Calluna* is a frequent component of calcareous rock face vegetation in the Highlands, sometimes in habitats where the feeding roots could hardly avoid contact with free calcium carbonate, and the species undoubtedly grows at times on soils which have a high content of exchangeable calcium (see Tables 66, 67). In the herb-rich Callunetum there is usually an intimate mixture of *Calluna* and calcicolous herbs and, although the soil may vary slightly within a small space, there is no sign that the *Calluna* is rooted in leached pockets or horizons. The abundance of calcicolous mosses alone suggests that the surface horizons of these soils have a good calcium status. It has been noted too that *Erica tetralix* is often abundant in mire communities on fairly rich soils adjoining calcareous flushes, especially in the Eastern Highlands.

The three *Vaccinia* may all be found on quite rich soils and *V. uliginosum* grows luxuriantly on many calcareous crags, along with calcicoles such as *Dryas octopetala*, sometimes in contrast to its scarcity or absence on adjacent acidic rocks. The growth of *Arctostaphylos uva-ursi* on a strongly calcareous sugar limestone soil has already been described (p. 50). *Empetrum hermaphroditum* is seldom absent from *Dryas* communities and it is one of the chief components of the mixed dwarf shrub communities with *Dryas*, *Juniperus communis* and *Salix repens* on blown shell sand at Bettyhill in Sutherland (see Fig. 27, p. 151). The *Empetrum* may be slightly chlorotic but is otherwise normal in appearance.

The occurrence of these interesting mixed communities of calcifuges and calcicoles may sometimes be due to sudden changes in soil conditions within a small space. For instance, on Ben Hope *Dryas* is abundant in a moss mat of *Rhacomitrium lanuginosum* and the common hypnaceous species of calcifuge dwarf shrub heath. The mosses grow on a leached surface layer whereas the *Dryas* roots penetrate deeply into the calcareous substratum. In cliff face habitats differences in degree of enrichment by irrigation and addition of disintegrated mineral fragments produce considerable and sudden changes in soil laterally. Pronounced soil gradients from oligotrophic to eutrophic are also often associated with changing influence of wind-blown sand (Figs. 6, p. 49, and 27, p. 151), or with rapid spatial change in calcite content of parent rock.

Juncus squarrosus and *Nardus stricta* are normally regarded as plants of acidic, base-deficient soils, but the herb-rich Juncetum squarrosi and Nardetum subalpinum so widespread in Breadalbane occur on soils with a pH range of 5·6–6·0 and exchangeable calcium content of 69–300 mg./100 gm. Even on acidic mountains both species are often associated with irrigation and this is particularly noticeable when the grazing intensity is low and ericaceous communities predominant. Several species of *Carex*, notably *C. rostrata*, *C. nigra* and *C. panicea*, and other mire plants such as *Juncus acutiflorus* have a wide tolerance of lime-status, and occur as dominants in habitats ranging from markedly oligotrophic to definitely eutrophic. Despite their prominence in the particular communities they have no value as differential species and the vegetation has to be characterised in terms of subsidiary species.

After disregarding the unreliable indicator species there remain many which, within the Highlands, give a good indication of particular ranges of soil pH and calcium status and these may be used to assess soil fertility (with regard to these factors) in the field. These indicators can be arranged in groups (Tables 69–73) according to the range of their requirements; the selection is based on laboratory soil analyses for described communities, supplemented by field correlations between vegetation, soil and parent rock, i.e. observation of species' abundance on or restriction to soils whose trophic levels (as defined on p. 169) have been established, and their association with parent material of approximately known base-content. In this context, soil analyses have to be considered in relation to the particular stand rather than the nodum as a whole, for some indicator species are present only in the richer or poorer stands of a nodum with variable soils. Again, our single soil samples (per stand) may not always give a true measure of soil conditions for shallow or deep-rooted species.

Since the method is partly subjective we do not claim to have established the limits of soil pH and calcium requirements for these species, but rather the optimum range. The abundance of these indicators rather than their mere presence is perhaps the best guide, and when any one of them occurs in quantity we believe that soil conditions will lie within the range prescribed.

Species named as indicators have mostly been encountered in the floristic analyses, but a few others which seem to be particularly good indicators, mainly rupestral bryophytes, have been included. Plants with uncertain soil requirements have been omitted, though some may with further study prove to be useful as indicators. While calcium has been regarded as the significant ion for 'calcicoles' some species may be general indicators for levels of base-status depending on other ions such as magnesium (see p. 166).

Indicators have been arranged in groups corresponding to the three soil trophic levels, as follows:

1. *Exacting calcicoles* (Table 69)

Species especially associated with parent materials containing large amounts of calcium carbonate and derived soils with a high content of exchangeable calcium (> 300 mg./100 gm.) and high pH (usually > 6·0). They include few common species but many of the local or rare montane vascular plants and cryptogams, especially those occurring chiefly or only on the main tract of calcareous Dalradian rocks (for a fuller list of the vascular species see Chapter 13, page 175, and Ferreira, 1959). Most of these plants appear to have a specific need for high calcium status and do not grow on other base-rich substrata (Ferreira, 1958).

2. *Calcicoles* (Table 70)

Species requiring at least moderately basic parent materials and derived soils containing over 30 mg. calcium/100 gm. and with a pH usually exceeding 4·8. They include the majority of species which distinguish mesotrophic and eutrophic noda. Many of them grow most abundantly on eutrophic soils but they are less demanding than the exacting calcicoles. Some, however, grow equally well on base-rich soils in which other elements, notably magnesium, replace calcium as the predominant cation, and these are termed basiphiles by Ferreira (1958).

These are perhaps the most useful species for pointing out the 'better' soils, especially when the parent material is not obviously calcareous or when pedogenic factors such as irrigation and drift composition are variable.

3. *Calcifuges* (Table 71)

Species which grow on rocks lacking free calcium carbonate and soils with little exchangeable calcium (< 30 mg./100 gm.) and low pH (usually < 4·5). They include species confined to oligotrophic noda and many are reliable indicators of the poorest soils. Some are particularly associated with acidic peat and mor humus but others contribute to the formation of more fertile moder humus on acidic soils. Many rupestral lichens might be added to the list.

We have distinguished a fourth group of species (Table 72) which avoid the very poorest soils (< 15 mg. Ca/100 gm. and pH < 4·5), especially those with mor humus, although they grow on the 'better' oligotrophic substrata. Some of these grow on meso-trophic and eutrophic soils as well but others evidently have an intermediate range of base-tolerance and avoid calcareous soils. Such plants are useful for indicating the least infertile sites in areas of predominantly poor rocks and soils which can nowhere support the more demanding calcicoles.

We have not tried to pick out a group of species growing on all but strongly cal-careous substrata, but give a final list (Table 73) of those which appear to be completely indifferent, growing over a wide range of soil calcium status and acidity.

Floristic variety of vegetation gives another broader indication of soil fertility. In general there is a fairly good direct correlation between average number of species in a nodum and average calcium status and pH of the soil. Although this relationship does not hold good throughout, especially when contrasting habitat complexes are compared (e.g. Vaccineto-Callunetum hepaticosum, av. 37 spp., and Caricetum saxatilis, av. 24 spp.), the floristically-rich noda (av. > 40 spp.) are all markedly calcicolous. Number of indicator species as well as their individual abundance is naturally the best guide.

Chapter 13

PLANT GEOGRAPHICAL FACTORS

WHEN lists are selected for a particular dominant the distribution of this dominant determines that of the resulting nodum as with *Dryas octopetala* and *Juniperus nana* heaths and *Carex saxatilis* and *Schoenus nigricans* mires. On the other hand the irregular distribution of many species and the relict status of some, especially in the montane element, accounts for a certain amount of floristic heterogeneity within various noda. This is supported by the experience that when a nodum is defined on the basis of lists drawn from the whole of the Highlands it may not have sufficient uniformity to rank as an association (pp. 7,8). If this nodum is then sub-divided geographically the subsidiary groups may often be distinguished as local associations.

Such regional variation in floristics is due not only to the presence or absence of certain species but also to local differences in their range of habitat preference. *Campanula rotundifolia, Helianthemum chamaecistus, Geranium sylvaticum* and *Heracleum sphondylium* are scarce or absent from upland communities north of the Great Glen. The last two are important members of the Tall Herb *nodum* within their geographical range so that lists from the whole of the Highlands give the *nodum* non-uniformity for these two species alone. Similarly, *Plantago maritima* is a usual member of several noda in the Western Highlands but becomes increasingly rare eastwards and apparently confined to soils of high base-status.

Phytosociology is thus linked to phytogeography and a treatment of the distribution of vegetation types in the Highlands involves some discussion of factors governing plant distribution—climate, soil and the changes in both during the Quaternary period. The subject is too large to develop at length but will be exemplified by a brief discussion of the vascular montane flora.

Due to the prevalence of lime-deficient soils throughout the Highlands the most widespread and abundant montane species are either calcifuge or indifferent to calcium status. Some of these occur in nearly every important massif of the Highlands and so appear as constants in a number of noda. They include:

Alchemilla alpina	Luzula spicata
Carex bigelowii	Lycopodium alpinum
C. pauciflora	L. selago
Empetrum hermaphroditum	Salix herbacea
Epilobium anagallidifolium	Saxifraga stellaris
Gnaphalium supinum	Sibbaldia procumbens
Juncus trifidus	Vaccinium uliginosum
Loiseleuria procumbens	

Except perhaps in the North-west Highlands, *Alchemilla alpina* and *Sibbaldia procumbens* are seemingly not completely indifferent to calcium status and usually grow most abundantly on mountains with calcareous rocks. *Sibbaldia* is especially associated with ground where snow-cover is greater than average.

A few species with comparable soil requirements, such as *Arctostaphylos uva-ursi*, *Chamaepericlymenum suecicum* and *Rubus chamaemorus* are widespread, but much more abundant in some districts than others, and they are least plentiful in the South-west Highlands. *Lycopodium annotinum*, *Betula nana* and *Arctous alpina* are more local, though often abundant, and the last two occur mainly to the north of the Great Glen (cf. distribution of the shrub-rich facies of Calluneto-Eriophoretum, Map 28). *Athyrium alpestre* and *Cryptogramma crispa* are local because they depend largely on late snow-lie, but both occur in most rocky corries where snow accumulates. Rarities especially associated with late snow-beds or their springs and flushes include *Alopecurus alpinus*, *Deschampsia alpina* and *Cerastium cerastoides*, and these have a scattered distribution, mainly on the highest hills.

There is a comparable group of widespread and often common calcicoles† which occur on nearly all the major outcrops of calcareous rocks. Because of the lesser extent of suitable substrata, however, they are never as prominent as the calcifuge and indifferent species in the vegetation as a whole. Some of these species may grow at times on acidic soils but they are most characteristic of calcareous rocks. This group consists of:

Alchemilla filicaulis	Rubus saxatilis
A. wichurae	Saussurea alpina
Asplenium viride	Saxifraga aizoides
Cochlearia alpina	S. hypnoides
Galium boreale	S. oppositifolia
Juncus triglumis	Sedum rosea
Oxyria digyna	Silene acaulis
Polygonum viviparum	Thalictrum alpinum
Polystichum lonchitis	

Some of these occur as constants in mesotrophic and eutrophic noda and they are frequently present (though in lower constancy classes) in many noda associated with basic soils.

There follows another group of calcicoles which have a wide distribution in the Highlands but are always local or rare. These are constants only in the few instances where stands are deliberately selected for their presence. This group contains:

Ajuga pyramidalis*	Cerastium alpinum
Alchemilla glomerulans	C. edmonstonii*
Cardaminopsis petraea*	Cherleria sedoides*
Carex atrata	Cochlearia micacea
C. capillaris	Draba incana
C. rupestris	Dryas octopetala
C. saxatilis*	Epilobium alsinifolium
C. vaginata	Equisetum variegatum

† We have followed, with a few exceptions, the separation of the montane flora into calcicole and calcifuge or indifferent groups made by Ferreira (1959)

Juncus castaneus
Phleum commutatum
Poa alpina
P. balfourii
P. glauca
Potentilla crantzii
Rhinanthus borealis

Sagina saginoides
Salix lapponum*
Salix myrsinites
Saxifraga nivalis
S. rivularis (rare)
Tofieldia pusilla
Veronica alpina*

Species marked with an asterisk may be regarded as indifferent but in some districts show a marked preference for calcareous rocks.

Some plants in this list have their headquarters on the Ben Lawers schist and other calcareous rocks in Breadalbane and Clova.

The following is a list of calcicolous rarities which are more or less confined to these two districts although a few of them have outlying stations elsewhere on limestone or other strongly calcareous rocks.

Agropyron donianum
Alchemilla conjuncta
Astragalus alpinus
Bartsia alpina
Carex atrofusca
C. grahami
C. microglochin
C. norvegica
Cystopteris montana
Draba rupestris
Erigeron borealis
Gentiana nivalis
Homogyne alpina
Juncus alpinus
J. biglumis

Kobresia simpliciuscula
Minuartia rubella
Myosotis alpestris
Oxytropis campestris
Sagina intermedia
Salix arbuscula
S. lanata
S. reticulata
Saxifraga cernua
Sedum villosum
Sesleria caerulea
Thlaspi alpestre
Veronica fruticans
Woodsia alpina
W. ilvensis

There remains a small number of species, both calcifuge and calcicole, which are rare and have highly relict distributions. The calcicoles of this group have distributions quite different from those of the foregoing list. In the list which follows, the region of occurrence is indicated and single station plants are denoted by an asterisk.

Arabis alpina (W. Central)*
Arenaria norvegica (Western)
Artemisia norvegica (N. Western)
Carex lachenalii (Central)
C. rariflora (E. Central)
Cicerbita alpina (E. Central)
Diapensia lapponica (W. Central)*
Gnaphalium norvegicum (all but S.W.)
Koenigia islandica (Western)

Luzula arcuata (Central & N. Western)
Minuartia verna (Central)
Oxytropis halleri (all but W. Central)
Phyllodoce caerulea (E. Central)*
Poa flexuosa (Central)
P. x jemtlandica (Central)
Saxifraga cespitosa (Central)
S. hirculus (Eastern)
Viscaria alpina (E. Central)*

Within the Highlands richness of the montane flora (i.e. number of species) in any one locality depends mainly on two factors, altitude and the calcium carbonate content of the soil parent material, but as MacGillivray (1855) first pointed out, the *area* of suitable ground appears to be important in this context as well. Since calcicoles far outnumber calcifuge and indifferent species in the Scottish montane flora, the floristically rich hills are those with large areas of calcareous rocks. Moreover all such hills have areas of lime-deficient rocks and soils in addition so that they also support a proportion of the other element, whereas the reverse is not true. On both calcareous and non-calcareous mountains richness of the montane flora generally depends on the range of altitude so that the highest hills usually yield the largest number of species. Some of the rarer species appear to need conditions which are associated with high altitude although other widespread montane plants, especially dwarf shrubs, evidently have an upper altitudinal limit (p. 51). The richest hills of all are therefore those which are high and have calcareous rocks outcropping extensively at all altitudes, but especially above 2500 ft. (763 m.).

The importance of high altitude for many montane plants is shown by the relatively poor flora of low-lying limestone areas such as that of Glen Tilt. The coastal limestones and shell-sand areas of the North-west are somewhat richer and some species grow there in great abundance; nevertheless they have a much smaller number of species than the southern districts of Breadalbane and Clova. The main areas of calcareous rocks in the Highlands are indicated by the map showing distribution of calcicolous vegetation (Fig. 30). Outside the last two districts they are never extensive at high levels and this is particularly true of the West-central and North-east Highlands. After Breadalbane and Clova the most notable localities for calcicoles are limited areas in Glencoe and the Ben Nevis and Ben Alder massifs; outlying parts of the Cairngorms; the Beinn Dearg-Seana Bhraigh group; Ben More Assynt; Ben Hope; scattered basic igneous hills in Western Argyll and the Inner Hebrides; the dolomitic limestone at Kishorn, Knockan, Inchnadamph and Durness; and the blown shell sand at Bettyhill.

Many montane species have become less abundant as a result of biotic influences but most of the local and rare species seem to be climatic relicts. Some species are rare because their special habitats (e.g. late snow-beds) are infrequent, but many are absent from a high proportion of places where the habitat appears to be suitable in every way. Discontinuous distributions of this kind are to be explained in terms of climatic change during the Post-glacial period. The gradual restriction of once widespread montane species to high ground and specialised habitats as the climate became warmer and wetter has been established by palaeo-ecological work (cf. Godwin, 1949, 1956). The critical period for the montane flora was evidently the Post-glacial Climatic Optimum when the climate was rather warmer than at present and the forest and scrub zones reached their highest levels. The subsequent fall in temperature would theoretically be matched by a downward shift in the altitudinal limits of the various zones although there is little supporting evidence for this.

Dahl (1951) has shown that in Fennoscandia there is a close correlation between the geographical distribution limits of montane plants in lowland stations and isotherms of maximum summer temperature, with the critical temperature varying over a range of at least 7° C for different species. The implication is very clearly that the lower limits to the range of these species are controlled directly or indirectly by summer warmth. In a climate which is marginal for a montane flora some species would thus tend to be rarer and confined to higher levels than others. Applying this idea to the Climatic Optimum in the Highlands some of the most warmth-sensitive species of the original Late-glacial flora would be eliminated altogether and others would survive only in scattered localities at high levels. The more warmth-tolerant species would remain more widespread and abundant over a greater altitudinal range and between these extremes there would be all degrees of 'relictness'. In the process of becoming relict the actual localities in which a particular species survives evidently depend a good deal on chance. The extent of suitable habitat may be important in this context; for instance, a relict calcicole will have a greater chance of survival in an extensive area of calcareous rocks and soils than in an area with a limited occurrence of suitable substrata. As Patton (1923) pointed out, when conditions for growth of the montane flora become sub-optimal, plant disease may be a potent cause of decline or extinction, giving relict distributions.

When Dahl's temperature classes and distribution maps are compared with the distribution of the same species in Britain, certain discrepancies are found. For instance *Saxifraga stellaris* and *Sedum rosea* ('limiting' temperature in Fennoscandia 25° C) are among the commonest British montane species, whereas *Gentiana nivalis* and *Gnaphalium norvegicum* ('limiting' temperature 28° C) are among the rarest. The considerable differences in oceanicity between Britain and Fennoscandia (perhaps acting in some cases through the effect on snow-cover regime) might account for differences in ecological behaviour of the same species in the two regions.

In the Highlands high altitude relicts include *Luzula arcuata*, *Saxifraga rivularis*, *Carex atrofusca*, *C. rariflora*, *C. lachenalii*, *Gnaphalium norvegicum*, *Cystopteris montana*, *Juncus biglumis*, *Poa flexuosa* and *P. x. jemtlandica*, and these may well be warmth-sensitive species. Examples of montane plants which are widespread both geographically and altitudinally are *Sedum rosea*, *Saxifraga oppositifolia*, *S. hypnoides*, *S. aizoides*, *S. stellaris*, *Silene acaulis*, *Salix herbacea*, *Alchemilla alpina*, *Carex bigelowii* and *Oxyria digyna*, and these may be presumed to be relatively tolerant of summer warmth in Britain. At present it is not possible to separate warmth-sensitive species from those which need prolonged snow-cover, for both groups are confined to high levels. The physiological significance of prolonged snow-cover may differ in various species, and apparent dependence on this factor may be merely coincidental in some.

Another important factor in the distribution of montane plants is the ability of the various species to maintain their populations and to spread both vegetatively and by seed. This depends largely on climate and some of the highly relict species are probably unable to spread by seed under present conditions while others are so reduced in abundance that their seeding potential is too low to allow any increase in the populations. Nearly all the common and many of the local montane species are able to spread by seed and readily colonise any new habitats which are formed by erosion. It is probable that many of the rarest species have been unable to spread downwards since the Climatic Optimum whereas the more abundant ones are those that extended their lower limits as the climate became cooler and colonised favourable habitats which were produced by human activities such as forest and scrub clearance. The present altitudinal limits of some of the rarer species, e.g. *Gnaphalium norvegicum*, therefore may not be a good indication of their actual climatic tolerances.

Special circumstances, such as per-glacial survival, could be invoked to explain the localisation of some relict species such as *Arenaria norvegica* or *Cicerbita alpina*. Nevertheless, plant dispersal often appears to be sufficiently imperfect as to produce an irregular distribution during a period of migration, and the element of chance in the process introduces anomalies which are largely unaccountable.

BIBLIOGRAPHY

ALBRECHT, W. A. (1957). 'Soil fertility and biotic geography.' *Geogr. Rev.*, **47**, 86–105.

ANDERSON, M. L. (1950). *The selection of tree species*. Edinburgh.

BEIJERINCK, W. (1940). *Calluna: a monograph on the Scotch heather*. Amsterdam.

BRAUN-BLANQUET, J. (1932). *Plant sociology* (Trans. Fuller and Conard). New York and London.

BRAUN-BLANQUET, J., SISSINGH, G. and VLIEGER, J. (1939). *Prodromus der Pflanzengesellschaften 6. Klasse der Vaccinio-Piceetea*. Montpellier.

BROCKMANN-JEROSCH, H. (1913). 'Der Einfluss des Klimacharakters auf die Verbreitung der Pflanzen und Pflanzengesellschaften.' *Engler's Bot. Jb.*, **49**, 19–43.

BURGES, A. (1951). 'The ecology of the Cairngorms. III. The *Empetrum-Vaccinium* zone.' *J. Ecol.*, **39**, 271–284.

CLAPHAM, A. R., TUTIN, T. G. and WARBURG, E. F. (1957). *Flora of the British Isles*. Cambridge.

Climatological atlas of the British Isles (1952). Meteorological Office, London.

CRAMPTON, C. B. (1911). *The vegetation of Caithness considered in relation to the geology*. Cambridge.

CRAMPTON, C. B. and MACGREGOR, M. (1913). 'The plant ecology of Ben Armine, Sutherlandshire.' *Scot. geogr. Mag.*, **29**, 169–192, 256–266.

CROMPTON, E. (1958). 'Hill soils and their production potential.' *J. Brit. Grassl. Soc.*, **13**, 229–237.

DAHL, E. (1951). 'On the relation between summer temperature and the distribution of alpine vascular plants in the lowlands of Fennoscandia.' *Oikos*, **3**, 22–52.

DAHL, E. (1956). *Rondane: mountain vegetation in south Norway and its relation to the environment.*' Oslo.

DAMANN, A. W. H. (1957). 'The south-Swedish Calluna-heath and its relation to the Calluneto-Genistetum.' *Bot. Notiser*, **110**, 363.

DARLING, F. F. (1947). *Natural history in the Highlands and Islands*. London.

DARLING, F. F. (1955). *West Highland survey: an essay in human ecology*. Oxford.

DU RIETZ, G. E. (1930). 'Classification and nomenclature of vegetation.' *Svensk bot. Tidskr.*, **24**, 489–503.

DURNO, S. E. and McVEAN, D. N. (1959). 'Forest history of the Beinn Eighe Nature Reserve.' *New Phytol.*, **58**, 228–236.

EVANS, E. PRICE (1932). 'Cader Idris: a study of certain plant communities in south-west Merionethshire.' *J. Ecol.*, **20**, 1–52.

FERREIRA, R. E. C. (1958). A comparative ecological and floristic study of the vegetation of Ben Hope, Ben Loyal, Ben Lui and Glas Maol in relation to the geology. *Unpublished thesis, University of Aberdeen.*

FERREIRA, R. E. C. (1959). 'Scottish mountain vegetation in relation to geology.' *Trans. bot. Soc. Edinb.*, **37**, 229–250.

FRASER, G. K. (1933). 'Studies of certain Scottish moorlands in relation to tree growth.' *Forestry Comm. Bull. no. 15.* London.

GIMINGHAM, C. H. (1949). 'The effects of grazing on the balance between *Erica cinerea* and *Calluna vulgaris* in upland heath, and their morphological responses.' *J. Ecol.*, **37**, 100–119.

GJAEREVOLL, O. (1949). 'Snøleievegetasjonen i Oviksfjellene.' *Acta. phytogeogr. suec.*, *25*.

GJAEREVOLL, O. (1956). *The plant communities of the Scandinavian alpine snow beds*. Trondheim.

GODWIN, H. (1949). 'The spreading of the British flora.' *J. Ecol.*, **37**, 140–147.

GODWIN, H. (1956). *The history of the British flora*. Cambridge.

GREIG-SMITH, P. (1950). 'Evidence from hepatics on the history of the British flora.' *J. Ecol.*, **38**, 320–344.

GREEN, F. H. W. (1959). 'Four years' experience in attempting to standardise measurements of potential evapo-transpiration in the British Isles, and the ecological significance of the results.' *Hannoversch-Münden Symposium*, **1**, 92–100 (*Int. Ass. Sci. Hydrol., Pub. No. 48*).

HANDLEY, W. R. C. (1954). 'Mull and mor formation in relation to forest soils.' *Forestry Comm. Bull. no. 23*, London.

HANSEN, H. M. (1930). *Studies on the vegetation of Iceland*. Copenhagen.

HEDDLE, R. G. and OGG, W. G. (1936). 'Irrigation experiments on a Scottish hill pasture.' *J. Ecol.*, **24**, 220–231.

HOLDGATE, M. W. (1955a). 'The vegetation of some springs and wet flushes on Tarn Moor near Orton, Westmorland.' *J. Ecol.*, **43**, 80–89.

HOLDGATE, M. W. (1955b). 'The vegetation of some British upland fens.' *J. Ecol.*, **43**, 389–403.

HULTEN, E. (1950). *Atlas of the distribution of vascular plants in N.W. Europe*. Stockholm.

INGRAM, M. (1958). 'The ecology of the Cairngorms. IV. The *Juncus* zone: *Juncus trifidus* communities.' *J. Ecol.*, **46**, 707–737.

JEFFERIES, T. A. (1915). 'Ecology of the purple heath grass.' *J. Ecol.*, **3**, 93–101.

JONES, E. W. (1958). 'An annotated list of British hepatics.' *Trans. Brit. bryol. Soc.*, **3**, 353–374.

KNABEN, G. (1950). *Botanical investigations in the middle districts of western Norway*. Bergen.

KRAJINA, V. (1933). 'Die Pflanzengesellschaften des Mlýnica-Tales in den Vysoké Tatry.' 1 Teil. *Beih. bot. Zbl.*, **50**, 774–957.

KUBIENA, W. L. (1953). *The soils of Europe*. Madrid.

LEACH, W. (1930). 'A preliminary account of the vegetation of some non-calcareous British screes.' *J. Ecol.*, **18**, 321–332.

LOWE, J. (1897). *The yew-trees of Great Britain and Ireland*. New York.

MACGILLIVRAY, W. (1855). *The natural history of Deeside and Braemar*. London.

McVEAN, D. N. (1955). 'Notes on the vegetation of Iceland.' *Trans. bot. Soc. Edinb.*, **36**, 320–338.

McVEAN, D. N. (1956). 'Ecology of *Alnus glutinosa* (L.) Gaertn. V. Notes on some British alder populations.' *J. Ecol.*, **44**, 321–330.

McVEAN, D. N. (1958a). 'Snow cover and vegetation in the Scottish Highlands.' *Weather*, **13**, 197–200.

McVEAN, D. N. (1958b). 'Island vegetation of some west Highland fresh-water lochs.' *Trans. bot. Soc. Edinb.*, **37**, 200–208.

MACVICAR, S. M. (1926). *The students' handbook of British hepatics*. Eastbourne.

METCALFE, G. (1950). 'The ecology of the Cairngorms. II. The mountain Callunetum.' *J. Ecol.*, **38**, 46–74.

NICHOLSON, I. A. and ROBERTSON, R. A. (1958). 'Some observations on the ecology of an upland grazing in north-east Scotland, with special reference to Callunetum.' *J. Ecol.*, **46**, 239–270.

NORDHAGEN, R. (1927–8). *Die Vegetation und Flora des Sylenegebeites*. Oslo.

NORDHAGEN, R. (1943). *Sikilsdalen og Norges Fjellbeiter*. Bergen.

OSTENFELD, C. H. (1908). 'The land-vegetation of the Faeroes.' *Botany of the Faeroes*. III. Copenhagen.

OSVALD, H. (1949). 'Notes on the vegetation of British and Irish mosses.' *Acta phytogeogr. suec.*, *26*.

PATTON, D. (1922). 'Variations in the vegetation along the outcrop of the Lawers-Caenlochan Schist.' *Rep. bot. Exch. Cl. Manchr.*, **6**, 797–807.

PATTON, D. (1923). 'The Vegetation of Beinn Laoigh (Ben Lui).' *Rep. bot. Exch. Cl. Manchr.*, **7**, 268–319.

PEARSALL, W. H. (1938). 'The soil complex in relation to plant communities. III. Moorlands and bogs.' *J. Ecol.*, **26**, 298–315.

PEARSALL, W. H. (1941). 'The "mosses" of the Stainmore district.' *J. Ecol.*, **29**, 161–175.

PEARSALL, W. H. (1950). *Mountains and moorlands*. London.

PEARSALL, W. H. (1956). 'Two blanket-bogs in Sutherland.' *J. Ecol.*, **44**, 493–516.

13

Pigott, C. D. (1956). 'The vegetation of Upper Teesdale in the north Pennines.' *J. Ecol.*, **44**, 545–586.

Poore, M. E. D. (1954). 'Phytosociology of the Breadalbane district of Perthshire.' *University of Cambridge thesis*.

Poore, M. E. D. (1955a). 'The use of phytosociological methods in ecological investigations. II. Practical issues involved in an attempt to apply the Braun-Blanquet system.' *J. Ecol.*, **43**, 245–269.

Poore, M. E. D. (1955b). 'The use of phytosociological methods in ecological investigations. III. Practical applications.' *J. Ecol.*, **43**, 606–651.

Poore, M. E. D. and McVean, D. N. (1957). 'A new approach to Scottish mountain vegetation.' *J. Ecol.*, **45**, 401–439.

Praeger, R. L. (1909). *A tourist's flora of the west of Ireland*. Dublin.

Ratcliffe, D. A. (1959). 'The vegetation of the Carneddau, North Wales. I. Grasslands, heaths and bogs.' *J. Ecol.*, **47**, 371–413.

Ratcliffe, D. A. and Walker, D. (1958). 'The Silver Flowe, Galloway, Scotland.' *J. Ecol.*, **46**, 407–445.

Richards, P. W. (1938). 'The bryophyte communities of a Killarney oakwood.' *Ann. bryol.*, Hague, **11**, 108–130.

Richards, P. W. and Wallace, E. C. (1950). 'An annotated list of British mosses.' *Trans. Brit. bryol. Soc.*, **1**, App. 1–31.

Robinson, G. W. (1949). *Soils: their origin, constitution and classification*. London.

Sjörs, H. (1948). 'Myrvegetation i Bergslagen.' *Acta phytogeogr. suec.*, *21*.

Smith, R. (1900). 'Botanical survey of Scotland. II. North Perthshire district.' *Scot. geogr. Mag.*, **16**, 441–467

Smith, W. G. (1912). '*Anthelia*: an arctic-alpine plant association.' *Scot. bot. Rev.*, **1**, 81–89.

Smith, W. G. (1918). 'The distribution of *Nardus stricta* in relation to peat.' *J. Ecol.*, **6**, 1–13.

Spence, D. N. (1957). 'Studies on the vegetation of Shetland. I. The serpentine debris vegetation in Unst.' *J. Ecol.*, **45**, 917–945.

Spence, D. N. (1960). 'Studies on the vegetation of Shetland. III. Scrub in Shetland and in South Uist, Outer Hebrides.' *J. Ecol.*, **48**, 73–95.

Steindorsson, S. (1951). *Skra um Islensk grodurhverfi. (A list of Icelandic plantsociations examined and defined.)* Akureyri.

Steven, H. M. and Carlisle, A. (1959). *The native pinewoods of Scotland*. Edinburgh.

Tamm, O. (1950). *Northern coniferous forest soils*. Oxford.

Tansley, A. G. (1949). *The British Islands and their vegetation*. Cambridge.

Tüxen, R. (1937). 'Die Pflanzengesellschaften Nordwestdeutschlands.' *Mitt. Flor.-Soziolog. Arbeits-Gemeinschaft in Niedersachsen*, Heft 3.

Tveitnes, A. (1945). 'Fjellbeitne i Hordaland.' *Tidsskr. norske Landbr.*, **52**, 47–63, 95–128.

Vestergren, T. (1902). 'Om den olikformiga snöbetäckningens inflytande pa vegetationen i Sarekfjällen.' *Bot. Notiser*, 241–268.

Wace, N. M. and Holdgate, M. W. (1958). 'The vegetation of Tristan da Cunha.' *J. Ecol.*, **46**, 593–620.

Walters, S. M. (1954). 'The distribution maps scheme.' *Proc. bot. Soc. Brit. Is.*, **1**, 121–130.

Warren Wilson, J. (1952). 'Vegetation patterns associated with soil movement on Jan Mayen island.' *J. Ecol.*, **40**, 249–264.

Warren Wilson, J. (1958). 'Dirt on snow patches.' *J. Ecol.*, **46**, 191–198.

Watson, W. (1953). *Census catalogue of British lichens*. London.

Watt, A. S. and Jones, E. W. (1948). 'The ecology of the Cairngorms. I. The environment and the altitudinal zonation of the vegetation.' *J. Ecol.*, **36**, 283–304.

Webb, D. A. (1947). 'The vegetation of Carrowkeel, a limestone hill in north-west Ireland.' *J. Ecol.*, **35**, 105–129.

Wilson, A. (1955). 'The altitudinal range of British plants.' *Northw. Nat. N.S.*, **1**, Supplement.

Yapp, W. B. (1953). 'The high level woodlands of the English Lake District.' *Northw. Nat. N.S.*, **1**, 190–207, 370–383.

FLORISTIC ANALYSES
NOTES ON FLORISTIC TABLES

1. The reference number of each floristic list is divided into an upper line giving the initial of the recorder's name and the year of the record and a lower line giving that recorder's serial number in any year.

2. The map reference is a full eight-figure Ordnance Survey grid reference, northings being given in the upper line and eastings in the lower. A separate list of locality names is provided for the floristic analyses.

3. The altitude of the stand is given in feet without the metric equivalent but the altitudinal range of each nodum is given in metres in the text.

4. Aspect is given in degrees to the nearest cardinal point as a rule but on one or two occasions compass bearings are given correct to one degree.

5. The figure for vegetation cover does not distinguish between plots with bare rock and those with unvegetated soil. This aspect is dealt with in the text.

6. Where the vegetation is divided into layers of different heights the average height of the tallest component has been given.

7. The species are listed in blocks as follows: trees, shrubs and dwarf shrubs; ferns and fern allies; grasses; sedges and all other monocotyledons; dicotyledon forbs; mosses; liverworts; lichens; algae or fungi where these have been recorded. The lists are in alphabetical order within each block. A few species are not considered with the group to which they belong in the strict sense; thus, *Thymus drucei* will be found with the forbs and not the shrubs.

8. The Domin 10-point scale of combined cover and abundance (see p. 6) has been used throughout, with the addition of a plus sign for species present in the same community immediately surrounding the sample plot but not in the plot itself. Where the cover of several species of grasses or mosses has been estimated together the combined number has been italicised and repeated for each of the species concerned.

9. Except in Table 8 the presence of tree species in canopy of woodland plots has not been recorded. Tree seedlings have been recorded as members of the woodland floor community in the usual way.

10. All nodum and facies constants have been printed in heavy type.

11. In general each table consists of one *nodum* or one association, the facies being separated by one blank column, but two closely related noda have often been placed in one table with two blank columns separating them. On the other hand, the facies of one or two associations have been presented in a separate table and cross references given. Isolated lists of vegetation types not studied in detail have been put alongside noda to which they are most closely related.

12. Where it has been necessary to compare two noda closely, as in Table 44, the constancy and the average dominance of the species are given in adjacent columns, constancy being given on a ten-point scale and dominance obtained by adding together all the Domin numbers and dividing by the number of occurrences of the species.

13. Total number of species recorded for each nodum is given in brackets after 'Number of species'; average number per stand and numbers of species in constancy classes V and IV are also given.

Except for *Festuca ovina* agg., aggregate species have not been included in figures for constancy classes V and IV, as more than one segregate, with different ecological requirements, may be involved.   When recorded separately, micro-species of *Alchemilla vulgaris* agg. have, however, been used in this way.

14. In the 'critical' genera *Hieracium, Euphrasia* and *Taraxacum* it has often been impossible to provide a specific name, since immature and non-flowering individuals were so frequently involved. Many of our records are referred merely to the aggregate species *Euphrasia officinalis* and *Taraxacum officinalis. Festuca ovina* and *F. vivipara* have also been estimated in the aggregate.

15. *Sphagnum nemoreum* often includes forms referable to *S. rubellum* and the second has been separated in the Tables only when it was present abundantly and as well-defined forms.

16. *Sphagnum subsecundum* and its varieties have been lumped in the Tables but are distinguished in footnotes.

17. It is not known with certainty if true *Cladonia leucophaea* occurs within the area of the survey. All *C. rangiferina* forms (K+ and K−) have therefore been presented as an aggregate.

18. Throughout the tables and the text the following abbreviated forms have normally been used:

Betula pubescens . . .	B. pubescens ssp. odorata
Juniperus communis . .	J. communis ssp. communis
J. nana	J. communis ssp. nana
Veronica humifusa . . .	V. serpyllifolia ssp. humifusa
Peltidea leucophlebia .	P. aphthosa var. leucophlebia
Trichophorum caespitosum .	T. caespitosum ssp. germanicum
Pohlia glacialis . . .	P. albicans var. glacialis
Hypnum cupressiforme . .	H. cupressiforme var. ericetorum

Table 3: Characteristic Species of the Higher Units of Classification

Classification Unit		Characteristic Species		
Order	Alliance	Exclusive	Selective	Preferential
Vaccinio-Piceetalia Pine and birch forest and related vegetation		Pinus sylvestris Betula pubescens Juniperus communis Quercus spp.	Ptilium crista-castrensis Genista anglica Juniperus nana	Vaccinium vitis-idaea
Caricetalia curvulae Chionophobous oligo-trophic grass, moss and dwarf-shrub montane heaths	Loiseleurieto-Arctostaphylion (Nardeto-Agrostion)	Alectoria nigricans A. ochroleuca Cetraria nivalis Carex caryophyllea Helianthemum chamaecistus* see p. 9	Rhacomitrium lanuginosum Loiseleuria procumbens Cerania vermicularis (strongly)	
Deschampsieto-Myrtilletalia Chionophilous or season-ally wet oligotrophic montane heaths	Phyllodoco-Vaccinion Nardeto-Caricion bigelowii Deschampsio-Anthoxanthion	Phyllodoce caerulea Cetraria hiascens Cladonia delessertii C. alpicola	Vaccinium uliginosum (weakly) Dicranum fuscescens (weakly)	Deschampsia caespitosa (weakly) Rhytidiadelphus squarrosus (weakly)
Salicetalia herbaceae Extreme chionophilous or short growing season montane heaths and meadows	Cassiopeto-Salicion herbaceae Ranunculeto-Oxyrion	Moerckia blyttii Veronica alpina	Dicranum starkei Polytrichum norvegicum Conostomum tetragonum Oligotrichum hercynicum Pleuroclada albescens	
Elyno-Seslerietalia Chionophobous and calci-colous grass and dwarf-shrub montane heaths	Kobresio-Dryadion	Asplenium viride Koeleria gracilis Carex atrata C. rupestris Anthyllus vulneraria Rhytidium rugosum	Dryas octopetala Salix reticulata Veronica fruticans Solorina saccata	Distichium capillaceum Thuidium abietinum Camptothecium lutescens
Adenostyletalia Oligotrophic to eutrophic tall herb and fern meadows or montane willow scrub	Lactucion alpinae	Salix lanata Cryptogramma crispa	Salix lapponum Athyrium alpestre	
Oxycocco-Ledetalia palustris Ombrogenous bogs	Oxycocco-Empetrion hermaphroditi	Betula nana Sphagnum fuscum Oxycoccus microcarpus Omphalia umbellifera	Rubus chamaemorus Eriophorum vaginatum Polytrichum alpestre	
Montio-Cardaminetalia Montane spring communities	Mniobryo-Epilobion hornemanni Cratoneureto-Saxifragion aizoidis	Montia lamprosperma Stellaria alsine Bryum weigelii Splachnum vasculosum	Poa annua Cerastium cerastoides Poa pratensis Cardamine pratensis	Philonotis fontana
Scheuchzerietalia Oligotrophic mires	Leucoscheuzerion	Sphagnum lindbergii	Sphagnum recurvum	Carex curta (weakly) Sphagnum teres
Caricetalia fuscae Mesotrophic to eutrophic mires	Caricion canescentis-fuscae Caricion atrofuscae-saxatilis Schoenion ferruginei	Cinclidium stygium Acrocladium giganteum Camptothecium nitens Mnium pseudopunctatum Sphagnum warnstorfianum S. contortum Acrocladium trifarium Pinguicula lusitanica Potamogeton polygoni-folius Schoenus nigricans Eriophorum latifolium	Carex saxatilis (strongly) C. hostiana	Aneura pinguis Drepanocladus revolvens

Table 4: Pinetum Hylocomieto-Vaccinetum [myrtillosum (1–10); triquetrosum (11–14)]

	1	2	3	4	5	6	7	8	9	10	11	12	13	14
Reference number	MX8	MX9	MX10	MX11	MX12	MX13	MX14	MX15	MX16	M57 026 8896	M57 057 8226	M57 025 8895	MX17	MX18
Map reference	—	—	—	—	—	—	—	—	—	2454	3985	2453	—	—
Altitude (feet)	900	900	900	900	900	1700	1700	50	500	700	750	600	—	—
Aspect (degrees)	—	—	—	—	—	—	—	—	—	—	—	180	—	—
Slope (degrees)	—	—	—	—	—	—	—	—	—	—	—	5	—	—
Cover (per cent)	—	—	—	—	—	—	—	—	—	100	100	100	—	—
Height (centimetres)	—	—	—	—	—	—	—	—	—	10	—	—	—	—
Plot area (square metres)	16	16	16	16	16	16	16	16	16	16	4	16	4	4
Betula pubescens	.	.	.	.	.	.	.	.	.	.	.	1	.	.
Calluna vulgaris	4	3	2	3	1	+	+	3	3	1	1	.	1	2
Empetrum nigrum	5	3	+	+	+	5	4	.	+	2	.	.	.	.
Erica cinerea	.	.	.	+	.	.	.	3	3	2	.	.	.	.
E. tetralix	3	3	2	.	.	.	.	.	.	2	.	.	.	.
Juniperus communis	+	.	.	.	.	.	.	.	.	.	.	.	.	.
Pinus sylvestris	.	.	.	.	.	.	.	.	1	.	.	+	.	.
Sorbus aucuparia	.	.	.	.	.	.	.	2	3	.	2	2	.	.
Vaccinium myrtillus	6	8	6	4	6	7	8	7	7	8	.	2	+	.
V. vitis-idaea	5	4	5	8	5	7	4	3	4	4	.	.	1	+
Blechnum spicant	+	.	.	.	.	.	+	+	.	.	+	.	.	.
Pteridium aquilinum	.	.	.	.	+	.	.	+	2	.	.	.	.	+
Agrostis tenuis	.	.	.	.	1	.	.	.	.	.	.	2	.	.
Deschampsia flexuosa	.	.	3	.	6	2	3	3	4	+	3	5	.	3
Molinia caerulea	.	+	.	.	.	2	.	.	.	.	.	.	.	.
Goodyera repens	2	.	.	3	2	.	.	.	.	.	2	.	1	1
Listera cordata	1	.	.	.	.	.	.	+	.	.	+	.	.	.
Luzula multiflora	.	.	2	1	.	.	.	.	.	.	.	3	.	.
L. pilosa	.	.	.	.	3	.	.	.	.	.	.	3	.	.
Galium hercynicum	.	.	.	.	.	3	.	.	.	.	.	1	.	.
Lathyrus montanus	.	.	.	.	.	+	.	.	.	.	.	.	.	.
Melampyrum pratense	+	1	1	.	3	2	.	+	3	3	2	.	.	1
Oxalis acetosella	.	.	.	.	.	+	.	.	+	.	.	4	.	.
Potentilla erecta	.	.	.	.	.	.	.	.	1	.	.	.	.	.
Trientalis europaea	.	.	.	.	.	.	.	.	.	.	1	.	.	.
Viola riviniana	.	.	.	.	.	+	.	.	.	.	.	.	.	.
Campylopus flexuosus	.	1	+	.	.	3	3	.	2	.	.	.	+	2
Dicranum majus	.	.	.	.	.	.	.	.	.	.	.	3	.	.
D. scoparium	2	1	.	1	.	.	.	2	.	.	3	.	3	1
Hylocomium splendens	5	6	4	6	5	7	6	6	8	5	3	9	8	7
Hypnum cupressiforme	1	.	.	.	.	+	.	.	.	.	2	.	.	.
Leucobryum glaucum	.	+	.	.	.	+	.	.	.	.	.	.	.	.
Plagiothecium undulatum	.	.	.	1	4	.	3	1	.	.	+	2	.	.
Pleurozium schreberi	.	2	2	2	1	3	.	1	4	+	4	2	2	.
Pseudoscleropodium purum	.	.	.	2	.	.	.	.	.	.	3	.	.	.
Ptilium crista-castrensis	+	.	.	2	.	.	4	6	+	.	.	.	.	.
Rhytidiadelphus loreus	2	1	1	.	.	5	4	.	.	.	2	.	3	1
R. triquetrus	.	.	4	+	1	.	.	.	.	.	8	3	3	6
Sphagnum acutifolium agg.	1	2	.	+	.	+	+	3	2	.	.	.	.	.
Thuidium tamariscinum	.	.	.	.	.	.	.	.	+	+	.	.	.	.
Lepidozia reptans	.	.	.	.	.	.	.	.	.	.	.	1	.	.
Lophocolea bidentata	2	.	.	2	+	.	.	.	.	.	1	1	.	.
Lophozia longidens	.	.	.	.	.	.	.	.	.	.	.	.	+	.
Scapania gracilis	.	.	.	.	.	.	.	.	.	.	.	.	+	.
Cladonia deformis	1	.	.	.	.	.	.	.	.	.	.	.	1	1
Number of species (45)	18	14	13	17	18	14	12	17	18	13	15	17	13	11

(Average 14)

Constancy class V 4
  ,,   ,, IV 3

LOCALITIES

1–5, 13, 14. Rothiemurchus, Inverness-shire; 6, 7. Glen Quoich, Aberdeenshire; 8, 9. Beinn Eighe Ross-shire; 10, 11. Amat Wood, Bonar Bridge, Sutherland; 11. Curr Wood, Dulnain Bridge, Inverness-shire.

Table 5: Pinetum Vaccineto-Callunetum

	1	2	3	4	5	6	7	8	9
Reference number	M55 039	M55 040	R36 007	M58 045	M57 027	M58 058	M58 062	58 57	M58 070
Map reference	8652 1999	8645 2006	8645 2004	8312 2225	8898 2463	8075 2899	8078 2984	8075 2930	8042 2883
Altitude (feet)	150	150	150	600	700	850	1300	1000	1300
Aspect (degrees)	325	360	360	360	360	–	–	–	
Slope (degrees)	5	3	5	20	8	0	0	0	0
Cover (per cent)	100	100	100	100	100	100	100	100	100
Height (centimetres)	60	60	65	60	30	–	–	–	–
Plot area (square metres)	16	16	4	8	16	4	4	4	4
Betula pubescens	+	+	.	.	.	.	.	.	.
Calluna vulgaris	6	7	8	7	7	4	5	7	8
Empetrum nigrum	.	3	.	1	2	.	.	+	3
Erica cinerea	.	.	.	+	.	.	.	.	.
E. tetralix	1	3	.	1	.	+	.	.	.
Ilex aquifolium	.	+	.	.	.	.	.	.	.
Pinus silvestris	1	+	.	1	.	.	.	1	.
Sorbus aucuparia	2	1	.	.	1	.	.	.	.
Vaccinium myrtillus	6	5	4	4	6	7	7	5	6
V. vitis idaea	3	3	3	3	3	3	4	6	3
Blechnum spicant	.	.	.	2	1	.	1	.	1
Pteridium aquilinum	1	2	1	2	.	.	2	.	.
Deschampsia flexuosa	2	1	1	3	1	3	3	3	3
Listera cordata	+	.	.	2	.	.	.	1	1
Luzula multiflora	.	.	.	.	.	+	.	.	.
Melampyrum pratense	2	1	.	.	.	.	.	.	.
Oxalis acetosella	.	.	.	.	.	.	1	.	.
Aulacomnium palustre	.	.	.	1	3	.	.	.	2
Dicranum majus	3	3	1	3	2	.	1	.	+
D. scoparium	.	1	1	.	.	2	.	3	.
Hylocomium splendens	3	5	7	4	3	4	8	9	5
H. umbratum	.	.	2	.	.	.	.	.	.
Hypnum cupressiforme	.	.	2	1	.	.	2	1	.
Plagiothecium undulatum	2	2	2	3	2	3	2	+	2
Pleurozium schreberi	.	.	3	2	.	3	2	4	2
Polytrichum commune	.	.	.	.	.	.	+	.	.
P. formosum	.	.	.	.	.	.	.	.	3
Ptilium crista-castrensis	1	2	3	4	+	9	3	4	4
Rhytidiadelphus loreus	3	1	3	.	2	.	4	2	2
Sphagnum girgensohnii	.	+	.	.	5	+	.	.	+
S. nemoreum	7	8	7	.	8	.	2	.	2
S. palustre	+	.	.	.	.	.	.	.	.
S. quinquefarium	7	.	7	.	.	.	2	+	7
S. russowii	.	.	.	.	8	.	.	.	.
Thuidium tamariscinum	3	+	2	.	2	.	.	.	.
Anastrepta orcadensis	.	.	.	3	.	.	.	.	.
Calypogeia trichomanis	.	.	.	3	3	.	2	.	3
Cephalozia bicuspidata	.	.	.	.	3	.	.	.	.
Cephaloziella sp.	.	.	.	3	.	.	.	.	.
Frullania tamarisci	+	.	2	.	.	.	.	.	.
Herberta hutchinsiae	.	+	.	.	.	.	.	.	.
Leptoscyphus taylori	1	.	.	4	.	.	.	.	.
Lophocolea bidentata	.	.	.	1	.	2	.	.	.
Lophozia floerkii	.	.	.	2	3	.	.	.	.
L. obtusa	.	.	.	.	.	.	3	.	.
L. ventricosa	.	.	.	2	.	.	.	3	2
Mastigophora woodsii	+	.	.	.	.	.	.	.	.
Plagiochila asplenioides	.	.	.	.	.	.	2	.	.
Scapania gracilis	.	.	2	.	.	.	.	.	.
Cladonia carneola	.	.	.	.	.	.	1	.	.
C. coccifera	.	.	.	.	.	.	.	2	.
C. cornuta	.	.	.	.	.	.	1	2	.
C. floerkeana	.	.	.	.	.	.	.	1	.
C. furcata	.	.	.	1	.	.	.	.	.
C. gracilis	.	.	.	1	.	.	.	.	.
C. impexa	.	.	.	1	.	.	.	1	.
C. pyxidata	.	+	.	.	.	1	1	.	.
C. rangiferina agg.	.	.	.	.	.	.	.	1	.
C. squamosa	.	.	.	.	.	1	.	2	.
Peltigera horizontalis	.	.	.	.	1	.	.	.	.
Number of species (60)	23	23	19	29	20	15	23	22	20

(Average 22)

Constancy class V 7
     ,,   ,, IV 4

LOCALITIES

1–3. Coille na Glas Leitire, Loch Maree, Ross-shire; 4. Mullardoch, Glen Cannich, Inverness-shire; 5. Amat Wood, Bonar Bridge, Ross-shire; 6. Loch an Eilein, Rothiemurchus, Inverness-shire; 7. Glenmore, Inverness-shire; 8. Iron Bridge, Rothiemurchus, Inverness-shire; 9. Invereshie, Inverness-shire.

Table 6: Birchwoods and related communities—1. Betuletum Oxaleto-Vaccinetum
4. Fern dominated

	1	2	3	4	5	6	7	8	9	10	11	12	13	14	15
Reference number	R57 223	M56 012	R57 001	P55 018	R57 222	M56 031	M56 004	P55 008	R57 137	TE 220	TE 221	P55 010	M56 005	P55 009	P55 007
Map reference	7768 3242	8655 1994	9460 2238	9189 2090	7768 3242	7904 3141	8690 1917	9159 2090	7858 2453	8191 2128	8255 2238	919– 208–	8695 1917	9159 2090	919– 208–
Altitude (feet)	1700	100	100	100	1700	1600	500	250	1500	1250	900	50	100	250	50
Aspect (degrees)	45	45	45	360	45	315	—	45	180	315	125	360	—	45	360
Slope (degrees)	25	5	20	45	25	2	—	30	30	24	13	35	—	40	35
Cover (per cent)	100	100	100	95	100	100	—	—	100	100	100	100	—	100	95
Height (centimetres)	35	10	—	50	20	60	—	—	—	—	—	70	—	—	60
Plot area (square metres)	4	4	4	4	4	16	4	4	4	4	4	4	4	4	4
Betula pubescens				+											
Calluna vulgaris		+	3	4		2									
Corylus avellana				1			1	+							
Empetrum hermaphroditum						1									
Erica cinerea				3					2					1	
Juniperus communis						8									
Lonicera periclymenum				4				4							
Rubus fruticosus agg.												1			1
R. idaeus					2		2								
R. saxatilis							+								
Salix aurita												1			+
Sorbus aucuparia	2	2	2	+	2		1	+	1	2	2	2	+	1	2
Ulmus glabra							1								
Vaccinium myrtillus	9	7	6	5	4	6	3	1	3	4	6		+		
V. vitis-idaea	1				2	5					2				
Athyrium alpestre															
A. filix-foemina												1			1
Blechnum spicant		1	3	3		1	+	5	2	2	2	2	3	4	3
Cystopteris fragilis															
Dryopteris austriaca			4	1											
Hymenophyllum wilsonii			2					+							
Lycopodium annotinum								1							
Pteridium aquilinum		+	+	5					4	2		3		5	3
Thelypteris dryopteris	2							3						+	
T. oreopteris								1				9		3	8
T. phegopteris															1
Agrostis canina			+		2										
A. stolonifera											2				
A. tenuis		3			4	3	1	2	6	3			4	3	
Anthoxanthum odoratum		1	2		3	4		6	4	3	3	7	5	5	4
Deschampsia caespitosa							5					3		1	2
D. flexuosa	3	4	5	3	3	3	2	2		4	5			2	1
Festuca ovina agg.										4					
Holcus lanatus		2										2	4		4
H. mollis											2				
Nardus stricta															
Poa pratensis															
Carex binervis															
C. pilulifera															
C. sylvatica				+								1			2
Endymion non-scriptus		+		1				2					2	2	2
Luzula campestris															
L. multiflora			+						1	2					
L. pilosa						3									
L. sylvatica	3		5		9						1				
Alchemilla alpina						+									
Anemone nemorosa						3						1	1	4	2
Angelica sylvestris															
Armeria maritima															
Campanula rotundifolia									3						
Cardamine hirsuta															
Cerastium vulgatum															1
Circaea intermedia															
Cirsium heterophyllum															
C. palustre															
Conopodium majus								2				2	3	2	
Digitalis purpurea												1			+
Euphrasia scotica															
Euphrasia sp.									2						
Filipendula ulmaria															
Fragaria vesca							1								
Galium hercynicum	1	4	+	1	3	3		2	4	3	2	2	2	2	2
Geranium robertianum															
G. sylvaticum															
Geum rivale								+							
Hieracium sp.															

(1–11); 2. Betula-herb nodum (12–20); 3. Vaccinium-Luzula treeless facies (21–26); treeless facies (27–30)

16	17	18	19	20	21	22	23	24	25	26	27	28	29	30	
R57	M58	R58	TE	TE	R57	R57	R58	R58	M57	R56	M56	M57	R57	M58	
024	004	004	206	210	213	260	039	065	033	078	139	050	256	055	Reference number
9432	9553	9556	8216	8221	7761	7749	7807	8481	7536	8519	7973	7654	7745	8433	
2272	2575	2592	2192	2206	3250	3271	3190	2077	2164	1923	2908	2174	3291	1845	Map reference
150	150	150	1600	1400	2000	2050	2700	2000	1900	2200	2500	1000	1000	150	Altitude (feet)
45	45	270	360	360	45	315	360	270	360	360	360	270	45	–	Aspect (degrees)
18	5	15	35	24	40	35	38	35	45	30	35	35	33	0	Slope (degrees)
100	100	100	95	95	100	100	100	100	100	100	100	100	100	100	Cover (per cent)
–	–	–	–	–	70	20	–	–	15	50	90	30	–	150	Height (centimetres)
4	16	4	4	4	4	4	4	4	4	4	4	4	4	4	Plot area (square metres)
·	·	·	1	1	·	2	·	·	·	·	·	·	·	·	Betula pubescens
·	·	·	·	·	·	·	·	·	·	·	·	·	·	·	Calluna vulgaris
·	·	·	·	·	·	·	·	·	·	·	·	·	·	·	Corylus avellana
·	·	·	·	·	·	3	·	·	·	1	·	·	·	·	Empetrum hermaphroditum
·	·	·	·	·	·	·	·	·	·	·	·	·	·	·	Erica cinerea
·	·	·	·	·	·	·	·	·	·	·	·	·	·	·	Juniperus communis
·	·	·	·	·	·	·	·	·	·	·	·	·	·	·	Lonicera periclymenum
·	·	·	+	·	·	·	·	·	·	·	·	·	·	·	Rubus fruticosus agg.
·	·	·	·	·	·	·	·	·	·	·	·	·	·	·	R. idaeus
·	·	·	·	·	·	·	1	·	·	·	·	·	·	·	R. saxatilis
·	·	·	·	·	·	·	·	·	·	·	·	·	·	·	Salix aurita
2	·	1	·	2	·	·	·	·	·	·	·	·	·	·	**Sorbus aucuparia**
·	·	·	·	·	·	·	·	·	·	·	·	·	·	·	Ulmus glabra
·	·	·	·	1	4	5	6	7	8	5	4	·	·	·	**Vaccinium myrtillus**
·	·	·	·	·	3	·	·	·	·	2	·	·	·	·	V. vitis-idaea
·	·	·	·	·	3	·	·	·	·	·	2	·	·	·	Athyrium alpestre
2	+	2	3	3	2	3	2	2	1	2	4	3	2	·	A. filix-foemina
·	·	1	·	·	·	·	·	·	·	·	·	·	·	·	**Blechnum spicant**
1	·	·	·	·	·	·	·	·	·	·	·	·	·	·	Cystopteris fragilis
·	·	·	·	·	·	·	1	3	·	4	2	·	·	·	Dryopteris austriaca
·	·	·	·	·	·	·	·	·	·	·	·	·	·	·	Hymenophyllum wilsonii
·	·	·	·	·	·	·	·	·	·	·	·	·	·	·	Lycopodium annotinum
·	5	1	·	2	·	·	·	·	·	·	·	·	3	9	Pteridium aquilinum
2	·	·	·	·	·	2	·	3	·	·	·	·	·	·	Thelypteris dryopteris
·	·	·	·	·	3	·	2	·	2	·	7	9	8	·	T. oreopteris
·	·	·	·	·	3	·	·	4	·	·	·	·	·	·	T. phegopteris
3	5	4	4	4	3	·	·	·	+	2	·	3	2	·	Agrostis canina
·	·	·	·	·	·	·	·	·	·	·	·	·	·	·	A. stolonifera
7	1	5	·	·	5	4	·	2	·	·	·	3	8	3	A. tenuis
5	5	5	2	3	2	2	3	3	·	·	·	·	2	·	**Anthoxanthum odoratum**
·	4	·	·	·	5	3	5	2	·	4	1	·	·	·	Deschampsia caespitosa
4	·	·	·	1	3	4	4	4	3	6	·	·	·	·	**D. flexuosa**
·	·	2	1	4	·	4	3	3	·	3	·	2	4	·	Festuca ovina agg.
3	·	·	·	·	·	·	·	·	·	·	·	3	·	1	Holcus lanatus
·	·	·	1	3	·	·	·	·	·	·	·	·	·	·	H. mollis
·	·	·	·	·	·	4	·	·	·	·	·	·	2	·	Nardus stricta
·	·	2	·	·	·	·	·	·	·	·	·	·	·	·	Poa pratensis
·	·	·	2	·	·	·	·	·	·	·	·	·	·	·	Carex binervis
·	·	·	·	·	·	·	·	·	·	·	·	1	·	·	C. pilulifera
·	·	·	·	·	·	·	·	·	·	·	·	·	·	·	C. sylvatica
3	4	4	·	·	·	·	·	·	·	·	·	·	·	·	Endymion non-scriptus
1	·	·	·	·	·	·	·	·	·	·	·	·	·	·	Luzula campestris
·	·	1	·	·	·	·	·	·	·	·	·	·	·	·	L. multiflora
·	·	·	·	·	·	·	·	·	·	·	·	·	1	·	L. pilosa
4	·	·	·	·	6	8	6	6	3	6	4	·	·	·	**L. sylvatica**
·	·	·	·	·	3	3	3	2	·	·	·	·	·	·	Alchemilla alpina
·	+	·	2	·	1	·	·	·	·	·	·	·	·	·	Anemone nemorosa
·	·	·	·	·	1	·	·	·	·	·	·	·	·	·	Angelica sylvestris
·	·	·	·	·	·	·	·	·	·	2	·	·	·	·	Armeria maritima
·	·	·	2	2	·	·	·	·	·	·	·	1	·	·	Campanula rotundifolia
·	·	·	·	·	·	·	·	·	·	·	·	·	·	2	Cardamine hirsuta
·	·	·	·	·	·	·	·	·	·	·	·	2	·	·	Cerastium vulgatum
·	·	·	·	·	·	·	·	·	·	·	·	·	·	5	Circaea intermedia
·	·	·	·	·	·	·	·	·	·	·	2	·	·	·	Cirsium heterophyllum
·	·	·	·	·	·	·	·	·	·	·	1	·	·	·	C. palustre
4	2	·	·	·	·	·	·	·	·	·	·	·	·	·	Conopodium majus
·	·	·	·	·	·	·	·	·	·	·	·	·	·	·	Digitalis purpurea
·	·	·	·	·	·	·	·	2	·	·	·	·	·	·	Euphrasia scotica
·	2	·	·	·	·	·	·	·	·	·	·	·	·	·	Euphrasia sp.
·	·	·	·	·	·	·	·	·	·	·	·	·	·	·	Filipendula ulmaria
·	·	·	·	·	·	·	·	·	·	·	·	·	·	·	Fragaria vesca
3	·	1	3	3	4	4	4	3	·	4	3	3	5	3	**Galium hercynicum**
·	·	·	·	·	·	·	·	·	·	·	·	2	·	·	Geranium robertianum
·	·	·	2	·	·	·	·	·	·	·	·	·	·	·	G. sylvaticum
·	·	·	·	·	·	·	·	·	·	·	·	·	·	·	Geum rivale
·	·	·	1	1	·	·	·	·	·	·	·	·	·	·	Hieracium sp.

Table 6

	1	2	3	4	5	6	7	8	9	10	11	12	13	14	15
Hypericum pulchrum	.	.	.	.	.	.	.	.	2	.	.	1	.	.	1
Lathyrus montanus	.	.	.	.	.	1	.	.	1	.	.	.	.	.	.
Lotus corniculatus	.	.	.	.	.	.	.	.	2	.	.	.	.	.	.
Lysimachia nemorum	.	.	.	.	.	.	.	.	.	.	.	1	3	.	.
Melampyrum pratense	.	+	.	1	2	2	.	.	.	1	.	.	.	.	.
Oxalis acetosella	1	3	3	3	3	2	2	2	2	3	3	3	3	2	3
Plantago lanceolata	.	.	.	.	.	.	.	.	3	.	.	.	.	.	.
Polygala serpyllifolia	.	.	.	.	.	.	.	.	.	.	.	.	.	.	.
Polygonum viviparum	.	.	.	.	.	2	.	.	.	.	.	.	.	.	.
Potentilla erecta	.	3	3	3	.	2	1	2	4	1	1	2	3	2	3
Primula vulgaris	.	.	.	.	.	.	.	.	2	3	.	2	3	2	2
Pyrola media	.	.	.	.	.	+	.	.	.	.	.	.	.	.	.
Prunella vulgaris	.	.	.	.	.	.	.	.	2	2	.	2	2	1	1
Ranunculus acris	.	.	.	.	.	.	.	.	.	.	.	.	2	.	.
R. ficaria	.	.	.	.	.	.	.	.	2	.	.	3	.	1	1
R. repens	.	.	.	.	.	.	.	.	.	.	.	1	.	.	1
Rhinanthus minor	.	.	.	.	.	.	.	.	.	.	.	.	.	.	.
Rumex acetosa	.	.	.	.	.	.	.	.	.	.	.	1	.	1	+
Sanicula europaea	.	.	.	.	.	3	.	.	.	.	.	.	.	.	.
Solidago virgaurea	.	.	.	.	.	.	2	.	.	.	.	.	.	.	.
Succisa pratensis	.	2	.	.	.	4	.	.	3	.	.	.	3	.	.
Taraxacum officinalis agg.	.	.	.	.	.	.	.	.	.	.	.	.	.	.	.
Teucrium scorodonia	.	.	.	.	.	.	4	.	.	.	.	.	.	.	.
Thymus drucei	.	.	.	.	.	.	.	.	2	.	.	.	.	.	.
Trientalis europaea	.	.	.	.	.	2	.	.	.	.	.	.	.	.	.
Veronica chamaedrys	.	.	.	.	.	+	.	.	.	.	.	.	.	.	.
V. officinalis	.	.	.	.	.	4	.	4	4	.	.	.	.	.	.
V. riviniana	.	.	3	.	.	+	4	2	4	.	.	2	4	2	2
Atrichum undulatum	.	.	.	.	.	.	.	.	.	.	.	.	.	.	1
Brachythecium rutabulum	.	.	.	.	.	2	.	.	.	.	.	2	.	.	1
Breutelia chrysocoma	.	.	.	1	.	.	.	.	.	.	.	2	.	1	+
Dicranum fuscescens	.	.	.	.	.	.	.	.	.	1	3	.	.	.	.
D. majus	4	2	3	2	.	.	1	3	.	2	3	2	2	3	3
D. scoparium	3	.	+	.	.	3	.	3	.	.	.	.	.	.	.
Eurhynchium praelongum	1	.	.	.	.	.	.	.	.	.	.	1	.	.	2
E. striatum	.	.	.	.	.	.	.	2	.	.	.	.	.	2	1
Hookeria lucens	.	.	.	.	.	.	.	.	.	.	.	2	.	.	2
Hylocomium brevirostre	.	.	.	.	.	.	5	.	.	.	.	.	4	.	.
H. splendens	6	3	4	5	3	3	4	.	7	6	6	7	.	1	1
H. umbratum	.	4	3	.	.	.	.	.	.	.	.	.	5	.	.
Hypnum callichroum	.	.	.	.	.	.	.	.	.	.	.	.	.	.	.
H. cupressiforme	1	.	3	.	.	.	.	.	.	.	2	2	3	+	2
Isothecium myosuroides	.	.	+	.	.	.	.	.	.	.	.	.	.	.	.
Mnium hornum	1	.	2	.	.	.	.	.	.	2	2	2	1	1	1
M. punctatum	.	.	.	.	.	.	.	.	.	.	.	.	.	.	.
M. undulatum	.	.	.	.	.	.	.	.	.	.	.	2	2	.	2
Plagiothecium denticulatum	.	.	.	.	.	.	.	.	.	.	.	.	.	.	.
P. undulatum	3	1	3	3	.	.	.	1	.	1	1	2	.	2	2
Pleurozium schreberi	4	2	3	2	1	1	.	.	4	3	4	1	.	.	1
Polytrichum alpinum	.	.	.	.	.	.	.	.	.	.	.	.	.	.	.
P. commune	.	3	.	.	.	2	.	.	.	.	.	.	.	.	.
P. formosum	3	2	2	.	2	.	.	1	3	3	4	2	.	1	2
Pseudoscleropodium purum	.	.	2	.	.	.	.	2	.	.	.	2	.	.	1
Ptilium crista-castrensis	4	2	3	.	.	6	.	.	.	.	.	.	.	.	.
Rhacomitrium lanuginosum	.	.	.	.	.	.	.	.	.	.	.	.	.	.	.
Rhytidiadelphus loreus	.	5	3	1	2	2	.	.	3	.	.	.	.	.	.
R. squarrosus	.	.	.	.	3	.	.	1	4	4	3	2	.	2	1
R. triquetrus	.	.	3	.	.	2	.	1	4	.	.	.	2	.	2
Sphagnum girgensohnii	.	.	.	.	.	.	.	.	.	.	.	.	.	.	.
S. nemoreum	.	.	3	.	.	.	.	.	.	1	.	.	.	.	.
S. palustre	.	.	.	6	.	.	.	.	.	.	.	2	.	.	.
S. quinquefarium	.	3	.	6	.	.	.	.	.	.	.	.	2	.	.
Thuidium tamariscinum	3	4	5	5	.	3	6	8	.	2	6	7	4	7	10
Alicularia scalaris	.	.	.	.	.	.	.	.	.	.	.	.	.	.	.
Anastrepta orcadensis	.	1	.	.	.	.	.	.	.	.	.	.	.	.	.
Aplozia sp.	.	.	.	.	.	.	.	.	.	.	.	2	.	.	+
Bazzania tricrenata	.	.	2	.	.	1	.	.	.	.	.	.	.	.	.
Calypogeia trichomanis	.	.	2	.	.	.	.	.	.	.	.	.	.	1	.
Chiloscyphus polyanthus	.	.	3	.	.	.	.	.	.	.	.	.	.	.	.
Diplophyllum albicans	.	.	.	.	.	.	.	.	.	.	.	.	.	.	.
Lepidozia reptans	.	.	2	.	.	.	.	.	.	.	.	.	.	.	.
L. trichoclados	.	.	1	.	.	.	.	.	.	.	.	.	.	.	.
Lophocolea bidentata	.	.	3	.	.	.	.	.	.	.	.	.	.	.	.
Lophozia barbata	.	.	.	.	.	.	.	.	.	.	.	.	.	.	.
L. floerkii	+	.	.	.	.	.	.	.	.	.	.	.	.	.	.
L. lycopodioides	.	.	.	.	.	.	.	.	.	.	.	.	.	.	.
L. quinquedentata	.	.	.	.	.	.	.	.	.	.	.	.	.	.	.
Lophozia sp.	.	.	.	2	.	.	.	+	.	.	.	2	.	.	2
L. ventricosa	.	1	.	.	.	.	.	.	.	.	.	.	.	.	.
Pellia epiphylla	.	.	.	.	.	.	.	.	.	.	.	2	.	.	2
Plagiochila asplenioides	.	2	.	.	.	.	.	.	.	.	.	2	.	1	2
P. spinulosa	.	.	.	.	.	.	1	.	.	.	.	.	.	.	.
Pleurozia purpurea	.	.	.	.	.	.	.	.	.	.	.	.	.	.	.
Ptilidium ciliare	.	.	.	.	.	.	.	.	.	.	.	.	.	.	.
Saccogyna viticulosa	.	.	2	.	.	.	.	.	.	.	.	.	.	.	.
Scapania gracilis	.	.	.	.	.	.	.	.	.	.	.	.	.	.	.
S. nimbosa	.	.	.	.	.	.	.	.	.	.	.	.	.	.	.
S. ornithopodioides	.	.	.	.	.	.	.	.	.	.	.	.	.	.	.

(*continued*)

Group 1

16	17	18	19	20	21	22	23	24	25	26	27	28	29	30	Species
·	·	·	·	·	·	·	·	·	·	·	·	·	·	·	Hypericum pulchrum
·	·	·	·	·	·	·	·	·	·	·	·	·	·	·	Lathyrus montanus
·	·	·	·	·	·	·	·	·	·	·	·	·	·	·	Lotus corniculatus
·	3	3	1	1	·	·	·	·	·	·	·	1	·	·	Lysimachia nemorum
·	·	·	·	·	·	·	·	·	3	·	·	·	·	·	Melampyrum pratense
3	4	4	3	3	3	3	3	2	·	2	2	3	3	6	**Oxalis acetosella**
·	·	·	1	3	·	·	·	·	·	·	·	1	·	·	Plantago lanceolata
·	·	·	·	2	·	·	·	·	·	·	·	·	·	·	Polygala serpyllifolia
·	·	·	·	·	·	·	·	·	·	·	·	·	·	·	Polygonum viviparum
4	2	3	·	3	·	·	·	·	2	3	1	2	3	1	**Potentilla erecta**
·	4	3	·	·	·	·	·	·	·	·	·	1	·	·	Primula vulgaris
·	·	·	·	·	·	·	·	·	·	·	·	·	·	·	Pyrola media
·	·	·	2	·	·	·	·	·	·	·	·	2	·	·	Prunella vulgaris
·	·	2	3	2	2	·	·	·	·	·	·	·	·	4	Ranunculus acris
·	1	·	·	·	·	·	·	·	·	·	·	·	·	·	R. ficaria
·	2	·	·	·	·	·	·	·	·	·	·	·	·	·	R. repens
·	·	·	·	·	·	·	·	1	·	·	·	·	·	·	Rhinanthus minor
·	·	·	·	·	3	·	1	3	·	4	3	·	3	·	Rumex acetosa
·	·	·	·	·	·	·	·	·	·	·	·	·	·	·	Sanicula europaea
·	·	·	·	·	·	·	1	2	5	·	·	·	·	·	Solidago virgaurea
·	·	·	·	·	·	·	·	·	2	3	·	2	·	·	Succisa pratensis
·	·	·	1	·	·	·	·	·	·	·	·	·	·	·	Taraxacum officinalis agg.
·	·	·	·	·	·	·	·	·	·	·	·	3	·	·	Teucrium scorodonia
·	·	·	·	·	·	·	·	·	·	·	·	·	·	·	Thymus drucei
·	·	·	·	·	·	·	·	·	·	·	·	·	·	·	Trientalis europaea
·	·	2	·	·	·	·	·	·	·	·	·	·	·	·	Veronica chamaedrys
·	·	2	1	1	1	·	·	·	·	·	·	2	·	·	V. officinalis
2	3	4	1	5	3	+	·	·	+	·	2	3	3	3	**V. riviniana**

Group 2

16	17	18	19	20	21	22	23	24	25	26	27	28	29	30	Species
·	·	·	1	·	·	·	·	·	·	·	·	·	·	·	Atrichum undulatum
·	·	·	·	·	·	·	·	·	·	·	·	·	·	·	Brachythecium rutabulum
·	·	·	·	·	·	·	1	·	·	·	·	1	·	·	Breutelia chrysocoma
·	·	·	·	·	·	·	·	·	·	·	·	·	·	·	Dicranum fuscescens
1	·	2	·	·	3	3	3	3	1	2	4	·	2	·	**D. majus**
·	·	·	1	·	·	3	·	1	·	3	·	1	2	·	D. scoparium
·	·	·	·	·	·	·	·	·	·	·	7	·	·	3	Eurhynchium praelongum
·	·	·	·	·	·	·	·	·	·	·	·	·	·	·	E. striatum
·	·	·	·	·	·	·	·	·	·	·	·	·	·	·	Hookeria lucens
·	·	·	·	·	·	·	·	·	·	·	·	·	·	·	Hylocomium brevirostre
3	3	3	4	4	4	4	4	4	2	6	2	3	3	4	**H. splendens**
4	·	·	·	·	·	·	·	·	·	·	·	·	·	·	H. umbratum
·	·	·	·	·	·	·	1	·	·	·	2	·	·	·	Hypnum callichroum
·	·	·	1	·	2	2	·	·	2	3	·	·	1	·	H. cupressiforme
·	·	·	·	·	·	·	·	·	·	·	·	·	·	·	Isothecium myosuroides
·	1	1	·	·	3	·	·	2	·	2	·	2	2	·	Mnium hornum
·	·	·	·	·	·	·	·	·	·	3	·	·	·	·	M. punctatum
3	·	2	·	·	·	·	·	·	·	·	·	·	·	·	M. undulatum
·	·	·	·	·	2	·	·	·	·	·	2	·	2	·	Plagiothecium denticulatum
1	·	·	·	·	2	2	3	5	2	2	3	·	·	·	**P. undulatum**
2	·	·	·	·	2	3	3	·	1	4	·	·	3	·	**Pleurozium schreberi**
·	·	·	·	·	·	·	·	·	·	·	1	·	·	·	Polytrichum alpinum
·	·	·	3	3	2	4	3	2	·	3	·	·	·	·	P. commune
2	·	2	3	3	·	·	·	·	·	·	·	·	·	·	P. formosum
·	4	4	·	·	·	·	·	·	·	·	·	1	·	3	Pseudoscleropodium purum
·	·	·	·	·	3	·	·	·	·	1	·	·	·	·	Ptilium crista-castrensis
·	·	·	·	·	·	·	·	2	·	·	·	·	·	·	Rhacomitrium lanuginosum
3	·	1	·	·	2	2	4	5	4	5	4	3	·	3	**Rhytidiadelphus loreus**
3	·	3	1	2	2	3	·	·	·	2	·	·	3	3	R. squarrosus
·	4	3	·	·	·	·	·	·	·	·	·	·	·	·	R. triquetrus
·	·	·	·	·	·	2	·	·	·	1	·	·	·	·	Sphagnum girgensohnii
·	·	·	·	·	2	·	3	2	7	·	·	·	·	·	S. nemoreum
·	·	·	·	·	·	·	·	·	·	·	·	·	·	·	S. palustre
·	·	·	·	·	·	·	·	·	·	3	·	·	·	·	S. quinquefarium
6	5	7	·	·	·	·	3	·	3	4	·	5	·	8	**Thuidium tamariscinum**

Group 3

16	17	18	19	20	21	22	23	24	25	26	27	28	29	30	Species
·	·	·	·	·	·	·	·	·	·	·	+	·	·	·	Alicularia scalaris
·	·	·	·	·	·	·	·	1	3	·	·	·	·	·	Anastrepta orcadensis
·	·	·	·	·	·	·	1	·	·	·	·	·	·	·	Aplozia sp.
·	·	·	·	·	·	·	·	·	3	·	·	·	·	·	Bazzania tricrenata
·	·	·	1	·	·	·	1	·	·	·	·	·	·	·	Calypogeia trichomanis
·	·	2	·	·	1	·	·	·	·	·	·	·	·	·	Chiloscyphus polyanthus
·	·	·	4	·	1	·	·	·	·	·	1	2	·	·	Diplophyllum albicans
·	·	·	·	·	·	·	·	·	·	·	·	·	·	·	Lepidozia reptans
·	·	·	·	·	·	·	·	·	·	·	·	·	·	·	L. trichoclados
2	1	·	·	·	2	·	·	·	3	·	·	·	·	4	Lophocolea bidentata
·	·	·	·	·	·	·	·	·	·	·	·	·	1	·	Lophozia barbata
·	·	·	·	·	·	·	·	·	·	·	·	·	·	·	L. floerkii
·	·	·	·	·	·	1	·	·	·	·	3	·	·	·	L. lycopodioides
·	·	·	·	·	·	·	1	·	·	·	·	·	·	·	L. quinquedentata
·	·	·	·	·	·	·	·	1	·	·	·	·	·	·	Lophozia sp.
·	·	·	·	2	·	·	·	·	·	·	·	·	·	·	L. ventricosa
·	·	·	·	·	·	·	·	·	·	·	·	·	·	·	Pellia epiphylla
·	2	·	·	·	·	·	·	·	·	·	·	·	·	·	Plagiochila asplenioides
·	·	·	·	·	·	·	·	·	·	·	·	·	·	·	P. spinulosa
·	·	·	·	·	·	·	·	2	·	·	·	·	·	·	Pleurozia purpurea
·	·	·	·	·	·	2	·	·	·	·	·	·	1	·	Ptilidium ciliare
·	·	·	·	·	·	·	·	·	·	·	·	·	·	·	Saccogyna viticulosa
·	·	·	·	·	·	·	·	2	·	·	·	·	·	·	Scapania gracilis
·	·	·	·	·	·	·	·	2	·	·	·	·	·	·	S. nimbosa
·	·	·	·	·	·	·	·	2	·	·	·	·	·	·	S. ornithopodioides

Table 6

	1	2	3	4	5	6	7	8	9	10	11	12	13	14	15
Cladonia coccifera	·	·	·	·	·	·	·	·	·	·	·	·	·	·	·
C. gracilis	·	·	·	·	·	·	·	·	·	·	·	·	·	·	·
C. impexa	·	·	·	·	·	·	·	·	·	·	·	·	·	·	·
C. macilenta	·	·	·	·	·	·	·	·	·	1	·	·	·	·	·
C. rangiferina agg.	·	·	·	·	·	·	·	·	·	·	·	·	·	·	·
C. squamosa	·	·	·	·	·	·	·	·	·	·	·	·	·	·	·
C. sylvatica	·	·	·	·	·	·	·	·	·	·	·	·	·	·	·
Peltigera canina	·	·	·	·	·	·	·	·	·	·	·	·	·	·	·
Number of species (162)	22	26	39	27	18	31	25	31	31	23	24	43	30	31	48

(Average 28)

Constancy class V   10
   ,,   ,,   IV   6

LOCALITIES

1. Glen Doll, Angus; 2. Beinn Eighe, Ross-shire; 3. Laxford Bridge, Sutherland; 4. Inverpolly, Sutherland; 5. Glen Doll, Angus; 6. Braemar, Aberdeenshire; 7. Strath Lungard, Ross-shire; 8. Inverpolly, Sutherland; 9. Creag Meagaidh, Inverness-shire; 10,11. Glen Affric, Inverness-shire; 12. Inverpolly, Sutherland; 13. Strath Lungard, Ross-shire; 14,15. Inverpolly, Sutherland; 16. Leitir an Staca, Sutherland; 17,18. Tongue,

(continued)

16	17	18	19	20	21	22	23	24	25	26	27	28	29	30	
.	.	.	.	.	.	.	.	.	.	.	2	.	.	.	Cladonia coccifera
.	.	.	.	.	.	.	.	.	1	.	.	1	.	.	C. gracilis
.	.	.	.	.	.	.	.	.	1	.	.	.	.	.	C. impexa
.	.	.	.	.	.	.	.	.	.	.	.	.	.	.	C. macilenta
.	.	.	.	.	.	.	.	.	1	.	.	.	.	.	C. rangiferina agg.
.	.	.	.	.	.	.	.	.	.	.	1	.	.	.	C. squamosa
.	.	.	.	.	.	.	.	.	1	.	.	.	.	.	C. sylvatica
.	.	.	.	.	.	.	.	.	.	.	.	.	.	+	Peltigera canina
28	24	27	28	25	38	30	25	26	34	36	25	29	27	18	Number of species (162)

(Average 33)   (Average 32)   (Average 25)

Constancy class V   7
    „   „   IV   10

Sutherland; 19,20. Glen Affric, Inverness-shire; 21. Glen Doll, Angus; 22. Glen Clova, Angus; 23. Corrie Kander, Aberdeenshire; 24. Achnashellach, Ross-shire; 25. Bidean nam Bian, Argyllshire 26. Liathach, Ross-shire; 27. Liathach, Ross-shire; 28. Glen Nevis, Inverness-shire, 29. Glen Clova, Angus; 30. Kishorn, Ross-shire.

Table 7: Moss communities of birchwoods—1. 'Immature' type (1–5); 2. 'Mature' type (6–10)

	1	2	3	4	5	6	7	8	9	10
Map reference			943 227					943 227		
Altitude (feet)			250–500					250–500		
Aspect (degrees)			45					45		
Slope (degrees)			>40					<30		
Cover (per cent)			100					100		
Plot area (square metres)			1					1		
Betula pubescens						1				
Calluna vulgaris								1		
Sorbus aucuparia			2				1	1	1	2
Vaccinium myrtillus					3					4
Blechnum spicant						2				
Hymenophyllum wilsonii*	5	6	4	7	4			3		
Agrostis canina									2	
A. tenuis									3	
Anthoxanthum odoratum						4	4	3	4	3
Deschampsia flexuosa	3	1	4			4	3	4	4	3
Festuca vivipara								2		
Luzula sylvatica										3
Galium hercynicum	3					3	3	2	3	4
Oxalis acetosella	2		3	3		3	2	4	3	2
Potentilla erecta						4		2		3
Rumex acetosa									2	
Dicranodontium longirostre*					4					
Dicranum majus		2	3		3	3	1			2
D. scoparium		3	2	2	3					
Isothecium myosuroides	2	4		7	4					
Hylocomium splendens	3	2	6			3	3	4	2	3
H. umbratum*	2		3		3	8	4	4	2	2
Hypnum callichroum*									4	
H. cupressiforme			3	2	4	1		2	3	
Mnium hornum						1		4		
Plagiothecium undulatum	1	1						4		
Pleurozium schreberi			3	2	3	3	1	4	3	3
Polytrichum formosum						3		3		
Ptilium crista-castrensis										5
Rhacomitrium lanuginosum						3		2		
Rhytidiadelphus loreus	3	3	6	4	4	3	4	4	7	8
Sphagnum nemoreum	6					5		4		
Thuidium tamariscinum	5	4	4		5	4	9	4	7	3
Anastrepta orcadensis*	5	3	3		3	3	2	4	2	2
Bazzania tricrenata*	4	4	2							
Calypogeia trichomanis								1		
Diplophyllum albicans	3	3			3			3		
Frullania tamarisci		2						2		
Lepidozia reptans		2								
Lophocolea bidentata		2		2						
Lophozia quinquedentata			2		3	2				
Plagiochila asplenioides			1	3						
P. spinulosa*					4					
Saccogyna viticulosa*			3			3		3	2	
Scapania gracilis*	2	6	3	3	4		3	3	2	
Peltigera canina	2							3		
Number of species	16	16	18	10	16	21	13	27	18	16

(Average 15)   (Average 19)

Number of species (30)   Number of species (38)

* Oceanic species.

LOCALITY. 1–10. Loch Stack, Sutherland.

Table 8: Fraxinus-Brachypodium provisional nodum (1–4); Hazel scrub (5)

	1 MX 11	2 MX 12	3 MX 13	4 MX 14	5 MX 15
Reference number	11	12	13	14	15
Map reference	–	–	–	–	–
Altitude (feet)	–	–	–	–	–
Aspect (degrees)	–	–	–	–	–
Slope (degrees)	–	–	–	–	–
Cover (per cent)	–	–	–	–	–
Plot area (square metres)	4	4	4	4	4
Betula pubescens	×	×	×	×	.
Corylus avellana	×	×	×	×	+
Fraxinus excelsior	×	×	×	×1	.
Populus tremula	.	.	.	.	1
Prunus padus	+	.	.	.	1
P. spinosa	.	.	.	.	1
Quercus robur	+	.	.	.	.
Rosa canina agg.	.	.	.	.	1
Rubus idaeus	.	.	.	.	1
R. saxatilis	.	.	.	.	+
Salix capraea	.	.	.	×	.
Sorbus aucuparia	+	×	×	×	×
Ulmus glabra	.	.	.	×	.
Asplenium viride	+	.	.	.	.
Athyrium filix-foemina	.	.	.	.	+
Dryopteris borreri	.	.	.	.	1
Polypodium vulgare	.	+	1	.	.
Pteridium aquilinum	.	.	.	.	2
Thelypteris oreopteris	+	.	.	.	.
Agrostis tenuis	3	1	3	2	2
Anthoxanthum odoratum	2	1	3	.	.
Brachypodium sylvaticum	5	5	6	8	3
Dactylis glomerata	3	1	2	2	3
Deschampsia caespitosa	.	+	+	3	3
Helictotrichon pratense	+	3	2	.	.
Molinia caerulea	.	.	.	1	.
Carex binervis	.	.	.	1	.
C. flacca	.	.	.	1	.
C. pulicaris	.	.	.	+	.
C. sylvatica	+	4	+	.	.
Endymion non-scriptus	5	6	3	.	4
Epipactis atrorubens	.	.	.	3	.
Listera ovata	.	.	2	.	.
Orchis fuchsii	.	.	.	.	1
Scilla verna	.	.	.	.	+
Ajuga reptans	.	.	.	.	+
Angelica sylvestris	.	.	.	2	2
Anemone nemorosa	.	2	.	.	.
Allium ursinum	3	.	.	.	.
Bellis perennis	.	1	.	.	.
Cardamine flexuosa	+	.	.	.	.
Centaurea nigra	.	.	.	1	+
Chrysanthemum leucanthemum	.	.	.	.	+
Chrysosplenium oppositifolium	+	.	.	.	.
Circaea intermedia	6	+	5	.	.
Cirsium heterophyllum	.	.	.	5	.
C. palustre	.	.	.	.	+
Conopodium majus	1	.	.	.	3
Filipendula ulmaria	2	3	3	3	3
Fragaria vesca	1	4	2	.	1
Geum urbanum	.	.	.	1	.
Glechoma hederacea	3	1	.	.	.
Hypericum pulchrum	.	.	.	1	.
Hypochaeris radicata	.	.	.	.	1
Lysimachia nemorum	2	3	4	+	1
Oxalis acetosella	3	3	4	.	.
Potentilla erecta	.	2	.	.	1
Prunella vulgaris	+	3	1	.	+
Primula vulgaris	6	6	4	2	.
Ranunculus acris	2	.	.	3	1
R. ficaria	.	.	.	.	2
Rumex acetosa	.	.	.	.	+
Sagina procumbens	+	.	.	.	.
Sanicula europaea	2	.	.	.	1
Senecio jacobaea	.	.	.	1	.
Stachys sylvatica	.	.	.	2	.
Succisa pratensis	.	.	.	.	+
Teucrium scorodonia	.	.	.	1	.
Taraxacum officinalis agg.	.	.	.	2	2
Trollius europaeus	.	.	.	.	2
Urtica dioica	.	.	.	.	+
Valeriana officinalis	.	.	.	.	+
Veronica chamaedrys	1	2	1	.	1
Vicia sepium	.	.	.	.	+
Viola riviniana	2	3	1	1	2
Atrichum undulatum	1	.	1	.	.
Barbula sp.	.	.	.	1	.
Ctenidium molluscum	1	.	1	1	.
Dicranum majus	.	.	.	1	.
Fissidens taxifolius	1	.	.	4	.
Eurhynchium praelongum	.	.	.	2	.
E. striatum	.	.	.	.	5
Isothecium myurum	1	.	2	1	.
Hylocomium splendens	.	.	.	3	.
Pseudoscleropodium purum	1	.	1	2	.
Rhytidiadelphus loreus	.	.	.	2	.
R. squarrosus	1	.	.	1	.
R. triquetrus	2	.	.	4	1
Thuidium tamariscinum	2	.	1	4	3
Aneura pinguis	.	.	.	3	.
Aplozia crenulata	.	.	.	1	.
Lobaria pulmonaria	1	.	.	.	.
Number of species (92)	41	26	27	43	45
			(Average 36)		

× = present in 25 square metres surrounding plot.
+ for tree species = present as above with seedlings in 4 square metre plot.

LOCALITIES 1,2. Sleat, Isle of Skye; 3. Strath Suardal, Skye; 4. Rassal, Loch Kishorn, Ross-shire; 5. Bettyhill, Sutherland.

Table 9: Juniperus-Thelypteris provisional nodum

	1	2	3	4		1	2	3	4
Reference number . . .	R57 186	R57 185	M58 056	R58 187	Anemone nemorosa . . .	.	.	.	1
Map reference . . .	8047 2749	8046 2760	8253 2837	8038 2737	Cardamine flexuosa . . .	2	2	.	.
Altitude . . .	1600	1400	1500	1800	C. hirsuta . . .	.	.	2	.
Aspect (degrees) . .	180	—	45	90	**Galium hercynicum** . .	2	4	3	3
Slope (degrees) . .	30	0	45	20	**Oxalis acetosella** . .	2	4	3	2
Cover (per cent) . .	100	100	100	100	Potentilla erecta . .	.	2	.	3
Height (centimetres) . .	120	120	100	90	Ranunculus acris . .	.	+	.	.
Plot area (square metres) .	4	4	4	4	Rumex acetosa . .	.	+	.	.
					Urtica dioica . .	2	.	+	.
Calluna vulgaris . . .	2	.	.	5	Viola riviniana . .	.	3	.	.
Empetrum hermaphroditum . .	1	.	.	.					
Juniperus communis . .	9	9	9	6	Ceratodon purpureus . .	.	.	1	.
Rubus idaeus . . .	.	.	1	.	Climacium dendroides . .	.	.	+	.
Vaccinium myrtillus . .	5	3	5	3	Dicranum majus . .	2	.	8	3
V. vitis-idaea . .	3	5	4	3	**D. scoparium** . .	3	8	8	3
					Hylocomium brevirostre .	.	.	8	.
Athyrium filix-foemina . .	+	.	.	.	H. splendens . .	4	8	.	3
Blechnum spicant . .	1	.	5	5	Hypnum cupressiforme . .	3	3	8	.
Dryopteris austriaca . .	.	.	1	.	Isothecium myosuroides .	2	.	.	.
D. filix-mas . .	1	1	.	.	Mnium hornum . .	.	.	.	3
Lycopodium annotinum . .	.	.	.	4	M. longirostrum . .	3	3	.	.
Polypodium vulgare . .	.	.	1	.	Plagiothecium sylvaticum .	.	.	8	.
Polystichum lobatum . .	.	.	1	.	P. undulatum . .	.	.	2	2
Thelypteris dryopteris . .	.	2	3	.	Pleurozium schreberi . .	3	.	.	3
T. oreopteris . .	.	.	.	5	Pseudoscleropodium purum .	3	8	.	3
T. phegopteris . .	1	.	5	.	Ptilium crista-castrensis .	5	.	3	.
					Rhytidiadelphus loreus .	2	.	.	2
Agrostis canina . .	.	.	.	3	R. squarrosus . .	2	2	.	.
A. tenuis . .	1	3	.	.	R. triquetrus . .	5	8	8	.
Anthoxanthum odoratum . .	.	.	2	.	Sphagnum girgensohnii .	.	.	.	5
Deschampsia flexuosa . .	2	.	.	.	**Thuidium tamariscinum** .	5	8	8	5
Festuca ovina agg. . .	.	.	1	.					
F. rubra . .	.	1	.	.	Lophocolea bidentata . .	1	.	3	2
Holcus lanatus . .	.	3	.	.	Lophozia barbata . .	2	.	.	.
H. mollis . .	.	.	2	.	L. floerkii . .	.	.	1	.
					L. hatcheri . .	.	.	1	.
Carex binervis . .	.	.	.	2	L. obtusa . .	+	.	.	.
Juncus effusus . .	.	.	.	1	Plagiochila asplenioides .	.	.	3	.
Luzula pilosa . .	2	2	.	.					
L. sylvatica . .	.	.	.	2	Nephromium parile . .	.	.	1	1
					Number of species (65) .	32	24	34	36
							(Average 29)		

LOCALITIES
1,2,4. Kingussie, Inverness-shire; 3. Slochd Summit, Inverness-shire.

Table 10: Salix lapponum-Luzula sylvatica nodum

	1	2	3	4	5	6	7	8	9	10	11
Reference number	R57 220	R57 210	R57 239a	R57 239b	R58 053	R58 060	R58 079	R57 090	R58 099	R58 022	R59 044
Map reference	7744 3277	7759 3338	7742 3255	7742 3255	8809 2230	8881 2328	8326 2162	7789 2650	7499 2643	7763 3174	7408 2592
Altitude (feet)	2400	2400	2500	2500	2200	2500	2600	2400	2200	3000	2300
Aspect (degrees)	45	135	45	45	360	360	90	360	45	90	90
Slope (degrees)	30	45	40	40	35	45	35	35	40	45	45
Cover (per cent)	100	100	100	100	100	100	100	100	100	100	100
Height (centimetres)	90	—	60	60	—	60	60	60	—	—	15
Plot area (square metres)	4	4	4	4	2	4	4	4	4	4	4
Calluna vulgaris	.	.	.	.	.	3	.	.	.	.	.
Empetrum hermaphroditum	.	.	+	2	.	.	.	.	3	2	3
Salix arbuscula	.	.	.	.	.	.	.	.	.	.	6
S. lanata	.	.	5	7	.	.	.	.	.	4	.
S. lapponum	8	8	7	5	5	8	6	9	.	+	.
S. myrsinites	.	.	.	.	.	.	.	8	8	.	.
S. phylicifolia	.	.	.	.	.	.	5	.	.	.	.
S. reticulata	.	.	+	+	.	.	.	.	.	3	.
Vaccinium myrtillus	2	3	4	6	4	3	3	.	.	4	5
V. uliginosum	+	.	.	.	.	.	.	.	.	.	.
V. vitis-idaea	.	.	.	.	3	.	.	.	3	3	2
Dryopteris austriaca	.	1	3	+	.	.	.	1	.	.	.
Lycopodium selago	.	.	.	.	.	.	.	.	.	+	.
Selaginella selaginoides	.	.	.	.	.	2	.	.	.	.	2
Thelypteris phegopteris	2	.	.	.	.	.	.	.	.	.	.
Agrostis canina	2	.	3	3	.	3	2	.	3	.	3
A. tenuis	.	.	.	.	2	2	.	3	.	.	3
Anthoxanthum odoratum	.	.	.	.	.	2	.	.	.	.	3
Deschampsia caespitosa	4	1	4	3	3	3	.	3	2	.	2
D. flexuosa	.	3	3	3	2	2	.	.	3	.	3
Festuca rubra	3	.	.	.	.	.	.	3	2	.	.
F. ovina agg.	.	.	.	.	3	3	2	3	3	3	4
Nardus stricta	.	.	.	.	.	3	.	.	.	.	.
Carex atrata	.	.	.	.	.	.	.	.	.	1	.
C. bigelowii	.	.	.	.	1	.	.	.	.	.	.
C. binervis	.	2	.	.	.	.	1	.	.	.	.
C. curta	2	.	.	.	.	.	.	.	.	.	.
Coeloglossum viride	.	.	.	.	.	.	1	.	.	1	.
Luzula sylvatica	1	7	8	7	4	4	3	3	+	.	4
Alchemilla alpina	2	.	.	.	.	.	.	3	2	3	4
A. glabra	6	.	1	2	.	.	4	.	.	1	2
A. vestita	.	.	.	.	.	.	.	+	.	.	.
Angelica sylvestris	.	.	.	.	5	3	4	.	.	2	.
Caltha palustris	4	.	.	.	.	.	2	.	.	.	.
Campanula rotundifolia	1	2	.	.	.	.	.	.	.	1	3
Cardamine pratensis	1	.	.	.	.	.	.	.	.	.	.
Chrysosplenium oppositifolium	3	.	.	.	.	.	.	.	.	.	.
Cirsium palustre	.	.	.	.	.	.	2	.	.	.	.
Cochlearia alpina	.	.	.	.	2	.	.	.	.	.	.
Crepis paludosa	.	.	.	.	.	.	2	.	.	.	.
Epilobium anagallidifolium	1	.	.	.	.	2	.	1	.	.	.
Euphrasia officinalis agg.	.	.	.	.	.	2	.	.	.	.	2
Filipendula ulmaria	3	.	.	.	.	.	3	.	.	.	.
Galium boreale	.	.	.	.	.	.	3	.	.	.	.
G. hercynicum	.	3	+	2	.	.	.	.	1	3	3
Geranium sylvaticum	.	1	.	.	.	.	.	.	2	.	.
Geum rivale	6	.	.	.	4	3	1	2	2	2	.
Melandrium rubrum	.	.	.	.	.	.	2	.	.	.	.
Oxalis acetosella	.	2	3	3	2	3	.	1	.	.	.
Oxyria digyna	.	.	.	.	3	.	.	1	2	+	.
Polygonum viviparum	.	.	.	.	.	1	.	3	1	.	3
Ranunculus acris	.	.	.	.	2	3	2	.	.	.	2
Rhinanthus minor	.	.	.	.	.	+	2	.	.	.	.
Rumex acetosa	2	2	4	3	3	2	3	2	.	+	.
Saussurea alpina	.	2	.	.	5	.	3	.	2	+	.
Saxifraga aizoides	.	.	.	.	.	.	.	3	.	2	.
S. hypnoides	.	.	.	.	.	.	.	.	2	3	.
S. oppositifolia	.	.	.	.	.	.	.	.	.	2	1
S. stellaris	1	.	.	.	.	.	.	1	.	.	.
Sedum rosea	3	2	.	.	4	1	.	.	1	3	.
Solidago virgaurea	.	.	.	.	.	.	1	.	1	+	.
Succisa pratensis	.	.	.	.	.	2	4	1	.	.	.
Taraxacum officinalis agg.	.	.	.	.	.	.	.	2	.	.	.
Thalictrum alpinum	.	.	.	.	2	2	.	2	2	2	3
Thymus drucei	.	.	.	.	.	2	.	.	2	.	3
Trollius europaeus	.	.	.	.	.	3	.	.	.	.	.
Valeriana officinalis	.	.	.	.	.	3	4	.	.	.	.
Viola riviniana	.	.	.	+	2	2	.	2	2	2	3
Acrocladium cuspidatum	2	.	.	.	.	.	.	.	.	.	.
Atrichum undulatum	.	.	2	+	.	.	.	.	.	.	.
Aulacomnium palustre	.	.	.	.	.	3	2	.	.	.	.
Brachythecium rutabulum	4	.	.	.	.	.	.	.	.	.	.
Dicranum bonjeani	1	.	2	+	.	.	.	.	.	.	.
D. majus	+	.	3	2	2	.	.	.	.	3	.
D. scoparium	.	3	+	2	2	.	.	.	3	3	3
Drepanocladus uncinatus	2	.	2	2	.	.	.	.	.	1	.

Table 10 (*continued*)

	1	2	3	4	5	6	7	8	9	10	11
Eurhynchium praelongum	·	2	·	·	·	·	·	·	·	·	·
Hylocomium splendens	4	2	3	5	7	7	4	7	7	8	4
Hypnum callichroum	·	·	+	2	·	·	·	·	·	·	·
H. cupressiforme	·	·	·	·	·	·	·	·	·	·	3
Mnium hornum	2	5	3	2	1	·	·	2	2	·	2
M. punctatum	2	2	2	2	2	1	·	3	·	·	1
M. undulatum	·	·	·	·	2	2	3	·	2	·	·
Philonotis fontana	·	·	·	·	·	1	·	·	·	·	·
Plagiothecium denticulatum	·	3	·	·	·	·	·	·	·	·	·
P. elegans	·	·	+	2	·	·	·	·	·	·	·
P. undulatum	·	2	2	3	3	·	·	·	·	·	·
Pleurozium schreberi	·	·	+	1	2	·	2	·	4	2	3
Polytrichum alpinum	·	·	2	+	1	·	·	·	·	2	2
Pseudoscleropodium purum	·	2	·	·	·	·	1	·	·	·	2
Ptilium crista-castrensis	·	·	·	·	3	2	·	·	4	4	·
Rhacomitrium lanuginosum	·	·	·	·	·	·	·	·	·	3	3
Rhytidiadelphus loreus	3	·	1	3	3	3	2	7	3	1	3
R. squarrosus	·	·	2	3	·	2	3	·	·	·	·
R. triquetrus	3	·	·	·	5	·	3	·	4	1	2
Sphagnum girgensohnii	2	5	4	4	·	4	·	4	·	·	·
S. nemoreum	·	·	+	2	·	·	·	·	+	·	·
S. palustre	·	·	3	3	·	2	·	2	·	·	·
S. papillosum	2	·	·	·	·	·	·	·	·	·	·
S. plumulosum	·	+	2	+	3	·	·	2	·	·	·
S. recurvum	+	·	·	·	·	2	·	·	·	·	·
S. russowii	·	+	1	+	·	1	·	·	·	·	·
S. squarrosum	2	·	·	·	·	·	·	4	·	·	·
S. subsecundum*	2	4	·	·	·	·	·	2	·	·	·
S. teres	3	·	·	·	·	2	+	·	·	·	·
Thuidium tamariscinum	·	2	+	+	3	2	5	2	4	·	+
Aneura multifida	·	·	·	·	·	·	·	1	·	·	·
A. pinguis	2	·	·	·	·	·	·	·	·	·	·
Chiloscyphus polyanthus	2	·	1	+	·	·	·	·	·	·	·
Lophocolea bidentata	1	1	1	+	·	1	3	·	·	·	·
Lophozia quinquedentata	·	·	2	2	3	·	·	2	2	·	2
L. lycopodioides	·	·	+	1	·	·	·	·	1	2	·
Lophozia sp.	·	1	·	·	·	·	·	·	·	·	·
Pellia sp.	4	·	·	·	·	·	·	3	·	·	·
Plagiochila asplenioides	1	·	·	·	·	·	·	1	·	·	1
Ptilidium ciliare	3	·	1	1	·	·	·	1	2	3	2
Cladonia furcata	·	·	·	·	·	·	·	·	2	·	·
C. pyxidata	·	·	+	1	·	·	·	·	·	·	·
Peltigera canina	·	·	·	·	·	2	4	·	+	·	·
Number of species (119)	43	29	42	42	36	42	37	36	37	37	38

(Average 38)

Constancy class V 8
       ,,   ,,   IV 19

* Var. auriculatum in 1, 8.
  ,,   inundatum in 2.

LOCALITIES

1. Winter Corrie, Driesh, Clova, Angus; 2. Loch Brandy, Clova; 3,4. Glen Fiadh, Clova; 5. Beinn Enaiglair, Braemore, Ross-shire; 6. Toll Lochan, Freevater Forest, Ross-shire; 7. Sgurr na Lapaich, Glen Cannich, Ross-shire; 8. Coire Chuirn, Drumochter, Inverness-shire; 9. Carn Gorm, Glen Lyon, Perthshire; 10. Caenlochan, Angus; 11. Meall nan Tarmachan, Perthshire.

Table 11A: Herb-rich facies of Callunetum vulgaris

	1	2	3	4	5		1	2	3	4	5
Reference number	R56 059	R56 085	R58 142	R58 143	R58 144	Galium boreale	3	3	.	.	.
						G. hercynicum	.	.	.	1	.
Map reference	8676 2030	8807 2203	8027 1331	7968 1337	8038 1365	Gentianella campestris	.	.	1	.	.
						Geum rivale	2	+	.	.	.
Altitude (feet)	800	1100	150	300	50	Hieracium pilosella	.	.	.	1	3
Aspect (degrees)	135	270	315	180	315	Hypericum pulchrum	3	+	2	2	.
Slope (degrees)	27	18	35	10	5	Hypochaeris radicata	1	.	3	.	.
Cover (per cent)	100	100	100	100	100	Lathyrus montanus	.	3	2	1	.
Height (centimetres)	30	30	15	10	7	Leontodon autumnalis	.	.	2	.	1
Plot area (square metres)	16	16	4	4	4	L. hispidus	.	.	.	.	2
						Linum catharticum	.	2	1	3	3
Calluna vulgaris	7	7	5	7	8	**Lotus corniculatus**	2	+	2	3	3
Dryas octopetala	.	.	3	.	.	Lysimachia nemorum	2	.	.	.	.
Empetrum nigrum	.	.	.	.	3	Parnassia palustris	.	.	.	.	1
Erica cinerea	3	2	5	3	3	**Plantago lanceolata**	4	4	3	3	3
E. tetralix	.	3	.	.	.	P. maritima	.	2	4	4	3
Salix repens	.	+	.	.	3	Polygala serpyllifolia	.	2	3	3	1
						Potentilla erecta	5	5	4	5	.
Blechnum spicant	2	+	.	.	.	Primula vulgaris	2	+	+	.	.
Pteridium aquilinum	2	.	.	.	.	Prunella vulgaris	.	.	3	3	1
Selaginella selaginoides	1	2	.	.	.	Ranunculus acris	2	2	.	.	.
						Rhinanthus minor agg.	.	.	1	.	.
Agrostis canina	3	3	2	1	3	Succisa pratensis	5	5	4	4	.
A. tenuis	.	3	4	2	.	Taraxacum officinalis agg.	.	1	.	.	.
Anthoxanthum odoratum	1	2	4	3	3	Thalictrum alpinum	.	2	.	.	.
Cynosurus cristatus	.	.	.	.	3	**Thymus drucei**	3	3	4	3	3
Deschampsia flexuosa	.	.	2	.	.	Trifolium pratense	.	.	1	.	2
Festuca ovina agg.	5	4	3	4	2	T. repens	.	.	1	2	3
F. rubra	4	2	4	3	3	Trollius europaeus	4	2	+	.	.
Holcus lanatus	.	.	.	1	.	Vicia sepium	.	+	.	.	.
Koeleria gracilis	.	.	3	3	3	Viola riviniana	4	4	3	2	.
Molinia caerulea	3	4	1	3	.						
Nardus stricta	.	.	3	+	.	Acrocladium cuspidatum	1	2	.	.	.
Sieglingia decumbens	1	3	3	4	3	Breutelia chrysocoma	4	4	.	.	.
						Ctenidium molluscum	3	3	.	.	3
Carex binervis	2	.	.	.	.	Dicranum scoparium	.	.	.	1	.
C. flacca	.	.	4	.	.	Drepanocladus uncinatus	1	.	.	.	.
C. panicea	3	4	4	3	2	Fissidens osmundoides	.	.	.	.	2
C. pilulifera	.	.	1	2	.	Hylocomium splendens	5	5	.	2	2
C. pulicaris	2	4	2	3	.	Hypnum cupressiforme	3	.	.	3	1
Luzula campestris	.	.	.	.	2	Pleurozium schreberi	.	3	.	.	.
Orchis ericetorum	.	.	1	.	.	Pseudoscleropodium purum	4	3	.	2	1
Trichophorum caespitosum	.	1	.	.	.	Rhytidiadelphus loreus	3	.	.	.	.
						R. squarrosus	1	3	.	1	.
Alchemilla alpina	+	+	.	.	.	R. triquetrus	.	3	.	.	2
A. xanthochlora	.	2	.	.	.	Thuidium delicatulum	3	.	.	.	.
Anemone nemorosa	3	2	.	.	.	T. tamariscinum	.	3	.	.	.
Angelica sylvestris	.	.	1	.	.						
Antennaria dioica	.	.	2	.	1	Frullania tamarisci	2	.	1	1	2
Anthyllis vulneraria	.	.	.	.	3						
Cirsium heterophyllum	4	3	.	.	.	Number of species (85)	43	50	42	36	36
Euphrasia officinalis agg.	.	3	3	3	3			(Average 41)			
Filipendula ulmaria	2	.	.	.	.						

LOCALITIES

1. Slioch, Loch Maree, Ross-shire; 2. Beinn Enaiglair, Inverlael, Ross-shire; 3. Monadh Dubh, Isle of Rhum, Inverness-shire; 4. Harris, Isle of Rhum, Inverness-shire; 5. Kilmory, Isle of Rhum, Inverness-shire.

	1	2	3	4	5	6	7	8	9	10	11	12
Reference number	R57 131	P52 017	P52 022	P52 101	P52 105	P52 020	M57 054a	M57 054b	M57 054c	M57 056	M57 058	M57 075
Map reference	7999 2692	7504 2755	7507 2750	7500 2780	7501 2780	7152 2751	807– 291–	807– 291–	807– 291–	8012 2858	8226 3065	8024 3232
Altitude (feet)	1000	1050	1350	1225	1300	1300	1000	1000	1000	1000	1200	1600
Aspect (degrees)	180	–	120	270	270	150	–	–	–	–	–	–
Slope (degrees)	5	2	2	2	2	2	0	0	0	0	0	0
Cover (per cent)	100	100	100	100	100	90	100	100	100	100	100	100
Height (centimetres)	40	30	30	25	25	20	12	45	30	40	30	20
Plot area (square metres)	4	4	3	4	4	4	4	4	4	4	4	4
Betula pubescens										2		
Calluna vulgaris	9	10	10	10	9	9	9	10	10	10	9	9
Empetrum hermaphroditum												1
Erica cinerea	2		2		5					+	2	
E. tetralix			1									
Genista anglica												+
Juniperus communis									1			1
Larix decidua												
Pinus sylvestris									+	1		
Sorbus aucuparia		1										
Vaccinium myrtillus	1	3		3	3		2	2		3		3
V. vitis-idaea			1			3	2	3	3	3	3	2
Blechnum spicant												
Lycopodium clavatum											1	
Pteridium aquilinum												
Agrostis canina	1				2							
A. tenuis										1	2	
Deschampsia flexuosa				2	3			2	2	3	2	3
Festuca ovina agg.	2	2	3			3						
Sieglingia decumbens											+	
Carex binervis						1						
C. panicea												1
C. pilulifera						1						
Juncus squarrosus												
Listera cordata		1	3		3	3						
Luzula pilosa		2										
Trichophorum caespitosum			2	1		2	+					
Campanula rotundifolia	1	1									+	
Galium hercynicum	1	1									3	
Hypericum pulchrum		1										
Polygala serpyllifolia												
Potentilla erecta	2		2		3			1		+	3	+
Succisa pratensis	+											
Trientalis europaea			1								3	
Aulacomnium palustre									1			
Breutelia chrysocoma												
Dicranum scoparium	2	2	2	1	1	3	1	3	2	3	1	2
Hylocomium splendens	8	8	7	4	5		2	6	7	4	8	2
Hypnum cupressiforme	3	4	3		6	6	2	6	3	7	3	2
Plagiothecium undulatum												
Pleurozium schreberi	4	7	8	6	3	2	3	5	6	1	4	9
Polytrichum alpestre										2		
P. commune				2						1		1
P. formosum			3									
Pseudoscleropodium purum									+			
Rhacomitrium lanuginosum				1		1						
Rhytidiadelphus loreus	2	2	1	3	5							3
R. squarrosus	2	1	1									
R. triquetrus	4	3							1			
Sphagnum nemoreum												
Thuidium tamariscinum								1	+			
Aneura multifida												
Calypogeia trichomanis												
Cephalozia bicuspidata												
Diplophyllum albicans												
Lepidozia setacea												
Leptoscyphus taylori												
Lophocolea sp.		2										
Lophozia floerkii												
L. ventricosa					1							
Ptilidium ciliare												3
Scapania gracilis												
S. umbrosa												
Cladonia coccifera							1	1				
C. furcata												1
C. crispata						3						
C. glauca										2		
C. gracilis			1		1	1						
C. impexa	1		2	5		2	7	4	3	4		3
C. pyxidata			1		1	2	3		1			
C. squamosa			1					3	1	3		
C. sylvatica				4	1							
C. uncialis						2	3	1	1			1
Hypogymnia physodes							3					
Peltigera canina	1								+			
P. polydactyla		2									1	
Number of species (76)	18	18	20	12	15	18	14	14	17	19	16	19

(Average 17)

Constancy class V 5
" " IV 4

vulgaris

13	14	15	16	17	
M57	R57	R57	M57	P52	Reference number
061	002	006	103	102	Map reference
7884	9443	9361	8406	–	
3336	2250	2318	1868	–	
1700	450	790	400	1300	Altitude (feet)
315	360	270	180	270	Aspect (degrees)
5	30	30	8	2	Slope (degrees)
100	100	100	100	100	Cover (per cent)
25	30	35	20	25	Height (centimetres)
4	4	4	4	4	Plot area (square metres)
.	.	.	.	.	Betula pubescens
10	9	8	10	10	**Calluna vulgaris**
.	.	.	.	.	Empetrum hermaphroditum
2	3	2	3	.	Erica cinerea
.	.	.	1	.	E. tetralix
2	.	.	.	.	Genista anglica
.	.	.	.	.	Juniperus communis
.	.	.	.	.	Larix decidua
.	.	.	.	.	Pinus sylvestris
.	.	.	.	.	Sorbus aucuparia
3	3	3	.	2	Vaccinium myrtillus
3	.	.	.	.	V. vitis-idaea
+	.	.	1	.	Blechnum spicant
.	.	.	.	.	Lycopodium clavatum
.	.	.	2	.	Pteridium aquilinum
.	.	.	.	.	Agrostis canina
.	.	.	.	.	A. tenuis
2	3	3	3	.	Deschampsia flexuosa
.	.	.	.	.	Festuca ovina agg.
.	.	.	.	.	Sieglingia decumbens
.	.	.	.	.	Carex binervis
.	.	.	.	.	C. panicea
.	.	1	.	.	C. pilulifera
1	.	.	.	.	Juncus squarrosus
2	.	.	.	1	Listera cordata
.	.	.	.	.	Luzula pilosa
.	.	.	+	1	Trichophorum caespitosum
.	.	.	.	.	Campanula rotundifolia
.	.	2	.	.	Galium hercynicum
.	.	.	+	.	Hypericum pulchrum
.	.	.	1	.	Polygala serpyllifolia
+	1	2	3	.	Potentilla erecta
.	.	.	2	.	Succisa pratensis
1	.	.	.	.	Trientalis europaea
.	.	.	.	.	Aulacomnium palustre
.	.	.	3	.	Breutelia chrysocoma
3	3	2	3	1	**Dicranum scoparium**
2	4	8	3	.	**Hylocomium splendens**
5	6	3	8	3	**Hypnum cupressiforme**
.	3	3	1	.	Plagiothecium undulatum
8	3	4	2	6	**Pleurozium schreberi**
.	.	.	.	.	Polytrichum alpestre
2	.	2	.	2	P. commune
.	.	.	.	.	P. formosum
.	.	.	.	.	Pseudoscleropodium purum
.	.	.	.	.	Rhacomitrium lanuginosum
.	3	5	2	2	Rhytidiadelphus loreus
.	.	.	.	.	R. squarrosus
.	.	.	.	.	R. triquetrus
.	3	+	.	.	Sphagnum nemoreum
.	.	.	1	.	Thuidium tamariscinum
.	1	.	.	.	Aneura multifida
.	1	2	.	.	Calypogeia trichomanis
.	.	1	.	.	Cephalozia bicuspidata
.	2	+	1	.	Diplophyllum albicans
.	3	.	.	.	Lepidozia setacea
.	3	.	.	.	Leptoscyphus taylori
.	.	.	.	.	Lophocolea sp.
1	.	2	.	.	Lophozia floerkii
.	.	2	.	.	L. ventricosa
.	.	.	.	2	Ptilidium ciliare
.	.	2	.	.	Scapania gracilis
.	.	+	.	.	S. umbrosa
.	2	.	.	.	Cladonia coccifera
.	.	.	.	.	C. furcata
.	.	.	.	.	C. crispata
.	.	.	.	.	C. glauca
.	.	.	.	.	C. gracilis
2	.	.	1	4	C. impexa
1	.	.	.	.	C. pyxidata
3	2	.	.	.	C. squamosa
.	.	.	.	3	C. sylvatica
.	.	.	.	2	C. uncialis
.	.	.	.	.	Hypogymnia physodes
.	.	4	.	.	Peltigera canina
.	.	.	.	.	P. polydactyla
20	19	23	21	13	Number of species (76)

LOCALITIES

1. Glen Banchor, Newtonmore, Inverness-shire; 2–5. Schiehallion, Perthshire; 6. Comrie, Perthshire; 7–9. Rothiemurchus, Cairngorms; 10. Invereshie, Cairngorms; 11. Carn Dearg, Grantown, Inverness-shire; 12. Corndavon Lodge, Cairngorms; 13. Druim Cholzie, Glen Muick, Aberdeenshire; 14. Laxford Bridge, Sutherland; 15. Strath nan Caran, Glendhu Forest, Sutherland; 16. Loch Kishorn, Ross-shire.

Table 12: Arctostaphyleto-Callunetum

	1	2	3	4	5	6	7	8
Reference number	R57 134	R57 184	R57 197	R57 299	M58 018	M58 071	R58 090	R58 094
Map reference	8003 2690	8029 2759	7997 2596	7636 2859	7553 2768	8038 2863	8189 2933	7901 2674
Altitude (feet)	1200	1200	2000	1400	1200	900	750	1000
Aspect (degrees)	180	180	90	180	90	—	—	135
Slope (degrees)	20	15	35	15	8	0	7	17
Cover (per cent)	100	100	100	100	100	100	100	100
Height (centimetres)	30	30	35	—	—	15	—	22
Plot area (square metres)	4	4	4	4	4	4	4	4
Arctostaphylos uva-ursi	7	6	3	5	7	8	6	7
Calluna vulgaris	8	8	8	7	7	7	8	8
Empetrum hermaphroditum	+	·	3	·	·	·	·	·
Erica cinerea	3	3	4	6	4	1	·	3
E. tetralix	·	2	·	·	·	·	·	·
Genista anglica	+	+	·	·	·	1	3	2
Juniperus communis	·	1	·	·	·	·	·	·
Sorbus aucuparia	·	·	·	·	·	·	·	1
Vaccinium myrtillus	3	·	5	·	·	+	·	2
V. vitis-idaea	2	3	4	3	·	1	4	3
Blechnum spicant	·	·	2	·	·	·	·	·
Lycopodium clavatum	·	·	·	·	+	·	·	·
Agrostis canina	·	·	·	·	3	·	·	·
A. tenuis	3	3	·	3	·	·	·	3
Anthoxanthum odoratum	1	·	·	·	3	·	·	2
Deschampsia flexuosa	2	3	3	3	3	3	3	3
Festuca ovina agg.	3	3	·	·	·	1	3	·
Sieglingia decumbens	·	·	·	·	2	·	·	·
Carex pilulifera	·	·	·	·	1	·	·	·
Listera cordata	·	·	·	·	+	·	·	·
Luzula campestris	·	·	·	·	·	+	·	2
L. multiflora	·	2	·	·	·	·	2	·
Anemone nemorosa	·	·	·	1	2	·	·	·
Antennaria dioica	·	·	·	·	1	·	·	·
Campanula rotundifolia	·	·	·	·	2	·	·	2
Galium hercynicum	2	2	1	·	2	·	·	·
Hypericum pulchrum	·	·	·	·	·	·	·	1
Hypochaeris radicata	·	·	·	·	·	·	1	·
Lathyrus montanus	2	+	·	+	+	+	3	2
Lotus corniculatus	1	2	·	·	1	+	3	+
Polygala serpyllifolia	·	·	·	·	1	·	·	·
Potentilla erecta	3	3	·	2	2	·	3	3
Pyrola media	1	2	+	2	3	·	+	+
Ramischia secunda	·	·	4	·	·	·	·	·
Solidago virgaurea	·	·	·	·	2	·	·	·
Succisa pratensis	·	·	·	·	·	·	+	1
Trientalis europaea	1	2	·	·	·	·	·	·
Veronica officinalis	·	1	·	·	·	·	·	·
Viola riviniana	+	1	·	2	+	·	+	3
Dicranum scoparium	·	1	3	3	2	2	·	2
Hylocomium splendens	3	7	6	·	1	·	4	3
Hypnum cupressiforme	1	4	3	5	4	3	3	3
Plagiothecium undulatum	·	·	1	·	·	·	·	·
Pleurozium schreberi	3	4	6	·	·	·	2	4
Polytrichum alpestre	·	·	·	·	2	·	·	·
P. commune	·	1	·	·	·	·	·	·
Pseudoscleropodium purum	·	3	·	1	·	·	·	3
Rhacomitrium lanuginosum	·	·	3	·	·	·	·	·
Rhytidiadelphus loreus	3	2	4	1	·	·	·	·
R. squarrosus	·	1	·	·	·	·	·	·
R. triquetrus	3	2	·	·	·	·	·	2
Lophocolea bidentata	·	·	·	·	·	·	2	·
Lophozia floerkii	·	1	·	·	·	·	·	·
L. quinquedentata	·	·	1	·	·	·	·	·
L. ventricosa	·	·	1	·	·	·	·	·
Cladonia bellidiflora	·	·	2	·	·	·	·	·
C. coccifera	·	·	·	·	1	·	·	2
C. floerkeana	·	·	·	·	·	·	·	2
C. gracilis	·	·	·	·	·	1	2	·
C. impexa	·	·	·	·	1	3	3	3
C. pyxidata	·	·	2	·	·	·	·	·
C. squamosa	·	·	·	·	·	1	·	·
Peltigera canina	·	·	1	·	·	2	4	·
Number of species (63)	23	29	23	16	26	17	21	28
				(Average 23)				

Constancy class V 8
„ „ IV 7

LOCALITIES

1. Glen Banchor, Inverness-shire; 2. Allt Mor, Kingussie, Inverness-shire; 3. Glen Markie, Inverness-shire; 4. Tulach Hill, Blair Atholl, Perthshire; 5. Keltney Burn, Perthshire; 6. Glen Feshie, Inverness-shire; 7. Boat of Garten, Inverness-shire; 8. Dalwhinnie, Inverness-shire.

Table 13: Vaccineto-Callunetum [hepaticosum (1–11); suecicosum (12–19)]

	1	2	3	4	5	6	7	8	9	10	11	12	13	14	15	16	17	18	19
Reference number	R57 012	R57 034	R59 003	R59 005	R59 006	R56 008	R56 101	R56 090	R56 077	R56 062	R58 069	M56 038	M56 039	R56 035	M56 066	M56 091	R57 277	R57 313	R57 097
Map reference	9454 2357	9491 2338	9275 2213	9108 2047	8451 1813	8607 1999	8729 2199	8829 2073	8580 1922	8588 1940	8450 2079	8619 1973	8654 1978	8833 2228	8576 2246	8796 2241	7971 2579	7558 2844	7727 2507
Altitude (feet)	1250	1300	1550	1350	1450	1170	1850	2000	1900	1300	2100	1450	1450	1800	1900	2000	1850	1900	2600
Aspect (degrees)	45	360	30	360	30	360	45	360	360	360	360	360	45	360	45	45	45	45	135
Slope (degrees)	20	35	35	35	35	30	30	30	25	35	35	30	25	25	25	30	15	25	10
Cover (per cent)	100	100	100	100	100	100	95	97	90	100	100	90	100	100	100	100	100	100	100
Height (centimetres)	60	35	35	50	25	40	—	—	—	40	—	30	30	23	30	30	60	60	30
Plot area (square metres)	4	4	4	4	4	4	4	4	4	4	4	4	4	4	4	4	4	4	4
Calluna vulgaris	9	8	8	9	9	8	6	8	6	8	8	8	8	6	8	8	9	9	9
Empetrum hermaphroditum	3	2	3	·	3	4	5	5	4	3	4	1	2	6	2	3	4	·	4
E. nigrum	·	·	·	·	·	·	·	·	·	·	·	·	·	·	·	·	·	2	·
Erica cinerea	·	·	·	4	·	·	·	·	·	·	·	·	·	·	·	·	·	·	·
Sorbus aucuparia	1	·	·	·	·	·	·	·	·	·	·	1	+	1	·	·	·	·	·
Vaccinium myrtillus	4	4	5	3	5	4	4	4	4	5	5	3	3	5	3	3	3	3	4
V. uliginosum	·	·	·	·	·	·	4	4	6	·	+	·	·	·	·	·	2	·	3
V. vitis-idaea	3	·	·	·	·	2	+	·	2	3	2	·	1	3	·	·	2	3	3
Blechnum spicant	·	·	2	3	·	·	·	+	·	2	·	·	+	·	1	2	·	·	2
Hymenophyllum wilsonii	+	·	·	·	·	·	·	·	1	·	·	·	·	·	·	·	·	·	·
Lycopodium selago	·	·	·	·	1	·	·	·	·	·	·	·	·	·	·	+	·	·	·
Agrostis canina	·	·	·	2	·	·	1	·	·	·	·	·	·	·	1	·	·	·	·
Anthoxanthum odoratum	·	·	·	·	·	·	·	·	·	·	·	·	·	·	2	·	·	·	·
Deschampsia flexuosa	2	3	3	3	3	3	3	3	2	3	3	2	3	4	3	2	+	2	3
Molinia caerulea	·	·	·	·	·	·	·	·	·	·	·	·	·	·	·	·	·	·	·
Nardus stricta	·	·	1	·	1	·	·	·	·	·	·	·	·	·	·	·	·	·	2
Carex bigelowii	·	·	1	·	·	·	3	1	2	·	·	·	·	1	·	·	·	·	1
Eriophorum vaginatum	·	·	·	2	·	·	·	·	·	·	·	·	+	2	2	1	3	1	·
Juncus squarrosus	·	·	·	·	·	·	·	·	·	·	·	·	+	+	·	·	·	·	·
J. trifidus	·	·	·	·	·	·	·	·	2	·	·	·	·	·	·	·	·	·	·
Listera cordata	2	2	1	1	·	·	·	2	·	2	·	·	2	·	3	·	3	1	·
Luzula sylvatica	2	·	·	·	·	·	·	+	·	·	2	·	1	2	1	·	·	·	·
Trichophorum caespitosum	·	·	·	2	·	·	·	2	·	·	·	·	1	·	1	·	·	·	·
Chamaepericlymenum suecicum	·	·	·	·	·	·	·	·	·	·	·	4	3	4	3	4	+	·	3
Galium hercynicum	·	·	·	2	·	·	·	·	·	·	·	1	·	3	+	·	·	·	·
Melampyrum pratense	2	·	2	·	3	·	3	2	2	3	1	1	+	·	·	·	1	·	2
Potentilla erecta	·	3	3	3	·	1	·	1	·	2	·	3	2	2	2	1	·	·	·
Rubus chamaemorus	·	·	2	·	·	·	·	·	·	·	·	3	4	2	3	+	3	3	+
Solidago virgaurea	·	·	2	2	1	·	1	·	1	2	+	·	·	·	·	·	·	·	·
Campylopus flexuosus	·	·	·	·	1	·	·	·	·	·	·	·	·	·	·	·	·	·	·
Dicranodontium uncinatum	+	3	3	1	2	·	3	+	+	2	·	1	·	·	1	·	·	·	·
Dicranum fuscescens	·	·	·	·	·	·	·	·	·	·	·	·	·	·	·	·	·	·	2
D. majus	2	·	2	·	2	1	3	2	·	2	2	·	·	2	·	·	·	2	·
D. scoparium	2	2	·	2	2	2	3	1	2	·	2	2	3	1	1	1	2	·	·
Hylocomium splendens	4	3	4	3	4	4	6	4	3	4	3	3	5	7	7	4	7	3	3
Hypnum cupressiforme	4	3	2	3	1	1	3	2	2	3	1	1	1	3	·	·	3	·	·
Plagiothecium undulatum	3	1	·	2	2	2	2	3	2	3	4	3	1	3	1	2	1	·	·
Pleurozium schreberi	2	·	3	2	3	2	4	3	3	3	2	1	4	3	2	3	3	3	4
Polytrichum alpinum	·	·	1	2	·	·	·	·	1	·	·	·	·	·	·	·	·	·	·
P. commune	·	·	·	·	·	·	·	·	·	·	·	·	·	·	2	·	1	·	·
Ptilium crista-castrensis	2	·	·	·	·	·	1	·	·	·	1	·	·	+	·	·	·	·	·
Rhacomitrium lanuginosum	3	3	2	3	3	3	6	4	7	3	3	2	·	·	·	4	·	·	2
Rhytidiadelphus loreus	4	3	4	3	4	3	4	4	3	4	3	3	4	6	3	3	5	3	5
Sphagnum fuscum	·	·	·	·	·	·	·	·	·	·	·	·	·	·	·	·	+	·	·
S. nemoreum	4	5	5	5	4	6	4	5	4	6	·	2	·	3	6	4	5	9	5
S. plumulosum	·	4	·	2	3	2	·	·	·	·	·	·	·	·	·	1	·	·	·
S. quinquefarium	·	3	·	·	·	2	·	·	4	3	3	4	·	·	4	·	·	·	·
S. russowii	·	·	·	·	·	·	·	·	·	·	·	·	·	2	·	·	·	2	3	2
S. tenellum	·	4	·	·	·	4	·	·	·	·	+	·	·	·	·	·	·	·	·
Thuidium tamariscinum	3	1	·	·	·	·	·	·	·	·	·	·	·	·	·	·	·	·	·
Anastrepta orcadensis	3	3	2	2	2	2	3	4	4	4	3	2	1	2	2	3	3	3	3
Anastrophyllum donianum	·	3	+	1	·	1	·	4	3	·	+	·	·	·	·	·	·	·	·
Bazzania tricrenata	4	4	3	+	3	1	3	4	3	4	3	2	2	·	3	2	·	·	·
B. pearsoni	·	3	5	4	3	3	2	4	4	+	4	·	·	·	·	·	·	·	·
Calypogeia cf. neesiana	·	·	·	·	·	·	·	·	·	·	·	1	1	·	1	·	·	·	·
C. trichomanis	·	·	·	·	·	·	·	·	·	·	·	·	·	·	·	·	1	·	1
Diplophyllum albicans	2	3	2	2	3	1	2	3	·	2	3	·	1	·	2	1	·	·	·

Table 13 (continued)

	1	2	3	4	5	6	7	8	9	10	11	12	13	14	15	16	17	18	19
Frullania tamarisci	·	·	·	·	·	1	·	·	·	·	·	·	·	·	·	·	·	·	·
Herberta hutchinsiae	4	6	3	5	5	3	·	2	+	5	·	5	·	·	·	·	·	·	·
Jamesoniella carringtonii	1	4	3	3	3	2	2	3	3	2	3	2	·	·	·	·	·	·	·
Lepidozia pearsoni	3	·	3	·	2	·	3	·	·	·	3	1	3	·	·	2	+	·	·
L. reptans	·	·	·	·	·	1	·	3	2	3	·	·	·	·	·	·	·	·	·
L. setacea	·	·	·	·	·	·	·	·	·	·	·	·	·	·	1	·	·	·	·
L. trichoclados	·	2	1	·	1	·	·	·	·	·	·	·	·	·	·	·	·	·	·
Leptoscyphus taylori	3	·	3	3	3	1	2	2	3	1	3	·	·	1	·	3	·	·	·
Lophozia floerkii	·	·	2	·	·	·	·	·	·	·	·	·	1	·	·	·	·	3	3
L. quinquedentata	2	2	·	·	2	·	·	·	1	·	2	·	·	·	·	·	·	·	·
L. ventricosa	·	·	·	·	·	·	·	·	·	·	·	·	·	·	2	·	·	·	·
Mastigophora woodsii	5	6	5	4	3	2	·	5	3	4	6	·	·	·	·	·	·	·	·
Plagiochila spinulosa	+	·	·	·	·	·	·	·	·	·	·	·	·	·	·	·	·	·	·
Pleurozia purpurea	3	4	3	4	4	3	·	3	3	4	3	2	·	·	·	·	·	·	·
Ptilidium ciliare	·	·	2	·	·	·	2	2	3	·	·	·	·	·	2	·	2	2	2
Scapania gracilis	3	3	2	2	3	2	2	3	2	4	3	·	·	·	·	·	·	·	·
S. nimbosa	·	2	·	·	3	·	·	2	3	2	2	·	·	·	·	·	·	·	·
S. ornithopodioides	3	3	3	2	3	2	2	3	3	4	2	·	·	·	·	·	·	·	·
Cladonia bellidiflora	·	·	·	·	·	·	1	·	1	·	1	1	·	·	·	·	·	1	2
C. coccifera	·	·	·	·	·	·	1	·	·	1	·	·	·	·	·	·	·	·	·
C. gracilis	·	·	1	·	·	·	2	·	2	1	1	1	·	·	·	·	·	·	2
C. impexa	·	·	2	2	2	4	·	·	·	2	·	2	2	·	·	3	·	·	·
C. rangiferina agg.	·	·	·	·	·	·	·	·	·	·	·	1	·	·	1	·	·	·	1
C. pyxidata	·	·	·	·	·	·	·	·	·	·	·	·	1	1	·	·	·	·	2
C. squamosa	·	·	·	·	·	·	·	·	·	·	1	1	·	1	·	·	·	·	·
C. sylvatica	·	3	·	·	·	·	3	3	3	·	2	2	·	2	·	2	·	3	2
C. uncialis	·	3	2	1	2	2	2	2	2	2	2	2	1	1	1	2	·	·	2
Peltigera canina	·	·	·	·	·	·	·	·	·	·	1	·	·	·	·	·	1	·	·
Number of species (85)	35	34	40	36	38	35	34	39	42	39	39	34	33	31	33	29	25	21	28

(Average 37)

(Average 29)

(Overall average 33)

Constancy class V 12 }
     ,, IV 7 } for the whole association.

LOCALITIES

1. Meall Horn, Reay Forest, Sutherland; 2. Foinaven, Reay Forest, Sutherland; 3. Quinag, Sutherland; 4. Ben More Coigach, Ross-shire; 5. Beinn Bhan, Applecross, Ross-shire; 6. Beinn Eighe, Ross-shire; 7. Carn na Criche, Fannich Forest, Ross-shire; 8. An Teallach, Dundonnell Forest, Ross-shire; 9,10. Liathach, Torridon, Ross-shire; 11. Sgurr a' Chaorachain, Monar Forest, Ross-shire; 12,13. Beinn Eighe, Ross-shire; 14. Beinn Dearg, Ross-shire; 15. Sgurr a' Ghlas Leathaid, Ross-shire; 16. Beinn Enaiglair, Ross-shire; 17. Glen Markie, Inverness-shire; 18. Farragon Hill, Perthshire; 19. Ben Alder, Inverness-shire.

Table 14: Juniperetum nanae [hepaticosum (1–7); lichenosum (8–10)]

	1	2	3	4	5	6	7	8	9	10
Reference number	R58 001	M55 010	M55 011	M55 012	M55 016	M55 018	R57 053	M56 079	R57 044	R57 048
Map reference	9503 2366	8618 1992	8618 1992	8618 1992	8615 1984	8556 1973	9495 2337	9186 2228	9436 2313	9591 2302
Altitude (feet)	1050	1350	1350	1350	1650	1850	1400	1550	1250	1400
Aspect (degrees)	45	360	360	360	135	315	135	–	225	225
Slope (degrees)	20	2	2	2	2	2	20	0	20	15
Cover (per cent)	100	100	100	100	100	100	97	75	95	100
Height (centimetres)	12	5	5	5	5	5	10	5	20	8
Plot area (square metres)	4	4	4	4	2	4	4	4	4	4
Arctostaphylos uva-ursi	3	3	4	5	4	2	3	4	6	.
Arctous alpina	+	2	.	.	+	3	3	4	.	.
Calluna vulgaris	8	5	5	5	4	6	7	5	6	6
Empetrum hermaphroditum	.	.	.	.	4	1	+	4	.	.
E. nigrum	2	.	.	.	.	.	.	.	.	.
Erica cinerea	4	2	4	.	.	2	4	.	4	6
Juniperus nana	4	7	7	8	7	7	7	4	6	8
Vaccinium myrtillus	.	.	.	.	2	.	3	2	.	.
V. uliginosum	.	.	.	.	3	.	.	.	.	.
Lycopodium selago	1	2	1	.	.	1	.	.	.	1
Agrostis canina	.	.	.	.	.	.	.	.	.	3
A. tenuis	.	.	.	.	.	.	1	.	.	.
Deschampsia flexuosa	2	3	3	3	3	2	3	3	.	3
Festuca ovina agg.	.	.	.	.	.	.	.	2	.	3
Molinia caerulea	.	.	2	1	.	.	2	.	.	.
Nardus stricta	.	.	.	.	.	.	.	.	.	2
Carex panicea	.	.	.	.	.	.	.	.	.	3
C. pilulifera	.	.	.	.	.	.	.	1	.	3
Luzula campestris	.	.	.	.	.	.	.	.	.	1
Orchis ericetorum	1	2	.	.	2	2	2	.	.	.
Trichophorum caespitosum	1	3	3	1	.	2	.	2	2	1
Antennaria dioica	.	.	.	.	.	.	.	+	.	.
Euphrasia brevipila	.	.	1	3	.	.	.	.	.	.
Polygala serpyllifolia	.	.	.	.	.	.	.	.	.	1
Potentilla erecta	2	.	2	.	.	2	3	.	2	3
Solidago virgaurea	.	.	.	.	.	1	1	2	.	.
Succisa pratensis	.	.	.	2	.	.	.	.	.	1
Thymus drucei	.	.	.	.	.	.	.	.	.	3
Viola riviniana	.	.	.	.	.	.	.	.	.	3
Campylopus flexuosus	.	.	.	1	.	1	1	.	.	.
Dicranum scoparium	1	.	.	.	.	.	2	1	.	.
Eurhynchium praelongum	.	.	.	.	.	.	.	1	.	.
Hylocomium splendens	1	.	.	1	.	.	2	.	.	2
H. umbratum	1	.	.	.	.	.	.	.	.	.
Hypnum cupressiforme	3	1	3	1	2	2	3	3	3	4
Isothecium myosuroides	.	.	.	.	.	.	.	.	.	4
Pleurozium schreberi	2	.	.	.	1	.	2	.	2	.
Rhacomitrium lanuginosum	4	3	3	2	+	2	4	4	3	2
Rhytidiadelphus loreus	1	.	.	.	.	.	2	.	.	2
Sphagnum nemoreum	.	.	.	2	.	2	3	.	.	.
Anastrophyllum donianum	.	.	.	.	.	.	1	.	.	.
Bazzania tricrenata	2	.	.	.	.	.	1	.	.	.
Diplophyllum albicans	2	1	1	.	.	.	2	.	1	1
Frullania tamarisci	1	.	.	.	.	1	2	1	.	1
Herberta hutchinsiae	4	.	.	.	.	.	4	.	.	.
Herberta sp. nov.	.	5	4	4	1	2	.	.	.	.
Jamesoniella carringtoni	3	.	.	.	.	.	3	.	.	.
Leptoscyphus taylori	.	.	.	.	.	.	1	.	.	.
Lophozia floerkii	.	.	.	.	.	.	.	2	.	.
L. quinquedentata	.	.	.	.	.	.	1	.	.	.
Nowellia curvifolia	.	.	.	.	.	.	2	.	.	.
Plagiochila asplenioides	.	.	.	.	.	.	.	2	.	.
P. spinulosa	3	.	.	.	.	.	.	.	.	.
Pleurozia purpurea	4	4	4	3	1	2	3	.	.	.
Ptilidium ciliare	.	.	.	.	1	.	.	.	.	.
Scapania gracilis	3	.	.	.	.	.	3	2	.	.
Sphenolobus minutus	.	.	.	.	.	.	2	.	.	.
Cetraria aculeata	.	.	.	.	.	.	.	2	.	2
C. islandica	.	.	.	.	.	.	.	.	.	2
Cladonia coccifera	1	.	.	.	.	.	1	.	.	.
C. gracilis	1	.	.	.	1	1	2	.	2	2
C. impexa	+	4	5	4	4	3	4	.	.	.
C. pyxidata	.	.	.	.	.	1	.	.	1	.
C. rangiferina agg.	.	.	.	.	.	.	2	1	3	2
C. sylvatica	3	.	.	.	.	.	3	5	5	3
C. uncialis	2	3	3	3	3	3	3	1	.	2
Sphaerophorus globosus	.	1	2	.	.	2	3	2	1	.
Number of species (67)	31	17	18	17	18	24	40	25	16	30

(Average 24)   (Overall average 24)   (Average 24)

Constancy class V 8
    ,,   ,,   IV 7

LOCALITIES

1. Conamheall, Loch Etiboll, Sutherland; 2–5. Beinn Eighe, Ross-shire; 6. Sgurr Dubh, Coulin Forest, Ross-shire; 7. Foinaven, Reay Forest, Sutherland; 8. Meallan Liath Mor, Canisp, Sutherland; 9. Arcuil, Reay Forest, Sutherland; 10. Farmheall, Parphe, Sutherland.

Table 15: Arctoeto-Callunetum (1-11); Loiseleuria-Empetrum provisional nodum (12,13)

	1	2	3	4	5	6	7	8	9	10	11	12	13
Reference number	M54 005	P54 006	P54 014	M55 001	M55 002	M55 008	M56 001	M56 002	M56 016	R56 016	R56 047	M56 023	M56 069
Map reference	2550 9270	2550 9270	2248 8780	1975 8540	1988 8545	1971 8642	1876 8515	2464 8652	1975 8489	8302 2004	8790 2361	7952 2975	8037 2968
Altitude (feet)	1780	1700	2000	2300	1800	2000	2000	2200	1800	2200	2200	3300	3300
Aspect (degrees)	315	270	–	360	90	270	45	157	90	180	225	350	–
Slope (degrees)	1	3	0	2	2	2	2	3	5	3	5	5	0
Cover (per cent)	100	95	100	100	100	100	100	100	90	75	100	60	50
Height (centimetres)	2	3	1	2	2	3	1	5	3	1	1	1	2
Plot area (square metres)	4	4	4	1	4	1	4	4	4	4	4	4	6
Arctostaphylos uva-ursi	.	.	.	+	1	.	.	.	+	.	+	.	.
Arctous alpina	4	4	4	5	4	5	+	4	4	5	4	.	.
Calluna vulgaris	8	8	7	7	6	7	7	6	7	6	7	+	.
Empetrum hermaphroditum	5	4	4	3	4	2	4	4	5	3	4	6	6
Erica cinerea	2	.	.	.	.	.	.	.	.	.	.	.	.
Juniperus nana	.	.	.	2	3	4	.	.	+	.	.	.	.
Loiseleuria procumbens	4	3	+	+	4	4	4	3	4	3	2	8	4
Salix herbacea	.	.	.	.	.	3	3	.	.	3	+	.	.
S. repens	.	.	+	.	.	.	.	.	.	.	.	.	.
Vaccinium myrtillus	1	2	1	.	3	.	.	2	.	.	2	3	4
V. uliginosum	.	.	+	.	.	+	.	.	.	.	.	.	.
V. vitis-idaea	3	1	.	.	.	.	.	3	.	.	3	+	.
Lycopodium alpinum	+	+	.	+	.	+	.	.	.	.	.	1	2
L. selago	1	1	+	3	.	1	2	+	+	+	.	2	.
Agrostis canina	.	.	.	.	.	.	3	.	.	3	.	.	.
A. tenuis	.	.	1	.	.	.	.	.	.	.	.	.	.
Deschampsia flexuosa	3	2	.	1	3	.	.	.	.	3	2	3	.	2
Festuca ovina agg.	2	2	.	2	.	3	2	.	.	3	.	.	.
Nardus stricta	.	.	.	+	+	.	.	.	.	.	.	.	.
Carex bigelowii	+	2	.	3	2	.	2	2	.	2	3	4	3
C. panicea	4	.	3	.	.	3	.	.	.	.	.	.	.
C. pilulifera	.	.	.	.	.	.	.	2	2	.	.	.	.
Juncus squarrosus	.	.	.	.	+	.	.	.	.	.	.	.	.
J. trifidus	.	.	.	.	.	.	.	.	.	.	.	2	4
Luzula multiflora	.	.	1	.	.	.	.	.	.	.	.	.	.
Trichophorum caespitosum	+	.	1	.	.	.	1	.	.	.	.	1	.
Antennaria dioica	2	1	+	.	.	.	1	+	.	3	.	.	.
Euphrasia frigida	1	+	+	.	.	.	.	.	.	.	.	.	.
E. officinalis agg.	.	.	.	.	.	.	.	.	2	.	.	.	.
Galium hercynicum	.	.	.	2	.	1	.	.	.	.	.	.	.
Hieracium holosericeum	.	.	.	.	.	+	.	.	1	.	.	.	.
Lotus corniculatus	+	+	.	.	.	.	.	.	.	.	.	.	.
Pinguicula vulgaris	+	+	.	.	.	+	.	.	.	.	.	.	.
Potentilla erecta	.	.	+	.	.	1	.	.	.	.	.	.	.
Solidago virgaurea	.	.	.	.	.	1	1	.	.	.	.	.	.
Thymus drucei	.	.	+	.	.	.	.	.	.	.	.	.	.
Dicranum fuscescens	.	.	.	.	.	.	.	.	.	1	.	1	.
D. scoparium	.	.	.	.	.	.	.	.	.	.	.	2	1
Hypnum cupressiforme	.	.	.	.	.	.	1	.	.	.	.	2	.
Pleurozium schreberi	.	.	1	.	.	.	.	.	+	.	.	2	.
Polytrichum alpinum	.	.	.	.	.	.	.	1	.	2	.	.	.
P. piliferum	.	.	.	.	.	.	.	2	.	2	.	1	.
Rhacomitrium lanuginosum	1	3	5	2	2	1	3	3	3	6	3	2	4
Alicularia scalaris	.	.	.	.	.	.	.	1	.	.	.	.	.
Diplophyllum albicans	.	.	.	.	.	.	2	1	.	.	.	.	.
Frullania tamarisci	.	.	.	.	.	.	2	.	.	.	.	.	.
Lophozia floerkii	.	.	.	.	.	.	1	.	.	1	1	.	.
Pleurozia purpurea	.	.	.	3	.	2	.	.	.	.	.	.	.
Ptilidium ciliare	.	.	.	.	.	.	.	.	.	.	.	2	1
Alectoria nigricans	.	2	1	.	.	.	2	2	2	1	2	1	.
A. ochroleuca	.	.	.	.	.	.	.	1	.	2	+	.	.
Cerania vermicularis	.	1	.	.	.	.	.	.	.	.	.	.	.
Cetraria aculeata	1	2	3	.	.	1	3	3	2	2	3	3	.
C. islandica	2	1	1	2	1	1	1	3	2	1	3	3	3
C. nivalis	.	.	.	.	.	.	.	.	.	.	.	2	+
Cladonia bellidiflora	.	.	.	1	1	.	.	.	.	.	1	2	.
C. subcervicornis	.	.	.	.	.	.	1	.	.	.	.	1	.
C. coccifera	.	.	.	.	1	.	1	.	.	1	2	.	.
C. gracilis	.	1	.	.	.	.	.	1	1	2	3	1	3
C. pyxidata	1	.	.	1	.	.	1	.	.	.	1	2	.
C. rangiferina	.	.	.	.	.	.	.	.	5	.	3	3	.
C. sylvatica	.	5	5	5	4	3	4	5	3	3	6	4	1
C. uncialis	.	3	1	4	3	3	3	4	3	2	4	2	1
Hypogymnia physodes	.	.	.	.	.	.	1	.	.	.	.	.	.
cf. Lecidea granulosa	.	.	.	.	.	.	.	.	.	.	.	+	.
Ochrolechia frigida	.	3	1	1	1	1	3	1	1	4	5	2	2

Table 15 (*continued*)

					1	2	3	4	5	6	7	8	9	10	11	12	13
Parmelia omphalodes	.	.	.	.	.	1	.	.	.	.	1	1	.	.	.	.	.
P. saxatilis	.	.	.	.	.	.	.	.	.	.	2	.	.	.	.	.	.
Platysma glaucum	.	.	.	.	3	3	+	3	3	3	4	3	3	3	3	.	.
P. lacunosum	.	.	.	.	+	1	2	.	.	+	+	+	+	.	.	.	.
Psoroma hypnorum	.	.	.	.	1	.	.	.	.	.	.	.	.	.	.	.	.
Sphaerophorus globosus	.	.	.	.	1	3	3	2	1	2	2	1	1	3	3	1	.
Stereocaulon evolutoides	.	.	.	.	.	.	.	.	.	.	.	.	1	.	.	.	.
S. vesuvianum	.	.	.	.	.	.	.	+	.	.	.	.	.	.	.	.	.
Number of species (74)	.	.	.	.	26	29	26	24	21	29	29	28	20	29	31	28	13

(Average 26)

Constancy class V 13 } for the association.
„ „ IV 7 }

LOCALITIES

1,2. Ben Klibreck, Sutherland; 3. Beinn Dearg, Braemore, Ross-shire; 4. Sgor nan Lochan Uaine, Coulin Forest, Ross-shire; 5. Loch Gobhlach, Coulin Forest, Ross-shire; 6. Beinn Eighe, Ross-shire; 7. Ben Damph, Ross-shire; 8. Ben Wyvis, Ross-shire; 9. Carn Eididh, Fuar Tholl, Coulin Forest, Ross-shire; 10. Sron na Gaoithe, Killilan Forest, Kintail; 11. Beinn a' Chaisteil, Strath Vaich, Ross-shire; 12. Devil's Point, Cairntoul, Cairngorms; 13. Creag an Leth Choin, Cairngorms.

Table 16: Cladineto-Callunetum [typicum (1–10);

	1	2	3	4	5	6	7	8	9	10
Reference number	XI	M55	M56	R56	R56	R56	M56	X2	M57	M58
	–	050	024	048	027	036	103	–	062	003
Map reference	–	8606	7955	8790	8815	8825	8010	–	7777	9284
	–	1986	2966	2361	2241	2235	3046	–	3145	3005
Altitude (feet)	–	2650	3100	2200	2600	2500	3200	–	2500	2300
Aspect (degrees)	–	90	135	225	180	180	135	–	270	90
Slope (degrees)	–	12	5	8	23	13	4	–	3	4
Cover (per cent)	–	95	90	100	100	97	100	–	90	100
Height (centimetres)	–	3	2	5	8	4	8	–	–	8
Plot area (square metres)	–	4	4	4	4	4	4	–	–	4
Arctostaphylos uva-ursi	.	.	.	.	.	.	.	.	.	.
Calluna vulgaris	7	7	8	8	9	8	8	6	7	5
Empetrum hermaphroditum	2	5	4	5	4	3	5	3	5	5
Erica tetralix	.	.	.	.	.	.	.	.	.	.
Loiseleuria procumbens	2	.	1	.	.	.	.	3	1	+
Rubus chamaemorus	.	.	.	.	.	.	.	.	.	3
Salix herbacea	.	.	.	2	.	.	.	.	.	2
Vaccinium myrtillus	3	3	.	2	2	.	3	.	.	2
V. uliginosum	.	4	.	.	.	.	1	.	.	.
V. vitis-idaea	2	.	.	2	+	2	.	3	+	.
Lycopodium alpinum	.	+	+	.	.	.	2	.	.	.
L. selago	1	+	.	.	1	.	+	+	.	.
Agrostis canina	.	.	.	.	.	1	.	.	.	.
A. tenuis	.	.	.	.	.	.	.	.	.	.
Deschampsia flexuosa	+	1	.	3	3	3	.	1	3	3
Festuca ovina agg.	.	3	.	.	.	.	.	.	.	.
Molinia caerulea	.	2	.	.	.	.	.	.	.	.
Nardus stricta	.	2	.	.	.	.	.	.	.	.
Carex bigelowii	3	3	3	3	3	3	3	+	.	2
C. panicea	.	.	.	.	.	.	.	.	.	.
C. pilulifera	.	.	.	.	.	2	1	.	.	.
Eriophorum vaginatum	.	.	.	.	+	.	.	.	.	.
Juncus squarrosus	.	1	.	.	.	1	.	.	.	.
J. trifidus	3	1	4	.	.	.	2	.	.	.
Narthecium ossifragum	.	2	.	.	.	.	.	.	.	.
Trichophorum caespitosum	.	+	.	.	.	.	+	.	.	.
Antennaria dioica	.	2	.	.	.	.	.	.	.	.
Potentilla erecta	.	2	.	.	.	.	.	.	.	.
Solidago virgaurea	.	2	.	.	.	.	.	.	.	.
Campylopus flexuosus	.	.	.	.	.	1	.	.	.	.
Dicranum scoparium	.	+	.	2	2	.	.	.	.	.
Hylocomium splendens	.	.	.	.	3	3	.	.	.	.
Hypnum cupressiforme	.	.	.	3	3	3	.	.	.	.
Pleurozium schreberi	.	.	.	3	3	2	.	.	.	3
Polytrichum alpinum	.	.	.	.	1	.	.	.	.	3
P. piliferum	1	.	.	.	.	.	.	.	.	.
Rhacomitrium lanuginosum	+	3	+	3	3	3	2	.	.	3
Rhytidiadelphus loreus	.	.	.	.	3	.	.	.	.	.
Anastrepta orcadensis	.	.	.	.	2	.	.	.	.	.
Diplophyllum albicans	.	.	.	.	2	.	.	.	+	.
Lophozia alpestris	.	.	.	.	.	.	.	+	.	.
Ptilidium ciliare	.	.	.	2	3	1	2	2	.	1
Alectoria nigricans	3	.	2	1	.	.	.	3	3	2
A. ochroleuca	3	.	2	.	.	.	.	.	.	2
Cerania vermicularis	1	.	.	.	.	.	.	.	.	.
Cetraria aculeata	4	.	2	3	1	.	2	1	4	1
C. islandica	2	3	2	3	.	3	3	1	3	2
C. nivalis	.	.	3	.	.	.	+	2	.	.
Cladonia bellidiflora	2	2	1	.	1	2	.	2	2	1
C. coccifera	.	.	2	.	2	2	.	.	.	.
C. floerkeana	.	.	.	.	.	.	.	.	.	.
C. gracilis	3	.	2	3	3	3	3	2	.	.
C. impexa	.	.	.	.	.	.	.	.	1	.
C. pyxidata	1	.	.	.	2	2	1	.	.	.
C. rangiferina agg.	.	.	3	3	4	4	3	.	.	1
C. squamosa	.	.	.	.	.	.	1	.	.	.
C. sylvatica	5	3	5	6	5	6	4	4	.	6
C. uncialis	4	3	4	4	2	4	3	3	3	4
Ochrolechia frigida	4	1	3	.	.	3	2	4	1	1
Platysma glaucum	.	.	1	.	.	.	.	.	4	.
Sphaerophorus globosus	3	.	.	2	+	1	.	4	+	.
Number of species (61)	23	25	19	22	26	24	22	19	14	20

(Overall

Constancy Class V 6
    „   „ IV 6

LOCALITIES

2. Beinn Eighe, Ross-shire; 3. Cairntoul, Cairngorms; 4. Beinn a' Chaisteil, Strath Vaich, Ross-shire; 5. Iorguill, Inverlael Forest, Ross-shire; 6. Beinn Dearg, Ross-shire; 7. Beinn a' Chaoruinn, Cairngorms; 9. Glas Maol, Aberdeenshire; 10. Morven, Caithness; 11. Sron na Lairige,

arctostaphyletosum (11–13); sylvaticosum (14–18)]

11	12	13	14	15	16	17	18	
M56	M57	M58	R57	P55	P55	M56	M57	Reference number
141	087	089	172	026	027	125	088	
8035	7905	8047	7970	8023	8023	8125	7912	Map reference
2953	2978	2965	2601	2883	2883	3253	2964	
2400	2500	2400	2500	2500	2500	2300	2900	Altitude (feet)
—	270	315	360	360	360	—	135	Aspect (degrees)
0	3	2	10	20	20	0	2	Slope (degrees)
100	100	100	100	100	100	100	100	Cover (percentage)
7	—	—	5	5	5	6	—	Height (centimetres)
4	4	4	4	4	4	4	4	Plot area (square metres)
5	5	5	·	·	·	·	·	**Arctostaphylos uva-ursi**
7	7	8	8	7	7	4	4	**Calluna vulgaris**
·	·	+	2	3	3	1	·	**Empetrum hermaphroditum**
·	·	+	·	·	·	·	·	Erica tetralix
·	·	·	·	1	·	·	·	Loiseleuria procumbens
·	·	·	·	·	·	·	·	Rubus chamaemorus
·	·	·	·	·	·	·	·	Salix herbacea
·	·	·	2	·	2	·	·	Vaccinium myrtillus
·	·	·	·	·	·	·	·	V. uliginosum
·	·	·	1	·	·	·	·	V. vitis-idaea
·	·	·	·	·	1	·	1	Lycopodium alpinum
2	+	·	·	·	1	·	·	L. selago
·	·	·	·	·	·	·	·	Agrostis canina
·	·	·	·	·	·	+	·	A. tenuis
·	·	·	3	3	3	2	·	**Deschampsia flexuosa**
·	·	·	·	·	·	·	·	Festuca ovina agg.
·	·	·	·	·	·	·	·	Molinia caerulea
·	·	·	·	·	·	·	·	Nardus stricta
·	1	·	3	1	1	·	2	**Carex bigelowii**
2	2	·	·	·	·	·	·	C. panicea
·	1	·	·	·	·	·	1	C. pilulifera
·	·	·	·	·	·	·	·	Eriophorum vaginatum
·	·	·	·	·	·	·	·	Juncus squarrosus
·	·	·	·	·	·	·	·	J. trifidus
·	·	·	·	·	·	·	·	Narthecium ossifragum
2	2	1	·	·	·	·	2	Trichophorum caespitosum
·	·	·	·	·	·	·	·	Antennaria dioica
·	·	·	·	·	·	·	·	Potentilla erecta
·	·	·	·	·	·	·	·	Solidago virgaurea
·	·	·	·	·	·	·	·	Campylopus flexuosus
·	·	1	1	·	·	·	·	Dicranum scoparium
·	·	·	·	·	·	·	·	Hylocomium splendens
·	·	2	2	1	1	·	·	Hypnum cupressiforme
1	·	·	1	·	·	·	·	Pleurozium schreberi
·	·	·	2	·	·	1	·	Polytrichum alpinum
·	·	·	·	·	·	·	·	P. piliferum
1	·	1	2	2	2	1	·	**Rhacomitrium lanuginosum**
·	·	·	·	·	·	·	·	Rhytidiadelphus loreus
·	·	1	·	·	·	·	·	Anastrepta orcadensis
·	·	·	·	·	1	·	·	Diplophyllum albicans
·	·	·	·	·	·	·	·	Lophozia alpestris
1	·	·	1	·	1	·	·	Ptilidium ciliare
1	·	2	·	·	1	2	·	Alectoria nigricans
·	+	·	·	·	·	·	·	A. ochroleuca
·	·	·	·	·	·	·	·	Cerania vermicularis
2	3	2	2	1	2	3	·	**Cetraria aculeata**
3	3	3	2	3	3	1	2	C. islandica
·	1	·	·	2	2	·	·	C. nivalis
·	·	·	·	·	1	·	·	**Cladonia bellidiflora**
1	·	·	1	·	·	·	·	C. coccifera
·	·	·	·	·	1	·	·	C. floerkeana
3	3	·	2	·	2	·	·	C. gracilis
·	3	·	·	·	·	·	·	C. impexa
·	·	·	·	·	·	·	·	C. pyxidata
3	2	4	5	4	3	2	3	**C. rangiferina agg.**
·	·	·	·	·	·	·	·	C. squamosa
6	5	6	6	7	7	8	8	**C. sylvatica**
4	4	2	2	3	3	2	1	**C. uncialis**
1	2	·	2	·	1	1	·	**Ochrolechia frigida**
1	·	+	·	·	·	·	·	Platysma glaucum
·	·	·	·	·	1	·	·	Sphaerophorus globosus
18	16	16	20	14	23	13	9	Number of species (61)

average 19)

Cairngorms; 12. Beinn Bhrotain, Cairngorms; 13. Creag an Leth Choin, Cairngorms; 14. Glen Banchor, Inverness-shire; 15,16. Geal Charn, Monadhliath; 17. Little Corr Riabhach, Ladder Hills, Aberdeenshire; 18. Beinn Bhrotain, Cairngorms.

Table 17: Rhacomitreto-Callunetum [empetrosum (1–7); arctostaphyletosum (8–13)]; related western Calluna-Arctostaphylos communities (14,15)

	1	2	3	4	5	6	7	8	9	10	11	12	13	14	15
Reference number	R56 012	M56 009	R56 105	R56 038	R56 074	R57 011	R57 019	R57 033	R57 037	R57 073	R57 087	R56 099	M55 007	R56 010	R56 081
Map reference	8613 2173	8423 1778	8303 1987	8825 2235	8732 2031	9458 2308	9592 2310	9496 2342	9348 2374	8690 2055	8815 2215	8742 2212	8639 1939	8555 1953	8567 1973
Altitude (feet)	2100	2000	2400	2550	2150	1450	1500	1000	1000	1050	1600	1350	2000	400	800
Aspect (degrees)	90	270	90	—	270	45	360	315	360	—	—	—	—	270	360
Slope (degrees)	5	3	20	4	30	5	15	20	5	5	0	5	0	15	12
Cover (per cent)	100	95	100	100	100	100	90	75	100	95	95	95	100	70	95
Height (centimetres)	—	3	5	3	8	3	5	5	5	5	9	9	2	—	16
Plot area (square metres)	4	4	4	4	4	4	4	4	4	4	4	4	1	4	4
Arctostaphylos uva-ursi								+		3	5	2		4	6
Arctous alpina								5	5	4	5	6			
Calluna vulgaris	6	8	8	7	8	8	7	6	7	7	7	7	7	6	7
Empetrum hermaphroditum	3	3	4	4	4	5	4			3		3	5		
E. nigrum	3								2						
Erica cinerea							+		4		3	2		3	5
Juniperus nana						3	2	4					3		
Loiseleuria procumbens				3									5		
Salix herbacea		+													
Vaccinium myrtillus			2		3	3	3	2		2					
V. uliginosum						2									
V. vitis-idaea	2	+		1											
Lycopodium alpinum				+	3									1	
L. selago		3		+	+	1		1	+		+		1	1	
Agrostis canina		3		2	3			2	2						2
Deschampsia flexuosa	2		3		4	2	3	3		2					3
Festuca ovina agg.					2		3		3	1			2	3	3
Molinia caerulea															
Nardus stricta					+	3	1		2				1		
Carex bigelowii	2		3	3	2		3						+		
C. binervis								+	2	1					
C. panicea			3								2				
C. pilulifera			2				2	+							
Juncus trifidus				2											
Orchis ericetorum											2				3
Trichophorum caespitosum			1		+				2	3	3	2		4	3
Alchemilla alpina			+	2	+										
Antennaria dioica		3		1	+								3	3	2
Galium hercynicum													3		
Hieracium holosericeum				+											
Potentilla erecta					2	2		2		2			1	1	4
Solidago virgaurea				1	2	2	+	+					1	2	3
Succisa pratensis		2													
Breutelia chrysocoma															2
Campylopus flexuosus														1	
Dicranum fuscescens			1			2									
D. scoparium			1	2		2			2	2	2	1			2
Hylocomium splendens			3	1	1	2			2	2					
Hypnum cupressiforme		2	1	3	3	3		3	3	4	3	3	2	2	3
Pleurozium schreberi			3	1	2	3				3	2	3			
Pohlia nutans												1			
Polytrichum alpinum	1								3	3		1			
P. piliferum		+		2											
Rhacomitrium lanuginosum	6	5	7	7	7	6	7	7	7	7	6	6	4	5	8
Rhytidiadelphus loreus			3		2					2	2	1		1	
Sphagnum tenellum															
Anastrepta orcadensis					1	2			1						
Bazzania tricrenata						3									
Diplophyllum albicans				2		3		1	2		2	2		1	1
Frullania tamarisci						1			2	2	1	2			2
Herberta hutchinsiae						4		+							
Jamesoniella carringtoni						3									
Leptoscyphus taylori						2									
Lophozia floerkii				1											
L. quinquedentata					1										
Mastigophora woodsii						3									
Plagiochila spinulosa					2										
Pleurozia purpurea				1	2			3							
Ptilidium ciliare		1	2	3	2										
Scapania gracilis						2				2	2				3
S. nimbosa						3									
S. ornithopodioides						+									

Table 17 (*continued*)

	1	2	3	4	5	6	7	8	9	10	11	12	13	14	15
Alectoria nigricans	1	.	2	2	.	.	2	.	.	.	.	2	.	.	.
Cetraria aculeata	2	.	3	3	.	.	.	.	3	3	3	3	.	2	.
C. islandica	2	2	3	3	2	.	1	.	3	3	.	2	2	.	.
Cladonia cervicornis	.	.	.	.	.	.	.	.	.	1	.	.	.	.	.
C. coccifera	.	.	.	1	2	.	.	.	.	2	2	2	.	1	.
C. gracilis	2	.	1	2	1	.	.	2	3	3	2	3	.	.	.
C. impexa	.	.	.	.	.	.	.	.	.	6	.	.	.	3	3
C. pyxidata	1	1	.	1	.	3	.	.	.	2	.	.	1	.	.
C. rangiferina agg.	.	.	.	3	.	3	.	.	2	1	2	.	.	.	.
C. sylvatica	5	2	3	5	4	4	3	3	5	.	5	5	3	.	.
C. uncialis	5	3	2	4	4	3	3	3	3	4	3	3	3	3	3
Coriscium viride	.	.	.	.	.	.	+	.	.	.	.	.	.	.	.
Icmadophila ericetorum	.	.	.	.	.	.	.	.	.	.	.	.	.	2	.
Ochrolechia frigida	3	2	.	4	+	.	3	.	.	.	3	4	+	.	.
Platysma glaucum	1	3	.	.	.	.	3	.	.	.	.	3	+	1	.
Pycnothelia papillaria	.	.	.	.	.	.	.	.	.	.	.	3	.	3	.
Sphaerophorus globosus	3	1	1	2	.	2	2	.	3	1	2	3	1	.	.
Glaeocapsa magna	.	.	.	.	.	.	.	.	.	.	.	.	.	1	.
Number of species (80)	19	19	23	32	31	34	20	19	27	31	22	24	22	23	20

(Overall average 23)

Constancy class V 7 ⎱ for the association.
   ,,   ,, IV 4 ⎰

LOCALITIES

1. Fionn Bheinn, Loch a' Chroisg Forest, Ross-shire; 2. Bealach nam Bo, Applecross, Ross-shire; 3. Sguman Coinntich, Killilan Forest, Kintail; 4. Beinn Dearg, Inverlael, Ross-shire; 5. Beinn Tarsuinn, Fisherfield Forest, Ross-shire; 6. Arcuil, Reay Forest, Sutherland; 7. Farmheall, Parphe, Sutherland; 8. Foinaven, Reay Forest, Sutherland; 9. Loch Eas na Maoile, Reay Forest, Sutherland; 10. Loch an Sgeireach, Kinlochewe Forest, Ross-shire; 11. Beinn Enaiglair, Braemore, Ross-shire; 12. Allt a' Mhadaidh, Fannich Forest, Ross-shire; 13. Beinn a' Chearcaill, Kinlochewe Forest, Ross-shire; 14. Lochan an Iasgair, Glen Torridon, Ross-shire; 15. Sgurr Dubh, Coulin Forest, Ross-shire.

Table 18: Vaccinetum chionophilum

	1	2	3	4	5	6	7	8	9	10	11	12	13
Reference number	M57 060	M57 071	M57 073	M56 099	M56 100	M56 118	M56 123	PX4	P54 005	R57 075	R57 078	R57 198	R58 068
Map reference	7876 3408	8036 3223	8038 3216	7778 3140	7780 3144	8999 3017	8127 3254	797– 290–	7974 3154	7861 2440	7987 2568	7997 2598	8450 2079
Altitude (feet)	2400	2500	2500	2100	2400	2500	2200	–	2400	2500	2300	2000	2100
Aspect (degrees)	360	180	135	45	270	90	45	–	165	90	90	270	45
Slope (degrees)	45	30	25	50	40	45	8	–	12	30	35	35	30
Cover (per cent)	100	100	100	100	100	100	100	–	100	100	100	100	100
Height (centimetres)	12	25	14	15	13	15	15	–	18	–	–	20	–
Plot area (square metres)	4	4	4	4	4	4	4	1	4	4	4	4	4
Calluna vulgaris	I	I	+	.	.	.	3	3	.	.	.	I	.
Empetrum hermaphroditum	2	4	+	2	2	4	2	I	2	3	3	2	3
Vaccinium myrtillus	8	8	7	10	9	6	8	9	7	9	9	9	10
V. uliginosum	.	.	4	.	.	5	.	.	7	.	.	.	+
V. vitis-idaea	.	4	.	I	2	.	4	3	.	.	.	+	2
Blechnum spicant	+	3	3	2	+	2	4	I	3	3	4	3	2
Dryopteris austriaca	.	.	.	I	.	.	.	+	.	.	.	.	.
D. borreri	.	.	.	I	.	.	.	.	.	.	.	.	.
Lycopodium clavatum	.	.	.	+	.	.	.	.	.	.	.	.	.
L. selago	I	.	.	.	.	.	.	.	.	.	.	.	.
Agrostis canina	.	.	.	.	.	.	.	.	.	3	I	2	.
A. tenuis	.	.	3	.	.	.	.	.	+	.	I	.	.
Anthoxanthum odoratum	.	.	.	.	.	.	3	.	.	3	I	.	.
Deschampsia caespitosa	.	.	.	.	.	.	.	.	.	.	2	.	.
D. flexuosa	3	3	2	3	4	4	3	4	.	4	3	3	3
Festuca ovina agg.	.	.	.	.	+	.	.	.	.	2	.	.	.
Molinia caerulea	.	.	.	.	.	.	.	.	2	.	.	.	.
Nardus stricta	I	+	I	2	I	+	.	.	4	3	I	I	.
Carex bigelowii	2	+	.	.	.	3	2	.	.	3	2	.	I
C. binervis	.	.	.	.	.	.	.	.	.	+	.	.	.
C. pilulifera	.	.	.	.	.	.	.	.	.	.	I	.	.
Juncus squarrosus	.	.	.	.	.	.	.	+	.	.	.	.	.
Luzula multiflora	.	.	.	.	.	.	.	.	.	.	2	I	.
L. sylvatica	.	.	.	+	.	3	.	.	.	.	+	2	2
Alchemilla alpina	.	.	.	2	+	2	.	.	2	3	3	.	.
Chamaepericlymenum suecicum	+	+	I	.	3	.	+	3	3	3	.	.	+
Euphrasia sp.	.	.	.	.	.	.	.	.	.	2	.	.	.
Galium hercynicum	.	2	I	3	3	3	3	3	2	3	3	I	3
Melampyrum pratense	.	.	3	I	I	+	.	.	2	.	.	.	2
Oxalis acetosella	.	.	.	3	.	.	3	+	.	3	I	2	.
Potentilla erecta	.	.	2	+	.	2	.	.	3	.	.	I	.
Rubus chamaemorus	.	.	.	.	.	.	.	I	.	.	.	.	2
Rumex acetosa	.	.	.	.	I	3	.	.	.	+	3	.	.
Trientalis europaea	.	.	3	.	.	.	.	.	2	.	.	.	.
Viola palustris	.	.	.	.	.	.	.	.	+	2	.	.	.
Dicranella heteromalla	.	.	.	.	.	.	.	.	.	I	.	.	.
Dicranodontium uncinatum	.	I	.	.	.	.	.	.	.	.	.	.	.
Dicranum fuscescens	2	.	.	.	.	3	.	.	.	3	3	.	.
D. majus	.	I	.	I	.	2	.	.	.	2	.	3	3
D. scoparium	5	2	2	4	.	.	.	3	+	.	.	.	I
Hylocomium splendens	.	4	2	5	2	5	2	5	.	5	6	6	6
H. umbratum	.	.	.	.	.	.	.	.	.	2	I	.	.
Hypnum callichroum	.	.	.	.	.	.	.	.	.	2	.	.	.
H. cupressiforme	.	.	.	.	•	.	.	3	.	.	.	.	.
Isothecium myosuroides	.	.	.	.	.	.	I	.	.	.	.	.	.
Leucobryum glaucum	.	.	.	.	.	.	.	.	+	.	.	.	.
Plagiothecium striatellum	.	.	.	.	.	.	.	.	.	.	I	I	.
P. undulatum	.	.	.	.	.	2	.	.	.	.	3	.	3
Pleurozium schreberi	3	6	7	6	7	I	4	3	8	5	6	6	4
Polytrichum alpinum	2	I	2	.	.	.	.	.	.	2	2	.	.
P. commune	.	.	.	.	4	2	4	4	.	.	.	3	.
Pohlia sp.	.	I	.	.	.	.	.	.	.	.	.	.	.
Ptilium crista-castrensis	.	.	.	.	.	.	.	.	.	.	I	2	3
Rhacomitrium canescens	.	.	.	.	.	.	.	.	.	2	.	.	.
R. fasciculare	.	.	.	.	.	I	.	.	.	.	.	.	.
R. lanuginosum	3	.	.	.	.	2	.	.	.	.	.	.	.
Rhytidiadelphus loreus	4	.	2	I	I	.	2	4	.	5	6	4	5
R. squarrosus	.	.	.	.	I	6	.	.	.	.	.	.	.
Sphagnum girgensohnii	.	.	.	.	.	.	.	.	.	.	.	.	3
S. nemoreum	I	.	.	.	.	.	.	6	+	.	I	3	4
S. quinquefarium	.	.	+	.	.	.	I	6	.	.	.	2	4
Thuidium tamariscinum	.	.	.	.	.	.	.	.	.	.	2	5	3
Anastrepta orcadensis	.	.	.	.	.	.	.	.	.	2	.	I	4
Bazzania tricrenata	.	.	.	.	.	.	.	.	.	.	.	.	3
Calypogeia trichomanis	.	I	.	.	.	I	.	.	.	.	.	.	.
Diplophyllum albicans	.	I	.	.	.	.	.	.	.	.	I	.	.
Lepidozia pearsoni	.	I	.	.	.	.	.	.	.	.	.	.	3

Table 18 (*continued*)

	1	2	3	4	5	6	7	8	9	10	11	12	13
Lophozia alpestris	I	.	.	.	.	.	.	.	.	.	.	.	.
L. floerkii	3	.	I	.	.	.	.	I	.	.	.	.	3
L. lycopodioides	.	4	.	.	.	.	.	.	.	.	.	.	.
L. quinquedentata	.	.	.	.	.	.	.	.	.	.	.	.	4
Ptilidium ciliare	.	2	2	I	I	.	+	.	3	3	2	.	2
Scapania ornithopodioides	.	.	.	.	.	.	.	.	.	.	.	.	2
Cetraria islandica	3	2	.	.	.	+	.	.	3	.	.	.	.
Cladonia bellidiflora	I	.	.	.	.	+	.	I	I	.	.	.	.
C. carneola	.	.	.	.	.	I	.	.	.	.	.	.	.
C. coccifera	.	.	.	.	.	I	.	.	.	.	.	.	.
C. gracilis	I	I	.	.	.	.	.	.	+	.	I	.	.
C. impexa	.	3	.	.	.	.	.	.	.	.	.	.	.
C. pyxidata	.	I	I	.	.	.	.	.	.	I	.	.	.
C. rangiferina agg.	.	I	.	.	.	.	.	.	.	.	.	.	.
C. squamosa	.	.	.	.	.	.	.	.	.	2	I	.	.
C. sylvatica	I	3	I	.	.	I	.	.	2	I	.	.	.
C. uncialis	I	.	.	.	.	I	.	.	.	I	.	.	.
Coriscium viride	I	.	.	.	.	.	.	.	.	.	.	.	.
Number of species (85)	27	25	23	21	19	32	15	21	24	37	30	20	31

(Average 25)

Constancy class V   8
   ,,   ,,   IV   3

LOCALITIES

1. Mount Keen, Aberdeenshire; 2,3. Brown Cow Hill, Aberdeenshire; 4. The Cairnwell, Perthshire; 5. Meall Odhar, Cairnwell; 6. Coire Etchachan, Aberdeenshire; 7. Meikle Corr Riabhach, Aberdeenshire; 8. Head of Loch Einich, Inverness-shire; 9. Craig an Dail Beag, Aberdeenshire; 10. Creag Meagaidh, Inverness-shire; 11,12. Glen Markie, Inverness-shire; 13. Sgurr a' Chaorachain. Monar Forest, Ross-shire.

15

Table 19: Vaccineto-Empetretum (1–16); Empetrum-hypnaceous Vaccinium-Nardus

	1	2	3	4	5	6	7	8	9	10	11
Reference number	M56 014	M56 056	M56 063	M56 071	R56 026	P52 054	P52 057	P52 059	M57 097	R57 098	R57 221
Map reference	8584 1935	8483 2085	8558 2265	9156 2295	8807 2222	7532 2721	7548 2715	7547 2714	7772 3115	7728 2506	7741 3276
Altitude (feet)	2000	2800	2700	2250	2600	2550	2500	2400	2850	2700	2600
Aspect (degrees)	360	315	135	315	360	350	210	210	315	112	45
Slope (degrees)	10	15	10	30	10	15	5	25	2	30	20
Cover (per cent)	80	100	100	100	99	100	100	100	100	100	100
Height (centimetres)	6	5	8	5	–	10	5	5	–	15	10
Plot area (square metres)	4	4	1	4	4	16	4	4	4	4	4
Calluna vulgaris	.	.	.	.	.	.	.	.	.	.	.
Empetrum hermaphroditum	7	8	10	8	8	6	9	8	8	7	5
Phyllodoce caerulea	.	.	.	.	.	.	.	.	.	.	.
Salix herbacea	.	.	.	.	.	.	.	.	.	.	.
Vaccinium myrtillus	4	5	3	4	5	7	5	5	4	7	7
V. uliginosum	.	.	.	.	.	.	.	.	.	5	6
V. vitis-idaea	.	1	2	.	.	3	.	3	3	.	3
Blechnum spicant	.	.	.	1	.	.	.	.	.	1	.
Lycopodium alpinum	.	.	.	+	.	.	.	.	.	.	.
L. selago	+	.	.	.	.	.	.	.	.	.	.
Agrostis canina	.	.	.	.	2	.	.	.	.	.	.
A. tenuis	.	.	1	.	.	.	.	.	.	.	.
Anthoxanthum odoratum	.	.	.	2	.	.	.	.	.	.	.
Deschampsia caespitosa	.	.	.	.	2	.	.	.	.	.	.
D. flexuosa	3	3	.	3	3	.	.	.	3	3	3
Festuca ovina agg.	.	.	2	3	2	3	.	.	.	.	.
F. rubra	.	.	.	.	.	.	.	.	.	.	.
Nardus stricta	.	.	.	2	.	.	.	.	.	2	.
Carex bigelowii	3	3	3	2	3	1	.	.	2	2	.
C. binervis	.	.	.	.	.	.	.	.	.	.	.
C. echinata	.	.	.	.	.	.	.	.	.	.	.
C. pilulifera	.	.	.	2	.	.	.	.	.	.	.
Juncus squarrosus	.	.	.	.	.	.	.	.	.	.	.
J. trifidus	.	.	.	.	.	.	.	.	.	.	.
Luzula multiflora	.	.	.	2	.	.	.	.	.	.	.
L. sylvatica	+	.	.	.	.	.	.	.	.	.	.
Alchemilla alpina	.	.	.	2	2	.	.	.	.	.	.
Chamaepericlymenum suecicum	.	.	.	.	.	.	.	.	.	.	.
Galium hercynicum	.	.	.	2	.	.	.	.	.	2	.
Melampyrum pratense	.	.	.	.	.	2	.	.	.	.	.
Oxalis acetosella	.	+	.	.	1	.	.	.	.	.	.
Potentilla erecta	.	.	.	+	.	.	.	.	.	.	.
Rubus chamaemorus	.	.	.	.	.	3	.	.	.	.	2
Rumex acetosa	.	.	.	.	1	.	.	.	.	2	.
Succisa pratensis	.	.	.	+	.	.	.	.	.	.	.
Dicranodontium uncinatum	.	.	.	.	.	.	.	.	.	.	.
Dicranum fuscescens	.	1	.	.	.	.	.	.	.	2	.
D. majus	.	.	.	2	2	.	.	.	.	2	.
D. scoparium	2	.	.	.	2	3	1	1	1	.	2
Hylocomium splendens	3	1	3	4	6	5	.	.	2	7	5
Hypnum cupressiforme	2	.	.	2	2	.	.	.	.	.	.
Plagiothecium striatellum	.	.	.	.	.	.	.	.	.	.	.
P. undulatum	.	.	.	1	.	1	.	.	.	2	.
Pleurozium schreberi	1	.	.	.	1	4	5	6	6	7	8
Pohlia nutans	.	.	.	.	.	.	1	.	.	.	.
Polytrichum alpinum	.	1	.	2	2	.	.	.	1	.	4
P. commune	.	.	.	.	.	3	.	.	.	.	.
P. cf. gracile	.	.	.	.	.	.	.	.	.	.	.
P. urnigerum	.	.	.	.	1	.	.	.	.	.	.
Ptilium crista-castrensis	.	.	.	.	.	.	.	.	.	+	.
Rhacomitrium lanuginosum	4	.	2	2	2	2	2	1	1	.	.
Rhytidiadelphus loreus	3	7	5	5	6	3	.	.	1	3	3
Sphagnum fuscum	.	.	.	.	.	6	.	.	.	.	.
S. nemoreum	.	3	.	.	3	6	.	.	.	.	.
S. quinquefarium	2	.	.	3	.	.	.	.	.	.	.
Anastrepta orcadensis	4	1	.	2	4	1	.	.	.	.	.
Anastrophyllum donianum	3	.	.	.	.	.	.	.	.	.	.
A. jorgensenii	.	.	.	.	.	.	.	.	.	.	.
Bazzania tricrenata	.	.	.	4	.	.	.	.	.	.	.
B. pearsoni	.	.	.	.	.	.	.	.	.	.	.
Blepharostoma trichophyllum	.	.	.	.	.	1	.	.	.	.	.
Diplophyllum albicans	.	+	.	.	1	.	.	.	.	.	.
Herberta hutchinsiae	4	.	.	.	.	.	.	.	.	.	.
Jamesoniella carringtoni	2	.	.	.	.	.	.	.	.	.	.
Leptoscyphus anomalus	.	.	.	.	.	3	.	.	.	.	.
L. taylori	2	.	.	.	.	.	.	.	.	.	.
Lophozia floerkii	.	+	.	2	.	.	.	.	.	1	.

moss communities (17,18);   Hepatic-rich Vaccineto-Empetretum (19);
communities (20,21)

12	13	14	15	16	17	18	19	20	21	
R57	M57	M56		M56	R58	M58	R56	R58	R58	Reference number
178	070	137	PX7	065	012	001	064	059	010	
7919	7806	7740	797−	8568	9286	9308	8730	8874	9502	Map reference
2503	3191	2626	290−	2252	3004	2595	2065	2342	2480	
2600	3000	2200	−	2200	2300	2250	2050	2600	2800	Altitude (feet)
180	360	45	−	45	360	45	360	90	90	Aspect (degrees)
30	10	40	−	50	35	18	30	10	15	Slope (degrees)
100	100	100	−	100	100	100	90	100	100	Cover (per cent)
−	−	10	−	15	9	6	20	10	8	Height (centimetres)
4	4	4	1	4	4	4	16	4	4	Plot area (square metres)
.	.	3	3	+	.	.	.	.	.	Calluna vulgaris
8	8	5	5	7	6	6	8	5	6	**Empetrum hermaphroditum**
.	.	6	.	.	.	.	.	.	.	Phyllodoce caerulea
.	4	.	.	.	.	.	.	.	.	Salix herbacea
5	4	7	7	8	5	3	5	5	4	**Vaccinium myrtillus**
.	+	2	3	.	.	.	+	2	.	V. uliginosum
5	.	3	.	2	4	3	.	3	3	V. vitis-idaea
.	.	2	1	2	.	.	2	.	.	Blechnum spicant
.	.	+	.	.	.	.	3	+	.	Lycopodium alpinum
.	.	1	.	.	.	.	+	.	.	L. selago
3	.	1	.	.	.	3	2	.	.	Agrostis canina
.	.	.	.	.	.	.	2	3	2	A. tenuis
.	.	.	3	.	.	.	.	.	.	Anthoxanthum odoratum
.	.	.	.	.	.	.	.	.	.	Deschampsia caespitosa
3	3	.	3	2	4	3	3	3	3	D. flexuosa
3	.	.	.	.	.	.	3	1	3	Festuca ovina agg.
.	1	.	.	.	.	.	.	.	.	F. rubra
1	.	2	.	1	.	2	3	7	5	Nardus stricta
2	3	.	.	.	2	2	2	3	3	Carex bigelowii
.	.	1	.	.	.	.	.	.	.	C. binervis
.	.	.	1	.	.	.	.	.	.	C. echinata
.	.	2	.	.	.	.	.	.	.	C. pilulifera
.	.	.	.	+	.	.	.	2	.	Juncus squarrosus
.	2	.	.	.	.	.	+	.	.	J. trifidus
.	.	.	.	2	.	.	.	.	.	Luzula multiflora
.	.	+	.	.	.	.	1	.	.	L. sylvatica
1	1	3	.	2	.	.	3	.	.	Alchemilla alpina
.	.	+	3	3	.	.	.	1	.	Chamaepericlymenum suecicum
1	.	1	1	2	2	.	2	2	3	Galium hercynicum
.	.	.	.	1	.	.	.	1	.	Melampyrum pratense
.	.	.	1	.	.	.	.	.	.	Oxalis acetosella
2	.	3	.	1	.	.	1	2	2	Potentilla erecta
.	.	.	2	.	.	.	.	.	.	Rubus chamaemorus
.	.	.	.	.	.	.	.	.	.	Rumex acetosa
.	.	.	.	.	.	.	.	.	.	Succisa pratensis
.	.	.	.	.	.	.	3	.	.	Dicranodontium uncinatum
.	5	.	.	.	.	.	3	.	.	Dicranum fuscescens
.	.	2	.	.	.	.	3	.	.	D. majus
1	.	.	3	1	1	.	3	1	1	D. scoparium
4	.	3	4	3	8	5	3	5	3	**Hylocomium splendens**
1	.	.	.	1	.	.	2	2	3	Hypnum cupressiforme
.	.	.	.	.	.	.	.	.	.	Plagiothecium striatellum
.	.	.	.	.	.	.	2	3	.	P. undulatum
7	4	5	3	2	5	2	2	3	3	**Pleurozium schreberi**
.	.	.	.	.	.	.	.	.	.	Pohlia nutans
1	2	.	.	.	.	1	2	.	.	Polytrichum alpinum
.	.	1	2	.	.	4	.	1	.	P. commune
.	.	.	2	.	.	.	.	.	.	P. cf. gracile
.	.	.	.	.	.	.	.	.	.	P. urnigerum
.	.	.	.	.	.	.	.	.	.	Ptilium crista-castrensis
2	2	.	.	.	3	2	6	3	3	Rhacomitrium lanuginosum
3	3	4	4	5	4	8	3	5	3	**Rhytidiadelphus loreus**
.	.	.	.	.	.	.	.	.	.	Sphagnum fuscum
2	.	.	7	.	.	.	5	2	2	S. nemoreum
.	.	.	7	.	.	.	.	.	.	S. quinquefarium
.	.	.	.	1	2	1	3	.	2	Anastrepta orcadensis
.	.	.	.	.	.	.	4	1	.	Anastrophyllum donianum
.	.	.	.	.	.	.	.	.	2	A. jorgensenii
.	.	.	.	.	.	.	3	.	3	Bazzania tricrenata
.	.	.	.	.	.	.	3	.	.	B. pearsoni
.	.	.	.	.	.	.	.	.	.	Blepharostoma trichophyllum
.	.	.	.	.	.	.	3	.	2	Diplophyllum albicans
.	.	.	.	.	.	.	.	.	.	Herberta hutchinsiae
.	.	.	.	.	.	.	3	.	2	Jamesoniella carringtoni
.	.	.	.	.	.	.	.	.	.	Leptoscyphus anomalus
.	.	.	.	.	.	.	3	.	.	L. taylori
.	2	.	.	.	.	1	.	.	.	Lophozia floerkii

Table 19

	1	2	3	4	5	6	7	8	9	10	11
L. hatcheri	.	.	.	.	.	.	.	.	.	.	.
L. quinquedentata	.	.	.	.	.	.	.	.	.	.	.
L. ventricosa	.	.	.	.	.	1	.	.	.	.	.
Mastigophora woodsii	3	.	.	.	.	.	.	.	.	.	.
Pleurozia purpurea	2	.	.	.	.	.	.	.	.	.	.
Ptilidium ciliare	.	1	3	1	1	1	2	2	2	1	2
Scapania nimbosa	2	.	.	.	.	.	.	.	.	.	.
S. ornithopodioides	1	.	.	.	.	.	.	.	.	.	.
Microhepatics	.	.	.	.	.	.	.	.	.	.	.
Cetraria aculeata	.	.	.	.	.	.	.	.	+	.	.
C. islandica	.	2	1	.	.	.	1	3	2	.	2
Cladonia bellidiflora	.	.	.	.	.	1	.	.	1	.	.
C. coccifera	.	.	.	.	1	.	.	.	.	.	.
C. gracilis	.	.	.	.	1	2	1	.	.	.	.
C. impexa	+	.	.	.	.	.	.	.	.	.	.
C. pyxidata	1	.	.	.	.	.	1	.	.	.	.
C. rangiferina agg.	.	.	.	.	.	2	.	3	2	.	.
C. squamosa	.	.	.	.	.	.	.	2	1	.	1
C. sylvatica	2	2	.	3	3	3	3	7	3	1	1
C. uncialis	2	.	.	1	1	.	1	.	.	.	.
Peltigera canina	.	.	.	.	.	.	.	.	.	.	.
Number of species (88)	26	17	11	29	29	25	13	10	17	19	14

(Average 20)

Constancy class V 7 }for the association.
        ,, ,, IV 5 }

LOCALITIES

1. Liathach, Torridon, Ross-shire; 2. Sgurr nan Ceanaichean, Achnashellach, Ross-shire; 3. Sgurr a' Mhuillinn, Achnasheen, Ross-shire; 4. Ben More Assynt, Ross-shire; 5. Beinn Enaiglair, Inverlael, Ross-shire; 6,7,8. Schiehallion, Perthshire; 9. Carn nan Sac, Cairnwell hills, Aberdeenshire; 10. Ben Alder, Inverness-shire; 11. Driesh, Glen Clova, Angus; 12. A'Bhuideanach, Laggan, Inverness-shire; 13. Coire

(*continued*)

215

12	13	14	15	16	17	18	19	20	21	
·	·	·	·	I	·	·	·	·	·	L. hatcheri
·	·	·	·	·	I	·	I	I	·	L. quinquedentata
·	·	·	·	·	·	·	·	2	·	L. ventricosa
·	·	·	·	·	·	·	3	·	·	Mastigophora woodsii
·	·	·	·	·	·	·	+	·	·	Pleurozia purpurea
I	3	3	·	2	·	2	·	3	2	**Ptilidium ciliare**
·	·	·	·	·	·	·	3	·	·	Scapania nimbosa
·	·	·	·	·	·	·	2	·	·	S. ornithopodioides
·	·	·	I	·	·	·	·	·	·	*Microhepatics*
·	·	·	·	·	I	·	·	·	3	Cetraria aculeata
·	I	·	·	·	I	I	2	3	3	C. islandica
·	·	I	·	·	·	·	·	·	I	Cladonia bellidiflora
·	·	I	·	·	·	·	·	·	·	C. coccifera
·	·	·	·	I	·	·	I	I	3	C. gracilis
·	·	·	·	·	·	·	2	·	·	C. impexa
·	·	·	·	·	I	·	·	I	·	C. pyxidata
·	3	I	·	·	I	·	·	·	3	C. rangiferina agg.
·	·	·	·	·	·	·	·	·	·	C. squamosa
2	4	2	·	I	2	3	·	3	4	**C. sylvatica**
I	I	2	·	·	·	·	3	I	3	C. uncialis
·	·	·	·	·	3	·	·	·	·	Peltigera canina
22	20	29	18	27	19	18	44	33	30	Number of species (88)

Kander, Aberdeenshire; 14. Sow of Atholl, Perthshire; 15. Glen Einich, Inverness-shire; 16. Sgurr a' Ghlas Leathaid, Achnasheen, Ross-shire; 17. Morven, Caithness; 18. Ben Klibreck, Sutherland; 19. Mullach Coire Mhic Fhearchair, Ross-shire; 20. Carn Ban, Freevater Forest, Ross-shire; 21. Ben Hope, Sutherland.

Table 20: Cladineto-Vaccinetum [sylvaticosum

	1	2	3	4	5	6	7	8	9	10
Reference number	P55 029	P55 030	M56 125	M57 080	R57 277	R57 276	R57 264	R57 266	R57 283	R57 280
Map reference	8023 2883	8023 2883	8125 3253	7768 3107	7841 3220	7832 3217	7738 3269	7738 3253	7722 2572	7758 3348
Altitude (feet)	2500	2500	2300	3150	3050	3150	3000	2700	2700	2800
Aspect (degrees)	—	—	—	45	180	360	315	—	45	315
Slope (degrees)	—	—	0	3	10	15	15	0	5	10
Cover (per cent)	—	—	100	100	100	100	—	100	100	100
Height (centimetres)	—	—	8	—	—	—	3	—	—	—
Plot area (square metres)	1	1	4	4	4	4	4	4	4	4
Calluna vulgaris	·	·	1	·	·	·	·	·	·	·
Empetrum hermaphroditum	·	3	4	1	4	5	3	3	3	2
Juniperus nana	·	·	·	·	·	·	·	·	·	·
Loiseleuria procumbens	1	·	·	·	·	·	·	·	·	·
Vaccinium myrtillus	4	3	3	4	4	4	7	6	3	7
V. uliginosum	·	·	·	·	4	3	·	·	·	·
V. vitis-idaea	·	·	·	·	4	4	4	4	5	3
Lycopodium alpinum	·	·	·	·	·	·	·	·	·	·
L. selago	·	·	·	·	·	·	·	·	·	·
Agrostis canina	·	·	·	·	·	·	·	·	·	3
Deschampsia flexuosa	3	3	3	3	2	3	·	4	3	2
Festuca ovina agg.	·	·	·	·	·	·	·	3	·	2
Nardus stricta	·	·	·	·	·	·	·	·	·	·
Carex bigelowii	2	3	·	3	4	3	3	3	3	3
C. pilulifera	·	·	·	·	·	·	·	·	·	·
Juncus trifidus	·	·	·	·	·	·	·	·	·	2
Trichophorum caespitosum	·	·	·	·	·	·	·	·	·	·
Galium hercynicum	·	·	·	2	·	·	·	1	1	·
Solidago virgaurea	·	·	·	·	·	·	·	·	·	·
Campylopus flexuosus	·	·	·	·	·	·	·	2	·	·
Dicranum fuscescens	·	·	·	2	3	3	3	2	3	2
D. scoparium	1	1	·	·	·	·	·	·	·	·
Hylocomium splendens	·	·	·	·	·	·	·	·	·	·
Pleurozium schreberi	2	2	·	·	2	2	2	·	3	1
Polytrichum alpinum	·	·	1	·	3	·	·	·	1	·
P. commune	·	·	·	·	·	·	·	·	·	·
Rhacomitrium lanuginosum	2	·	2	2	2	2	3	1	3	·
Rhytidiadelphus loreus	1	·	·	·	·	·	·	·	·	·
Alicularia scalaris	1	·	·	·	·	·	·	·	·	·
Anastrepta orcadensis	·	·	·	·	·	·	·	·	·	2
Lophozia floerkii	·	·	·	·	·	·	·	·	·	·
L. ventricosa	·	·	·	·	·	·	·	·	·	2
Ptilidium ciliare	1	1	+	·	1	2	1	1	2	·
Alectoria nigricans	·	·	·	1	2	·	·	+	3	3
Cerania vermicularis	·	·	·	·	·	·	·	1	1	·
Cetraria aculeata	·	·	3	+	2	+	·	2	8	+
C. islandica	2	2	3	3	4	3	3	3	2	3
C. nivalis	2	·	·	·	2	·	·	·	·	·
Cladonia bellidiflora	·	·	·	·	1	2	2	2	1	2
C. coccifera	·	·	·	·	2	·	·	·	+	·
C. foliacea	·	·	·	·	·	·	·	·	+	·
C. gracilis	2	1	·	1	4	4	3	3	8	3
C. pyxidata	·	·	·	·	1	1	2	·	1	·
C. rangiferina agg.	3	3	3	6	8	8	6	7	8	7
C. squamosa	·	·	1	·	·	·	·	·	·	·
C. sylvatica	9	9	9	7	8	8	7	7	8	5
C. tenuis	·	·	·	·	·	·	·	·	·	·
C. uncialis	2	1	2	4	2	3	4	3	8	4
Coriscium viride	·	·	·	·	·	+	·	·	·	·
Icmadophila ericetorum	·	·	·	·	·	·	·	·	·	·
Ochrolechia frigida	·	·	·	+	+	2	2	1	3	2
Sphaerophorus globosus	·	·	·	·	·	·	·	·	·	·
Number of species (52)	16	12	16	14	22	20	17	21	25	19

(Average 18)

(Overall average 19)

Constancy class V 11
   ,,   ,, IV 6

LOCALITIES

1,2. Geal Charn, Monadhliath hills, Inverness-shire; 3. Ladder Hills, Banffshire; 4. Carn a'Gheoidh, Cairnwell hills, Perthshire; 5. Lochnagar, Aberdeenshire; 6. Fafernie, Glen Muick, Aberdeenshire; 7. Driesh, Glen Clova, Angus; 8. Mayar, Glen Clova, Angus; 9. An Sgulan, Dalnaspidal, Perthshire; 10. Green Hill, Glen Clova, Angus; 11. Carn a' Chlarsaich, Cairnwell hills, Perthshire; 12. Carn a'Gheoidh, Cairnwell hills, Perthshire; 13. An Socach, Cairnwell hills, Aberdeenshire; 14. Craig Derry, Cairngorms; 15. Meall Odhar, Glas Maol, Aberdeenshire;

(1–10); typicum (11–16); empetrosum (17–23)]

11	12	13	14	15	16	17	18	19	20	21	22	23	
M57	M57	M57	M56	M57	R58	M57	M56	M56	M56	R57	M58	M58	Reference number
078	079	096	032	063	110	059	025	104	029	091	066	060	
7783	7769	7803	7981	7774	7508	7871	7955	8010	7980	7787	8042	8033	Map reference
3071	3100	3095	3045	3152	2650	3409	2953	3046	2995	2651	3009	2971	Altitude (feet)
2700	2900	3000	2800	2700	3000	3000	3100	3200	3500	2800	3700	3250	
—	—	—	108	—	180	360	225	135	180	360	—	90	Aspect (degrees)
0	0	0	2	0	5	8	10	6	5	5	0	10	Slope (degrees)
100	100	100	100	100	100	100	90	100	100	100	100	100	Cover (per cent)
—	—	—	1	—	—	—	5	8	5	—	4	5	Height (centimetres)
4	4	4	4	4	4	4	4	4	4	4	4	4	Plot area (square metres)
.	.	.	.	.	.	.	.	+	.	.	.	.	Calluna vulgaris
+	3	2	+	+	2	7	8	7	8	7	7	8	**Empetrum hermaphroditum**
.	.	.	.	.	.	.	+	.	.	.	.	.	Juniperus nana
.	.	1	.	.	.	.	.	.	.	.	.	.	Loiseleuria procumbens
4	5	5	3	5	6	6	4	5	3	6	4	3	**Vaccinium myrtillus**
.	.	.	.	.	.	.	.	6	4	.	5	4	V. uliginosum
3	3	.	3	3	3	.	4	.	.	3	.	3	V. vitis-idaea
.	.	.	.	.	.	.	.	2	.	.	+	.	Lycopodium alpinum
.	.	.	.	.	.	1	1	.	.	.	+	+	L. selago
.	.	.	3	.	3	.	.	.	.	.	.	.	Agrostis canina
3	2	2	3	2	4	3	3	2	.	3	2	3	**Deschampsia flexuosa**
.	.	.	.	1	2	.	.	.	.	2	.	.	Festuca ovina agg.
+	.	.	1	.	.	.	+	1	3	.	.	.	Nardus stricta
6	5	3	4	6	4	+	3	4	3	2	3	3	**Carex bigelowii**
.	.	.	.	.	.	.	.	2	.	.	.	.	C. pilulifera
.	.	1	.	.	.	.	.	.	.	.	3	.	Juncus trifidus
.	.	.	.	.	.	.	.	.	.	.	1	.	Trichophorum caespitosum
1	.	.	3	1	3	.	.	.	.	.	.	.	Galium hercynicum
.	.	.	.	.	.	.	.	.	.	.	.	1	Solidago virgaurea
.	.	.	.	.	.	.	.	.	.	.	.	.	Campylopus flexuosus
.	4	4	5	5	1	.	.	.	.	3	3	.	Dicranum fuscescens
.	.	.	3	.	1	2	1	2	.	2	.	2	D. scoparium
.	.	.	.	.	.	.	1	.	.	.	.	1	Hylocomium splendens
.	.	.	.	3	2	4	1	2	.	3	.	1	Pleurozium schreberi
2	2	+	2	1	.	.	.	.	.	1	.	.	Polytrichum alpinum
.	.	.	+	.	.	.	.	.	.	.	.	.	P. commune
4	1	2	4	3	3	.	3	1	4	2	2	2	**Rhacomitrium lanuginosum**
.	.	.	.	.	.	3	.	.	.	3	.	2	Rhytidiadelphus loreus
.	.	.	.	.	.	.	.	.	.	.	.	.	Alicularia scalaris
.	.	.	.	.	.	.	.	.	.	2	.	.	Anastrepta orcadensis
.	.	.	.	.	.	.	.	.	.	2	.	.	Lophozia floerkii
.	.	.	.	.	.	.	.	.	.	.	.	.	L. ventricosa
.	1	3	2	.	2	3	2	3	.	3	3	2	Ptilidium ciliare
2	+	1	.	2	1	.	+	.	.	.	.	.	Alectoria nigricans
1	.	.	.	.	.	.	1	.	.	.	.	.	Cerania vermicularis
4	2	.	1	3	.	2	3	2	.	.	.	.	Cetraria aculeata
2	3	3	2	3	1	3	4	3	4	3	3	3	**C. islandica**
.	.	.	1	.	.	.	3	1	.	.	.	.	C. nivalis
2	.	3	2	2	3	.	2	.	+	.	2	.	Cladonia bellidiflora
.	.	.	.	.	.	1	.	3	2	.	.	1	C. coccifera
.	.	.	.	.	.	.	.	.	.	.	.	.	C. foliacea
1	3	2	2	2	4	2	2	2	2	2	1	2	**C. gracilis**
.	+	1	1	.	.	.	2	.	.	.	2	1	C. pyxidata
1	3	4	3	1	5	3	5	4	5	7	1	5	**C. rangiferina agg.**
.	.	.	1	.	.	1	.	.	.	.	.	.	C. squamosa
3	6	5	3	6	5	5	5	4	6	7	6	6	**C. sylvatica**
.	.	.	3	.	.	.	.	.	.	.	.	.	C. tenuis
3	3	3	4	.	3	2	2	3	1	2	5	2	**C. uncialis**
.	1	.	.	.	.	.	.	.	.	.	.	1	Coriscium viride
.	.	.	.	.	.	.	.	.	1	.	.	.	Icmadophila ericetorum
2	3	2	2	1	3	+	3	2	+	.	1	1	**Ochrolechia frigida**
1	.	.	.	.	.	.	.	.	.	.	.	.	Sphaerophorus globosus
20	19	19	26	19	21	18	25	22	15	20	20	23	Number of species (52)

(Average 20) (Average 20)

16. Meall Garbh, Glen Lyon, Perthshire; 17. Mount Keen, Aberdeenshire; 18. Cairntoul, Aberdeenshire; 19. Beinn a'Chaoruinn, Cairngorms; 20. Ben Macdhui, Cairngorms; 21. Meall a'Chaoruinn, Drumochter, Inverness-shire; 22. Cairngorm, Inverness-shire; 23. Creag an Leth Choin, Cairngorms.

Table 21 : Festuceto-Vaccinetum [cladin

	1	2	3	4	5	6	7	8	9	10	11	12	13
Reference number	M57 077	P52 031	P52 032	P52 061	R57 265	R57 139	R57 155	R57 304	R57 314	P52 178	P52 180	P52 179	R58 106
Map reference	7776 3071	7396 2633	7397 2632	7436 2614	7738 3262	7862 2445	7965 2598	7634 2949	7553 2840	7409 2652	7409 2651	7409 2651	7496 2640
Altitude (feet)	2800	2800	2900	2850	2750	2400	2500	2400	2530	2500	2550	2550	2750
Aspect (degrees)	90	190	90	150	360	225	180	270	360	170	170	170	180
Slope (degrees)	3	30	15	15	25	20	20	30	30	5	5	3	10
Cover (per cent)	100	100	100	70	100	100	100	100	100	90	90	100	100
Height (centimetres)	–	5	4	5	–	–	–	10	–	20	15	15	–
Plot area (square metres)	4	4	4	4	4	4	4	4	4	5	2	5	4
Empetrum hermaphroditum	2	.	.	.	4	5	5	3	5	1	.	.	.
Loiseleuria procumbens	.	.	.	.	+	.	.	.	.	.	.	.	.
Saiix herbacea	.	.	.	.	4	.	.	.	.	.	.	.	.
Vaccinium myrtillus	4	6	7	6	5	6	4	8	7	9	9	.	6
V. uliginosum	.	.	.	.	.	.	.	.	.	.	.	.	.
V. vitis-idaea	3	2	2	3	3	4	4	3	3	3	3	3	2
Lycopodium alpinum	2	.	.	.	.	.	.	3	.	.	.	2	+
L. selago	.	.	.	.	.	.	.	.	1	.	.	.	.
Agrostis canina	.	.	1	.	4	3	3	3	3	.	.	.	3
A. tenuis	.	3	3	.	.	3	2	.	.	.	2	1	3
Anthoxanthum odoratum	.	.	.	.	.	2	.	.	.	.	.	.	.
Deschampsia caespitosa	.	.	.	.	.	.	.	.	.	.	.	.	.
D. flexuosa	.	.	.	.	3	3	3	3	.	.	.	.	3
Festuca ovina agg.	6	7	6	6	4	3	5	4	4	5	5	5	4
Nardus stricta	.	1	.	.	.	2	1	1	.	1	.	1	.
Poa pratensis	.	.	.	.	.	.	.	.	.	.	.	.	.
Carex bigelowii	6	1	4	6	4	3	2	3	3	2	3	3	4
C. pilulifera	.	3	.	1	.	2	4	2	.	3	1	2	3
Juncus squarrosus	.	1	.	.	.	.	.	.	.	2	.	.	.
J. trifidus	.	.	.	.	2	.	.	.	.	.	.	.	.
Luzula campestris	+	.	.	.	.	.	.	.	.	.	.	.	.
L. multiflora	.	.	.	.	.	1	1	.	.	.	.	.	.
L. spicata	.	.	.	.	.	.	.	.	.	.	.	.	.
Achillea millefolium	.	.	.	.	.	.	.	.	.	.	.	.	.
Alchemilla alpina	1	4	3	1	7	5	5	6	5	1	2	8	6
Antennaria dioica	.	.	.	.	.	.	.	.	.	.	.	.	.
Campanula rotundifolia	.	.	.	.	.	.	.	2	1	.	.	.	.
Cerastium vulgatum	.	1	.	.	.	.	.	.	.	.	.	.	.
Euphrasia sp.	.	.	.	.	.	.	1	.	.	.	.	.	.
Galium hercynicum	+	4	4	4	2	.	.	2	2	3	2	2	3
Hieracium sp.	.	.	.	.	.	2	.	.	.	.	.	.	.
Lotus corniculatus	.	.	.	.	.	.	.	.	.	.	.	.	.
Polygonum viviparum	.	.	.	.	.	.	.	.	.	.	.	.	.
Potentilla erecta	.	.	.	.	.	.	.	.	.	.	.	.	.
Solidago virgaurea	.	.	.	.	.	.	.	.	.	.	.	.	.
Succisa pratensis	.	.	.	.	.	.	.	.	.	.	.	.	.
Thymus drucei	.	.	.	.	.	.	.	.	.	.	.	.	.
Viola palustris	.	.	.	.	.	.	.	.	.	.	.	.	.
V. riviniana	.	.	.	.	.	.	.	1	.	.	.	.	.
Dicranum fuscescens	.	1	3	2	3	.	.	.	.	1	.	1	2
D. majus	.	.	.	.	.	.	.	.	1	.	.	.	.
D. scoparium	.	.	.	2	2	3	.	3	2	.	1	1	2
Hylocomium brevirostre	.	.	.	.	.	.	.	.	.	.	.	.	.
H. splendens	.	.	.	.	.	2	3	1	2	.	.	.	.
Hypnum cupressiforme	.	1	.	.	.	.	.	2	+	.	.	.	.
Pleurozium schreberi	.	3	5	4	3	4	4	3	4	7	6	3	3
Pohlia nutans	.	1	.	.	2	.	.	.	.	.	.	1	.
Polytrichum alpinum	.	.	3	1	1	.	1	2	2	.	2	2	1
P. commune	.	3	.	.	.	.	.	.	.	.	.	.	.
P. juniperinum	.	.	.	.	.	.	.	.	.	1	.	.	.
P. piliferum	.	.	.	.	2	.	.	.	.	.	.	.	2
Rhacomitrium canescens	.	.	.	.	.	.	.	.	.	.	.	.	.
R. lanuginosum	.	.	2	3	3	3	3	3	3	1	.	2	3
Rhytidiadelphus loreus	.	.	1	.	.	3	3	2	2	.	.	.	.
R. squarrosus	.	.	.	.	.	.	.	.	.	.	.	.	.
Alicularia scalaris	.	.	.	.	.	.	.	.	.	.	.	1	.
Anastrepta orcadensis	.	.	.	.	.	.	.	.	.	.	.	.	.
Lophozia alpestris	.	.	.	.	.	.	.	.	.	.	.	1	.
L. floerkii	.	.	.	.	3	.	1	.	.	.	.	.	.
L. hatcheri	.	.	.	.	.	.	.	.	.	.	.	.	1
L. lycopodioides	.	.	.	.	.	.	.	.	.	.	.	1	.
Pellia epiphylla	.	1	.	.	.	.	.	.	.	.	.	.	•
Ptilidium ciliare	1	1	3	2	2	.	2	2	2	.	3	2	2
Scapania gracilis	.	.	.	.	.	.	.	.	.	.	.	.	.

osum (1–13); rhacomitrosum (14–24)]

14	15	16	17	18	19	20	21	22	23	24	
R58	R58	R57	R58	R58	R58	R58	P52	M57	R57	R58	Reference number
047	136	055	075	109	033	009	099	099	099	116	
8805	7272	7858	8809	8463	7511	7781	7454	7761	7726	7431	Map reference
2218	2263	2384	2253	2119	2641	1843	2670	3090	2502	2638	
2500	2500	3300	2950	2600	2700	2500	2650	2600	3500	3500	Altitude (feet)
225	360	90	180	315	45	360	240	180	90	270	Aspect (degrees)
25	5	25	28	35	28	15	3	5	25	25	Slope (degrees)
100	100	100	100	100	100	100	70	100	100	100	Cover (per cent)
—	—	—	—	—	—	—	7	—	8	—	Height (centimetres)
4	4	4	4	4	4	4	4	4	4	4	Plot area (square metres)
2	·	·	4	·	·	·	·	3	4	·	Empetrum hermaphroditum
·	·	·	·	·	·	·	·	·	·	·	Loiseleuria procumbens
·	1	1	·	·	·	·	·	·	·	·	Salix herbacea
4	4	4	6	5	6	4	1	7	5	3	**Vaccinum myrtillus**
·	·	·	·	·	·	·	·	·	3	·	V. uliginosum
3	3	·	·	3	3	·	2	2	·	2	**V. vitis-idaea**
·	1	3	1	·	·	·	·	·	3	·	Lycopodium alpinum
·	·	·	1	·	·	·	·	·	·	·	L. selago
3	3	3	3	3	1	3	·	+	·	3	**Agrostis canina**
3	2	2	·	·	3	3	·	·	3	4	A. tenuis
·	·	·	3	·	·	3	·	2	·	·	Anthoxanthum odoratum
·	·	4	3	·	·	3	·	·	·	4	Deschampsia caespitosa
2	2	3	4	4	3	3	·	2	3	3	**D. flexuosa**
5	7	·	3	5	6	5	7	4	·	5	**Festuca ovina agg.**
·	3	4	4	3	·	2	·	1	7	·	Nardus stricta
·	·	·	·	·	·	·	·	·	·	3	Poa pratensis
4	3	5	4	3	3	·	3	2	3	4	**Carex bigelowii**
·	2	·	3	2	3	3	3	3	2	·	C. pilulifera
·	·	3	·	·	·	·	·	·	·	·	Juncus squarrosus
·	·	·	·	·	·	·	·	·	·	·	J. trifidus
·	·	·	·	·	·	·	·	·	·	·	Luzula campestris
·	3	2	·	·	·	·	·	2	·	·	L. multiflora
·	1	·	·	·	·	·	·	·	·	·	L. spicata
2	·	·	·	·	·	·	·	·	·	·	Achillea millefolium
5	5	3	4	5	4	4	7	5	3	8	**Alchemilla alpina**
3	·	·	3	·	·	·	·	·	·	·	Antennaria dioica
·	·	·	·	·	·	·	·	·	·	3	Campanula rotundifolia
·	·	·	·	·	·	·	·	·	·	·	Cerastium vulgatum
2	1	·	2	3	·	·	·	1	·	·	Euphrasia sp.
3	4	5	4	2	3	4	2	1	1	4	**Galium hercynicum**
·	·	·	·	1	·	·	·	·	·	·	Hieracium sp.
+	·	·	·	·	·	·	·	·	·	·	Lotus corniculatus
·	3	·	·	·	·	·	·	·	·	·	Polygonum viviparum
·	3	·	3	·	·	4	·	·	·	·	Potentilla erecta
·	·	·	·	·	·	·	·	·	1	·	Solidago virgaurea
·	·	·	1	·	·	·	·	·	·	·	Succisa pratensis
4	·	·	3	4	·	4	·	·	·	·	Thymus drucei
·	·	·	·	·	3	3	·	·	·	·	Viola palustris
·	3	·	3	·	·	·	·	2	·	3	V. riviniana
·	·	·	·	·	·	·	1	·	3	3	Dicranum fuscescens
·	·	·	·	·	·	·	·	·	·	·	D. majus
·	3	4	·	·	1	3	·	·	3	·	D. scoparium
1	·	·	·	·	·	·	·	·	·	·	Hylocomium brevirostre
2	3	2	3	3	3	3	·	1	1	4	**H. splendens**
·	2	·	·	3	·	2	·	2	·	·	Hypnum cupressiforme
1	4	3	2	·	5	·	1	7	3	3	**Pleurozium schreberi**
·	·	·	·	·	·	·	1	·	·	·	Pohlia nutans
1	2	3	2	1	2	3	·	1	·	3	**Polytrichum alpinum**
·	·	·	·	·	·	·	·	·	·	·	P. commune
·	·	·	·	·	·	·	1	·	·	·	P. juniperinum
·	·	·	·	·	·	·	1	·	·	·	P. piliferum
·	·	1	·	·	·	·	·	·	·	·	Rhacomitrium canescen
7	5	6	4	5	1	5	4	1	5	3	**R. lanuginosum**
2	3	3	3	2	1	5	·	2	1	2	**Rhytidiadelphus loreu**
·	·	·	·	·	3	3	·	·	·	1	R. squarrosus
·	·	·	·	·	·	·	·	·	·	·	Alicularia scalaris
·	1	·	·	·	2	·	·	·	1	·	Anastrepta orcadensis
·	·	·	·	·	·	·	·	·	·	·	Lophozia alpestris
·	·	3	·	·	·	·	·	·	3	·	L. floerkii
·	·	1	·	·	·	·	·	·	·	·	L. hatcheri
·	·	·	·	·	·	·	·	·	·	·	L. lvcopodioides
·	·	·	·	·	·	·	·	·	·	·	Pellia epiphylla
1	1	·	2	·	2	2	1	·	1	2	**Ptilidium ciliare**
·	·	·	·	1	·	·	·	·	·	·	Scapania gracilis

Table 21

	1	2	3	4	5	6	7	8	9	10	11	12	13
Alectoria nigricans .	2	·	·	·	·	·	·	·	·	·	·	1	·
Cerania vermicularis	·	·	1	1	·	·	·	·	·	·	·	2	·
Cetraria aculeata .	4	·	1	·	2	3	2	·	2	1	·	3	1
C. islandica .	·	·	1	·	3	1	1	1	1	1	1	1	·
Cladonia alpicola .	·	·	1	·	·	·	·	·	·	·	·	·	·
C. bellidiflora .	·	·	·	·	1	2	1	1	1	·	·	2	2
C. coccifera .	·	·	·	·	·	·	·	·	·	·	·	·	2
C. gracilis .	1	2	1	1	2	3	3	3	2	·	·	3	4
C. impexa .	·	1	1	·	·	·	·	·	·	·	·	·	·
C. pyxidata .	·	·	·	·	·	·	1	·	2	·	·	·	·
C. rangiferina agg.	3	3	3	3	3	3	5	3	2	5	4	5	4
Cladonia squamosa.	·	1	·	1	·	·	·	·	·	·	·	3	·
C. sylvatica .	5	3	3	4	3	5	5	6	5	7	6	8	4
C. uncialis .	2	2	2	3	2	3	2	·	2	1	4	4	4
Ochrolechia frigida.	2	·	·	·	·	2	1	·	·	·	·	·	2
Peltigera canina .	·	·	·	·	·	·	·	·	·	·	·	·	·
Platysma glaucum .	·	·	·	·	·	·	·	·	·	·	·	1	·
Sphaerophorus globosus .	·	1	1	·	·	2	1	·	·	3	·	·	·
Number of species (82) .	17	25	24	19	28	27	32	26	27	21	16	30	27

(Average 24)

Constancy class V   11

    ,,   ,,   IV   8

(Overall average 25)

LOCALITIES

1. Carn a' Chlarsaich, Cairnwell hills, Perthshire; 2,3,4,10,11,12,21,24. Ben Lawers, Perthshire; 5. Driesh, Glen Clova, Angus; 6. Creag Meagaidh, Laggan, Inverness-shire; 7. Glen Markie, Monadhliath, Inverness-shire; 8. Ben Vrackie, Perthshire; 9. Farragon Hill, Perthshire; 13,19. Carn Gorm, Glen Lyon, Perthshire; 14. Beinn Enaiglair, Braemore, Ross-shire; 15. Ben Lui, Argyll; 16. Beinn a' Chaoruinn, Laggan,

(continued)

14	15	16	17	18	19	20	21	22	23	24	
·	·	·	·	·	·	·	·	·	·	·	Alectoria nigricans
2	·	·	·	·	·	·	·	·	·	·	Cerania vermicularis
·	1	·	2	2	·	·	1	·	·	·	Cetraria aculeata
1	2	1	1	1	1	1	1	1	3	·	**C. islandica**
·	·	·	·	·	·	·	·	·	·	·	Cladonia alpicola
·	·	·	·	·	·	·	·	2	·	·	C. bellidiflora
·	·	·	2	·	·	·	·	·	·	1	C. coccifera
·	2	·	3	3	1	·	1	·	2	·	**C. gracilis**
·	·	·	·	·	·	·	·	2	·	·	C. impexa
2	1	·	·	·	·	·	·	+	2	·	C. pyxidata
·	·	·	3	·	·	·	2	1	2	·	**C. rangiferina agg.**
·	·	·	·	·	·	·	·	·	·	·	Cladonia squamosa
2	·	·	3	2	2	2	2	3	2	2	**C. sylvatica**
3	2	·	2	2	·	·	1	2	3	+	**C. uncialis**
·	·	·	1	·	·	·	·	·	·	·	Ochrolechia frigida
1	·	·	·	·	·	·	·	·	·	·	Peltigera canina
·	·	·	·	·	·	·	·	·	·	·	Platysma glaucum
3	·	·	·	·	·	·	1	·	·	·	Sphaerophorus globosus
29	33	21	30	30	21	24	20	28	27	24	Number of species (82)

(Average 26)

Inverness-shire; 17. Beinn Dearg, Braemore, Ross-shire; 18. Maoile Lunndaih, Monar Forest, Ross-shire; 20. Beinn Odhar Beag, Glenfinnan, Inverness-shire; 22. Carn Bhinnein, Cairnwell hills, Perthshire; 23. Ben Alder, Inverness-shire.

Table 22: Rhacomitreto-Empetretum (1–11); Empetrum-hypnaceous moss communities (12, 13)

	1	2	3	4	5	6	7	8	9	10	11	12	13
Reference number	R56 025	M55 043	R56 072	M56 043	M55 046	M56 092	M56 119	M56 131	M55 007	R56 083	R57 051	R58 012	M58 001
Map reference	8807 2222	8634 1975	8735 2057	8601 1972	8604 1985	8000 3008	8011 3020	7852 3256	8426 1785	8734 1983	9477 2338	9286 3004	9308 2595
Altitude (feet)	2550	2500	3300	2250	2800	3200	3600	3450	2400	2700	2300	2300	2250
Aspect (degrees)	360	315	135	360	90	315	90	225	315	360	135	360	45
Slope (degrees)	35	2	10	2	10	10	4	5	10	20	5	35	18
Cover (per cent)	95	100	90	95	100	100	90	100	90	100	95	100	100
Height (centimetres)	–	2	–	12	2	10	10	8	7	–	–	9	6
Plot area (square metres)	4	4	4	4	4	4	4	4	4	4	4	4	4
Calluna vulgaris	.	.	.	.	.	.	.	+	.	.	.	.	.
Empetrum hermaphroditum	7	6	3	6	7	4	7	2	8	7	6	6	6
Loiseleuria procumbens	.	.	.	.	.	.	.	+	+	.	.	.	.
Vaccinium myrtillus	3	2	3	4	3	4	3	4	+	4	4	5	3
V. uliginosum	.	2	.	2	5	.	.	.	.	4	.	.	.
V. vitis-idaea	+	.	.	.	.	.	.	.	+	.	.	4	3
Lycopodium alpinum	.	.	.	.	.	.	.	.	.	+	.	.	.
L. selago	1	.	.	.	.	+	1	.	2	2	.	.	.
Agrostis canina	.	.	.	.	3	.	.	.	.	.	.	.	3
Anthoxanthum odoratum	.	.	.	+	.	.	.	.	.	.	.	.	.
Deschampsia flexuosa	.	2	4	1	1	3	.	1	.	4	4	4	3
Festuca ovina agg.	3	1	.	.	.	.	.	.	3	3	.	.	.
F. rubra	.	.	.	.	.	.	.	.	1	.	.	.	.
Nardus stricta	.	.	.	+	3	1	.	.	2	.	2	.	2
Carex bigelowii	3	3	3	2	2	3	3	3	3	3	2	2	2
Juncus trifidus	.	.	5	5	3	6	6	7	.	2	.	.	.
Alchemilla alpina	.	.	.	.	.	1	.	.	.	3	.	.	.
Armeria maritima	.	2	.	+	.	.	.	.	.	.	.	.	.
Chamaepericlymenum suecicum	.	.	.	+	.	.	.	.	.	.	.	.	.
Cherleria sedoides	.	.	3	.	.	.	.	.	.	.	.	.	.
Galium hercynicum	.	.	.	.	.	.	.	.	.	.	2	2	.
Potentilla erecta	.	.	.	1	1	.	.	.	.	.	.	.	.
Silene acaulis	.	.	.	.	.	2	.	.	.	.	.	.	.
Solidago virgaurea	.	.	.	2	+	.	.	.	.	.	.	.	.
Dicranodontium uncinatum	.	.	.	1	.	.	.	.	.	.	.	.	.
Dicranum fuscescens	.	1	.	.	.	2	1	.	2	.	.	.	.
D. scoparium	1	.	1	.	.	.	.	2	1	1	.	1	.
Hylocomium splendens	2	.	.	.	.	.	.	.	4	1	.	8	5
Hypnum cupressiforme	2	.	.	2	.	.	.	.	2	3	1	.	.
Plagiothecium undulatum	.	.	.	.	.	.	.	.	2	.	.	.	.
Pleurozium schreberi	1	2	.	.	.	2	.	.	.	1	.	5	2
Polytrichum alpinum	2	.	.	1	.	1	.	.	2	.	.	.	1
P. commune	.	.	.	.	.	.	.	.	.	.	.	.	4
Rhacomitrium lanuginosum	9	8	9	8	7	8	6	9	4	8	8	3	2
Rhytidiadelphus loreus	2	1	.	.	.	.	.	.	4	.	.	4	8
Sphagnum nemoreum	3	.	2	.	.	.	.	.	.	.	.	.	.
S. quinquefarium	.	.	.	.	.	.	.	.	2	.	.	.	.
Alicularia scalaris	.	1	.	.	.	.	.	.	.	.	.	.	.
Anastrepta orcadensis	.	1	1	.	.	2	.	.	3	3	2	2	1
Anastrophyllum donianum	.	.	.	1	.	.	.	.	.	.	.	.	.
Bazzania tricrenata	3	.	.	.	.	.	.	.	.	.	.	.	.
Diplophyllum albicans	3	.	.	1	.	.	.	.	1	2	.	.	.
Jamesoniella carringtoni	1	.	.	.	.	.	.	.	2	.	.	.	.
Leptoscyphus taylori	1	.	.	.	.	.	.	.	.	.	.	.	.
Lophozia floerkii	.	.	.	2	.	3	.	1	.	.	.	.	1
L. quinquedentata	.	1	.	.	.	.	.	.	.	.	.	1	.
Pleurozia purpurea	3	.	.	1	.	.	.	.	.	1	.	.	6
Ptilidium ciliare	2	1	1	.	.	3	.	.	2	.	.	.	2
Scapania gracilis	.	.	.	.	.	.	.	.	.	2	1	.	.
S. ornithopodioides	.	.	.	.	.	.	.	.	2	.	.	.	.
S. subalpina	.	.	.	.	.	.	.	.	1	.	.	.	.
Alectoria nigricans	.	+	.	.	.	.	.	.	.	.	.	.	.
Cerania vermicularis	.	.	1	.	.	.	.	.	2	.	.	.	.
Cetraria aculeata	.	1	2	1	.	.	.	.	3	2	3	1	.
C. islandica	2	3	2	3	2	3	4	2	1	2	3	1	1
C. nivalis	.	.	.	.	.	.	.	2	.	.	.	.	.
Cladonia bellidiflora	1	.	.	.	.	+	2	.	1	.	.	.	.
C. coccifera	3	.	.	.	.	.	+	.	1	.	.	.	.
C. degenerans	.	.	.	.	.	.	.	2	.	.	.	.	.
C. floerkeana	.	.	.	.	.	.	.	.	1	.	.	.	.
C. gracilis	3	1	+	1	.	.	.	3	1	2	1	2	.
C. impexa	.	.	.	.	.	.	.	.	2	.	.	.	.

Table 22 (*continued*)

	1	2	3	4	5	6	7	8	9	10	11	12	13
Cladonia pyxidata	.	1	2	.	.	.	.	1	.	1	.	1	.
C. rangiferina agg.	2	2	.	1	.	1	+	.	1	.	1	1	.
C. squamosa	.	.	.	.	.	.	.	1	.	.	.	.	.
C. sylvatica	3	.	1	2	3	3	1	2	3	4	3	2	3
C. tenuis	.	3	.	.	.	.	.	.	.	.	.	.	.
C. uncialis	3	1	3	2	3	2	2	4	3	3	3	.	.
Ochrolechia frigida	.	.	2	.	.	+	.	1	1	.	2	.	.
O. tartarea	.	.	.	.	.	.	2	.	.	.	.	.	.
Peltigera canina	.	.	.	.	.	.	.	.	.	.	.	3	.
Sphaerophorus globosus	.	1	.	.	.	.	.	.	+	.	2	.	.
Stereocaulon evolutoides	.	2	.	.	.	.	.	.	.	.	.	.	.
Number of species (73)	27	24	19	25	16	22	17	18	35	24	18	19	18

(Average 23)

Constancy class V   8
  ,,   ,,   IV   5

LOCALITIES

1. Beinn Enaiglair, Braemore, Ross-shire; 2,4,5. Beinn Eighe, Ross-shire; 3. Mullach Coire Mhic Fhearchair, Fisherfield Forest, Ross-shire; 6. Loch Etchachan, Cairngorms; 7. Beinn Mheadhoin, Cairngorms; 8. Lochnagar, Aberdeenshire; 9. Sgurr a' Chaorachain, Applecross, Ross-shire; 10. Beinn Lair, Letterewe, Ross-shire; 11. Foinaven, Reay Forest, Sutherland; 12. Morven, Caithness; 13. Ben Klibreck, Sutherland.

Table 23: Dryas octopetala heaths—1. Dryas-Salix reticulata nodum (1–6); 4. Unclassified Dryas

	1	2	3	4	5	6	7	8	9	10
Reference number	R57 253	R57 215	R57 066	M58 012	R58 135	R57 228	M54 001	M56 073	M56 010a	M56 010b
Map reference	7767 3240	7763 3242	8867 2285	7357 2389	7274 2263	7772 3185	9676 2421	9191 .2303	8451 1885	8451 1885
Altitude (feet)	2300	2250	2550	3000	2300	2800	100	1700	1050	1050
Aspect (degrees)	45	360	225	180	360	180	270	225	315	315
Slope (degrees)	40	50	15	50	50	45	40	25	50	50
Cover (per cent)	80	100	100	90	100	100	80	95	75	75
Height (centimetres)	–	5	–	–	–	–	4	4	4	4
Plot area (square metres)	4	4	4	2	4	4	4	4	1	2
Arctostaphylos uva-ursi	.	.	.	.	.	.	.	.	.	.
Betula pubescens	.	.	.	.	.	.	.	.	.	1
Calluna vulgaris	.	.	.	.	.	2	.	.	.	.
Dryas octopetala	8	+	4	8	4	8	4	7	6	5
Empetrum hermaphroditum	3	1	2	.	.	.	.	.	1	.
E. nigrum	.	.	.	.	.	.	.	.	.	.
Juniperus nana	.	.	.	.	.	.	.	.	.	.
Rubus saxatilis	.	.	.	.	.	.	.	.	.	.
Salix aurita	.	.	.	.	.	.	.	.	.	.
S. arbuscula	.	.	.	4	.	.	.	.	.	.
S. herbacea	.	.	+	+	.	.	.	.	.	.
S. lapponum	.	.	+	.	.	.	.	.	.	.
S. myrsinites	2	.	.	.	.	.	.	.	.	.
S. repens	.	.	.	1	.	.	.	.	.	.
S. reticulata	3	8	3	4	6	3	.	.	.	.
Sorbus aucuparia	.	.	.	.	.	.	.	.	.	1
Vaccinium myrtillus	2	.	1	.	.	.	.	.	.	.
V. uliginosum	4	.	.	1	4	.	.	.	.	.
V. vitis-idaea	2	1	2	.	.	3	.	.	.	.
Asplenium viride	2	.	.	.	2	.	.	.	1	+
Botrychium lunaria	.	.	.	.	.	1	.	.	.	.
Equisetum variegatum	.	.	.	.	.	1	.	.	.	.
Lycopodium selago	.	.	.	.	.	1	.	.	.	2
Selaginella selaginoides	1	2	1	2	2	1	1	3	3	2
Agrostis canina	.	.	.	.	.	2	.	.	.	.
A. tenuis	.	.	2	.	.	2	+	.	.	.
Anthoxanthum odoratum	.	.	2	.	.	.	.	.	.	.
Deschampsia caespitosa	.	2	4	2	2	2	.	.	.	.
D. flexuosa	.	.	.	.	.	.	.	.	.	.
Festuca ovina agg.	3	3	4	2	4	5	5	3	4	4
F. rubra	.	3	.	.	.	.	2	.	.	.
Helictotrichon pratense	.	.	.	.	.	3	.	.	.	.
Holcus lanatus	.	.	.	.	.	.	.	.	.	.
Koeleria gracilis	.	.	.	.	.	.	2	.	.	.
Nardus stricta	.	.	.	.	.	.	.	.	.	.
Sesleria caerulea	.	.	.	.	.	.	.	.	.	.
Sieglingia decumbens	.	.	.	.	.	.	4	.	.	.
Carex atrata	.	.	2	+	2	.	.	.	.	.
C. bigelowii	.	.	2	3	.	.	.	.	.	.
C. binervis	.	.	2	.	.	.	.	.	.	.
C. capillaris	.	.	+	2	2	1	.	4	.	.
C. demissa	.	.	.	.	.	.	.	1	.	.
C. flacca	.	.	.	.	3	.	.	.	2	2
C. hostiana	.	.	.	.	.	.	.	.	.	.
C. panicea	.	.	.	.	.	.	.	1	.	.
C. pilulifera	.	.	.	.	.	1	.	.	.	.
C. pulicaris	.	.	.	4	.	2	.	3	.	.
C. rupestris	.	.	.	.	.	3	6	2	5	4
Coeloglossum viride	.	3	1	1	.	1	.	.	.	.
Epipactis atrorubens	.	.	.	.	.	.	+	.	.	.
Listera ovata	.	.	.	.	.	.	.	.	.	.
Luzula campestris	.	.	.	1	.	.	.	.	.	.
L. multiflora	.	.	3	.	1	2	.	.	.	.
L. sylvatica	.	.	4	.	.	.	.	.	.	.
L. spicata	.	.	1	1	.	1	.	.	.	.
Orchis mascula	.	.	.	.	.	.	.	.	.	.
Juncus trifidus	.	.	2	.	.	.	.	.	.	.
Schoenus nigricans	.	.	.	.	.	.	.	.	.	.
Tofieldia pusilla	.	.	.	.	.	.	.	.	.	.
Achillea millefolium	.	.	3	.	.	.	.	.	.	.
Alchemilla alpina	.	.	3	4	2	3	.	1	1	2
A. filicaulis	.	1	.	2	.	.	.	2	.	.
A. glabra	.	.	.	.	.	.	.	.	.	.
A. vestita	.	.	.	.	.	2	.	.	.	.
A. wichurae	.	.	2	.	.	.	.	.	.	.
Anemone nemorosa	.	.	.	.	.	.	.	.	.	.
Angelica sylvestris	.	+	3	2	1	.	.	.	1	.
Antennaria dioica	3	.	.	.	.	3	+	.	.	.

2. Dryas-Carex rupestris nodum (7–12); 3. Dryas-Carex flacca nodum (13–18); communities (19, 20)

11	12	13	14	15	16	17	18	19	20	
M57	M54	P54	P54	M54	M57	M57	R57	R57	R57	Reference number
076	002	001	002	004	037	016	338	255	117	
7782	9604	9605	9612	9652	7567	8027	8028	7767	7744	Map reference
3128	2453	2705	2696	2388	2108	1330	1330	3240	2463	
2750	150	50	200	200	1500	200	150	2100	3000	Altitude (feet)
—	225	360	180	135	360	270	270	45	360	Aspect (degrees)
0	30	5	2	5	40	10	38	55	45	Slope (degrees)
100	90	100	100	100	100	95	100	85	100	Cover (per cent)
5	3	8	5	8	—	—	—	—	—	Height (centimetres)
4	4	4	4	4	4	4	4	4	4	Plot area (square metres)
·	·	·	·	3	·	·	·	·	·	Arctostaphylos uva-ursi
·	·	·	·	·	·	·	·	·	·	Betula pubescens
·	1	·	·	·	2	4	5	3	·	Calluna vulgaris
7	8	9	9	6	5	8	6	7	6	**Dryas octopetala**
4	·	1	·	·	·	·	·	3	·	Empetrum hermaphroditum
·	·	3	3	4	·	·	·	·	·	E. nigrum
·	·	·	·	4	·	·	·	·	·	Juniperus nana
·	·	·	·	·	·	·	·	+	·	Rubus saxatilis
·	·	·	·	·	+	·	·	·	·	Salix aurita
·	·	·	·	·	·	·	·	·	·	S. arbuscula
·	·	·	·	·	·	·	·	·	·	S. herbacea
·	·	·	·	·	·	·	·	·	·	S. lapponum
·	·	·	·	·	+	·	·	·	·	S. myrsinites
·	·	3	2	1	·	·	·	·	·	S. repens
·	·	·	·	·	·	·	·	·	·	**S. reticulata**
·	·	·	·	·	·	·	·	·	·	Sorbus aucuparia
·	·	·	·	·	·	·	·	3	·	Vaccinium myrtillus
1	·	·	·	·	·	·	·	·	·	V. uliginosum
1	·	·	·	·	·	·	·	3	·	V. vitis-idaea
·	·	·	·	·	·	·	·	2	·	Asplenium viride
·	·	·	·	·	·	·	·	·	·	Botrychium lunaria
·	·	·	·	·	·	·	·	·	·	Equisetum variegatum
·	·	·	·	·	·	·	·	·	·	Lycopodium selago
3	·	+	·	3	3	·	·	2	·	**Selaginella selaginoides**
·	·	·	·	·	·	·	·	2	·	Agrostis canina
·	1	·	·	3	3	·	3	·	·	A. tenuis
·	·	·	·	·	3	3	3	2	·	Anthoxanthum odoratum
·	·	·	·	·	1	·	·	3	1	Deschampsia caespitosa
·	·	·	·	·	1	·	·	·	·	D. flexuosa
6	5	2	·	6	3	3	4	4	3	**Festuca ovina agg.**
3	·	·	·	1	·	·	4	2	·	F. rubra
·	·	·	1	4	·	·	·	·	·	Helictotrichon pratense
·	·	·	·	·	·	·	2	·	·	Holcus lanatus
·	3	+	·	1	·	·	·	·	·	Koeleria gracilis
·	·	·	·	·	1	·	·	·	·	Nardus stricta
+	·	·	·	·	·	·	·	·	·	Sesleria caerulea
·	2	·	·	·	1	·	3	·	·	Sieglingia decumbens
·	·	·	·	·	·	·	·	·	1	Carex atrata
·	·	·	·	·	·	·	·	·	·	C. bigelowii
·	·	·	·	·	·	·	·	·	·	C. binervis
5	·	·	·	·	1	·	·	3	·	C. capillaris
·	·	·	·	·	·	·	·	·	·	C. demissa
·	4	6	6	5	3	5	4	·	·	**C. flacca**
·	·	·	·	·	2	·	·	·	·	C. hostiana
·	·	·	·	+	·	1	·	·	·	C. panicea
·	·	·	·	·	·	·	·	·	·	C. pilulifera
·	·	·	·	·	3	3	3	2	·	C. pulicaris
3	5	·	·	·	·	·	·	·	·	**C. rupestris**
·	·	·	·	·	·	·	·	1	·	Coeloglossum viride
·	·	·	·	·	·	·	·	·	·	Epipactis atrorubens
·	·	·	·	1	·	·	·	·	·	Listera ovata
·	·	1	·	1	·	·	·	·	·	Luzula campestris
·	·	·	·	·	·	·	·	2	1	L. multiflora
·	·	·	·	·	·	·	·	·	·	L. sylvatica
·	·	·	·	·	·	·	·	·	·	L. spicata
·	·	·	·	2	·	·	·	·	·	Orchis mascula
·	+	·	·	·	·	·	·	·	·	Juncus trifidus
·	·	·	·	2	·	·	·	·	·	Schoenus nigricans
+	·	·	·	·	2	·	·	·	·	Tofieldia pusilla
·	·	·	·	·	·	·	·	·	·	Achillea millefolium
·	·	·	·	·	3	·	·	3	·	Alchemilla alpina
·	·	·	·	·	·	·	·	·	·	A. filicaulis
·	·	·	·	·	·	·	·	3	·	A. glabra
·	·	·	·	·	·	·	·	1	·	A. vestita
·	·	·	·	·	·	·	·	·	·	A. wichurae
·	·	·	·	·	1	·	·	·	·	Anemone nemorosa
·	·	·	·	·	·	·	1	·	·	Angelica sylvestris
·	2	+	·	2	1	·	·	3	·	Antennaria dioica

Table 23

	1	2	3	4	5	6	7	8	9	10
Anthyllis vulneraria	·	·	·	·	·	·	1	·	·	·
Arabis hirsuta	·	·	·	·	·	·	·	·	·	·
Armeria maritima	·	·	2	·	2	·	·	·	·	·
Astragalus alpinus	·	·	·	·	·	·	·	·	·	·
Bartsia alpina	·	·	·	+	·	·	·	·	·	·
Bellis perennis	·	·	·	·	·	·	+	1	·	·
Campanula rotundifolia	2	·	·	2	3	1	1	·	·	·
Cerastium alpinum	·	·	1	·	·	·	·	·	·	·
C. vulgatum	·	·	2	·	·	·	·	·	·	·
Cherleria sedoides	·	·	2	2	2	·	·	·	·	·
Daucus carota	·	·	·	·	·	·	+	·	·	·
Erigeron borealis	·	·	·	·	·	·	·	·	·	·
Euphrasia brevipila	·	·	·	·	·	·	·	2	·	·
E. frigida	·	·	·	·	·	·	·	·	·	·
Euphrasia sp.	2	3	2	·	·	3	·	·	·	·
Filipendula ulmaria	·	·	·	·	·	·	·	·	·	·
Galium boreale	1	·	·	·	·	·	·	2	1	·
G. hercynicum	·	·	·	·	·	·	·	2	·	·
G. verum	·	·	·	·	·	·	·	·	·	·
Gentianella amarella	·	·	·	·	·	·	·	·	·	·
G. campestris	·	·	·	·	·	2	·	·	·	·
Geranium sylvaticum	·	1	·	·	·	·	·	·	·	·
Geum rivale	·	·	4	·	·	·	·	1	·	·
Heracleum sphondylium	·	·	·	·	·	·	·	·	·	·
Hieracium pilosella	·	·	·	·	·	·	2	·	·	·
Hieracium sp.	2	2	·	·	2	2	·	·	1	·
Hypericum pulchrum	·	·	·	·	·	1	·	·	·	·
Hypochaeris radicata	·	·	·	·	·	·	·	·	·	·
Lathyrus montanus	·	·	·	·	·	·	+	·	·	·
Linum catharticum	·	·	·	·	·	·	3	3	1	+
Lotus corniculatus	·	·	·	·	·	1	1	·	·	·
Parnassia palustris	·	2	·	·	·	2	·	·	·	·
Pinguicula vulgaris	·	1	·	1	1	·	1	·	·	·
Leontodon autumnalis	·	·	·	·	·	·	·	·	·	·
Plantago coronopus	·	·	·	·	·	·	·	·	·	·
P. lanceolata	·	·	·	·	·	2	2	·	·	·
P. maritima	·	·	·	·	·	·	3	2	4	·
P. media	·	·	·	·	·	·	·	·	·	·
Polygala serpyllifolia	·	·	·	·	·	·	·	·	·	·
P. vulgaris	·	·	·	·	·	·	1	·	·	·
Polygonum viviparum	·	3	3	3	3	2	·	2	3	3
Potentilla crantzii	·	·	·	3	·	·	·	·	·	·
P. erecta	·	·	·	·	·	·	·	·	·	·
Prunella vulgaris	·	·	·	·	·	·	2	·	·	·
Pyrola rotundifolia	·	2	·	·	1	+	·	·	·	·
Ramischia secunda	2	·	·	·	·	·	·	·	·	·
Ranunculus acris	·	·	3	·	·	1	·	1	·	·
Rhinanthus minor	·	·	2	·	·	·	·	·	·	·
Rumex acetosa	·	·	3	·	·	·	·	·	·	·
Saussurea alpina	·	·	4	·	2	·	·	·	·	·
Saxifraga aizoides	·	3	+	2	3	·	2	1	+	1
S. hypnoides	·	·	1	·	·	·	·	·	·	·
S. oppositifolia	3	2	3	2	3	2	·	·	·	·
Sedum rosea	·	·	2	·	1	·	·	·	·	·
Senecio jacobaea	·	·	·	·	·	·	+	·	·	·
Silene acaulis	4	2	4	4	3	4	·	·	·	·
Solidago virgaurea	2	·	·	·	·	·	·	·	1	·
Succisa pratensis	3	+	2	·	·	3	2	·	3	3
Taraxacum officinalis agg.	·	·	·	·	·	·	·	+	·	·
Thalictrum alpinum	·	2	4	3	3	·	·	2	·	·
Thymus drucei	3	1	5	3	2	·	3	3	3	3
Trifolium pratense	·	·	·	·	·	·	·	·	·	·
T. repens	·	·	·	·	·	·	·	·	·	1
Trollius europaeus	·	·	·	·	·	·	·	·	·	1
Veronica fruticans	·	+	·	·	·	2	·	·	·	·
Viola riviniana	·	·	·	·	·	3	1	2	1	1
Acrocladium cuspidatum	·	·	2	·	2	·	·	·	·	·
Anoectangium compactum	·	·	·	·	2	·	·	·	·	·
Anomobryum filiforme	1	·	·	·	·	·	·	·	·	·
Blindia acuta	·	·	·	·	2	·	·	·	·	·
Breutelia chrysocoma	·	·	4	·	·	·	·	·	·	4
Camptothecium lutescens	·	·	+	·	·	·	·	·	·	·
Campylium protensum	·	·	·	·	3	·	·	·	·	·
Campylopus fragilis	·	·	·	·	·	2	·	·	·	·
Ctenidium molluscum	3	4	3	1	5	·	1	·	4	3
Dicranum majus	·	·	2	·	·	·	·	·	·	·
D. scoparium	·	2	·	·	2	·	·	·	·	·
Distichium capillaceum	2	3	·	·	1	·	·	·	4	1
Ditrichum flexicaule	3	7	3	·	3	2	1	2	·	·
Drepanocladus uncinatus	·	4	2	·	3	·	·	·	·	·
Encalypta streptocarpa	1	·	·	·	·	·	·	·	·	·
Entodon orthocarpus	·	·	3	·	·	·	·	·	·	·
Fissidens adianthoides	·	2	·	·	3	·	·	·	1	1
F. cristatus	·	·	·	·	·	·	·	·	·	·
F. osmundoides	·	·	·	·	2	1	·	·	·	·
F. taxifolius	·	·	·	·	·	·	·	·	·	·
Hylocomium splendens	3	4	4	1	3	2	·	·	1	3
Hypnum cupressiforme	·	·	·	1	·	1	3	·	·	1
Isopterygium pulchellum	·	1	·	·	·	·	·	·	·	·
Mnium orthorrhynchum	·	·	·	·	·	1	·	·	·	·

(continued)

11	12	13	14	15	16	17	18	19	20	
·	·	·	·	I	·	·	·	·	·	Anthyllis vulneraria
·	·	·	·	·	·	·	·	2	·	Arabis hirsuta
·	·	·	·	·	·	·	·	·	·	Armeria maritima
·	·	·	·	·	·	·	·	2	·	Astragalus alpinus
·	·	·	·	·	·	·	·	·	·	Bartsia alpina
·	2	+	I	·	·	·	·	·	·	Bellis perennis
3	·	2	·	2	·	·	·	2	·	Campanula rotundifolia
·	·	·	·	·	·	·	·	·	·	Cerastium alpinum
·	·	·	I	·	·	·	·	·	·	C. vulgatum
·	·	·	·	·	·	·	·	·	I	Cherleria sedoides
·	·	·	·	·	·	·	·	·	·	Daucus carota
·	·	·	·	·	·	·	·	2	·	Erigeron borealis
·	·	·	·	·	·	·	·	·	·	Euphrasia brevipila
3	·	·	·	·	·	·	·	·	·	E. frigida
·	2	·	·	·	2	I	I	2	·	Euphrasia sp.
·	·	·	·	·	I	·	·	2	·	Filipendula ulmaria
2	·	·	·	·	3	·	·	·	·	Galium boreale
2	I	·	·	·	·	·	·	·	·	G. hercynicum
·	·	I	2	·	·	·	·	·	·	G. verum
·	2	·	·	·	·	·	·	·	·	Gentianella amarella
·	·	·	·	·	·	·	·	·	·	G. campestris
·	·	·	·	·	·	·	·	·	·	Geranium sylvaticum
·	·	·	·	·	2	·	·	I	·	Geum rivale
·	·	·	·	·	·	·	·	2	·	Heracleum sphondylium
·	2	·	·	·	·	·	·	2	·	Hieracium pilosella
·	·	·	·	·	·	I	2	2	·	Hieracium sp.
·	3	·	·	·	I	2	2	I	·	Hypericum pulchrum
·	+	·	·	·	·	2	3	·	·	Hypochaeris radicata
·	·	·	·	·	·	·	·	·	·	Lathyrus montanus
·	3	I	·	3	3	3	3	3	·	Linum catharticum
·	I	I	+	·	·	·	3	3	·	Lotus corniculatus
·	·	·	·	·	3	·	·	2	·	Parnassia palustris
I	·	·	·	·	2	·	·	·	·	Pinguicula vulgaris
·	·	·	·	·	2	·	2	·	·	Leontodon autumnalis
·	·	·	·	·	·	·	I	·	·	Plantago coronopus
·	3	+	+	3	3	3	4	·	·	**P. lanceolata**
·	3	I	·	2	2	2	4	·	·	P. maritima
·	·	+	·	·	·	·	·	·	·	P. media
·	·	·	·	·	·	I	2	·	·	Polygala serpyllifolia
·	·	I	+	2	·	·	·	·	·	P. vulgaris
2	·	2	·	·	·	·	·	2	3	Polygonum viviparum
·	·	·	·	·	·	·	·	·	·	Potentilla crantzii
I	2	·	·	·	3	·	4	·	·	P. erecta
·	3	·	·	·	3	I	I	2	·	Prunella vulgaris
·	·	·	·	·	·	·	·	·	·	Pyrola rotundifolia
·	·	·	·	·	·	·	·	·	·	Ramischia secunda
·	·	·	·	·	·	·	2	2	·	Ranunculus acris
·	·	·	·	·	I	·	·	I	·	Rhinanthus minor
·	·	·	·	·	·	·	·	·	·	Rumex acetosa
4	·	·	·	·	+	·	·	·	·	Saussurea alpina
+	·	·	·	·	I	·	·	I	3	Saxifraga aizoides
·	·	·	·	·	·	·	·	·	·	S. hypnoides
2	·	·	·	·	·	·	·	3	I	S. oppositifolia
·	·	·	·	·	·	·	·	·	·	Sedum rosea
·	·	·	·	·	·	·	·	·	·	Senecio jacobaea
·	·	·	·	·	2	·	·	3	6	**Silene acaulis**
·	·	·	·	·	·	·	·	·	·	Solidago virgaurea
·	3	·	·	3	·	3	4	3	·	Succisa pratensis
·	·	·	·	·	I	I	2	·	·	Taraxacum officinalis agg.
I	·	·	·	3	2	·	·	·	·	Thalictrum alpinum
3	3	3	3	3	3	3	4	3	·	**Thymus drucei**
·	·	·	·	·	·	I	3	·	·	Trifolium pratense
·	·	I	·	·	·	I	·	·	·	T. repens
·	·	·	·	·	·	·	·	·	·	Trollius europaeus
·	·	·	·	·	·	·	·	I	·	Veronica fruticans
·	2	+	+	3	3	I	2	3	·	**Viola riviniana**
·	·	·	·	·	·	·	·	·	·	Acrocladium cuspidatum
·	·	·	·	·	·	·	·	·	·	Anoectangium compactum
·	·	·	·	·	·	·	·	·	·	Anomobryum filiforme
·	·	·	·	·	·	·	·	·	·	Blindia acuta
·	·	·	·	·	5	·	·	·	·	Breutelia chrysocoma
·	·	I	2	·	·	·	·	·	·	Camptothecium lutescens
·	·	·	·	·	·	·	·	I	·	Campylium protensum
·	·	·	·	·	·	·	·	·	·	Campylopus fragilis
3	+	·	·	2	4	·	·	2	3	Ctenidium molluscum
·	·	·	·	·	·	·	·	·	·	Dicranum majus
·	·	·	·	·	·	·	·	·	·	D. scoparium
·	·	·	·	·	·	·	·	·	·	Distichium capillaceum
4	+	3	3	3	·	·	·	·	·	Ditrichum flexicaule
·	·	·	·	·	·	·	·	·	·	Drepanocladus uncinatus
·	·	·	·	·	·	·	·	·	·	Encalypta streptocarpa
·	·	·	·	·	·	·	·	·	·	Entodon orthocarpus
·	·	·	·	·	·	·	·	·	·	Fissidens adianthoides
·	·	I	I	·	·	·	·	·	·	F. cristatus
·	·	·	·	·	·	·	·	·	·	F. osmundoides
·	I	·	·	·	·	·	·	·	·	F. taxifolius
I	·	2	·	·	·	·	·	3	3	**Hylocomium splendens**
·	I	·	·	3	·	·	·	·	·	Hypnum cupressiforme
·	·	·	·	·	·	·	·	·	·	Isopterygium pulchellum
·	·	·	·	·	·	·	·	·	2	Mnium orthorrhynchum

Table 23

	1	2	3	4	5	6	7	8	9	10
Mnium sp.	·	·	·	·	·	·	·	·	·	·
M. undulatum	·	·	1	·	·	·	·	·	·	·
Neckera crispa	·	·	·	·	·	·	1	·	·	·
Eurhynchium striatum	·	·	1	·	·	·	·	·	·	·
Orthothecium rufescens	·	·	·	1	2	·	·	·	·	·
O. intricatum	·	1	·	·	·	·	·	·	·	·
Plagiobryum zierii	·	·	·	·	·	·	·	·	·	·
Philonotis fontana	·	·	·	·	1	·	·	·	·	·
Plagiopus oederi	·	·	·	·	3	·	·	·	·	·
Pleurozium schreberi	·	·	·	·	·	·	·	·	·	·
Pohlia cruda	·	·	·	·	·	1	·	·	·	·
Polytrichum alpinum	·	·	·	·	1	·	·	·	·	·
P. urnigerum	·	·	·	·	·	1	·	·	·	·
Pseudoscleropodium purum	·	·	3	1	·	·	·	·	·	·
Meesia uliginosa	·	·	+	·	1	·	·	·	·	·
Ptilium crista-castrensis	·	3	3	·	1	·	·	·	·	·
Rhacomitrium canescens	·	2	3	·	·	1	·	·	·	·
R. lanuginosum	2	·	3	1	5	·	1	2	·	3
Rhytidiadelphus loreus	·	1	·	·	·	·	·	·	·	·
R. squarrosus	·	1	2	·	·	·	·	·	·	·
R. triquetrus	2	4	3	·	4	2	·	·	·	·
Rhytidium rugosum	·	·	4	·	·	2	·	·	·	·
Saelania glaucescens	·	·	·	·	·	·	·	·	·	·
Thuidium abietinum	·	·	·	·	·	1	·	·	·	1
T. delicatulum	·	·	·	·	3	·	·	·	·	1
T. recognitum	·	·	·	·	·	2	·	·	·	·
T. tamariscinum	·	·	1	·	·	·	·	·	·	·
Tortella tortuosa	3	2	·	2	·	2	3	5	3	3
Aneura pinguis	·	·	·	·	1	·	·	·	·	·
Frullania tamarisci	·	·	·	·	1	2	·	·	·	1
Herberta adunca	·	·	·	·	2	·	·	·	·	1
Lejeunea patens	·	·	·	·	1	·	·	·	·	·
Lophocolea bidentata	·	·	·	·	·	·	·	·	·	·
Lophozia bicrenata	·	·	·	·	·	·	·	·	1	·
L. floerkii	2	·	·	·	·	·	·	·	·	·
L. quinquedentata	·	2	·	·	3	·	·	·	·	·
Metzgeria hamata	·	·	·	·	3	·	·	·	·	·
M. pubescens	·	3	·	·	·	·	·	·	·	·
Plagiochila asplenioides	1	2	1	·	2	·	·	·	·	1
Preissia quadrata	·	1	·	·	·	·	·	·	·	1
Ptilidium ciliare	1	·	·	·	·	·	·	·	·	·
Scapania aspera	·	2	·	·	3	·	·	·	·	·
S. cf. calcicola	·	·	·	1	·	·	·	·	·	·
S. nemorosa	·	·	·	·	·	·	·	·	·	1
S. undulata	·	·	·	·	·	·	·	·	·	·
Alectoria nigricans	·	·	·	·	·	·	·	·	·	·
Cerania vermicularis	·	·	·	·	·	·	·	·	·	·
Cetraria aculeata	·	·	·	·	·	·	·	·	·	·
C. islandica	·	·	·	·	2	2	·	·	·	·
Cladonia gracilis	2	·	·	·	·	·	·	·	·	·
C. pyxidata	2	·	·	·	·	·	·	·	·	·
C. rangiformis	·	·	·	·	·	·	1	·	·	·
C. sylvatica	2	·	·	·	·	·	·	·	·	·
Leptogium sp.	·	·	·	·	·	·	·	·	·	·
Peltidea leucophlebia	·	·	·	·	·	·	·	·	2	·
Peltigera canina	·	·	1	·	·	·	·	·	·	·
Solorina saccata	·	·	·	·	·	·	1	2	1	·
Number of species (215)	36	45	65	37	59	54	36	29	27	31

(Average 49)   (Average 32)

(Overall

LOCALITIES

1,2,19. Glen Doll, Clova, Angus; 3. Seana Bhraigh, Ross-shire; 4. Creag Mhor, Loch Lyon, Perthshire; 5. Ben Lui, Argyll; 6. Caenlochan Glen, Angus; 7. Smoo Cave, Durness, Sutherland; 8. Between Conival and Breabag Tarsuinn, Ben More Assynt, Sutherland; 9,10. Glas Cnoc,

(*continued*)

11	12	13	14	15	16	17	18	19	20	
·	·	1	·	·	·	·	·	·	·	Mnium sp.
·	·	·	·	·	·	·	·	·	·	M. undulatum
·	·	·	·	·	·	·	·	·	·	Neckera crispa
·	·	·	·	·	·	·	·	·	·	Eurhynchium striatum
·	·	·	·	·	·	·	·	·	1	Orthothecium rufescens
·	·	·	·	·	·	·	·	·	·	O. intricatum
·	·	·	·	·	·	·	·	·	1	Plagiobryum zierii
·	·	·	·	·	·	·	·	·	·	Philonotis fontana
·	·	·	·	·	·	·	·	·	·	Plagiopus oederi
·	·	·	·	4	·	·	·	·	·	Pleurozium schreberi
·	·	·	·	·	·	·	·	·	·	Pohlia cruda
·	·	·	·	·	·	·	·	·	·	Polytrichum alpinum
·	·	·	·	·	·	·	·	·	·	P. urnigerum
·	·	1	1	1	2	·	·	1	·	Pseudoscleropodium purum
·	·	·	·	·	·	·	·	·	·	Meesia uliginosa
·	·	·	·	·	·	·	·	·	·	Ptilium crista-castrensis
·	·	·	·	·	·	·	·	·	2	Rhacomitrium canescens
1	·	·	·	·	1	·	·	·	6	R. lanuginosum
·	·	·	·	·	·	·	·	·	·	Rhytidiadelphus loreus
·	·	·	·	·	·	·	·	·	·	R. squarrosus
·	·	4	·	1	2	·	·	3	·	R. triquetrus
2	·	·	·	·	·	·	·	·	·	Rhytidium rugosum
·	·	·	·	·	·	·	·	1	·	Saelania glaucescens
·	·	·	·	·	·	·	·	·	·	Thuidium abietinum
·	·	3	·	3	·	·	·	·	·	T. delicatulum
·	·	·	·	·	·	·	·	·	·	T. recognitum
·	·	·	·	·	·	·	·	·	·	T. tamariscinum
2	+	·	·	·	·	·	·	2	2	**Tortella tortuosa**
·	·	·	·	·	·	·	·	·	·	Aneura pinguis
·	·	+	·	·	·	·	·	1	·	Frullania tamarisci
·	·	·	·	·	·	·	·	·	·	Herberta adunca
·	·	·	·	·	·	·	·	·	·	Lejeuna patens
·	·	1	·	·	·	·	·	·	·	Lophocolea bidentata
·	·	·	·	·	·	·	·	·	·	Lophozia bicrenata
·	·	·	·	·	·	·	·	·	·	L. floerkii
·	·	·	·	·	·	·	·	·	·	L. quinquedentata
·	·	·	·	·	·	·	·	·	·	Metzgeria hamata
·	·	·	·	·	·	·	·	·	·	M. pubescens
·	·	+	·	·	·	·	·	1	·	Plagiochila asplenioides
·	·	·	·	·	·	·	·	·	·	Preissia quadrata
·	·	·	·	·	·	·	·	1	·	Ptilidium ciliare
·	·	·	·	·	·	·	·	·	·	Scapania aspera
·	·	·	·	·	·	·	·	·	·	S. cf. calcicola
·	·	·	·	·	·	·	·	·	·	S. nemorosa
·	·	+	·	1	·	·	·	·	·	S. undulata
2	·	·	·	·	·	·	·	·	·	Alectoria nigricans
2	·	·	·	·	·	·	·	·	·	Cerania vermicularis
3	·	·	·	·	·	·	·	·	·	Cetraria aculeata
2	·	·	·	·	·	·	·	·	·	C. islandica
1	·	·	·	·	·	·	·	·	·	Cladonia gracilis
·	·	·	·	·	·	·	·	1	·	C. pyxidata
·	·	·	·	+	·	·	·	·	·	C. rangiformis
1	·	·	·	·	·	·	·	·	·	C. sylvatica
·	1	·	·	·	·	·	·	·	·	Leptogium sp.
·	·	·	·	·	1	·	·	·	·	Peltidea leucophlebia
·	·	+	·	·	·	·	·	2	·	Peltigera canina
·	·	·	·	·	·	·	·	2	·	Solorina saccata
35	32	36	16	36	48	22	30	59	18	Number of species (215)

(Average 31)

average 38)

Kishorn, Ross-shire; 11. The Cairnwell, Perthshire; 12. Heilam, Sutherland; 13,14. Bettyhill, Sutherland; 15. Borralie, Sutherland; 16. Meall Mor, Glencoe, Argyll; 17,18. Monadh Dubh, Isle of Rhum; 20. Coire na Coichille, Ardverikie, Inverness-shire.

Table 24: Species-poor

	1	2	3	4	5	6	7	8	9	10
Reference number	R57 036	R58 011	R58 063	R58 049	R58 029	R58 082	R58 076	R57 082	R57 317	M57 012
Map reference	9390 2322	9288 2574	8838 2263	8814 2222	7800 1854	8316 2198	8467 2079	7860 2443	7783 2983	8003 1339
Altitude (feet)	600	2000	2500	1750	2000	900	1000	2100	1500	100
Aspect (degrees)	45	270	180	–	360	180	–	270	270	203
Slope (degrees)	27	30	20	2	25	10	0	20	25	33
Cover (per cent)	100	100	100	100	100	100	100	100	100	100
Height (centimetres)	–	–	–	–	--	7	–	–	–	–
Plot area (square metres)	4	4	4	4	4	4	4	4	4	4
Empetrum hermaphroditum	.	.	.	.	.	.	.	.	.	.
Vaccinium myrtillus	.	2	3	.	2	2	.	3	2	2
Blechnum spicant	.	.	.	.	2	.	.	1	.	.
Dryopteris filix-mas	.	.	.	.	.	.	.	.	.	.
Lycopodium selago	.	.	.	.	.	.	.	.	.	.
Agrostis canina	4	4	6	2	5	2	3	7	+	5
A. tenuis	6	7	6	8	4	8	7	7	7	2
Anthoxanthum odoratum	5	4	5	4	5	3	5	3	3	4
Deschampsia caespitosa	2	3	.	.	3	.	.	2	.	.
D. flexuosa	.	.	3	.	.	.	.	1	.	2
Festuca ovina agg.	.	4	5	4	5	7	5	5	7	6
F. rubra	.	.	.	.	.	.	.	.	3	.
Holcus lanatus	4	.	.	.	.	.	2	.	.	.
Molinia caerulea	.	.	.	.	.	.	3	.	.	.
Nardus stricta	.	2	5	.	4	.	3	4	.	.
Sieglingia decumbens	.	.	.	.	.	3	4	.	.	4
Carex bigelowii	.	1	3	.	.	.	.	.	.	.
C. binervis	3	.	.	2	1	.	.	2	.	.
C. demissa	.	.	.	2	.	.	.	.	.	.
C. echinata	.	.	.	3	2	.	.	.	.	.
C. nigra	.	.	.	.	.	.	.	.	.	.
C. panicea	.	.	.	3	2	.	3	.	.	.
C. pilulifera	.	.	3	2	3	3	3	3	2	.
C. pulicaris	.	.	.	2	.	.	.	.	.	.
Endymion non-scriptus	1	.	.	.	.	.	.	.	.	.
Eriophorum angustifolium	.	.	2	.	.	.	.	.	.	.
Juncus effusus	+	.	.	1	.	.	.	.	.	.
J. squarrosus	.	1	4	3	2	.	3	3	.	.
Luzula campestris	3	.	.	.	.	3	.	.	3	.
L. multiflora	.	.	3	3	3	.	3	1	.	3
L. sylvatica	1	2	.	.	.	.	.	2	.	.
Orchis ericetorum	.	1	.	.	.	.	.	.	.	.
Trichophorum caespitosum	.	.	.	.	2	3	.	.	.	.
Achillea millefolium	.	.	.	.	.	.	3	.	.	.
A. ptarmica	.	.	.	.	.	.	.	.	.	.
Alchemilla alpina	.	.	3	.	.	.	.	.	.	.
A. vestita	.	.	.	.	.	.	.	.	.	.
Campanula rotundifolia	.	.	.	.	.	.	.	.	.	.
Cerastium vulgatum	.	.	.	.	.	.	.	1	.	1
Euphrasia sp.	.	.	.	.	.	.	.	1	.	3
Galium hercynicum	4	3	5	2	4	4	3	4	5	4
G. verum	.	.	.	.	.	.	.	.	.	.
Lathyrus montanus	.	.	.	.	.	.	.	.	.	2
Leontodon autumnalis	2	+	.	1	2	.	.	.	.	.
Linum catharticum	.	.	.	.	.	.	.	.	.	.
Lotus corniculatus	.	.	.	.	.	.	.	.	.	1
Oxalis acetosella	.	.	.	.	.	.	.	.	.	.
Pedicularis sylvatica	.	.	.	.	.	.	.	.	.	.
Plantago lanceolata	1	.	.	2	.	.	.	.	.	4
Prunella vulgaris	.	.	.	.	.	.	.	.	.	.
Polygala serpyllifolia	.	.	.	.	.	.	.	.	.	3
Polygonum viviparum	.	.	.	.	.	.	.	4	.	.
Potentilla erecta	3	3	4	4	5	5	4	5	3	5
Ranunculus acris	3	+	.	3	.	.	2	.	.	.
R. ficaria	2	.	.	.	.	.	.	.	.	.
R. flammula	.	.	.	1	.	.	.	.	.	.
Rumex acetosa	3	.	.	.	.	.	.	.	.	+
Sedum anglicum	.	.	.	.	.	.	.	.	.	3
Succisa pratensis	1	.	.	1	.	.	3	.	.	.
Taraxacum officinalis agg.	.	.	.	1	.	.	.	.	.	.
Thymus drucei	.	2	.	.	.	.	.	.	.	5
Trifolium repens	4	.	.	.	.	.	.	.	.	2
Veronica chamaedrys	.	.	.	.	.	.	.	.	.	.
V. officinalis	.	.	.	.	.	.	.	.	.	3
Viola riviniana	+	3	2	4	4	.	3	3	2	3
Antitrichia curtipendula	.	.	.	.	.	.	.	.	.	1
Dicranella heteromalla	.	.	.	.	.	.	.	.	.	.
Dicranum fuscescens	.	.	.	.	.	.	.	.	.	.
D. majus	.	.	.	.	.	.	.	.	.	.
D. scoparium	.	.	.	.	.	.	.	.	.	.
Drepanocladus uncinatus	.	.	.	.	.	.	.	.	.	.
Hylocomium splendens	4	7	5	5	4	4	4	5	3	3

Agrosto-Festucetum

11	12	13	14	15	16	17	18	19	20	
R58	R57	R57	R57	R57	R57	R57	R58	M56	R56	Reference number
005	074	334	059	005	217	158	108	074	060	
9498	7861	8009	8724	9361	7754	7969	7511	9191	8687	Map reference
2565	2442	1330	2220	2318	3280	2602	2641	2303	2201	
300	2250	1000	1200	780	1100	2550	2700	1700	2400	Altitude (feet)
—	90	315	—	270	45	315	45	225	360	Aspect (degrees)
2	12	28	0	30	30	25	30	40	35	Slope (degrees)
100	100	100	100	100	100	100	100	100	100	Cover (per cent)
—	—	—	—	10	8	—	—	12	—	Height (centimetres)
4	4	4	4	4	4	4	4	4	4	Plot area (square metres)
·	·	·	·	·	·	2	·	·	·	Empetrum hermaphroditum
·	·	3	·	·	4	3	·	·	3	Vaccinium myrtillus
·	·	2	·	·	·	·	·	·	3	Blechnum spicant
·	·	·	·	·	1	·	·	·	·	Dryopteris filix-mas
·	·	·	·	·	·	1	·	·	·	Lycopodium selago
·	9	3	5	5	3	2	·	·	·	**Agrostis canina**
7	9	5	8	7	7	5	7	6	5	**A. tenuis**
4	4	5	3	4	4	·	3	5	3	**Anthoxanthum odoratum**
·	3	·	·	·	·	3	3	1	4	Deschampsia caespitosa
·	·	5	+	·	·	2	3	·	3	D. flexuosa
4	5	5	4	3	7	4	3	6	5	**Festuca ovina agg.**
·	·	·	·	·	·	·	·	·	1	F. rubra
·	·	·	·	2	·	·	·	·	·	Holcus lanatus
·	·	·	·	·	·	·	·	·	·	Molinia caerulea
1	3	3	2	·	·	3	3	·	3	Nardus stricta
4	·	·	·	·	·	·	·	·	·	Sieglingia decumbens
·	·	·	·	·	·	3	·	·	3	Carex bigelowii
·	2	3	·	·	·	·	·	·	·	C. binervis
·	·	·	·	·	·	·	·	·	·	C. demissa
·	2	·	2	·	·	·	·	·	·	C. echinata
·	·	4	3	2	·	·	·	·	·	C. nigra
·	·	3	2	·	·	·	·	·	·	C. panicea
1	·	3	+	2	2	·	·	·	3	C. pilulifera
·	·	·	·	·	·	·	·	·	·	C. pulicaris
·	·	·	·	·	·	·	·	·	·	Endymion non-scriptus
·	1	·	·	·	·	·	·	·	·	Eriophorum angustifolium
·	·	·	·	·	·	·	·	·	·	Juncus effusus
·	3	4	2	·	·	·	·	·	·	J. squarrosus
4	·	·	·	3	2	·	·	·	·	Luzula campestris
·	2	3	3	·	·	·	·	2	·	L. multiflora
·	·	3	·	·	·	·	·	1	3	L. sylvatica
·	·	·	+	·	·	·	·	·	·	Orchis ericetorum
·	2	·	·	·	·	·	·	·	·	Trichophorum caespitosum
3	·	·	·	·	·	·	·	·	·	Achillea millefolium
·	·	·	2	·	·	·	·	·	·	A. ptarmica
·	·	·	·	·	·	·	2	·	2	Alchemilla alpina
·	·	·	·	·	·	·	·	·	2	A. vestita
·	2	·	·	·	3	·	·	·	·	Campanula rotundifolia
+	·	·	·	·	2	·	3	2	2	Cerastium vulgatum
·	·	·	2	·	2	1	1	1	3	Euphrasia sp.
5	3	3	3	5	4	5	5	3	2	**Galium hercynicum**
·	·	·	·	·	2	·	·	·	·	G. verum
·	·	·	·	·	·	·	·	·	·	Lathyrus montanus
·	2	·	·	·	·	·	·	·	·	Leontodon autumnalis
·	·	·	·	·	·	·	·	2	·	Linum catharticum
·	·	·	·	·	·	·	·	·	·	Lotus corniculatus
·	·	·	·	·	1	2	2	1	·	Oxalis acetosella
·	·	1	·	·	·	·	·	·	·	Pedicularis sylvatica
3	·	·	2	·	·	·	·	·	·	Plantago lanceolata
1	·	·	·	·	·	·	·	·	·	Prunella vulgaris
·	·	·	2	·	2	·	·	·	·	Polygala serpyllifolia
·	·	·	·	·	·	·	·	·	·	Polygonum viviparum
3	4	5	3	3	3	3	·	·	5	**Potentilla erecta**
2	2	·	2	·	·	·	·	3	3	Ranunculus acris
·	·	·	·	·	·	·	·	·	·	R. ficaria
·	·	·	·	·	·	·	·	·	·	R. flammula
3	·	1	·	·	·	·	·	2	2	Rumex acetosa
·	·	·	·	·	·	·	·	·	·	Sedum anglicum
·	·	·	+	·	·	·	·	·	·	Succisa pratensis
·	3	·	·	·	·	·	·	1	·	Taraxacum officinalis agg.
·	·	·	·	·	·	·	·	4	·	Thymus drucei
3	·	·	·	·	·	·	·	4	·	Trifolium repens
·	·	·	·	·	1	·	·	2	·	Veronica chamaedrys
·	·	·	·	·	·	·	4	·	4	V. officinalis
1	3	·	4	+	2	·	·	1	4	**Viola riviniana**
·	·	·	·	·	·	·	·	·	·	Antitrichia curtipendula
·	·	·	·	·	·	1	·	·	·	Dicranella heteromalla
·	·	·	·	·	·	2	·	·	·	Dicranum fuscescens
·	·	·	·	·	·	·	·	·	1	D. majus
3	·	·	·	·	2	1	·	+	2	D. scoparium
·	·	·	·	·	·	·	2	·	·	Drepanocladus uncinatus
5	3	3	3	4	4	4	2	3	6	**Hylocomium splendens**

Table 24

	1	2	3	4	5	6	7	8	9	10
Hypnum cupressiforme	·	·	3	2	·	1	3	·	·	3
Mnium hornum	·	·	·	·	·	·	·	·	·	1
M. punctatum	·	·	·	1	·	·	·	·	·	·
M. undulatum	·	·	·	·	·	·	·	·	·	·
Plagiothecium undulatum	·	·	2	·	1	·	·	·	·	·
Pleurozium schreberi	·	·	·	·	1	3	·	4	2	2
Polytrichum alpinum	·	·	·	·	·	·	·	2	3	3
P. commune	3	·	·	·	2	·	3	·	·	·
P. juniperinum	·	·	·	·	·	·	·	·	·	2
P. piliferum	·	·	·	·	·	·	·	·	·	+
Pseudoscleropodium purum	2	3	·	4	·	3	4	3	·	·
Rhacomitrium canescens	·	·	·	·	·	·	·	·	·	·
R. lanuginosum	·	·	·	·	·	·	·	·	·	1
Rhytidiadelphus loreus	·	3	·	·	1	·	·	3	·	3
R. squarrosus	3	4	5	3	2	3	3	3	4	·
R. triquetrus	3	3	·	·	·	·	·	·	1	·
Sphagnum nemoreum	·	·	·	·	2	·	·	·	·	·
Thuidium tamariscinum	8	3	·	2	3	2	3	·	·	·
Anastrepta orcadensis	·	·	·	·	·	·	·	·	·	·
Calypogeia trichomanis	·	·	·	·	·	·	·	·	·	·
Frullania tamarisci	·	·	·	·	·	·	·	·	·	2
Lophocolea bidentata	·	·	·	2	·	·	2	·	·	·
Lophozia barbata	·	·	·	·	·	·	·	·	·	·
L. floerkii	·	·	2	·	·	·	·	·	·	·
L. incisa.	·	·	·	·	·	·	·	·	·	·
Ptilidium ciliare	·	·	·	·	·	·	·	·	2	·
Cetraria aculeata	·	·	·	·	·	·	·	·	·	1
Cladonia rangiferina agg.	·	·	·	·	·	·	·	·	·	·
C. sylvatica	·	·	·	·	·	·	·	·	·	·
C. tenuis	·	·	·	·	·	·	·	·	·	·
Peltigera canina	·	·	·	·	·	·	1	·	·	·
Number of species (103)	26	24	20	30	27	16	27	25	17	34

(Average 25)

Constancy class V 9
    „   „ IV 4

LOCALITIES

1. Loch na Mucnaich, Reay Forest, Sutherland; 2. Ben Klibreck, Sutherland; 3. Eididh nan Clach Geala, Inverlael Forest, Ross-shire; 4. Beinn Enaiglair, Braemore, Ross-shire; 5. Beinn Odhar Mhor, Glenfinnan, Inverness-shire; 6. Mullach na Maoile, Glen Cannich, Inverness-shire; 7. Allt a' Chonais, Achnashellach, Ross-shire; 8,12. Creag Meagaidh, Laggan, Inverness-shire; 9. Glen Tilt, Perthshire; 10.13, Fionchra

(*continued*)

11	12	13	14	15	16	17	18	19	20	
3	·	·	·	·	1	1	·	·	·	Hypnum cupressiforme
1	·	3	·	·	·	2	·	·	·	Mnium hornum
·	·	·	·	·	·	·	·	·	·	M. punctatum
2	·	·	·	·	·	·	·	·	·	M. undulatum
·	·	4	·	·	·	·	·	·	·	Plagiothecium undulatum
·	·	1	·	1	4	6	3	3	2	Pleurozium schreberi
·	·	·	·	·	·	4	4	3	3	Polytrichum alpinum
4	·	3	1	3	1	·	·	·	·	P. commune
·	·	·	·	·	·	·	·	·	·	P. juniperinum
·	·	·	·	·	·	·	·	·	·	P. piliferum
·	·	2	2	2	·	·	·	·	·	Pseudoscleropodium purum
·	·	·	·	·	·	·	·	·	3	Rhacomitrium canescens
·	·	·	·	·	·	·	·	·	2	R. lanuginosum
·	·	2	·	4	·	5	·	6	3	Rhytidiadelphus loreus
4	3	2	3	3	·	·	8	·	4	**R. squarrosus**
·	·	·	·	2	4	·	·	·	·	R. triquetrus
·	·	·	·	·	·	·	·	·	·	Sphagnum nemoreum
5	·	3	3	8	·	·	·	3	3	Thuidium tamariscinum
·	·	·	·	·	·	1	·	·	·	Anastrepta orcadensis
·	·	·	1	·	·	·	·	·	·	Calypogeia trichomanis
·	·	·	·	·	·	·	·	·	·	Frullania tamarisci
·	·	·	2	·	1	·	·	·	·	Lophocolea bidentata
·	·	·	·	·	3	·	·	·	·	Lophozia barbata
·	·	·	·	·	1	·	·	·	·	L. floerkii
·	·	·	·	·	·	1	·	·	·	L. incisa
·	·	·	·	·	3	1	·	·	·	Ptilidium ciliare
·	·	·	·	·	·	·	·	·	·	Cetraria aculeata
·	·	·	·	·	1	·	·	·	·	Cladonia rangiferina agg.
·	·	·	·	·	2	·	·	·	·	C. sylvatica
·	·	·	·	·	1	·	·	·	·	C. tenuis
·	·	·	·	·	2	·	·	1	+	Peltigera canina
25	21	27	30	19	34	24	17	26	33	Number of species (103)

Isle of Rhum; 11. Ben Loyal, Sutherland; 14. Allt a' Mhadaidh, Fannich Forest, Ross-shire; 15. Strath nan Caran, Glendhu Forest, Sutherland; 16. Braedownie, Clova, Angus; 17. Glen Banchor, Monadhliath, Inverness-shire; 18. Carn Gorm, Glen Lyon, Perthshire; 19. Ben More Assynt, Sutherland; 20. Slioch, Ross-shire.

Table 25: Alchemilleto-Agrosto-Festucetum

	1	2	3	4	5	6	7	8	9	10
Reference number	R58 030	R57 200	R57 305	R56 067	R56 094	R57 171	M57 052	R57 196	R57 088	R57 216
Map reference	7793 1853	8006 2602	7634 2949	8723 2061	8734 2157	7964 2597	7695 2175	7995 2597	7796 2643	7754 3280
Altitude (feet)	2400	2100	2400	1900	1700	2400	1800	1900	1900	1100
Aspect (degrees)	45	270	270	225	90	225	270	270	–	45
Slope (degrees)	30	38	27	30	35	32	45	35	0	30
Cover (per cent)	90	100	100	95	95	100	100	95	100	95
Height (centimetres)	–	–	–	–	–	–	–	–	–	–
Plot area (square metres)	4	4	4	4	4	4	4	4	4	4
Calluna vulgaris	·	·	·	·	1	·	1	·	2	2
Empetrum hermaphroditum	·	1	·	1	2	4	·	2	·	·
Salix herbacea	·	·	1	·	·	·	·	·	·	·
Sorbus aucuparia	·	·	·	·	·	·	·	1	·	·
Vaccinium myrtillus	3	·	2	3	2	3	+	2	·	·
V. uliginosum	·	·	·	·	·	·	·	·	·	·
V. vitis-idaea	·	·	3	+	·	3	·	2	+	·
Blechnum spicant	2	+	·	·	3	·	·	·	·	·
Botrychium lunaria	·	·	·	·	·	·	3	·	·	·
Lycopodium alpinum	·	·	·	+	·	3	·	·	·	·
L. selago	·	·	·	·	·	·	·	·	·	·
Selaginella selaginoides	2	·	2	3	3	2	3	1	1	·
Thelypteris dryopteris	·	2	·	·	·	·	·	·	·	·
T. oreopteris	·	·	·	·	2	·	·	·	·	·
Agrostis canina	2	·	·	3	5	·	3	·	·	·
A. tenuis	4	3	3	4	4	3	3	3	5	4
Anthoxanthum odoratum	3	2	1	4	4	·	3	3	4	2
Deschampsia caespitosa	2	·	1	·	3	·	·	·	·	·
D. flexuosa	·	·	·	3	2	·	1	·	·	·
Festuca ovina agg.	5	5	7	5	5	4	5	5	5	7
F. rubra	3	3	+	·	·	·	·	3	1	·
Nardus stricta	3	·	·	3	4	3	·	1	2	·
Sieglingia decumbens	·	·	·	·	·	·	·	·	·	2
Carex bigelowii	·	·	·	·	·	1	·	·	·	·
C. binervis	·	·	·	·	3	·	·	·	·	·
C. caryophyllea	·	3	·	·	·	·	·	·	·	·
C. panicea	·	·	·	·	·	·	·	2	·	·
C. pilulifera	1	·	·	·	3	1	1	1	·	3
C. pulicaris	2	3	·	·	2	·	·	1	·	·
Juncus squarrosus	2	·	·	·	·	·	·	·	2	·
J. trifidus	·	·	·	·	·	·	·	·	·	·
Luzula campestris	·	·	·	·	·	·	·	·	·	·
L. multiflora	2	·	·	2	2	1	2	·	3	2
L. spicata	·	·	·	·	·	·	·	·	·	·
L. sylvatica	·	·	·	·	·	·	1	·	·	·
Trichophorum caespitosum	·	·	·	·	2	·	·	·	·	·
Achillea millefolium	·	·	1	·	·	·	·	·	4	·
Alchemilla alpina	4	6	7	7	5	8	6	6	7	7
A. glabra	·	·	3	·	·	·	·	·	1	·
A. vestita	4	·	·	·	·	·	·	·	3	·
A. xanthochlora	·	·	·	+	·	·	·	·	·	3
Angelica sylvestris	·	·	·	·	1	·	·	·	·	·
Antennaria dioica	·	·	·	+	·	·	·	·	·	·
Armeria maritima	·	·	·	·	·	·	·	·	·	·
Campanula rotundifolia	·	3	2	·	·	3	2	1	·	+
Cardamine flexuosa	·	·	·	·	·	·	·	·	1	·
Cerastium alpinum	·	·	·	·	·	·	·	·	·	·
C. vulgatum	·	·	·	·	·	·	·	·	·	·
Cherleria sedoides	·	·	·	·	·	·	·	·	·	·
Cirsium palustre	·	·	·	·	·	·	·	·	·	1
Euphrasia sp.	·	·	·	3	2	2	3	·	2	3
Galium boreale	·	·	2	·	·	·	·	·	·	·
G. hercynicum	3	3	2	3	3	3	3	1	2	·
G. verum	·	·	1	·	·	·	·	·	+	3
Gentianella campestris	·	·	·	·	·	·	·	·	·	3
Geranium sylvaticum	·	·	·	·	·	·	+	·	·	·
Geum rivale	3	·	1	·	1	·	+	·	·	·
Gnaphalium supinum	·	·	·	·	·	·	2	·	·	1
Hieracium holosericeum	·	·	·	·	·	·	·	·	·	·
Hypericum pulchrum	·	·	·	·	1	·	·	·	·	·
Leontodon autumnalis	·	·	·	·	1	·	·	·	·	·
Linum catharticum	·	·	·	1	·	·	·	·	·	2
Lotus corniculatus	·	·	·	·	·	·	1	·	·	·
Oxalis acetosella	·	3	·	·	·	·	·	1	·	·
Pinguicula vulgaris	·	·	·	·	1	·	·	·	·	·
Plantago maritima	·	·	·	·	+	·	·	·	·	·
Polygala serpyllifolia	1	·	·	2	·	·	·	·	·	·
Polygonum viviparum	4	·	2	·	·	·	·	·	·	·
Potentilla crantzii	·	·	2	·	·	·	·	·	·	·
P. erecta	4	·	·	4	3	2	·	·	·	·
Prunella vulgaris	2	·	1	·	·	·	·	·	2	3
Ranunculus acris	2	·	·	+	3	·	3	·	2	1
Rumex acetosa	·	·	·	·	2	·	2	·	2	·
Saxifraga aizoides	·	·	·	·	·	·	·	1	·	2

(1–14); Rhacomitrium-rich facies (15–19)

11	12	13	14	15	16	17	18	19	
R57	R58	P52	M56	M55	M56	M56	R56	M57	Reference number
070	107	095	042	003	006	046	071	028	Map reference
7985	7509	7380	8605	8595	8417	8730	8733	7320	
2590	2640	2582	1975	1966	1793	1983	2058	2134	
1500	2800	2700	2150	2700	2350	2650	2750	2700	Altitude (feet)
270	45	70	315	135	135	180	90	180	Aspect (degrees)
45	40	10	5	30	30	14	35	3	Slope (degrees)
100	100	90	100	100	100	100	98	100	Cover (per cent)
—	—	20	1	5	3	8	—	—	Height (centimetres)
4	4	4	1	4	4	4	4	4	Plot area (square metres)
·	·	·	·	+	·	·	·	·	Calluna vulgaris
2	·	·	1	2	+	3	·	·	Empetrum hermaphroditum
·	·	·	·	·	·	·	·	·	Salix herbacea
·	·	·	·	·	·	·	·	·	Sorbus aucuparia
·	4	4	2	3	3	·	2	·	Vaccinium myrtillus
·	·	·	·	+	·	·	·	·	V. uliginosum
·	3	·	·	·	2	·	·	3	V. vitis-idaea
·	·	1	·	1	·	+	·	·	Blechnum spicant
·	·	2	·	·	·	·	·	·	Botrychium lunaria
·	·	·	+	2	+	2	1	·	Lycopodium alpinum
·	·	·	1	+	·	·	·	·	L. selago
·	2	·	2	·	·	·	·	·	Selaginella selaginoides
·	·	·	·	·	·	·	·	·	Thelypteris dryopteris
·	·	·	·	·	·	·	·	·	T. oreopteris
·	2	·	·	4	5	·	3	·	Agrostis canina
5	4	2	4	·	·	5	3	7	**A. tenuis**
2	2	6	2	3	2	·	2	·	**Anthoxanthum odoratum**
·	1	5	·	2	2	2	·	·	Deschampsia caespitosa
·	3	·	·	2	·	2	·	·	D. flexuosa
5	6	6	3	3	4	5	5	6	**Festuca ovina agg.**
·	·	·	·	·	·	·	·	·	F. rubra
1	·	·	1	3	1	3	·	1	Nardus stricta
·	·	·	·	·	·	·	·	·	Sieglingia decumbens
·	·	3	3	4	2	3	·	4	Carex bigelowii
·	·	·	·	·	·	·	·	·	C. binervis
·	·	·	·	·	·	·	·	·	C. caryophyllea
·	·	·	·	·	·	·	·	·	C. panicea
1	·	1	3	·	3	3	·	3	C. pilulifera
·	·	·	·	·	·	·	·	·	C. pulicaris
·	·	·	·	·	·	·	·	·	Juncus squarrosus
·	·	·	·	+	·	2	·	·	J. trifidus
3	·	·	·	·	2	·	·	·	Luzula campestris
·	2	·	·	1	·	·	·	2	L. multiflora
·	1	·	·	·	·	·	·	2	L. spicata
·	·	·	·	·	+	·	·	·	L. sylvatica
·	·	·	1	·	·	1	·	·	Trichophorum caespitosum
·	1	·	·	·	·	·	·	·	Achillea millefolium
8	7	5	4	2	4	3	6	3	**Alchemilla alpina**
·	2	·	·	·	·	·	·	·	A. glabra
·	·	·	·	·	·	·	·	·	A. vestita
·	·	·	·	·	·	·	·	·	A. xanthochlora
·	·	·	·	·	·	·	·	·	Angelica sylvestris
·	·	·	2	+	·	·	·	·	Antennaria dioica
·	·	·	·	·	·	·	3	·	Armeria maritima
·	3	3	·	·	·	·	·	2	Campanula rotundifolia
·	·	·	·	·	·	·	·	·	Cardamine flexuosa
·	+	2	·	·	·	·	·	·	Cerastium alpinum
2	·	·	·	·	·	·	·	·	C. vulgatum
·	·	·	·	·	·	·	4	·	Cherleria sedoides
·	·	·	·	·	·	·	·	·	Cirsium palustre
3	2	·	·	1	·	2	·	2	Euphrasia sp.
·	·	·	·	·	·	·	·	·	Galium boreale
4	·	3	2	4	3	2	4	4	**G. hercynicum**
·	·	·	·	·	·	·	·	·	G. verum
·	·	·	·	·	·	·	·	·	Gentianella campestris
·	·	·	·	·	·	·	·	·	Geranium sylvaticum
·	·	·	·	·	·	·	·	·	Geum rivale
·	·	·	·	+	·	·	+	·	Gnaphalium supinum
·	·	·	·	·	·	1	·	·	Hieracium holosericeum
·	·	·	·	·	·	·	·	·	Hypericum pulchrum
·	·	·	·	·	·	·	·	·	Leontodon autumnalis
·	·	·	·	·	·	·	·	·	Linum catharticum
·	2	·	·	·	·	·	·	·	Lotus corniculatus
·	·	1	·	·	·	·	·	·	Oxalis acetosella
·	·	·	·	·	·	·	·	·	Pinguicula vulgaris
·	·	·	·	·	·	·	·	·	Plantago maritima
2	·	·	·	·	·	+	·	·	Polygala serpyllifolia
·	3	·	·	·	·	·	·	·	Polygonum viviparum
·	3	·	·	·	·	·	·	·	Potentilla crantzii
3	3	1	+	4	2	3	·	4	P. erecta
·	·	·	·	·	·	·	·	·	Prunella vulgaris
·	·	1	2	·	·	·	·	·	Ranunculus acris
·	·	2	·	·	·	·	3	·	Rumex acetosa
·	·	·	·	·	·	·	·	·	Saxifraga aizoides

Table 25

	1	2	3	4	5	6	7	8	9	10
Saxifraga hypnoides	.	3	.	.	.	.	.	.	+	.
S. oppositifolia	.	.	3	.	.	.	.	5	.	.
Sibbaldia procumbens	.	.	.	2	.	.	.	.	.	.
Silene acaulis	.	.	.	.	.	.	.	.	.	.
Solidago virgaurea	.	.	.	.	.	.	.	.	.	.
Succisa pratensis	.	.	.	1	2	.	1	.	.	.
Taraxacum officinalis agg.	.	.	.	.	.	.	.	.	2	1
Thalictrum alpinum	4	.	1	.	2	2	3	.	.	.
Thymus drucei	5	.	5	6	6	3	6	5	5	6
Trifolium repens	.	.	.	.	.	.	.	.	4	3
Trollius europaeus	2	.	.	.	.	.	.	.	.	.
Veronica officinalis	.	1	.	.	.	.	.	2	.	1
V. serpyllifolia	.	1	.	.	.	.	.	.	.	.
Viola palustris	.	.	.	.	.	.	.	.	.	.
V. riviniana	3	1	2	4	4	+	3	3	2	3
Acrocladium cuspidatum	.	.	.	.	.	.	.	.	.	1
Atrichum undulatum	.	.	.	.	.	.	.	.	.	2
Breutelia chrysocoma	.	.	.	.	4	.	3	2	.	.
Campylopus fragilis	1	.	.	.	1	.	.	.	.	.
Ctenidium molluscum	3	.	.	.	3	.	4	.	.	.
Dicranella heteromalla	.	.	.	.	.	.	.	.	.	.
Dicranum scoparium	2	2	.	.	.	3	.	1	.	.
Drepanocladus uncinatus	.	.	.	.	2	.	.	.	.	1
Hylocomium splendens	4	5	3	4	3	4	.	7	4	2
Hypnum callichroum	1	.	.	.	.	.	.	.	.	.
H. cupressiforme	.	.	.	3	3	1	.	.	.	2
Leucobryum glaucum	.	.	.	.	.	2	.	.	.	.
Mnium punctatum	.	.	.	.	.	.	.	.	1	1
M. undulatum	.	.	.	.	.	.	.	.	2	.
Plagiothecium undulatum	.	.	.	.	.	.	.	.	.	.
Pleurozium schreberi	.	4	3	3	2	4	1	+	2	1
Pohlia nutans	.	.	.	.	.	.	.	.	1	.
Polytrichum alpinum	.	5	.	2	2	1	2	.	3	.
P. commune	.	.	.	.	.	.	.	.	.	.
P. piliferum	.	.	.	.	.	.	.	.	.	.
P. urnigerum	.	.	.	2	1	.	.	.	.	.
Pseudoscleropodium purum	3	.	.	2	.	.	.	3	.	.
Ptilium crista-castrensis	+	+	.	.	.	.	.	.	.	.
Rhacomitrium canescens	.	.	2	3	.	.	.	1	2	3
R. fasciculare	.	.	.	.	1	.	.	.	.	.
R. lanuginosum	.	.	2	2	3	5	2	2	.	.
Rhodobryum roseum	.	.	.	.	.	.	.	.	1	.
Rhytidiadelphus loreus	.	7	3	3	2	3	2	3	+	.
R. squarrosus	2	.	3	2	3	.	.	3	4	3
R. triquetrus	4	2	3	.	.	.	1	3	.	.
Sphagnum plumulosum	.	.	.	.	2	.	.	.	.	.
Thuidium delicatulum	4	.	.	3	2	.	.	.	.	.
T. tamariscinum	.	.	.	.	.	.	1	3	4	.
Anastrepta orcadensis	.	.	.	.	.	.	.	.	.	.
Diplophyllum albicans	.	.	.	.	1	1	.	.	.	.
Frullania tamarisci	1	.	.	.	.	.	.	.	.	.
Herberta adunca	+	.	.	.	.	.	.	.	.	.
Lophocolea bidentata	.	.	.	.	.	.	.	.	.	1
Lophozia floerkii	.	.	.	.	2	.	.	.	.	.
L. hatcheri	.	.	.	.	.	.	.	.	1	.
L. lycopodioides	.	.	.	.	.	.	.	.	.	.
Pellia sp.	.	.	.	.	1	.	.	.	.	.
Ptilidium ciliare	.	.	1	3	1	1	1	.	.	.
Cetraria aculeata	.	.	.	.	.	.	.	.	.	.
C. islandica	.	.	1	.	.	.	.	.	.	.
Cladonia bellidiflora	.	.	.	.	.	1	.	.	.	.
C. coccifera	.	.	.	2	.	.	.	.	.	.
C. gracilis	.	.	.	.	.	2	.	.	.	.
C. impexa	.	.	.	2	.	.	.	.	.	.
C. pyxidata	2	.	.	.	.	.	.	.	.	.
C. rangiferina agg.	.	.	.	.	.	3	.	.	.	.
C. squamosa	.	.	.	.	.	.	.	.	.	.
C. sylvatica	.	.	2	.	1	3	.	.	.	.
C. uncialis	.	.	.	2	.	2	.	.	.	.
Coriscium viride	.	.	.	.	.	.	.	.	.	.
Ochrolechia frigida	.	.	.	.	.	.	.	.	.	.
Peltigera canina	1	2	.	3	.	.	.	.	.	1
Sphaerophorus globosus	.	.	.	.	.	.	.	.	.	.
Number of species (147)	41	25	34	41	54	34	35	33	38	35

(Average 34)

Constancy class V 9 ⎫ for lists 1-14.
     „   „ IV 5 ⎭

LOCALITIES

1. Beinn Odhar Mhor, Glenfinnan, Inverness-shire; 2,6,8,11. Glen Markie, Monadhliath, Inverness-shire; 3. Ben Vrackie, Perthshire; 4,18, Mullach Coire Mhic Fhearchair, Fisherfield Forest, Ross-shire; 5. Druim Reidh, Fannich Forest, Ross-shire; 7. Meall Cumhann, Glen Nevis, Inverness-shire; 9. Coire Chuirn, Drumochter, Inverness-shire; 10. The Scorrie, Clova, Angus; 12. Invervar, Glen Lyon, Perthshire; 13. Meall

11	12	13	14	15	16	17	18	19	
·	·	1	·	·	·	·	·	·	Saxifraga hypnoides
·	·	·	·	·	·	·	·	·	S. oppositifolia
·	·	·	·	·	·	·	2	1	Sibbaldia procumbens
·	2	2	·	·	·	·	+	·	Silene acaulis
·	·	2	·	·	·	·	·	·	Solidago virgaurea
·	·	·	·	1	·	2	·	·	Succisa pratensis
·	·	·	·	·	·	·	·	·	Taraxacum officinalis agg.
·	2	·	5	·	·	·	·	·	Thalictrum alpinum
+	4	4	5	2	4	3	2	3	**Thymus drucei**
·	·	1	·	·	·	·	·	·	Trifolium repens
·	·	·	·	·	·	·	·	·	Trollius europaeus
2	·	·	·	·	·	·	·	·	Veronica officinalis
·	·	·	·	·	·	·	·	·	V. serpyllifolia
·	·	·	·	2	·	·	·	4	Viola palustris
·	·	1	2	·	·	3	·	3	**V. riviniana**
·	·	·	·	·	·	·	·	·	Acrocladium cuspidatum
·	·	·	·	·	·	·	·	·	Atrichum undulatum
·	·	·	·	·	·	·	·	·	Breutelia chrysocoma
·	·	·	·	·	·	·	·	·	Campylopus fragilis
·	·	·	·	·	·	·	·	·	Ctenidium molluscum
·	·	·	·	·	1	·	·	·	Dicranella heteromalla
+	·	1	·	·	1	·	2	1	Dicranum scoparium
·	·	·	·	·	·	·	·	·	Drepanocladus uncinatus
4	3	1	1	4	3	1	3	·	**Hylocomium splendens**
·	·	·	·	·	·	·	·	·	Hypnum callichroum
·	·	·	·	·	2	·	·	·	H. cupressiforme
·	·	·	·	·	·	·	·	·	Leucobryum glaucum
·	·	·	·	·	·	·	·	·	Mnium punctatum
·	·	·	·	·	·	·	·	·	M. undulatum
·	·	·	·	·	1	·	·	·	Plagiothecium undulatum
4	2	3	·	·	·	2	3	·	**Pleurozium schreberi**
·	·	·	·	·	·	·	·	·	Pohlia nutans
·	·	4	·	·	3	·	3	3	Polytrichum alpinum
·	·	·	·	·	·	1	·	·	P. commune
·	1	·	·	·	4	·	+	·	P. piliferum
·	·	·	·	·	·	·	·	·	P. urnigerum
·	·	·	·	·	·	·	·	·	Pseudoscleropodium purum
·	·	·	·	·	·	·	·	·	Ptilium crista-castrensis
·	·	·	·	·	·	·	·	·	Rhacomitrium canescens
·	·	·	·	·	·	·	·	·	R. fasciculare
·	·	1	4	6	7	7	8	4	**R. lanuginosum**
·	·	·	·	·	·	·	·	·	Rhodobryum roseum
3	·	1	·	4	1	·	3	2	Rhytidiadelphus loreus
3	·	4	·	·	·	·	·	·	R. squarrosus
·	·	·	·	·	·	·	·	·	R. triquetrus
·	·	·	·	·	·	·	·	·	Sphagnum plumulosum
·	·	·	·	·	·	·	·	·	Thuidium delicatulum
1	·	·	·	·	·	·	·	·	T. tamariscinum
·	·	·	·	·	·	1	·	·	Anastrepta orcadensis
·	1	·	·	·	·	1	·	·	Diplophyllum albicans
·	·	·	·	·	·	·	·	·	Frullania tamarisci
·	·	1	·	·	·	·	·	·	Herberta adunca
·	·	·	·	·	·	·	·	·	Lophocolea bidentata
·	·	·	·	·	·	·	·	·	Lophozia floerkii
·	·	·	·	·	·	·	·	·	L. hatcheri
·	·	·	·	·	·	1	·	·	L. lycopodioides
·	·	·	·	·	·	·	·	·	Pellia sp.
·	2	1	·	·	·	·	2	·	Ptilidium ciliare
·	·	·	·	·	·	1	·	·	Cetraria aculeata
·	·	·	·	1	1	3	1	·	C. islandica
·	·	·	·	·	·	·	·	·	Cladonia bellidiflora
·	·	·	·	·	2	·	+	·	C. coccifera
·	3	·	·	·	1	2	·	1	C. gracilis
·	·	·	·	·	·	·	·	·	C. impexa
·	·	1	·	·	2	·	·	1	C. pyxidata
·	·	·	·	·	1	·	·	2	C. rangiferina agg.
·	·	·	·	·	1	·	·	·	C. squamosa
·	3	1	·	·	2	3	·	+	C. sylvatica
·	·	·	1	1	3	3	2	2	**C. uncialis**
·	·	·	·	·	·	·	1	·	Coriscium viride
·	·	·	·	·	·	·	·	+	Ochrolechia frigida
·	1	·	·	·	·	·	·	·	Peltigera canina
·	·	·	·	·	+	·	·	·	Sphaerophorus globosus
22	31	33	24	30	35	33	26	27	Number of species (147)

(Average 30)

nan Tarmachan, Killin, Perthshire; 14,15. Beinn Eighe, Ross-shire; 16. Sgurr a' Chaorachain, Applecross, Ross-shire; 17. Ben Lair, Ross-shire; 19. Beinn Eunaich, Dalmally, Argyll.

Table 26: Species-rich Agrosto-Festucetum

	1	2	3	4	5	6	7	8	9	10	11	12	13	14	15	16
Reference number	R56 044	R57 166	R58 084	R57 071	R57 028	R57 072	R57 252	R57 254	R57 004	R57 244	R57 035	R56 057	R57 023	R57 316	M56 048	R56 118
Map reference	8809 2232	7905 2562	8317 2197	7982 2589	9447 2243	7858 2450	7767 3241	7767 3240	9361 2318	7781 3288	9398 2319	8632 2061	9391 2368	7788 2983	8723 1992	8179 1916
Altitude (feet)	2250	1000	1000	1500	500	1750	2050	2100	775	1400	550	300	2000	1500	2300	1650
Aspect (degrees)	360	180	180	—	45	180	45	45	—	270	180	135	45	270	90	360
Slope (degrees)	28	28	15	0	20	40	40	38	0	28	30	33	30	37	12	35
Cover (per cent)	98	100	100	100	100	100	100	100	100	100	100	100	100	95	100	100
Height (centimetres)	—	—	—	4	3	—	16	6	4	3	4	4	—	—	8	—
Plot area (square metres)	16	4	4	4	4	4	4	4	4	4	4	16	4	4	4	16
Betula sp. (seedling)	·	2	·	·	·	1	·	·	·	·	·	·	·	·	·	·
Calluna vulgaris	·	3	·	·	3	2	2	3	·	3	·	·	·	·	1	3
Dryas octopetala	·	·	·	·	·	·	·	3	·	·	·	·	·	·	·	·
Empetrum hermaphroditum	·	·	·	·	·	·	·	2	·	·	·	·	·	·	4	2
Helianthemum chamaecistus	·	4	·	·	·	·	·	·	·	4	·	·	·	5	·	·
Rubus idaeus	·	·	·	·	·	2	·	·	·	·	·	·	·	1	·	·
R. saxatilis	·	·	·	·	·	·	·	·	·	·	·	·	·	·	·	·
Salix phylicifolia	·	·	·	·	·	·	·	·	·	·	·	·	·	·	·	·
Sorbus aucuparia (seedling)	·	·	·	·	·	·	·	·	·	·	·	·	·	·	·	·
Vaccinium myrtillus	1	·	·	·	·	2	2	3	·	·	·	·	·	3	·	·
V. vitis-idaea	·	·	·	·	·	1	2	2	·	·	·	·	·	·	·	·
Blechnum spicant	·	·	·	·	·	·	·	·	·	·	·	·	·	·	·	2
Botrychium lunaria	·	·	·	·	·	·	·	·	·	·	·	·	·	·	·	·
Lycopodium alpinum	·	·	·	·	·	·	·	·	·	·	·	·	·	·	1	·
L. selago	·	·	·	·	·	·	·	·	1	·	·	·	·	·	·	·
Pteridium aquilinum	·	·	2	·	·	+	·	·	·	·	·	·	·	·	·	·
Selaginella selaginoides	3	·	·	·	3	·	·	·	·	·	·	1	2	·	3	3
Agrostis canina	3	·	·	·	3	4	2	·	2	2	3	·	3	·	·	3
A. tenuis	4	4	5	8	2	3	5	3	4	7	4	7	8	3	4	4
Anthoxanthum odoratum	2	3	·	3	3	3	5	3	·	3	3	4	3	·	2	3
Briza media	·	·	·	·	·	·	·	·	·	·	·	·	·	3	·	·
Cynosurus cristatus	·	·	3	·	·	·	·	·	2	·	·	3	·	·	·	·
Deschampsia caespitosa	5	·	·	·	·	2	5	4	·	·	·	·	3	·	·	2
D. flexuosa	4	·	·	·	·	·	·	·	·	·	·	·	4	·	·	·
Festuca ovina agg.	7	6	5	3	5	5	5	3	7	8	4	6	4	7	5	5
F. rubra	7	3	3	3	3	3	2	·	7	2	5	5	4	+	·	·
Helictotrichon pratense	·	·	·	·	·	·	·	·	·	·	·	·	·	3	·	·
Holcus lanatus	·	·	3	4	·	·	·	·	·	·	·	3	·	·	·	·
Molinia caerulea	·	·	·	·	1	·	·	·	·	·	·	·	·	·	·	·
Nardus stricta	4	·	2	·	4	·	4	5	4	3	4	·	4	·	·	3
Poa pratensis	·	·	3	·	·	·	·	·	2	·	·	·	·	·	·	·
Sieglingia decumbens	·	6	4	·	3	3	·	2	4	·	4	3	·	·	·	·
Carex bigelowii	3	·	·	·	·	·	·	·	·	·	·	·	2	·	·	·
C. binervis	3	·	·	·	·	·	·	·	·	·	·	·	·	·	·	3
C. capillaris	·	·	·	·	·	·	·	4	·	·	·	·	·	·	·	·
C. caryophyllea	·	3	·	·	·	·	1	3	3	·	·	·	·	3	·	·
C. demissa	+	1	·	·	2	·	·	·	·	·	·	·	·	·	·	·
C. dioica	·	·	·	·	·	·	·	·	3	·	·	·	·	·	·	·
C. flacca	·	3	·	·	·	·	·	2	·	·	·	·	·	3	·	·
C. hostiana	·	·	·	·	·	·	·	·	·	·	·	·	·	·	·	·
C. lepidocarpa	·	·	·	·	·	·	·	·	·	·	·	·	·	·	·	·
C. nigra	·	·	·	·	·	·	·	·	3	·	2	·	·	·	·	·
C. pallescens	·	·	·	·	·	2	·	·	·	·	·	·	·	·	·	3
C. panicea	·	·	·	·	3	2	·	·	2	·	4	·	·	·	2	3
C. pilulifera	2	·	1	·	2	2	2	·	·	·	·	·	·	·	1	2
C. pulicaris	4	2	·	·	3	2	·	3	·	·	2	·	·	·	·	2
Coeloglossum viride	2	·	·	·	·	·	·	2	·	·	·	·	1	·	·	1
Juncus articulatus	·	·	·	·	·	·	·	·	·	·	·	·	·	·	·	·
J. kochii	·	·	·	·	·	·	·	·	1	·	·	·	·	·	·	·
Luzula campestris	·	·	3	3	1	·	·	·	2	·	2	1	·	·	·	·
L. multiflora	·	·	·	·	·	+	3	1	·	·	·	·	·	·	1	1
L. spicata	1	·	·	·	·	·	·	1	·	·	·	·	·	·	·	·
L. sylvatica	1	·	·	·	·	·	2	·	·	·	·	·	3	·	·	1
Narthecium ossifragum	·	·	·	·	1	·	·	·	·	·	·	·	·	·	·	·
Orchis mascula	·	·	·	·	·	·	·	·	·	·	·	·	·	·	·	·
Achillea millefolium	2	·	6	6	·	+	·	·	·	2	·	3	·	·	·	·
Alchemilla alpina	3	·	·	·	·	3	3	4	·	3	·	·	·	2	4	5
A. filicaulis	·	·	·	·	·	·	·	·	·	·	2	·	·	·	2	·
A. glabra	·	·	·	·	·	·	3	3	·	·	·	·	3	3	·	·
A. vestita	·	·	3	·	·	2	2	3	2	·	3	2	·	·	·	2
A. wichurae	·	·	·	·	·	·	·	·	·	·	·	·	·	·	·	·
A. xanthochlora	·	·	·	·	·	·	·	·	·	·	·	·	·	·	·	·
Anemone nemorosa	·	·	·	·	·	·	·	·	·	·	·	·	·	·	·	·
Antennaria dioica	·	+	·	·	·	+	·	3	·	·	·	·	·	·	1	·
Arabis hirsuta	·	·	·	·	·	·	·	1	·	·	·	·	·	·	·	·
Armeria maritima	3	·	·	·	·	·	·	·	·	·	·	·	·	·	·	·
Bartsia alpina	·	·	·	·	·	·	·	·	·	·	·	·	·	·	·	·
Bellis perennis	·	·	5	3	·	·	·	1	5	·	4	4	·	·	·	·
Campanula rotundifolia	·	3	·	·	·	2	2	3	·	·	·	·	·	·	·	·
Cardamine pratensis	·	·	·	·	·	·	·	·	·	·	·	·	·	·	·	·
Cerastium vulgatum	·	·	2	2	·	·	1	·	·	1	1	3	2	2	·	·
Cherleria sedoides	2	·	·	·	·	·	·	·	·	·	·	·	·	·	·	·

(1–16); Saxifrageto-Agrosto-Festucetum (17–28)

17	18	19	20	21	22	23	24	25	26	27	28	
R57	R57	R57	R57	R58	R58	R57	R57	R57	R57	R57	R57	Reference number
309	212	298	021	128	101	318	296	154	286	292	312	
7692	7761	7642	9425	7275	7448	7774	7633	7962	7479	7641	7689	Map reference
2962	3253	2859	2355	2261	2660	2973	2940	2597	2987	2876	2966	
1800	1400	1500	1150	2000	2300	1300	1700	2200	1850	1100	2150	Altitude (feet)
135	45	270	225	360	360	315	180	180	270	360	315	Aspect (degrees)
25	25	25	35	40	35	28	5	18	35	38	15	Slope (degrees)
100	100	100	95	100	100	100	100	100	95	100	100	Cover (per cent)
—	17	—	—	—	—	—	—	—	—	—	4	Height (centimetres)
4	4	4	4	4	4	4	4	4	4	4	4	Plot area (square metres)
·	·	·	·	·	·	I	I	·	·	2	·	*Betula* sp. (seedling)
·	2	·	2	·	·	·	I	2	·	·	·	*Calluna vulgaris*
·	·	·	·	2	·	·	·	·	·	·	·	*Dryas octopetala*
·	·	·	·	·	·	·	·	·	·	·	·	*Empetrum hermaphroditum*
·	·	3	·	·	·	·	·	·	·	2	2	*Helianthemum chamaecistus*
·	·	·	·	·	·	·	·	·	2	·	·	*Rubus idaeus*
·	·	·	·	·	·	·	·	·	+	·	·	*R. saxatilis*
·	·	·	3	·	·	·	·	·	·	·	·	*Salix phylicifolia*
·	·	·	·	·	·	·	·	·	I	·	·	*Sorbus aucuparia* (seedling)
·	·	·	·	·	I	·	·	·	·	·	·	*Vaccinium myrtillus*
·	·	·	·	·	·	·	·	·	·	·	·	*V. vitis-idaea*
·	·	·	·	·	·	·	·	·	·	·	·	*Blechnum spicant*
·	·	·	+	·	·	·	·	·	·	·	·	*Botrychium lunaria*
·	·	·	·	·	·	·	·	·	·	·	·	*Lycopodium alpinum*
·	·	·	·	·	·	·	·	·	·	·	·	*L. selago*
·	·	·	·	·	·	·	·	·	·	·	·	*Pteridium aquilinum*
2	3	+	3	2	2	3	·	3	·	2	2	**Selaginella selaginoides**
·	8	2	3	3	4	·	2	2	2	3	+	**Agrostis canina**
5	8	·	3	4	4	4	·	·	3	·	4	**A. tenuis**
·	2	·	3	4	I	·	·	·	2	·	·	**Anthoxanthum odoratum**
2	3	·	·	·	·	2	I	·	·	3	·	*Briza media*
·	·	·	·	·	·	·	·	·	·	·	·	*Cynosurus cristatus*
2	·	2	·	2	3	2	·	·	I	2	·	*Deschampsia caespitosa*
·	·	·	·	·	·	·	·	·	·	·	·	*D. flexuosa*
4	4	4	5	5	5	5	5	7	5	4	5	**Festuca ovina agg.**
3	·	2	3	3	3	4	·	·	·	3	·	*F. rubra*
·	·	·	2	·	·	·	·	·	I	3	·	*Helictotrichon pratense*
·	·	·	·	·	·	·	·	·	·	·	·	*Holcus lanatus*
·	·	·	·	·	·	·	·	·	·	·	·	*Molinia caerulea*
3	3	·	3	·	4	2	·	2	·	·	·	*Nardus stricta*
·	·	·	·	·	·	·	·	·	·	·	·	*Poa pratensis*
I	3	·	·	·	·	3	·	I	·	·	·	*Sieglingia decumbens*
·	·	·	·	·	·	·	·	·	·	·	·	*Carex bigelowii*
·	·	·	·	·	·	·	·	·	·	·	·	*C. binervis*
·	·	·	2	2	3	·	·	·	·	3	+	*C. capillaris*
·	·	·	·	·	·	2	·	·	2	·	2	*C. caryophyllea*
3	·	2	+	3	·	·	3	·	·	·	·	*C. demissa*
·	·	·	·	·	·	·	·	·	·	·	·	*C. dioica*
·	·	·	2	3	·	·	·	·	·	5	·	*C. flacca*
·	·	·	·	·	·	·	·	2	·	·	·	*C. hostiana*
·	·	·	·	2	·	·	·	·	2	·	·	*C. lepidocarpa*
·	·	·	·	2	·	·	·	·	·	·	·	*C. nigra*
·	·	·	·	·	·	·	·	·	·	·	·	*C. pallescens*
5	5	6	3	2	3	5	5	5	·	5	·	**C. panicea**
·	·	·	·	·	·	·	·	·	·	·	·	*C. pilulifera*
3	3	3	3	4	5	4	3	2	2	2	2	**C. pulicaris**
I	·	·	·	·	·	·	·	·	·	·	·	*Coeloglossum viride*
·	·	·	·	·	·	·	·	·	·	·	·	*Juncus articulatus*
·	·	·	·	·	·	·	·	I	·	·	·	*J. kochii*
·	·	·	·	·	·	·	·	·	·	·	·	*Luzula campestris*
·	·	·	I	·	·	·	·	·	·	·	2	*L. multiflora*
·	·	·	2	·	·	·	·	·	·	·	·	*L. spicata*
·	·	·	·	·	·	·	·	·	·	·	·	*L. sylvatica*
·	·	I	·	·	·	·	·	·	·	·	·	*Narthecium ossifragum*
·	·	·	·	·	·	·	·	·	·	·	·	*Orchis mascula*
·	+	2	·	·	·	·	·	·	2	·	·	*Achillea millefolium*
·	2	·	3	3	3	·	·	·	2	·	·	*Alchemilla alpina*
·	·	·	3	·	·	·	·	·	·	·	·	*A. filicaulis*
4	3	5	·	3	5	3	·	3	I	·	5	*A. glabra*
·	·	·	·	5	·	3	2	5	·	·	2	*A. vestita*
·	2	·	·	4	5	·	·	·	·	·	·	*A. wichurae*
·	·	3	·	·	·	·	·	·	·	·	·	*A. xanthochlora*
·	·	·	·	I	·	·	·	·	·	·	·	*Anemone nemorosa*
·	·	·	·	·	·	·	·	·	·	·	·	*Antennaria dioica*
·	·	·	·	·	·	·	·	·	·	·	·	*Arabis hirsuta*
·	·	·	·	·	·	·	·	·	·	·	·	*Armeria maritima*
·	·	·	I	·	·	·	·	·	·	·	·	*Bartsia alpina*
3	·	·	·	·	I	·	·	·	3	·	·	*Bellis perennis*
·	3	·	3	3	2	·	I	2	·	·	2	*Campanula rotundifolia*
·	·	·	·	·	·	·	·	·	·	·	2	*Cardamine pratensis*
·	·	·	·	2	·	·	2	I	·	·	·	*Cerastium vulgatum*
·	·	·	·	·	·	·	·	·	·	·	·	*Cherleria sedoides*

Table 26

	1	2	3	4	5	6	7	8	9	10	11	12	13	14	15	16
Cirsium heterophyllum							5									
C. palustre												2				
C. vulgare												2				
Conopodium majus											3					
Crepis paludosa																
Euphrasia sp.			3	3		3	2	2	3	3	3	3		2		2
Filipendula ulmaria						2	2							2		2
Fragaria vesca														2		
Galium boreale								2						+	+	2
G. hercynicum			3	4	3		2	1		1		3	3			2
G. verum		3				+				1				2		
Gentianella campestris						1		1								
Geranium sylvaticum							2	2								
Geum rivale	3						2	2					3	+		3
Heracleum sphondylium							2									
Hieracium pilosella		3				2		2				2				
Hieracium sp.						1		3								
Hypericum pulchrum								2		1						
Hypochaeris radicata		1									1					
Lathyrus montanus					1	2		1								
Leontodon autumnalis					3				3		3		2			
Linum catharticum					2	1		3				2		3		
Lotus corniculatus		4				4	2	3				3		3		
Lysimachia nemorum											3		3			
Mercurialis perennis							2	1						2		
Oxalis acetosella	1							2				2				
Oxytropis campestris																
Parnassia palustris								3								
Pinguicula vulgaris	1															
Plantago lanceolata		3	4		4	4			5	3	5	5		3		
P. maritima											1				1	
Polygala serpyllifolia						2	2		2						1	
Polygonum viviparum	3	3				4		3		3				3		
Potentilla crantzii																
P. erecta		4	2		3	4	3	2		3	2				2	4
P. sterilis												3				
Primula vulgaris					4	1										
Prunella vulgaris		3	4	3	4	3	2	3	3	2	4	3		2		1
Ranunculus acris	3		3	4	2	3		2	4		4	4	4	3	+	2
R. ficaria									+		2					
Rhinanthus minor agg.								2								
Rumex acetosa			2	3					+		3	4	3			
Sagina procumbens											2	1				
Saussurea alpina															3	
Saxifraga aizoides																
S. hypnoides																
S. oppositifolia	4															
Sedum rosea	1															
Senecio jacobaea			1						2		1					
Silene acaulis	5							3							1	
Solidago virgaurea								1								
Succisa pratensis		3			3	3		3		1					2	3
Taraxacum officinalis agg.	3				3	1		4		3				2		
Teucrium scorodonia						1										
Thalictrum alpinum	3				4								3		3	3
Thymus drucei	3	5	2		4	5	3	5	+	5		3	2	4	3	
Trifolium repens		3	4	4					3		2	5				5
Trollius europaeus					1										3	2
Valeriana officinalis													2			+
Veronica chamaedrys											2	3				
V. officinalis		2		2			1			1		2				
Vicia sepium						1	1									
Viola lutea											1					
V. palustris	3															
V. riviniana		3	2	3	3	4	3	5						4	2	3
Acrocladium cuspidatum		2							2		2	2	2			
Anomobryum filiforme																
Antitrichia curtipendula																
Atrichum undulatum			2									1				
Aulacomnium turgidum															2	
Barbula fallax									1		3					
Brachythecium glareosum																
Breutelia chrysocoma	2				4								3			4
Bryum pallens																
B. pseudotriquetrum									3		3					
Campylium protensum									4		1					
C. stellatum	3															
Campylopus fragilis					3	1										
Climacium dendroides																
Cratoneuron commutatum																
Ctenidium molluscum	3				3			2	6		4	3	3	2	2	
Dicranum scoparium		2		1		2	1			1		2			1	2
Distichium capillaceum																
Ditrichum flexicaule	3								3					2	1	
Drepanocladus uncinatus	2			3									2			
Entodon orthocarpus														2		
Fissidens adianthoides	3															
F. cristatus						2								1		
F. osmundoides	1								2							1
Hylocomium splendens	2	3	3	3	4	2	4	3		1		5	6	4	2	5

(continued)

17	18	19	20	21	22	23	24	25	26	27	28	
·	·	·	·	4	·	·	·	·	·	·	·	Cirsium heterophyllum
·	1	·	·	·	·	·	·	·	·	·	·	C. palustre
·	·	·	·	·	·	·	·	·	1	·	·	C. vulgare
·	·	·	·	·	·	·	·	·	·	·	·	Conopodium majus
·	·	·	+	3	·	·	·	·	·	·	·	Crepis paludosa
2	2	2	·	2	3	·	·	3	3	·	2	Euphrasia sp.
·	1	·	+	·	·	·	·	·	·	·	·	Filipendula ulmaria
·	·	·	·	·	·	·	2	·	2	+	·	Fragaria vesca
·	·	·	1	·	·	·	·	+	·	·	2	Galium boreale
·	·	·	·	2	1	·	·	1	·	·	·	G. hercynicum
2	2	·	·	·	·	·	2	·	·	+	·	G. verum
·	·	·	·	·	·	·	·	1	3	·	·	Gentianella campestris
·	+	·	·	·	·	·	·	·	·	·	·	Geranium sylvaticum
·	·	·	·	3	2	·	·	3	3	·	3	Geum rivale
·	·	·	·	·	·	·	·	·	·	·	·	Heracleum sphondylium
·	2	·	·	·	·	·	·	·	·	·	·	Hieracium pilosella
·	1	·	+	2	1	2	·	·	1	·	·	Hieracium sp.
·	·	·	·	·	·	·	·	·	1	·	·	Hypericum pulchrum
·	·	·	2	·	·	·	·	·	·	·	·	Hypochaeris radicata
·	·	·	·	·	·	·	·	·	·	·	·	Lathyrus montanus
3	2	1	2	·	·	3	·	·	·	·	·	Leontodon autumnalis
2	2	1	2	2	2	·	2	2	2	2	+	**Linum catharticum**
·	2	2	·	·	·	2	3	·	1	·	2	Lotus corniculatus
·	·	·	3	·	·	·	·	·	·	·	·	Lysimachia nemorum
·	·	·	·	·	·	·	·	·	3	·	·	Mercurialis perennis
·	·	·	·	1	·	·	·	·	·	·	·	Oxalis acetosella
·	·	·	·	·	·	·	·	1	·	2	·	Oxytropis campestris
·	·	·	·	·	·	·	·	·	·	2	·	Parnassia palustris
·	·	·	2	·	·	·	·	1	·	2	·	Pinguicula vulgaris
5	4	1	5	1	·	5	·	·	·	·	·	Plantago lanceolata
·	·	·	4	·	·	·	·	·	·	·	·	P. maritima
·	2	·	·	·	·	·	·	1	·	·	·	Polygala serpyllifolia
4	3	4	·	3	4	3	4	·	2	3	3	**Polygonum viviparum**
·	·	·	·	·	·	·	2	·	·	·	3	Potentilla crantzii
2	3	2	3	·	2	3	2	4	·	2	·	P. erecta
·	·	·	·	·	·	·	1	·	·	·	·	P. sterilis
·	·	·	1	·	·	·	·	·	·	·	·	Primula vulgaris
3	+	2	3	4	·	4	2	2	2	2	·	**Prunella vulgaris**
3	2	1	3	4	·	3	·	3	1	+	1	**Ranunculus acris**
·	·	·	·	·	·	·	·	·	·	·	·	R. ficaria
·	3	·	·	·	·	·	·	·	·	·	·	Rhinanthus minor agg.
·	·	·	·	·	·	·	·	·	·	·	·	Rumex acetosa
·	·	·	·	·	·	·	·	·	·	·	·	Sagina procumbens
·	·	·	·	·	·	·	·	·	·	·	·	Saussurea alpina
5	2	6	+	3	2	4	8	4	4	4	4	**Saxifraga aizoides**
·	·	·	·	·	·	·	·	·	·	·	+	S. hypnoides
·	3	·	3	·	1	·	·	·	3	·	3	S. oppositifolia
·	·	·	·	·	·	·	·	·	·	·	·	Sedum rosea
·	·	·	2	·	·	·	1	·	·	·	·	Senecio jacobaea
·	·	·	4	·	2	·	·	·	·	·	·	Silene acaulis
·	·	·	·	·	·	·	·	·	·	·	·	Solidago virgaurea
·	3	·	2	·	·	2	·	·	1	·	·	Succisa pratensis
3	·	·	2	2	2	·	·	·	·	·	·	Taraxacum officinalis agg.
·	·	·	·	·	·	·	·	·	·	·	·	Teucrium scorodonia
·	·	·	4	3	2	·	·	2	·	·	·	Thalictrum alpinum
2	4	4	5	4	4	4	4	5	4	4	5	**Thymus drucei**
·	·	·	1	·	·	2	·	+	·	·	·	Trifolium repens
·	·	·	2	·	·	·	·	·	·	·	1	Trollius europaeus
·	·	·	·	·	·	·	·	·	·	·	·	Valeriana officinalis
·	·	·	·	·	·	·	·	·	·	·	·	Veronica chamaedrys
·	·	1	·	·	·	·	·	2	1	·	·	V. officinalis
·	·	·	·	·	·	·	·	·	·	·	·	Vicia sepium
·	·	·	·	·	·	·	·	·	·	·	·	Viola lutea
·	·	·	·	·	·	·	·	·	·	·	·	V. palustris
·	1	2	3	4	3	2	2	3	3	3	·	**V. riviniana**
2	·	·	·	1	1	2	·	·	·	·	·	Acrocladium cuspidatum
·	·	·	·	·	1	·	·	·	·	·	·	Anomobryum filiforme
·	·	·	+	·	·	·	·	·	·	·	·	Antitrichia curtipendula
·	·	·	·	·	·	·	·	·	·	·	·	Atrichum undulatum
·	·	·	·	·	·	·	·	·	·	·	·	Aulacomnium turgidum
·	·	·	·	·	·	·	·	·	·	·	·	Barbula fallax
·	·	·	·	·	·	1	·	·	·	·	·	Brachythecium glareosum
·	·	·	1	3	·	·	·	·	·	·	·	Breutelia chrysocoma
·	·	·	·	·	·	·	·	1	·	·	·	Bryum pallens
1	·	3	2	·	·	·	·	·	·	·	·	B. pseudotriquetrum
·	·	2	2	·	2	·	·	·	·	1	·	Campylium protensum
·	·	·	·	·	2	·	·	·	·	·	·	C. stellatum
·	·	·	·	·	·	·	·	·	·	·	·	Campylopus fragilis
·	·	·	·	·	2	·	·	3	·	·	·	Climacium dendroides
3	·	2	·	·	·	·	·	·	·	2	·	Cratoneuron commutatum
3	1	4	4	4	3	3	2	3	1	3	2	**Ctenidium molluscum**
·	·	·	·	·	·	·	·	1	·	2	1	Dicranum scoparium
·	·	·	·	·	·	2	·	·	·	·	·	Distichium capillaceum
·	·	3	4	·	·	3	3	·	1	3	4	Ditrichum flexicaule
·	·	·	2	3	2	·	1	·	1	·	1	Drepanocladus uncinatus
·	2	·	·	·	·	1	·	2	3	·	1	Entodon orthocarpus
·	1	2	·	·	2	·	·	·	·	·	·	Fissidens adianthoides
·	·	·	·	·	·	·	·	·	·	·	·	F. cristatus
3	·	·	3	·	·	·	·	·	·	·	·	F. osmundoides
·	·	2	4	4	1	·	·	2	5	5		**Hylocomium splendens**

Table 26

	1	2	3	4	5	6	7	8	9	10	11	12	13	14	15	16
Hypnum callichroum													2			
H. hamulosum	3															
H. cupressiforme			3	4								3		3	1	2
Mnium cuspidatum													2			
M. hornum				1												
M. orthorrhynchum													2			1
M. punctatum									2		1					
M. undulatum			3											1		
Neckera complanata																
Oligotrichum hercynicum				1												
Pleurozium schreberi						1	4									
Polytrichum alpinum	1		3				1		+	2		2	3			1
P. commune					3					2		3		2		3
Pseudoscleropodium purum	1	3	3			2				2		3				
Ptilium crista-castrensis										2						
Rhacomitrium canescens		2				2									2	2
R. lanuginosum	2															
Rhodobryum roseum												2	3			3
Rhytidiadelphus loreus	2			2	3			1				2	3			1
R. squarrosus	+	4		3		3	3	1	+	2	+	5	3	4		3
R. triquetrus	3	2		1		3		3						4	2	
Sphagnum nemoreum								1								
Thuidium delicatulum	2			3	2	2		1	+		2		3	4		3
T. tamariscinum			3		3									4	1	3
Trichostomum brachydontium																
Tortella tortuosa	2					2	1				2			3		
Weissia controversa																
Alicularia scalaris								1								2
Anastrepta orcadensis																2
Bazzania tricrenata																1
Calypogeia fissa						2									2	
Chiloscyphus polyanthus														2		1
Frullania tamarisci	1					1									2	
Herberta adunca	1															
Lophocolea bidentata			2				3	1	1		1					
Lophozia floerkii	1					1	1									
L. hatcheri																
L. lycopodioides			2				1									
L. quinquedentata									2				3			
Madotheca platyphylla													2			
Pellia fabbroniana													2			
Plagiochila asplenioides	3					1		1								
Preissia quadrata																
Ptilidium ciliare																
Scapania aspera															1	
S. crassiretis																
S. gracilis			3													
S. nemorosa				2												
Cetraria aculeata															1	
C. islandica														2		
Cladonia gracilis														1		
C. pyxidata						2									2	
Peltidea leucophlebia	1															
Peltigera canina				2	3	+		2	+	1		2				
Solorina saccata																

| Number of species 1–16 (179) | 57 | 33 | 33 | 31 | 41 | 58 | 47 | 63 | 39 | 35 | 37 | 43 | 41 | 40 | 41 | 51 |

(Average 43)

Constancy class V	9
,, ,, IV	7

LOCALITIES

1. Beinn Enaiglair, Braemore, Ross-shire; 2. Kinlochlaggan, Inverness-shire; 3. Mullach na Maoile, Glen Cannich, Inverness-shire; 4,25. Glen Markie, Monadhliath, Inverness-shire; 5. Laxford Bridge, Sutherland; 6. Creag Meagaidh, Laggan, Inverness-shire; 7,8,18. Glen Doll, Clova, Angus; 9. Strath nan Caran, Glendhu Forest, Sutherland; 10. Capel Mounth, Clova, Angus; 11. Loch Stack, Sutherland; 12. Abhainn Bruachaig, Kinlochewe Forest, Ross-shire; 13. Carn Dearg, Reay Forest, Sutherland; 14. Falls of Tarf, Glen Tilt, Perthshire; 15. Beinn Lair

(*continued*)

17	18	19	20	21	22	23	24	25	26	27	28	
·	·	·	·	·	·	·	·	·	·	·	·	Hypnum callichroum
·	·	·	·	·	·	·	·	·	·	·	·	H. hamulosum
·	1	·	·	·	·	·	2	2	3	·	3	H. cupressiforme
·	·	·	·	·	·	·	·	·	·	·	1	Mnium cuspidatum
·	·	·	·	·	·	·	·	·	·	·	·	M. hornum
·	·	·	·	·	·	·	·	·	·	·	2	M. orthorrhynchum
·	·	·	2	·	·	1	·	·	·	·	·	M. punctatum
·	·	·	1	3	2	·	·	1	·	·	·	M. undulatum
·	·	·	·	·	·	·	·	·	·	·	·	Neckera complanata
·	·	·	·	·	·	·	·	·	·	·	·	Oligotrichum hercynicum
·	·	·	2	·	·	·	·	·	·	·	·	Pleurozium schreberi
·	·	·	2	·	·	·	·	·	·	·	·	Polytrichum alpinum
·	·	·	·	·	·	·	·	·	·	·	·	P. commune
·	·	·	2	·	·	2	·	2	·	3	·	Pseudoscleropodium purum
·	·	·	2	·	·	·	·	·	·	·	·	Ptilium crista-castrensis
·	·	2	3	·	·	·	1	·	2	·	5	Rhacomitrium canescens
·	·	·	·	·	·	·	·	1	·	·	2	R. lanuginosum
·	·	·	·	·	·	·	·	·	·	·	1	Rhodobryum roseum
·	·	·	·	·	·	·	·	1	·	·	·	Rhytidiadelphus loreus
·	1	2	2	3	3	·	·	2	·	·	2	**R. squarrosus**
·	3	1	4	3	2	·	·	2	5	·	2	R. triquetrus
·	·	·	2	·	·	·	2	1	·	·	·	Sphagnum nemoreum
1	·	·	2	·	·	2	1	·	·	·	·	Thuidium delicatulum
·	·	·	3	3	·	·	·	·	·	·	·	T. tamariscinum
·	·	3	·	·	·	·	·	·	·	·	·	Trichostomum brachydontium
·	·	4	3	·	·	3	2	·	3	3	2	Tortella tortuosa
·	·	·	·	·	·	·	·	2	·	·	·	Weissia controversa
·	·	·	·	·	·	·	·	·	·	·	·	Alicularia scalaris
·	·	·	·	·	·	·	·	·	·	·	·	Anastrepta orcadensis
·	·	·	·	·	·	·	·	·	·	·	·	Bazzania tricrenata
·	·	·	·	·	·	·	·	·	·	·	·	Calypogeia fissa
·	·	·	·	·	·	·	·	·	·	·	·	Chiloscyphus polyanthus
·	·	·	3	·	·	·	·	·	2	3	2	Frullania tamarisci
·	·	·	·	·	·	·	·	·	·	·	·	Herberta adunca
·	·	·	2	·	·	·	·	·	·	·	·	Lophocolea bidentata
·	·	·	·	·	·	·	·	·	·	·	·	Lophozia floerkii
·	·	·	·	·	·	·	·	·	·	·	2	L. hatcheri
·	·	·	·	·	·	·	·	·	·	·	·	L. lycopodioides
·	·	·	2	2	·	·	·	·	1	·	2	L. quinquedentata
·	·	·	·	1	·	·	·	·	·	·	·	Madotheca platyphylla
·	·	·	·	·	·	·	·	·	·	·	·	Pellia fabbroniana
·	·	·	2	1	·	·	·	·	·	1	·	Plagiochila asplenioides
·	·	·	·	·	·	1	1	·	·	·	·	Preissia quadrata
·	·	·	·	·	·	·	·	·	·	·	2	Ptilidium ciliare
·	·	·	·	·	2	·	·	·	1	2	·	Scapania aspera
·	·	·	·	·	·	·	·	·	·	·	·	S. crassiretis
·	·	·	·	·	·	·	·	·	·	·	·	S. gracilis
·	1	·	·	·	·	·	·	·	·	·	·	S. nemorosa
·	·	·	·	·	·	·	·	1	·	·	2	Cetraria aculeata
·	·	·	·	·	·	·	·	·	·	·	·	C. islandica
·	·	·	·	·	·	·	·	·	·	·	1	Cladonia gracilis
·	·	1	1	·	·	·	·	·	2	1	2	C. pyxidata
·	·	·	2	·	·	·	·	1	·	·	2	Peltidea leucophlebia
·	·	·	·	1	·	·	·	·	1	·	·	Peltigera canina
·	·	·	·	·	·	·	·	·	·	·	1	Solorina saccata
32	43	35	62	56	45	42	33	45	53	41	50	Number of species 17–28 (153)

(Average 44)

Constancy class V   13
       ,,   ,, IV   10

Letterewe, Ross-shire; 16. Sgurr Mhic Bharraich, Loch Duich, Ross-shire; 17. Allt Loch Valigan, Blair Atholl, Perthshire; 19. Tulach Hill, Blair Atholl, Perthshire; 20. Saval More, Reay Forest, Sutherland; 21. Ben Lui, Argyll; 22. Ben Lawers, Perthshire; 23. Glen Tilt, Perthshire; 24. Ben Vrackie, Perthshire; 26. Loch Loch, Perthshire; 27. Creag Odhar, Shierglas, Blair Atholl, Perthshire; 28. Meall Breac, Blair Atholl, Perthshire.

Table 27: Thalictrum-Ctenidium provisional nodum

	1	2	3	4	5	6
Reference number	M55 009	M56 011	M56 015	M56 102	M57 002	R58 007
Map reference	8630 1980	8454 1904	8458 1958	7778 3145	7383 2423	9387 2802
Altitude (feet)	1700	1250	550	2500	2750	1250
Aspect (degrees)	180	225	270	270	135	135
Slope (degrees)	3	5	10	15	30	25
Cover (per cent)	100	100	100	100	100	90
Height (centimetres)	1	2	1	2	·	·
Plot area (square metres)	1	2	2	2	1	4
Calluna vulgaris	·	·	2	·	·	3
Salix sp.	·	·	·	1	·	·
Vaccinium myrtillus	·	·	·	·	·	1
Botrychium lunaria	+	+	·	·	·	·
Pteridium aquilinum	·	·	1	·	·	·
Selaginella selaginoides	2	2	2	2	3	·
Agrostis canina	·	·	·	·	+	4
A. tenuis	·	3	·	4	3	4
Anthoxanthum odoratum	·	3	2	·	1	3
Deschampsia caespitosa	·	·	·	2	1	·
D. flexuosa	·	·	1	·	·	2
Festuca ovina agg.	4	4	5	1	5	5
F. rubra	·	·	·	·	·	3
Koeleria gracilis	·	3	·	·	·	·
Nardus stricta	·	2	·	+	2	3
Sieglingia decumbens	4	·	1	·	1	2
Carex capillaris	·	·	·	2	3	·
C. demissa	·	·	·	2	1	·
C. hostiana	3	·	·	·	·	·
C. panicea	·	5	5	·	·	4
C. pilulifera	·	1	·	·	·	·
C. pulicaris	3	1	4	3	4	4
Trichophorum caespitosum	·	·	1	·	·	·
Alchemilla alpina	·	·	·	+	4	4
A. filicaulis	3	2	2	4	·	3
A. glabra	·	·	·	+	4	·
Anemone nemorosa	·	·	·	·	1	·
Antennaria dioica	·	·	1	·	·	·
Bellis perennis	1	1	3	1	4	·
Campanula rotundifolia	·	·	1	+	·	·
Cherleria sedoides	·	·	·	·	+	·
Euphrasia sp.	·	·	1	3	2	·
Galium boreale	·	·	4	·	·	1
G. hercynicum	·	·	·	·	1	2
Geum rivale	2	·	·	·	·	·
Hieracium pilosella	·	·	3	·	·	·
Hieracium sp.	·	·	1	·	·	·
Linum catharticum	·	·	2	2	·	·
Lotus corniculatus	·	·	1	·	·	·
Lysimachia nemorum	1	·	·	·	·	·
Pinguicula vulgaris	·	·	+	·	2	·
Plantago lanceolata	·	2	3	·	·	3
P. maritima	·	2	2	·	·	·
Polygonum viviparum	·	·	·	3	3	·
Potentilla erecta	2	3	3	1	·	2
Prunella vulgaris	2	3	3	2	3	·
Ranunculus acris	1	3	·	·	2	·
R. repens	·	2	·	·	·	·
Saxifraga aizoides	·	·	·	2	2	·
S. oppositifolia	·	·	·	·	2	·
Succisa pratensis	1	1	·	·	·	·
Sibbaldia procumbens	·	·	·	·	1	·
Silene acaulis	·	·	·	·	2	·
Taraxacum sp.	·	+	·	4	·	·
Thalictrum alpinum	7	5	6	6	5	5
Thymus drucei	2	3	3	2	4	3
Trifolium repens	1	·	·	·	·	·
Trollius europaeus	2	·	·	+	·	1
Veronica chamaedrys	1	·	·	·	·	·
Viola riviniana	+	·	2	·	1	·
Blindia acuta	·	·	·	·	2	·
Bryum pseudotriquetrum	1	·	·	·	·	·
Campylium protensum	·	·	·	·	1	2
Cratoneuron commutatum	·	·	·	2	·	·
Ctenidium molluscum	3	4	2	6	3	4
Distichium capillaceum	·	·	1	·	·	·
Ditrichum flexicaule	1	·	·	1	1	1
Drepanocladus uncinatus	·	·	·	·	1	·
Fissidens adianthoides	·	3	·	·	·	·
F. osmundoides	·	·	2	·	2	3
Hylocomium splendens	·	·	1	·	2	3
Hypnum cupressiforme	·	·	1	·	·	2
Pleurozium schreberi	·	·	·	·	1	·
Pseudoscleropodium purum	·	·	·	·	·	3
Rhacomitrium aquaticum	·	+	·	·	·	·
R. canescens	·	·	·	·	3	·
R. lanuginosum	·	·	·	·	·	1
Rhytidiadelphus squarrosus	·	·	·	·	1	·
R. triquetrus	·	·	·	·	1	·
Thuidium delicatulum	·	·	·	·	2	·
T. tamariscinum	·	·	·	·	·	2
Tortella tortuosa	1	2	·	·	1	3
Trichostomum brachydontium	·	·	1	·	·	·
Aneura sp.	·	·	·	·	1	·
Plagiochila asplenioides	·	·	1	·	·	1
Ptilidium ciliare	·	·	·	·	1	·
Scapania cf. subalpina	·	·	1	·	·	·
Cetraria islandica	·	·	·	·	1	·
Cladonia cervicornis	·	·	·	·	2	·
Peltidea leucophlebia	·	·	·	·	1	·
Number of species (90)	24	26	34	27	48	32

(Average 32)

LOCALITIES

1. Beinn Eighe, Ross-shire; 2. Glas Cnoc, Loch Kishorn, Ross-shire; 3. Cnoc nan Each, Strathcarron, Ross-shire; 4. Meall Odhar, Cairnwell, Aberdeenshire; 5. Ben Heasgarnich, Perthshire; 6. Ben Griam More, Sutherland.

Table 28: Nardetum sub-alpinum (1–14); Juncetum

	1	2	3	4	5	6	7	8	9	10	11	12	13	14
Reference number	P52 013	P52 014	P52 015	P52 091	P52 106	P52 158	R57 076	R57 240	R57 260	R57 259	R57 290	R58 031	R58 086	R56 075
Map reference	7388 2638	7391 2636	7393 2636	—	7501 2780	—	7962 2582	7769 3289	7751 3272	7746 3290	7715 2869	7791 1853	8318 2190	8739 2032
Altitude (feet)	1500	2000	2150	2200	1300	1850	1250	1200	1750	1000	1450	2700	1200	1600
Aspect (degrees)	140	140	180	140	320	150	270	270	325	45	225	90	180	360
Slope (degrees)	10	3	4	5	3	3	10	25	20	32	5	25	15	30
Cover (per cent)	100	100	100	100	100	100	100	100	100	100	100	100	100	100
Height (centimetres)	15	—	15	15	15	20	—	17	—	—	15	—	—	—
Plot area (square metres)	4	8	4	4	2	4	4	4	4	4	4	4	4	4
Calluna vulgaris	2	.	.	.	.	.	.	.	.	.	2	.	3	.
Empetrum hermaphroditum	.	.	.	.	.	.	.	.	.	.	.	.	.	.
Vaccinium myrtillus	3	1	1	3	3	5	.	3	.	.	3	.	.	2
V. vitis-idaea	.	.	.	.	.	.	.	.	.	.	.	.	.	1
Blechnum spicant	.	.	.	.	.	.	.	.	.	.	.	1	.	2
Botrychium lunaria	.	.	1	.	.	.	.	.	.	.	.	.	.	.
Selaginella selaginoides	.	.	.	.	.	.	.	.	.	.	.	.	.	2
Agrostis canina	.	3	.	2	.	.	5	6	7	7	6	3	2	5
A. stolonifera	.	.	.	2	.	.	.	.	.	.	.	.	.	.
A. tenuis	4	2	3	1	2	3	5	6	7	7	6	3	4	5
Anthoxanthum odoratum	4	4	3	4	3	3	4	2	2	3	3	.	3	3
Deschampsia caespitosa	1	1	.	1	.	1	.	.	.	.	2	4	.	4
D. flexuosa	.	.	.	.	1	.	+	3	3	3	.	3	.	4
Festuca ovina agg.	5	7	7	3	4	3	6	6	4	7	4	.	3	5
F. rubra	.	.	.	.	.	.	.	.	.	2	2	.	.	.
Holcus lanatus	.	.	.	.	.	.	.	.	.	.	.	.	3	.
Molinia caerulea	.	.	.	.	.	.	.	.	.	.	.	.	3	.
Nardus stricta	9	9	8	8	7	8	5	7	7	5	8	9	7	5
Sieglingia decumbens	.	.	.	.	.	.	.	3	.	.	3	.	.	.
Carex bigelowii	.	.	.	.	.	.	.	.	.	.	.	3	.	.
C. binervis	1	.	.	2	2	2	2	.	2	.	2	.	.	4
C. echinata	.	.	.	.	.	.	.	.	.	.	.	.	.	.
C. nigra	.	.	.	.	.	.	.	.	.	.	.	.	.	.
C. panicea	.	1	.	2	4	.	3	.	.	.	3	.	3	.
C. pilulifera	3	1	2	2	3	2	5	2	.	3	2	4	2	3
C. vaginata	.	.	.	.	.	.	.	.	.	.	.	.	.	.
Eriophorum angustifolium	.	.	.	.	.	.	.	.	.	.	.	.	.	.
Juncus effusus	.	.	.	.	.	.	.	.	.	.	2	.	.	.
J. squarrosus	.	4	.	1	2	4	.	.	.	.	3	.	6	3
Luzula campestris	.	.	.	.	.	.	3	3	.	3	.	.	.	.
L. multiflora	1	2	3	2	2	2	.	.	2	.	.	1	2	3
L. pilosa	.	.	.	.	.	.	.	.	3	.	.	.	.	.
L. sylvatica	.	.	.	.	.	.	.	.	.	.	.	.	.	2
Narthecium ossifragum	.	.	.	.	.	.	.	.	.	.	.	2	1	2
Trichophorum caespitosum	.	.	.	.	.	.	.	.	.	.	.	2	2	2
Achillea millefolium	1	.	3	.	.	.	.	.	.	.	2	.	.	.
Anemone nemorosa	1	.	1	2	1	.	.	.	.	.	.	.	.	.
Armeria maritima	.	.	.	.	.	.	.	.	.	.	.	.	.	.
Campanula rotundifolia	.	.	3	3	.	.	.	2	.	.	.	.	.	.
Cerastium vulgatum	.	.	1	.	.	.	.	.	.	.	.	.	.	.
Chamaepericlymenum suecicum	.	.	.	.	.	.	.	.	.	.	.	.	.	.
Euphrasia sp.	.	.	.	.	.	.	.	.	.	.	.	.	2	1
Galium hercynicum	2	4	4	3	3	3	5	4	4	5	3	3	.	3
Lathyrus montanus	.	.	.	.	.	.	.	.	.	.	.	.	1	.
Leontodon autumnalis	.	.	.	.	.	.	.	.	.	.	2	.	1	.
Melampyrum pratense	.	.	.	.	.	.	.	.	.	.	.	.	.	.
Oxalis acetosella	.	.	.	.	1	.	.	.	2	.	.	.	.	2
Pedicularis sylvatica	.	.	.	.	1	.	.	.	.	.	.	.	.	.
Pinguicula vulgaris	.	.	.	.	.	.	.	.	.	.	.	.	.	.
Plantago lanceolata	1	.	.	.	.	.	.	.	.	.	2	.	.	.
Polygala serpyllifolia	1	.	.	.	2	.	.	.	.	.	1	.	3	.
Polygonum viviparum	.	.	1	.	.	.	.	.	.	.	3	.	.	.
Potentilla erecta	3	3	3	3	3	3	3	2	3	3	4	4	4	2
Ranunculus acris	.	.	.	.	1	.	.	.	.	.	2	.	2	.
Rubus chamaemorus	.	.	.	.	.	.	.	.	.	.	.	.	.	.
Rumex acetosa	.	.	.	.	1	.	.	.	.	3	.	.	.	.
Succisa pratensis	.	.	.	.	.	.	.	.	.	.	.	.	3	.
Thymus drucei	1	.	2	3	.	.	.	.	.	.	.	.	.	.
Trifolium repens	.	.	1	2	.	.	.	.	.	.	1	.	.	.
Veronica officinalis	1	.	1	.	.	.	.	.	1	.	.	.	.	.
Viola palustris	3	.	2	3	.	1	.	.	.	.	.	.	3	.
V. riviniana	1	.	.	.	2	.	.	3	2	.	2	4	4	3
Atrichum undulatum	.	.	.	.	.	.	.	.	.	.	1	.	.	.
Aulacomnium palustre	.	.	.	.	.	.	.	.	.	.	.	.	.	.
Breutelia chrysocoma	.	.	.	.	.	.	.	.	.	.	.	.	.	2
Dicranum majus	.	.	.	.	.	.	.	.	.	.	.	.	.	.
D. scoparium	.	.	.	.	.	.	.	.	3	.	1	.	.	1
Hylocomium splendens	6	.	.	.	5	2	3	4	4	1	4	1	2	5
Hypnum cupressiforme	.	.	.	.	.	.	.	2	2	.	2	.	1	2
Mnium hornum	.	.	.	.	.	.	.	.	.	.	2	.	2	.
M. cf. stellare	.	.	.	.	2	.	.	.	.	.	.	.	.	.
M. punctatum	.	.	.	.	.	.	.	.	.	.	.	.	2	.

squarrosi sub-alpinum (15–24); Juncus squarrosus bogs (25–28)

15	16	17	18	19	20	21	22	23	24	25	26	27	28	
P52	P52	P52	R58	P52	P52	P52	R57	R57	R57	R57	R57	R57	M56	Reference number
177	182	030	067	113	112	111	291	179	084	177	064	017	019	
7409	7410	7394	8451	7403	7403	7393	7730	7920	7866	7917	8735	9447	8461	Map reference
2653	2650	2634	2079	2654	2654	2655	2867	2503	2441	2502	2211	2360	2055	
2475	2575	2450	2000	2100	1750	1650	1800	2700	2400	2500	1600	2250	2650	Altitude (feet)
190	170	170	360	150	120	150	180	180	225	180	360	45	—	Aspect (degrees)
4	2	8	10	3	3	5	3	33	13	25	10	8	0	Slope (degrees)
100	100	100	100	100	100	100	100	100	100	100	100	100	100	Cover (per cent)
30	20	10	—	15	20	20	18	—	—	—	—	—	8	Height (centimetres)
10	4	4	4	2	2	4	4	4	4	4	4	4	4	Plot area (square metres)
·	·	·	·	·	·	·	·	·	·	2	2	·	·	Calluna vulgaris
·	·	·	·	·	·	·	·	·	·	2	3	·	·	Empetrum hermaphroditum
3	3	2	·	1	·	1	·	3	·	·	5	·	2	**Vaccinium myrtillus**
·	·	·	·	·	·	·	1	·	·	·	2	·	·	V. vitis-idaea
·	·	·	·	·	·	·	·	·	·	·	·	·	·	Blechnum spicant
·	·	·	·	·	·	·	·	·	·	·	·	·	·	Botrychium lunaria
·	·	·	·	·	·	·	·	·	·	2	·	·	·	Selaginella selaginoides
1	2	3	4	·	3	3	3	5	3	·	·	3	·	**Agrostis canina**
·	·	·	·	·	·	·	·	·	·	·	·	·	·	A. stolonifera
3	·	·	4	·	·	·	·	5	·	3	2	·	·	**A. tenuis**
3	·	4	3	2	4	1	3	4	4	·	·	·	·	**Anthoxanthum odoratum**
·	·	·	·	·	·	·	·	·	·	·	·	·	·	Deschampsia caespitosa
3	2	2	3	2	·	3	3	3	4	·	3	2	·	**D. flexuosa**
4	4	5	3	8	3	5	3	3	4	3	2	·	·	**Festuca ovina agg.**
·	·	·	·	·	·	·	·	·	·	·	·	·	·	F. rubra
·	·	·	·	·	·	·	·	·	·	·	·	·	·	Holcus lanatus
·	·	·	·	·	·	·	·	·	·	·	·	·	·	Molinia caerulea
2	4	·	3	1	5	6	7	7	5	3	·	·	1	**Nardus stricta**
·	·	·	·	·	·	·	·	·	·	·	·	·	·	Sieglingia decumbens
2	3	·	3	·	·	·	·	4	5	·	·	3	·	Carex bigelowii
·	·	·	·	·	·	·	+	·	·	·	·	·	·	C. binervis
·	·	·	·	·	·	·	·	·	·	3	·	·	·	C. echinata
·	·	·	·	·	·	·	·	·	·	·	2	·	3	C. nigra
·	·	2	·	·	·	·	·	·	·	·	·	·	·	C. panicea
·	·	·	·	·	2	·	·	·	·	·	·	·	·	**C. pilulifera**
·	·	·	·	·	·	·	·	·	·	1	·	·	·	C. vaginata
·	·	·	·	·	·	·	2	·	·	3	·	·	·	Eriophorum angustifolium
·	·	·	·	·	·	·	·	·	·	·	·	·	·	Juncus effusus
9	9	9	7	6	7	6	7	7	8	8	8	8	8	**J. squarrosus**
·	·	·	·	·	·	·	·	·	·	·	·	·	·	Luzula campestris
·	·	·	3	2	·	2	·	·	·	·	1	·	·	L. multiflora
·	·	·	·	·	·	·	·	·	·	·	·	·	·	L. pilosa
·	·	·	·	·	·	·	·	·	·	·	·	·	·	L. sylvatica
·	·	·	·	·	·	·	·	·	·	3	·	·	·	Narthecium ossifragum
·	·	·	·	·	·	·	·	·	·	4	3	·	·	Trichophorum caespitosum
·	·	·	·	·	·	·	·	·	·	·	·	·	·	Achillea millefolium
·	·	·	·	·	·	·	·	·	·	·	·	·	·	Anemone nemorosa
·	·	·	·	·	·	·	·	·	·	·	·	4	·	Armeria maritima
·	·	·	·	·	·	·	·	·	·	·	·	·	·	Campanula rotundifolia
·	·	·	·	·	·	·	·	·	·	·	·	·	·	Cerastium vulgatum
·	·	·	·	·	·	·	·	·	·	·	4	·	·	Chamaepericlymenum suecicum
·	·	·	·	·	·	·	·	·	·	2	·	·	·	Euphrasia sp.
5	3	4	5	4	3	3	5	3	4	·	3	3	3	**Galium hercynicum**
·	·	·	·	·	·	·	·	·	·	·	·	·	·	Lathyrus montanus
·	·	·	·	·	·	·	·	·	·	·	·	·	·	Leontodon autumnalis
·	·	·	·	·	·	·	·	·	·	·	1	·	·	Melampyrum pratense
·	·	·	·	·	·	·	·	·	·	·	·	·	·	Oxalis acetosella
·	·	·	·	·	·	·	·	·	·	·	·	·	·	Pedicularis sylvatica
·	·	·	·	·	·	·	·	·	·	2	·	·	·	Pinguicula vulgaris
·	·	·	·	·	·	·	·	·	·	·	·	·	·	Plantago lanceolata
·	·	·	·	·	·	·	·	·	·	·	·	·	·	Polygala serpyllifolia
·	·	·	·	·	·	·	·	·	·	·	·	·	·	Polygonum viviparum
·	·	3	4	·	·	1	3	·	·	4	4	2	3	**Potentilla erecta**
·	·	·	·	·	·	·	·	·	·	·	·	·	·	Ranunculus acris
·	·	·	·	·	·	·	·	·	2	·	·	·	·	Rubus chamaemorus
·	·	3	·	·	·	·	·	·	·	·	·	·	·	Rumex acetosa
·	·	·	·	·	·	·	·	·	·	3	·	·	·	Succisa pratensis
·	·	·	·	·	·	·	·	·	·	·	·	·	·	Thymus drucei
·	·	·	·	·	·	·	·	·	·	·	·	·	·	Trifolium repens
·	·	·	·	·	·	·	·	·	·	·	·	·	·	Veronica officinalis
·	·	·	·	·	·	·	·	·	·	2	·	·	·	Viola palustris
·	·	·	·	·	·	·	·	·	·	·	·	·	·	V. riviniana
·	·	·	·	·	·	·	·	·	·	·	·	·	·	Atrichum undulatum
·	·	·	·	·	·	·	·	·	·	3	·	·	3	Aulacomnium palustre
·	·	·	·	·	·	·	·	·	·	·	·	·	·	Breutelia chrysocoma
·	·	·	·	·	·	·	·	·	·	·	2	·	·	Dicranum majus
1	·	·	·	·	2	·	·	·	·	·	·	·	1	D. scoparium
2	1	·	5	·	·	·	2	4	3	4	4	·	6	**Hylocomium splendens**
·	·	·	·	·	·	·	·	·	·	1	·	·	·	Hypnum cupressiforme
·	·	·	·	·	·	·	·	·	·	·	·	·	·	Mnium hornum
·	·	·	·	·	·	·	·	·	·	·	·	·	·	M. cf. stellare
·	·	·	·	·	·	·	·	·	·	·	·	·	·	M. punctatum

Table 28

	1	2	3	4	5	6	7	8	9	10	11	12	13	14
Mnium undulatum	.	.	.	.	.	.	.	.	.	.	1	.	.	.
Plagiothecium undulatum	.	.	.	.	.	.	.	.	2	.	.	.	.	2
Pleurozium schreberi	5	6	4	.	4	3	2	5	.	4	.	.	2	2
Polytrichum alpestre	.	.	.	.	.	.	.	.	.	.	.	.	.	.
P. alpinum	3	1	.	1	.	.	.	.	.	3	.	.	.	2
P. commune	.	.	3	.	1	.	.	1	2	.	.	.	.	2
Pseudoscleropodium purum	1	.	.	1	.	.	2	.	.	.	1	.	3	.
Rhacomitrium lanuginosum	.	.	.	.	.	.	.	.	.	.	.	.	.	.
Rhytidiadelphus loreus	.	.	.	.	.	.	1	+	.	.	.	2	2	4
R. squarrosus	4	6	6	1	1	3	2	3	3	3	3	3	3	2
R. triquetrus	1	.	.	1	.	.	.	.	.	.	.	.	.	.
Sphagnum cuspidatum	.	.	.	.	.	.	.	.	.	.	.	.	.	.
S. nemoreum	.	.	.	.	.	.	.	.	.	.	.	.	.	3
S. papillosum	.	.	.	.	.	.	.	.	.	.	.	.	.	.
S. russowii	.	.	.	.	.	.	.	.	.	.	.	.	.	+
S. auriculatum	.	.	.	.	.	.	.	.	.	.	.	.	.	2
S. inundatum	.	.	.	.	.	.	.	.	.	.	.	.	.	.
Thuidium tamariscinum	.	.	.	.	.	.	3	.	.	.	.	.	2	5
Anastrepta orcadensis	.	.	.	.	.	.	.	.	.	.	.	.	.	1
Calypogeia trichomanis	.	.	.	.	.	.	.	.	.	.	.	.	2	.
Diplophyllum albicans	.	.	.	.	.	.	.	.	.	.	2	.	.	2
Lepidozia pearsoni	.	.	.	.	.	.	.	.	.	.	.	.	.	.
Leptoscyphus taylori	.	.	.	.	.	.	.	.	.	.	.	.	.	.
Lophocolea bidentata	.	.	.	.	.	.	.	1	.	2	1	2	2	.
Lophozia barbata	.	.	.	.	.	.	.	2	.	1	.	.	.	.
L. floerkii	.	.	.	.	.	.	.	.	.	.	.	.	.	.
L. quinquedentata	.	.	.	.	.	.	.	.	.	2	.	.	.	.
L. ventricosa	.	.	.	.	.	.	.	.	.	.	.	.	.	.
Ptilidium ciliare	.	.	.	.	.	.	1	.	3	.	2	.	.	1
Scapania gracilis	.	.	.	.	.	.	.	.	.	.	.	.	.	2
Cetraria islandica	.	.	.	.	.	.	.	.	.	.	.	.	.	.
Cladonia pyxidata	.	.	.	.	.	.	1	.	.	.	.	.	.	.
C. subsquamosa	.	.	.	.	.	.	.	.	.	.	.	.	.	.
C. sylvatica	.	.	.	.	.	.	.	1	.	.	.	.	.	.
C. uncialis	.	.	.	.	.	.	.	.	.	.	.	.	.	.
Number of species	26	16	22	26	23	17	23	24	18	26	29	18	33	41

(Average 24)

Constancy class V   9
      ,,   ,, IV   4

LOCALITIES

1–6,15–17,19–21. Ben Lawers, Perthshire; 7. Glen Markie, Monadhliath, Inverness-shire; 8. Carn Derg, Glen Clova, Angus; 9,10. Kilbo Burn, Clova, Angus; 11,22. Allt Slanaidh, Glen Tilt, Perthshire; 12. Beinn Odhar Mhor, Glenfinnan, Inverness-shire; 13. Mullach na Maoile, Glen Cannich, Inverness-shire; 14. Beinn Tarsuinn, Letterewe, Ross-shire; 18. Sgurr a' Chaorachain, Monar Forest, Ross-shire; 23,25. A' Bhuid-

(continued)

15	16	17	18	19	20	21	22	23	24	25	26	27	28	
·	·	·	·	·	·	·	·	·	·	·	·	·	·	Mnium undulatum
·	·	·	3	·	·	·	2	3	3	·	2	·	·	Plagiothecium undulatum
4	5	1	3	1	·	1	3	2	2	3	·	1	·	**Pleurozium schreberi**
·	·	·	·	·	·	·	·	·	·	·	·	2	·	Polytrichum alpestre
·	·	·	·	·	·	·	·	3	2	·	2	·	·	P. alpinum
1	4	1	3	·	·	·	·	·	·	2	·	·	2	P. commune
·	·	·	·	·	·	·	·	·	·	·	·	·	·	Pseudoscleropodium purum
1	·	·	·	·	·	·	·	·	·	·	·	3	·	Rhacomitrium lanuginosum
·	·	·	4	·	·	·	2	·	·	3	3	3	4	**Rhytidiadelphus loreus**
2	4	4	4	3	2	5	3	4	4	2	·	·	·	**R. squarrosus**
·	·	·	·	·	·	·	·	·	·	·	·	·	·	R. triquetrus
·	·	·	·	·	·	·	·	·	·	·	·	2	·	Sphagnum cuspidatum
·	·	·	·	·	·	·	·	·	3	·	4	4	2	S. nemoreum
·	·	·	·	·	·	·	·	·	·	4	2	4	·	S. papillosum
·	·	·	·	·	·	·	·	·	·	7	·	·	·	S. russowii
·	·	·	·	·	·	·	·	·	·	·	·	·	·	S. auriculatum
·	·	·	·	·	·	·	·	·	·	+	·	·	·	S. inundatum
·	·	·	·	·	·	·	·	·	·	·	2	1	·	Thuidium tamariscinum
·	·	·	·	·	·	·	·	·	1	·	2	·	·	Anastrepta orcadensis
·	·	·	·	·	·	·	·	·	·	3	2	·	·	Calypogeia trichomanis
·	·	·	·	·	·	·	·	·	·	·	·	4	·	Diplophyllum albicans
·	·	·	·	·	·	·	·	·	·	·	2	·	·	Lepidozia pearsoni
·	·	·	·	·	·	·	·	·	·	·	·	4	·	Leptoscyphus taylori
1	·	·	·	·	3	1	3	·	·	·	·	·	·	Lophocolea bidentata
·	·	·	·	·	·	·	·	1	·	·	·	·	·	Lophozia barbata
1	1	·	·	·	·	·	3	1	·	·	2	·	·	L. floerkii
·	·	·	·	·	·	·	·	·	·	·	·	·	·	L. quinquedentata
·	·	·	·	·	·	·	·	·	·	·	·	·	1	L. ventricosa
3	2	2	·	·	·	·	3	·	2	2	1	2	1	**Ptilidium ciliare**
·	·	·	·	·	·	·	·	·	·	·	·	3	·	Scapania gracilis
·	·	·	·	·	·	·	·	·	·	·	·	1	1	Cetraria islandica
1	·	·	·	·	·	·	·	·	·	·	·	·	·	Cladonia pyxidata
·	·	·	·	·	·	·	·	·	·	·	·	1	·	C. subsquamosa
1	·	·	·	·	·	·	·	·	·	·	·	·	+	C. sylvatica
·	·	·	·	·	·	·	·	·	·	·	·	2	+	C. uncialis
21	14	13	17	10	9	13	19	18	18	28	29	20	19	Number of species

(Average 15)   (Average 24)

Constancy class V   9
    ,,   ,,   IV   4

heanach, Laggan, Inverness-shire; 24. Creag Meagaidh, Laggan, Inverness-shire; 26. Sgurr Mor, Fannich, Ross-shire; 27. Meall Horn, Reay Forest, Sutherland; 28. Sgurr na Feartaig, Achnashellach, Ross-shire.

Table 29: Species-rich Nardetum sub-alpinum (1–8); Species-rich

	1	2	3	4	5	6	7	8	9	10	11
Reference number	R58 132	R58 104	R58 100	R57 160	R57 241	R57 203	R57 218	R57 232	R58 113	R58 137	R58 098
Map reference	7276 2260	7498 2642	7457 2661	7855 2443	7768 3288	7744 3327	7753 3280	7755 3252	7450 2643	7275 2262	7498 2645
Altitude (feet)	1500	2300	1750	1700	1250	1600	1350	1500	2250	2000	2200
Aspect (degrees)	360	45	270	90	270	225	45	90	360	360	45
Slope (degrees)	20	30	5	20	28	20	40	5	10	10	10
Cover (per cent)	100	100	100	100	100	100	100	100	100	100	100
Height (centimetres)	–	–	–	24	–	–	30	24	–	–	–
Plot area (square metres)	4	4	4	4	4	4	4	4	4	4	4
Calluna vulgaris	·	·	·	·	·	1	·	·	·	·	·
Empetrum hermaphroditum	·	3	·	·	·	·	·	·	·	·	·
E. nigrum	·	·	·	·	·	·	·	·	·	·	·
Erica tetralix	·	·	·	·	·	·	·	·	·	·	2
Salix aurita	·	·	·	2	·	·	·	·	·	·	·
S. herbacea	·	·	·	·	·	·	·	·	·	·	·
Vaccinium myrtillus	·	2	·	·	·	·	·	·	·	·	·
Equisetum palustre	·	2	·	1	2	·	·	·	·	·	·
E. sylvaticum	·	·	·	·	·	·	·	·	·	·	1
E. variegatum	·	·	·	·	·	·	·	·	·	·	·
Lycopodium selago	·	·	·	·	·	·	·	·	·	·	·
Selaginella selaginoides	·	3	·	1	·	·	·	·	1	2	2
Agrostis canina	5	3	3	2	4	3	4	·	3	3	3
A. stolonifera	·	·	·	·	·	3	·	3	·	·	·
A. tenuis	5	2	3	4	4	2	3	3	3	·	·
Anthoxanthum odoratum	5	3	4	3	4	·	3	5	3	3	3
Arrhenatherum elatius	·	·	·	·	·	·	3	·	·	·	·
Briza media	·	·	·	·	1	·	1	·	·	·	·
Deschampsia caespitosa	·	3	3	·	·	·	2	·	·	·	·
Festuca ovina agg.	3	5	3	3	4	3	3	4	4	4	4
F. rubra	4	3	·	·	2	·	·	·	·	·	·
Holcus lanatus	·	·	·	2	3	2	4	4	·	·	·
Molinia caerulea	·	·	·	5	1	·	·	·	·	·	·
Nardus stricta	7	7	7	8	8	7	5	8	4	4	6
Phleum commutatum	·	·	·	·	·	·	·	·	·	·	·
Sesleria caerulea	·	·	·	·	·	·	·	·	·	·	·
Sieglingia decumbens	·	·	·	·	·	·	·	2	·	·	·
Carex aquatilis	·	·	·	·	·	·	·	·	·	·	·
C. bigelowii	·	·	·	·	·	·	·	·	·	·	·
C. binervis	·	2	·	·	·	2	·	·	·	·	·
C. demissa	·	2	3	·	·	·	·	·	·	·	2
C. dioica	·	·	·	·	·	·	·	·	+	·	·
C. echinata	·	2	3	3	4	3	4	4	2	3	3
C. flacca	·	·	·	·	·	·	3	2	·	·	·
C. hostiana	2	·	·	·	·	·	·	·	·	·	2
C. nigra	·	·	·	3	·	2	·	3	1	4	·
C. panicea	4	·	4	4	4	3	3	3	3	4	4
C. pulicaris	4	3	3	1	3	·	4	2	2	3	1
C. saxatilis	·	·	·	·	·	·	·	·	·	·	·
C. vaginata	·	·	·	·	·	·	·	·	·	·	·
Coeloglossum viride	·	·	·	·	·	·	·	·	·	·	·
Eriophorum angustifolium	·	2	·	·	2	4	·	1	·	·	2
Juncus acutiflorus	·	·	·	·	2	·	·	·	·	3	·
J. articulatus	·	·	·	·	·	·	·	·	·	·	·
J. effusus	·	·	·	·	·	·	·	·	3	·	·
J. kochii	·	·	2	·	·	3	·	1	+	·	2
J. squarrosus	3	2	5	3	3	7	2	3	8	7	7
J. triglumis	·	·	·	·	·	·	·	·	·	·	·
Luzula multiflora	3	3	1	2	3	1	·	3	+	·	1
L. sylvatica	·	·	·	·	·	·	2	·	·	·	·
Narthecium ossifragum	·	·	·	2	·	·	·	·	·	1	2
Orchis ericetorum	·	·	·	·	·	·	·	·	·	·	·
Trichophorum caespitosum	·	·	·	2	·	2	·	·	·	·	·
Triglochin palustre	·	·	·	·	·	·	·	·	·	·	·
Achillea ptarmica	·	·	·	·	2	·	·	2	·	·	·
Alchemilla alpina	·	3	·	·	·	·	2	·	·	·	·
A. filicaulis	·	·	·	·	·	·	·	3	·	·	·
A. glabra	3	·	3	·	·	·	·	·	3	4	2
A. vestita	·	3	3	·	·	·	·	·	·	·	·
A. wichurae	·	4	·	·	·	·	·	·	·	·	·
A. xanthochlora	·	·	·	·	·	·	2	·	·	·	·
Anemone nemorosa	·	·	·	·	·	·	·	·	·	·	·
Angelica sylvestris	1	·	·	·	·	·	2	·	·	·	·
Caltha palustris	·	·	·	·	·	·	·	1	·	·	·
Campanula rotundifolia	2	3	·	·	2	·	·	·	·	·	·
Cardamine flexuosa	·	·	·	·	·	1	·	·	·	·	·
C. pratensis	·	·	·	·	·	·	·	·	·	·	·
Cerastium vulgatum	2	1	2	·	1	·	·	·	2	2	·
Cirsium heterophyllum	·	·	·	·	·	·	5	·	·	·	·
C. palustre	·	·	·	·	2	·	·	·	·	·	·
Crepis paludosa	2	·	·	·	·	·	·	·	·	3	·
Epilobium palustre	·	·	2	·	·	·	·	·	2	1	·
Euphrasia sp.	3	2	3	3	·	2	·	1	·	3	2
Filipendula ulmaria	2	·	·	·	·	·	4	·	·	·	·

Juncetum squarrosi sub-alpinum (9–11); Hypno-Caricetum alpinum (12–23)

12	13	14	15	16	17	18	19	20	21	22	23	
R58	R58	R58	R58	R58	R58	R58	R58	R58	R58	R57	R59	Reference number
019	124	114	118	021	077	037	133	102	064	142	010	
7336	7401	7450	7378	7753	8321	7801	7275	7441	8481	7868	7394	Map reference
2489	2521	2643	2566	3149	2167	3162	2263	2645	2072	2435	2588	
2250	2700	2250	2500	1800	2000	2000	1700	3200	1000	2600	2750	Altitude (feet)
360	360	360	135	315	45	270	360	360	270	180	90	Aspect (degrees)
12	15	10	10	25	20	7	25	7	5	20	25	Slope (degrees)
100	100	100	100	100	100	100	100	100	100	100	100	Cover (per cent)
—	—	—	—	—	20	—	—	—	—	—	—	Height (centimetres)
4	4	4	4	4	4	4	4	4	4	4	4	Plot area (square metres)
·	·	·	·	·	·	·	·	·	·	·	·	Calluna vulgaris
2	·	·	·	+	·	·	·	·	·	·	·	Empetrum hermaphroditum
·	·	·	·	·	·	2	·	·	·	·	·	E. nigrum
·	·	·	·	·	·	·	·	·	·	·	·	Erica tetralix
·	·	·	·	·	·	+	·	·	·	·	·	Salix aurita
·	·	·	·	·	·	·	1	·	·	·	·	S. herbacea
·	·	·	·	·	·	·	·	·	·	·	·	Vaccinium myrtillus
·	·	·	2	·	·	·	·	·	·	·	5	Equisetum palustre
·	·	·	·	·	·	·	·	·	·	·	·	E. sylvaticum
·	·	2	·	·	·	·	·	·	·	·	·	E. variegatum
2	·	·	·	·	·	·	·	·	·	·	·	Lycopodium selago
2	3	1	3	1	1	2	3	3	1	·	3	**Selaginella selaginoides**
2	3	2	·	·	·	·	·	·	3	4	4	**Agrostis canina**
·	·	·	·	·	·	·	·	·	·	·	·	A. stolonifera
·	3	·	·	·	·	+	·	·	3	2	3	**A. tenuis**
·	·	·	2	2	·	·	4	·	·	·	·	**Anthoxanthum odoratum**
·	·	·	·	·	·	·	·	·	·	·	·	Arrhenatherum elatius
·	·	·	3	·	3	·	·	·	·	·	·	Briza media
·	·	2	2	·	·	·	·	·	·	4	·	Deschampsia caespitosa
1	3	3	4	3	2	·	5	3	2	4	4	**Festuca ovina agg.**
1	3	3	5	·	·	3	3	·	·	3	·	F. rubra
·	·	·	2	·	·	·	·	·	3	·	·	Holcus lanatus
·	·	·	·	·	·	2	·	·	·	4	·	Molinia caerulea
5	3	5	·	3	3	2	4	·	2	+	+	**Nardus stricta**
·	·	·	·	·	·	2	·	·	·	·	·	Phleum commutatum
·	1	·	·	·	·	·	·	·	·	·	·	Sesleria caerulea
·	·	·	·	·	·	·	·	·	2	·	·	Sieglingia decumbens
·	·	·	·	·	8	·	·	·	·	·	·	Carex aquatilis
·	·	·	·	·	·	·	·	·	·	7	·	C. bigelowii
·	·	·	·	·	·	·	·	·	·	·	·	C. binervis
4	3	2	3	·	+	·	·	2	·	·	·	C. demissa
4	·	·	·	·	2	·	2	·	·	·	·	C. dioica
·	·	4	·	+	5	5	4	·	5	5	·	**C. echinata**
·	·	·	·	·	·	·	·	·	·	·	·	C. flacca
·	·	·	·	·	·	·	·	·	·	·	·	C. hostiana
3	9	5	7	5	4	8	7	5	5	·	7	**C. nigra**
4	3	3	4	4	4	3	3	3	3	·	3	**C. panicea**
5	4	3	3	4	4	2	4	5	2	·	4	**C. pulicaris**
·	·	·	·	·	·	·	·	3	·	4	1	C. saxatilis
·	·	·	·	·	·	·	·	·	·	2	·	C. vaginata
·	·	·	·	·	·	1	·	·	·	·	·	Coeloglossum viride
4	·	2	2	3	3	3	4	·	2	4	1	**Eriophorum angustifolium**
·	·	1	·	·	·	2	1	·	·	·	·	Juncus acutiflorus
·	2	·	3	6	·	·	·	·	3	·	·	J. articulatus
·	·	·	·	·	·	·	·	·	2	·	·	J. effusus
3	·	3	·	4	·	3	·	·	·	·	·	J. kochii
4	·	·	3	3	1	3	·	·	2	·	·	**J. squarrosus**
·	·	·	·	·	·	·	1	·	·	·	2	J. triglumis
·	·	·	3	1	2	·	·	·	2	3	·	**Luzula multiflora**
·	·	·	·	·	·	·	·	·	·	·	·	L. sylvatica
3	·	·	·	3	·	1	·	·	·	·	·	Narthecium ossifragum
·	·	·	·	·	·	·	·	·	·	2	·	Orchis ericetorum
3	·	·	·	·	·	·	·	·	·	·	·	Trichophorum caespitosum
·	·	·	·	1	3	·	·	·	·	·	·	Triglochin palustre
·	·	·	·	·	·	·	·	·	·	·	·	Achillea ptarmica
·	·	·	·	·	·	·	·	·	·	·	·	Alchemilla alpina
·	·	·	·	·	·	·	·	·	·	·	·	A. filicaulis
·	4	3	2	·	·	4	2	·	·	·	·	A. glabra
·	·	·	·	·	·	·	·	·	·	·	·	A. vestita
·	·	·	·	·	·	·	·	·	·	·	·	A. wichurae
2	·	·	3	2	·	·	·	·	·	·	·	A. xanthochlora
1	·	·	·	·	·	·	·	·	·	·	·	Anemone nemorosa
·	·	·	·	·	·	·	·	·	·	·	·	Angelica sylvestris
·	1	·	3	2	1	·	·	·	·	3	·	Caltha palustris
1	·	2	·	·	·	·	·	·	·	·	·	Campanula rotundifolia
·	·	·	·	·	·	·	·	·	·	·	·	Cardamine flexuosa
·	·	·	2	·	2	·	·	·	·	·	·	C. pratensis
·	·	·	1	·	1	·	·	·	·	2	·	Cerastium vulgatum
·	·	·	·	·	·	·	·	·	·	·	·	Cirsium heterophyllum
·	·	·	·	·	·	·	·	·	·	·	·	C. palustre
·	·	·	·	·	3	·	4	·	·	·	·	Crepis paludosa
·	·	·	·	·	1	·	2	·	2	·	·	Epilobium palustre
·	2	·	3	1	3	·	3	3	3	·	3	Euphrasia sp.
·	·	·	·	·	1	·	·	·	·	·	·	Filipendula ulmaria

Table 29

	1	2	3	4	5	6	7	8	9	10	11
Galium boreale	·	1	·	·	·	·	·	·	·	·	·
G. hercynicum	2	2	1	2	2	·	2	1	+	·	·
G. verum	·	·	·	·	·	·	3	·	·	·	·
Geranium sylvaticum	·	1	·	·	·	·	·	·	·	·	·
Geum rivale	·	2	·	·	·	·	3	·	·	3	·
Hypericum pulchrum	·	·	·	·	·	·	1	·	·	·	·
Lathyrus montanus	·	·	·	·	·	·	2	·	·	·	·
Leontodon autumnalis	3	·	3	3	+	3	·	3	2	3	3
Linum catharticum	·	·	1	·	·	·	2	·	2	·	2
Lysimachia nemorum	·	·	·	·	·	·	3	·	·	·	2
Oxalis acetosella	1	·	·	·	·	·	·	·	·	·	·
Parnassia palustris	·	·	·	·	·	·	·	·	·	3	·
Pedicularis sylvatica	·	·	·	·	·	·	·	·	·	·	·
Pinguicula vulgaris	·	·	·	2	·	·	·	·	2	·	2
Plantago lanceolata	3	·	·	4	2	·	·	·	·	·	·
Polygala serpyllifolia	·	·	·	2	·	·	·	·	·	·	·
Polygonum viviparum	1	3	3	3	·	·	·	·	3	3	2
Potentilla erecta	·	2	3	3	3	3	3	3	3	3	3
Prunella vulgaris	+	·	+	2	·	·	3	·	·	3	1
Ranunculus acris	3	2	+	3	3	·	3	3	1	3	·
R. flammula	·	·	2	·	·	·	·	2	·	·	·
Rhinanthus minor agg.	·	·	·	2	·	·	·	·	·	2	·
Rumex acetosa	·	·	·	·	·	·	·	·	·	·	·
Sagina procumbens	·	·	·	·	·	·	·	·	·	·	·
Saxifraga aizoides	·	·	·	·	·	·	·	·	·	·	·
S. oppositifolia	·	·	·	·	·	·	·	·	·	·	·
S. stellaris	·	·	·	·	·	·	·	·	·	·	·
Senecio jacobaea	·	·	·	·	·	·	·	2	·	·	·
Silene acaulis	·	1	·	·	·	·	·	·	·	·	·
Stellaria graminea	·	·	+	·	·	·	·	·	·	·	·
Succisa pratensis	·	·	·	3	2	·	3	3	·	·	·
Taraxacum officinalis agg.	3	·	2	1	1	·	·	3	·	1	1
Thalictrum alpinum	3	2	+	·	·	·	·	·	3	3	3
Thymus drucei	·	3	·	·	·	·	·	·	·	·	·
Trifolium repens	·	·	3	+	3	·	1	·	3	·	·
Veronica chamaedrys	·	·	·	·	·	·	2	·	·	·	·
V. officinalis	·	·	·	·	2	·	·	·	·	·	·
Vicia sepium	2	·	·	·	·	·	·	·	·	2	·
Viola palustris	·	·	2	3	3	·	·	·	1	3	3
V. riviniana	3	3	·	·	2	·	·	3	·	3	·
Acrocladium cuspidatum	2	·	3	·	·	·	2	3	4	·	3
A. stramineum	·	·	·	·	·	2	·	·	·	·	·
Atrichum undulatum	·	·	1	·	·	·	1	·	·	·	·
Aulacomnium palustre	·	·	·	1	·	1	·	·	2	·	3
Brachythecium rivulare	2	·	·	·	·	·	·	·	3	·	·
Breutelia chrysocoma	·	·	·	·	·	·	·	·	·	·	·
Bryum pseudotriquetrum	·	·	1	·	·	·	·	·	2	2	1
Camptothecium nitens	·	·	·	·	·	·	·	·	·	·	·
Campylium stellatum	·	·	·	·	·	·	·	·	1	·	3
Cinclidium stygium	·	·	·	·	·	·	·	·	·	·	·
Climacium dendroides	·	·	2	·	·	·	2	1	·	·	·
Cratoneuron commutatum	·	·	·	·	·	·	·	·	·	·	·
C. filicinum	·	·	·	·	·	·	·	·	·	·	·
Ctenidium molluscum	·	·	1	·	·	·	·	·	·	·	·
Dicranum bonjeani	·	·	·	·	·	·	1	·	·	·	·
D. scoparium	·	·	·	·	·	·	·	·	·	·	·
Drepanocladus revolvens	·	·	·	·	·	·	·	·	·	·	2
D. uncinatus	·	·	·	·	·	·	·	·	·	·	·
Fissidens adianthoides	·	·	·	·	·	·	·	·	·	·	·
Hylocomium brevirostre	·	·	·	·	·	·	·	·	·	·	·
H. splendens	4	4	2	3	3	1	3	2	3	5	3
Mnium hornum	·	·	·	·	1	·	·	·	·	·	·
M. pseudopunctatum	·	·	·	·	2	2	·	2	4	·	3
M. punctatum	2	·	3	·	·	·	·	·	·	4	·
M. seligeri	·	·	·	·	·	·	·	·	2	1	·
M. undulatum	3	·	·	·	2	·	1	·	3	2	3
Philonotis calcarea	·	·	·	·	·	·	·	·	·	·	·
P. fontana	·	·	2	·	·	·	·	·	4	2	4
Pleurozium schreberi	·	2	·	·	·	·	·	·	·	·	·
Polytrichum alpinum	·	2	·	·	·	·	·	·	·	·	·
P. commune	·	·	·	·	·	·	·	·	·	·	·
Pseudoscleropodium purum	3	2	·	3	3	·	·	2	·	·	·
Ptilium crista-castrensis	1	·	·	·	·	·	·	·	·	·	·
Rhacomitrium lanuginosum	·	1	·	·	·	·	·	·	·	·	·
Rhytidiadelphus loreus	·	2	·	·	·	·	·	·	·	·	·
R. squarrosus	4	·	2	2	3	3	2	3	2	3	+
R. triquetrus	·	3	·	·	·	·	·	·	1	3	·
Sphagnum contortum	·	·	·	·	·	·	·	·	·	·	2
S. girgensohnii	·	1	·	·	·	4	·	·	+	·	·
S. nemoreum	·	·	·	·	·	·	·	·	·	·	·
S. palustre	·	·	·	3	·	·	·	·	·	·	·
S. plumulosum	·	2	·	2	·	·	·	·	·	·	3
S. recurvum	·	·	·	·	·	1	·	·	·	·	·
S. russowii	·	1	·	·	·	·	·	·	·	·	·
S. squarrosum	·	·	·	·	·	1	·	·	·	·	·
S. auriculatum	·	·	·	·	·	3	·	·	·	·	·
S. teres	·	·	·	·	·	·	·	·	+	·	·
S. warnstorfianum	·	2	·	·	·	·	·	·	+	·	4
Thuidium delicatulum	·	·	·	·	·	·	·	·	·	·	·
T. tamariscinum	3	3	·	1	4	2	·	1	·	2	·

(continued)

12	13	14	15	16	17	18	19	20	21	22	23	
.	.	.	.	.	.	.	.	.	.	.	.	Galium boreale
.	.	.	.	.	.	.	3	.	.	.	2	G. hercynicum
.	.	.	.	.	.	.	.	.	.	.	.	G. verum
.	.	.	.	.	.	.	.	.	.	.	.	Geranium sylvaticum
.	2	.	2	3	.	.	1	.	.	3	.	Geum rivale
.	.	.	.	.	.	.	.	.	.	.	.	Hypericum pulchrum
.	+	.	.	.	.	.	.	.	.	.	.	Lathyrus montanus
.	+	3	1	+	4	2	3	.	3	2	+	**Leontodon autumnalis**
2	.	2	3	1	.	.	2	.	.	.	.	Linum catharticum
.	.	.	.	.	3	.	.	.	3	.	.	Lysimachia nemorum
.	1	.	.	.	.	.	.	.	.	.	.	Oxalis acetosella
.	.	.	.	.	3	.	3	.	.	3	.	Parnassia palustris
.	.	.	.	.	.	.	.	.	1	.	.	Pedicularis sylvatica
2	.	2	2	2	+	.	1	2	.	.	2	Pinguicula vulgaris
.	.	.	.	.	.	.	2	.	3	.	.	Plantago lanceolata
.	.	.	.	.	.	.	.	.	.	.	.	Polygala serpyllifolia
2	3	3	3	3	+	3	3	3	.	3	4	**Polygonum viviparum**
3	.	.	4	3	2	2	4	.	4	.	.	**Potentilla erecta**
.	.	.	.	3	3	2	2	.	1	.	.	Prunella vulgaris
.	.	2	.	4	3	2	3	.	3	.	.	**Ranunculus acris**
1	.	.	.	.	2	.	.	.	2	.	.	R. flammula
.	.	.	.	.	+	.	1	.	1	.	.	Rhinanthus minor agg.
.	.	.	.	1	.	1	.	.	.	2	.	Rumex acetosa
.	.	.	.	.	.	1	.	.	.	.	.	Sagina procumbens
.	.	.	.	+	.	.	.	.	.	.	3	Saxifraga aizoides
.	.	.	.	.	.	.	.	1	.	.	.	S. oppositifolia
.	.	.	.	.	.	.	.	.	.	+	.	S. stellaris
.	.	.	.	.	.	.	.	.	.	.	.	Senecio jacobaea
.	.	.	.	.	.	.	.	.	.	.	.	Silene acaulis
.	.	.	.	.	.	.	.	.	.	.	.	Stellaria graminea
2	.	.	.	.	2	.	.	.	5	.	.	Succisa pratensis
2	1	.	.	+	.	.	3	.	.	1	.	Taraxacum officinalis agg.
4	3	3	3	4	4	.	3	4	.	3	4	**Thalictrum alpinum**
2	3	.	.	.	.	.	.	.	.	.	.	Thymus drucei
.	.	.	.	3	+	3	.	.	2	.	.	Trifolium repens
.	.	.	.	.	.	.	.	.	.	.	.	Veronica chamaedrys
.	.	.	.	.	.	.	.	.	.	.	.	V. officinalis
.	.	.	.	.	.	.	.	.	.	..	.	Vicia sepium
.	3	2	.	.	.	.	3	3	.	4	3	Viola palustris
.	.	.	.	.	.	.	.	.	.	.	.	V. riviniana
2	2	3	4	3	5	3	3	.	2	.	2	**Acrocladium cuspidatum**
.	.	.	.	.	.	.	.	.	.	.	.	A. stramineum
.	.	.	.	.	.	.	.	.	.	.	.	Atrichum undulatum
1	.	.	.	2	.	.	.	.	.	+	.	Aulacomnium palustre
.	2	.	.	.	3	.	.	.	2	.	.	Brachythecium rivulare
.	.	.	.	.	2	.	3	.	2	.	.	Breutelia chrysocoma
4	3	4	3	.	.	3	.	1	.	.	4	Bryum pseudotriquetrum
3	.	.	5	.	.	.	.	.	.	.	+	Camptothecium nitens
3	.	3	4	.	.	.	.	1	.	.	3	Campylium stellatum
.	2	1	2	.	.	.	1	1	.	.	3	Cinclidium stygium
.	.	.	.	.	.	3	.	.	.	.	.	Climacium dendroides
.	2	4	4	.	.	3	.	.	.	.	4	Cratoneuron commutatum
.	2	.	.	.	.	.	.	.	.	.	.	C. filicinum
4	1	.	.	.	3	1	.	5	1	.	.	Ctenidium molluscum
.	.	.	.	.	.	.	.	.	.	.	3	Dicranum bonjeani
.	.	.	.	.	.	.	2	2	.	.	.	D. scoparium
3	5	5	4	.	.	.	1	2	.	.	3	Drepanocladus revolvens
2	.	.	.	.	.	.	.	.	.	.	.	D. uncinatus
1	2	1	3	.	.	.	.	.	.	.	3	Fissidens adianthoides
.	.	.	.	.	.	.	2	.	.	.	.	Hylocomium brevirostre
3	3	4	.	3	4	+	4	3	4	5	3	**H. splendens**
.	.	.	.	.	.	.	1	1	.	.	.	Mnium hornum
.	.	1	2	1	.	2	1	1	.	.	.	M. pseudopunctatum
.	.	.	.	.	3	1	.	.	.	.	.	M. punctatum
.	.	.	.	.	.	.	.	.	.	.	2	M. seligeri
.	1	.	4	2	2	3	1	.	1	.	.	**M. undulatum**
.	.	.	3	.	.	.	.	.	.	.	.	Philonotis calcarea
2	2	4	3	2	1	2	.	1	.	+	2	**P. fontana**
.	.	.	.	.	.	.	.	.	.	.	.	Pleurozium schreberi
.	.	.	.	.	.	.	.	2	.	+	.	Polytrichum alpinum
.	.	.	.	.	.	.	.	.	1	.	.	P. commune
.	.	.	2	3	.	2	.	.	1	.	.	Pseudoscleropodium purum
.	.	.	.	.	.	.	3	.	.	.	.	Ptilium crista-castrensis
.	.	.	.	.	.	.	.	3	.	.	3	Rhacomitrium lanuginosum
.	.	.	.	.	.	.	3	2	.	3	.	Rhytidiadelphus loreus
3	2	2	.	2	4	+	3	.	3	6	1	**R. squarrosus**
2	2	1	.	1	4	.	3	3	.	.	3	R. triquetrus
.	.	.	.	.	.	.	.	.	.	.	.	Sphagnum contortum
.	.	.	.	.	.	.	.	.	.	+	.	S. girgensohnii
.	.	.	.	.	.	.	.	.	.	3	.	S. nemoreum
.	.	.	.	.	.	.	.	.	3	.	.	S. palustre
3	.	.	.	.	.	.	3	3	.	.	.	S. plumulosum
1	.	.	.	.	.	.	.	.	.	+	.	S. recurvum
1	.	.	.	.	.	.	.	.	.	.	.	S. russowii
.	.	.	.	.	.	.	.	.	.	.	.	S. squarrosum
.	.	.	.	.	.	.	.	.	4	.	.	S. auriculatum
.	.	.	.	.	.	.	.	.	.	.	.	S. teres
.	.	.	.	2	.	.	4	4	.	.	.	S. warnstorfianum
.	.	.	.	1	.	.	.	.	.	.	.	Thuidium delicatulum
.	.	.	.	.	2	.	5	.	2	.	.	T. tamariscinum

Table 29

	1	2	3	4	5	6	7	8	9	10	11
Aneura cf. sinuata	·	·	1	·	·	2	·	1	1	·	2
A. pinguis	·	·	·	1	·	·	·	·	2	1	·
Calypogeia trichomanis	·	·	·	·	·	·	·	·	·	·	2
Chiloscyphus pallescens	·	·	·	·	·	·	·	·	·	·	2
C. polyanthus	·	·	·	·	·	·	·	2	·	2	·
Lophocolea bidentata	2	·	·	2	2	2	1	3	2	3	·
Lophozia bantriensis	·	·	·	·	·	·	·	·	·	·	·
L. lycopodioides	·	2	·	·	·	·	·	·	·	·	·
L. quinquedentata	·	2	·	·	·	·	·	·	·	·	·
Pellia fabbroniana	·	·	1	·	·	2	1	1	3	·	3
Ptilidium ciliare	·	1	·	·	·	·	·	·	·	·	·
Scapania dentata	·	·	1	·	·	·	·	·	·	2	·
S. irrigua	·	·	·	·	·	3	·	·	·	·	3
S. nemorosa	·	·	·	·	·	·	·	·	·	1	·
Cladonia sylvatica	·	·	·	·	·	·	·	·	·	·	·
Peltidea aphthosa	·	·	·	·	·	·	·	·	·	·	·
Number of species	39	50	43	42	40	33	44	40	48	42	47

Number of species 128

(Average 43)

Number of species 73

(Average 46)

Lists 1–8 and 9–11 should be studied in conjunction with the species-poor facies of the two associations (Table 28).

LOCALITIES

1,10,19. Ben Lui, Argyll; 2,11. Carn Gorm, Glen Lyon, Perthshire; 3,9,14. Inverinain Burn, Glen Lyon, Perthshire; 4,22. Creag Meagaidh, Laggan, Inverness-shire; 5. Cairn Derg, Glen Clova, Angus; 6. Corrie Burn, Clova, Angus; 7. Braedownie, Clova, Angus; 8. Glen Fiadh, Clova, Angus; 12. Meall na Samhna, Glen Lochay, Perthshire; 13. Meall Ghaordie, Glen Lyon, Perthshire; 15. Creag Chaillaich, Killin,

(continued)

12	13	14	15	16	17	18	19	20	21	22	23	
3	.	.	.	.	.	.	I	I	.	.	.	Aneura cf. sinuata
.	.	I	I	.	.	.	I	.	.	.	2	A. pinguis
I	.	.	.	.	.	.	I	.	.	.	.	Calypogeia trichomanis
.	.	.	.	.	.	.	.	.	.	.	.	Chiloscyphus pallescens
2	.	.	.	.	.	.	.	.	.	.	.	C. polyanthus
.	.	.	.	I	I	.	2	.	I	.	.	Lophocolea bidentata
.	2	.	.	.	.	.	.	.	.	.	.	Lophozia bantriensis
.	.	.	.	.	.	.	.	.	.	.	.	L. lycopodioides
3	.	I	.	.	.	.	.	.	.	.	.	L. quinquedentata
.	.	.	.	.	I	2	.	I	.	.	.	Pellia fabbroniana
.	.	.	.	+	.	.	.	.	.	.	3	Ptilidium ciliare
.	.	.	.	.	.	.	.	.	.	.	.	Scapania dentata
I	.	.	.	.	.	.	.	.	.	.	.	S. irrigua
.	.	.	.	.	.	.	I	.	.	.	.	S. nemorosa
.	.	.	.	.	.	.	.	I	.	.	.	Cladonia sylvatica
.	.	.	.	.	.	.	.	I	.	.	.	Peltidea aphthosa
49	38	36	31	48	50	41	61	36	44	32	37	Number of species

Number of species 139

(Average 42)

Constancy class V   14
    ,,   ,, IV   9

Perthshire; 16. Glas Maol, Perthshire; 17. Sgurr na Lapaich, Glen Cannich, Inverness-shire; 18. Carn an Tuirc, Glen Clunie, Aberdeenshire; 20. Meall Garbh, Ben Lawers, Perthshire; 21. Sgurr nan Ceannaichean, Achnashellach, Ross-shire; 23. Meall nan Tarmachan, Killin, Perthshire.

Table 30: Deschampsietum caespitosae alpinum [species-poor facies commun

	1	2	3	4	5	6	7	8
Reference number	R57 022	R57 056	R57 081	R57 063	M58 046	R57 206	R57 161	R56 114
Map reference	9393 2365	9457 2353	7989 2565	8720 2210	8342 2166	7758 3337	7868 2433	8188 2020
Altitude (feet)	1800	1600	2850	2350	2500	2400	2900	3000
Aspect (degrees)	45	45	90	360	90	90	135	45
Slope (degrees)	30	35	35	35	35	40	35	30
Cover (per cent)	100	100	100	100	100	100	100	100
Height (centimetres)	–	–	–	–	15	–	15	–
Plot area (square metres)	4	4	4	4	4	4	4	4
Calluna vulgaris	.	.	.	.	.	.	.	.
Rubus idaeus	.	.	.	.	.	.	.	.
Vaccinium myrtillus	.	3	2	3	1	2	.	2
V. vitis-idaea	.	.	.	.	.	.	.	.
Athyrium filix-foemina	.	.	.	.	.	.	.	.
Blechnum spicant	1	.	.	2	2	.	.	2
Dryopteris abbreviata	.	.	.	.	.	.	.	.
D. austriaca	.	.	+	2	.	.	.	.
D. filix-mas	.	.	.	.	.	.	.	.
Lycopodium selago	.	.	.	.	.	.	.	.
Polystichum lonchitis	.	.	.	.	.	.	.	.
Selaginella selaginoides	.	.	.	.	.	.	.	.
Thelypteris dryopteris	.	.	.	.	.	.	.	.
T. oreopteris	.	.	.	.	.	.	1	.
Agrostis canina	4	4	.	2	2	3	.	3
A. tenuis	8	6	4	5	3	4	7	5
Anthoxanthum odoratum	4	4	4	3	4	4	4	3
Deschampsia caespitosa	5	4	8	6	7	8	7	6
D. flexuosa	4	5	3	3	2	.	.	4
Festuca ovina agg.	.	2	.	3	3	3	.	.
F. rubra	.	.	.	.	.	1	.	.
Helictotrichon pratense	.	.	.	.	.	.	.	.
Holcus mollis	.	.	.	.	.	.	.	.
Nardus stricta	.	2	+	5	.	6	3	3
Phleum commutatum	.	.	.	.	.	.	1	.
Poa pratensis	.	.	.	.	.	1	.	.
Carex bigelowii	3	3	1	.	2	.	.	3
C. binervis	.	.	.	3	.	.	.	.
C. capillaris	.	.	.	.	.	.	.	.
C. flacca	.	.	.	.	.	.	.	.
C. lepidocarpa	.	.	.	.	.	.	.	.
C. panicea	.	.	.	.	.	.	.	.
C. pilulifera	.	.	.	.	.	.	.	1
C. pulicaris	.	.	.	.	.	.	.	.
Coeloglossum viride	.	.	.	.	.	.	.	.
Juncus trifidus	.	.	.	.	.	.	.	.
Luzula multiflora	.	.	.	2	1	.	2	2
L. spicata	.	.	.	.	.	.	.	.
L. sylvatica	4	4	.	3	2	.	.	.
Orchis mascula	.	.	.	.	.	.	.	.
Trichophorum caespitosum	.	.	.	.	2	.	.	.
Achillea millefolium	.	.	.	.	.	.	.	.
Alchemilla alpina	.	3	3	3	+	3	3	2
A. filicaulis	.	.	.	.	.	.	2	.
A. glabra	.	.	+	.	.	2	.	.
A. vestita	.	.	.	.	.	.	.	.
Angelica sylvestris	.	.	.	.	.	1	.	.
Armeria maritima	.	.	.	.	.	.	.	.
Campanula rotundifolia	.	.	.	.	.	2	.	.
Cerastium alpinum	.	.	.	.	.	.	+	.
C. vulgatum	.	.	+	1	.	.	.	.
Cirsium heterophyllum	.	.	.	.	.	.	.	.
Crepis paludosa	.	.	.	.	.	.	.	.
Epilobium anagallidifolium	.	.	.	.	.	.	.	.
Euphrasia sp.	.	.	.	3	.	.	3	.
Filipendula ulmaria	.	.	.	.	.	+	.	.
Galium boreale	.	.	.	.	.	.	.	.
G. hercynicum	4	3	4	3	2	3	3	4
Geranium sylvaticum	.	.	.	.	.	2	.	.
Geum rivale	.	.	.	.	.	.	.	.
Gnaphalium supinum	.	.	.	.	.	.	.	.
Heracleum sphondylium	.	.	.	.	.	.	.	.
Hieracium sp.	.	.	.	.	.	.	.	.
Hypericum pulchrum	.	.	.	.	.	.	.	.
Lathyrus montanus	.	.	.	.	.	.	.	.
Leontodon autumnalis	.	.	.	.	.	.	.	.
Linum catharticum	.	.	.	.	.	.	.	.
Mercurialis perennis	.	.	.	.	.	.	.	.
Oxalis acetosella	3	3	3	3	.	3	.	.
Parnassia palustris	.	.	.	.	.	.	.	.
Polygonum viviparum	.	.	.	.	.	.	.	.
Potentilla erecta	.	3	2	.	3	.	.	4

(1–8); species-rich facies (9–16)]; Unclassified Deschampsia caespitosa
ities (17,18)

9	10	11	12	13	14	15	16	17	18	
R58 046	R58 008	R57 087	R58 016	R57 268	R57 225	R57 251	R56 055	M57 098	R57 162	Reference number
8809 2229	9502 2475	7866 2433	7272 2270	7765 3175	7773 3238	7768 3241	8583 1931	7992 2995	7875 2429	Map reference
2250	2000	2800	2000	2750	1900	1900	2600	4000	3600	Altitude (feet)
360	270	45	360	90	45	45	360	–	–	Aspect (degrees)
40	40	30	40	38	40	37	35	0	2	Slope (degrees)
100	100	90	100	100	100	100	95	90	100	Cover (per cent)
23	–	–	23	–	23	40	–	12	35	Height (centimetres)
4	4	4	4	4	4	4	4	4	4	Plot area (square metres)
	I					4				Calluna vulgaris
						3				Rubus idaeus
2	3			I	4	2	I			Vaccinium myrtillus
	2					2				V. vitis-idaea
					+					Athyrium filix-foemina
					3	I				Blechnum spicant
						2				Dryopteris abbreviata
		2			2					D. austriaca
					3					D. filix-mas
							I			Lycopodium selago
				+						Polystichum lonchitis
2	I	I	I	2						Selaginella selaginoides
					2					Thelypteris dryopteris
					4					T. oreopteris
3	3		3	2	3	2	2			**Agrostis canina**
4	4	5	4		6	4	4		3	**A. tenuis**
	3	5	4	4	4	3	3			**Anthoxanthum odoratum**
7	5	6	6	8	5	5	8	10	10	**Deschampsia caespitosa**
4	3	2	3		4	3	5	I		**D. flexuosa**
4	4	3	3	4		4	4		3	Festuca ovina agg.
2	4	4	4	3		2				F. rubra
				3						Helictotrichon pratense
					4					Holcus mollis
	5	4								Nardus stricta
		3								Phleum commutatum
										Poa pratensis
2		2	3				2	I	I	Carex bigelowii
										C. binervis
				I						C. capillaris
				4						C. flacca
				I						C. lepidocarpa
2	3									C. panicea
2				4						C. pilulifera
3										C. pulicaris
			I							Coeloglossum viride
							2			Juncus trifidus
2		2		2		I	I			Luzula multiflora
		I					2			L. spicata
3	3		3	2	5		4			L. sylvatica
	I									Orchis mascula
										Trichophorum caespitosum
2										Achillea millefolium
3	2	3	3	+	4	5	2			**Alchemilla alpina**
	3	3		5						A. filicaulis
			3	5		3				A. glabra
2				5	2					A. vestita
I	2		2		4					Angelica sylvestris
			I				+			Armeria maritima
		I	2		3	3				Campanula rotundifolia
		I								Cerastium alpinum
2	+	2		2		2	I		I	C. vulgatum
						5				Cirsium heterophyllum
			2		I					Crepis paludosa
		2								Epilobium anagallidifolium
3		3		I			3			Euphrasia sp.
2		2	3	3						Filipendula ulmaria
			2							Galium boreale
2		4			3	3	4		4	**G. hercynicum**
				2	3					Geranium sylvaticum
3	3		2	4	3					Geum rivale
								I		Gnaphalium supinum
					3					Heracleum sphondylium
			I		3					Hieracium sp.
	2				I					Hypericum pulchrum
					3					Lathyrus montanus
	2									Leontodon autumnalis
				2						Linum catharticum
					+					Mercurialis perennis
3			3	3	2	3	2			Oxalis acetosella
				2						Parnassia palustris
2		2		3						Polygonum viviparum
					3	3	+			Potentilla erecta

Table 30

	1	2	3	4	5	6	7	8
Prunella vulgaris								
Ranunculus acris				3	2	1		
Rumex acetosa	5	4	4	3		3	2	3
Sagina procumbens								
Saxifraga aizoides								
S. hypnoides								
S. oppositifolia								
S. stellaris								
Sedum rosea								
Sibbaldia procumbens			+				5	
Succisa pratensis						1		
Taraxacum officinalis agg.				1				
Thalictrum alpinum				3				
Thymus drucei								
Trollius europaeus								
Veronica alpina								
V. chamaedrys								
V. fruticans						2		
V. officinalis								
V. serpyllifolia			+					
Vicia sepium						+		
Viola palustris	1		3				3	4
V. riviniana		2		2	3	3		
Acrocladium cuspidatum								
Atrichum undulatum								
Breutelia chrysocoma								
Campylopus schwarzii								
Ctenidium molluscum								
Dicranella heteromalla								
Dicranum bonjeani								3
D. majus								
D. scoparium		3	2	2				
D. starkei								
Drepanocladus uncinatus			1					
Fissidens adianthoides								
Hookeria lucens								
Hylocomium splendens	6	5	4	5	3	1		4
Hypnum callichroum								
H. cupressiforme								
Mnium affine								
M. hornum		2						
M. punctatum					2			
M. rostratum								
M. undulatum								
Oligotrichum hercynicum								
Plagiothecium denticulatum								
P. undulatum				3	1			
Pleurozium schreberi	3		2	1	1			3
Pohlia sp.								
Polytrichum alpinum	3	4	1	3	1		2	4
P. urnigerum								
Pseudoscleropodium purum								
Ptilium crista-castrensis		3						
Rhacomitrium canescens							3	3
R. lanuginosum								
Rhytidiadelphus loreus	5	5	3	4	3			7
R. squarrosus	3	3	5	2	3	3	4	3
R. triquetrus	2							
Sphagnum girgensohnii					2			
S. nemoreum		3		3				
S. palustre					1			
S. plumulosum								
S. russowii					1			
S. squarrosum						6		
S. auriculatum						1		
Thuidium tamariscinum	4	5						
Alicularia scalaris								
Anastrepta orcadensis		3		3				3
Aneura pinguis		2						
Bazzania tricrenata								
Calypogeia trichomanis								
Chiloscyphus polyanthus								
Diplophyllum albicans						1		
Lophocolea bidentata								
Lophozia alpestris								3
L. floerkii								
L. lycopodioides	2		2					
L. quinquedentata				2				
L. ventricosa								
Mastigophora woodsii		3						
Pellia epiphylla								
P. fabbroniana								
Plagiochila asplenioides								
P. spinulosa								2
Ptilidium ciliare		2	2					
Scapania gracilis		2						

(*continued*)

	9	10	11	12	13	14	15	16	17	18	
	·	2	·	·	·	·	·	·	·	·	Prunella vulgaris
	3	3	2	4	3	1	·	3	·	·	**Ranunculus acris**
	3	3	4	2	3	2	3	4	·	·	**Rumex acetosa**
	·	·	1	·	·	·	·	·	·	·	Sagina procumbens
	·	1	·	·	2	·	·	·	·	·	Saxifraga aizoides
	·	·	+	2	2	·	·	·	·	·	S. hypnoides
	2	1	·	2	·	·	·	·	·	·	S. oppositifolia
	·	·	1	·	·	·	·	+	·	·	S. stellaris
	−	·	1	2	·	·	·	·	·	·	Sedum rosea
	−	·	3	·	·	·	·	·	·	·	Sibbaldia procumbens
	·	·	·	·	·	2	·	·	·	·	Succisa pratensis
	1	·	3	·	2	2	·	·	·	·	Taraxacum officinalis agg.
	3	3	·	3	·	·	·	·	·	·	Thalictrum alpinum
	4	3	·	·	·	·	+	·	·	·	Thymus drucei
	·	2	·	2	·	·	·	·	·	·	Trollius europaeus
	·	·	2	·	·	·	·	·	·	·	Veronica alpina
	·	·	·	·	·	2	·	·	·	·	V. chamaedrys
	·	·	·	·	1	·	·	·	·	·	V. fruticans
	·	·	·	·	1	·	3	·	·	·	V. officinalis
	·	·	·	·	·	·	·	·	·	·	V. serpyllifolia
	·	·	·	·	·	·	·	·	·	·	Vicia sepium
	·	·	·	·	·	·	·	·	·	·	Viola palustris
	3	3	2	2	3	3	3	·	·	·	**V. riviniana**
	·	·	·	·	3	·	·	·	·	·	Acrocladium cuspidatum
	2	·	·	·	·	·	·	·	·	·	Atrichum undulatum
	·	2	·	3	·	·	·	·	·	·	Breutelia chrysocoma
	·	·	·	·	·	·	·	2	·	·	Campylopus schwarzii
	2	2	·	2	·	1	·	·	·	·	Ctenidium molluscum
	·	·	1	·	·	·	·	3	·	·	Dicranella heteromalla
	·	·	·	·	1	·	·	·	·	·	Dicranum bonjeani
	2	·	·	·	·	3	3	3	·	·	D. majus
	·	·	·	1	·	·	·	3	·	·	D. scoparium
	·	·	·	·	·	·	·	·	3	·	D. starkei
	·	1	3	2	1	1	·	·	·	·	Drepanocladus uncinatus
	·	1	·	3	·	·	·	·	·	·	Fissidens adianthoides
	·	·	·	2	·	·	·	·	·	·	Hookeria lucens
	4	3	4	3	3	4	4	4	·	3	**Hylocomium splendens**
	1	·	2	·	3	1	·	2	·	·	Hypnum callichroum
	·	·	·	2	·	2	·	2	·	·	H. cupressiforme
	2	·	·	·	·	·	·	·	·	·	Mnium affine
	1	·	·	3	·	·	1	2	·	·	M. hornum
	1	·	·	2	·	·	·	1	·	·	M. punctatum
	·	·	·	·	3	1	·	·	·	·	M. rostratum
	2	1	·	2	2	·	·	·	·	·	M. undulatum
	·	·	·	·	·	·	·	2	2	·	Oligotrichum hercynicum
	1	·	·	·	·	·	·	·	·	·	Plagiothecium denticulatum
	1	·	·	3	·	1	2	2	·	·	P. undulatum
	·	·	·	·	·	·	·	2	·	3	Pleurozium schreberi
	·	·	·	·	·	·	·	·	3	·	Pohlia sp.
	3	2	2	2	·	2	1	4	2	3	**Polytrichum alpinum**
	·	3	·	·	·	·	·	·	·	·	P. urnigerum
	2	3	·	2	·	·	·	·	·	·	Pseudoscleropodium purum
	·	·	·	3	·	·	2	·	·	·	Ptilium crista-castrensis
	·	2	·	·	·	·	·	·	·	·	Rhacomitrium canescens
	·	·	·	·	·	·	·	2	·	·	R. lanuginosum
	3	2	4	4	·	2	3	4	·	3	**Rhytidiadelphus loreus**
	2	3	3	3	·	3	3	2	·	3	**R. squarrosus**
	3	3	2	3	3	·	·	·	·	·	R. triquetrus
	·	·	·	·	·	·	·	·	·	·	Sphagnum girgensohnii
	·	·	1	2	·	·	·	3	·	·	S. nemoreum
	·	·	·	·	·	·	·	·	·	·	S. palustre
	1	·	·	·	·	·	·	·	·	·	S. plumulosum
	·	·	·	·	·	·	·	·	·	·	S. russowii
	1	·	·	·	·	·	·	2	·	·	S. squarrosum
	·	·	·	·	·	·	·	2	·	·	S. auriculatum
	3	3	·	3	1	3	·	2	·	·	Thuidium tamariscinum
	·	·	·	·	·	·	·	1	·	·	Alicularia scalaris
	·	·	·	·	·	·	·	3	·	·	Anastrepta orcadensis
	·	1	·	·	·	·	·	·	·	·	Aneura pinguis
	·	·	·	·	·	·	·	3	·	·	Bazzania tricrenata
	1	·	·	·	·	·	·	·	·	·	Calypogeia trichomanis
	·	·	·	·	·	1	·	·	·	·	Chiloscyphus polyanthus
	·	·	2	1	·	·	·	2	·	·	Diplophyllum albicans
	2	2	·	2	2	1	3	·	·	·	Lophocolea bidentata
	·	·	·	·	·	·	·	·	3	·	Lophozia alpestris
	·	·	·	·	·	·	·	·	·	·	L. floerkii
	·	·	3	·	·	2	2	·	·	·	L. lycopodioides
	2	·	·	2	·	·	2	·	·	·	L. quinquedentata
	·	·	·	·	·	·	·	3	·	·	L. ventricosa
	·	·	·	·	·	·	·	·	·	·	Mastigophora woodsii
	·	·	·	·	·	·	·	1	·	·	Pellia epiphylla
	2	1	·	2	·	·	·	·	·	·	P. fabbroniana
	·	·	·	1	2	·	1	·	·	·	Plagiochila asplenioides
	·	·	·	1	·	·	·	·	·	·	P. spinulosa
	·	·	·	·	·	·	·	·	·	2	Ptilidium ciliare
	·	·	·	·	·	·	·	·	·	·	Scapania gracilis

Table 30

	1	2	3	4	5	6	7	8
S. nimbosa	.	.	.	.	.	.	.	.
S. ornithopodioides	.	2	.	.	.	.	.	.
Cladonia bellidiflora	.	.	.	.	.	.	.	1
C. coccifera	.	.	.	.	.	.	.	1
C. gracilis	.	.	.	.	.	.	.	.
C. impexa	.	.	.	.	1	.	.	.
C. rangiferina	.	.	.	.	.	.	.	1
C. sylvatica	.	.	.	.	.	.	.	2
C. uncialis	.	.	.	.	.	.	.	2
Peltidea leucophlebia	.	.	.	.	.	.	.	.
Peltigera canina	.	.	.	.	.	.	.	.
Number of species (169)	20	31	27	33	32	24	18	31

(Average 27)

Constancy class V 12 } for the association.
   ,,   ,, IV 8

LOCALITIES

1. Carn Dearg, Reay Forest, Sutherland; 2. Meall Horn, Reay Forest, Sutherland; 3. Geal Charn, Monadhliath, Inverness-shire; 4. Sgurr Mor, Fannich, Ross-shire; 5. Sgurr na Lapaich, Glen Cannich, Inverness-shire; 6. Loch Brandy, Clova, Angus; 7,11,18. Craig Meagaidh, Laggan, Inverness-shire; 8. Beinn Fhada, Kintail, Inverness-shire; 9. Beinn Enaiglair, Braemore, Ross-shire; 10. Ben Hope, Sutherland;

(*continued*)

9	10	11	12	13	14	15	16	17	18	
.	.	.	.	.	.	.	+	.	.	S. nimbosa
.	.	.	.	.	.	.	2	.	.	S. ornithopodioides
.	.	.	.	.	.	.	2	.	.	Cladonia bellidiflora
.	.	.	.	.	.	.	.	.	.	C. coccifera
.	.	.	.	.	.	.	1	.	.	C. gracilis
.	.	.	.	.	.	.	.	.	.	C. impexa
.	.	.	.	.	.	.	.	.	.	C. rangiferina
1	.	.	.	.	.	.	.	.	.	C. sylvatica
.	.	.	.	.	.	.	.	.	.	C. uncialis
1	.	.	.	.	.	.	.	.	.	Peltidea leucophlebia
1	.	1	1	.	.	.	.	.	.	Peltigera canina
58	47	46	55	47	52	39	53	9	12	Number of species (169)
			(Average 50)							

12. Ben Lui, Perthshire; 13. Caenlochan Glen, Angus; 14,15. Glen Doll, Angus; 16. Liathach, Torridon, Ross-shire; 17. Aonach Beag, Nevis hills, Inverness-shire.

Table 31: Luzula sylvatica Grassland nodum

	1	2	3	4	5	6	7
Reference number	M58 029	M58 040	M58 049	M57 013	M58 005	R58 009	R58 013
Map reference	–	–	7633 1537	8006 1338	9472 2584	9502 2475	7396 2321
Altitude (feet)	1400	1200	1700	1750	1800	2000	2200
Aspect (degrees)	90	360	180	315	90	270	270
Slope (degrees)	15	3	5	3	40	40	28
Cover (per cent)	100	100	100	100	100	100	95
Height (centimetres)	20	–	14	–	–	–	15
Plot area (square metres)	4	4	4	4	4	4	4
Empetrum nigrum	.	.	.	+	.	.	.
Vaccinium myrtillus	.	.	4	+	4	5	6
V. vitis-idaea	.	.	.	.	+	3	.
Blechnum spicant	.	.	.	.	1	2	.
Agrostis canina	.	.	.	.	.	+	4
A. tenuis	3	2	2	.	3	4	2
Anthoxanthum odoratum	1	3	.	3	.	3	2
Deschampsia caespitosa	.	.	.	.	.	5	2
D. flexuosa	.	3	2	2	2	3	4
Festuca ovina agg.	.	.	2	3	.	4	3
F. rubra	.	3	.	.	.	3	.
Nardus stricta	.	.	2	4	2	+	1
Carex bigelowii	2	.	.	.	.	.	+
C. binervis	1	.	+	.	.	.	.
C. echinata	.	.	.	1	.	.	.
C. nigra	.	.	2	2	.	.	.
Eriophorum angustifolium	.	.	.	.	.	.	.
E. vaginatum	.	.	.	1	.	.	.
Juncus squarrosus	.	.	6	2	3	.	.
Luzula multiflora	1	.	.	.	.	.	.
L. sylvatica	9	8	8	8	8	5	5
Alchemilla alpina	.	.	.	.	.	2	2
Cerastium vulgatum	1	1	.	.	.	.	.
Galium hercynicum	.	.	3	.	2	.	3
Melampyrum pratense	.	.	.	.	1	.	.
Oxalis acetosella	.	.	.	.	3	.	2
Potentilla erecta	3	3	3	4	2	.	.
Ranunculus acris	.	.	.	.	.	2	.
Rumex acetosa	4	4	.	2	2	2	1
R. acetosella	+	+	.	.	.	.	.
Dicranum scoparium	.	.	1	.	1	2	1
Eurhynchium praelongum	.	.	.	1	.	.	.
Hylocomium splendens	.	.	3	2	3	5	4
Hypnum cupressiforme	.	.	1	.	.	3	3
Mnium hornum	.	.	.	.	.	2	.
Plagiothecium sylvaticum	.	.	.	.	1	.	.
P. undulatum	.	.	3	.	2	.	3
Pleurozium schreberi	.	.	3	2	1	3	3
Polytrichum alpinum	.	.	.	.	.	3	.
P. commune	.	.	2	+	2	.	4
Pseudoscleropodium purum	.	.	.	3	3	1	.
Ptilium crista-castrensis	.	.	.	.	.	.	2
Rhacomitrium lanuginosum	.	.	1	.	.	3	.
Rhytidiadelphus loreus	2	.	3	1	4	6	4
R. squarrosus	1	1	2	7	4	3	.
R. triquetrus	.	.	.	.	.	2	.
Thuidium tamariscinum	.	.	.	.	.	4	.
Anastrepta orcadensis	.	.	.	.	.	1	2
Diplophyllum albicans	.	.	.	.	.	1	.
Frullania tamarisci	.	.	.	.	.	1	.
Lophocolea bidentata	.	.	.	1	.	.	.
Lophozia ventricosa	.	.	1	.	.	.	.
Ptilidium ciliare	.	.	1	.	.	.	.
Cladonia gracilis	.	.	.	.	.	2	.
C. pyxidata	.	.	.	.	.	.	2
C. sylvatica	.	.	.	.	+	.	.
Peltigera canina	.	.	.	.	+	1	.
Number of species (57)	12	10	22	22	24	32	24

(Average 21)

LOCALITIES

1. Conachair, St. Kilda; 2. Mullach Bi, St. Kilda; 3. Ben Hiant, Ardnamurchan; 4. Fionchra, Isle of Rhum; 5. Ben Loyal, Sutherland; 6. Ben Hope, Sutherland; 7. Ben Dorain, Bridge of Orchy, Argyll.

Table 32: Low-alpine Nardus noda—1. Nardus-Trichophorum nodum Pleurozium nodum (12–16); 4. Nardus-

	1	2	3	4	5	6	7	8	9	10	11
Reference number	M56 028	M56 030	M56 106	M56 027	M56 036	M55 044	M55 030	M55 041	R57 190	R57 083	M55 024
Map reference	7978 2998	7980 2995	8013 3047	8002 3016	8609 1989	8636 1975	8598 1985	8635 1978	7781 2655	7866 2441	8608 1989
Altitude (feet)	3600	3500	3400	2750	2000	2750	2200	2700	2900	2400	2100
Aspect (degrees)	180	180	135	135	45	315	360	135	45	225	90
Slope (degrees)	5	3	5	12	5	2	2	2	3	5	2
Cover (per cent)	95	90	100	100	100	100	100	100	100	100	100
Height (centimetres)	2	2	10	5	10	10	12	8	–	–	7
Plot area (square metres)	4	4	4	4	4	4	4	4	4	4	4
Calluna vulgaris				4	2						3
Empetrum hermaphroditum	+	4	4	4	1	3	4	2			2
Erica cinerea				4							
Juniperus nana				+	1		+				+
Loiseleuria procumbens	+	+		5	+						
Salix herbacea					+						
Vaccinium myrtillus	4	4	4		3	1	2	2	3		2
V. uliginosum			4	3	4	4	3	4			
V. vitis-idaea											
Lycopodium alpinum		2	1	4	3	+		3			
L. selago				1	2			2			3
Agrostis canina										4	
A. tenuis				1		3	2		3		4
Deschampsia caespitosa											
D. flexuosa				2		+	3		3	1	1
Festuca ovina agg.										3	
Molinia caerulea				4						3	2
Nardus stricta	9	7	5	3	6	9	8	8	6	7	4
Carex bigelowii	3	3	3			1	3	2	3	2	
C. panicea								1			
C. pilulifera			3							2	
Eriophorum angustifolium									+	2	
E. vaginatum											+
Juncus squarrosus					1	2	+	1			1
Luzula multiflora										1	
L. sylvatica							+				
Narthecium ossifragum				2	1			2	2	3	3
Orchis ericetorum					2						
Trichophorum caespitosum	4	5	5	5	5	2	4	5	8	7	8
Alchemilla alpina	1										
Euphrasia frigida								1			
Galium hercynicum					+		2		2	1	
Leontodon autumnalis											
Melampyrum pratense							1				
Potentilla erecta			2	3	3	3	2	3		4	5
Rumex acetosa											
Solidago virgaurea					2		1				
Succisa pratensis					2						
Viola palustris											
V. riviniana										3	
Dicranodontium uncinatum											
Dicranum fuscescens			1								
D. scoparium			2					1		1	
Hylocomium splendens										4	
Hypnum cupressiforme						1	1	+		4	
Leucobryum glaucum			1								
Plagiothecium undulatum											
Pleurozium schreberi			2			1		+		3	
Polytrichum alpinum									3		
P. commune							1				+
P. gracile											
P. juniperinum								1			
Rhacomitrium lanuginosum	2	6	2	1	7	4	4	5			+
Rhytidiadelphus loreus						1	1	1		2	
R. squarrosus										3	
Sphagnum compactum									1	2	
S. nemoreum										2	2
S. russowii											
Alicularia scalaris								1			
Anastrepta orcadensis							4	1			
Anastrophyllum donianum						4					
Bazzania triangularis							4				
B. tricrenata											
Calypogeia trichomanis											
Diplophyllum albicans	1					1					
Leptoscyphus taylori						1					
Lophozia alpestris								1			
L. floerkii	2		1					1			
Pleurozia purpurea					3	3					
Ptilidium ciliare						3		+			
Scapania gracilis											
S. nemorosa						3					
S. nimbosa											

(1–8); 2. Related Trichophorum-Nardus communities (9–11); 3. Nardus-Rhacomitrium provisional nodum (17–19)

12	13	14	15	16	17	18	19	
P52	P52	M57	R56	R56	R57	M55	M55	Reference number
007	063	029	116	023	040	005	029	
7397	7424	7323	8194	8748	9329	8639	8598	Map reference
2567	2615	2136	2008	2009	2408	1932	1985	
2650	3100	2800	2900	3100	2300	2300	2200	Altitude (feet)
240	50	180	315	135	–	–	360	Aspect (degrees)
3	2	5	7	10	0	0	2	Slope (degrees)
100	100	100	100	100	100	100	100	Cover (per cent)
12	8	–	–	–	–	12	12	Height (centimetres)
2	2	4	4	4	4	4	4	Plot area (square metres)
·	·	·	·	·	·	+	·	Calluna vulgaris
·	·	·	1	·	·	1	4	**Empetrum hermaphroditum**
·	·	·	·	·	·	·	·	Erica cinerea
·	·	·	·	·	·	·	·	Juniperus nana
·	·	·	·	·	·	·	·	Loiseleuria procumbens
·	·	·	·	·	·	·	·	Salix herbacea
·	·	2	3	3	2	3	3	**Vaccinium myrtillus**
·	·	·	·	·	·	·	·	V. uliginosum
·	·	·	1	·	·	+	·	V. vitis-idaea
·	·	·	·	2	·	1	·	Lycopodium alpinum
·	·	·	·	·	·	·	·	L. selago
·	·	·	3	·	·	·	·	Agrostis canina
2	·	1	·	·	·	·	3	A. tenuis
·	·	5	3	6	·	·	·	Deschampsia caespitosa
·	1	+	3	3	·	·	·	D. flexuosa
·	·	3	3	·	·	·	·	Festuca ovina agg.
·	·	·	·	·	·	·	·	Molinia caerulea
9	9	8	8	8	6	8	9	**Nardus stricta**
3	3	·	3	3	3	2	3	**Carex bigelowii**
·	·	2	·	·	·	·	·	C. panicea
·	·	2	·	·	·	·	·	C. pilulifera
·	·	·	·	·	·	·	·	Eriophorum angustifolium
·	·	·	·	·	·	·	·	E. vaginatum
·	·	1	2	·	·	+	·	Juncus squarrosus
·	·	·	·	·	·	·	·	Luzula multiflora
·	·	·	·	1	·	·	·	L. sylvatica
·	·	·	·	·	·	·	·	Narthecium ossifragum
·	·	·	·	·	·	·	·	Orchis ericetorum
·	·	·	·	·	·	2	·	**Trichophorum caespitosum**
·	·	·	·	2	·	·	·	Alchemilla alpina
·	·	·	2	·	·	·	·	Euphrasia frigida
4	3	1	3	3	3	4	1	**Galium hercynicum**
·	·	·	1	·	·	·	·	Leontodon autumnalis
·	·	·	·	·	·	·	·	Melampyrum pratense
·	·	3	3	1	·	1	3	Potentilla erecta
1	·	·	·	·	·	·	·	Rumex acetosa
·	·	·	·	·	·	·	2	Solidago virgaurea
·	·	·	·	·	·	·	·	Succisa pratensis
·	·	·	3	2	·	·	·	Viola palustris
·	·	2	·	·	·	·	·	V. riviniana
·	·	·	·	·	·	1	·	Dicranodontium uncinatum
·	3	·	·	·	·	·	·	Dicranum fuscescens
1	1	·	3	2	·	·	2	D. scoparium
·	·	4	6	5	2	·	·	Hylocomium splendens
·	·	·	3	·	2	1	1	**Hypnum cupressiforme**
·	·	·	·	·	·	·	·	Leucobryum glaucum
1	·	·	3	·	·	·	·	Plagiothecium undulatum
5	2	1	3	3	3	3	·	**Pleurozium schreberi**
·	2	·	3	3	2	·	·	Polytrichum alpinum
2	·	·	·	·	·	·	+	P. commune
·	·	·	·	·	·	1	·	P. gracile
·	·	·	·	·	·	·	·	P. juniperinum
·	3	1	3	3	8	5	5	**Rhacomitrium lanuginosum**
2	3	3	4	5	2	2	1	**Rhytidiadelphus loreus**
5	·	2	·	2	·	·	·	R. squarrosus
·	·	·	·	·	·	·	·	Sphagnum compactum
·	·	·	3	·	·	2	·	S. nemoreum
·	·	·	2	·	·	·	·	S. russowii
·	·	·	·	·	·	·	·	Alicularia scalaris
·	1	·	3	·	2	·	3	Anastrepta orcadensis
·	·	·	2	·	·	·	·	Anastrophyllum donianum
·	·	·	·	·	·	·	3	Bazzania triangularis
·	·	·	·	·	1	·	·	B. tricrenata
·	·	·	2	·	·	·	·	Calypogeia trichomanis
·	·	·	·	·	·	·	·	Diplophyllum albicans
·	·	·	·	·	·	·	·	Leptoscyphus taylori
·	·	·	·	·	·	·	·	Lophozia alpestris
·	·	·	1	4	1	·	·	L. floerkii
·	·	·	·	·	·	·	2	Pleurozia purpurea
2	1	3	3	4	2	1	·	**Ptilidium ciliare**
·	·	·	·	·	2	2	·	Scapania gracilis
·	·	·	·	·	·	·	3	S. nemorosa
·	·	·	1	·	·	·	·	S. nimbosa

Table 32

	1	2	3	4	5	6	7	8	9	10	11
Cetraria aculeata	.	.	.	.	.	I	.	.	.	.	.
C. islandica	3	3	3	3	3	3	2	3	.	.	I
C. bellidiflora	3	2	.	I	.	2	I	2	.	.	.
C. coccifera	.	I	.	I	.	.	.	.	.	.	.
C. gracilis	I	.	+	2	.	3	I	.	.	.	.
C. impexa	.	.	.	.	.	.	4	.	.	.	.
C. pyxidata	2	.	.	.	.	I	.	+	.	.	.
C. rangiferina agg.	I	.	2	I	2	I	2	.	.	.	.
C. sylvatica	I	3	.	2	3	.	.	.	.	.	+
C. tenuis	.	.	.	.	.	I	.	3	.	.	.
C. uncialis	I	3	2	4	3	2	2	3	.	.	2
Ochrolechia frigida	.	.	.	+	.	+	.	.	.	.	.
O. tartarea	.	.	.	+	.	.	.	.	.	.	.
Sphaerophorus globosus	.	.	.	.	.	.	.	.	.	.	.
Number of species	17	13	19	25	24	27	28	31	11	21	20

Number of species 62 (Average 23) Number of species 36 (Average 17)

LOCALITIES

1,2. Ben Macdhui, Cairngorms; 3. Beinn a' Chaoruinn, Cairngorms; 4. Coire Etchachan, Cairngorms; 5-8,11,19. Beinn Eighe, Ross-shire; 9. A' Bhuideanach Bheag, Drumochter, Inverness-shire; 10. Creag Meagaidh, Laggan, Inverness-shire; 12. Meall nan Tarmachan,

(continued)

12	13	14	15	16	17	18	19	
·	·	·	·	·	·	·	+	Cetraria aculeata
·	1	·	2	1	3	3	3	**C. islandica**
·	·	·	·	·	·	·	1	C. bellidiflora
·	·	·	·	·	·	·	·	C. coccifera
·	·	·	·	2	1	·	1	C. gracilis
·	·	·	·	·	·	·	4	C. impexa
·	·	·	·	·	·	·	·	C. pyxidata
·	·	·	·	·	·	·	2	C. rangiferina agg.
·	3	·	1	2	2	·	·	C. sylvatica
·	·	·	·	·	·	1	·	C. tenuis
·	·	·	·	1	2	2	1	**C. uncialis**
·	·	·	·	·	·	·	·	Ochrolechia frigida
·	·	·	·	·	·	·	·	O. tartarea
·	·	·	·	·	·	·	+	Sphaerophorus globosus
12	14	18	33	24	19	23	25	Number of species

Number of species 46
(Average 20)

Number of species 41
(Average 22)

Perthshire; 13. Ben Lawers, Perthshire; 14. Beinn Eunaich, Dalmally, Argyll; 15. Beinn Fhada, Kintail, Ross-shire; 16. A' Mhaighdean, Fisherfield Forest, Ross-shire; 17. Ben Hee, Sutherland; 18. Beinn a' Chearcaill, Kinlochewe Forest, Ross-shire.

Table 33: Nardetum medio-alpinum

	1	2	3	4	5	6
Reference number	M56 108	M57 081	M57 091	M58 061	M58 063	M58 068
Map reference	7986 2995	8022 3138	7924 2958	8023 2984	8047 3011	8043 3006
Altitude (feet)	4000	3500	3550	3900	3700	4000
Aspect (degrees)	180	—	90	90	90	360
Slope (degrees)	4	0	2	4	4	5
Cover (per cent)	100	100	100	100	100	95
Height (centimetres)	5	—	—	8	—	10
Plot area (square metres)	4	4	4	4	4	4
Vaccinium myrtillus	.	.	.	.	3	.
Lycopodium selago	.	.	.	.	2	.
Deschampsia caespitosa	.	.	.	+	.	.
D. flexuosa	2	2	3	.	.	.
Nardus stricta	10	10	10	10	10	10
Carex bigelowii	3	3	3	3	3	3
Juncus trifidus	+	.	.	.	.	.
Trichophorum caespitosum	.	2	.	1	.	.
Galium hercynicum	.	2	.	.	.	.
Dicranum fuscescens	1	2	2	7	5	3
D. scoparium	3	.	.	.	.	5
D. starkei	1	.	.	.	.	.
Pohlia nutans	2	.	.	.	.	.
Polytrichum alpinum	1	1	.	.	.	1
P. norvegicum	+	.	.	.	.	.
Rhacomitrium heterostichum	1	.	.	.	.	.
R. lanuginosum	.	2	1	.	2	2
Diplophyllum albicans	.	.	.	.	4	2
Lepidozia sp.	.	.	1	.	.	.
Lophozia alpestris	1	1	.	.	.	1
L. floerkii	.	.	.	1	3	3
Lophozia sp.	.	.	1	.	.	.
Pleuroclada albescens	.	1	.	.	.	.
Ptilidium ciliare	2	3	1	4	.	2
Cetraria hiascens	2	2	1	2	+	1
C. islandica	1	3	2	2	3	3
Cladonia bellidiflora	2	3	3	3	2	3
C. coccifera	.	.	1	.	.	.
C. delessertii	+	2	2	+	3	3
C. gracilis	.	2	1	2	.	1
C. pyxidata	1	.	.	2	1	2
C. rangiferina agg.	.	.	1	.	1	.
C. sylvatica	2	2	3	2	2	3
C. uncialis	.	2	2	1	.	.
Ochrolechia frigida	.	1	.	.	.	.
Number of species (35)	19	19	15	15	15	16

(Average 16·5)

Constancy class V 8
,, ,, IV 0

LOCALITIES

1. Allt Clach nan Taillear, Ben Macdhui, Cairngorms; 2. Ben Avon, Cairngorms; 3. Beinn Bhrotain, Cairngorms; 4. Cairnlochan, Cairngorms; 5,6. Cairngorm, Inverness-shire.

Table 34: Polytricheto-Caricetum bigelowii [rhytidiadelphetosum (1–

	1	2	3	4	5	6	7	8	9
Reference number	P52 214	P52 224	P52 225	P52 229	P52 088	M56 110	M56 111	M56 117	M56 127
Map reference	7418 2640	7415 2642	7415 2642	7415 2642	7413 2633	7986 2995	7999 2991	7985 3093	7851 3219
Altitude (feet)	2850	3350	3300	3300	3250	4000	4100	3800	3300
Aspect (degrees)	–	350	320	320	120	180	–	45	90
Slope (degrees)	0	5	10	10	7	2	0	4	3
Cover (per cent)	80	100	80	80	100	100	100	100	100
Height (centimetres)	–	–	–	–	–	5	5	5	2
Plot area (square metres)	4	4	4	4	4	4	4	4	4
Empetrum hermaphroditum									
Salix herbacea	3	1	2	3		3	3		
Vaccinium myrtillus	1								
V. uliginosum									1
Lycopodium selago					1				
Agrostis canina									
A. tenuis	4	3	3	3	4				1
Anthoxanthum odoratum					6				
Deschampsia alpina							3	2	
D. caespitosa	1	3	4	3	3	4			
D. flexuosa									2
Festuca ovina agg.	4	1	2	2					2
Nardus stricta					3	2	1	1	
Poa trivialis									
Carex bigelowii	3	2	3		2	4	10	6	9
Juncus trifidus								1	
Luzula spicata						+		+	
Alchemilla alpina	2	2	2	2	3				
Cerastium vulgatum	1		1	2					
Cherleria sedoides	1		4	6					
Euphrasia frigida	2		3						
Euphrasia sp.				3					
Galium hercynicum	3	2	4	3	3				
Gnaphalium supinum	1	1							
Oxalis acetosella	2		2	3					
Rumex acetosa	3		3	3	3				
Saxifraga stellaris		1							
Silene acaulis			2						
Trientalis europaea									
Viola palustris	3	2	3	3					
Conostomum tetragonum		1				1	1	+	
Dicranum fuscescens									
D. molle									
D. scoparium			4	2		3	2	2	
D. starkei		2							4
Ditrichum homomallum			1						
Drepanocladus uncinatus									
Hylocomium splendens	2		3	3					
Oligotrichum hercynicum		2							
Pleurozium schreberi	5		3	2	3				
Pohlia nutans		3	1					1	
Polytrichum alpinum	8	9	8	9	7	7	3	7	4
P. norvegicum									
Rhacomitrium canescens									
R. fasciculare							1		
R. heterostichum		4			3		3		
R. lanuginosum		1	1						
Rhytidiadelphus loreus	5	1	3	4					
R. squarrosus	1				6				
Sphagnum compactum		1							
S. russowii	1	2		1					
Alicularia scalaris	1	4		1					
Cephalozia ambigua		1							
C. bicuspidata		1	1						
Diplophyllum albicans	1	2							
Leptoscyphus taylori									
Lophozia alpestris	1					1	2	2	
L. floerkii									
Lophozia sp.									
L. ventricosa		2							
Pleuroclada albescens		1						1	
Ptilidium ciliare		1	1					1	2
Cetraria hiascens							2	2	2
C. islandica		2	1				1		+
Cladonia bellidiflora		3		1					3
C. cervicornis									
C. coccifera								1	1
Cladonia degenerans								2	
C. delessertii									

5); typicum (6–16)]; Related Deschampsia caespitosa community (17)

10	11	12	13	14	15	16	17	
M56	M57	R57	R57	R57	R57	R57	M57	Reference number
105	043	165	263	105	193	281	044	
8013	7715	7874	7737	7720	7780	7757	7715	Map reference
3046	2197	2425	3267	2494	2654	3350	2197	
3400	4050	3600	2950	3600	2950	2800	4050	Altitude (feet)
135	270	180	360	360	45	–	180	Aspect (degrees)
30	3	3	12	3	5	0	5	Slope (degrees)
100	100	100	100	100	100	100	100	Cover (per cent)
3	–	–	–	–	–	–	35	Height (centimetres)
4	4	4	4	4	4	4	4	Plot area (square metres)
+	·	·	·	·	·	·	·	Empetrum hermaphroditum
·	·	·	6	·	·	·	·	Salix herbacea
·	·	·	·	·	·	+	·	Vaccinium myrtillus
·	·	·	·	·	·	·	·	V. uliginosum
+	·	·	·	·	2	·	·	Lycopodium selago
·	·	·	·	·	·	+	·	Agrostis canina
·	·	·	3	3	·	·	·	A. tenuis
·	·	·	·	·	·	·	·	Anthoxanthum odoratum
·	·	·	·	·	·	·	·	Deschampsia alpina
1	2	·	·	2	·	2	8	D. caespitosa
·	2	·	2	3	6	2	·	D. flexuosa
·	·	·	·	·	·	2	·	Festuca ovina agg.
2	·	·	·	·	·	·	·	Nardus stricta
·	·	·	3	·	·	·	·	Poa trivialis
9	8	9	8	8	8	9	4	Carex bigelowii
2	·	·	·	·	·	·	·	Juncus trifidus
1	·	·	·	·	·	·	·	Luzula spicata
·	·	·	·	·	·	·	·	Alchemilla alpina
·	·	·	·	·	·	·	·	Cerastium vulgatum
·	·	·	·	·	·	·	·	Cherleria sedoides
·	·	·	·	·	·	·	·	Euphrasia frigida
·	·	·	·	·	·	·	·	Euphrasia sp.
·	·	·	2	·	·	·	·	Galium hercynicum
1	·	·	·	·	·	·	+	Gnaphalium supinum
·	·	·	·	·	·	·	·	Oxalis acetosella
·	·	·	·	·	·	·	·	Rumex acetosa
·	·	·	·	1	·	·	·	Saxifraga stellaris
+	·	·	·	·	·	·	·	Silene acaulis
·	·	·	2	·	·	·	·	Trientalis europaea
·	·	·	·	·	·	·	·	Viola palustris
·	·	·	·	·	·	·	·	Conostomum tetragonum
·	1	3	4	3	2	4	3	Dicranum fuscescens
·	3	·	·	·	·	·	·	D. molle
2	1	·	·	·	·	·	4	D. scoparium
·	·	·	·	·	·	·	3	D. starkei
·	·	·	·	·	·	·	·	Ditrichum homomallum
·	1	·	2	·	·	·	·	Drepanocladus uncinatus
·	1	·	·	·	·	·	·	Hylocomium splendens
·	·	·	·	·	·	·	·	Oligotrichum hercynicum
·	·	·	3	·	·	·	·	Pleurozium schreberi
3	·	·	·	·	1	·	·	Pohlia nutans
3	7	5	6	5	7	6	3	Polytrichum alpinum
·	·	+	·	·	·	·	·	P. norvegicum
1	·	·	·	1	·	·	3	Rhacomitrium canescens
·	3	·	·	1	·	·	4	R. fasciculare
1	·	·	·	·	·	·	·	R. heterostichum
2	2	2	·	2	1	·	2	R. lanuginosum
·	·	·	1	·	·	·	·	Rhytidiadelphus loreus
·	·	·	1	·	·	·	·	R. squarrosus
·	·	·	·	·	3	·	·	Sphagnum compactum
·	·	·	·	·	·	·	·	S. russowii
·	·	·	·	·	·	·	·	Alicularia scalaris
·	·	·	·	·	·	·	·	Cephalozia ambigua
·	·	·	·	·	·	·	·	C. bicuspidata
·	·	·	·	·	·	·	·	Diplophyllum albicans
·	·	·	·	·	1	·	·	Leptoscyphus taylori
·	·	·	·	·	·	·	·	Lophozia alpestris
3	·	·	·	3	·	·	·	L. floerkii
·	·	·	·	·	1	·	·	Lophozia sp.
·	·	·	·	·	·	·	·	L. ventricosa
·	·	·	·	·	·	·	·	Pleuroclada albescens
·	3	3	4	3	·	4	3	Ptilidium ciliare
·	·	·	1	·	·	2	·	Cetraria hiascens
·	2	1	2	·	3	3	1	C. islandica
3	3	3	·	3	2	·	·	Cladonia bellidiflora
·	·	·	·	1	·	·	·	C. cervicornis
·	·	·	·	·	·	·	·	C. coccifera
·	3	·	·	·	·	·	·	Cladonia degenerans
·	3	·	·	·	·	·	3	C. delessertii

Table 34

	1	2	3	4	5	6	7	8	9
C. destricta	.	1	.	.	.	.	.	.	.
C. floerkeana	.	.	.	.	.	.	.	.	.
C. gracilis	.	.	2	.	.	.	.	.	.
C. pyxidata	.	1	.	.	.	.	.	.	1
C. rangiferina agg. . .	.	.	.	.	.	.	.	.	.
C. squamosa . . .	.	.	.	.	.	.	.	.	2
C. sylvatica	.	.	.	.	.	1	.	1	3
C. uncialis . . .	.	.	.	.	.	.	.	.	1
Crocynia sp. . . .	.	.	.	.	.	.	.	.	.
Ochrolechia frigida . .	.	.	.	.	.	.	.	.	1
Peltidea leucophlebia . .	1	.	.	.	.	.	.	.	.
Stereocaulon evolutoides . .	.	.	.	.	.	.	.	.	.
Number of species (81) . .	25	32	26	21	12	10	12	16	16

(Average 23)

(Overall

Constancy class V   2 } for the association.
    „   „   IV   0 }

LOCALITIES

1–5. Ben Lawers, Perthshire; 6,7. Ben Macdhui, Cairngorms; 8. Beinn a' Bhuird, Cairngorms; 9. Lochnagar, Aberdeenshire; 10. Beinn a' Chaoruinn, Cairngorms; 11,17. Aonach Beag, Nevis hills, Inverness-shire; 12. Creag Meagaidh, Inverness-shire; 13. Driesh, Clova, Angus;

(*continued*)

10	11	12	13	14	15	16	17	
·	·	·	·	·	·	·	·	C. destricta
·	I	·	·	·	·	·	·	C. floerkeana
·	·	·	I	I	·	·	·	C. gracilis
·	I	3	I	I	I	·	I	C. pyxidata
·	·	·	·	+	·	·	·	C. rangiferina agg.
·	·	·	·	·	·	·	·	C. squamosa
+	3	3	2	5	·	2	·	C. sylvatica
·	I	+	I	·	2	2	·	C. uncialis
I	·	·	·	·	·	·	·	Crocynia sp.
·	·	·	·	·	·	·	·	Ochrolechia frigida
·	·	·	·	·	·	·	·	Peltidea leucophlebia
I	·	·	·	·	·	·	·	Stereocaulon evolutoides
20	20	11	20	18	14	12	14	Number of species (81)

(Average 15)

average 19)

14. Ben Alder, Inverness-shire; 15. Meall a' Chaoruinn, Drumochter, Inverness-shire; 16. Green Hill, Clova, Angus.

Table 35: Dicraneto-

	1	2	3	4	5	6	7	8	9
Reference number	P52 012	P52 058	P52 164	P52 175	P52 183	P52 184	P52 185	P52 191	P52 192
Map reference	7439 2673	7548 2714	7496 2691	7416 2635	7411 2648	7411 2646	7411 2646	7512 2687	7512 2687
Altitude (feet)	3200	3500	3100	3750	2675	2800	2800	3300	3250
Aspect (degrees)	345	—	120	100	60	60	120	40	40
Slope (degrees)	10	0	2	12	4	4	1	4	4
Cover (per cent)	90	100	90	100	90	100	100	100	90
Height (centimetres)	3	5	3	—	2	12	7	2	5
Plot area (square metres)	2	0·5	1	1	4	2	4	4	4
Crataegus monogyna*	·	·	·	·	1	·	·	·	·
Vaccinium myrtillus	4	4	·	·	1	1	1	2	1
Lycopodium selago	·	·	·	2	·	·	·	1	·
Agrostis canina	·	·	·	·	·	·	·	·	·
A. tenuis	2	·	1	4	·	5	·	4	6
Deschampsia caespitosa	·	·	·	·	·	·	·	·	·
D. flexuosa	5	·	1	2	·	·	·	·	·
Festuca ovina agg.	2	·	5	·	5	6	4	4	6
Nardus stricta	·	·	·	·	·	2	·	·	·
Carex bigelowii	3	9	9	2	·	5	4	7	4
Alchemilla alpina	1	·	·	·	·	·	·	·	·
Galium hercynicum	1	·	·	·	4	3	·	·	2
Rumex acetosa	·	·	·	·	·	·	·	·	·
Saxifraga stellaris	·	·	·	1	·	·	·	·	·
Viola palustris	·	·	·	·	·	·	·	·	·
Dicranum fuscescens	7	4	3	9	9	9	9	6	10
D. scoparium	·	·	·	·	1	·	·	·	·
Drepanocladus uncinatus	·	·	·	·	·	·	·	·	·
Hylocomium splendens	·	·	·	·	·	·	·	·	·
Oligotrichum hercynicum	·	·	·	3	·	·	·	·	·
Pleurozium schreberi	·	·	2	·	·	5	·	·	·
Pohlia nutans	1	·	1	·	·	·	·	·	·
Polytrichum alpestre	·	·	·	·	·	·	·	·	·
P. alpinum	1	·	3	4	·	3	2	1	3
P. norvegicum	·	·	1	·	·	·	·	·	·
Rhacomitrium fasciculare	·	·	·	·	·	·	·	·	·
R. lanuginosum	3	1	3	1	1	3	3	6	·
Sphagnum compactum	·	·	·	·	·	·	·	·	·
Alicularia scalaris	1	·	·	·	·	·	·	·	·
Diplophyllum albicans	·	·	1	·	·	·	·	·	·
Lophozia alpestris	·	·	1	·	·	·	·	·	·
L. floerkii	·	·	·	4	·	·	·	·	·
L. ventricosa	·	·	·	·	·	·	·	·	·
Ptilidium ciliare	·	·	2	·	·	·	·	·	·
cf. Biatora uliginosa	·	·	·	·	·	·	·	·	·
Cetraria aculeata	1	·	·	·	1	1	·	·	·
C. islandica	·	1	·	·	3	2	2	2	2
Cladonia alpicola	·	·	1	·	1	·	3	2	·
C. bellidiflora	1	2	3	·	3	·	3	3	·
C. coccifera	1	·	·	·	·	·	·	·	·
C. floerkeana	·	·	·	·	·	·	·	·	·
C. gracilis	·	·	·	·	·	·	·	1	·
C. pyxidata	·	·	·	·	·	·	·	·	·
C. rangiferina agg.	·	·	·	·	·	·	·	·	·
C. squamosa	1	2	·	·	·	·	·	·	·
C. sylvatica	1	·	3	·	·	1	2	3	·
C. uncialis	2	1	2	·	·	1	·	1	·
Ochrolechia frigida	·	·	·	·	·	·	·	·	·
Stereocaulon evolutoides	·	·	1	1	·	·	·	·	·
Number of species (49)	18	8	18	11	11	14	10	14	8

(Average 13·5)

Constancy class V   5
    ,,   ,, IV   4

*seedling

LOCALITIES

1–9. Ben Lawers, Perthshire; 10. Ben Wyvis, Ross-shire; 11. Glas Maol, Caenlochan, Angus; 12. Ben Alder, Inverness-shire; 13. Aonach Mor, Ben Alder hills, Inverness-shire; 14. A' Bhuideanach Bheag, Drumochter, Inverness-shire; 15. Creag Meagaidh, Inverness-shire; 16. Driesh, Clova, Angus; 17. Ben Avon, Cairngorms; 18,19. Green Hill, Clova, Angus.

Caricetum bigelowii

10	11	12	13	14	15	16	17	18	19	
M56	M57	R57	R57	R57	R57	R57	M57	R57	R57	Reference number
003	064	106	112	192	163	262	083	281a	281b	
8684	7768	7714	7746	7780	7874	7736	8015	7757	7757	Map reference
2463	3164	2494	2476	2654	2426	3267	3130	3350	3350	
3400	3500	3650	3500	2950	3600	3000	3500	2800	2800	Altitude (feet)
−	−	−	45	45	135	360	360	−	−	Aspect (degrees)
0	0	0	10	5	5	3	3	0	0	Slope (degrees)
95	100	100	100	100	100	100	100	100	100	Cover (per cent)
5	−	−	−	−	−	−	−	−	−	Height (centimetres)
4	4	4	4	4	4	4	4	4	4	Plot area (square metres)
.	.	.	.	.	.	.	.	.	.	Crataegus monogyna*
.	.	.	.	.	.	5	.	1	2	Vaccinium myrtillus
.	.	.	.	.	.	.	+	.	.	Lycopodium selago
.	.	.	.	.	.	.	.	2	+	Agrostis canina
.	.	5	.	3	+	.	.	.	.	A. tenuis
+	.	.	3	.	.	.	.	.	.	Deschampsia caespitosa
2	.	.	3	5	.	3	1	+	5	D. flexuosa
.	.	.	.	.	+	3	.	3	+	Festuca ovina agg.
.	.	.	1	.	.	.	.	.	.	Nardus stricta
9	8	8	9	8	9	8	7	8	7	**Carex bigelowii**
.	.	.	.	.	.	.	.	.	.	Alchemilla alpina
.	.	.	.	2	.	.	.	.	.	Galium hercynicum
.	.	2	.	.	2	.	.	.	.	Rumex acetosa
.	.	.	.	.	.	.	.	.	.	Saxifraga stellaris
.	.	+	.	.	.	.	.	.	.	Viola palustris
4	9	8	9	7	7	6	7	6	8	**Dicranum fuscescens**
1	.	.	.	.	.	.	.	.	.	D. scoparium
2	.	.	.	.	.	.	.	.	.	Drepanocladus uncinatus
2	.	.	.	.	.	.	.	.	.	Hylocomium splendens
.	.	.	.	.	.	.	.	.	.	Oligotrichum hercynicum
2	.	.	.	.	.	+	.	.	.	Pleurozium schreberi
.	1	.	.	.	.	.	1	.	.	Pohlia nutans
.	.	.	.	.	.	4	.	.	.	Polytrichum alpestre
2	2	3	2	2	3	3	3	3	+	P. alpinum
.	.	.	1	.	.	.	1	.	.	P. norvegicum
.	.	.	3	.	.	.	.	.	.	Rhacomitrium fasciculare
3	1	.	1	2	2	3	.	2	1	**R. lanuginosum**
.	.	.	.	1	.	.	.	.	.	Sphagnum compactum
.	.	.	.	.	.	.	.	.	.	Alicularia scalaris
.	.	.	.	.	.	.	.	.	.	Diplophyllum albicans
1	.	.	.	.	.	.	.	.	.	Lophozia alpestris
.	2	.	4	.	.	.	.	.	.	L. floerkii
.	.	.	.	1	.	.	.	.	.	L. ventricosa
4	3	5	3	.	5	.	.	.	.	Ptilidium ciliare
1	.	.	.	.	.	.	.	.	.	cf. Biatora uliginosa
.	.	.	.	.	.	.	.	2	+	Cetraria aculeata
3	3	+	.	2	1	2	.	3	+	C. islandica
.	.	.	.	.	.	.	.	.	.	Cladonia alpicola
3	2	2	.	2	3	3	2	2	2	**C. bellidiflora**
2	.	.	.	.	.	.	.	.	.	C. coccifera
+	.	1	.	.	.	.	.	.	.	C. floerkeana
1	2	1	.	1	1	2	.	3	+	C. gracilis
1	1	1	.	.	2	.	1	2	1	C. pyxidata
3	.	.	.	.	.	2	.	3	+	C. rangiferina agg.
3	.	.	.	.	.	.	.	.	.	C. squamosa
3	1	3	2	3	+	4	.	4	3	C. sylvatica
1	2	.	.	2	.	3	.	4	3	C. uncialis
2	.	.	.	.	.	.	.	2	+	Ochrolechia frigida
.	.	.	.	.	.	.	.	.	.	Stereocaulon evolutoides
24	13	13	12	14	13	15	9	17	16	Number of species (49)

Table 36: Cladineto-Juncetum trifidi

	1	2	3	4	5	6	7	8
Reference number	M56 116a	M56 116b	M56 116c	M57 067	M57 084	M57 095	M58 064	M58 067
Map reference	7987 3093	7988 3094	7988 3094	7791 3192	8024 3136	7802 3093	8046 3011	8042 3009
Altitude (feet)	3750	3700	3700	3300	3700	3000	3700	3500
Aspect (degrees)	90	–	–	–	270	–	–	45
Slope (degrees)	10	–	–	–	5	–	–	5
Cover (per cent)	100	100	100	100	95	90	95	95
Height (centimetres)	15	12	12	–	–	–	–	–
Plot area (square metres)	4	2	1	1	4	4	4	4
Empetrum hermaphroditum	.	.	.	.	.	1	.	2
Salix herbacea	.	.	.	.	.	.	.	3
Vaccinium myrtillus	2	4	.	.	+	.	+	+
Lycopodium alpinum	.	.	.	.	.	.	1	+
L. selago	.	.	.	1	.	.	.	.
Agrostis tenuis	.	.	.	+	.	.	.	.
Deschampsia caespitosa	2	.	.	.	.	.	.	.
D. flexuosa	.	2	.	.	2	2	.	2
Festuca ovina agg.	.	.	.	2	2	.	1	3
Nardus stricta	2	2	.	1	.	.	.	.
Carex bigelowii	4	3	3	4	3	4	3	4
C. pilulifera	1	.	.	.	.	.	.	.
Juncus trifidus	7	6	9	7	7	6	7	7
Luzula spicata	3	.	.	.	1	.	.	.
Alchemilla alpina	2	.	.	.	.	.	+	.
Silene acaulis	1	.	.	.	.	.	.	.
Dicranum fuscescens	1	.	.	.	.	.	1	1
Oligotrichum hercynicum	.	1	.	.	.	.	.	.
Pohlia nutans	1	.	.	.	.	.	2	1
Polytrichum alpinum	.	.	.	2	.	.	1	1
P. piliferum	.	.	1	.	2	2	1	.
Rhacomitrium lanuginosum	.	.	1	1	6	2	3	2
Gymnomitrium concinnatum	.	1	.	.	.	.	.	.
Lophozia alpestris	.	.	.	.	.	.	1	.
L. floerkii	1	4	2	.	.	.	1	.
Ptilidium ciliare	3	.	.	.	.	.	2	2
Alectoria nigricans	.	.	.	.	.	5	.	.
Cerania vermicularis	.	.	.	.	+	2	.	.
Cetraria aculeata	.	.	1	.	.	4	.	.
C. hiascens	.	.	2	.	.	.	1	3
C. islandica	3	3	3	2	3	2	3	3
C. nivalis	1	.	.	.	.	.	.	.
Cladonia bellidiflora	2	2	3	3	2	3	2	.
C. coccifera	.	.	1	.	.	.	.	.
C. crispata	2	.	1	.	.	.	.	.
C. floerkeana	.	.	.	.	1	.	1	.
C. delessertii	.	.	.	.	.	.	2	2
C. foliacea	.	.	.	.	1	1	.	2
C. gracilis	.	4	3	6	2	1	5	3
C. pyxidata	.	2	2	2	2	2	3	2
C. rangiferina agg.	3	.	.	.	.	2	2	4
C. sylvatica	4	3	2	1	2	1	5	7
C. uncialis	2	3	2	3	3	3	6	4
Lecidea cf. uliginosa	.	.	2	.	.	.	.	.
Ochrolechia frigida	.	1	1	.	.	3	1	3
O. tartarea	.	.	.	1	.	2	.	.
Sphaerophorus fragilis	.	.	.	.	.	1	.	.
Stereocaulon evolutoides	+	.	.	.	.	.	.	.
Number of species (48)	21	15	17	15	17	20	25	23

(Average 19)

Constancy class V 8
     „   „ IV 3

LOCALITIES

1-3. South Beinn a' Bhuird, Cairngorms; 4,7,8. Cairngorm, Inverness-shire; 5. Ben Avon, Banffshire; 6. An Socach, Cairnwell hills. Aberdeenshire.

Table 37: Juncus trifidus-Festuca ovina nodum

	1	2	3	4	5	6	7	8	9	10	11	12	13	14
Reference number	R56 041	R56 050	R56 052	R56 084	M56 076	R56 024	M56 047	M55 045	M55 031	R57 065	R57 014	MX19	P52 089	P52 090
Map reference	8700 2218	8805 2252	8816 2256	8733 1981	9169 2332	8746 2013	8743 1982	8636 1975	8598 1985	–	9454 2349	–	7413 2633	7413 2633
Altitude (feet)	2750	2800	3300	2800	1900	2750	2800	2750	2200	2850	2250	2400	3550	3700
Aspect (degrees)	360	–	–	315	–	135	–	360	–	–	–	–	250	180
Slope (degrees)	10	–	–	5	–	12	–	2	–	–	–	–	15	5
Cover (per cent)	40	55	40	40	30	30	20	25	60	50	25	30	50	30
Height (centimetres)	–	–	–	–	–	–	–	5	7	–	–	–	3	5
Plot area (square metres)	4	4	12	4	4	4	4	2	4	4	4	10	2	2
Arctous alpina	3	·	·	·	·	·	·	·	·	·	·	·	·	·
Empetrum hermaphroditum	·	·	·	·	1	1	·	1	2	·	+	·	·	·
Loiseleuria procumbens	1	·	·	2	+	·	+	2	+	·	·	·	·	·
Salix herbacea	4	+	+	3	·	·	2	3	3	3	4	4	·	·
Vaccinium myrtillus	2	2	·	·	2	1	·	2	3	·	·	·	·	·
V. uliginosum	·	·	·	·	·	·	·	·	3	+	·	·	·	·
V. vitis-idaea	3	·	·	·	·	·	·	·	·	+	·	·	·	·
Lycopodium selago	·	·	·	·	·	·	·	·	·	·	·	·	1	·
Agrostis canina	2	2	·	3	1	3	·	·	·	3	3	3	·	·
A. tenuis	·	·	·	·	·	·	·	·	3	·	·	·	·	·
Deschampsia flexuosa	4	3	3	3	·	3	1	·	1	3	3	2	·	·
Festuca ovina agg.	2	4	3	4	4	3	2	2	2	3	4	2	5	7
F. rubra	·	·	·	·	·	·	·	·	·	·	·	2	·	·
Carex bigelowii	3	3	2	+	·	·	+	2	1	2	·	1	2	3
C. pilulifera	·	·	·	2	1	·	·	·	·	·	·	·	·	·
Juncus trifidus	4	3	4	3	3	3	3	4	4	3	4	1	·	·
Luzula spicata	3	1	2	·	+	3	+	+	·	2	·	·	2	3
Achillea millefolium	3	·	·	·	1	·	·	·	·	·	3	·	·	·
Alchemilla alpina	5	3	4	3	1	3	2	+	·	3	3	2	1	·
Antennaria dioica	3	3	·	4	2	·	1	1	3	3	1	·	·	·
Armeria maritima	·	3	3	2	·	3	1	1	·	2	3	1	·	·
Artemisia norvegica	·	·	·	·	·	·	·	·	·	3	3	·	·	·
Cherleria sedoides	·	5	3	·	+	4	·	·	·	+	3	+	·	·
Euphrasia frigida	·	·	·	·	·	1	·	·	·	1	+	·	·	·
Gnaphalium supinum	3	·	2	2	2	3	·	·	·	2	3	·	·	·
Hieracium holosericeum	1	+	·	·	·	·	·	·	1	·	·	·	·	·
Plantago maritima	·	·	·	2	3	·	2	·	·	·	3	·	·	·
Potentilla erecta	·	·	·	·	3	·	·	·	·	·	·	·	·	·
Sibbaldia procumbens	·	·	2	+	1	4	·	·	·	2	·	·	·	·
Silene acaulis	2	3	3	+	+	·	1	·	·	3	2	·	·	·
Solidago virgaurea	·	+	·	1	·	·	1	1	1	+	1	+	·	·
Polygonum viviparum	2	·	·	·	·	·	·	·	·	3	3	·	·	·
Succisa pratensis	1	·	·	3	2	·	2	·	2	·	·	+	·	·
Taraxacum officinalis agg.	·	·	·	·	2	·	·	·	·	·	·	·	·	·
Thymus drucei	3	3	·	5	3	3	2	·	+	3	·	3	·	·
Andreaea rupestris	·	·	·	·	·	·	·	·	·	·	·	·	·	3
Aulacomnium turgidum	·	2	·	·	·	·	·	·	·	·	·	·	·	·
Conostomum tetragonum	·	·	·	·	·	1	·	·	·	·	·	·	·	·
Dicranella heteromalla	·	·	·	·	·	3	·	·	·	·	·	·	2	·
Diphyscium foliosum	·	·	·	1	·	1	·	·	·	·	·	·	·	·
Dicranum scoparium	·	2	·	·	·	·	·	·	·	·	·	1	·	·
Hylocomium splendens	·	1	·	·	·	·	·	·	·	·	·	·	·	·
Hypnum cupressiforme	·	1	·	·	·	·	·	·	·	·	·	·	·	·
H. hamulosum	·	1	·	·	·	·	·	·	·	·	·	·	·	·
Oligotrichum hercynicum	2	·	+	·	·	3	·	·	·	·	·	·	3	2
Pleurozium schreberi	2	·	·	·	·	·	·	·	·	·	·	·	·	·
Polytrichum alpinum	·	2	·	·	·	1	·	·	·	·	2	·	3	·
P. piliferum	3	·	2	2	3	3	2	·	·	2	2	1	2	3
P. urnigerum	·	·	·	·	·	·	·	·	1	·	·	·	·	·
Rhacomitrium fasciculare	3	·	·	·	·	3	·	·	·	·	·	·	3	·
R. heterostichum	3	2	3	3	·	3	·	·	·	·	·	·	·	·
R. lanuginosum	6	5	5	4	1	4	1	3	4	6	2	2	5	2
Alicularia scalaris	·	·	2	·	·	2	·	·	·	3	2	·	5	4
Diplophyllum albicans	·	·	·	·	·	·	·	·	·	·	2	·	5	4
Gymnomitrium concinnatum	·	·	2	·	·	4	·	·	·	3	3	1	5	4
G. coralloides	·	·	·	·	·	·	·	·	·	·	·	·	5	4
Lophozia floerkii	·	·	·	·	·	·	·	·	·	·	·	1	·	·
Ptilidium ciliare	·	2	·	·	·	·	·	·	·	·	·	·	·	·
Alectoria nigricans	·	·	·	·	·	·	·	·	·	1	·	·	·	·
Cerania vermicularis	1	·	+	·	·	·	·	·	·	+	·	·	1	1
Cetraria aculeata	·	2	·	·	·	1	·	·	·	+	2	·	1	3
C. islandica	·	3	1	·	·	1	·	·	·	·	·	·	1	3
Cladonia bellidiflora	·	·	·	·	·	·	·	2	2	·	·	+	·	1
C. coccifera	·	·	2	·	·	2	·	·	·	·	·	·	2	1
C. destricta	·	·	·	·	·	·	·	·	·	·	·	·	·	2
C. floerkeana	·	·	·	·	·	·	·	·	·	·	·	·	·	1
C. gracilis	·	·	·	·	·	·	1	·	·	·	·	·	·	·
C. pyxidata	·	3	·	·	·	·	·	·	·	·	·	·	·	·
C. squamosa	·	·	·	·	·	·	·	·	·	·	·	·	·	2

(1–12); Related Festuca ovina communities (13, 14)

	1	2	3	4	5	6	7	8	9	10	11	12	13	14
C. subcervicornis	·	·	·	·	·	·	·	3	·	1	·	·	·	·
C. uncialis	1	2	2	·	·	·	·	·	·	1	2	·	·	·
Lecidea sp.	·	·	·	·	·	1	·	·	·	·	·	·	·	·
Ochrolechia frigida	2	4	·	3	1	·	2	3	3	3	3	·	·	·
Parmelia omphalodes	1	·	·	·	·	·	·	·	·	·	·	·	·	·
Platysma glaucum	·	+	·	·	·	·	·	2	·	·	2	·	·	·
Solorina crocea	3	·	+	·	·	2	·	·	·	1	·	·	·	·
Sphaerophorus globosus	2	3	·	·	·	·	·	2	1	3	2	·	·	·
Stereocaulon vesuvianum	·	·	·	5	·	1	3	·	·	·	·	·	·	·
Number of species (78)	32	32	23	24	24	31	19	18	19	34	27	23	19	19

(Average 25·5)

Constancy class V   6
    ,,   ,,   IV   12

LOCALITIES

1. Creachan Rairigidh, Fannich Forest, Ross-shire; 2,3. Beinn Dearg, Inverlael, Ross-shire; 4,7. Beinn Lair, Letterewe, Ross-shire; 5. Ben More Assynt, Sutherland; 6. A' Mhaighdean, Fisherfield Forest, Ross-shire; 8,9. Beinn Eighe, Ross-shire; 10,12. Ross-shire (2 localities); 11. Meall Horn, Reay Forest, Sutherland; 13,14. Ben Lawers, Perthshire.

	1	2	3	4	5	6	7	8	9	10	11
Reference number	R57 267	R58 134	R57 086	R57 237	R57 224	R57 230	M57 053	R59 009	R57 219	R57 130	R57 207
Map reference	7765 3175	7275 2261	7866 2433	7753 3245	7774 3238	7748 3249	7695 2176	7397 2194	7745 3278	7999 2598	7758 3337
Altitude (feet)	2750	2000	2800	2300	1850	2350	1900	2350	2000	2000	2400
Aspect (degrees)	90	360	45	135	135	360	270	120	45	250	90
Slope (degrees)	45	45	35	35	45	35	45	40	35	50	60
Cover (per cent)	100	100	100	100	100	95	100	100	100	100	80
Height (centimetres)	27	40	45	20	25	20	20	40	–	–	–
Plot area (square metres)	4	4	4	4	4	4	4	4	4	4	4
Betula sp.					4						
Calluna vulgaris				2	3	2	+				1
Empetrum hermaphroditum							+				
Juniperus communis				2							
Rubus idaeus				3							
R. saxatilis	4	2	3	3		2	1	2	2		1
Salix capraea					+						
S. herbacea											
S. lapponum				1		4				4	
Vaccinium myrtillus	2	3	2	3	3	3	3	2	2		2
V. vitis-idaea	2		2	3			3	2			
Asplenium viride											
Athyrium alpestre											
A. filix-foemina											
Blechnum spicant											
Botrychium lunaria											
Cystopteris fragilis											
Dryopteris austriaca											
D. filix-mas										3	
Lycopodium selago											
Polystichum lonchitis	3			1	3					2	
Selaginella selaginoides						+		1	1		2
Thelypteris dryopteris		1	3								
T. oreopteris											
T. phegopteris									2		
Agrostis canina	1		1		2	+			3		
A. stolonifera											
A. tenuis			2	3		3			3		
Anthoxanthum odoratum	2	2		2	3		2	3	3		
Deschampsia caespitosa	4	3	2	2	3	4	3	4	3	2	4
D. flexuosa		3									
Festuca ovina agg.	3	2	3	4		3		2	4	2	4
F. rubra		3	2			2			2	1	
Helictotrichon pratense								2			
Melica nutans	+										
Nardus stricta				4					1	3	
Poa alpina											
P. balfourii						2					
Carex atrata						3					
C. bigelowii			1								
C. binervis					1				2		
C. flacca	2			3	2			3	3	3	4
C. panicea											
C. pilulifera				1							
C. pulicaris				2	1	+			+	3	2
Coeloglossum viride			+			+	+				
Juncus squarrosus											
Luzula multiflora			2								
L. spicata											
L. sylvatica	4	3		3	4	4	2	4	3	3	3
Orchis mascula							1	1			
Achillea millefolium											
Alchemilla alpina	+		2	2		2			2	3	3
A. filicaulis			6			5	1				
A. glabra	5	4		4	5	5		5	4	3	5
A. vestita	3			2	3	+					
A. wichurae								5	2		
Anemone nemorosa		1			+				2		
Angelica sylvestris	4	3	4	2		4	3	4	4	3	2
Antennaria dioica										1	
Arabis hirsuta	1										
Armeria maritima											
Caltha palustris											
Campanula rotundifolia	2			2				3	1	2	
Cardamine flexuosa											
Cicerbita alpina											
Cirsium heterophyllum	5	+		4				4			
C. palustre											
Cochlearia alpina		2	3								
Crepis paludosa		2				+					2
Draba incana	2								2		
Epilobium montanum		1									
Euphrasia scotica											
Euphrasia sp.	1		3		1	2					

Herb nodum

12	13	14	15	16	17	18	19	20	21	22	
M56	P52	R58	R56	R57	R56	R56	R57	R58	M56	M57	Reference number
140	066	038	098	055	061	063	062	073	075	022	
7973	7435	7807	8808	9458	8616	8584	8721	8451	9191	8005	Map reference
2908	2489	3190	2230	2351	1918	1916	2211	2133	2318	1339	
2500	2400	2800	2300	1700	1200	2000	2350	2800	1600	1500	Altitude (feet)
45	340	360	360	45	360	360	340	45	225	360	Aspect (degrees)
45	–	35	45	35	35	40	40	40	70	80	Slope (degrees)
100	–	100	100	100	95	100	95	100	100	100	Cover (per cent)
37	–	90	60	50	60	60	50	50	38	30	Height (centimetres)
4	8	4	16	4	16	16	16	4	8	4	Plot area (square metres)
·	·	·	·	·	·	·	·	·	·	·	Betula sp.
·	·	·	2	·	+	·	·	·	+	·	Calluna vulgaris
·	1	·	·	·	·	·	·	·	·	·	Empetrum hermaphroditum
·	·	·	·	·	·	·	·	·	·	·	Juniperus communis
·	·	·	·	·	·	·	·	·	·	·	Rubus idaeus
·	·	·	3	+	·	·	3	3	3	·	R. saxatilis
·	·	·	·	·	·	·	·	·	·	·	Salix capraea
·	·	·	1	·	·	·	·	·	·	·	S. herbacea
·	·	·	·	·	·	·	·	·	·	·	S. lapponum
·	4	·	4	·	2	3	3	3	6	·	Vaccinium myrtillus
·	2	·	·	·	·	·	·	·	1	·	V. vitis-idaea
·	1	·	·	·	·	·	·	·	·	·	Asplenium viride
·	·	4	·	·	·	·	·	+	·	·	Athyrium alpestre
·	·	·	·	2	·	·	·	·	·	·	A. filix-foemina
·	·	·	·	·	1	·	·	·	1	·	Blechnum spicant
·	1	·	·	·	·	·	·	·	·	·	Botrychium lunaria
·	1	·	·	·	·	·	·	·	·	·	Cystopteris fragilis
·	·	2	·	·	·	·	2	4	·	·	Dryopteris austriaca
·	·	·	·	·	·	·	·	·	2	·	D. filix-mas
·	1	·	·	·	·	1	·	·	·	·	Lycopodium selago
·	·	·	·	·	·	·	·	·	2	·	Polystichum lonchitis
·	·	·	1	2	1	1	1	·	·	·	Selaginella selaginoides
·	·	+	·	·	·	·	·	·	·	·	Thelypteris dryopteris
·	·	·	·	+	·	·	·	·	·	·	T. oreopteris
·	·	3	·	+	3	·	·	·	·	·	T. phegopteris
1	·	·	3	4	5	·	3	·	·	·	Agrostis canina
·	3	·	·	·	·	·	·	·	·	·	A. stolonifera
·	·	·	·	3	·	3	1	·	·	·	A. tenuis
·	·	·	3	3	4	3	1	·	·	·	Anthoxanthum odoratum
·	2	3	3	5	4	5	4	5	·	·	**Deschampsia caespitosa**
·	·	3	3	3	3	3	3	4	3	·	D. flexuosa
·	3	·	4	3	4	5	3	·	1	·	Festuca ovina agg.
·	·	·	3	·	·	·	·	·	·	·	F. rubra
·	·	·	·	·	·	·	·	·	·	·	Helictotrichon pratense
·	·	·	·	·	·	·	·	·	·	·	Melica nutans
·	·	·	·	2	2	·	·	·	·	·	Nardus stricta
·	1	·	·	·	·	·	·	·	·	·	Poa alpina
·	·	·	·	·	·	·	·	·	·	·	P. balfourii
·	·	·	·	·	·	·	·	·	·	·	Carex atrata
·	·	·	1	3	·	3	2	·	·	·	C. bigelowii
·	·	·	3	4	3	·	·	·	·	·	C. binervis
·	·	·	·	·	·	·	·	·	·	3	C. flacca
·	·	·	·	3	3	1	·	·	·	·	C. panicea
·	·	·	·	·	·	·	·	·	·	·	C. pilulifera
·	·	·	2	·	3	·	·	·	·	·	C. pulicaris
·	·	·	2	·	·	·	1	·	·	·	Coeloglossum viride
·	·	·	·	·	2	·	·	·	·	·	Juncus squarrosus
·	·	·	·	·	·	·	·	·	·	·	Luzula multiflora
·	·	·	·	·	·	·	1	·	·	·	L. spicata
5	7	3	4	4	3	5	4	4	4	5	**L. sylvatica**
·	·	·	·	·	·	·	·	·	·	+	Orchis mascula
·	·	·	3	·	·	·	·	·	1	·	Achillea millefolium
·	3	·	3	·	2	2	2	2	·	·	Alchemilla alpina
·	·	·	·	·	3	+	4	·	·	·	A. filicaulis
6	2	3	·	·	·	·	·	4	2	·	A. glabra
·	2	·	·	4	·	·	·	·	·	·	A. vestita
·	2	·	3	·	·	·	·	·	·	·	A. wichurae
·	3	·	·	·	·	·	·	·	·	·	Anemone nemorosa
3	3	·	3	3	4	4	5	·	3	3	**Angelica sylvestris**
·	·	·	·	·	·	·	·	·	·	·	Antennaria dioica
·	·	·	·	·	·	·	·	·	·	·	Arabis hirsuta
·	·	·	·	·	2	3	+	·	·	·	Armeria maritima
·	·	·	·	·	4	4	·	·	·	·	Caltha palustris
·	1	·	·	·	·	·	·	·	·	·	Campanula rotundifolia
·	·	·	·	·	·	·	·	·	·	1	Cardamine flexuosa
·	·	9	·	·	·	·	·	·	·	·	Cicerbita alpina
·	·	·	·	·	·	·	·	5	·	·	Cirsium heterophyllum
·	·	·	·	·	·	·	·	·	2	·	C. palustre
·	2	·	·	·	·	·	·	·	·	1	Cochlearia alpina
·	·	·	·	·	·	+	·	·	·	·	Crepis paludosa
·	·	·	3	·	·	·	+	·	·	·	Draba incana
·	·	·	·	·	·	·	·	·	1	1	Epilobium montanum
·	·	·	·	·	2	2	·	·	·	·	Euphrasia scotica
·	·	·	·	·	·	?	?	?	?	·	Euphrasia sp.

Table 38

	1	2	3	4	5	6	7	8	9	10	11
Filipendula ulmaria	5	4	·	5	3	·	5	4	2	·	3
Fragaria vesca	·	·	·	1	3	·	·	·	·	·	·
Galium boreale	3	·	·	2	4	3	·	·	·	·	2
G. hercynicum	·	·	·	3	·	·	·	1	2	·	·
Geranium sylvaticum	4	3	5	3	4	4	7	3	4	5	3
Geum rivale	4	5	3	4	4	4	3	4	3	3	3
Heracleum sphondylium	3	3	·	3	3	·	·	2	4	·	3
Hieracium sp.	·	·	·	·	1	2	·	1	1	1	1
Hypericum pulchrum	·	·	·	·	·	·	·	·	·	·	·
Lathyrus montanus	·	·	·	·	·	·	·	·	·	·	·
Linum catharticum	·	·	·	3	2	2	·	2	·	·	·
Listera ovata	·	+	·	·	·	·	·	·	·	·	·
Lotus corniculatus	·	·	·	2	·	·	3	·	·	·	·
Melandrium rubrum	4	3	3	·	·	·	·	3	·	·	+
Mercurialis perennis	·	4	·	4	·	·	·	3	·	·	·
Oxalis acetosella	·	·	·	·	·	·	·	·	·	·	·
Oxyria digyna	+	·	4	+	·	2	·	·	·	3	+
Pinguicula vulgaris	·	·	·	·	·	·	·	·	·	·	1
Plantago lanceolata	·	·	·	2	·	·	·	·	·	·	·
Polygonum viviparum	·	·	3	·	1	2	·	·	·	·	·
Potentilla crantzii	·	·	·	·	·	·	·	·	·	·	·
P. erecta	2	·	·	3	3	·	·	·	3	4	·
Prunella vulgaris	·	·	·	3	·	·	·	·	·	·	·
Pyrola rotundifolia	·	·	·	1	1	·	·	·	·	·	·
Ranunculus acris	·	1	2	·	·	2	+	·	·	·	·
Rhinanthus minor agg.	·	·	·	·	·	·	·	1	1	1	·
Rumex acetosa	·	3	4	·	·	·	2	·	·	+	·
Saussurea alpina	3	+	·	·	·	·	+	·	3	5	3
Saxifraga aizoides	·	·	·	·	·	3	·	·	·	3	3
S. hypnoides	·	2	2	·	·	·	·	·	·	·	·
S. oppositifolia	·	·	1	·	·	·	·	·	·	1	·
S. stellaris	·	·	·	·	·	·	·	·	·	·	·
Sedum rosea	4	4	7	+	4	2	2	2	+	2	·
Solidago virgaurea	2	3	·	3	·	·	2	3	·	+	·
Succisa pratensis	1	·	·	4	6	4	3	4	7	4	5
Taraxacum officinalis agg.	·	·	1	·	·	2	·	1	2	·	·
Thalictrum alpinum	·	·	·	·	·	2	·	·	·	2	·
Thymus drucei	·	·	·	3	·	·	·	2	·	2	·
Trollius europaeus	4	4	·	·	+	·	+	·	4	3	3	4
Tussilago farfara	2	·	·	·	·	4	·	·	·	·	2
Valeriana officinalis	3	5	·	·	·	·	2	2	·	·	+
Veronica chamaedrys	·	·	·	·	·	·	·	·	·	·	·
V. officinalis	·	·	·	1	·	·	·	·	·	·	·
Vicia sepium	·	·	·	·	·	·	·	·	·	·	·
V. sylvatica	·	·	·	·	3	·	·	+	·	·	·
Viola lutea	·	·	·	·	·	·	·	·	·	·	·
V. riviniana	3	·	·	3	2	3	3	2	3	3	2
Acrocladium cuspidatum	·	·	·	·	·	+	·	·	1	1	·
Antitrichia curtipendula	·	·	·	·	·	·	·	·	·	·	·
Atrichum undulatum	·	·	·	·	·	·	·	2	2	·	·
Bartramia pomiformis	·	·	·	·	·	·	·	·	·	·	·
Brachythecium rivulare	·	·	·	·	·	·	·	·	·	·	·
B. rutabulum	2	·	·	·	·	·	·	1	·	·	·
Breutelia chrysocoma	·	2	·	·	·	3	·	·	3	·	·
Bryum pseudotriquetrum	·	·	·	·	·	·	·	·	·	·	·
Camptothecium sericeum	·	2	·	·	·	·	·	·	·	·	·
Campylium protensum	·	·	1	·	·	2	·	·	·	·	·
C. stellatum	·	·	·	·	·	·	·	·	2	2	·
Cratoneuron commutatum	·	·	·	·	·	+	·	·	·	·	·
Ctenidium molluscum	2	2	3	·	1	3	4	·	3	5	1
Dicranum bonjeani	·	·	·	1	·	·	·	·	·	·	·
D. majus	2	·	·	·	·	1	·	·	2	·	·
D. scoparium	2	·	1	·	·	2	1	·	·	2	1
Ditrichum flexicaule	·	·	·	·	1	+	·	·	·	·	·
Drepanocladus revolvens	·	·	·	·	·	·	·	·	·	3	2
D. uncinatus	2	·	·	·	1	+	·	·	3	3	·
Eurhynchium praelongum	·	·	·	·	·	·	·	·	·	·	·
E. piliferum	·	·	·	·	·	·	·	·	·	·	·
Fissidens adianthoides	·	·	·	·	·	1	·	·	·	·	2
F. osmundoides	·	·	·	1	·	·	·	·	·	·	·
Hookeria lucens	·	1	·	·	·	·	·	·	2	·	1
Hylocomium brevirostre	·	1	·	·	·	·	·	·	·	·	·
H. splendens	2	4	4	3	3	3	·	3	2	4	2
H. umbratum	·	·	1	·	·	·	·	·	·	·	·
Hypnum callichroum	·	·	·	·	·	·	·	·	·	·	·
H. cupressiforme	1	·	·	·	·	·	·	·	3	·	·
H. hamulosum	·	·	·	·	·	·	·	·	·	3	·
Isopterygium elegans	·	·	·	1	·	·	·	·	·	·	·
Isothecium myurum	·	·	·	·	·	·	·	·	·	·	·
Leptodontium recurvifolium	·	·	·	·	·	·	·	·	·	·	·
Mnium hornum	·	2	·	·	·	·	·	·	·	·	1
M. longirostrum	·	·	·	2	·	·	·	·	·	·	·
M. pseudopunctatum	·	·	·	·	·	·	·	·	·	·	·
M. punctatum	·	1	2	·	·	+	·	·	·	·	2
M. seligeri	·	3	·	·	·	·	·	·	·	·	·
M. undulatum	2	3	3	·	·	1	·	2	·	·	·
Neckera crispa	·	1	·	·	·	·	·	·	·	·	·
Philonotis fontana	·	·	·	·	·	·	·	·	·	·	2
Plagiothecium denticulatum	·	1	·	·	·	·	·	·	·	·	·

(continued)

12	13	14	15	16	17	18	19	20	21	22	
·	2	·	·	3	·	·	·	·	3	3	Filipendula ulmaria
·	·	·	·	·	·	·	·	·	·	·	Fragaria vesca
·	·	·	·	·	·	·	·	·	·	·	Galium boreale
·	·	2	·	1	2	2	·	3	·	·	G. hercynicum
3	·	+	·	·	·	·	·	·	·	·	Geranium sylvaticum
6	3	·	2	3	3	2	3	·	2	2	**Geum rivale**
·	4	·	·	·	·	·	·	·	·	·	Heracleum sphondylium
·	1	·	·	·	·	·	·	·	·	·	Hieracium sp.
·	·	·	·	·	·	·	·	·	2	·	Hypericum pulchrum
·	·	·	·	·	·	·	·	·	+	·	Lathyrus montanus
·	·	·	·	·	·	·	·	·	·	·	Linum catharticum
·	·	·	·	·	·	·	·	·	·	·	Listera ovata
·	·	·	·	·	·	·	·	·	·	·	Lotus corniculatus
4	·	·	·	·	·	·	·	·	·	·	Melandrium rubrum
·	·	·	·	·	·	·	·	·	·	·	Mercurialis perennis
2	3	·	·	·	·	2	·	3	·	·	Oxalis acetosella
+	2	+	2	+	·	·	3	·	·	·	Oxyria digyna
·	·	·	·	·	·	·	·	·	·	·	Pinguicula vulgaris
·	·	·	·	·	·	·	·	·	·	·	Plantago lanceolata
·	1	·	1	·	·	·	·	·	·	·	Polygonum viviparum
·	1	·	·	·	·	·	·	·	·	·	Potentilla crantzii
·	·	·	3	3	·	·	·	·	2	·	P. erecta
·	·	·	·	·	·	·	·	·	·	·	Prunella vulgaris
·	·	·	·	·	·	·	·	·	·	·	Pyrola rotundifolia
·	3	·	1	3	3	3	3	2	·	5	Ranunculus acris
·	·	·	·	·	·	·	2	·	·	2	Rhinanthus minor agg.
2	3	2	2	3	·	2	2	3	3	3	Rumex acetosa
·	·	4	3	4	4	5	3	·	·	·	Saussurea alpina
·	1	·	·	·	·	·	·	·	·	·	Saxifraga aizoides
·	2	·	·	·	·	2	·	·	·	4	S. hypnoides
·	·	·	·	·	·	·	2	·	·	·	S. oppositifolia
·	·	·	·	·	·	·	2	·	·	·	S. stellaris
2	4	3	4	4	3	4	4	5	4	1	**Sedum rosea**
·	·	·	3	+	4	3	2	·	3	·	Solidago virgaurea
·	·	·	2	5	3	·	·	·	·	3	Succisa pratensis
·	·	·	3	·	·	·	3	·	·	2	Taraxacum officinalis agg.
·	2	·	3	3	·	·	2	·	·	·	Thalictrum alpinum
·	2	·	4	·	2	·	2	·	·	·	Thymus drucei
·	·	·	4	5	4	4	5	·	+	·	Trollius europaeus
·	·	·	·	·	·	·	·	·	·	·	Tussilago farfara
·	·	·	·	3	2	·	·	·	3	·	Valeriana officinalis
·	·	·	·	·	·	·	·	·	2	·	Veronica chamaedrys
·	·	·	·	·	·	·	·	3	·	·	V. officinalis
·	·	·	·	·	·	·	·	·	1	·	Vicia sepium
·	·	·	·	·	·	·	·	·	·	·	V. sylvatica
·	·	·	·	·	·	·	·	·	·	·	Viola lutea
2	·	·	2	·	1	·	·	·	·	·	V. riviniana
·	1	·	·	3	2	·	·	1	·	·	Acrocladium cuspidatum
·	·	·	·	·	·	·	·	·	1	·	Antitrichia curtipendula
·	·	·	·	·	·	·	·	·	·	·	Atrichum undulatum
·	·	·	·	·	·	·	·	·	1	·	Bartramia pomiformis
·	·	·	·	3	·	·	·	·	·	·	Brachythecium rivulare
·	·	·	·	·	·	·	·	1	·	·	B. rutabulum
·	·	·	4	2	5	3	2	·	·	·	Breutelia chrysocoma
·	·	·	·	·	·	·	·	·	·	·	Bryum pseudotriquetrum
·	·	·	·	·	·	·	·	·	·	·	Camptothecium sericeum
·	·	·	·	·	·	·	·	·	·	·	Campylium protensum
·	·	·	·	·	·	·	·	·	·	·	C. stellatum
·	·	·	·	·	·	·	·	·	·	·	Cratoneuron commutatum
·	1	·	·	3	3	·	2	·	·	·	Ctenidium molluscum
·	·	·	·	·	·	·	·	·	·	·	Dicranum bonjeani
·	1	2	3	·	2	2	2	·	1	·	D. majus
·	·	·	·	1	·	3	3	2	·	·	D. scoparium
·	1	·	·	·	·	·	·	·	·	·	Ditrichum flexicaule
·	·	·	·	2	·	·	2	2	·	·	Drepanocladus revolvens
4	·	·	·	·	2	1	·	·	3	2	D. uncinatus
											Eurhynchium praelongum
·	·	·	·	·	·	·	·	·	·	7	E. piliferum
·	·	·	·	·	·	·	·	·	·	·	Fissidens adianthoides
·	·	·	·	·	·	·	·	·	·	·	F. osmundoides
·	·	·	·	·	·	·	1	·	·	·	Hookeria lucens
·	·	·	·	·	·	·	·	·	·	·	Hylocomium brevirostre
2	3	4	5	3	4	5	4	5	2	·	**H. splendens**
·	·	·	1	1	·	·	1	3	·	·	H. umbratum
·	·	·	2	·	·	·	3	2	·	·	Hypnum callichroum
·	·	·	1	·	2	·	·	·	2	·	H. cupressiforme
·	·	·	·	·	·	·	·	·	·	·	H. hamulosum
·	·	·	·	·	·	·	·	·	·	·	Isopterygium elegans
·	·	·	·	·	·	·	·	·	·	·	Isothecium myurum
·	·	·	·	2	1	·	1	·	·	·	Leptodontium recurvifolium
·	·	·	·	·	3	2	2	·	1	·	Mnium hornum
1	·	·	·	·	·	·	·	·	·	·	M. longirostrum
·	1	·	·	·	·	·	·	·	·	·	M. pseudopunctatum
·	·	·	2	2	3	2	3	1	·	·	M. punctatum
·	·	·	·	•	·	•	•	·	•	·	M. seligeri
·	1	·	·	2	2	·	·	·	1	1	M. undulatum
·	·	·	·	·	·	·	·	·	·	·	Neckera crispa
·	1	·	·	·	·	·	·	·	·	5	Philonotis fontana
·	1	·	·	·	·	·	·	1	·	·	Plagiothecium denticulatum

Table 38

	1	2	3	4	5	6	7	8	9	10	11
Plagiothecium undulatum			+						4		
Pleurozium schreberi											
Polytrichum alpinum	1										
P. commune											
Pseudoscleropodium purum	1	3		1		1	3	1		1	1
Ptilium crista-castrensis		3								3	
Rhacomitrium canescens										1	
R. lanuginosum											
Rhodobryum roseum	3		2	2							
Rhytidiadelphus loreus	1	4	3				3		2		2
R. squarrosus	2	5	2	2		2		1	2		2
R. triquetrus	2	5	5	3	1	3	3	3		3	1
Rhytidium rugosum											
Sphagnum girgensohnii											
S. nemoreum											
S. plumulosum											
S. papillosum											
S. quinquefarium											
S. squarrosum											
S. auriculatum									3		
Thuidium tamariscinum		4		1	3	4	8		6	2	2
Tortella tortuosa				1	1	2			1		
Trichostomum tenuirostre											
Alicularia scalaris											
Anastrepta orcadensis											
Aneura pinguis											1
A. cf. sinuata											2
Bazzania tricrenata											
Blepharostoma trichophyllum											
Calypogeia trichomanis											
Chiloscyphus polyanthus					2	+			2		
Diplophyllum albicans			1						2		
Herberta adunca											
Jamesoniella carringtoni											
Lophocolea bidentata	3	3	2	1					2		2
Lophozia barbata											
L. floerkii					1						
L. incisa											
L. lycopodioides	1										
L. quinquedentata	2	+	2			3					
Madotheca platyphylla		2									
Mastigophora woodsii											
Metzgeria hamata											
Pellia fabbroniana						+			1		2
Plagiochila asplenioides	2	2	2	2	1	2		2	1	1	1
P. spinulosa											
Pleurozia purpurea											
Ptilidium ciliare			1								
Scapania aspera										1	
S. gracilis											
S. nimbosa											
S. ornithopodioides											
Cladonia gracilis											
C. impexa											
C. pyxidata											
C. rangiferina											
C. sylvatica											
C. uncialis											
Peltidea aphthosa											1
P. leucophlebia					2						
Peltigera canina							1				
Number of species (225)	54	53	45	56	44	60	31	45	54	49	49

Constancy class V   6
    ,,   ,,   IV   14

LOCALITIES

1. Caenlochan, Angus; 2. Ben Lui, Argyll; 3. Creag Meagaidh, Laggan, Inverness-shire; 4,6. Glen Fiadh, Clova, Angus; 5. Glen Doll, Clova, Angus; 7. Meall Cumhan, Glen Nevis, Inverness-shire; 8. Meall nan Tarmachan, Killin, Perthshire; 9. Winter Corrie, Driesh, Clova, Angus; 10. Glen Markie, Monadhliath, Inverness-shire; 11. Loch Brandy, Clova, Angus; 12. Loch Einich, Cairngorms; 13. Glen Lyon, Perth-

(*continued*)

12	13	14	15	16	17	18	19	20	21	22	
·	1	1	3	3	·	3	2	3	·	·	Plagiothecium undulatum
·	3	·	3	·	·	·	·	·	·	·	Pleurozium schreberi
·	3	·	3	2	·	·	2	1	·	·	Polytrichum alpinum
·	·	2	·	·	·	·	·	·	1	·	P. commune
1	·	·	·	·	·	·	·	·	·	·	Pseudoscleropodium purum
2	1	·	3	·	·	·	·	·	·	·	Ptilium crista-castrensis
·	·	·	·	·	·	·	·	·	·	·	Rhacomitrium canescens
·	1	·	·	·	·	·	1	·	1	·	R. lanuginosum
·	·	·	·	·	·	·	·	·	·	·	Rhodobryum roseum
3	1	5	3	3	3	5	3	3	3	·	Rhytidiadelphus loreus
·	·	3	·	3	3	2	3	5	·	·	R. squarrosus
2	1	·	3	2	·	·	3	3	3	·	R. triquetrus
·	1	·	·	·	·	·	·	·	·	·	Rhytidium rugosum
·	·	·	·	·	·	·	·	3	·	·	Sphagnum girgensohnii
·	·	·	4	2	·	2	3	3	·	·	S. nemoreum
·	·	·	2	·	1	2	3	·	·	·	S. plumulosum
·	·	·	·	·	·	·	4	·	·	·	S. papillosum
·	·	·	·	·	·	2	·	·	·	·	S. quinquefarium
·	·	·	·	·	·	1	·	·	·	·	S. squarrosum
·	·	·	·	·	2	2	·	1	·	·	S. auriculatum
·	1	2	2	6	5	4	·	·	3	1	Thuidium tamariscinum
·	·	·	·	·	·	·	·	·	·	·	Tortella tortuosa
·	·	·	1	·	·	·	·	·	·	·	Trichostomum tenuirostre
·	·	·	·	2	·	·	1	·	·	·	Alicularia scalaris
·	·	·	3	·	·	2	·	·	·	·	Anastrepta orcadensis
·	·	·	·	·	·	·	·	·	·	·	Aneura pinguis
·	·	·	·	·	·	1	·	·	·	·	A. cf. sinuata
·	·	·	3	·	2	3	2	·	·	·	Bazzania tricrenata
·	1	·	·	·	·	·	·	·	·	·	Blepharostoma trichophyllum
·	·	·	·	·	·	2	·	·	·	·	Calypogeia trichomanis
·	·	·	·	·	·	·	·	·	·	·	Chiloscyphus polyanthus
·	·	·	2	2	·	3	2	·	·	·	Diplophyllum albicans
·	·	·	·	2	2	·	·	·	·	·	Herberta adunca
·	·	·	3	·	·	2	2	·	·	·	Jamesoniella carringtoni
·	·	·	·	3	·	·	1	3	·	·	Lophocolea bidentata
·	·	·	·	·	·	·	·	·	·	·	Lophozia barbata
·	·	·	·	·	·	·	·	·	·	·	L. floerkii
·	·	·	·	·	·	·	1	·	·	·	L. incisa
·	·	·	·	·	·	·	·	1	·	·	L. lycopodioides
·	·	·	·	·	·	·	2	2	·	·	L. quinquedentata
·	·	·	·	·	·	·	·	·	·	·	Madotheca platyphylla
·	·	·	2	·	2	4	·	·	·	·	Mastigophora woodsii
·	·	·	·	·	·	·	2	·	·	·	Metzgeria hamata
·	·	·	·	·	·	·	2	·	·	·	Pellia fabbroniana
·	·	·	·	·	·	·	·	·	·	·	Plagiochila asplenioides
·	·	·	·	2	·	·	·	·	·	·	P. spinulosa
·	·	·	·	·	·	3	·	·	·	·	Pleurozia purpurea
·	·	·	·	·	·	·	·	·	·	·	Ptilidium ciliare
·	·	·	·	·	·	·	·	·	·	·	Scapania aspera
·	·	·	·	·	·	·	2	·	·	·	S. gracilis
·	·	·	2	·	·	·	·	·	·	·	S. nimbosa
·	·	·	3	·	·	3	2	·	·	·	S. ornithopodioides
·	·	·	·	·	1	·	·	·	·	·	Cladonia gracilis
·	·	·	·	·	·	1	·	·	·	·	C. impexa
·	·	·	·	·	·	·	·	·	1	·	C. pyxidata
·	·	·	·	·	1	·	·	·	·	·	C. rangiferina
·	1	·	3	·	·	·	2	·	·	·	C. sylvatica
·	·	·	1	·	·	·	2	·	·	·	C. uncialis
·	·	·	·	·	·	·	·	·	·	·	Peltidea aphthosa
·	·	·	·	·	·	·	·	·	1	·	P. leucophlebia
·	1	·	2	3	1	·	1	·	1	1	Peltigera canina
19	56	21	56	57	58	57	69	37	43	22	Number of species (225)

(Average 47)

shire; 14. Corrie Kander, Aberdeenshire; 15. Beinn Enaiglair, Inverlael, Ross-shire; 16. Meall Horn, Reay Forest, Sutherland; 17. Carn na Feola, Beinn Dearg, Torridon; 18. Liathach, Torridon, Ross-shire; 19. Sgurr Mor, Fannich Forest, Ross-shire; 20. Maoile Lunndaih, Monar Forest, Ross-shire; 21. Ben More Assynt, Sutherland; 22. Fionchra, Isle of Rhum.

Table 39: Cryptogrammeto-Athyrietum chionophilum

	1	2	3	4	5	6	7	8	9	10
Reference number	M56 135	M56 146	R56 068	R58 017	R57 095	M56 138	M56 115	R58 070	M57 035	M57 031
Map reference	8980 3010	8003 3013	8732 2059	7265 2268	7713 2496	8718 2205	8976 3095	8449 2077	7543 2147	7307 2072
Altitude (feet)	3000	3000	2750	3100	3550	2800	3500	2700	3200	3300
Aspect (degrees)	270	360	—	45	90	45	135	45	45	90
Slope (degrees)	10	50	0	35	25	35	25	35	50	35
Cover (per cent)	90	50	50	100	60	60	50	95	75	80
Height (centimetres)	35	15	—	—	—	10	15	—	—	8
Plot area (square metres)	4	4	4	4	4	4	4	4	4	4
Empetrum hermaphroditum	.	2	.	.	.	.	.	.	.	.
Vaccinium myrtillus	+	2	2	.	.	.	.	.	+	.
V. uliginosum	.	2	.	.	.	.	.	.	.	.
Athyrium alpestre	8	5	4	5	4	3	3	2	2	.
Blechnum spicant	.	4	2	2	+	.	.	.	+	.
Cryptogramma crispa	.	.	5	4	6	5	6	7	6	7
Dryopteris austriaca	2	.	.	.	.	.	.	2	.	.
D. spinulosa	.	.	3	.	.	.	.	.	.	.
Lycopodium selago	.	1	1	.	+	+	.	.	.	.
Thelypteris dryopteris	.	.	.	.	.	.	.	.	3	.
T. oreopteris	.	.	3	.	.	.	.	.	.	.
T. phegopteris	.	.	3	2	.	.	.	+	.	.
Agrostis tenuis	.	.	2	3	.	.	.	2	.	2
Anthoxanthum odoratum	.	.	.	3	.	.	.	3	.	.
Deschampsia caespitosa	.	.	2	3	3	3	4	4	3	3
D. flexuosa	1	3	3	3	1	+	.	4	2	+
Festuca ovina agg.	.	.	2	.	.	1	.	.	.	.
Nardus stricta	2	.	2	3	.	1	.	3	.	1
Carex bigelowii	1	1	1	2	3	.	2	.	.	.
Juncus trifidus	+	.	3	.	.	.	2	.	.	.
Luzula multiflora	.	.	.	.	.	.	.	2	.	.
L. spicata	.	.	.	1	.	+	.	.	.	.
L. sylvatica	.	.	.	+	.	.	.	.	.	.
Trichophorum caespitosum	1	1	.	.	.	.	.	.	.	.
Alchemilla alpina	+	3	4	3	+	1	.	3	2	2
Campanula rotundifolia	.	3	.	.	.	.	.	.	.	.
Cerastium vulgatum	.	.	.	.	.	1	.	2	.	.
Epilobium anagallidifolium	.	.	.	.	.	2	.	2	+	.
Euphrasia frigida	.	.	1	.	.	.	.	1	.	.
Galium hercynicum	1	2	3	3	+	2	2	3	3	1
Gnaphalium supinum	.	.	.	1	+	.	1	.	.	1
Oxalis acetosella	.	.	.	.	.	2	.	3	3	.
Oxyria digyna	.	.	.	.	.	2	.	.	.	.
Potentilla erecta	.	.	.	+	.	.	.	.	.	.
Rubus chamaemorus	1	.	.	.	.	.	.	.	.	.
Rumex acetosa	.	.	.	3	2	1	.	3	2	1
Saxifraga stellaris	.	.	.	2	1	3	.	.	1	2
Sibbaldia procumbens	.	.	2	.	.	.	.	.	.	+
Succisa pratensis	1	.	.	.	.	.	.	.	.	.
Viola palustris	.	2	.	1	3	.	3	3	3	.
V. riviniana	.	.	2	.	.	.	.	.	.	.
Dicranella heteromalla	.	.	.	2	.	.	.	.	.	.
Dicranum fuscescens	6	.	.	.	1	.	2	.	.	2
D. majus	.	.	3	.	.	7	.	3	1	.
D. scoparium	1	.	3	4	2	.	.	3	.	.
D. starkei	.	.	.	2	.	7	2	2	3	.
Drepanocladus uncinatus	.	.	.	.	1	.	.	.	.	.
Eurhynchium praelongum	3	.	.	.	.	.	2	.	.	3
Hylocomium splendens	.	.	3	2	.	7	.	4	2	3
H. umbratum	.	.	.	3	.	7	.	3	.	.
Hypnum callichroum	1	.	4	3	4	7	.	3	3	2
Mnium punctatum	.	.	.	.	.	7	.	2	2	.
Oligotrichum hercynicum	.	.	+	1	.	7	.	.	.	.
Plagiothecium denticulatum	3	.	.	.	3	.	1	.	.	.
P. sylvaticum	.	.	2	.	.	7	.	.	3	3
P. undulatum	.	.	.	3	.	7	.	3	3	.
Pleurozium schreberi	.	.	2	2	.	7	1	.	.	2
Pohlia nutans	.	.	.	.	.	.	.	.	.	2
Polytrichum alpinum	3	.	.	4	1	7	3	3	1	4
P. norvegicum	.	.	.	.	.	.	+	.	.	.
P. piliferum	.	.	.	.	.	.	1	.	.	.
P. urnigerum	.	.	1	.	.	.	.	2	2	1
Pseudoscleropodium purum	.	.	.	.	.	7	.	.	.	.
Rhacomitrium aquaticum	.	.	3	.	.	.	.	.	.	.
R. canescens	.	.	3	.	2	.	.	.	1	6
R. fasciculare	.	.	.	.	.	.	3	.	.	.
R. heterostichum	.	4	.	.	.	.	.	.	.	.
R. lanuginosum	.	.	4	.	2	.	1	3	.	.
Rhytidiadelphus loreus	.	.	3	7	1	7	+	5	4	2
R. squarrosus	.	.	2	2	3	.	.	3	.	4
Sphagnum auriculatum	.	.	.	.	.	7	.	.	.	.
S. nemoreum	1	.	3	.	.	7	.	4	.	.

Table 39 (*continued*)

	1	2	3	4	5	6	7	8	9	10
Alicularia scalaris	·	·	·	·	·	7	·	·	·	·
Anastrepta orcadensis	·	·	·	·	·	·	·	3	1	·
Anastrophyllum donianum	·	·	4	·	·	·	·	·	·	·
Anthelia julacea	·	·	3	·	·	·	·	·	·	·
Aplozia sphaerocarpa	·	·	1	·	·	·	·	·	·	·
Bazzania tricrenata	·	·	3	·	·	7	·	·	·	·
B. trilobata	·	·	·	·	·	7	·	·	·	·
Calypogeia trichomanis	·	·	·	·	·	7	·	·	·	·
Diplophyllum albicans	·	·	4	2	·	7	·	·	2	·
Leptoscyphus taylori	·	·	3	·	·	·	·	1	·	·
Lophozia alpestris	·	·	·	·	·	·	2	·	2	·
L. floerkii	2	·	3	4	1	7	2	4	3	1
L. obtusa	·	·	·	·	·	·	·	·	1	·
L. quinquedentata	·	·	2	·	·	·	·	·	·	·
L. ventricosa	·	·	·	·	·	·	·	·	1	·
Marsupella emarginata	·	·	·	·	·	7	·	·	·	·
Pellia epiphylla	·	·	·	·	·	7	·	·	·	·
Ptilidium ciliare	·	·	·	·	·	·	1	·	·	·
Scapania nimbosa	1	·	·	·	·	·	·	·	·	·
S. cf. curta	·	·	·	·	·	·	·	·	1	·
S. ornithopodioides	·	·	·	·	·	7	·	·	·	·
Microhepatics	·	2	·	·	·	·	·	·	·	·
Cetraria islandica	·	1	1	·	·	1	·	·	·	·
Cladonia bellidiflora	1	1	·	·	2	+	3	2	2	1
C. coccifera	·	·	·	1	·	·	·	·	·	·
C. gracilis	·	·	1	·	·	·	·	2	1	1
C. pyxidata	·	·	·	·	1	·	·	·	·	·
C. squamosa	1	·	·	·	·	·	·	·	·	·
Crocynia cf. neglecta	·	·	·	·	·	·	1	·	·	·
Peltigera canina	·	·	·	·	·	·	·	2	·	2
Stereocaulon vesuvianum	·	·	1	·	·	·	·	·	·	·
Number of species (102)	23	17	46	33	26	42	23	38	34	27

(Average 31)

Constancy class V 11
  ,,   ,, IV 11

LOCALITIES

1. Derry Cairngorm, Aberdeenshire; 2. Coire Etchachan, Cairngorms, Aberdeenshire; 3. Mullach Coire Mhic Fhearchair, Fisherfield Forest, Ross-shire; 4. Ben Lui, Perthshire; 5. Ben Alder, Inverness-shire; 6. Sgurr Mor, Fannich Forest, Ross-shire; 7. South Beinn a' Bhuird, Cairngorms; 8. Sgurr Choinnich, Monar Forest, Ross-shire; 9. Bidean nam Bian, Glencoe, Argyll; 10. Ben Cruachan, Argyll.

Table 40: Dwarf Herb nodum (1–20);

	1	2	3	4	5	6	7	8	9	10
Reference number	R57 108	R57 118	R57 227	M56 078	M57 048	R56 022	R56 040	R56 051	R56 108	R56 030
Map reference	7727 2482	7746 2465	7772 3185	9195 2325	7714 2199	8746 2012	8689 2233	8807 2250	8194 2010	8837 2252
Altitude (feet)	2800	3000	2800	2800	3900	2650	2750	2700	2900	2350
Aspect (degrees)	360	360	180	90	45	135	135	270	325	–
Slope (degrees)	10	35	40	45	40	7	12	27	15	0
Cover (per cent)	100	100	95	90	95	100	100	98	100	92
Height (centimetres)	–	–	–	4	–	3	–	–	–	–
Plot area (square metres)	4	4	4	4	4	4	4	4	4	4
Dryas octopetala	.	.	4	.	.	.	.	.	.	.
Empetrum hermaphroditum	.	.	2	.	.	2	4	3	.	2
Salix arbuscula	.	.	.	.	.	.	.	.	.	.
S. herbacea	.	.	.	.	.	.	.	.	.	3
S. reticulata	.	.	3	.	.	.	.	.	.	.
Vaccinium myrtillus	1	.	2	.	.	.	1	2	.	.
V. vitis-idaea	2	.	2	.	.	1	3	2	.	.
Botrychium lunaria	.	.	.	.	.	.	.	.	.	.
Lycopodium alpinum	.	.	.	.	.	1	.	.	.	.
L. selago	.	.	.	+	.	+	.	1	.	1
Selaginella selaginoides	2	3	.	3	3	2	3	3	3	3
Agrostis canina	3	2	.	.	.	2	4	4	3	5
A. tenuis	4	3	.	6	.	5	+	3	3	3
Anthoxanthum odoratum	.	.	3	2	.	3	.	.	.	2
Deschampsia caespitosa	4	4	3	3	.	5	5	4	5	1
D. flexuosa	.	.	.	.	.	3	.	3	3	.
Festuca ovina agg.	6	3	5	4	1	5	6	6	4	5
F. rubra	.	3	2	.	.	.	.	.	2	.
Helictotrichon pratense	.	.	3	.	.	.	.	.	.	.
Nardus stricta	3	.	2	.	.	4	.	3	3	4
Poa alpina	.	.	.	2	1	.	.	.	.	.
P. pratensis	.	.	.	.	.	.	.	.	.	.
Sieglingia decumbens	.	.	.	.	.	.	.	.	.	.
Carex bigelowii	3	2	.	2	.	3	4	4	5	2
C. capillaris	.	3	3	.	.	.	.	.	.	.
C. demissa	.	.	.	.	.	.	.	.	.	1
C. lachenalii	.	.	.	.	2	.	.	.	.	.
C. panicea	.	.	.	.	.	.	.	.	.	3
C. pilulifera	.	.	.	.	.	2	3	1	.	3
C. pulicaris	.	.	5	.	+	.	.	.	.	3
C. saxatilis	.	.	.	.	+	.	.	.	.	.
C. vaginata	.	.	.	.	2	.	.	.	.	.
Juncus biglumis	.	.	.	.	2	.	.	.	.	.
J. trifidus	2	1	.	.	.	.	.	3	2	.
J. triglumis	.	1	.	.	.	.	.	.	.	.
Luzula multiflora	2	.	2	1	.	.	1	.	.	.
L. spicata	.	1	.	.	2	.	1	2	2	1
L. sylvatica	.	.	2	.	.	.	.	.	.	1
Tofieldia pusilla	.	.	2	.	.	.	.	.	.	.
Trichophorum caespitosum	1	.	.	.	.	.	.	.	.	.
Achillea millefolium	.	.	.	3	.	.	.	+	.	.
Alchemilla alpina	3	2	1	5	4	2	4	4	4	4
A. filicaulis	.	.	2	3	4	.	.	.	.	.
A. glabra	.	.	.	.	.	.	.	.	.	.
A. vestita	.	.	.	.	.	.	.	.	.	.
A. vulgaris agg.	.	.	.	.	.	.	.	.	.	.
A. wichurae	.	.	.	.	.	.	.	.	.	.
Angelica sylvestris	.	.	2	.	.	.	.	.	.	.
Antennaria dioica	.	.	.	.	.	.	.	.	.	2
Armeria maritima	.	2	.	1	.	1	4	3	.	.
Bellis perennis	.	.	1	.	.	.	.	.	.	.
Campanula rotundifolia	3	.	.	.	.	.	.	.	.	.
Cardamine pratensis	.	.	.	.	.	.	.	.	.	.
Cerastium alpinum	.	.	.	.	2	.	.	.	.	.
C. vulgatum	.	2	.	1	.	.	.	.	.	.
Cherleria sedoides	.	+	.	4	.	8	.	3	.	.
Cochlearia alpina	.	.	.	.	4	.	.	.	.	.
Draba rupestris	.	.	.	.	.	.	.	.	.	.
Epilobium anagallidifolium	.	.	.	3	3	.	.	.	.	.
Euphrasia frigida	.	.	.	2	3	.	.	.	.	.
Euphrasia sp.	3	3	3	.	.	.	.	.	2	.
Galium hercynicum	3	.	.	.	.	1	1	.	2	2
Gentianella campestris	.	.	1	.	.	.	.	.	.	.
Geranium sylvaticum	.	.	2	.	.	.	.	.	.	.
Geum rivale	.	1	2	.	.	.	.	.	.	.
Gnaphalium supinum	.	.	.	2	2	.	.	2	.	2
Hieracium pilosella	.	.	2	.	.	.	.	.	.	.
Hieracium sp.	.	.	2	.	.	.	.	.	.	.
Leontodon autumnalis	+	.	.	.	.	.	1	.	.	3
Linum catharticum	.	.	3	.	.	.	.	.	.	.
Myosotis alpestris	.	.	.	.	.	.	.	.	.	.
Oxyria digyna	.	.	.	.	2	.	.	.	.	.
Parnassia palustris	.	.	2	.	.	.	.	.	.	.

Related Alchemilla vulgaris community (21)

11	12	13	14	15	16	17	18	19	20	21	
P52 078	P52 080	P52 081	P52 086	P52 087	P52 195	P52 065	R58 130	M56 045	R57 068	R57 119	Reference number
7414 2632	7414 2632	7412 2632	7408 2630	7408 2630	7411 2633	7418 2612	7274 2263	8728 1985	8876 2295	7745 2463	Map reference
3250	3250	3350	3100	3250	2900	3050	2300	2450	2650	2900	Altitude (feet)
150	150	150	160	110	200	310	360	270	300	45	Aspect (degrees)
8	8	8	12	15	15	10	20	5	40	20	Slope (degrees)
90	80	90	100	—	100	100	100	100	100	90	Cover (per cent)
4	3	10	10	5	10	5	—	2	—	5	Height (centimetres)
4	4	4	4	2	4	4	4	1	4	4	Plot area (square metres)
.	.	.	.	.	.	.	4	.	3	.	Dryas octopetala
.	.	.	.	.	.	.	4	.	.	.	Empetrum hermaphroditum
.	.	.	.	.	.	.	4	.	.	.	Salix arbuscula
.	.	.	.	.	.	3	.	.	.	1	S. herbacea
.	.	.	.	.	.	.	.	.	.	.	S. reticulata
.	.	.	.	.	.	.	.	.	1	.	Vaccinium myrtillus
.	.	.	.	.	.	.	.	.	.	.	V. vitis-idaea
.	2	.	1	.	.	.	.	.	.	.	Botrychium lunaria
.	.	.	.	.	.	.	.	4	.	.	Lycopodium alpinum
2	1	.	.	.	.	1	.	.	.	1	L. selago
1	3	3	2	.	2	2	3	3	2	3	**Selaginella selaginoides**
.	.	.	.	.	.	.	.	.	.	3	Agrostis canina
3	3	3	2	3	4	3	3	4	4	4	**A. tenuis**
.	.	2	3	4	.	.	.	.	1	.	Anthoxanthum odoratum
2	2	1	3	2	2	.	3	1	4	4	**Deschampsia caespitosa**
.	.	.	.	.	.	.	.	.	.	.	D. flexuosa
3	3	3	3	4	1	7	6	4	4	.	**Festuca ovina agg.**
.	.	.	.	.	.	.	6	.	2	4	F. rubra
.	.	.	.	.	.	.	3	.	.	.	Helictotrichon pratense
.	3	3	4	3	2	.	2	.	.	3	Nardus stricta
.	.	.	.	.	.	.	.	.	.	2	Poa alpina
.	.	.	.	.	.	.	2	.	.	.	P. pratensis
.	.	.	.	.	.	.	.	.	3	.	Sieglingia decumbens
1	.	.	.	.	.	2	.	2	3	1	Carex bigelowii
.	.	1	.	.	.	.	3	.	.	2	C. capillaris
.	.	.	.	.	.	.	.	2	.	.	C. demissa
.	.	.	.	.	.	.	.	.	.	.	C. lachenalii
.	.	.	.	.	.	.	.	3	1	.	C. panicea
.	.	.	.	.	4	.	.	.	.	.	C. pilulifera
.	.	.	.	.	2	.	3	3	.	.	C. pulicaris
.	.	.	.	.	.	.	.	.	.	.	C. saxatilis
.	.	.	.	.	.	.	2	.	.	.	C. vaginata
.	.	.	.	.	.	.	.	.	.	.	Juncus biglumis
.	.	.	.	.	.	.	.	.	.	.	J. trifidus
.	.	.	.	.	.	.	.	.	.	.	J. triglumis
.	.	.	.	.	.	.	.	.	3	.	Luzula multiflora
2	1	2	1	2	.	3	.	2	2	.	L. spicata
.	.	.	.	.	.	.	2	.	.	.	L. sylvatica
.	.	.	.	.	.	.	.	.	.	.	Tofieldia pusilla
.	.	.	.	.	.	.	.	.	.	.	Trichophorum caespitosum
.	.	.	.	.	2	.	.	.	4	.	Achillea millefolium
8	5	7	4	4	3	3	4	3	3	3	**Alchemilla alpina**
.	.	.	.	.	.	.	.	3	.	.	A. filicaulis
.	.	.	.	3	.	.	3	.	.	.	A. glabra
.	.	.	.	3	.	.	3	.	.	5	A. vestita
2	3	4	2	3	3	.	.	.	.	.	A. vulgaris agg.
.	.	.	.	.	.	.	.	.	3	.	A. wichurae
.	.	.	.	.	.	.	1	.	.	.	Angelica sylvestris
.	.	.	.	.	.	.	2	1	.	.	Antennaria dioica
.	.	.	.	.	.	.	2	+	3	.	Armeria maritima
.	.	.	.	.	.	.	.	.	.	.	Bellis perennis
2	3	.	2	3	2	3	2	.	.	.	Campanula rotundifolia
.	1	.	2	.	.	.	.	.	.	.	Cardamine pratensis
2	2	3	3	2	2	1	.	.	2	.	Cerastium alpinum
2	1	.	2	3	1	1	1	.	+	1	C. vulgatum
2	3	4	2	3	2	1	2	.	6	.	Cherleria sedoides
.	.	.	.	.	.	.	.	.	.	.	Cochlearia alpina
.	.	.	3	.	.	.	.	.	.	.	Draba rupestris
1	2	2	2	2	.	.	.	.	.	1	Epilobium anagallidifolium
.	.	.	.	.	.	.	.	.	.	.	Euphrasia frigida
2	3	3	3	2	3	.	2	2	3	2	Euphrasia sp.
3	3	2	3	1	.	2	.	.	.	.	Galium hercynicum
.	.	.	.	.	.	.	.	.	.	.	Gentianella campestris
.	.	.	.	.	.	.	.	.	.	.	Geranium sylvaticum
.	.	.	.	.	.	.	.	.	+	1	Geum rivale
2	.	.	.	1	1	.	.	.	.	1	Gnaphalium supinum
.	.	.	.	.	.	.	.	.	.	.	Hieracium pilosella
.	.	.	.	.	.	.	.	.	.	.	Hieracium sp.
.	.	.	.	.	.	.	.	.	1	.	Leontodon autumnalis
.	.	.	.	.	.	.	.	.	.	.	Linum catharticum
.	.	3	1	.	.	.	.	.	.	.	Myosotis alpestris
.	.	.	.	.	.	.	.	.	.	.	Oxyria digyna
.	.	.	.	.	.	.	.	.	.	.	Parnassia palustris

Table 40

	1	2	3	4	5	6	7	8	9	10
Pinguicula vulgaris	·	·	1	·	·	·	·	·	·	·
Plantago maritima	·	·	·	·	·	·	·	·	·	2
Polygonum viviparum	3	3	3	3	2	·	·	3	·	3
Potentilla erecta	·	·	·	·	·	·	·	·	3	1
Ranunculus acris	·	·	2	3	4	·	·	2	·	3
Rhinanthus minor agg.	·	·	·	·	·	·	·	·	·	·
Rumex acetosa	·	·	·	1	2	·	+	·	·	·
Sagina procumbens	·	2	·	·	·	·	·	·	·	·
S. saginoides	·	·	·	2	2	·	·	·	·	·
Saussurea alpina	2	·	·	·	·	·	·	·	·	·
Saxifraga aizoides	·	2	2	·	2	·	·	·	·	·
S. hypnoides	·	2	·	·	3	·	·	·	·	·
S. oppositifolia	·	3	·	1	4	·	·	·	·	·
S. stellaris	·	·	·	2	2	·	·	·	·	·
Sedum rosea	·	·	·	2	1	·	·	·	·	·
Sibbaldia procumbens	·	·	·	4	4	2	4	3	3	2
Silene acaulis	8	8	6	5	+	·	7	5	8	8
Solidago virgaurea	·	·	·	·	·	·	+	·	·	+
Succisa pratensis	·	·	2	·	·	·	·	·	1	1
Taraxacum officinalis agg.	·	·	·	2	2	·	·	·	·	·
Thalictrum alpinum	3	3	1	+	·	·	·	3	+	3
Thymus drucei	3	3	3	1	·	4	4	5	4	2
Trollius europaeus	·	·	·	·	·	·	·	·	·	+
Veronica alpina	·	1	·	·	2	·	·	·	·	·
V. serpyllifolia	·	·	·	1	2	·	·	·	·	·
Viola lutea	·	·	·	·	·	·	·	·	·	1
V. palustris	·	+	·	2	·	2	2	3	3	1
V. riviniana	·	·	3	3	·	·	·	·	·	·
Andreaea alpina	·	·	·	·	·	·	·	·	2	·
cf. Arctoa fulvella	·	·	·	·	·	·	·	·	·	·
Aulacomnium turgidum	·	·	·	·	·	2	4	3	·	·
Bartramia ithyphylla	·	·	·	·	·	·	·	·	·	·
Blindia acuta	·	·	·	·	1	·	·	·	·	·
Brachythecium rivulare	·	·	·	1	·	·	·	·	·	·
Breutelia chrysocoma	·	·	·	·	·	·	·	·	·	1
Bryum pseudotriquetrum	·	2	·	·	·	·	·	·	·	·
Bryum sp.	·	·	2	·	·	·	·	·	·	·
Campylium protensum	·	·	2	·	·	·	·	·	·	·
C. stellatum	·	·	·	·	·	·	·	·	·	3
Campylopus flexuosus	·	·	·	·	·	·	·	1	·	·
Climacium dendroides	·	·	·	·	·	·	·	·	·	·
Ctenidium molluscum	2	3	2	5	3	·	·	·	·	3
Dichodontium pellucidum	·	·	·	·	1	·	·	·	·	·
Dicranum fuscescens	·	·	·	·	·	·	·	·	·	·
D. scoparium	1	·	·	·	·	2	2	3	2	3
D. starkei	·	·	·	·	2	·	·	·	·	·
Distichium capillaceum	·	·	·	·	·	·	·	·	·	·
Ditrichum flexicaule	·	·	3	·	·	·	·	·	·	·
Drepanocladus uncinatus	2	3	·	·	·	·	3	2	·	3
Entodon orthocarpus	·	·	·	·	·	·	·	·	·	·
Fissidens osmundoides	·	·	·	·	·	·	·	·	·	·
Gymnostomum recurvirostrum	·	·	·	·	·	·	·	·	·	·
Hylocomium splendens	4	·	2	·	4	3	3	4	2	3
H. pyrenaicum	·	·	·	·	·	·	·	·	·	·
Hypnum cupressiforme	2	·	·	·	·	2	1	3	·	3
H. callichroum	·	·	·	·	·	1	·	·	·	·
H. hamulosum	·	·	·	2	·	·	2	2	+	2
Isothecium myosuroides	·	·	·	·	·	·	·	·	·	·
Leucobryum glaucum	·	·	·	·	·	·	·	·	·	1
Oligotrichum hercynicum	·	·	·	·	·	·	·	·	·	·
Oncophorus virens	·	·	·	·	·	·	·	·	·	·
Plagiobryum zierii	·	1	1	·	·	·	·	·	·	·
Pleurozium schreberi	2	·	·	·	3	2	·	3	2	·
Pohlia cruda	·	1	·	·	·	·	·	·	·	·
P. nutans	·	·	·	·	3	·	·	·	·	·
Polytrichum alpinum	1	·	·	3	2	3	3	2	2	2
P. urnigerum	·	·	·	·	3	·	·	·	·	·
Pseudoleskea incurvata	·	·	·	·	·	·	·	·	·	·
Pseudoscleropodium purum	·	·	·	·	·	·	·	·	·	3
Ptilium crista-castrensis	·	·	·	·	·	·	·	·	·	·
Rhacomitrium aquaticum	·	·	·	·	·	·	·	·	2	·
R. canescens	·	3	·	·	·	·	·	·	·	3
R. fasciculare	·	·	·	1	2	1	·	·	3	·
R. heterostichum	·	·	·	·	·	·	·	·	·	·
R. lanuginosum	3	·	·	·	·	3	5	6	5	3
Rhodobryum roseum	·	·	·	·	·	·	·	·	·	·
Rhytidiadelphus loreus	1	·	·	·	3	3	2	3	2	2
R. squarrosus	3	1	·	2	·	3	·	·	·	1
R. triquetrus	·	·	3	·	·	·	·	·	·	1
Sphagnum nemoreum	·	·	·	·	·	·	·	·	1	·
Thuidium abietinum	·	·	3	·	·	·	·	·	·	·
T. delicatulum	·	·	·	·	·	·	·	·	·	·
T. tamariscinum	·	·	3	·	·	·	·	·	·	·
Trichostomum tenuirostre	·	·	·	·	·	·	·	·	·	·
Tortella tortuosa	·	2	2	·	·	·	·	·	·	·
Alicularia scalaris	·	·	1	1	·	·	·	1	·	·
Aneura pinguis	·	·	1	·	·	·	·	·	·	·
Anthelia julacea	·	·	·	·	1	·	·	·	·	·
Blepharostoma trichophyllum	·	1	·	·	·	·	·	·	·	·

(continued)

11	12	13	14	15	16	17	18	19	20	21	
·	·	·	·	·	·	·	·	·	1	·	Pinguicula vulgaris
·	·	·	·	·	·	·	·	3	·	·	Plantago maritima
·	1	3	·	·	3	3	4	·	4	3	Polygonum viviparum
·	·	·	·	·	·	·	·	·	·	·	Potentilla erecta
·	·	·	1	1	1	·	·	·	2	·	Ranunculus acris
·	·	1	·	·	·	·	·	·	·	·	Rhinanthus minor agg.
·	2	2	·	1	·	·	·	·	3	·	Rumex acetosa
·	·	·	·	·	·	·	·	·	·	·	Sagina procumbens
·	1	1	3	·	·	·	·	·	·	·	Sagina saginoides
·	·	·	·	·	·	·	·	·	1	·	Saussurea alpina
·	·	·	1	·	·	·	·	·	·	1	Saxifraga aizoides
·	·	1	1	·	·	·	2	·	·	·	S. hypnoides
·	·	1	·	1	·	·	3	·	3	3	S. oppositifolia
·	·	·	·	·	·	·	·	·	·	·	S. stellaris
·	·	·	·	·	1	·	·	·	+	·	Sedum rosea
4	3	3	4	3	3	1	·	4	2	3	**Sibbaldia procumbens**
·	3	2	·	·	4	4	6	3	5	2	**Silene acaulis**
·	·	·	·	·	·	·	·	·	·	·	Solidago virgaurea
·	·	·	·	·	·	·	·	1	·	·	Succisa pratensis
·	·	1	·	·	·	·	·	+	·	1	Taraxacum officinalis agg.
·	·	·	1	1	1	3	3	3	4	5	Thalictrum alpinum
3	3	3	3	4	3	·	3	3	4	3	**Thymus drucei**
·	·	·	·	·	1	·	·	·	·	·	Trollius europaeus
·	·	·	·	·	·	·	·	·	2	·	Veronica alpina
1	·	·	3	·	·	·	·	·	·	·	V. serpyllifolia
·	·	1	·	·	1	·	·	·	·	·	Viola lutea
2	·	·	3	1	·	·	·	2	·	·	V. palustris
·	·	·	2	·	·	·	3	·	·	·	V. riviniana
·	·	·	·	·	·	·	·	7	·	·	Andreaea alpina
1	·	·	·	·	·	·	·	·	·	·	cf. Arctoa fulvella
1	1	1	·	·	·	·	·	·	2	·	Aulacomnium turgidum
·	·	·	·	·	·	·	·	·	·	·	Bartramia ithyphylla
·	·	·	·	·	·	·	·	·	·	1	Blindia acuta
·	·	·	·	·	·	·	·	·	·	·	Brachythecium rivulare
·	·	·	·	·	·	·	·	·	·	·	Breutelia chrysocoma
·	·	·	·	·	1	·	·	·	2	·	Bryum pseudotriquetrum
·	·	·	·	·	·	·	·	·	·	·	Bryum sp.
·	·	·	·	·	·	·	3	·	1	·	Campylium protensum
·	·	·	·	·	·	·	·	·	·	1	C. stellatum
·	·	·	·	·	·	·	·	·	·	·	Campylopus flexuosus
·	·	·	·	·	1	·	·	·	·	·	Climacium dendroides
·	·	·	1	·	·	·	3	·	2	3	Ctenidium molluscum
·	·	·	·	·	·	·	·	·	·	·	Dichodontium pellucidum
·	·	·	·	·	·	1	·	·	·	·	Dicranum fuscescens
·	1	·	·	·	·	1	·	·	2	·	D. scoparium
·	·	·	·	·	·	·	·	·	·	·	D. starkei
·	·	·	·	·	·	·	2	·	·	·	Distichium capillaceum
·	·	·	·	·	·	·	3	·	1	·	Ditrichum flexicaule
·	·	·	·	·	·	·	2	·	2	1	Drepanocladus uncinatus
·	·	·	·	·	·	·	1	·	·	·	Entodon orthocarpus
·	·	·	·	·	·	·	·	·	·	4	Fissidens osmundoides
·	·	·	·	·	·	·	·	+	·	·	Gymnostomum recurvirostrum
·	·	·	2	1	2	3	·	3	·	·	Hylocomium splendens
·	·	·	·	·	·	·	·	·	2	·	H. pyrenaicum
·	·	·	·	·	·	·	3	·	2	·	Hypnum cupressiforme
·	·	·	·	·	·	·	·	·	1	·	H. callichroum
·	·	·	·	·	·	·	·	·	·	·	H. hamulosum
·	·	·	·	·	·	·	·	·	3	·	Isothecium myosuroides
·	·	·	·	·	·	·	·	·	·	·	Leucobryum glaucum
1	·	·	·	·	·	·	·	·	·	·	Oligotrichum hercynicum
·	·	·	·	·	·	·	·	·	·	4	Oncophorus virens
·	·	·	·	·	·	·	·	·	·	·	Plagiobryum zierii
1	·	·	2	1	·	5	·	·	·	·	Pleurozium schreberi
1	·	·	·	·	·	·	·	·	·	·	Pohlia cruda
1	1	·	·	·	·	·	·	·	·	·	P. nutans
3	3	3	3	3	2	3	·	+	2	·	**Polytrichum alpinum**
3	1	3	1	2	·	·	·	·	1	·	P. urnigerum
·	·	·	1	·	2	·	·	·	·	·	Pseudoleskea incurvata
·	·	·	·	·	·	·	3	·	·	·	Pseudoscleropodium purum
·	·	·	·	·	·	·	·	·	1	·	Ptilium crista-castrensis
·	·	·	·	·	·	·	·	2	·	·	Rhacomitrium aquaticum
1	4	3	6	5	5	·	3	·	·	4	R. canescens
·	·	·	·	·	·	·	·	·	·	·	R. fasciculare
1	·	1	·	·	·	·	·	·	·	·	R. heterostichum
3	·	·	·	·	·	5	3	1	4	2	R. lanuginosum
1	·	·	·	·	·	·	·	·	·	·	Rhodobryum roseum
·	·	·	·	·	·	·	·	·	2	·	Rhytidiadelphus loreus
1	·	·	1	5	1	·	·	·	2	·	R. squarrosus
·	·	·	·	·	3	·	3	·	3	2	R. triquetrus
·	·	·	·	·	·	·	·	·	·	·	Sphagnum nemoreum
·	·	·	·	·	·	·	·	·	·	·	Thuidium abietinum
·	·	·	·	·	·	·	3	·	2	·	T. delicatulum
·	·	·	·	·	1	·	·	·	·	·	T. tamariscinum
·	1	·	1	·	·	·	·	·	·	·	Trichostomum tenuirostre
·	·	·	·	·	1	·	4	·	1	1	Tortella tortuosa
2	1	2	·	·	·	·	·	·	·	1	Aliularia scalaris
·	·	·	·	·	·	·	·	·	·	1	Aneura pinguis
·	·	·	·	·	·	·	·	·	·	·	Anthelia julacea
·	·	·	·	·	·	·	·	·	·	·	Blepharostoma trichophyllum

Table 40

	1	2	3	4	5	6	7	8	9	10
Diplophyllum albicans	.	.	.	.	.	.	.	1	.	2
Frullania tamarisci	.	.	.	.	.	.	.	.	.	.
Lophozia alpestris	.	.	.	.	3	.	.	.	.	.
L. hatcheri	.	.	.	.	.	.	.	2	.	.
L. lycopodioides	.	.	.	.	.	.	.	.	.	.
L. quinquedentata	.	2	.	.	1	.	.	.	.	.
L. ventricosa	.	1	.	.	.	.	.	.	.	.
Marsupella emarginata	.	.	.	.	1	.	.	.	.	.
M. pearsoni	.	.	.	1	.	.	.	.	.	.
Pellia epiphylla	.	.	.	.	3	.	.	.	.	.
Plagiochila asplenioides	.	2	.	.	1	.	.	.	.	.
Preissia quadrata	.	1	.	.	.	.	.	.	.	.
Ptilidium ciliare	.	.	.	.	.	.	2	2	.	.
Scapania aspera	.	.	.	.	.	.	.	.	.	.
S. subalpina	.	.	.	1	.	.	.	.	.	.
Cetraria aculeata	.	.	.	.	.	.	.	.	.	.
C. islandica	.	.	.	.	.	2	2	3	1	.
Cladonia bellidiflora	.	.	.	.	.	.	.	1	.	.
C. coccifera	.	.	.	.	.	.	2	.	.	.
C. furcata	.	.	.	.	.	.	.	.	.	.
C. gracilis	.	.	1	.	.	1	1	.	.	.
C. pyxidata	.	.	1	.	.	.	.	.	.	2
C. sylvatica	.	.	.	.	.	.	.	.	.	.
C. uncialis	.	.	.	.	.	.	3	2	.	.
Ochrolechia frigida	.	.	.	1	.	.	2	.	.	.
Peltidea leucophlebia	.	1	.	.	.	.	.	.	.	.
Peltigera canina	.	.	.	1	.	+	.	.	.	.
Sphaerophorus globosus	.	.	.	.	.	.	1	1	.	.
Stereocaulon vesuvianum	.	.	.	.	.	.	.	.	.	.
Number of species (191)	32	42	51	44	46	35	38	46	33	52

(Avera

Constancy class V 9
     ,,   ,, IV 10

LOCALITIES

1. Ben Alder, Inverness-shire; 2. Ardverikie Forest, Inverness-shire; 3. Caenlochan Glen, Angus 4. Ben More Assynt, Sutherland;
5. Aonach Beag, Nevis range, Inverness-shire; 6. A'Mhaighdean, Fisherfield Forest, Ross-shire; 7. Meall Gorm, Fannich Forest, Ross-shire;
8. Beinn Dearg, Inverlael, Ross-shire; 9. Beinn Fhada, Kintail, Ross-shire; 10. Eididh nan Clach Geala, Inverlael, Ross-shire; 11-17. Ben

(continued)

11	12	13	14	15	16	17	18	19	20	21	
.	.	.	.	.	1	.	.	.	.	.	Diplophyllum albicans
.	.	.	.	.	.	.	2	.	2	.	Frullania tamarisci
.	.	.	.	.	.	.	.	.	.	.	Lophozia alpestris
.	.	.	.	.	.	.	.	.	.	.	L. hatcheri
.	.	.	.	.	1	.	.	.	.	.	L. lycopodioides
.	.	.	.	.	.	.	.	.	2	.	L. quinquedentata
.	.	.	.	.	.	.	.	.	.	.	L. ventricosa
.	.	.	.	.	.	.	.	.	.	.	Marsupella emarginata
.	.	.	.	.	.	.	.	.	.	.	M. pearsoni
.	.	.	.	.	.	.	.	.	.	.	Pellia epiphylla
.	.	.	.	.	.	.	.	.	1	.	Plagiochila asplenioides
.	.	.	.	.	.	.	.	.	.	.	Preissia quadrata
.	1	.	.	.	.	2	.	.	1	.	Ptilidium ciliare
.	.	.	.	.	.	.	2	.	.	.	Scapania aspera
.	.	.	.	.	.	.	.	.	.	.	S. subalpina
.	.	.	.	.	.	1	.	.	.	.	Cetraria aculeata
.	.	.	.	.	.	.	.	.	.	.	C. islandica
.	.	.	.	.	.	.	.	.	.	.	Cladonia bellidiflora
.	.	.	.	.	.	.	.	.	.	.	C. coccifera
1	.	.	.	.	.	.	.	.	.	.	C. furcata
.	.	.	.	.	.	.	.	.	.	.	C. gracilis
.	.	1	.	.	1	.	.	.	.	.	C. pyxidata
1	.	1	.	.	1	.	.	.	.	.	C. sylvatica
1	.	.	.	.	.	1	.	.	.	.	C. uncialis
.	.	.	.	.	.	.	.	1	.	.	Ochrolechia frigida
.	.	1	.	.	.	.	.	.	.	.	Peltidea leucophlebia
.	.	.	.	.	.	.	.	.	3	.	Peltigera canina
.	.	.	.	.	.	.	.	.	.	.	Sphaerophorus globosus
.	.	.	.	.	.	.	.	1	.	.	Stereocaulon vesuvianum
38	33	35	38	28	43	26	47	30	57	42	Number of species (191)

ge 39)

Lawers, Perthshire; 18. Ben Lui, Dalmally, Argyll; 19. Beinn Lair, Letterewe Forest, Ross-shire; 20. Seana Bhraigh, Strath Mulzie, Ross-shire; 21. Ardverikie Forest, Inverness-shire.

Table 41: Alchemilla-Sibbaldia nodum (1–12); Potentilla erecta facies (13–15)

	1	2	3	4	5	6	7	8	9	10	11	12	13	14	15
Reference number	M57 004	R57 141	R56 108	M55 023	M56 055	R57 170	M55 034	M56 018	M57 066	R58 111	M56 067	M55 036	M57 034	M55 042	M55 025
Map reference	7382 2415	7868 2437	8195 2010	8617 1975	8507 2102	7736 2451	8595 1965	8461 2055	7787 3185	7507 2632	9149 2289	8399 1953	7530 2160	8635 1978	8608 1989
Altitude (feet)	3300	2700	2900	2800	2850	2800	2900	2600	3300	2800	2100	3100	2900	2700	2200
Aspect (degrees)	90	180	315	45	315	360	90	270	225	180	270	45	180	180	90
Slope (degrees)	4	30	20	8	5	20	10	3	2	5	5	10	5	2	2
Cover (per cent)	100	85	95	95	100	100	90	75	100	100	100	95	95	100	100
Height (centimetres)	–	–	–	2	6	–	3	1	–	–	2	5	–	–	1
Plot area (square metres)	4	4	4	3	2	4	4	4	4	4	1	1	2	1	1
Empetrum hermaphroditum										2				+	1
Salix herbacea				1		3									
Vaccinium myrtillus		2		1							3	3	2		3
Blechnum spicant															+
Botrychium lunaria		2													
Lycopodium alpinum		3		1									2		
L. selago	1			1	+		1					1			
Selaginella selaginoides	1			1						2					
Thelypteris oreopteris							3								
Agrostis canina			4					3		4	7				4
A. tenuis		4	2	3	3	4	4	3	3	3		+	2	3	
Anthoxanthum odoratum		2									1				
Deschampsia caespitosa	5		5	3	5	4	+	6	6	4	2	2	5	5	2
D. flexuosa			3			3		2	+				2		
Festuca ovina agg.		3	3	1			3		1	4		3	4		
F. rubra										3					
Nardus stricta	+	4	3	1		3	4	+		2			3		2
Carex bigelowii			3	3	1		1	3		4		3	6	3	4
C. pilulifera			3		1		+				2		1		
C. pulicaris										4					
Juncus trifidus			3	4			2								
Luzula multiflora		1													
L. spicata		1	2		2										
Trichophorum caespitosum												+	1		+
Alchemilla alpina	5	4	3	6	5	5	3	4	6	5	4	4	4	5	
A. vestita		3								4					
Antennaria dioica															2
Armeria maritima				2							1				
Caltha palustris	1														
Cerastium vulgatum	1			2						2					
Epilobium anagallidifolium				3											
Euphrasia frigida				3							1	3			2
Euphrasia sp.	1	3	1	3		2		1		3					
Galium hercynicum	3			4		4	3		4		3	3	4		1
Gnaphalium supinum	3	1	3	4		5	4		2			3		1	
Polygala serpyllifolia															3
Polygonum viviparum	4			3								4			
Potentilla erecta		1						2			4		5	+	6
Ranunculus acris											+				
Rumex acetosa											1				
Saxifraga stellaris	+				1		+								
Sibbaldia procumbens	5	4	5	4	4	6	2	4	2	5	4	5			
Silene acaulis											2				
Succisa pratensis												+			1
Taraxacum officinalis agg.				1											
Thymus drucei	2	4		6	1			5			5			6	5
Viola palustris	3		1	2	3	3	3		1	3	2			3	
V. riviniana		3													
Andreaea alpina								+			1			2	
Ctenidium molluscum										1					
Dicranella heteromalla		2						1							
Dicranum fuscescens						1									
D. scoparium							2								
D. starkei							1					7			
Diphyscium foliosum		2													
cf. Ditrichum heteromallum				1											
Drepanocladus uncinatus	6									1					
Fissidens osmundoides										2					
Hylocomium splendens		2		1			1			2					
Oligotrichum hercynicum			3	3								2			
Pleurozium schreberi	2														
Pohlia nutans		1											2		
Polytrichum alpinum	3				3	2	+	1	3			3	3		1
P. commune					2										
P. piliferum		1						+							
P. urnigerum	2	3		1		3						2			
Rhacomitrium canescens		8							6	5					
R. fasciculare	3		5	4		3		2					7		
R. heterostichum											5				
R. lanuginosum		1	2		4		6	4	1			3	4	5	3
Rhytidiadelphus loreus			1	2		2						5			
R. squarrosus	1				3					3					
R. triquetrus										+					

Table 41 (*continued*)

	1	2	3	4	5	6	7	8	9	10	11	12	13	14	15
Sphagnum girgensohnii	.	.	.	.	.	2	.	.	.	.	.	.	.	.	.
Thuidium tamariscinum	.	.	.	.	5	.	.	.	.	.	.	.	.	.	.
Tortella tortuosa	.	.	.	.	.	.	.	.	.	.	+	.	.	.	.
Alicularia scalaris	.	3	.	.	.	4	.	.	.	.	.	3	.	.	.
Anthelia sp.	.	.	.	.	.	.	+	.	.	.	.	+	.	.	.
Diplophyllum albicans	.	.	.	.	.	1	.	.	.	.	.	.	.	.	.
Lophozia alpestris	.	.	.	4	.	.	.	.	.	.	.	.	.	.	.
L. floerkii	.	.	.	1	.	.	2	.	.	.	.	3	.	.	.
L. hatcheri	.	.	.	1	.	.	.	.	.	.	.	.	.	.	.
L. ventricosa	.	3	.	.	.	.	.	.	.	.	.	.	1	.	.
Moerckia blyttii	.	.	.	.	.	3	.	.	.	.	.	.	.	.	.
Ptilidium ciliare	.	.	.	.	.	.	.	.	.	.	.	1	.	.	.
Cetraria islandica	1	.	.	.	.	.	1	.	.	.	.	.	.	.	.
Cladonia bellidiflora	.	.	.	.	.	1	3	.	.	.	.	.	.	.	.
C. cervicornis	.	.	.	.	.	.	.	.	.	.	1	.	.	.	.
C. coccifera	.	1	.	.	.	.	.	.	.	.	.	.	.	.	.
C. pyxidata	.	2	.	.	.	.	.	.	.	.	.	.	.	.	.
C. rangiferina agg.	.	2	.	.	.	.	.	.	.	.	.	.	.	.	.
C. sylvatica	.	2	.	.	.	.	.	.	.	.	.	.	.	.	.
Peltidea leucophlebia	.	.	.	.	.	.	.	.	.	.	.	+	.	.	.
Peltigera canina	.	.	.	.	2	.	.	.	.	.	.	2	.	.	.
P. horizontalis	2	.	.	.	.	.	.	.	.	.	.	.	.	.	.
cf. Spilonema paradoxum	.	.	.	.	.	.	.	1	.	.	.	.	.	.	.
Number of species	23	31	18	29	23	19	26	18	12	26	16	27	19	11	17

(Average 22) (Average 16)

Constancy class V 4
„ „ IV 9

LOCALITIES

1. Ben Heasgarnich, Perthshire; 2. Creag Meagaidh, Inverness-shire; 3. Beinn Fhada, Kintail; 4,7,12,14,15. Beinn Eighe, Ross-shire; 5. Moruisg, Achnasheen, Ross-shire; 6. Beinn Eibhinn, Ardverikie Forest, Inverness-shire; 8. Sgurr na Feartaig, Achnashellach, Ross-shire; 9. Cairn of Claise, Aberdeenshire; 10. Meall Garbh, Glen Lyon, Perthshire; 11. Breabag, Ben More Assynt, Sutherland; 13. Bidean nam Bian, Glencoe, Argyll.

Table 42: Saxifragetum aizoidis (1–9); Mixed Saxifrage facies (10–13)

	1	2	3	4	5	6	7	8	9	10	11	12	13
Reference number	R58 125	R58 129	R58 117	R57 129	R57 315	R57 089	R57 201	R57 249	R58 066	R58 105	R58 123	R58 024	R57 214
Map reference	7407 2518	7275 2262	7374 2565	7997 2598	7554 2843	7793 2646	7757 3249	7764 3242	8481 2078	7498 2642	7407 2518	7761 3179	7762 3245
Altitude (feet)	2600	2200	2600	1850	2300	2100	2200	2100	2300	2400	2700	3000	2300
Aspect (degrees)	360	360	90	225	90	180	180	360	360	45	360	360	45
Slope (degrees)	50	50	45	48	50	40	70	25	50	50	45	40	35
Cover (per cent)	100	100	100	100	100	100	100	95	98	100	100	100	100
Height (centimetres)	—	—	—	—	—	—	—	—	—	—	—	—	—
Plot area (square metres)	4	4	4	4	4	4	4	4	4	4	4	4	4
Calluna vulgaris	.	.	.	.	.	1	1	.	.	.	.	.	.
Salix herbacea	.	.	.	.	.	.	.	.	.	.	.	3	.
S. lapponum	.	.	.	.	.	3	.	.	.	.	.	.	.
S. reticulata	.	.	.	.	.	.	.	.	.	.	.	2	.
Vaccinium myrtillus	.	.	.	.	.	.	.	.	.	.	.	3	1
V. vitis-idaea	.	.	.	.	2	.	.	.	.	.	.	.	.
Cystopteris fragilis	2	.	.	.	.	.	.	.	2	.	.	2	.
C. montana	2	3	.	.	.	.	.	.	.	.	.	.	.
Hymenophyllum wilsonii	.	.	.	.	.	.	.	.	1	.	.	.	.
Lycopodium selago	.	.	.	.	.	.	.	.	.	.	.	2	.
Polystichum lonchitis	.	.	.	.	.	1	.	.	.	.	.	.	.
Selaginella selaginoides	2	2	+	3	2	3	2	2	.	2	3	3	4
Agrostis canina	.	.	1	.	.	.	.	.	.	2	.	.	3
A. stolonifera	1	.	.	.	.	.	.	.	.	.	.	.	.
A. tenuis	3	.	.	1	.	3	3	.	2	3	3	1	3
Anthoxanthum odoratum	.	2	3	1	.	3	2	3	2	.	1	.	3
Deschampsia caespitosa	3	4	4	4	3	4	3	4	3	3	1	3	4
D. flexuosa	.	.	.	.	.	.	.	.	3	.	.	.	.
Festuca ovina agg.	1	.	2	4	4	3	4	3	3	4	3	2	3
F. rubra	5	4	5	4	2	5	3	5	3	4	4	4	5
Helictotrichon pratense	.	.	.	.	.	.	2	.	.	.	.	.	.
Nardus stricta	.	.	.	.	.	3	3	.	.	.	.	3	3
Poa balfourii	.	.	.	.	.	.	1	1	.	.	.	.	.
Carex bigelowii	.	.	.	.	.	.	.	.	.	.	.	.	2
C. capillaris	.	.	.	.	3	.	.	.	.	+	.	.	.
C. demissa	.	+	3	2	.	3	.	.	.	+	.	.	.
C. echinata	.	.	.	.	.	2	.	.	.	.	.	.	.
C. flacca	.	.	3	.	.	.	.	.	.	.	.	.	.
C. lepidocarpa	.	.	.	.	4	.	.	.	.	.	.	.	.
C. pulicaris	.	.	3	4	4	3	2	.	.	3	3	.	3
Juncus articulatus	.	.	.	.	.	2	.	.	.	.	.	.	.
J. biglumis	.	.	.	.	.	.	.	.	.	1	.	.	.
J. kochii	.	.	.	.	.	1	.	.	.	.	.	.	.
J. triglumis	1	.	1	.	1	3	.	.	.	2	.	.	.
Luzula multiflora	.	.	.	.	.	3	2	2	.	2	1	2	2
L. spicata	.	.	.	.	.	2	.	.	.	.	.	2	.
L. sylvatica	3	2	.	.	.	.	.	2	3	.	.	.	.
Achillea millefolium	.	.	.	.	2	.	.	.	.	.	.	.	.
Alchemilla alpina	.	.	.	3	2	3	3	3	3	3	3	4	2
A. filicaulis	.	.	5	.	.	.	.	.	.	.	5	.	5
A. glabra	4	4	5	3	4	.	3	3	1	2	5	.	2
A. vestita	.	.	.	.	.	.	.	.	.	.	.	.	2
A. wichurae	.	.	.	.	.	2	.	.	.	.	.	.	.
A. xanthochlora	.	.	.	.	.	3	.	2	.	.	.	.	.
Angelica sylvestris	.	3	.	.	.	.	.	.	3	.	.	.	.
Arabis hirsuta	.	.	.	.	.	.	.	1	.	.	.	.	.
Armeria maritima	.	2	.	.	.	.	.	.	.	.	.	.	.
Bellis perennis	.	.	.	.	2	.	.	.	.	.	.	.	.
Caltha palustris	.	.	.	.	.	.	.	.	.	.	.	.	1
Campanula rotundifolia	.	.	+	3	2	.	1	2	.	2	2	.	2
Cardamine flexuosa	.	.	.	.	.	.	.	1	.	.	.	.	.
C. pratensis	.	.	.	.	.	.	.	.	.	2	.	.	.
Cerastium alpinum	.	.	.	.	.	.	.	.	.	.	1	2	.
C. vulgatum	2	2	3	.	.	.	1	2	.	1	1	.	2
Cochlearia alpina	2	1	.	.	.	.	.	.	3	.	2	.	.
Crepis paludosa	.	2	2	.	.	3	.	.	.	.	.	.	.
Epilobium alsinifolium	.	.	.	.	.	.	+	2	.	.	.	.	.
E. anagallidifolium	.	.	.	.	.	2	.	.	.	.	1	.	.
Euphrasia officinalis agg.	2	1	2	3	2	1	3	2	2	.	2	.	2
Galium boreale	.	.	.	.	2	.	.	2	.	.	.	.	.
G. hercynicum	.	.	1	.	1	.	1	1	.	1	.	2	1
Geranium sylvaticum	.	1	2	.	.	.	1	.	.	.	.	.	.
Geum rivale	4	3	2	2	.	.	2	.	1	2	.	.	2
Heracleum sphondylium	2	.	.	.	.	.	.	1	.	.	.	.	.
Hieracium sp.	.	1	.	.	1	.	2	3	2	.	.	.	.
Linum catharticum	.	.	2	2	3	2	2	3	.	.	.	.	.

Table 42 (*continued*)

	1	2	3	4	5	6	7	8	9	10	11	12	13
Lotus corniculatus	.	.	2	.	.	.	2	.	.	.	.	.	.
Oxalis acetosella	2	.	.	.	.	.	.	.	2	.	.	1	1
Oxyria digyna	.	.	1	+	.	1	3	+	.	2	.	.	2
Parnassia palustris	3	1	3	2	1	3	3	3	.	.	.	.	.
Pinguicula vulgaris	1	1	+	2	1	3	2	1	.	.	.	.	1
Plantago lanceolata	.	.	.	.	.	.	3	1	.	.	.	.	.
Polygonum viviparum	3	2	2	2	3	3	+	3	1	3	3	3	3
Potentilla erecta	.	.	+	.	2	2	.	.	.	.	.	.	.
Prunella vulgaris	.	.	.	.	1	.	.	.	.	.	.	.	.
Pyrola rotundifolia	.	.	.	.	.	.	.	.	.	.	.	3	.
Ranunculus acris	3	2	2	.	2	2	1	3	3	.	.	3	.
Rhinanthus minor agg.	.	.	.	+	.	2	2	.	1	.	.	.	.
Rumex acetosa	.	.	.	.	.	.	.	3	3	.	.	.	.
Sagina procumbens	.	.	.	.	.	1	.	.	.	.	.	.	.
S. nodosa	.	.	.	.	.	.	.	1	.	.	.	.	.
Saxifraga aizoides	8	8	8	9	8	6	9	9	6	6	6	4	6
S. hypnoides	2	3	.	.	.	.	.	2	3	3	.	3	.
S. oppositifolia	1	2	.	3	3	+	3	3	6	5	6	4	2
S. stellaris	.	.	.	.	.	2	.	.	1	.	.	.	.
Sedum rosea	1	1	.	.	.	.	.	.	3	1	.	.	.
Sibbaldia procumbens	.	.	.	.	.	.	.	.	.	.	.	3	.
Silene acaulis	.	.	.	.	.	.	.	.	.	2	.	3	2
Succisa pratensis	.	.	.	.	.	3	3	.	.	.	.	.	.
Taraxacum officinalis agg.	.	.	2	2	.	2	+	.	.	.	.	2	3
Thalictrum alpinum	.	2	.	3	.	3	4	.	2	2	3	2	3
Thymus drucei	.	.	1	4	4	3	2	1	2	3	3	.	4
Trifolium repens	.	.	2	.	.	.	.	.	.	.	.	.	.
Tussilago farfara	.	.	.	.	.	.	.	+	.	.	.	.	.
Veronica alpina	.	.	.	.	.	.	.	.	.	.	.	3	.
Viola riviniana	.	.	3	4	2	3	1	2	.	.	3	.	1
Acrocladium cuspidatum	2	1	3	3	2	.	.	1	.	.	.	.	3
Atrichum undulatum	.	.	.	.	.	1	.	.	.	.	.	.	.
Bartramia halleriana	.	.	.	.	.	.	.	.	1	.	.	.	.
Blindia acuta	.	.	.	1	.	2	2	1	.	.	1	.	.
Brachythecium rivulare	5	.	.	.	.	.	.	.	.	.	2	.	.
Breutelia chrysocoma	.	2	.	.	.	2	.	.	3	.	.	.	.
Bryum pseudotriquetrum	3	3	.	2	2	3	.	1	.	3	2	.	3
Campylium protensum	.	.	.	2	.	.	3	.	.	1	.	.	2
C. stellatum	.	3	.	.	1	4	.	.	.	.	3	.	.
Climacium dendroides	.	.	.	.	2	.	.	.	.	.	.	.	.
Cratoneuron commutatum	4	6	.	2	2	.	.	2	.	2	2	.	.
C. filicinum	3	.	.	.	1	.	.	.	.	.	2	.	.
Ctenidium molluscum	2	3	2	4	3	2	3	3	.	.	6	1	2
Dichodontium pellucidum	.	2	.	.	.	.	.	.	.	.	.	.	.
Dicranum bonjeani	.	.	1	.	.	.	.	.	.	.	.	.	.
D. majus	.	.	.	.	.	.	.	2	.	.	.	.	.
D. scoparium	.	2	.	2	.	.	.	.	3	.	.	3	.
Ditrichum flexicaule	.	.	.	.	1	.	.	1	.	2	3	.	3
Drepanocladus uncinatus	.	1	.	3	.	.	.	3	1	.	2	2	1
Fissidens adianthoides	.	2	1	3	2	2	.	.	.	.	3	.	3
Hylocomium splendens	.	2	1	2	.	1	.	3	3	4	4	7	.
Hypnum callichroum	.	1	.	.	.	.	.	.	.	.	.	.	.
Isopterygium muellerianum	.	1	.	.	.	.	.	.	.	.	.	.	.
Mnium hornum	.	.	.	.	.	.	.	.	.	.	.	1	.
M. pseudopunctatum	2	3	.	.	.	.	.	.	.	.	.	.	.
M. punctatum	.	.	.	2	.	.	.	2	1	.	.	.	.
M. seligeri	.	1	.	.	3	.	.	.	.	.	.	.	.
M. undulatum	.	.	2	1	.	.	1	2	3	.	.	.	.
Philonotis fontana	3	3	.	1	.	4	.	2	.	.	3	.	2
Plagiobryum zierii	.	.	.	.	.	.	.	.	.	.	.	.	1
Pohlia albicans	2	.	.	.	.	.	.	.	.	.	.	.	.
Polytrichum alpinum	.	.	.	.	.	.	.	.	1	.	.	.	.
P. urnigerum	.	.	.	.	.	.	1	.	.	.	.	.	.
Pseudoscleropodium purum	.	.	.	1	.	.	.	.	.	.	.	.	.
Ptilium crista-castrensis	.	.	.	.	.	.	.	.	2	.	.	1	.
Rhacomitrium canescens	.	.	.	.	.	.	.	.	2	.	.	3	1
R. lanuginosum	.	.	.	.	.	.	.	.	1	.	.	2	.
Rhytidiadelphus loreus	.	.	.	.	.	.	.	.	2	2	.	4	.
R. squarrosus	.	.	.	1	.	.	.	.	2	.	2	3	3
R. triquetrus	+	3	2	2	1	.	.	3	5	4	4	3	3
Sphagnum nemoreum	.	.	.	.	.	.	.	.	1	.	.	.	.
Thuidium delicatulum	.	.	.	2	.	.	.	.	.	.	.	.	.
T. tamariscinum	.	2	.	2	.	.	.	.	3	3	4	.	.
Tortella tortuosa	.	.	.	+	.	.	.	1	.	.	.	.	.
Alicularia scalaris	.	.	.	.	.	2	.	.	1	.	.	1	.
Aneura cf. sinuata	.	.	1	.	.	.	.	1	.	.	.	.	.
A. pinguis	.	.	2	.	.	.	.	.	.	2	.	.	1
Aplozia sp.	.	.	.	.	.	.	.	.	.	.	.	.	1
A. riparia	.	.	.	.	.	1	.	.	.	.	.	.	.
Bazzania tricrenata	.	.	.	.	.	.	.	.	2	.	.	.	.
Chiloscyphus polyanthus	.	.	.	.	.	.	.	3	.	.	3	.	.
Diplophyllum albicans	.	.	.	.	.	.	.	.	2	.	.	2	.
Lophocolea bidentata	.	2	2	.	.	.	.	1	.	.	.	.	.

Table 42 (*continued*)

	1	2	3	4	5	6	7	8	9	10	11	12	13
Lophozia bantriensis* . . .	2	3	.	.	.	.	2	1	.	.	.	.	.
L. lycopodioides . . .	.	.	.	.	.	.	.	.	.	.	.	2	.
L. quadriloba	.	.	.	.	.	.	.	.	.	.	1	.	.
L. quinquedentata . . .	.	2	.	.	.	.	.	3	2	3	.	1	2
Metzgeria hamata . . .	.	1	.	.	.	.	.	.	.	.	.	.	•
Pellia fabbroniana . . .	1	1	.	.	.	2	1	2	.	1	.	.	2
Plagiochila asplenioides .	.	.	.	.	1	.	1	2	2	2	2	1	2
Preissia quadrata . . .	2	1	1	.	2	.	.	.	.	.	1	.	.
Ptilidium ciliare	.	.	.	.	.	.	.	.	.	.	.	1	.
Scapania aspera	.	.	.	.	.	.	.	.	.	.	2	.	.
S. gracilis	.	.	.	.	.	.	.	.	2	.	.	.	.
Cladonia sylvatica . . .	.	.	.	.	.	.	.	.	1	.	.	.	.
Peltigera canina . . .	.	1	.	.	.	.	.	.	2	.	.	3	.
P. leucophlebia . . .	.	.	.	.	.	.	.	.	2	.	.	.	.
Number of species (142) . .	38	51	43	44	44	51	46	61	50	40	44	45	48

(Average 47.5) (Average 44)

Constancy class V 12
   ,,   ,, IV 10

* Mostly forms close to *L. muelleri.*

LOCALITIES

1,11. Meall Ghaordie, Perthshire; 2. Ben Lui, Argyll; 3. Craig Chaillaich, Killin, Perthshire; 4. Glen Markie, Monadhliath, Inverness-shire; 5. Farragon Hill, Perthshire; 6. Coire Chuirn, Drumochter, Inverness-shire; 7. Glen Fiadh, Clova, Angus; 8,13. Glen Doll, Clova, Angus; 9. Sgurr nan Ceannaichean, Strathcarron, Ross-shire; 10. Carn Gorm, Glen Lyon, Perthshire; 12. Caenlochan, Angus.

Table 43: Cariceto-Rhacomitretum lanuginosi

	1	2	3	4	5	6	7	8	9	10	11
Reference number	P52 035	P52 117	P52 006	M57 032	M56 070	R57 045	M55 035	R57 052	M55 028	P55 003	R56 039
Map reference	7397 2630	—	7397 2567	7301 2096	9152 2283	9485 2338	8599 1952	9847 2335	8667 2465	9280 2203	8825 2235
Altitude (feet)	3100	2700	2700	3100	2350	2400	3100	2350	2600	2200	2550
Aspect (degrees)	—	—	—	—	45	360	—	180	270	195	—
Slope (degrees)	—	—	—	—	3	5	0	3	4	25	0
Cover (per cent)	100	100	100	100	75	100	100	90	100	100	100
Height (centimetres)	3	12	10	—	5	—	12	—	8	5	—
Plot area (square metres)	2	10	4	4	2	4	4	4	4	4	4
Empetrum hermaphroditum									1	1	+
Salix herbacea		3					2		4		
Vaccinium myrtillus		3	4		3	3	1	3	5	5	3
V. uliginosum							+				
V. vitis-idaea		2							+		
Lycopodium selago					3						
Agrostis canina	3					4		2	+	3	3
A. tenuis							2				
Deschampsia caespitosa				1			2				
D. flexuosa		3	7	1	2	4	3	3	3	1	3
Festuca ovina agg.		2	2	4	3	3		4	1		
Nardus stricta							+				
Carex bigelowii	4	3	6	4	+	3	5	3	4	3	4
C. pilulifera						2					1
Juncus squarrosus							+				
J. trifidus					+	+	6	7			
Luzula spicata		2				1	2	2			
Alchemilla alpina		1	2								1
Armeria maritima					3	6	+	4			
Cherleria sedoides					5	4		2			
Galium hercynicum	2	2	2			2	2	3	3	3	3
Potentilla erecta										3	
Rumex acetosa						2		1			
Silene acaulis						5		2			
Succisa pratensis								+			
Dicranodontium longirostre						+					
Dicranum fuscescens	2	3	3		2	4	2	2	2		
D. scoparium		1									
Hylocomium splendens									4	3	
Hypnum cupressiforme						3				2	
Plagiothecium undulatum						4					
Pleurozium schreberi		1	4						3	2	
Polytrichum alpinum	1	3	3	2		3	1	3	2		
P. urnigerum									2		
Rhacomitrium lanuginosum	10	10	6	10	8	6	8	9	8	9	10
Rhytidiadelphus loreus	1		1			5			2		
Alicularia scalaris		1			5						
Anastrophyllum donianum						1					
Diplophyllum albicans						2	1	3			
Lophozia ventricosa		1									
Ptilidium ciliare			1								
Alectoria nigricans									1		
Cerania vermicularis	1										
Cetraria aculeata		3	1					1			
C. islandica	2	2	2	3	2	2			1	3	
Cladonia alpicola	2										
C. bellidiflora		1		2							
C. coccifera							+				
C. gracilis		2	1								
C. pyxidata					+			3			
C. rangiferina agg.			1								
C. squamosa	1										
C. sylvatica			1		2				4		2
C. uncialis	3	3	1	2	1		1	3	1		3
Coriscium viride				+				1			
Ochrolechia frigida						1		3	+		1
Peltigera canina						1					
Sphaerophorus globosus						1		3			
Stereocaulon evolutoides									1		
S. vesuvianum							1				
Number of species (60)	12	21	18	10	17	23	21	23	22	13	12

(Average 16)

Constancy class V 6
,,   ,, IV 4

LOCALITIES

1–3. Ben Lawers, Perthshire; 4. Ben Cruachan, Argyll; 5. Breabag, Ben More Assynt, Sutherland; 6,8. Foinaven, Reay Forest, Sutherland; 7. Beinn Eighe, Ross-shire; 9. Ben Wyvis, Ross-shire; 10. Quinag (Cuineag), Sutherland; 11. Beinn Dearg, Inverlael, Ross-shire.

Table 44: Polygoneto-Rhacomitretum lanuginosi (1–11);

	1	2	3	4	5	6	7	8	9
Reference number	R56 031	R56 042	R56 045	R56 096	M56 020	M56 072	MX5	MX6	R57 013
Map reference	8797 2300	8700 2218	8777 2302	8712 2150	8466 2054	9162 2289	–	–	9457 2347
Altitude (feet)	2900	2750	2750	2850	2600	2500	3000	2800	2400
Aspect (degrees)	325	90	180	90	90	270	–	–	90
Slope (degrees)	15	10	5	12	8	8	–	–	7
Cover (per cent)	100	95	97	90	90	90	–	–	100
Height (centimetres)	–	–	–	–	2	2	–	–	–
Plot area (square metres)	4	4	4	4	4	4	4	4	4
Empetrum hermaphroditum	2	·	1	·	+	·	·	·	·
Loiseleuria procumbens	·	·	+	·	·	·	·	·	·
Salix herbacea	3	·	+	3	·	3	3	6	3
Vaccinium myrtillus	·	3	3	2	3	3	·	2	2
V. vitis-idaea	3	3	2	·	1	·	·	·	·
Lycopodium alpinum	3	·	·	·	·	·	·	·	·
L. selago	·	·	·	·	1	+	·	·	·
Selaginella selaginoides	3	·	·	·	2	·	·	·	·
Agrostis canina	3	4	3	3	2	1	·	·	3
A. tenuis	4	·	2	·	2	·	·	·	4
Deschampsia caespitosa	3	1	·	2	2	2	2	·	1
D. flexuosa	·	3	3	3	3	2	·	·	4
Festuca ovina agg.	·	5	·	5	2	3	3	3	4
Nardus stricta	3	1	·	·	·	·	·	·	·
Carex bigelowii	4	4	4	3	3	3	4	4	4
C. pilulifera	2	·	·	·	·	·	·	·	·
Coeloglossum viride	·	·	·	·	·	·	·	+	·
Juncus squarrosus	·	·	·	·	·	·	·	·	·
J. trifidus	1	2	3	3	·	3	3	+	·
Luzula multiflora	·	1	·	·	·	·	·	·	·
L. spicata	·	1	·	2	·	2	2	2	2
Achillea millefolium	·	·	·	3	·	·	·	·	4
Alchemilla alpina	4	3	3	4	3	+	+	·	3
Antennaria dioica	·	·	1	3	·	·	·	·	2
Armeria maritima	3	4	3	3	2	4	2	2	3
Cherleria sedoides	·	·	·	3	·	7	·	·	3
Cochlearia micacea	·	·	·	·	·	·	+	1	·
Euphrasia frigida	·	·	·	2	·	1	2	2	·
Galium hercynicum	2	2	·	·	·	3	3	·	·
Gnaphalium supinum	·	·	·	2	·	·	·	·	·
Leontodon autumnalis	·	·	·	·	·	·	·	·	·
Plantago maritima	·	·	·	·	·	·	·	·	3
Polygonum viviparum	3	3	+	3	·	3	3	3	4
Potentilla erecta	·	·	·	·	·	·	·	·	·
Ranunculus acris	·	·	·	·	·	·	·	+	·
Rumex acetosa	·	·	·	·	·	·	·	·	·
Saussurea alpina	·	·	·	·	·	·	·	4	·
Sedum rosea	·	·	·	·	·	·	·	+	·
Sibbaldia procumbens	3	·	·	3	·	·	·	·	·
Silene acaulis	3	4	4	3	5	·	2	2	5
Solidago virgaurea	·	1	·	·	·	·	·	1	·
Succisa pratensis	·	·	·	·	·	·	·	·	·
Thalictrum alpinum	·	·	·	·	·	·	·	+	·
Thymus drucei	5	2	3	3	3	·	1	+	2
Viola palustris	1	·	·	·	·	·	·	·	·
Aulacomnium turgidum	2	2	2	2	3	·	1	1	2
Breutelia chrysocoma	·	·	·	·	2	·	·	1	·
Campylopus flexuosus	·	·	·	·	·	·	·	·	2
Dicranum fuscescens	·	1	3	·	·	2	·	·	3
D. scoparium	2	1	3	·	2	·	·	·	·
Drepanocladus uncinatus	2	·	1	·	·	·	·	·	·
Grimmia patens	·	·	·	·	·	·	·	·	2
Hylocomium splendens	2	2	3	1	2	·	·	·	3
Hypnum cupressiforme	·	1	1	2	1	1	·	·	3
H. callichroum	2	·	·	·	·	·	·	·	3
H. hamulosum	·	1	1	·	4	·	1	1	·
Mnium hornum	·	·	·	·	·	·	·	·	·
M. punctatum	·	·	·	·	·	·	·	·	·
Oligotrichum hercynicum	·	·	·	1	·	·	·	·	·
Plagiothecium striatellum	·	2	·	·	·	2	·	1	·
P. undulatum	·	·	·	·	3	·	·	·	4
Pleurozium schreberi	2	2	3	·	·	·	1	1	·
Polytrichum alpinum	1	1	2	1	2	3	1	3	·
P. piliferum	1	1	·	1	·	·	·	·	·
P. urnigerum	·	·	·	·	·	·	·	1	·
Rhacomitrium aquaticum	·	·	·	1	·	·	·	·	·
R. fasciculare	·	·	·	·	·	·	·	·	·
R. lanuginosum	9	9	9	8	7	7	8	8	7
Rhytidiadelphus loreus	1	2	3	·	2	2	1	1	4
R. squarrosus	·	·	·	·	·	·	·	·	·

Cushion herb facies of Cariceto-Rhacomitretum (12–14)

10	11	A		B		12	13	14	
		C	D	C	D				
R57	R58					R56	R56	R57	Reference number
046	072					028	046	043	
9485	8462					8812	8782	9347	Map reference
2337	2133					2259	2299	2430	
2400	3100					3540	2800	2500	Altitude (feet)
180	45					360	360	315	Aspect (degrees)
15	5					4	3	20	Slope (degrees)
95	95					100	100	95	Cover (per cent)
–	–					–	–	–	Height (centimetres)
4	4					4	4	4	Plot area (square metres)
·	·	3	1	3	1	·	·	·	Empetrum hermaphroditum
·	·	·	·	1	+	·	·	·	Loiseleuria procumbens
4	3	3	3	8	3	·	3	3	Salix herbacea
·	2	9	3	7	3	·	3	3	Vaccinium myrtillus
·	·	2	1	4	2	·	2	·	V. vitis-idaea
·	·	·	·	1	3	·	·	·	Lycopodium alpinum
·	·	1	3	2	1	·	·	+	L. selago
·	·	·	·	2	2	·	·	·	Selaginella selaginoides
3	3	6	3	8	3	·	3	·	Agrostis canina
·	·	1	2	4	3	·	·	·	A. tenuis
3	3	2	1	8	2	2	·	·	Deschampsia caespitosa
5	4	10	3	7	3	·	4	2	D. flexuosa
4	4	4	2	8	3	3	5	4	Festuca ovina agg.
·	·	10	+	2	2	·	·	·	Nardus stricta
1	4	10	5	10	4	4	3	3	**Carex bigelowii**
·	·	2	2	1	2	·	·	·	C. pilulifera
·	·	·	·	1	+	·	·	·	Coeloglossum viride
·	·	1	+	·	·	·	·	·	Juncus squarrosus
2	·	4	4	8	3	·	·	·	J. trifidus
2	·	·	·	1	2	·	·	·	Luzula multiflora
2	1	3	2	7	2	·	·	·	L. spicata
4	+	·	·	3	4	·	·	·	Achillea millefolium
3	3	3	1	9	3	+	·	+	**Alchemilla alpina**
·	+	·	·	3	2	·	·	·	Antennaria dioica
3	5	4	4	10	3	4	3	4	**Armeria maritima**
4	·	3	3	4	4	5	·	5	Cherleria sedoides
·	·	·	·	2	1	·	·	·	Cochlearia micacea
·	3	·	·	4	2	·	·	·	Euphrasia frigida
3	2	9	3	5	3	·	2	·	Galium hercynicum
1	·	·	·	2	1	·	·	·	Gnaphalium supinum
·	+	·	·	1	+	·	·	·	Leontodon autumnalis
2	·	·	·	2	2	·	·	·	Plantago maritima
3	4	·	·	9	3	·	·	·	**Polygonum viviparum**
·	·	1	3	·	·	·	·	·	Potentilla erecta
3	·	·	·	2	1	·	·	·	Ranunculus acris
3	·	·	·	1	3	·	·	·	Rumex acetosa
·	1	·	·	1	4	·	·	·	Saussurea alpina
·	·	·	·	1	+	·	·	·	Sedum rosea
+	3	·	·	3	2	2	·	·	Sibbaldia procumbens
6	7	2	3	9	4	5	6	4	**Silene acaulis**
·	·	·	·	2	1	·	·	·	Solidago virgaurea
·	·	1	+	·	·	·	·	·	Succisa pratensis
·	4	·	·	1	2	·	·	·	Thalictrum alpinum
3	4	·	·	9	3	·	2	·	**Thymus drucei**
·	·	·	·	1	1	·	·	·	Viola palustris
·	3	·	·	8	2	·	3	·	Aulacomnium turgidum
2	·	·	·	3	2	·	·	·	Breutelia chrysocoma
·	1	·	·	1	2	·	·	·	Campylopus flexuosus
·	·	8	2	4	2	2	3	·	Dicranum fuscescens
3	2	2	1	5	2	·	·	3	D. scoparium
·	3	·	·	2	2	·	·	·	Drepanocladus uncinatus
·	·	·	·	1	2	·	·	·	Grimmia patens
3	3	2	3	7	2	·	2	·	Hylocomium splendens
2	3	2	2	7	2	·	1	3	Hypnum cupressiforme
3	3	·	·	3	3	·	·	·	H. callichroum
·	1	·	·	6	2	·	1	·	H. hamulosum
·	2	·	·	1	2	·	·	2	Mnium hornum
·	2	·	·	1	2	·	·	·	M. punctatum
·	·	·	·	1	1	1	·	·	Oligotrichum hercynicum
·	1	·	·	2	2	·	·	·	Plagiothecium striatellum
·	2	1	4	2	3	·	·	2	P. undulatum
2	1	4	2	6	2	·	2	·	Pleurozium schreberi
2	3	7	2	9	2	4	2	1	**Polytrichum alpinum**
·	·	·	·	3	1	·	·	·	P. piliferum
·	·	1	2	1	1	·	·	·	P. urnigerum
·	·	·	·	1	1	·	·	·	Rhacomitrium aquaticum
3	1	·	·	2	2	·	·	·	R. fasciculare
6	5	10	9	10	8	8	8	8	**R. lanuginosum**
4	3	4	2	9	2	·	2	2	**Rhytidiadelphus loreus**
·	2	·	·	1	2	·	·	·	R. squarrosus

Table 44

	1	2	3	4	5	6	7	8	9
Alicularia scalaris	·	·	·	I	·	·	·	·	·
Anastrophyllum donianum	·	·	·	·	·	·	·	·	·
Diplophyllum albicans	·	2	·	·	I	I	I	·	·
Frullania tamarisci	·	·	·	·	I	·	·	·	·
Gymnomitrium obtusum	·	·	·	2	·	·	·	·	·
Leptoscyphus taylori	·	·	·	·	I	·	·	·	·
Lophozia alpestris	·	·	·	·	·	·	·	2	·
L. hatcheri	I	·	·	·	·	·	·	I	·
L. lycopodioides	·	·	·	·	·	·	·	·	·
L. ventricosa	·	·	·	2	·	·	·	·	·
Ptilidium ciliare	3	I	2	I	2	I	·	2	·
Alectoria nigricans	·	·	·	·	·	·	·	·	·
Cerania vermicularis	·	·	·	I	·	·	+	·	·
Cetraria aculeata	2	I	I	·	I	·	+	·	·
C. islandica	3	2	2	·	3	2	+	I	2
Cladonia alpicola	·	·	·	·	·	·	·	·	·
C. bellidiflora	·	·	·	·	+	·	I	I	·
C. coccifera	2	·	·	I	·	·	·	·	·
C. gracilis	I	2	·	·	I	·	·	·	·
C. pyxidata	·	2	·	I	·	·	·	·	·
C. rangiferina agg.	I	·	2	·	·	·	·	·	·
C. squamosa	·	·	·	·	·	·	·	·	·
C. sylvatica	I	I	3	·	·	·	·	+	·
C. uncialis	3	2	2	2	I	·	2	2	2
Coriscium viride	·	·	·	·	·	·	·	·	·
Ochrolechia frigida	3	2	3	2	+	I	·	·	2
Peltidea leucophlebia	·	·	·	·	·	I	+	I	·
Peltigera canina	I	·	·	·	2	·	·	·	·
Pertusaria oculata	·	·	·	·	I	·	·	·	·
Platysma glaucum	·	·	·	·	·	I	·	·	·
Sphaerophorus globosus	2	2	2	2	I	+	2	2	2
Stereocaulon evolutoides	·	·	·	·	·	·	+	·	·
S. vesuvianum	·	·	·	·	·	·	·	·	·
Number of species	42	40	35	38	38	29	29	36	32

(Average 35)

Constancy class V   12
      ,,   ,, IV   9

A. Cariceto-Rhacomitretum lanuginosi.
B. Polygoneto-Rhacomitretum lanuginosi.
C. Constancy (scale: 1–10).
D. Dominance (scale: 1–10).

LOCALITIES

1,3,13. Am Faochagach, Strath Vaich, Ross-shire; 2. Creachan Rairigidh, Fannich Forest, Ross-shire; 4. Fannich Forest, Ross-shire; 5. Sgurr na Feartaig, Achnashellach, Ross-shire; 6. Creag Liath, Ben More Assynt, Sutherland; 7,8. Beinn Eighe, Ross-shire; 9. Creagan Meall Horn, Reay

(continued)

| 10 | 11 | A | | B | | 12 | 13 | 14 | |
		C	D	C	D				
·	·	2	1	1	1	·	·	·	Alicularia scalaris
·	·	1	1	·	·	·	·	·	Anastrophyllum donianum
·	2	3	2	4	1	1	·	2	Diplophyllum albicans
·	·	·	·	1	1	·	·	·	Frullania tamarisci
·	·	·	·	1	2	·	·	·	Gymnomitrium obtusum
·	·	·	·	1	1	·	·	·	Leptoscyphus taylori
·	·	·	·	1	2	·	·	·	Lophozia alpestris
·	·	·	·	2	1	·	·	·	L. hatcheri
·	1	·	·	1	1	·	·	·	L. lycopodioides
·	·	1	1	1	2	·	·	·	L. ventricosa
·	2	1	1	7	2	1	+	·	Ptilidium ciliare
·	·	1	1	·	·	·	·	·	Alectoria nigricans
·	·	1	1	2	1	·	·	·	Cerania vermicularis
1	1	3	1	6	1	·	·	2	Cetraria aculeata
2	2	8	2	9	2	3	2	2	**C. islandica**
·	·	1	2	·	·	·	·	·	Cladonia alpicola
·	·	2	1	3	1	1	·	1	C. bellidiflora
·	·	1	+	2	1	·	·	·	C. coccifera
·	1	2	1	3	1	2	·	·	C. gracilis
·	·	2	2	2	1	·	1	2	C. pyxidata
·	·	1	1	2	1	·	·	·	C. rangiferina agg.
·	·	1	1	·	·	·	·	·	C. squamosa
·	·	4	2	4	1	·	·	1	C. sylvatica
1	2	9	2	9	2	2	·	2	**C. uncialis**
·	·	2	1	·	·	·	·	2	Coriscium viride
1	2	4	1	8	2	·	2	·	Ochrolechia frigida
·	·	·	·	3	1	·	·	·	Peltidea leucophlebia
·	·	1	1	1	1	·	·	·	Peltigera canina
·	·	·	·	1	1	·	·	·	Pertusaria oculata
·	·	·	·	1	1	·	·	·	Platysma glaucum
·	2	2	2	9	2	·	2	·	**Sphaerophorus globosus**
·	·	1	1	1	+	·	·	·	Stereocaulon evolutoides
·	·	1	1	·	·	·	·	·	S. vesuvianum
36	48					18	25	25	Number of species

(Average 23)

Forest, Sutherland; 10. Foinaven, Reay Forest, Sutherland; 11. Maoile Lunndaih, Monar Forest, Ross-shire; 12. Beinn Dearg, Inverlael, Ross-shire; 14. Ben Hee, Sutherland.

Table 45: Deschampsieto-Rhytidiadelphetum

	1	2	3	4	5	6	7	8	9	10
Reference number	M57 030	M57 041	R57 109	R56 119	R56 070	R56 053	M56 083	M55 014	R57 180	M57 093
Map reference	7328 2137	7711 2197	7747 2481	8148 2017	8733 2059	8813 2252	8690 2466	8622 2148	7920 2493	7777 3176
Altitude (feet)	2900	3500	3350	3025	2600	3000	3000	2800	2800	3100
Aspect (degrees)	45	135	45	360	90	270	90	360	360	135
Slope (degrees)	30	5	35	20	35	23	10	3	10	3
Cover (per cent)	100	100	100	100	100	100	100	100	100	100
Height (centimetres)	—	20	—	—	—	—	5	6	—	—
Plot area (square metres)	4	4	4	4	4	4	4	4	4	4
Salix herbacea								+		
Vaccinium myrtillus				4	3	2		+		
V. vitis-idaea										
Blechnum spicant		1								
Lycopodium alpinum						1				
L. selago					1					
Selaginella selaginoides										
Agrostis canina					3		2	*3*	3	+
A. tenuis	3	2	3		5	4		*3*	5	4
Anthoxanthum odoratum	3				4					
Deschampsia caespitosa	5	8	9		3	5	4	2		5
D. flexuosa	3		2	5	5	4	2			
Festuca ovina agg.					2	3			3	
F. rubra								2		
Nardus stricta	1			2	2					
Poa pratensis									2	
Carex bigelowii				4	2	6	5	3	4	3
C. pilulifera					1					
Juncus trifidus										
Luzula multiflora		2				2				
L. spicata										
L. sylvatica					+					
Achillea millefolium										
Alchemilla alpina		+			2	2			1	2
A. filicaulis										2
A. glabra										
Armeria maritima								+		
Campanula rotundifolia									3	1
Cerastium alpinum										
C. edmonstonii									2	
C. vulgatum		2	2							
Cochlearia micacea										
Euphrasia frigida	2	3	2						1	3
Filipendula ulmaria										
Galium hercynicum	4	3	4	3	5	4	3	3	3	3
Geum rivale										
Gnaphalium supinum										
Leontodon autumnalis					2					
Oxalis acetosella	1									
Polygonum viviparum										
Potentilla erecta					2					
Pyrola cf. minor										3
Ranunculus acris										3
Rumex acetosa	5	1	3	2	3	4		+	4	3
Saussurea alpina										
Saxifraga hypnoides										
S. oppositifolia							1			
S. stellaris			3							
Sibbaldia procumbens						2				2
Silene acaulis										
Thalictrum alpinum										
Thymus drucei										
Trollius europaeus										
Veronica humifusa										1
V. officinalis										
Viola palustris		4		1		3			3	2
V. riviniana					3					
Aulacomnium turgidum										
Breutelia chrysocoma						2				
Campylopus flexuosus										
Climacium dendroides										
Ctenidium molluscum										
Dicranella heteromalla							1			
Dicranum fuscescens							2		2	
D. scoparium				3		2	2		3	
D. starkei										
Ditrichum flexicaule										
Drepanocladus uncinatus										
Hylocomium brevirostre										
H. splendens	6		3	4	3	5			4	
H. pyrenaicum										
H. umbratum			1							
Hypnum cupressiforme						2				

[typicum (1–13); triquetrosum (14–20)]

11	12	13	14	15	16	17	18	19	20	
M56	R57	R57	M55	M55	R56	M56	M55	M58	M57	Reference number
062	015	016	017	038	111	053	026	014	003	
8562	9450	9448	8605	8601	8194	8508	8618	7386	7382	Map reference
2257	2353	2359	1953	1952	2010	2102	1973	2414	2418	
2700	2540	2300	3100	3100	2900	2850	2900	3000	3100	Altitude (feet)
270	45	45	90	45	315	315	270	360	45	Aspect (degrees)
5	15	15	2	40	15	20	3	40	25	Slope (degrees)
100	100	100	100	100	100	100	100	100	100	Cover (per cent)
5	–	–	3	8	–	6	2	–	–	Height (centimetres)
4	4	4	1	1	4	4	2	4	4	Plot area (square metres)
·	·	·	2	3	2	+	·	+	·	Salix herbacea
·	3	4	·	·	·	1	·	·	·	Vaccinium myrtillus
3	·	·	·	·	·	·	·	·	·	V. vitis-idaea
·	·	·	·	·	·	·	·	·	·	Blechnum spicant
·	·	·	·	·	·	·	·	·	·	Lycopodium alpinum
·	·	·	·	·	1	·	·	·	·	L. selago
·	·	·	·	·	3	·	·	1	·	Selaginella selaginoides
·	·	·	·	4	4	·	·	3	2	Agrostis canina
3	5	4	·	·	2	·	4	·	2	A. tenuis
·	·	·	·	·	2	·	·	2	·	Anthoxanthum odoratum
2	5	·	6	7	3	2	6	4	5	Deschampsia caespitosa
1	3	4	·	·	·	·	·	·	2	D. flexuosa
3	·	·	3	2	2	2	2	3	·	Festuca ovina agg.
·	·	·	·	·	3	·	·	·	1	F. rubra
·	2	2	·	·	4	·	·	·	·	Nardus stricta
·	·	·	·	·	·	·	·	1	2	Poa pratensis
7	3	3	2	2	3	3	+	2	+	Carex bigelowii
·	·	·	·	·	·	·	·	·	·	C. pilulifera
·	·	·	·	·	·	1	·	·	·	Juncus trifidus
·	·	·	·	·	2	·	·	·	·	Luzula multiflora
·	·	·	·	·	1	1	·	·	·	L. spicata
·	·	·	·	·	·	·	·	·	·	L. sylvatica
·	·	·	·	·	2	·	2	·	·	Achillea millefolium
·	2	·	3	2	3	2	·	1	3	Alchemilla alpina
·	·	·	·	3	·	·	·	·	·	A. filicaulis
·	·	·	·	·	·	·	·	4	1	A. glabra
·	·	3	2	·	2	2	1	1	·	Armeria maritima
·	·	·	·	·	·	·	·	3	·	Campanula rotundifolia
·	·	·	·	·	·	·	·	2	·	Cerastium alpinum
·	·	·	2	·	·	·	·	·	·	C. edmonstonii
2	·	·	·	2	2	·	1	1	3	C. vulgatum
·	·	·	·	·	·	2	·	·	·	Cochlearia micacea
·	·	·	2	2	+	·	·	·	1	Euphrasia frigida
·	·	·	·	·	·	·	·	·	+	Filipendula ulmaria
4	3	3	4	3	2	·	3	2	3	Galium hercynicum
·	·	·	·	·	1	·	·	3	·	Geum rivale
·	·	·	2	·	2	·	·	·	·	Gnaphalium supinum
·	·	·	·	·	2	·	·	·	·	Leontodon autumnalis
·	·	·	+	·	·	·	1	2	2	Oxalis acetosella
·	1	·	3	2	4	1	·	3	2	Polygonum viviparum
·	1	3	·	·	2	·	·	·	·	Potentilla erecta
·	·	·	·	·	·	·	·	2	·	Pyrola cf. minor
·	·	·	4	3	2	2	2	3	1	Ranunculus acris
·	·	·	1	5	·	3	3	2	3	Rumex acetosa
·	·	·	·	·	·	·	+	·	·	Saussurea alpina
·	·	·	2	·	·	+	+	1	·	Saxifraga hypnoides
·	·	·	·	·	·	·	·	2	·	S. oppositifolia
·	·	·	·	·	·	·	·	·	·	S. stellaris
·	·	·	2	1	3	3	·	1	3	Sibbaldia procumbens
·	·	·	+	·	4	4	2	2	·	Silene acaulis
·	·	·	·	·	4	·	·	3	3	Thalictrum alpinum
·	·	·	+	3	4	3	·	3	·	Thymus drucei
·	·	·	·	·	2	·	·	1	·	Trollius europaeus
·	·	·	·	·	·	·	·	·	2	Veronica humifusa
·	·	·	·	1	·	·	·	·	·	V. officinalis
·	2	·	3	·	2	3	·	1	3	Viola palustris
·	·	·	·	·	·	·	·	·	·	V. riviniana
·	·	·	·	·	4	·	·	·	·	Aulacomnium turgidum
·	·	·	·	·	1	·	·	·	·	Breutelia chrysocoma
·	·	·	·	·	·	·	·	·	·	Campylopus flexuosus
·	·	·	·	·	2	·	·	3	·	Climacium dendroides
·	·	·	·	·	2	·	·	+	·	Ctenidium molluscum
·	·	·	·	·	·	·	·	·	·	Dicranella heteromalla
2	·	·	3	·	·	2	·	·	·	Dicranum fuscescens
·	·	2	1	·	·	·	·	·	·	D. scoparium
·	·	·	1	·	·	·	·	·	·	D. starkei
·	·	·	·	·	3	·	·	·	·	Ditrichum flexicaule
·	·	·	·	·	4	·	·	·	3	Drepanocladus uncinatus
·	·	·	·	·	·	·	·	3	·	Hylocomium brevirostre
3	5	5	3	2	6	1	6	5	3	H. splendens
·	·	·	·	·	2	·	·	·	·	H. pyrenaicum
·	·	·	·	·	2	·	·	·	2	H. umbratum
+	2	3	3	+	·	·	·	·	·	Hypnum cupressiforme

Table 45

	1	2	3	4	5	6	7	8	9	10
Hypnum callichroum	·	·	·	·	·	1	·	·	·	·
H. hamulosum	·	·	·	·	·	·	·	·	·	·
Oligotrichum hercynicum	·	·	·	·	·	·	·	·	·	·
Plagiothecium undulatum	·	·	·	·	·	·	·	·	·	·
Pleurozium schreberi	2	2	1	4	3	3	3	·	7	·
Pohlia cruda	·	·	·	·	·	·	·	·	·	·
Pohlia sp.	·	·	1	·	·	·	·	·	·	·
Polytrichum alpinum	4	2	3	3	4	4	2	2	5	2
P. gracile	·	·	·	·	·	·	·	·	·	·
Rhacomitrium canescens	·	+	·	·	·	1	·	·	·	2
R. lanuginosum	·	·	·	2	·	·	3	·	2	·
Rhytidiadelphus loreus	6	+	+	9	8	8	9	9	4	+
R. squarrosus	·	9	6	3	3	3	·	·	7	7
R. triquetrus	·	·	·	·	·	·	·	·	·	·
Sphagnum acutifolium agg.	·	·	·	·	·	·	·	1	·	·
Alicularia scalaris	·	·	·	·	·	·	·	·	·	·
Anastrepta orcadensis	·	·	·	3	·	3	·	·	1	·
Lophozia alpestris	·	·	·	·	·	·	·	·	·	·
L. floerkii	·	·	·	·	·	3	2	·	·	·
L. hatcheri	·	·	·	·	·	·	·	·	·	·
L. lycopodioides	·	·	·	·	·	·	·	·	1	·
Plagiochila asplenioides	·	·	·	·	·	·	·	·	·	·
Ptilidium ciliare	·	3	·	3	2	3	1	1	2	·
Cetraria aculeata	·	·	·	·	·	·	·	·	·	·
C. islandica	·	·	·	1	·	1	2	·	1	·
Cladonia bellidiflora	·	·	·	·	·	2	·	·	·	·
C. gracilis	·	·	·	·	·	·	·	·	·	·
C. rangiferina agg.	·	·	·	1	·	·	·	·	·	·
C. sylvatica	·	·	·	3	·	·	·	·	·	·
C. uncialis	·	·	·	2	·	·	·	·	·	·
Ochrolechia frigida	·	·	·	·	·	·	·	·	·	·
Peltidea leucophlebia	·	·	·	·	·	·	·	·	·	·
Peltigera canina	·	·	·	·	2	·	·	1	3	·
P. horizontalis	·	·	·	·	·	1	·	·	·	·
Number of species (107)	13	16	15	22	23	30	15	14	25	23

(Average 21)

Constancy class V 6
,,   ,,   IV 4

LOCALITIES

1. Beinn Eunaich, Dalmally, Argyll; 2. Aonach Beag, Glen Nevis, Inverness-shire; 3. Aonach Mor, Ben Alder group, Inverness-shire; 4. Saileag, Glen Shiel, Ross-shire; 5. Mullach Coire Mhic Fhearchair, Ross-shire; 6. Beinn Dearg, Inverlael, Ross-shire; 7. Ben Wyvis, Ross-shire; 8. Fionn Bheinn, Achnasheen, Ross-shire; 9. A 'Bhuidheanach, Laggan, Inverness-shire; 10. Caenlochan, Angus; 11. Sgurr a' Mhuillinn,

(continued)

11	12	13	14	15	16	17	18	19	20	
·	·	·	·	·	2	·	·	·	·	Hypnum callichroum
·	·	·	·	·	·	3	·	·	·	H. hamulosum
·	·	·	·	2	·	·	·	·	·	Oligotrichum hercynicum
·	2	·	·	·	·	·	2	·	·	Plagiothecium undulatum
·	2	4	2	·	2	·	·	·	1	Pleurozium schreberi
·	·	·	·	2	·	·	·	·	·	Pohlia cruda
·	·	·	·	·	·	·	·	·	·	Pohlia sp.
2	3	3	2	1	3	2	2	1	4	**Polytrichum alpinum**
·	·	·	·	4	·	·	·	·	·	P. gracile
·	·	·	·	·	4	·	·	·	·	Rhacomitrium canescens
2	2	4	2	+	·	3	·	·	·	R. lanuginosum
8	8	9	3	5	·	4	7	4	8	**Rhytidiadelphus loreus**
·	1	·	·	·	3	5	·	2	7	R. squarrosus
·	·	·	·	6	7	1	3	5	2	**R. triquetrus**
·	·	·	·	·	·	·	·	·	·	Sphagnum acutifolium agg.
·	·	·	·	1	·	1	·	·	·	Alicularia scalaris
2	2	2	·	·	·	1	·	·	·	Anastrepta orcadensis
·	·	·	·	·	·	1	·	·	·	Lophozia alpestris
1	·	2	·	·	·	·	·	·	2	L. floerkii
·	·	·	·	1	·	·	·	·	·	L. hatcheri
·	3	·	·	·	1	·	·	·	1	L. lycopodioides
·	·	·	·	·	·	·	·	1	·	Plagiochila asplenioides
3	1	2	·	·	·	·	·	·	1	Ptilidium ciliare
·	·	·	·	·	·	1	·	·	·	Cetraria aculeata
·	2	2	+	·	1	·	·	·	·	C. islandica
·	·	·	+	·	·	·	·	·	·	Cladonia bellidiflora
1	+	·	·	·	·	·	·	·	·	C. gracilis
·	·	·	·	·	·	·	·	·	·	C. rangiferina agg.
·	·	·	·	·	·	·	·	·	·	C. sylvatica
·	·	·	·	·	·	·	·	·	·	C. uncialis
·	·	·	·	·	·	2	·	·	·	Ochrolechia frigida
1	·	·	·	+	·	·	·	·	·	Peltidea leucophlebia
+	·	·	2	1	·	·	1	·	·	Peltigera canina
·	·	·	·	·	·	·	·	·	·	P. horizontalis
20	24	19	24	31	47	32	20	38	31	Number of species (107)

(Average 32)

Strath Bran, Ross-shire; 12, 13. Meall Horn, Reay Forest, Sutherland; 14. Ruadh Stac Mor, Beinn Eighe, Ross-shire; 15. A'Choinneach Mhor, Beinn Eighe, Ross-shire; 16. Beinn Fhada, Kintail, Ross-shire; 17. Moruisg, Strath Carron, Ross-shire; 18. Ruadh Stac Beag, Beinn Eighe, Ross-shire; 19, 20. Ben Heasgarnich, Glen Lyon, Perthshire.

Table 46: Polytricheto-Dicranetum starkei

	1	2	3	4	5	6	7	8	9	10
Reference number	M57 094	M56 113	M56 084	M56 087	M56 081	R56 120	R56 115	R57 114	M56 094	R57 110
Map reference	7983 2943	7975 3093	8690 2466	8813 2261	8690 2466	8146 2032	8194 2016	7746 2476	7997 3002	7748 2481
Altitude (feet)	3500	3400	3000	3200	3000	3000	3100	3500	3550	3350
Aspect (degrees)	90	135	90	45	90	360	360	360	45	45
Slope (degrees)	30	35	25	30	45	20	35	5	30	30
Cover (per cent)	100	100	80	80	90	90	95	90	100	75
Height (centimetres)	—	—	—	—	—	—	—	—	—	—
Plot area (square metres)	4	2	4	4	4	4	4	4	4	4
Athyrium alpestre	1	.	.	.	.	.	.	.	.	.
Blechnum spicant	.	.	.	.	.	1	+	.	.	.
Cryptogramma crispa	.	.	.	.	.	+	.	.	.	.
Lycopodium selago	.	.	.	2	1	1	.	.	+	.
Thelypteris oreopteris	.	.	.	.	.	2	.	.	.	.
Agrostis canina	.	.	.	+	.	.	.	.	.	.
A. tenuis	.	1	.	.	.	.	.	.	.	.
Deschampsia caespitosa	2	2	2	3	4	3	4	2	1	2
D. flexuosa	.	.	.	2	.	.	.	.	.	.
Festuca ovina agg.	.	.	.	.	.	.	.	1	.	.
F. rubra	.	.	.	.	.	.	2	.	.	.
Nardus stricta	.	1	1	.	.	2	1	.	.	.
Carex bigelowii	.	1	3	2	2	.	2	3	.	.
Alchemilla alpina	.	.	.	.	.	1	1	.	.	.
Cerastium cerastoides	+	.	.	.	.	.	.	.	.	+
Galium hercynicum	.	.	.	+	.	.	.	.	.	.
Gnaphalium supinum	.	1	3	3	3	3	2	.	.	.
Rumex acetosa	2	.	.	.	.	.	.	.	.	.
Saxifraga stellaris	3	.	+	2	1	3	3	2	1	1
Sibbaldia procumbens	.	.	.	3	.	.	.	.	.	.
Viola palustris	.	.	2	.	2	.	.	.	.	.
Acrocladium stramineum	.	.	.	.	.	.	2	.	.	.
Campylopus flexuosus	.	.	.	.	1	.	.	.	.	.
Conostomum tetragonum	.	.	3	.	.	3	.	4	+	.
Dicranum falcatum	1	.	.	.	.	.	.	.	6	.
D. starkei	8	8	8	8	7	7	6	7	2	8
Hypnum callichroum	.	.	.	.	.	1	.	.	.	.
Oligotrichum hercynicum	1	.	2	3	5	3	1	.	1	1
Pleurozium schreberi	.	.	.	.	.	2	.	.	.	.
Pohlia drummondii	.	4	.	.	.	.	3	.	.	3
P. ludwigii	3	.	.	.	.	.	.	.	6	.
P. nutans	.	.	1	.	1	3	.	3	.	.
Polytrichum alpinum	2	2	2	1	1	1	3	2	.	+
P. norvegicum	5	4	3	3	2	5	4	4	5	4
P. urnigerum	.	.	.	.	3	.	.	.	.	.
Rhacomitrium aquaticum	.	.	.	.	.	.	.	.	1	.
R. canescens	.	.	.	.	.	3	2	.	.	.
R. fasciculare	.	.	4	2	+	4	.	3	.	1
R. heterostichum	.	2	.	.	.	.	.	2	+	.
R. lanuginosum	.	1	.	.	.	3	.	.	.	.
Rhytidiadelphus loreus	.	.	.	+	1	2	2	.	.	.
R. squarrosus	.	.	.	.	.	.	1	.	.	.
Sphagnum nemoreum	.	.	.	.	.	.	1	.	.	.
Alicularia scalaris	2	.	.	2	1	4	5	.	3	.
Anthelia juratzkana	.	.	4	3	1	.	.	.	5	3
Cephalozia bicuspidata	.	.	.	1	.	.	.	.	1	.
Diplophyllum albicans	3	.	.	.	.	.	.	.	.	.
Gymnomitrium concinnatum	.	.	.	1	.	.	.	7	.	.
Lophozia alpestris	3	.	.	1	.	.	.	2	2	3
L. floerkii	.	4	2	4	5	5	6	.	.	.
Marsupella emarginata	.	.	.	.	.	4	.	.	.	.
Moerckia blyttii	.	.	.	2	.	3	.	.	.	.
Pleuroclada albescens	.	.	.	.	.	.	.	4	2	4
Scapania uliginosa	.	.	.	.	.	.	.	.	4	.
S. undulata	.	.	.	.	.	.	.	3	.	1
Cetraria islandica	.	.	+	.	+	.	.	.	.	.
Cladonia bellidiflora	.	.	3	1	.	1	.	1	.	.
C. delessertii	.	.	1	.	.	.	.	.	.	.
C. gracilis	.	.	1	.	.	.	.	.	.	.
C. pyxidata	.	.	1	1	.	.	.	.	.	.
C. uncialis	.	.	1	.	.	.	.	.	.	.
Solorina crocea	.	.	2	2	3	.	.	.	.	.
Stereocaulon evolutoides	.	.	+	1	.	.	.	.	.	.
S. vesuvianum	.	.	.	.	.	.	+	.	.	.
Number of species (64)	14	12	23	26	20	26	23	13	17	13

(Average 19)

Constancy class V 6
„   „   IV 4

LOCALITIES

1. Garbh Choire, Braeriach, Cairngorms; 2. South Beinn a' Bhuird, Cairngorms; 3,5. Ben Wyvis, Ross-shire; 4. Beinn Dearg, Braemore, Ross-shire; 6. Sgurr a' Bhealaich Deirg, Glen Shiel; 7, Beinn Fhada, Kintail Forest, Ross-shire; 8,10. Aonach Mor, Ben Alder hills, Inverness-shire; 9. Loch Etchachan, Cairngorms.

Table 47: Rhacomitreto-Dicranetum starkei

	1	2	3	4	5	6	7	8	9
Reference number	M56 129	R57 080	R57 115	M56 114	M57 082	M57 040	R57 096	M57 049	M56 121
Map reference	7845 3234	7989 2564	7747 2475	7975 3093	8015 3130	7711 2197	7714 2495	7714 2199	8013 3024
Altitude (feet)	3400	2950	3500	3400	3500	3500	3500	3900	3600
Aspect (degrees)	360	90	135	135	90	135	90	360	135
Slope (degrees)	20	28	18	35	10	15	25	60	15
Cover (per cent)	100	95	80	90	100	100	95	90	80
Height (centimetres)	–	–	–	–	–	–	–	–	–
Plot area (square metres)	4	4	4	4	4	4	4	4	4
Empetrum hermaphroditum	·	·	·	·	I	·	·	·	·
Loiseleuria procumbens	·	·	·	I	·	·	·	·	·
Salix herbacea	+	·	·	+	I	·	·	·	+
Vaccinium myrtillus	·	2	·	·	·	·	·	·	·
Athyrium alpestre	·	·	·	·	·	2	·	·	·
Blechnum spicant	·	·	·	·	·	I	·	·	·
Cryptogramma crispa	·	·	·	·	·	·	2	·	·
Dryopteris austriaca	·	·	·	+	·	·	·	·	·
Lycopodium selago	+	·	·	·	2	2	I	·	I
Agrostis tenuis	·	3	·	3	I	2	5	·	·
Anthoxanthum odoratum	·	3	·	·	·	·	·	·	·
Deschampsia caespitosa	I	2	3	3	·	4	3	3	2
D. flexuosa	I	2	·	·	·	·	·	·	·
Festuca ovina agg.	·	·	·	2	·	·	·	·	I
Nardus stricta	I	2	·	3	2	3	·	·	·
Poa alpina	·	·	·	·	·	·	·	I	·
Carex bigelowii	3	+	3	5	3	+	3	·	2
Juncus trifidus	·	·	·	3	2	·	·	·	4
Luzula spicata	·	·	I	·	·	·	·	·	·
Narthecium ossifragum	·	·	·	·	·	I	·	·	·
Alchemilla alpina	·	5	·	2	2	2	·	·	·
Epilobium anagallidifolium	·	·	·	·	·	·	·	3	·
Euphrasia frigida	·	I	·	·	·	2	·	3	·
Galium hercynicum	·	4	2	2	·	2	2	2	·
Gnaphalium supinum	·	4	4	5	7	3	3	6	6
Ranunculus acris	·	·	·	·	·	·	·	3	·
Saxifraga stellaris	·	·	·	+	+	3	I	2	·
Sibbaldia procumbens	·	4	·	·	·	5	8	I	·
Silene acaulis	·	·	·	+	·	·	·	·	I
Taraxacum officinalis agg.	·	·	·	·	·	·	·	I	·
Veronica alpina	·	·	·	·	·	·	·	2	·
Viola palustris	·	3	·	I	·	I	·	3	·
Andreaea nivalis	·	·	4	·	·	·	·	·	·
Conostomum tetragonum	4	·	I	I	2	I	·	·	2
Dicranum starkei	4	4	I	3	6	2	5	5	3
Dicranella heteromalla	·	2	·	·	·	·	·	·	·
Hylocomium splendens	·	·	·	·	·	2	·	·	·
Hypnum callichroum	·	·	·	·	·	·	·	2	·
Oligotrichum hercynicum	I	+	I	2	I	3	·	2	3
Pleurozium schreberi	·	3	·	·	·	·	·	·	·
Pohlia drummondii	5	·	·	·	·	·	·	·	·
P. ludwigii	·	·	·	·	2	·	·	·	·
P. nutans	·	4	·	3	·	I	·	·	2
Polytrichum alpinum	3	3	·	3	·	·	3	·	·
P. norvegicum	6	·	3	4	·	3	2	2	4
P. piliferum	·	2	·	·	·	·	·	·	·
P. urnigerum	·	2	·	·	·	·	·	2	·
Rhacomitrium aquaticum	·	·	·	·	·	·	·	·	I
R. canescens	·	5	8	·	I	I	7	7	·
R. fasciculare	·	·	2	2	6	3	2	·	·
R. heterostichum	6	4	·	5	6	3	·	2	7
R. lanuginosum	·	·	·	I	3	2	·	·	·
Rhytidiadelphus loreus	·	·	·	·	·	·	·	2	·
R. squarrosus	·	4	·	·	·	2	·	·	·
Alicularia scalaris	·	2	3	I	·	3	·	I	I
Anthelia juratzkana	·	·	3	·	·	3	·	·	·
Cephaloziella sp.	·	·	·	·	·	3	·	·	·
Gymnomitrium concinnatum	·	+	·	·	·	·	·	·	·
G. varians	·	·	I	·	·	·	·	·	·
Lophozia alpestris	2	I	·	·	·	·	·	I	3
L. floerkii	3	3	·	3	3	·	2	3	2
Marsupella emarginata	·	·	2	·	·	I	·	·	3
M. sullivantii	·	·	2	·	·	·	·	·	·
Moerckia blyttii	·	·	·	·	I	5	·	·	I
Ptilidium ciliare	·	2	·	·	·	·	·	·	·

Table 47 (*continued*)

	1	2	3	4	5	6	7	8	9
Cetraria islandica	.	1	.	.	1	1	.	.	.
Cladonia bellidiflora . . .	.	1	.	1	.	2	.	.	.
C. coccifera	.	1	.	.	.	.	.	.	.
C. uncialis	.	.	.	1	.	.	.	.	.
Crocynia sp.	1	.	.	.	.	.	.	.	.
Peltigera rufescens	.	.	.	.	.	.	.	3	.
Number of species (71) . . .	16	32	18	27	22	33	15	24	21

(Average 22)

Constancy class V 6
„ „ IV 6

LOCALITIES

1. Lochnagar, Aberdeenshire; 2. Geal Charn, Monadhliath, Inverness-shire; 3. Aonach Mor, Ben Alder hills, Inverness-shire; 4. South Beinn a' Bhuird, Cairngorms; 5. Ben Avon, Cairngorms; 6,8. Aonach Beag, Nevis hills, Inverness-shire; 7. Ben Alder, Inverness-shire; 9. Beinn Mheadhoin, Cairngorms.

Table 48: Gymnomitreto-Salicetum herbaceae (1–9); Exposed ground facies (10,11); Gymnomitrium varians facies (12–14)

	1	2	3	4	5	6	7	8	9	10	11	12	13	14
Reference number	P52 132	P52 169	P52 226	P52 227	M56 095	R57 113	R57 164	R58 018	M58 013	M58 011	R58 071	M58 065	M56 097	M57 090
Map reference	7415 2642	7414 2642	7145 2642	7415 2642	7995 3002	7748 2473	7874 2424	7263 2266	7384 2414	7453 2377	8448 2088	8046 3011	7994 2994	7923 2958
Altitude (feet)	3400	3175	3300	3300	3500	3600	3600	3680	3500	3000	3450	3650	4000	3450
Aspect (degrees)	–	350	320	320	45	180	180	225	90	–	360	90	45	90
Slope (degrees)	15	20	10	10	15	8	3	10	10	0	3	30	10	15
Cover (per cent)	80	90	90	90	80	100	100	85	95	80	70	90	95	90
Height (centimetres)	–	1	–	–	5	–	–	–	–	–	–	–	–	–
Plot area (square metres)	4	1	4	4	4	4	4	4	4	4	4	4	4	4
Empetrum hermaphroditum					+									
Salix herbacea	5	2	1	3	1	7	6	5	8	6	4	3		1
Lycopodium alpinum											1			
L. selago	1		2	1	3						1			
Agrostis canina			3	3				2	2	3				
Deschampsia alpina													+	+
D. caespitosa				2	4	1			3		2		+	
D. flexuosa	2	1			+	3		3			1			
Festuca ovina agg.	3	1	5	3		3	1		3		3			
Nardus stricta									+					
Carex bigelowii	3		1			4	1				3		1	
C. lachenalii					4									
Juncus trifidus					+							2		
Luzula arcuata												3	2	
L. spicata					1				1		2			
Alchemilla alpina				1	1			2	+	2				
Armeria maritima											3			
Cerastium cerastoides					3									
Galium hercynicum									1					
Gnaphalium supinum			1		4		+	+	1		3	4		2
Saxifraga stellaris					1								+	
Sibbaldia procumbens									1		2			
Silene acaulis					1						1			
Conostomum tetragonum	3	3	2		2	3	3	2	2		1	3		
Dicranella heteromalla						1	1							
Dicranum fuscescens					3									
D. starkei	5	3	3	3	3	2	3	2	6			1	3	
Diphyscium foliosum								1		1				
cf. Ditrichum zonatum				1										
Oligotrichum hercynicum	2	3	3	3	3	3	2	1				3	2	3
Pohlia drummondii					1								2	
P. nutans	3		1			1	1		1			2		
Polytrichum alpinum	3				1				3		1			
P. juniperinum	1													
P. norvegicum				4		3	+							
P. piliferum	1							2			1			1
P. urnigerum											1			
Rhacomitrium aquaticum											4		1	
R. canescens														3
R. fasciculare						7	5		4			3	1	
R. heterostichum	3	2	4	4	3	1	5							
R. lanuginosum	1	1	1	2	1	1		3	2	5	3			2
Alicularia scalaris	1	3	3	3	7	1	2		1		3	3		
Anthelia sp.	1													
Cephalozia ambigua	1	1												
C. bicuspidata			1											
cf. Cephaloziella byssacea												1		
Diplophyllum albicans	1	1	3	3										
D. taxifolium										3				
Gymnomitrium alpinum							1	2	3	2				
G. concinnatum	8	9	8	8	7	5	8	7	4	8	7			
G. varians							3					9	10	9
Lophozia alpestris	5	2	1	1		2	2		1	3		2	2	2
L. cf. attenuata				1										
L. floerkii					7		3			3				
L. ventricosa		1												
Moerckia blyttii					1									
Pleuroclada albescens		1	1		1									
Ptilidium ciliare							2			1				
Scapania sp.	1													
Cetraria aculeata											1			
C. islandica			1								1			
Cladonia bellidiflora	2				2	3	3	1	2		1	3		
C. coccifera					3									
C. degenerans					1									
C. delessertii													2	
C. foliacea											1			

Table 48 (*continued*)

	1	2	3	4	5	6	7	8	9	10	11	12	13	14
Cladonia gracilis	1	·	·	·	·	2	·	·	·	·	·	3	·	·
C. pyxidata	1	·	·	·	·	·	1	·	·	·	·	1	·	·
C. sylvatica	·	·	·	·	·	2	·	·	1	1	·	·	·	·
C. uncialis	1	·	·	1	·	·	·	2	2	2	·	·	·	·
Lecidea alpestris	2	·	·	1	·	·	·	·	·	·	·	1	·	·
Lecidea sp.	·	·	·	·	1	·	·	·	·	·	·	·	·	·
Ochrolechia gemminipara	1	·	·	·	·	·	·	·	·	·	·	1	·	·
O. tartarea	1	·	·	·	·	·	·	·	·	·	·	·	·	·
Solorina crocea	2	·	1	1	·	·	·	·	·	·	1	·	·	·
Stereocaulon evolutoides	·	·	·	·	·	·	·	·	·	2	·	·	·	·
S. vesuvianum	·	·	1	1	·	·	·	·	·	·	·	·	·	·
Number of species	29	15	21	21	31	20	19	15	23	24	15	21	11	9

(Average 21)

Constancy class V 7
„ „ IV 4

LOCALITIES

1–4. Ben Lawers, Perthshire; 5. Loch Etchachan, Cairngorms; 6. Aonach Mor, Ben Alder hills, Inverness-shire; 7. Creag Meagaidh, Laggan, Inverness-shire; 8. Ben Lui, Perthshire; 9. Beinn Heasgarnich, Perthshire; 10. Beinn a' Chreachain, Bridge of Orchy, Argyll; 11. Sgurr a' Chaorachain, Monar Forest, Ross-shire; 12. Cairngorm, Inverness-shire; 13. Ben Macdhui, Cairngorms; 14. Beinn Bhrotain, Cairngorms.

Table 49: Trichophoreto-Eriophoretum [typicum (1–12);

	1	2	3	4	5	6	7	8	9	10	11	12
Reference number	R57 025	P55 016	R56 015	R56 020	R57 029	R57 146a	R56 082	R57 146b	R57 069	R57 135	R57 049	R58 034
Map reference	9499 2282	9182 2069	8601 2022	8575 1968	9427 2242	7956 2574	8576 1976	7956 2574	7958 2581	8007 2690	9480 2240	7530 2290
Altitude (feet)	500	75	250	500	700	1100	300	1100	1200	1250	360	1000
Aspect (degrees)	45	–	–	–	180	–	–	–	270	90	–	–
Slope (degrees)	5	0	3	0	10	0	0	0	10	10	0	0
Cover (per cent)	100	100	100	100	100	100	100	100	100	100	100	100
Height (centimetres)	–	15	–	–	–	–	–	–	–	–	–	–
Plot area (square metres)	4	4	4	4	4	4	4	4	4	4	4	4
Betula nana	.	.	.	.	.	.	.	.	.	.	.	.
Calluna vulgaris	5	5	5	5	7	3	2	3	4	4	5	4
Erica tetralix	4	3	3	4	4	5	2	7	5	6	5	4
Myrica gale	3	2	3	3	4	4	.	5	4	6	.	4
Vaccinium myrtillus	.	.	.	.	.	.	.	.	.	.	.	.
Selaginella selaginoides	.	.	.	.	.	.	.	.	.	.	.	.
Agrostis canina	.	.	.	.	.	1	.	.	2	2	.	.
A. tenuis	.	.	.	.	.	.	.	.	.	.	.	.
Anthoxanthum odoratum	.	.	.	.	.	.	.	.	.	.	.	.
Festuca ovina agg.	.	.	.	1	.	.	.	.	1	.	.	.
Molinia caerulea	4	4	5	4	6	3	2	+	2	3	4	5
Nardus stricta	.	.	.	.	.	.	.	.	3	3	.	.
Sieglingia decumbens	.	.	.	.	.	.	.	.	.	.	.	.
Carex curta	.	.	.	.	.	.	.	.	.	.	.	.
C. demissa	.	.	.	.	.	.	.	.	.	.	.	.
C. echinata	.	.	.	.	2	.	1	.	2	2	.	.
C. hostiana	.	.	.	.	.	.	.	.	.	.	.	.
C. nigra	.	.	.	.	.	.	.	.	2	.	.	.
C. panicea	.	.	2	2	3	.	.	.	2	3	.	.
C. pauciflora	.	.	.	.	.	4	.	+	.	.	.	3
C. pulicaris	.	.	.	.	.	.	.	.	.	.	.	.
C. rostrata	.	.	.	2	.	.	.	.	.	.	.	.
Eriophorum angustifolium	4	2	2	3	3	3	5	3	3	3	3	3
E. vaginatum	3	4	5	4	2	3	4	3	2	+	4	4
Juncus bulbosus	.	.	.	.	.	2	.	.	1	.	.	.
J. effusus	.	.	.	.	.	.	.	.	.	3	.	.
J. squarrosus	.	.	.	.	.	.	.	3	5	.	.	.
Listera cordata	.	.	.	.	.	.	.	.	1	.	.	.
Luzula multiflora	.	.	.	.	.	.	.	.	.	.	.	.
Narthecium ossifragum	3	3	3	3	3	4	3	3	3	3	4	4
Orchis ericetorum	.	.	.	.	+	.	.	.	.	.	.	.
Trichophorum caespitosum	4	8	4	7	4	4	+	5	5	3	6	5
Drosera anglica	1	.	.	1	.	3	.	.	.	.	+	.
D. rotundifolia	2	3	1	3	+	2	3	+	.	.	3	3
Euphrasia sp.	.	.	.	.	.	.	.	.	.	.	.	.
Leontodon autumnalis	.	.	.	.	.	.	.	.	.	.	.	.
Pedicularis palustris	.	.	.	.	.	.	.	.	.	.	.	.
P. sylvatica	.	.	.	.	.	.	.	.	.	.	.	.
Pinguicula vulgaris	.	.	1	1	.	.	.	.	2	.	.	.
Polygala serpyllifolia	.	2	.	.	.	.	.	.	.	1	2	.
Potentilla erecta	3	3	1	2	3	.	.	.	.	3	2	.
Succisa pratensis	.	.	.	.	2	.	.	.	.	.	.	.
Viola palustris	.	.	.	.	.	.	.	.	.	.	.	.
Acrocladium cuspidatum	.	.	.	.	.	.	.	.	.	.	.	.
A. stramineum	.	.	.	.	.	.	.	.	.	.	.	.
Aulacomnium palustre	.	.	.	.	.	.	.	.	1	1	.	.
Breutelia chrysocoma	.	.	.	3	.	.	.	.	2	.	.	.
Campylopus atrovirens	.	.	.	.	.	.	.	.	.	.	3	.
C. flexuosus	.	.	.	1	.	.	.	.	.	.	.	.
Dicranum bonjeani	.	.	.	.	.	.	.	.	.	.	.	.
Drepanocladus exannulatus	.	.	.	.	.	.	.	.	1	.	.	.
D. revolvens	.	.	.	.	.	.	.	.	.	.	.	.
Hylocomium splendens	.	.	.	.	4	.	.	.	3	2	.	.
Hypnum cupressiforme	3	5	1	2	3	.	2	.	1	2	3	+
Mnium punctatum	.	.	.	.	.	.	.	.	1	.	.	.
Plagiothecium undulatum	.	.	.	.	.	.	.	.	3	.	.	.
Pleurozium schreberi	.	.	.	.	2	.	.	.	2	2	.	.
Polytrichum alpestre	.	.	.	.	.	.	.	.	.	.	.	.
P. commune	.	.	.	.	.	.	.	.	.	.	.	.
Pseudoscleropodium purum	.	.	.	.	.	.	.	.	.	.	.	.
Rhacomitrium lanuginosum	4	.	1	4	.	.	3	.	+	.	4	2
Rhytidiadelphus loreus	.	.	.	.	2	.	.	.	3	.	.	.
R. squarrosus	.	.	.	.	2	.	.	.	.	.	.	.
Sphagnum compactum	.	.	.	2	.	.	.	.	.	.	.	6
S. cuspidatum	1	.	.	.	.	4	5	.	.	.	.	.
S. girgensohnii	.	.	.	.	.	.	.	.	.	.	.	.
S. imbricatum	.	.	.	.	.	.	.	.	.	.	.	3
S. magellanicum	.	.	.	.	.	6	3	.	.	.	.	3
S. palustre	.	.	.	.	.	.	.	.	.	.	.	.

caricetosum (13–21)]; Rhacomitrium-rich community (22)

13	14	15	16	17	18	19	20	21	22	
R58	R57	R57	R57	R56	R58	R58	R57	P55	R57	Reference number
088	143	132	257	080	051	087	054	023	050	
8317	7947	8000	7746	8567	8816	8317	9405	7515	9480	Map reference
2191	2578	2690	3290	1973	2222	2191	2296	2539	2240	
1200	1000	1000	1000	800	1750	1200	150	1900	360	Altitude (feet)
—	—	—	45	—	—	180	—	—	—	Aspect (degrees)
0	2	0	28	3	0	7	5	5	—	Slope (degrees)
100	100	100	100	100	100	100	100	100	100	Cover (per cent)
—	—	—	—	—	—	—	—	—	—	Height (centimetres)
4	4	4	4	4	4	4	4	4	4	Plot area (square metres)
·	·	·	·	·	3	·	·	4	·	Betula nana
2	3	2	4	5	4	2	·	3	5	**Calluna vulgaris**
2	5	6	6	3	4	5	3	4	3	**Erica tetralix**
·	·	·	·	·	·	·	3	·	·	**Myrica gale**
·	·	·	2	·	·	·	·	·	·	Vaccinium myrtillus
3	3	·	·	·	3	3	·	·	·	Selaginella selaginoides
·	2	2	3	·	·	2	·	·	·	Agrostis canina
·	·	·	·	·	·	·	·	1	·	A. tenuis
·	2	·	3	·	·	·	·	·	·	Anthoxanthum odoratum
2	3	·	3	·	·	3	·	·	·	Festuca ovina agg.
4	·	3	4	5	5	5	3	3	3	**Molinia caerulea**
3	3	3	5	·	3	·	·	·	·	Nardus stricta
·	1	·	·	·	·	·	·	·	·	Sieglingia decumbens
·	·	·	·	·	·	·	3	·	·	Carex curta
·	·	·	·	·	2	·	·	·	·	C. demissa
7	4	2	5	3	4	5	·	5	·	**C. echinata**
·	3	·	·	·	·	·	·	·	·	C. hostiana
4	5	4	·	·	·	·	5	·	·	C. nigra
4	4	+	3	·	4	3	3	2	·	**C. panicea**
·	·	4	·	2	·	·	·	5	·	C. pauciflora
·	·	·	·	·	2	·	·	·	·	C. pulicaris
·	·	·	·	·	·	·	·	·	·	C. rostrata
4	3	4	+	4	3	4	3	+	3	**Eriophorum angustifolium**
·	·	·	·	5	·	4	·	·	4	**E. vaginatum**
3	4	·	3	·	4	1	2	·	·	Juncus bulbosus
·	2	·	·	·	·	·	3	·	·	J. effusus
5	3	4	3	3	2	·	·	·	·	J. squarrosus
·	1	·	2	·	·	·	·	·	·	Listera cordata
3	4	4	2	3	5	4	+	·	2	**Narthecium ossifragum**
2	·	·	·	·	·	·	·	·	·	Orchis ericetorum
2	·	2	·	7	2	4	·	·	4	**Trichophorum caespitosum**
·	·	·	·	·	·	·	·	·	·	Drosera anglica
+	1	2	1	2	1	3	1	·	·	**D. rotundifolia**
2	2	·	·	2	·	·	·	·	·	Euphrasia sp.
·	·	·	·	3	·	·	·	·	·	Leontodon autumnalis
·	1	·	·	·	·	·	·	·	·	Pedicularis palustris
3	·	·	·	·	·	·	·	·	·	P. sylvatica
·	2	·	·	·	3	2	·	1	·	Pinguicula vulgaris
·	·	·	·	2	2	·	·	·	·	Polygala serpyllifolia
5	3	1	2	3	3	3	·	2	3	**Potentilla erecta**
4	2	·	·	·	3	3	·	·	·	Succisa pratensis
1	·	·	1	·	2	·	·	·	·	Viola palustris
2	1	·	·	·	·	·	·	·	·	Acrocladium cuspidatum
3	·	·	·	2	1	·	·	·	·	A. stramineum
2	·	3	3	·	·	2	·	3	·	Aulacomnium palustre
·	4	·	·	·	3	3	·	·	·	Breutelia chrysocoma
·	·	·	·	·	·	·	·	·	·	Campylopus atrovirens
·	·	·	·	·	·	·	·	·	·	C. flexuosus
·	·	·	2	·	·	·	·	·	·	Dicranum bonjeani
·	·	·	·	·	·	·	·	·	·	Drepanocladus exannulatus
·	1	·	·	·	·	·	·	·	·	D. revolvens
2	4	1	2	·	3	3	·	·	·	Hylocomium splendens
·	4	·	3	2	1	·	·	·	2	**Hypnum cupressiforme**
·	·	·	2	·	·	·	·	·	·	Mnium punctatum
·	·	·	1	·	·	·	·	·	·	Plagiothecium undulatum
·	4	1	2	·	·	·	·	1	·	Pleurozium schreberi
·	·	·	3	·	·	·	·	·	·	Polytrichum alpestre
·	·	·	2	·	·	·	·	·	·	P. commune
·	·	·	·	·	3	1	·	·	·	Pseudoscleropodium purum
·	3	·	·	3	1	·	·	·	9	Rhacomitrium lanuginosum
·	·	·	·	·	·	·	·	·	·	Rhytidiadelphus loreus
1	·	·	·	2	1	·	·	·	·	R. squarrosus
·	·	·	·	3	·	·	·	·	·	Sphagnum compactum
·	·	·	·	·	·	·	·	·	·	S. cuspidatum
·	·	·	2	·	·	·	·	·	·	S. girgensohnii
·	·	·	·	·	·	·	·	·	·	S. imbricatum
·	·	·	·	·	·	·	·	·	·	S. magellanicum
·	·	·	8	·	3	4	·	9	·	S. palustre

Table 49

	1	2	3	4	5	6	7	8	9	10	11	12
Sphagnum papillosum	6	4	5	6	+	5	7	8	6	1	4	8
S. plumulosum	3	.	2	2	.	.	2	.	3	.	3	3
S. quinquefarium	.	.	.	.	.	.	.	.	.	.	.	.
S. recurvum	.	.	.	.	.	.	.	.	.	2	.	.
S. rubellum§	8	9	5	3	6	6	.	7	3	9	4	3
S. russowii	.	.	.	.	.	.	.	.	.	2	.	.
S. squarrosum	.	.	.	.	1	.	.	.	.	.	.	.
S. subsecundum†	3	.	.	1	.	.	6	.	3	+	.	.
S. tenellum	4	.	2	3	.	2	2	3	.	.	5	4
Thuidium tamariscinum	.	.	.	.	.	.	.	.	.	.	.	.
Aneura pinguis	.	.	.	.	.	.	.	.	.	.	.	.
Aneura sp.	.	.	.	.	.	.	.	.	.	.	.	.
Calypogeia trichomanis	1	.	.	.	.	.	.	+	1	1	.	.
Cephalozia sp.	.	.	.	.	.	2	.	.	.	.	.	.
Diplophyllum albicans	2	.	.	1	.	.	.	.	.	.	2	.
Lepidozia setacea	.	.	.	.	.	.	1	.	.	.	.	.
Leptoscyphus anomalus	.	1	.	.	.	2	.	2	.	.	.	.
L. taylori	2	.	.	.	.	.	.	.	.	.	2	.
Lophozia quinquedentata	.	.	.	.	.	.	.	.	.	.	.	.
L. ventricosa	.	.	.	.	.	.	.	.	1	.	.	2
Odontoschisma sphagni	3	+	1	3	1	3	.	2	.	.	2	2
Pellia epiphylla	.	.	.	.	.	.	.	.	.	.	.	.
Pleurozia purpurea	4	.	1	4	.	.	.	.	.	.	5	3
Scapania undulata	.	.	.	.	.	.	.	.	.	.	.	.
Cladonia gracilis	.	.	.	.	.	.	.	.	.	.	.	.
C. impexa	3	1	.	1	.	.	.	.	.	.	3	.
C. mitis	.	.	.	.	.	.	.	.	.	.	.	.
C. sylvatica	.	.	.	.	.	.	.	.	.	.	.	2
C. uncialis	2	1	.	2	.	.	.	.	1	.	3	1
Sphaerophorus fragilis	.	+	.	.	.	.	.	.	.	.	.	.
Number of species (64) (82)	26	19	20	32	20	20	17	18	35	25	26	22

(Average 23)

Constancy class V 12
    ,,   ,, IV 5
(Overall

Constancy class V 8 ⎱
    ,,   ,, IV 7 ⎰ for the association.

† Var. auriculatum in 7, 10, 14, 18, 21.   Var. inundatum in 1, 4, 11, 15, 19, 20, 21.
§ Including S. nemoreum.

LOCALITIES

1,11,22. Laxford Bridge, Sutherland; 2. Inverkirkaig, Sutherland; 3,4,7. Beinn Eighe, Ross-shire; 5. Ben Stack, Sutherland; 6,8,14. Glen Markie. Monadhliath, Inverness-shire; 9. Markie Burn, Monadhliath; 10,15. Glen Banchor, Inverness-shire; 12. Rannoch Moor, Argyll; 13,19.

(*continued*)

13	14	15	16	17	18	19	20	21	22	
•	4	4	+	7	5	•	3	•	•	**Sphagnum papillosum**
•	2	•	4	2	4	7	•	•	3	S. plumulosum
•	•	•	•	3	•	4	•	•	•	S. quinquefarium
•	•	8	+	•	•	2	•	•	•	S. recurvum
•	•	5	4	3	•	•	•	3	3	**S. rubellum**§
•	•	•	•	•	•	3	•	•	•	S. russowii
•	•	•	•	•	1	•	•	•	•	S. squarrosum
3	4	•	•	3	3	4	9	•	•	S. subsecundum†
•	•	•	•	4	•	•	•	•	•	S. tenellum
•	•	•	2	•	•	1	•	•	•	Thuidium tamariscinum
•	•	•	•	•	1	•	•	•	•	Aneura pinguis
1	•	•	•	•	•	•	•	•	•	Aneura sp.
1	•	1	3	•	•	•	•	•	•	Calypogeia trichomanis
•	•	•	•	•	•	•	•	•	•	Cephalozia sp.
•	1	•	•	2	•	•	•	•	•	Diplophyllum albicans
•	•	•	+	•	•	•	•	•	•	Lepidozia setacea
•	•	•	•	•	•	•	•	•	•	Leptoscyphus anomalus
•	•	•	•	•	•	•	•	•	•	L. taylori
•	•	•	1	•	•	•	•	•	•	Lophozia quinquedentata
•	•	•	•	•	•	•	•	•	•	L. ventricosa
•	•	•	2	•	•	•	•	•	2	Odontoschisma sphagni
•	•	1	•	•	•	•	•	•	•	Pellia epiphylla
•	•	•	3	•	•	•	•	•	2	Pleurozia purpurea
•	2	•	•	•	•	•	•	•	•	Scapania undulata
•	2	•	•	•	•	•	•	•	•	Cladonia gracilis
•	3	•	•	1	•	•	•	•	1	C. impexa
•	1	•	•	•	•	•	•	•	•	C. mitis
•	•	•	•	•	•	•	•	•	•	C. sylvatica
•	2	•	•	•	•	•	•	•	3	C. uncialis
•	•	•	•	•	•	•	•	•	•	Sphaerophorus fragilis
29	39	23	37	26	36	30	14	15	16	Number of species (64) (82)

(Average 28)

average 25·5)

Constancy class V   9
     „   „   IV   5

Mullach na Maoile, Glen Cannich, Inverness-shire; 16. White Haugh, Clova, Angus; 17. Sgurr Dubh, Coulin, Ross-shire; 18. **Beinn** Enaiglair, Braemore, Ross-shire; 20. Achfary, Sutherland; 21. Cam Creag, Loch Rannoch, Perthshire.

Table 50: Calluneto-Eriophoretum; [lichen-rich

	1	2	3	4	5	6	7	8	9	10
Reference number	R56 029	R56 037	R56 049	R56 100	R56 107	M56 026	M56 040	M56 058	M56 064	M56 069
Map reference	8833 2226	8825 2235	8790 2361	8736 2209	8302 2004	7889 3137	8656 1976	8517 2113	8559 2249	9146 2296
Altitude (feet)	1800	2500	2200	1600	2200	2500	1500	1850	2200	2000
Aspect (degrees)	360	180	135	360	180	90	45	—	270	45
Slope (degrees)	25	12	8	5	10	3	3	0	5	3
Cover (per cent)	100	98	100	100	100	100	100	100	100	100
Height (centimetres)	30	10	13	30	10	10	13	12	12	12
Plot area (square metres)	4	4	4	4	4	4	4	4	4	4
Arctous alpina	.	.	.	.	.	.	.	.	.	.
Betula nana	.	.	.	.	.	.	.	.	.	.
B. pubescens	.	.	.	.	.	.	.	.	.	.
B. verrucosa	.	.	.	.	.	.	.	.	.	.
Calluna vulgaris	8	6	8	7	6	8	5	7	4	6
Empetrum hermaphroditum	2	6	.	1	.	3	5	2	3	2
E. nigrum	.	.	4	.	6	.	.	.	.	.
Erica tetralix	.	.	.	2	.	.	.	.	.	.
Oxycoccus microcarpus	.	.	.	.	.	.	.	.	.	.
Vaccinium myrtillus	3	1	2	.	2	4	3	3	3	3
V. uliginosum	.	.	.	.	2	.	.	.	.	+
V. vitis-idaea	2	2	2	.	3	3	•	.	1	2
Deschampsia flexuosa	2	.	.	.	2	.	.	.	.	.
Nardus stricta	.	+	.	.	.	.	.	.	.	.
Carex bigelowii	.	3	3	.	3	.	.	.	4	3
C. binervis	1	.	.	.	.	.	.	.	.	.
Eriophorum angustifolium	2	.	.	3	.	.	4	.	1	.
E. vaginatum	7	4	5	6	5	3	4	6	7	6
Juncus squarrosus	4	4	4	3	6	.	2	3	+	1
Listera cordata	2	.	.	.	.	.	3	+	.	2
Narthecium ossifragum	.	.	.	4	.	.	.	.	.	.
Orchis ericetorum	+	.	.	.	.	.	.	.	.	.
Trichophorum caespitosum	.	1	.	6	3	.	.	2	.	.
Chamaepericlymenum suecicum	+	.	.	.	.	.	2	2	.	4
Galium hercynicum	.	.	.	.	.	.	.	1	.	.
Melampyrum pratense	.	.	.	.	.	.	.	2	1	.
Pinguicula vulgaris	.	.	1	2	1	.	.	+	.	+
Potentilla erecta	1	.	.	.	2	.	+	2	.	2
Rubus chamaemorus	.	3	3	.	3	5	3	3	4	2
Solidago virgaurea	.	.	.	.	2	.	.	.	.	.
Aulacomnium palustre	.	.	.	.	+	.	.	.	.	3
Campylopus flexuosus	.	.	.	.	.	1	.	.	.	.
Dicranum majus	2	.	.	.	.	.	.	.	.	.
D. scoparium	2	1	1	.	.	.	.	1	.	.
Eurhynchium praelongum	.	.	.	.	.	.	.	.	.	.
Hylocomium splendens	6	7	4	3	4	.	5	5	8	4
Hypnum cupressiforme	1	1	.	4	2	.	.	.	.	.
Plagiothecium undulatum	3	2	.	2	.	.	1	.	.	.
Pleurozium schreberi	3	4	4	3	4	+	.	1	3	.
Pohlia nutans	.	.	.	.	.	.	.	.	.	.
Polytrichum alpestre	.	.	.	.	.	.	.	.	.	.
P. commune	2	.	.	3	.	.	3	+	.	•
Rhacomitrium lanuginosum	.	3	3	1	5	.	.	2	4	.
Rhytidiadelphus loreus	4	4	2	3	3	.	4	2	.	3
R. squarrosus	.	.	.	.	.	.	.	.	.	.
Sphagnum fuscum	.	.	.	.	.	+	.	.	+	.
S. nemoreum	5	3	7	5	.	7	3	.	.	5
S. palustre	.	.	.	.	.	.	.	.	.	4
S. papillosum	.	.	.	7	.	.	.	.	.	.
S. plumulosum	.	.	.	3	.	.	.	.	.	.
S. quinquefarium	.	.	.	3	.	.	.	4	2	5
S. recurvum	.	.	.	.	.	.	.	4	4	5
S. rubellum	.	.	.	.	5	.	.	.	.	.
S. russowii	.	.	.	.	.	.	.	.	.	.
S. tenellum	.	.	.	2	.	.	.	.	.	.
Anastrepta orcadensis	3	3	.	.	1	.	.	.	.	.
Calypogeia trichomanis	.	.	.	.	2	.	.	.	.	.
Diplophyllum albicans	.	.	2	2	.	.	.	.	.	.
Lepidozia setacea	.	.	.	.	.	.	.	.	.	.
L. pearsoni	.	.	.	.	.	1	.	.	.	.
Leptoscyphus anomalus	.	.	.	1	.	1	.	.	.	.
L. taylori	.	.	.	.	2	.	.	.	.	.
Lophozia floerkii	.	.	.	.	3	.	.	.	.	2
L. ventricosa	.	.	.	.	.	.	.	.	.	.
Odontoschisma sphagni	.	.	2	.	.	.	.	.	.	.
Ptilidium ciliare	2	3	2	1	2	.	+	.	.	.
Scapania gracilis	.	.	.	1	.	.	.	.	.	.

facies (11–13); shrub-rich facies (14–21)]

11	12	13	14	15	16	17	18	19	20	21	
M56	P55	R59	M56	M56	M56	M54	X3	P54	M55	P55	Reference number
124	024	038	035	059	126	X		007	027	022	
8133	8090	8395	7988	8578	7869	9271	8778	—	8652	7552	Map reference
3253	2788	2830	3047	2248	3212	2559	2250	—	2448	2550	
2400	2300	1900	2800	1500	2200	1500	1700	1500	1800	1650	Altitude (feet)
135	180	90	270	360	360	450	—	270	225	45	Aspect (degrees)
5	10	5	2	10	3	5	—	3	2	5	Slope (degrees)
100	100	100	100	100	100	100	—	100	100	100	Cover (per cent)
6	12	12	10	22	17	15	—	20	12	30	Height (centimetres)
4	4	4	4	4	4	4	4	4	4	4	Plot area (square metres)
·	·	·	·	+	·	4	2	4	4	·	Arctous alpina
·	4	·	+	4	5	4	3	4	3	3	Betula nana
·	·	·	·	·	·	·	·	·	+	·	B. pubescens
·	·	·	·	·	·	·	·	·	+	·	B. verrucosa
2	6	5	7	7	8	6	6	9	7	8	**Calluna vulgaris**
3	3	4	3	3	3	3	3	·	3	·	**Empetrum hermaphroditum**
·	·	·	·	·	·	3	3	3	3	4	E. nigrum
·	·	4	·	·	·	2	·	1	1	1	Erica tetralix
·	3	3	·	·	·	·	·	·	·	3	Oxycoccus microcarpus
+	2	+	2	2	2	·	2	3	2	3	**Vaccinium myrtillus**
·	·	·	·	·	·	·	·	·	·	·	V. uliginosum
+	2	·	·	·	3	·	·	+	·	2	V. vitis-idaea
·	·	·	·	·	·	·	·	·	·	·	Deschampsia flexuosa
·	·	·	·	·	·	·	·	·	·	·	Nardus stricta
2	·	·	1	·	·	·	·	·	·	·	Carex bigelowii
·	·	·	·	·	·	·	·	·	+	·	C. binervis
·	·	·	·	1	1	·	3	4	·	·	Eriophorum angustifolium
4	6	5	4	6	3	5	·	·	6	7	**E. vaginatum**
·	5	·	·	+	·	7	6	4	1	·	Juncus squarrosus
·	·	·	·	2	·	·	+	·	·	·	Listera cordata
·	·	·	·	·	·	·	·	·	·	·	Narthecium ossifragum
·	·	·	·	·	·	·	·	·	·	·	Orchis ericetorum
·	·	·	·	·	·	·	·	3	+	·	Trichophorum caespitosum
·	·	·	·	·	·	+	·	·	·	·	Chamaepericlymenum suecicum
·	·	·	·	·	·	·	·	·	·	·	Galium hercynicum
·	·	·	·	+	·	·	·	·	·	·	Melampyrum pratense
·	·	·	·	·	·	·	·	·	+	·	Pinguicula vulgaris
·	·	·	·	·	·	·	1	1	·	·	Potentilla erecta
5	3	3	3	2	3	1	·	1	3	3	**Rubus chamaemorus**
·	·	·	·	·	·	·	·	·	·	·	Solidago virgaurea
·	·	·	·	2	2	·	1	·	·	·	Aulacomnium palustre
·	·	·	·	·	·	1	·	1	·	·	Campylopus flexuosus
·	·	·	·	·	·	·	·	·	·	·	Dicranum majus
1	·	·	2	·	3	·	1	·	·	·	D. scoparium
·	·	·	·	·	·	1	·	·	·	·	Eurhynchium praelongum
1	2	+	4	4	2	3	5	·	6	6	**Hylocomium splendens**
·	·	·	·	·	·	·	1	3	·	4	Hypnum cupressiforme
·	·	·	·	1	1	·	3	·	2	·	Plagiothecium undulatum
·	2	+	4	2	3	1	·	2	4	4	**Pleurozium schreberi**
1	·	·	·	·	·	·	·	·	·	·	Pohlia nutans
2	·	·	·	·	·	·	·	·	·	·	Polytrichum alpestre
·	·	·	·	1	·	·	·	·	·	·	P. commune
·	·	3	4	·	·	·	·	·	·	·	Rhacomitrium lanuginosum
1	·	·	2	3	2	·	2	·	4	3	Rhytidiadelphus loreus
·	·	·	·	·	·	3	·	·	·	·	R. squarrosus
+	·	4	1	·	+	·	·	·	+	·	Sphagnum fuscum
2	9	5	·	7	3	3	4	7	4	8	**S. nemoreum**
·	·	·	·	·	·	+	·	·	·	·	S. palustre
·	·	·	3	·	·	·	·	·	·	·	S. papillosum
·	·	·	·	·	·	·	·	·	·	·	S. plumulosum
·	·	·	·	·	·	·	·	·	·	·	S. quinquefarium
·	·	·	7	·	·	·	·	·	·	·	S. recurvum
·	·	·	·	·	·	·	·	·	·	·	S. rubellum
·	·	·	7	3	·	·	·	·	·	·	S. russowii
2	·	3	·	·	·	·	·	·	·	·	S. tenellum
·	·	·	·	·	·	·	·	·	·	·	Anastrepta orcadensis
1	·	1	·	·	1	·	·	·	1	·	Calypogeia trichomanis
·	·	·	·	·	·	1	1	·	·	·	Diplophyllum albicans
·	·	·	·	·	·	1	·	·	·	·	Lepidozia setacea
·	·	·	·	·	·	·	·	·	·	·	L. pearsoni
1	1	·	·	·	·	·	1	·	·	·	Leptoscyphus anomalus
·	·	3	·	·	·	1	·	·	·	·	L. taylori
·	·	·	·	1	·	·	·	·	·	·	Lophozia floerkii
·	·	2	1	·	3	·	·	·	1	·	L. ventricosa
·	·	·	·	·	·	·	·	·	·	·	Odontoschisma sphagni
1	1	2	1	·	6	·	·	·	1	2	Ptilidium ciliare
·	·	·	·	·	·	·	·	·	·	·	Scapania gracilis

Table 50

	1	2	3	4	5	6	7	8	9	10
Cetraria aculeata	.	.	2	.	.	.	.	.	.	.
C. islandica	.	.	.	.	2	.	.	.	.	.
Cladonia bellidiflora	1	1	.	.	.	.	.	.	.	.
C. coccifera	.	1	.	.	.	.	.	.	.	.
C. cf. deformis	.	.	.	.	.	.	.	.	.	.
C. gracilis	.	1	.	.	.	.	.	.	.	.
C. impexa	.	.	.	3	.	.	.	.	.	.
C. rangiferina agg.	.	3	.	.	.	.	.	1	.	.
C. squamosa	.	.	.	.	.	.	.	.	.	.
C. sylvatica	1	4	3	.	3	.	.	1	3	.
C. tenuis	.	.	.	.	.	.	.	.	.	.
C. uncialis	+	2	2	2	2	.	.	.	.	.
Ochrolechia tartarea . . .	+	.	.	.	.	.	.	.	.	.
Omphalia umbellifera . . .	.	.	.	.	.	2	.	.	3	2
Number of species (81) . . .	28	26	20	27	30	13	17	23	17	22

(Average 22)

Constancy class V 8
,, ,, IV 4

(Overall

LOCALITIES

1,2. Beinn Dearg, Ross-shire; 3. Beinn a' Chaisteil, Strath Vaich, Ross-shire; 4. Allt a' Mhadaidh, Fannich Forest, Ross-shire; 5. Sron na Gaoithe, Killilan Forest, Ross-shire; 6. Morrone, Braemar, Aberdeenshire; 7. Beinn Eighe, Ross-shire; 8. Moruisg, Achnasheen, Ross-shire; 9. Sgurr a' Mhuillinn, Ross-shire; 10. Ben More Assynt, Sutherland; 11. Meikle Corr Riabhach, Ladder Hills, Banffshire; 12. An

(continued)

11	12	13	14	15	16	17	18	19	20	21	
·	·	2	·	·	·	·	·	·	·	·	Cetraria aculeata
2	·	2	2	·	·	·	·	·	·	·	C. islandica
·	·	·	·	·	·	·	·	·	·	·	Cladonia bellidiflora
·	·	·	·	·	·	·	·	·	·	·	C. coccifera
·	·	·	·	·	2	·	·	·	·	·	C. cf. deformis
·	·	·	·	·	·	·	·	·	·	·	C. gracilis
·	·	·	2	·	2	·	3	+	3	·	C. impexa
3	3	9	1	·	·	·	·	·	·	1	C. rangiferina agg.
1	·	·	1	·	1	·	·	·	·	·	C. squamosa
8	6	9	2	·	·	·	+	3	·	·	C. sylvatica
+	·	·	·	·	·	·	·	·	·	·	C. tenuis
·	·	3	1	·	·	·	2	·	·	·	C. uncialis
·	·	2	·	·	·	·	·	·	·	·	Ochrolechia tartarea
1	·	·	·	+	·	·	·	·	·	·	Omphalia umbellifera
24	16	23	22	22	23	19	21	18	24	16	Number of species (81)

(Average 21)   (Average 20)

average 21)

Bhuidheanach, Monadhliath, Inverness-shire; 13. Carn nan tri-tighearnan, Cawdor, Nairnshire; 14. Moine Bhealaidh of Craig Derry, Cairngorms; 15. Sgurr a' Ghlas Leathaid, Achnasheen, Ross-shire; 16. Lochnagar, Aberdeenshire; 19. Ben Klibreck, Sutherland; 20. Ben Wyvis, Ross-shire; 21. Camghouran, Loch Rannoch, Perthshire.

Table 51: Empetreto-Eriophoretum

	1	2	3	4	5	6	7	8	9
Reference number	M56 033	M56 034	R56 104	M57 072	M57 092	R57 278	M58 016	R58 020	R58 058
Map reference	7987 3045	8002 3042	8303 1979	8045 3224	7778 3186	7838 3219	7497 2699	7334 2482	8856 2293
Altitude (feet)	2800	2800	2850	2700	3000	2800	3000	2750	2500
Aspect (degrees)	–	–	90	–	180	180	135	360	270
Slope (degrees)	0	0	5	0	2	15	2	12	3
Cover (per cent)	100	100	100	100	100	100	100	100	100
Height (centimetres)	5	5	–	–	–	–	–	–	–
Plot area (square metres)	4	4	4	4	4	4	4	4	4
Calluna vulgaris	.	.	1	1	.	.	.	.	.
Empetrum hermaphroditum	5	4	5	4	5	7	5	5	6
Oxycoccus microcarpus	1	.	.	.	.	.	.	.	.
Vaccinium myrtillus	.	3	2	2	3	4	3	3	3
V. uliginosum	3	+	3	.	4	5	.	2	5
V. vitis-idaea	4	.	2	3	2	.	4	4	3
Deschampsia flexuosa	.	1	.	.	1	.	.	3	.
Festuca ovina agg.	.	.	.	.	1	.	.	.	2
Nardus stricta	.	.	.	.	.	.	5	4	.
Carex bigelowii	+	1	4	+	2	2	3	3	4
C. nigra	.	.	.	1	.	.	.	.	.
Eriophorum angustifolium	3	.	4	.	2	3	3	3	4
E. vaginatum	6	7	5	6	7	5	2	5	5
Juncus squarrosus	.	.	+	.	.	2	.	.	+
Luzula multiflora	.	.	.	.	+	.	.	.	1
Trichophorum caespitosum	.	3	4	.	.	3	1	4	.
Chamaepericlymenum suecicum	.	+	.	.	.	.	.	.	2
Galium hercynicum	.	.	.	.	1	.	.	2	.
Pinguicula vulgaris	.	.	.	.	.	.	.	2	1
Potentilla erecta	.	.	.	.	.	.	.	2	1
Rubus chamaemorus	3	4	1	3	3	3	4	2	3
Trientalis europaea	.	.	.	.	+	.	.	.	.
Viola palustris	.	.	.	.	.	.	.	.	1
Aulacomnium palustre	3	2	2	3	3	.	.	.	.
Campylopus flexuosus	.	.	.	.	.	2	.	.	.
Dicranum fuscescens	.	.	.	1	.	.	1	.	.
D. majus	.	.	.	2	.	.	.	.	.
D. scoparium	.	.	.	3	.	2	2	3	.
Hylocomium splendens	.	.	3	.	.	1	.	3	3
Pleurozium schreberi	1	2	2	2	3	5	.	3	2
Pohlia nutans	1	.	.	.	.	.	1	.	.
Polytrichum alpestre	1	3	2	3	+	.	4	4	.
P. alpinum	.	.	1	.	.	.	.	2	3
P. commune	2	.	.	1	2	.	2	.	.
Rhacomitrium lanuginosum	.	.	4	1	1	2	1	2	4
Rhytidiadelphus loreus	.	.	3	2	3	.	.	3	3
Sphagnum fuscum	+	.	4	+	.	.	.	.	.
S. magellanicum	8	8	.	1	.	.	.	.	.
S. nemoreum	8	8	4	5	5	5	.	5	3
S. russowii	.	.	.	.	5	.	.	3	2
S. papillosum	8	.	8	.	.	.	9	7	7
S. plumulosum	.	.	3	5	.	.	1	.	4
S. tenellum	.	.	+	.	.	.	.	.	1
Anastrepta orcadensis	.	.	.	.	.	2	.	3	.
Diplophyllum albicans	.	.	.	.	.	.	.	.	2
Leptoscyphus anomalus	2	3	.	.	.	1	3	.	.
L. taylori	.	.	.	3	.	.	.	.	.
Lophozia floerkii	.	.	.	.	.	2	.	.	.
cf. L. porphyroleuca	1	.	.	.	.	.	.	.	.
L. ventricosa	.	.	.	3	+	.	1	2	1
Ptilidium ciliare	.	.	3	.	2	3	1	3	2
Cetraria aculeata	.	.	1	1	.	.	+	.	.
C. islandica	.	.	.	3	.	3	2	.	1
Cladonia bellidiflora	.	1	.	.	1	.	.	.	.
C. gracilis	.	.	.	1	1	.	2	.	.
C. rangiferina agg.	.	.	.	2	.	3	1	.	.
C. pyxidata	.	.	.	.	.	.	.	.	1
C. sylvatica	+	2	3	7	.	4	2	2	3
C. uncialis	+	2	.	.	.	.	2	.	3
Ochrolechia frigida	.	.	.	.	.	.	.	.	2
Omphalia umbellifera	+	3	.	2	.	.	.	.	.
Number of species (61)	22	19	26	28	25	22	26	27	33

(Average 25)

Constancy class V 8
,, ,, IV 5

LOCALITIES

1. Craig Derry, Cairngorms, Aberdeenshire; 2. Beinn a' Chaoruinn, Cairngorms, Aberdeenshire; 3. Sguman Coinntich, Killilan Forest, Ross-shire; 4. Brown Cow Hill, Glen Avon, Aberdeenshire; 5. Caenlochan, Angus; 6. Glen Muick, Aberdeenshire; 7. Carn Mairg, Glen Lyon, Perthshire; 8. Meall na Samhna, Glen Lochay, Perthshire; 9. Seana Bhraigh, Gleann Beag, Ross-shire.

Table 52: Trichophoreto-Callunetum (1–12); Molinieto-Callunetum

	1	2	3	4	5	6	7	8	9	10	11	12
Reference number	M56 144	M57 055	M57 086	R57 248	R57 008	R58 036	R58 052	R58 057	R58 085	R58 041	R59 041	R59 035
Map reference	8019 2937	8007 2862	7898 2995	7767 3250	9344 2331	— —	8817 2219	8828 2215	8317 2190	8952 2987	8475 3115	8415 2859
Altitude (feet)	2150	1400	1600	1400	1150	1000	1700	1500	1200	2000	900	1150
Aspect (degrees)	315	270	45	135	270	315	180	270	180	270	—	—
Slope (degrees)	5	5	4	7	5	5	10	15	10	10	0	0
Cover (per cent)	95	100	100	100	100	100	100	100	100	100	100	100
Height (centimetres)	12	10	12	20	—	—	20	—	—	20	—	—
Plot area (square metres)	4	4	4	4	4	4	4	4	4	4	4	4
Arctostaphylos uva-ursi		1										
Betula nana							3					
Calluna vulgaris	8	7	8	8	6	7	8	7	6	6	3	5
Erica cinerea			1									
E. tetralix	3	5	3	2	3	4	3	4	4	4	4	4
Genista anglica		1	3									
Myrica gale												
Pinus sylvestris		1										
Vaccinium myrtillus				3								
Lycopodium selago	+											
Agrostis canina												
A. tenuis												
Anthoxanthum odoratum												
Deschampsia flexuosa												
Molinia caerulea			2		3	+				3		
Nardus stricta												
Carex bigelowii			3									
C. binervis												
C. echinata										2		
C. panicea	1		+	2								
C. pilulifera												
Eriophorum angustifolium				2	3			2	3	3	3	
E. vaginatum					4				3		4	3
Juncus squarrosus				2			3	3		3		
Luzula multiflora				2								
Narthecium ossifragum				3			3	2	4	3	3	
Orchis ericetorum										3		
Trichophorum caespitosum	3	5	4	7	7	7	6	8	8	6	7	4
Antennaria dioica			2									
Drosera rotundifolia											3	
Hieracium sp.												
Pedicularis sylvatica										2		
Pinguicula vulgaris	+				1					2		
Polygala serpyllifolia										2		
Potentilla erecta			2	+	3					2		
Succisa pratensis												
Trientalis europaea												
Viola riviniana												
Campylopus flexuosus		1										
Dicranella heteromalla			1									
Dicranum scoparium		2		1		1						
Hylocomium splendens				3	2				2	1		
Hypnum cupressiforme		4		4	2	4	3	3	3			2
Leucobryum glaucum												
Plagiothecium undulatum				2								
Pleurozium schreberi	1			3		3	3					
Rhacomitrium lanuginosum	5				4	3	4	4		3		2
Rhytidiadelphus loreus				3	1							
Sphagnum compactum										4		
S. nemoreum				3	4	4		4				
S. palustre												
S. papillosum				3					3	3	9	
S. plumulosum									5	3		
S. rubellum									4	4	4	
S. russowii												
S. tenellum	+			2						4	3	
Thuidium tamariscinum												
Alicularia scalaris												
Anastrepta orcadensis							2					
Calypogeia trichomanis											1	
Cephalozia sp.					1						1	
Diplophyllum albicans				2				1				
Leptoscyphus anomalus				2						2		
L. taylori						2		1	1			
Lophocolea bidentata				2								
Lophozia floerkii								2				
L. ventricosa						1	2					
Odontoschisma sphagni				2								3
Pleurozia purpurea					4		3					
Ptilidium ciliare				1			2					
Scapania gracilis					2				1			

(13–21); Related Trichophorum community (22)

13	14	15	16	17	18	19	20	21	22	
R56	M57	R56	R57	M58	R58	R58	R58	R56	R59	Reference number
016	024	017	058	054	089	048	040	013	008	
8584	7996	8582	8804	8407	8317	8800	8939	8601	7303	Map reference
1998	1315	1990	2203	1862	2217	2203	2998	2022	2046	
650	600	600	1000	400	750	1000	2000	250	1700	Altitude (feet)
180	180	125	270	—	180	270	180	—	180	Aspect (degrees)
25	5	25	25	0	15	15	15	3	20	Slope (degrees)
100	100	100	100	100	100	100	100	100	100	Cover (per cent)
35	25	30	—	—	30	—	30	—	—	Height (centimetres)
4	4	4	4	4	4	4	4	4	4	Plot area (square metres)
.	.	.	.	.	.	.	.	.	.	Arctostaphylos uva-ursi
.	.	.	.	.	.	.	.	.	.	Betula nana
7	8	5	8	4	7	8	9	5	2	**Calluna vulgaris**
5	.	1	4	.	.	2	.	.	.	Erica cinerea
5	.	5	+	5	3	3	1	5	.	**E. tetralix**
.	.	.	.	.	.	.	.	.	.	Genista anglica
.	.	1	.	.	.	.	.	2	.	Myrica gale
.	.	.	.	.	.	.	.	.	.	Pinus sylvestris
.	1	.	.	3	.	.	.	.	2	Vaccinium myrtillus
.	.	.	.	.	.	.	.	.	.	Lycopodium selago
.	.	.	1	.	.	.	.	.	3	Agrostis canina
.	.	.	.	+	.	.	.	.	.	A. tenuis
.	+	.	.	.	.	.	.	.	3	Anthoxanthum odoratum
1	1	.	.	.	.	.	3	.	2	Deschampsia flexuosa
6	6	7	7	7	8	6	5	7	.	**Molinia caerulea**
.	1	.	2	.	.	.	.	.	4	Nardus stricta
.	.	.	.	.	.	.	.	.	.	Carex bigelowii
.	+	.	.	.	.	.	.	.	.	C. binervis
.	.	.	.	2	.	+	.	.	.	C. echinata
.	.	.	.	2	.	2	.	.	3	C. panicea
.	1	.	.	.	.	.	.	.	.	C. pilulifera
.	3	.	.	.	2	2	.	1	3	Eriophorum angustifolium
.	.	.	.	.	.	.	.	.	.	E. vaginatum
.	+	.	.	.	.	.	.	.	2	Juncus squarrosus
.	.	.	.	.	.	.	.	.	.	Luzula multiflora
.	.	2	.	3	.	.	.	2	3	Narthecium ossifragum
.	.	.	.	.	.	.	.	.	.	Orchis ericetorum
2	5	4	2	5	.	.	.	5	8	**Trichophorum caespitosum**
.	.	.	.	.	.	1	.	.	.	Antennaria dioica
1	.	.	.	.	.	.	.	.	.	Drosera rotundifolia
.	.	.	.	.	.	.	.	.	.	Hieracium sp.
.	.	.	.	.	.	.	.	.	2	Pedicularis sylvatica
.	.	.	.	.	.	.	.	.	.	Pinguicula vulgaris
1	3	1	.	.	3	.	.	.	.	Polygala serpyllifolia
2	3	2	2	4	4	3	3	2	5	**Potentilla erecta**
2	.	.	.	2	2	.	.	.	.	Succisa pratensis
.	.	.	.	.	3	.	.	.	.	Trientalis europaea
.	.	.	.	.	3	.	.	.	.	Viola riviniana
.	.	1	.	.	.	.	.	.	2	Campylopus flexuosus
.	.	.	.	.	.	.	.	.	.	Dicranella heteromalla
1	.	.	.	3	.	.	1	.	2	Dicranum scoparium
1	2	1	3	.	4	4	.	.	2	Hylocomium splendens
3	5	1	2	6	.	1	4	3	3	**Hypnum cupressiforme**
1	.	.	.	1	.	.	.	.	.	Leucobryum glaucum
.	.	.	.	1	3	4	.	.	.	Plagiothecium undulatum
1	2	.	2	.	2	2	2	.	2	Pleurozium schreberi
2	.	4	.	.	.	.	1	1	1	Rhacomitrium lanuginosum
1	2	.	3	.	.	3	.	.	.	Rhytidiadelphus loreus
.	.	.	.	3	.	.	.	1	.	Sphagnum compactum
1	7	.	.	.	.	6	.	.	.	S. nemoreum
.	.	.	.	.	2	.	.	.	.	S. palustre
.	.	.	.	.	2	.	.	.	3	S. papillosum
.	7	.	.	.	.	.	.	1	.	S. plumulosum
.	.	.	.	.	.	.	.	1	5	S. rubellum
.	.	.	.	.	2	.	.	1	.	S. russowii
1	.	1	.	.	.	.	.	1	.	S. tenellum
.	.	.	.	.	.	2	.	.	.	Thuidium tamariscinum
.	.	.	.	2	.	.	.	.	.	Alicularia scalaris
.	.	.	.	.	.	.	.	.	.	Anastrepta orcadensis
.	.	.	.	.	.	3	.	.	.	Calypogeia trichomanis
.	.	.	.	.	.	.	.	.	.	Cephalozia sp.
.	.	1	.	.	.	.	1	1	2	Diplophyllum albicans
.	.	.	.	.	.	.	.	.	.	Leptoscyphus anomalus
.	.	.	.	.	.	.	.	.	.	L. taylori
.	.	.	.	.	.	.	.	.	.	Lophocolea bidentata
.	.	.	.	.	.	.	.	.	.	Lophozia floerkii
.	.	.	.	.	.	2	.	.	.	L. ventricosa
1	1	2	.	.	.	.	.	1	.	Odontoschisma sphagni
.	.	.	.	.	.	.	.	.	.	Pleurozia purpurea
.	.	.	.	.	.	.	.	.	.	Ptilidium ciliare
.	.	1	.	.	.	.	.	.	.	Scapania gracilis

Table 52

	1	2	3	4	5	6	7	8	9	10	11	12
Cetraria aculeata . . .	2	.	7	.	.	.	.	.	.	.	.	2
C. islandica . . .	3	.	.	.	.	.	.	.	.	.	.	.
Cladonia carneola . . .	.	.	7	.	.	.	.	.	.	.	.	.
C. coccifera . . .	.	3	7	.	.	.	.	.	.	.	.	.
C. cornuta . . .	.	.	.	.	.	.	.	.	.	.	.	.
C. floerkeana . . .	.	2	7	.	.	.	.	.	.	.	.	.
C. gracilis . . .	1	5	7	.	.	.	.	.	.	.	.	.
C. impexa . . .	3	2	7	.	4	4	5	4	.	.	2	9
C. pyxidata . . .	.	2	7	2	1	.	.	.	.	1	.	1
C. rangiferina agg. .	1	.	.	.	.	.	5	.	.	.	.	3
C. squamosa . . .	.	.	7	.	.	.	.	.	.	.	.	.
C. sylvatica . . .	2	.	.	.	.	.	5	.	.	2	2	9
C. uncialis . . .	5	2	7	.	3	.	5	2	+	3	1	2
Icmadophila ericetorum . .	.	2	7	.	.	.	.	.	.	.	.	.
Ochrolechia frigida . .	1	.	.	.	.	.	.	.	.	.	.	.
Pycnothelia papillaria . .	.	+	.	.	.	.	.	.	.	.	.	.
Number of species (60) (55) .	17	17	21	22	22	12	18	14	12	23	17	12

(Average 17)

Constancy class V 4
 ,,   ,, IV 3

LOCALITIES

1. Glen Einich, Cairngorms, Inverness-shire; 2. Invereshie, Cairngorms, Inverness-shire; 3. Beinn Bhrotain, Cairngorms, Aberdeenshire; 4. Glen Doll, Clova, Angus; 5. Strath nan Caran, Glendhu Forest, Sutherland; 6. Rannoch Moor, Argyll; 7. Beinn Enaiglair, Inverlael, West Ross; 8. Beinn Dearg, Inverlael, West Ross; 9. Mullach na Maoile, Glen Cannich, Inverness-shire; 10, 20. Carn a' Mhaim, Cairngorms,

(continued)

13	14	15	16	17	18	19	20	21	22	
.	.	.	.	.	.	.	.	.	.	Cetraria aculeata
.	.	.	.	.	.	.	.	.	.	C. islandica
.	.	.	.	.	.	.	.	.	.	Cladonia carneola
1	.	1	.	.	.	.	1	.	.	C. coccifera
.	.	.	.	+	.	.	.	.	.	C. cornuta
.	.	.	.	.	.	.	.	.	.	C. floerkeana
.	.	.	.	.	.	.	2	.	.	C. gracilis
3	.	4	.	.	.	.	.	3	.	C. impexa
1	.	1	.	.	.	.	1	.	.	C. pyxidata
.	.	.	.	.	.	.	.	.	.	C. rangiferina agg.
1	.	.	.	.	.	.	.	.	.	C. squamosa
.	.	.	.	.	.	.	2	.	.	C. sylvatica
1	.	2	.	.	.	.	.	.	.	**C. uncialis**
.	.	.	.	.	.	.	.	.	.	Icmadophila ericetorum
.	.	.	.	.	.	.	.	.	.	Ochrolechia frigida
.	.	.	.	.	.	.	.	.	.	Pycnothelia papillaria
25	20	21	12	17	14	20	14	18	22	Number of species (60) (55)

(Average 18)

Constancy class V 5
" " IV 3

Aberdeenshire; 11. Moss of Bednawinny, nr. Dallas, Morayshire; 12. Carn a' Mhais Leathain, Cawdor, Nairnshire; 13,15,21. Beinn Eighe, West Ross; 14. Bloodstone Hill, Isle of Rhum, Inverness-shire; 16. Braemore, Loch Broom, West Ross; 17. Loch Kishorn, West Ross; 18. Mullardoch Glen Cannich, Inverness-shire; 19. Beinn Enaiglair, Inverlael, West Ross; 22. Ben Cruachan, Argyll.

Table 53: Molinia-Myrica nodum

Reference number	1	2	3	4	5	6	7	8	9
	R56 014	R58 095	R58 028	R58 093	M58 050	R58 044	R57 138	R58 147	R57 133
Map reference	8601 2022	7482 2657	7811 1863	7902 2675	7652 1735	8318 2225	7653 1732	7956 2575	8000 2690
Altitude (feet)	250	750	400	1000	500	700	400	1100	1050
Aspect (degrees)	90	—	360	90	270	—	180	90	90
Slope (degrees)	3	0	5	5	10	3	12	25	25
Cover (per cent)	100	100	100	100	100	100	100	100	100
Height (centimetres)	36	—	—	—	—	—	—	50	—
Plot area (square metres)	4	4	4	4	4	4	4	4	4
Calluna vulgaris	2	.	.	.	1	3	1	2	.
Erica tetralix	2	.	.	2	3	2	1	.	2
Myrica gale	5	7	5	7	5	7	5	3	8
Equisetum sylvaticum	.	.	.	.	.	.	.	.	2
Selaginella selaginoides	.	.	.	.	3	.	1	.	.
Agrostis canina	.	3	.	3	.	.	3	.	+
Deschampsia flexuosa	.	.	.	.	.	.	.	1	.
Festuca ovina agg.	.	.	.	3	.	.	3	.	+
Molinia caerulea	9	7	9	7	8	5	8	10	3
Nardus stricta	.	.	.	.	.	.	1	.	4
Sieglingia decumbens	.	.	.	.	.	.	2	.	.
Carex echinata	.	.	3	.	.	+	4	.	2
C. panicea	1	2	3	.	2	.	3	.	3
Eriophorum angustifolium	1	.	.	.	.	.	.	.	+
E. latifolium	.	.	.	.	+	.	.	.	.
Juncus acutiflorus	.	2	.	.	.	.	.	.	.
J. conglomeratus	.	.	1	.	.	.	.	.	.
J. squarrosus	.	.	.	.	.	.	.	.	4
Luzula multiflora	.	2	.	.	.	.	.	.	.
Narthecium ossifragum	1	.	4	.	2	2	2	.	3
Orchis ericetorum	1	.	2	.	.	.	.	.	.
Schoenus nigricans	.	.	.	.	3	.	.	.	.
Trichophorum caespitosum	2	.	3	.	2	4	1	.	.
Campanula rotundifolia	.	.	.	1	.	.	.	.	.
Drosera rotundifolia	.	.	.	.	1	1	.	.	+
Euphrasia micrantha	.	.	.	.	2	.	.	.	.
Galium hercynicum	.	1	.	3	.	.	.	3	.
Hypericum pulchrum	1	.	.	.	.	.	2	.	.
Pedicularis sylvatica	.	.	.	.	1	.	.	.	.
Pinguicula vulgaris	.	.	.	.	1	.	.	.	.
Polygala serpyllifolia	1	.	.	.	.	2	.	.	.
Potentilla erecta	1	2	3	3	3	3	3	2	3
Succisa pratensis	.	1	2	2	3	.	2	.	.
Viola riviniana	.	.	.	3	.	.	3	.	2
Acrocladium cuspidatum	.	.	.	.	2	.	.	.	3
Aulacomnium palustre	.	.	.	.	.	.	.	.	3
Breutelia chrysocoma	.	1	.	.	3	.	1	.	.
Campylium stellatum	.	.	.	.	3	.	.	.	.
Campylopus flexuosus	.	.	.	.	.	1	.	.	.
Ctenidium molluscum	.	.	.	.	.	.	1	.	.
Dicranum scoparium	1	.	.	.	.	.	.	1	.
Drepanocladus revolvens	.	.	.	.	2	.	.	.	.
Hylocomium splendens	2	3	.	3	.	2	1	3	1
Hypnum cupressiforme	1	2	.	.	2	3	3	3	.
Leucobryum glaucum	1	.	.	.	.	.	.	.	.
Plagiothecium undulatum	.	.	.	.	.	.	1	.	.
Pseudoscleropodium purum	.	2	.	2	.	.	3	.	.
Rhacomitrium lanuginosum	.	.	.	.	1	.	.	.	.
Rhytidiadelphus loreus	1	.	.	.	.	1	.	.	.
R. squarrosus	.	2	.	1	.	.	1	.	2
R. triquetrus	.	.	.	.	.	.	.	.	1
Sphagnum cuspidatum	.	.	.	.	2	.	.	.	.
S. nemoreum	3	.	.	.	3	4	.	.	.
S. papillosum	.	.	4	.	.	2	.	.	.
S. plumulosum	1	2	2	.	.	1	.	.	.
S. recurvum	.	.	.	.	1	.	.	.	.
S. russowii	.	3	.	.	.	.	.	.	.
S. strictum	.	.	.	.	.	.	2	.	.
S. teres	.	.	.	.	.	.	.	.	3
S. warnstorfianum	.	.	.	.	.	.	.	.	8
Thuidium tamariscinum	1	2	.	.	.	.	2	.	.
Aneura pinguis	.	.	.	.	2	.	.	.	1
Calypogeia trichomanis	.	.	.	.	.	2	1	.	.
Lophocolea bidentata	.	1	.	.	.	.	.	1	.
Cladonia impexa	.	.	.	.	1	.	.	.	.
Number of species (65)	18	17	12	13	27	18	27	10	24

(Average 18)

Constancy class V 3
     ,,   ,, IV 5

LOCALITIES

1. Beinn Eighe, Ross-shire; 2. Glen Lyon, Perthshire; 3. Glen Finnan, Inverness-shire; 4. Dalwhinnie, Inverness-shire; 5,7. Resipol, Sunart, Argyll: 6. Glen Cannich, Inverness-shire; 8. Glen Markie, Monadhliath, Inverness-shire; 9. Glen Banchor, Newtonmore, Inverness-shire.

Table 54: Sphagneto-Jun100etum effusi (1–9); Related Juncus acutiflorus community (10); Related Carex rostrata community (11); Sphagnum recurvum spring community (12)

	1	2	3	4	5	6	7	8	9	10	11	12
Reference number	R57 038	R57 204	R57 145	M57 001	M58 002	M58 043	R59 001	R59 030	R59 040	R58 131	R57 302	R57 175
Map reference	9358 2380	7745 3326	7952 2579	7396 2644	9347 2876	8261 2193	8679 2430	8203 3092	8466 3142	7278 2255	7628 2941	7987 2610
Altitude (feet)	950	1700	1000	1900	500	1500	1000	1500	900	1150	1600	2500
Aspect (degrees)	–	180	270	270	180	180	360	180	–	180	–	90
Slope (degrees)	0	20	5	3	4	3	15	5	2	3	3	25
Cover (per cent)	100	100	100	100	100	100	100	100	100	100	100	100
Height (centimetres)	60	–	70	35	–	–	–	–	–	–	–	–
Plot area (square metres)	4	4	4	4	4	4	4	4	4	4	4	4
Calluna vulgaris								2		1		
Erica tetralix								2				
Agrostis canina	4			1			3	3	3	3		
A. stolonifera			4		4	3		4	4		2	
A. tenuis	3											4
Anthoxanthum odoratum	2	2		2		1				2		
Deschampsia flexuosa				2								
Festuca ovina agg.		3			2					3	2	
F. rubra		2										
Holcus lanatus		5	2		1							
H. mollis						3	4	3	3			
Molinia caerulea	2									4		
Nardus stricta	2	3	3									
Carex echinata		3	3				2	3	3	3		4
C. nigra		3	4	3	3	2	3	3		1	3	
C. rostrata	3								5		5	
Eriophorum angustifolium	3	3	3	3		2	4	3				1
E. vaginatum	3			2								
Juncus acutiflorus										9		
J. kochii	3											
J. effusus	6	9	8	5	7	8	6	7	8			
J. squarrosus	3		2	3								
Luzula multiflora		2	2		1					2		
L. sylvatica	2				2							
Cardamine pratensis		1						1				
Cirsium palustre						1						
Digitalis purpurea						1						
Epilobium anagallidifolium												1
E. palustre		3	3			3		3		1	1	
Galium hercynicum		2	2	1	3	2	4	3	4	2	2	
G. palustre			2									
Leontodon autumnalis										1		
Potentilla erecta	2	2	3		1	2	2	3	2	4		
Ranunculus acris						3						
Rumex acetosa		3			1	3	3		2			
Saxifraga stellaris						1						
Stellaria alsine						1						
Succisa pratensis										+		
Taraxacum officinalis agg.						1						
Viola palustris		3	3		2	2				2	1	3
V. riviniana						1			+			
Acrocladium stramineum	3		1		1						2	
Atrichum undulatum						1						
Aulacomnium palustre	3		3		+			3		2	7	
Dicranum scoparium					+							
Eurhynchium praelongum					3	1						
Hylocomium splendens	3	1	2		4			2		1		
Hypnum cupressiforme					2							
Mnium hornum	2				+							
M. pseudopunctatum											2	
M. punctatum	1											
M. undulatum						1						
Philonotis fontana						1						
Plagiothecium undulatum				1	2							
Pleurozium schreberi	3											
Polytrichum commune	8	4	5	4	3	3	5	3	6	3	2	3
Pseudoscleropodium purum	1				1				1			
Rhytidiadelphus loreus										2		
R. squarrosus	3		3		3	1	2		1	2		
Sphagnum girgensohnii					4			2				
S. inundatum	2		2									
S. palustre	5	7	2	+	4	6	2	5		8	3	
S. recurvum	4	3	8	9	6	5	8	7	7		7	10
S. russowii										6		
S. squarrosum		3			1	3		1				
S. teres		7							3			
Thuidium tamariscinum								1				

Table 54 (*continued*)

	1	2	3	4	5	6	7	8	9	10	11	12
Alicularia scalaris	.	.	.	.	.	1	.	.	.	.	.	.
Calypogeia trichomanis	.	.	.	.	.	.	.	2	.	.	.	.
Cephalozia sp.	2	.	.	.	.	.	.	.	.	.	.	.
Lophocolea bidentata	.	.	.	.	3	1	.	.	1	.	2	.
Pellia epiphylla	.	.	.	.	.	2	.	.	.	.	.	.
Scapania irrigua	.	.	.	.	.	1	.	.	.	.	.	.
S. nemorosa	.	.	.	.	1	.	.	.	.	.	.	.
S. undulata	2	.	.	.	.	.	.	.	.	.	.	.
Peltigera canina	.	.	.	.	1	.	.	.	.	.	.	.
Number of species	29	22	22	13	29	31	13	23	15	23	13	7

(Average 22)

Constancy class V 7
   ,,   ,, IV 2

LOCALITIES

1. Allt Beithe, Reay Forest, Sutherland; 2. Loch Brandy, Clova, Angus; 3. Glen Markie, Monadhliath, Inverness-shire; 4. Ben Lawers, Perthshire; 5. Kinbrace, Sutherland; 6. Glen Affric, Inverness-shire; 7. Ben Wyvis, Ross-shire; 8. Sgor Gaoithe, Grantown-on-Spey, Moray-shire; 9. Souldow, nr. Dallas, Morayshire; 10. Ben Lui, Argyll; 11. Ben Vrackie, Perthshire; 12. Glen Banchor, Monadhliath, Inverness-shire.

Table 55: Sphagneto-Caricetum sub-alpinum (1–9); Sphagneto-

	1	2	3	4	5	6	7	8	9	10	11	12	13	14
Reference number	R57 245	R57 144	R57 174	R58 095	R58 122	R58 050	R58 078	R58 092	R58 006	M58 044	R57 182	R58 115	R57 269	R57 226
Map reference	7798 3291	7947 2578	7975 2603	7496 2654	7384 2518	8816 2221	8325 2163	8185 2964	9486 2548	8272 2173	7918 2490	7444 2647	7766 3173	7772 3230
Altitude (feet)	2150	1000	2400	1750	2000	1750	2400	730	300	2600	2750	3100	3150	2650
Aspect (degrees)	–	–	90	–	180	–	90	–	–	–	–	360	–	45
Slope (degrees)	2–3	0	10	3	12	0	20	0	0	0	5	15	5	10
Cover (per cent)	100	100	100	100	100	100	100	100	100	100	100	100	100	100
Height (centimetres)	–	–	–	–	–	–	–	–	–	–	–	–	–	–
Plot area (square metres)	4	4	4	4	4	4	4	4	4	4	4	4	4	4
Betula pubescens								1	3					
Empetrum hermaphroditum			2											
E. nigrum														
Erica tetralix							5							
Salix herbacea												2		
S. lapponum x atrocinerea										+				
Vaccinium myrtillus													2	1
V. vitis-idaea														
Equisetum arvense														
Selaginella selaginoides										+		2		
Agrostis canina			3	3					3	1	4		3	3
A. stolonifera		5						3				4		
A. tenuis					2		2		3	2				
Anthoxanthum odoratum				3	3	3	3		3	1	1			
Deschampsia alpina														
D. caespitosa														
D. flexuosa	3								2					
Festuca ovina agg.			4	3	2		2	3		1		4	2	
F. rubra								3				3		
Holcus lanatus									2					
Molinia caerulea		4	2				2		5					
Nardus stricta		2			3	4	3	1	2	3	3	+	2	2
Carex aquatilis														
C. bigelowii												4		1
C. curta	+						3			2	+		4	2
C. demissa		2												
C. dioica				2										
C. echinata	5	6	5	5	8	5	6	4		3	5	2	6	6
C. lachenalii														
C. nigra	5	6	+	7	3	5	5	8	3	8		2		
C. panicea		2		3		2	2		4					
C. rariflora														
C. rostrata	+		4				3							
C. saxatilis												3		
Eriophorum angustifolium	2	5	3		3	3	3	3	5	2	3	5	4	3
E. vaginatum	4		5									4		4
Juncus articulatus		2												
J. kochii		3	+				3	2					2	2
J. squarrosus	1	2		3	3	3		2						1
Luzula multiflora	+			1	2									2
Narthecium ossifragum			3		2		2	3	+					
Orchis ericetorum									+					
Trichophorum caespitosum					1									
Angelica sylvestris							1							
Epilobium anagallidifolium														
E. palustre														
Galium hercynicum				2	3									
Leontodon autumnalis							1							
Parnassia palustris							1							
Pinguicula vulgaris				2										1
Polygala serpyllifolia					1			3						
Polygonum viviparum							2			2		3		
Potentilla erecta		2	3	3	4	2	2	3	3					
P. palustris											3			
Ranunculus acris							3				1			
R. flammula			3											
Rubus chamaemorus														
Rumex acetosa														
Saxifraga stellaris										1	2		2	
Succisa pratensis								3						
Thalictrum alpinum												3		
Trientalis europaea	+													
Viola palustris	3	3	3			5	3			3	3	3	3	3
Acrocladium cuspidatum	1													
A. sarmentosum			2									3	1	2
A. stramineum	2			1		3				2		1		1
Aulacomnium palustre	1			3	1			5	+	2				
Dicranum scoparium												3		
Drepanocladus exannulatus		3						1		1	3			
D. revolvens														

Caricetum alpinum (10–20); Carex aquatilis-rariflora nodum (21–29)

15	16	17	18	19	20	21	22	23	24	25	26	27	28	29	
R57	R57	R57	RX8	R57	R58	M56	R57	R57	M57	M57	M57	R57	R57	M56	Reference number
211	067	279		195	120	132	231	194	065	069	068	271	272	134	
7762	8873	7768	8275	7789	7376	7849	7853	7789	7777	7795	7795	7778	7779	7773	Map reference
3340	2294	3340	2182	2659	2573	3220	3240	2659	3176	3183	3183	3231	3230	3171	
2550	2650	2450	3000	2700	2400	3250	3450	2700	3000	3200	3200	2400	2400	3200	Altitude (feet)
360	—	—	—	—	—	—	—	—	—	—	—	45	—	—	Aspect (degrees)
10	3	3	0	5	0	0	5	0	0	2	0	10	5	0	Slope (degrees)
100	75	100	100	100	100	100	100	100	100	100	100	100	100	100	Cover (per cent)
—	—	—	—	—	—	—	—	—	—	—	—	—	—	—	Height (centimetres)
4	9	4	4	4	4	4	4	4	4	4	4	4	4	4	Plot area (square metres)
·	·	·	·	·	·	·	·	·	·	·	·	·	·	·	Betula pubescens
·	·	·	·	·	·	·	·	·	·	·	·	·	·	·	Empetrum hermaphroditum
I	·	·	·	·	·	·	·	·	·	·	·	·	·	·	E. nigrum
·	·	·	·	·	·	·	·	·	·	·	·	·	·	·	Erica tetralix
·	·	·	·	·	·	·	3	·	·	·	·	·	·	·	Salix herbacea
·	·	·	·	·	·	·	·	·	·	·	·	·	·	·	S. lapponum x atrocinerea
·	·	·	·	·	·	·	3	·	·	·	·	·	·	·	Vaccinium myrtillus
I	·	·	·	·	·	·	·	·	·	·	·	·	·	·	V. vitis-idaea
·	·	·	·	·	·	·	·	·	+	·	·	·	·	·	Equisetum arvense
·	·	·	·	·	·	·	·	·	·	·	·	·	·	·	Selaginella selaginoides
·	·	·	2	·	3	·	·	·	·	·	·	5	3	·	Agrostis canina
·	·	3	·	·	·	·	·	·	·	·	·	·	4	·	A. stolonifera
·	·	·	·	·	·	·	·	·	2	·	·	·	·	·	A. tenuis
·	·	·	·	·	·	·	·	·	·	·	·	·	3	·	Anthoxanthum odoratum
·	3	·	·	·	·	·	·	·	·	·	·	·	·	4	Deschampsia alpina
·	·	·	·	+	·	·	·	·	·	·	·	·	·	·	D. caespitosa
·	·	2	·	·	·	·	·	·	·	·	·	·	·	·	D. flexuosa
·	2	1	·	·	3	·	2	2	·	·	·	·	·	2	Festuca ovina agg.
·	·	·	·	·	·	·	·	·	·	·	·	·	·	·	F. rubra
·	·	·	·	·	·	·	·	·	·	·	·	·	·	·	Holcus lanatus
·	·	·	·	·	·	·	·	·	·	·	·	·	·	·	Molinia caerulea
·	3	1	4	·	4	·	2	·	·	·	·	·	·	·	**Nardus stricta**
·	·	·	·	·	·	·	·	6	7	·	7	7	7	I	Carex aquatilis
·	3	·	3	3	·	+	6	·	+	3	2	·	·	3	C. bigelowii
·	·	5	1	4	·	7	·	6	7	2	·	·	·	5	C. curta
·	·	·	·	·	·	·	·	·	·	·	·	·	·	·	C. demissa
·	·	·	·	·	·	·	·	·	·	·	·	·	·	·	C. dioica
7	5	6	2	7	·	·	·	3	·	·	·	5	·	·	**C. echinata**
·	·	·	·	·	·	·	4	·	·	·	·	·	·	·	C. lachenalii
2	·	5	·	·	·	·	·	·	I	·	3	·	7	·	**C. nigra**
·	·	·	·	·	·	·	·	·	·	·	·	·	·	·	C. panicea
·	·	·	·	·	·	3	2	3	3	8	4	·	·	·	C. rariflora
·	·	·	·	·	5	·	·	·	·	·	·	·	·	·	C. rostrata
·	·	·	·	·	·	·	·	·	·	·	·	·	·	·	C. saxatilis
4	4	4	2	3	3	2	·	2	·	I	I	3	3	3	**Eriophorum angustifolium**
·	3	3	3	·	3	I	·	·	2	·	+	·	·	·	E. vaginatum
·	·	·	·	·	·	·	·	·	·	·	·	·	·	·	Juncus articulatus
3	·	·	3	·	·	·	·	·	·	·	·	·	·	·	J. kochii
·	·	·	·	·	·	·	·	·	·	·	·	·	·	·	J. squarrosus
·	·	I	·	·	·	·	·	I	·	·	·	2	·	I	Luzula multiflora
3	·	·	·	·	·	·	·	·	·	·	·	·	·	·	Narthecium ossifragum
·	·	·	·	·	·	·	·	·	·	·	·	·	·	·	Orchis ericetorum
3	·	I	·	·	·	·	·	·	·	·	·	2	·	·	Trichophorum caespitosum
·	·	·	·	·	·	·	·	3	·	·	·	·	+	3	Angelica sylvestris
·	·	·	I	·	·	2	·	·	·	·	·	·	·	·	Epilobium anagallidifolium
·	·	2	·	·	·	·	·	·	·	·	·	·	·	·	E. palustre
·	I	I	·	·	2	·	·	·	·	·	·	5	2	·	Galium hercynicum
·	·	·	·	·	·	·	·	·	·	·	·	·	I	·	Leontodon autumnalis
·	·	·	·	·	·	·	·	·	·	·	·	·	·	·	Parnassia palustris
I	·	·	·	·	·	·	·	·	·	·	·	·	·	·	Pinguicula vulgaris
·	·	·	·	·	·	·	·	·	·	·	·	·	·	·	Polygala serpyllifolia
·	·	·	·	·	·	·	·	·	·	·	·	·	4	·	Polygonum viviparum
·	·	·	·	·	·	·	·	·	·	·	·	·	2	·	**Potentilla erecta**
·	·	·	·	·	·	·	·	·	·	·	·	·	·	·	P. palustris
·	·	·	·	·	·	·	·	·	·	·	·	·	·	·	Ranunculus acris
·	·	·	·	·	·	·	·	·	·	·	·	·	·	·	R. flammula
·	·	·	·	·	·	2	·	2	·	·	·	·	·	·	Rubus chamaemorus
·	·	·	·	·	·	·	·	·	·	·	·	2	3	·	Rumex acetosa
·	+	·	·	2	·	I	·	·	·	·	·	·	·	·	Saxifraga stellaris
·	·	·	·	·	·	·	·	·	·	·	·	·	·	·	Succisa pratensis
·	·	·	·	·	·	·	·	·	·	·	·	·	·	·	Thalictrum alpinum
·	·	·	·	·	·	·	·	·	·	·	·	3	·	·	Trientalis europaea
2	·	2	3	·	4	3	·	3	·	·	·	·	3	2	**Viola palustris**
·	·	·	·	·	·	·	·	·	·	·	·	·	·	·	Acrocladium cuspidatum
·	2	·	·	·	·	2	·	·	·	2	·	·	·	·	A. sarmentosum
·	·	+	I	·	·	2	·	·	·	·	·	2	·	I	A. stramineum
·	·	·	3	I	·	·	·	·	·	·	·	·	·	·	Aulacomnium palustre
·	·	·	I	·	2	·	·	·	·	·	·	·	·	·	Dicranum scoparium
·	2	·	I	·	·	2	·	·	·	·	·	·	·	·	Drepanocladus exannulatus
·	·	·	·	·	·	·	·	·	·	5	5	·	·	·	D. revolvens

Table 55

	1	2	3	4	5	6	7	8	9	10	11	12	13	14
Hylocomium splendens								3	3			3		
Hypnum cupressiforme									+					
Mnium punctatum														
Philonotis fontana										1			1	2
Plagiothecium undulatum														
Pohlia nutans														
Polytrichum alpestre												2		2
P. commune	4				3	5	4	2		1	2	3	4	2
Pseudoscleropodium purum								1						
Rhacomitrium lanuginosum												1		
Rhytidiadelphus loreus									2			2		
R. squarrosus					2				2					
Sphagnum compactum														
S. cuspidatum														
S. girgensohnii							4		2	3	3	5	3	
S. lindbergii										2	3		9	6
S. magellanicum														
S. nemoreum			4											
S. palustre						8	2		8	5				
S. papillosum	5	2	8	6	3						4	3	3	6
S. plumulosum		3	3	4				5	+		4	3		3
S. recurvum	9	4	6	6	9	4	4		2	6	3	3	2	3
S. riparium														
S. russowii	3			4		4			3	1	3	2	3	3
S. squarrosum														
S. subsecundum*		9	2		1		8	5	4	2	8		4	5
S. tenellum														
S. teres											2		5	
S. warnstorfianum													3	
Thuidium tamariscinum								2	3					
Calypogeia trichomanis					1			1						
Diplophyllum albicans											3			
Lophozia ventricosa						2					2			
Pellia epiphylla										1	1		2	
Ptilidium ciliare												2		2
Scapania dentata													2	
S. irrigua														
S. uliginosa											3			
S. undulata	1													
Cladonia sylvatica												2		
C. uncialis														
	19	19	20	20	18	16	26	24	26	29	22	31	21	24

(Average 21)

Number of species (63)	Number of species (73)
Constancy class V 5	Constancy class V 7
" " IV 3	" " IV 7

* Var. auriculatum in 2, 3, 5, 9, 13, 14, 15, 16, 19, 22, 25. Var. inundatum in 2, 8, 9, 10, 11, 29.

LOCALITIES

1. Moulzie Burn, Clova, Angus; 2. Glen Markie, Monadhliath, Inverness-shire; 3. Glen Banchor, Monadhliath, Inverness-shire; 4. Carn Gorm, Glen Lyon, Perthshire; 5. Meall Ghaordie, Breadalbane, Perthshire; 6. Beinn Enaiglair, Inverlael, Ross-shire; 7. Sgurr na Lapaich, Glen Cannich, Inverness-shire; 8. Abernethy Forest, Inverness-shire; 9. Loch an Dithreibh, Ben Loyal, Sutherland; 10, 18. Tom a' Choinnich, Glen Affric, Inverness-shire; 11. A' Bhuidheanach, Laggan, Inverness-shire; 12. Ben Lawers, Perthshire; 13. Caenlochan Glen,

(continued)

335

15	16	17	18	19	20	21	22	23	24	25	26	27	28	29	
·	1	·	2	·	2	·	·	·	·	·	·	·	·	·	Hylocomium **splendens**
·	·	·	·	·	·	·	·	·	·	·	·	·	·	·	Hypnum cupressiforme
·	·	·	·	·	·	·	·	·	·	·	1	·	·	·	Mnium punctatum
·	2	·	·	·	·	·	·	·	·	·	·	·	·	·	Philonotis fontana
·	·	·	·	·	·	·	·	·	·	·	·	3	·	·	Plagiothecium undulatum
·	·	·	1	·	·	·	·	·	·	·	·	·	·	·	Pohlia nutans
·	·	2	·	·	3	·	·	·	4	4	·	·	·	3	Polytrichum alpestre
3	2	4	3	·	2	3	2	4	4	·	·	2	2	1	**P. commune**
·	·	·	·	·	·	·	·	·	·	·	·	·	·	·	Pseudoscleropodium purum
·	1	·	2	·	·	·	·	·	·	·	·	·	·	·	Rhacomitrium lanuginosum
·	1	·	2	·	·	·	·	·	·	·	·	·	·	·	Rhytidiadelphus loreus
·	·	·	·	·	·	·	·	·	·	·	·	3	·	·	R. squarrosus
·	·	·	·	·	·	·	4	·	9	4	·	·	·	9	Sphagnum compactum
·	·	·	·	3	·	·	·	·	·	·	·	·	·	·	S. cuspidatum
·	·	·	·	·	·	·	·	5	·	·	·	3	7	9	S. girgensohnii
5	7	·	2	·	·	·	3	·	9	·	·	·	·	·	S. lindbergii
2	·	·	·	·	·	·	·	·	9	·	·	·	·	·	S. magellanicum
·	2	·	5	·	·	·	·	·	9	·	·	·	·	9	S. nemoreum
·	·	·	·	·	·	·	·	·	·	·	+	·	·	·	S. palustre
5	4	3	8	3	10	·	8	·	9	·	5	·	+	9	**S. papillosum**
5	·	·	2	·	·	·	4	·	9	2	·	·	+	·	S. plumulosum
·	·	7	·	4	·	9	·	6	·	·	4	·	4	9	**S. recurvum**
·	·	·	6	·	·	·	·	·	·	·	·	·	·	·	S. riparium
3	·	1	·	3	3	·	3	·	·	·	·	·	+	·	**S. russowii**
·	·	·	·	·	·	·	·	7	·	·	·	·	·	·	S. squarrosum
5	5	·	·	7	·	·	3	·	·	7	·	·	4	·	S. subsecundum*
·	2	·	·	·	·	3	·	·	·	·	·	·	·	·	S. tenellum
·	·	·	·	·	·	·	·	3	·	·	·	·	7	·	S. teres
·	·	·	·	·	·	·	·	·	·	·	·	·	·	·	S. warnstorfianum
·	·	·	·	·	·	·	·	·	·	·	·	·	·	·	Thuidium tamariscinum
·	·	·	·	·	·	·	·	·	·	·	·	·	·	·	Calypogeia trichomanis
·	·	·	·	·	·	·	·	·	·	·	·	·	·	·	Diplophyllum albicans
·	·	·	·	·	·	·	·	·	3	·	·	·	·	1	Lophozia ventricosa
·	·	·	1	·	·	·	·	·	·	·	·	·	·	·	Pellia epiphylla
·	·	·	·	·	·	·	·	·	1	·	·	·	·	·	Ptilidium ciliare
·	2	·	·	·	·	·	·	·	·	·	·	·	·	·	Scapania dentata
·	·	·	·	·	·	·	·	·	2	·	·	·	·	·	S. irrigua
·	·	·	5	·	·	·	·	·	·	·	·	·	·	·	S. uliginosa
·	·	·	·	·	·	·	·	·	·	·	·	·	·	·	S. undulata
·	·	·	·	·	·	·	·	·	·	·	·	·	·	+	Cladonia sylvatica
·	+	·	·	·	·	·	·	·	·	·	·	·	·	·	C. uncialis
17	23	20	21	15	14	12	18	14	18	13	10	12	23	19	

(Average 21.5)   (Average 15.5)

Number of species (61)

Constancy class V   o
          ,,   ,,   IV   5

Angus; 14. Meikle Kilrannoch, Clova, Angus; 15. Green Hill, Clova, Angus; 16. Seana Bhraigh, Strath Mulzie, Ross-shire; 17. Burn of Longshank, Glen Esk, Angus; 19, 20. Coire Chuirn, Drumochter, Inverness-shire; 20. Beinn nan Eachan, Killin, Perthshire; 21, 22. Lochnagar, Aberdeenshire; 24–26. Cairn of Claise, Caenlochan, Angus; 27, 28. Glen Doll, Clova, Angus; 29. Glas Maol, Caenlochan, Angus.

Table 56: Juncus acutiflorus-Acrocladium cuspidatum nodum

	1	2	3	4	5	6
Reference number	M58 015	R57 282	R58 096	R58 112	R58 139	R58 126
Map reference	7475 2707	7734 3335	7483 2657	7476 2656	7875 2652	7275 2255
Altitude (feet)	900	1200	900	750	1150	1200
Aspect (degrees)	–	180	180	–	–	315
Slope (degrees)	0	25	15	3	0	5
Cover (per cent)	100	100	100	100	100	100
Height (centimetres)	60	–	60	–	–	–
Plot area (square metres)	4	4	4	4	4	4
Betula sp.				1		
Erica tetralix				2		
Salix aurita				1		
Thelypteris oreopteris		2				
Agrostis stolonifera					5	
A. tenuis	3			2	2	
Anthoxanthum odoratum				3		2
Briza media			2	3		
Festuca ovina agg.				2		
F. rubra		3	2	3		3
Holcus lanatus		3	4	3	3	3
Molinia caerulea	2		4	4	4	2
Nardus stricta		3	1	3		2
Poa pratensis	2					
Carex echinata		5		2		3
C. nigra			3	2		+
C. pallescens			1			
C. panicea		4	4	4	2	3
C. pulicaris				2		2
Eriophorum angustifolium				2		
Juncus acutiflorus	9	9	9	6	8	9
J. kochii				3		
J. effusus	2					
J. squarrosus		1		2		
Luzula multiflora				1		
Narthecium ossifragum				3		
Achillea ptarmica		3		3	+	
Ajuga reptans	3					
Caltha palustris					+	3
Cardamine hirsuta	1					
C. pratensis						+
Centaurea nigra			1			
Cirsium palustre	1	3		2		
Crepis paludosa	2			4		3
Drosera rotundifolia				1		
Epilobium palustre	3	+	3	2	2	1
Euphrasia officinalis agg.				2		3
Filipendula ulmaria			3			+
Galium hercynicum	3				3	
Leontodon autumnalis				2		3
Linum catharticum				1		
Lysimachia nemorum						3
Parnassia palustris						3
Pedicularis palustris				2	2	1
Plantago lanceolata						2
Potentilla erecta	3	3	3	4	2	3
P. palustris					+	
Prunella vulgaris		2	3	1		4
Ranunculus acris		2	3	1	1	4
R. flammula		2	2	2	2	2
Rhinanthus minor agg.					2	
Rumex acetosa	3					2
Succisa pratensis			2	4	3	3
Taraxacum officinalis agg.		1	2			3
Trifolium repens			1	2		1
Trollius europaeus			2			
Viola palustris	3	3			3	
Acrocladium cuspidatum	4	3	3	2	1	3
A. sarmentosum				2		
Atrichum undulatum		+	2			
Brachythecium rutabulum		2				
Breutelia chrysocoma				3		
Bryum pseudotriquetrum				2	1	2
Campylium stellatum				2		
Climacium dendroides						+
Drepanocladus fluitans					2	
D. revolvens				1		
Hylocomium splendens	+	2	1	2		4
Mnium pseudopunctatum						2
M. seligeri						2
M. undulatum	2		2			2
Philonotis fontana						2
Polytrichum commune				2		
Pseudoscleropodium purum		1			1	
Rhytidiadelphus squarrosus	5	3	2	1	2	3
Sphagnum contortum				7		
S. palustre	1				1	
S. recurvum					2	
S. squarrosum		3				+
S. warnstorfianum					7	
Thuidium tamariscinum		1		1		
Aneura multifida				1		
A. pinguis				2		
Calypogeia trichomanis			2			
Chiloscyphus polyanthus				1		2
Lophocolea bidentata	3	1	3	+		2
Pellia sp.		2	3	1	2	1
Number of species (87)	20	27	28	52	27	42

(Average 33)

LOCALITIES

1. Woodend, Glen Lyon, Perthshire; 2. Milton of Clova, Angus; 3,4. Invervar, Glen Lyon, Perthshire; 5. Dalwhinnie, Inverness-shire; 6. Ben Lui, Dalmally, Argyll.

Table 57: Carex rostrata-Sphagnum warnstorfianum nodum

	1	2	3	4	5	6	7	8	9	10
Reference number	R57 159	R57 294	R57 307	R57 301	R57 300	R57 275	R58 120	R59 007	R59 027	R59 029
Map reference	7972 2607	7627 2934	7639 2963	7628 2942	7628 2943	7779 3227	7379 2572	7355 2386	7783 3128	8200 3086
Altitude (feet)	2400	1400	2100	1600	1600	2700	2600	2750	2500	1500
Aspect (degrees)	360	–	–	–	–	45	–	45	270	–
Slope (degrees)	10	0	0	2	2	20	0	25	5	3
Cover (per cent)	100	100	100	100	100	100	100	100	100	100
Height (centimetres)	–	–	30	–	–	–	–	–	–	–
Plot area (square metres)	4	4	4	4	4	4	4	4	4	4
Betula sp.	.	.	+	.	.	.	.	.	.	.
Calluna vulgaris	.	.	1	.	.	.	.	.	.	.
Empetrum hermaphroditum	2	.	.	.	.	.	1	.	.	.
E. nigrum	.	.	3	.	.	.	.	.	.	.
Erica tetralix	.	4	3	2	2	.	.	.	.	.
Salix aurita	.	.	1	.	.	.	.	.	+	.
Equisetum palustre	.	.	.	.	.	.	.	.	3	.
Selaginella selaginoides	3	+	2	1	+	+	2	3	3	.
Agrostis canina	2	.	.	.	.	.	4	.	2	.
A. stolonifera	.	.	.	1	+	2	4	.	2	.
A. tenuis	.	.	.	.	.	.	.	4	.	.
Anthoxanthum odoratum	3	.	2	.	.	.	.	.	.	2
Deschampsia caespitosa	.	.	.	.	.	.	.	3	.	.
Festuca ovina agg.	3	3	3	2	3	.	4	5	3	.
F. rubra	.	.	.	.	.	.	.	3	.	.
Nardus stricta	3	.	2	3	.	.	3	4	4	4
Carex aquatilis	.	.	.	.	.	+	.	.	.	.
C. bigelowii	.	.	.	.	.	.	.	4	.	.
C. curta	.	.	.	.	.	3	.	.	2	.
C. demissa	.	2	8	.	2	.	.	.	2	.
C. echinata	5	.	8	.	.	4	4	3	4	4
C. nigra	4	.	8	+	4	.	.	2	4	.
C. panicea	2	4	8	.	.	2	2	3	.	4
C. pulicaris	2	.	3	.	.	.	.	.	3	.
C. rostrata	7	7	8	8	6	9	6	6	7	8
C. saxatilis	.	.	.	.	.	.	.	1	.	.
Eriophorum angustifolium	.	.	+	2	2	4	3	.	2	3
Juncus acutiflorus	.	.	.	.	2	.	.	.	.	.
J. articulatus	+	.	2	.	.	.	.	.	2	2
J. effusus	.	.	.	.	.	.	.	.	.	2
J. kochii	3	3	2	.	2	.	.	.	.	4
Luzula multiflora	.	.	1	.	.	.	.	1	2	.
L. sylvatica	.	.	.	.	1	.	.	.	.	.
Potamogeton polygonifolius	.	.	.	.	1	.	.	.	.	.
Alchemilla vulgaris agg.	.	.	+	.	.	.	.	2	.	2
Caltha palustris	.	.	.	.	.	.	.	2	3	.
Cardamine pratensis	2	.	.	.	.	.	.	.	1	.
Cerastium vulgatum	1	.	.	.	.	.	.	1	.	.
Cirsium palustre	.	.	.	.	.	.	.	.	.	2
Crepis paludosa	.	.	.	.	.	.	.	.	.	2
Drosera rotundifolia	.	1	.	.	.	.	.	.	.	.
Epilobium anagallidifolium	1	.	.	.	.	.	.	.	.	.
E. palustre	.	+	.	2	2	+	.	.	+	2
Euphrasia officinalis agg.	.	.	3	.	.	.	.	3	.	.
Galium hercynicum	.	2	.	1	+	.	1	3	.	3
Leontodon autumnalis	.	.	.	.	.	+	.	2	3	.
Linum catharticum	.	.	1	.	.	.	.	.	.	.
Parnassia palustris	.	.	.	.	.	.	.	3	.	.
Pedicularis palustris	.	.	.	+	1	.	.	.	.	.
Pinguicula vulgaris	.	1	.	.	.	.	.	.	2	.
Polygonum viviparum	.	.	3	.	.	2	.	3	3	.
Potentilla erecta	.	2	3	2	1	.	.	2	.	3
P. palustris	.	.	.	4	2	3	.	.	3	.
Ranunculus acris	.	.	.	.	.	.	.	4	.	.
Succisa pratensis	.	2	.	.	.	.	.	.	.	.
Thalictrum alpinum	2	.	3	.	.	.	.	3	2	.
Trientalis europaea	.	.	.	.	.	.	.	.	.	3
Viola palustris	3	.	3	2	3	4	4	3	3	4
Acrocladium cuspidatum	.	2	+	3	+	.	.	.	1	3
A. giganteum	.	.	.	.	+	.	.	.	.	.
A. sarmentosum	.	.	.	2	2	.	.	.	.	.
A. stramineum	.	1	.	2	2	.	1	.	3	1
Aulacomnium palustre	4	2	4	4	3	.	3	4	4	3
Brachythecium rutabulum	.	.	.	2	3	.	.	.	.	.
Bryum pseudotriquetrum	.	2	.	2	1	.	.	.	.	.
Camptothecium nitens	6	3	4	.	.	.	.	.	.	.
Campylium stellatum	.	3	3	.	.	.	.	.	.	3
Climacium dendroides	.	.	1	.	.	.	.	.	.	2
Ctenidium molluscum	.	2	.	.	.	.	.	.	.	.
Dicranella squarrosa	.	.	.	3	1	.	.	.	.	.

Table 57 (*continued*)

	1	2	3	4	5	6	7	8	9	10
Dicranum bonjeani	·	2	2	·	·	·	·	·	·	·
Drepanocladus fluitans	·	·	·	2	3	1	·	·	1	·
D. revolvens	·	2	2	4	2	·	·	·	·	·
Fissidens adianthoides	·	2	2	·	·	·	·	·	·	·
Hylocomium splendens	·	3	3	3	1	·	1	4	3	3
Hypnum cupressiforme	·	3	·	·	·	·	·	·	·	·
Mnium pseudopunctatum	3	2	+	3	3	·	·	2	3	3
Philonotis fontana	·	·	1	2	4	·	·	·	·	·
Pleurozium schreberi	·	2	·	·	·	·	·	·	1	·
Polytrichum commune	·	·	·	+	2	2	2	2	2	·
Pseudoscleropodium purum	·	+	·	·	·	·	·	·	·	1
Ptilium crista-castrensis	·	·	·	·	·	·	·	2	·	·
Rhytidiadelphus loreus	·	1	·	·	·	·	·	2	·	·
R. squarrosus	3	+	1	·	1	·	1	3	·	2
Sphagnum contortum	·	3	·	·	·	·	·	·	·	2
S. girgensohnii	·	+	·	+	3	·	·	·	·	+
S. nemoreum	4	·	·	·	·	·	3	2	·	·
S. palustre	·	4	·	+	3	·	·	·	·	+
S. papillosum	·	3	·	·	·	·	7	1	·	·
S. plumulosum	·	4	·	·	·	+	1	·	·	·
S. recurvum	·	2	·	4	4	4	·	·	6	·
S. russowii	·	1	·	·	2	·	·	·	·	·
S. squarrosum	·	·	·	3	1	9	1	·	·	·
S. subsecundum	·	·	·	3	8	5	3	·	·	·
S. teres	3	2	+	4	3	6	·	+	6	3
S. warnstorfianum	6	8	6	4	5	·	+	7	5	6
Thuidium tamariscinum	·	3	2	·	·	·	·	1	·	2
Aneura multifida	·	2	·	·	·	·	·	·	·	·
A. pinguis	·	2	·	·	2	·	·	·	3	2
Calypogeia trichomanis	·	2	2	1	·	·	·	·	·	2
Chiloscyphus polyanthus	·	·	·	2	1	·	·	·	·	·
Harpanthus flotowianus	·	·	·	·	·	·	·	·	2	·
Lophocolea bidentata	·	·	·	3	3	·	·	·	·	1
Lophozia bantriensis	·	1	·	·	·	·	·	·	·	·
L. quinquedentata	·	·	·	·	·	·	·	1	3	·
Pellia fabbroniana	·	·	1	3	3	·	·	·	3	3
Ptilidium ciliare	1	·	·	·	·	·	2	1	·	·
Scapania nemorosa	·	1	2	3	2	·	·	·	·	·
S. uliginosa	·	·	·	·	·	1	·	·	·	·
S. undulata	·	·	·	·	·	·	·	·	3	·
Number of species (110)	26	45	44	39	46	22	25	39	41	36

(Average 36)

Constancy class V 9
    ,,   ,,   IV 14

LOCALITIES

1. Glen Banchor, Monadhliath, Inverness-shire; 2–5. Ben Vrackie, Pitlochry, Perthshire; 6. Meikle Kilrannoch, Clova, Angus; 7. Beinn nan Eachan, Killin, Perthshire; 8. Creag Mhor, Forest of Mamlorn, Perthshire; 9. The Cairnwell, Aberdeenshire; 10. Baddoch, nr. Nethybridge, Inverness-shire.

Table 58: Carex panicea-Campylium stellatum nodum (1–18);

	1	2	3	4	5	6	7	8	9	10	11
Reference number	R57 288	R57 285	R57 308	R57 293	R57 341	R57 256	M56 101	R57 169	R57 311	R57 168	R56 056
Map reference	7625 2894	7728 2991	7690 2952	7637 2878	8029 1332	7745 3291	7780 3144	7908 2560	7690 2964	7908 2560	8633 2062
Altitude (feet)	1100	1600	1450	1250	100	1000	2400	1300	2000	1350	300
Aspect (degrees)	45	270	270	90	315	45	270	180	315	180	135
Slope (degrees)	5	15	30	3	35	25	5	25	5	20	5
Cover (per cent)	100	100	100	100	100	100	100	100	100	100	100
Height (centimetres)	–	–	–	–	–	–	13	–	–	–	–
Plot area (square metres)	4	4	4	4	4	4	4	4	4	4	16
Calluna vulgaris	.	.	.	.	.	.	.	.	.	2	.
Empetrum hermaphroditum	.	.	.	.	.	.	2	.	.	.	.
Erica tetralix	3	2	.	3	.	3	.	4	+	3	.
Salix sp.	.	.	.	.	.	.	.	.	.	.	.
Equisetum fluviatile	.	.	.	.	.	.	.	.	.	.	.
E. palustre	.	.	.	.	.	.	.	.	.	.	+
E. sylvaticum	+	.	.	.	.	.	.	.	.	.	.
E. variegatum	.	.	2	.	.	.	.	.	2	.	.
Selaginella selaginoides	1	+	+	2	2	2	2	2	1	2	2
Agrostis canina	.	.	.	.	.	2	.	.	.	2	.
Anthoxanthum odoratum	.	.	2	.	.	.	.	.	.	.	2
Briza media	+	2	.	3	.	.	.	.	+	.	.
Cynosurus cristatus	.	.	.	.	.	.	.	.	.	.	2
Deschampsia caespitosa	.	.	.	.	.	.	.	.	.	.	.
Festuca ovina agg.	.	.	3	.	.	2	.	4	2	2	3
F. rubra	.	.	2	.	4	.	.	.	.	2	5
Holcus lanatus	.	.	.	.	.	1	.	.	.	.	2
Molinia caerulea	3	.	.	3	.	3	.	4	.	3	4
Nardus stricta	.	.	2	.	.	2	.	.	1	2	.
Poa annua	.	.	.	.	.	.	.	.	.	.	.
Sieglingia decumbens	.	.	1	.	.	.	.	.	.	3	1
Carex bigelowii	.	.	.	.	.	.	2	.	.	.	.
C. capillaris	.	.	.	.	.	.	+	.	+	.	.
C. demissa	9	9	5	.	3	.	2	.	5	8	3
C. dioica	.	.	.	.	.	2	4	.	5	.	2
C. echinata	.	.	4	2	4	4	.	8	.	.	6
C. flacca	9	9	.	9	6	.	.	.	.	.	.
C. hostiana	9	9	.	9	.	.	7	.	8	.	3	3
C. lepidocarpa	.	.	.	9	.	.	.	.	.	.	.
C. nigra	.	9	4	.	5	.	.	8	3	.	3
C. panicea	9	9	7	9	6	7	3	8	5	7	4
C. pulicaris	3	9	4	9	3	.	.	3	2	.	3
C. rostrata	.	.	.	.	.	.	.	.	.	.	.
Coeloglossum viride	1	.	.	.	.	.	.	.	.	.	.
Eleocharis pauciflora	2	3	2	.	4	.	4	.	5	3	4
Eriophorum angustifolium	.	.	4	2	.	2	4	3	3	.	2
E. latifolium	3	.	.	4	.	.	.	2	.	.	.
Isolepis setacea	.	.	2	.	.	.	.	.	.	.	1
Juncus acutiflorus	.	.	.	.	.	.	.	.	.	.	.
J. alpinus	.	.	.	3	.	.	2	.	1	.	.
J. articulatus	3	3	3	2	5	.	3	.	3	3	5
J. effusus	.	.	.	.	.	.	2	.	.	.	.
J. kochii	2	3	3	.	.	4	.	3	.	1	3
J. squarrosus	.	.	.	.	.	4	.	.	.	.	.
J. triglumis	.	.	.	.	.	.	.	.	.	.	.
Luzula multiflora	.	.	.	.	.	.	.	.	.	.	.
Narthecium ossifragum	.	.	.	.	.	4	.	2	.	.	.
Orchis fuchsii	.	.	.	.	.	.	.	.	.	.	1
Tofieldia pusilla	3	.	.	2	.	.	3	.	2	.	.
Trichophorum caespitosum	3	.	.	.	.	3	3	.	.	.	.
Triglochin palustre	.	.	.	.	2	.	.	.	.	.	.
Achillea ptarmica	.	.	.	.	.	.	.	.	.	.	1
Alchemilla filicaulis	.	.	.	.	.	.	3	.	.	.	.
A. glabra	.	.	.	.	.	.	+	.	.	.	.
A. vestita	.	.	.	.	.	.	.	.	.	.	.
Angelica sylvestris	.	.	.	.	.	.	.	.	.	.	.
Bellis perennis	.	.	.	.	3	.	.	.	.	.	+
Caltha palustris	.	+	.	.	.	.	.	.	.	.	.
Cardamine pratensis	.	.	.	.	.	.	.	.	.	.	.
Cerastium vulgatum	.	.	.	.	.	.	.	.	.	.	.
Cirsium palustre	.	.	.	.	.	.	.	.	.	.	.
Crepis paludosa	.	.	.	.	.	.	.	.	.	.	.
Drosera rotundifolia	1	.	.	.	.	.	.	.	.	.	3
Epilobium alsinifolium	.	.	.	.	.	.	.	.	.	.	.
E. anagallidifolium	.	.	.	.	.	.	.	.	.	.	.
E. palustre	.	.	.	.	.	.	.	.	.	.	+
Euphrasia officinalis agg.	3	3	3	3	.	3	1	3	2	3	3
Galium hercynicum	.	.	.	.	.	.	.	.	.	.	.
Leontodon autumnalis	+	1	2	.	4	1	.	.	1	1	1
L. hispidus	.	+	.	.	.	.	.	.	.	.	.
Linum catharticum	3	.	3	+	.	.	2	.	.	2	+
Lysimachia nemorum	.	.	.	.	.	.	.	.	.	.	+
Parnassia palustris	.	.	.	.	3	.	.	.	.	.	3
Pedicularis palustris	2	.	2	2	.	.	.	.	.	.	3

Carex rostrata—brown moss nodum (19–22)

12	13	14	15	16	17	18	19	20	21	22	
R57	R57	R57	R57	R57	R57	R57	R57	R57	R57	R58	Reference number
295	150	151	167	242	202	229	152	297	306	119	Map reference
7633	7960	7960	7908	7768	7738	7774	7960	7639	7639	7379	
2940	2598	2598	2560	3288	3325	3184	2598	2861	2963	2572	
1650	2100	2100	1350	1250	1200	2800	2100	1450	2100	2600	Altitude (feet)
180	270	270	180	270	180	180	270	–	–	–	Aspect (degrees)
15	13	15	15	25	7	20	10	0	0	0	Slope (degrees)
100	100	100	95	85	95	100	100	100	100	100	Cover (per cent)
–	–	–	–	–	–	–	–	30	30	–	Height (centimetres)
4	4	4	4	4	4	4	4	4	4	4	Plot area (square metres)
·	·	·	·	·	·	·	·	·	·	·	Calluna vulgaris
·	·	·	·	·	·	·	·	·	·	·	Empetrum hermaphroditum
2	·	·	·	+	1	·	·	·	·	·	Erica tetralix
1	·	·	·	·	·	·	·	·	·	·	Salix sp.
·	·	·	·	·	·	·	·	·	+	·	Equisetum fluviatile
·	·	·	·	2	·	·	·	2	·	1	E. palustre
·	·	·	1	·	·	·	·	·	·	·	E. sylvaticum
·	·	·	·	·	·	·	·	·	·	·	E. variegatum
3	2	2	·	2	·	2	3	·	+	1	**Selaginella selaginoides**
3	2	·	·	·	·	3	·	·	·	·	Agrostis canina
·	·	·	·	·	2	2	·	·	·	·	Anthoxanthum odoratum
2	·	·	·	2	1	·	·	·	·	·	Briza media
·	·	·	·	·	·	·	·	·	·	·	Cynosurus cristatus
·	·	·	·	·	·	3	·	·	·	·	Deschampsia caespitosa
5	3	3	·	·	·	·	3	·	3	·	Festuca ovina agg.
·	1	1	·	·	·	3	·	·	·	·	F. rubra
·	·	·	·	2	1	·	·	·	·	·	Holcus lanatus
·	·	·	·	4	·	·	·	·	·	·	Molinia caerulea
·	·	·	·	4	1	·	·	·	2	2	Nardus stricta
·	·	·	·	·	·	1	·	·	·	·	Poa annua
·	·	·	·	·	·	·	·	·	·	·	Sieglingia decumbens
·	·	·	·	·	·	·	·	·	·	2	Carex bigelowii
·	·	·	·	·	·	·	·	·	·	·	C. capillaris
8	1	3	·	·	4	·	2	·	·	3	C. demissa
8	·	·	·	·	2	·	·	·	·	·	C. dioica
·	·	·	·	4	8	4	·	·	·	5	C. echinata
·	·	·	·	·	·	·	·	·	·	·	C. flacca
·	·	·	5	7	2	·	·	·	·	·	C. hostiana
·	·	·	·	·	·	·	·	5	7	·	C. lepidocarpa
8	9	·	3	·	·	8	·	2	5	2	C. nigra
8	3	3	4	7	4	3	3	5	4	4	**C. panicea**
8	2	2	2	+	·	3	·	·	2	2	C. pulicaris
·	+	·	3	·	·	·	7	5	5	7	**C. rostrata**
·	·	·	·	·	·	·	·	·	·	·	Coeloglossum viride
·	·	9	8	·	5	·	7	3	·	·	Eleocharis pauciflora
1	+	3	3	3	1	·	·	·	2	2	Eriophorum angustifolium
·	·	·	1	·	·	·	·	·	·	·	E. latifolium
·	·	·	·	·	·	·	·	·	·	·	Isolepis setacea
·	·	·	3	·	·	·	·	·	·	·	Juncus acutiflorus
2	·	·	·	·	·	·	·	·	·	·	J. alpinus
3	3	2	3	·	3	1	1	·	3	·	**J. articulatus**
·	·	·	·	·	·	·	·	·	·	·	J. effusus
2	·	·	2	4	5	·	3	·	3	2	J. kochii
·	·	·	·	4	·	·	1	·	·	·	J. squarrosus
·	·	·	·	·	·	2	·	·	·	·	J. triglumis
·	·	·	·	·	·	·	·	1	·	·	Luzula multiflora
·	·	·	·	1	3	·	·	·	·	·	Narthecium ossifragum
·	·	·	·	·	·	·	·	·	·	·	Orchis fuchsii
·	·	·	·	·	·	·	·	·	·	·	Tofieldia pusilla
·	·	·	·	·	·	·	·	·	·	·	Trichophorum caespitosum
·	·	·	·	·	·	·	·	·	·	·	Triglochin palustre
·	·	·	·	·	·	·	·	·	·	·	Achillea ptarmica
·	·	·	·	·	·	·	·	·	·	·	Alchemilla filicaulis
·	·	·	·	·	·	·	·	·	·	·	A. glabra
2	·	·	·	·	4	·	·	·	·	·	A. vestita
·	·	·	·	·	2	·	·	·	·	·	Angelica sylvestris
·	·	·	·	·	·	·	·	·	·	·	Bellis perennis
·	·	·	·	·	4	·	·	·	·	2	Caltha palustris
2	·	·	·	·	1	·	·	1	+	1	Cardamine pratensis
·	2	·	·	·	·	·	·	·	·	·	Cerastium vulgatum
·	·	·	·	1	·	·	·	·	·	·	Cirsium palustre
·	·	·	·	2	·	·	·	·	·	·	Crepis paludosa
·	·	·	1	·	·	·	·	·	·	·	Drosera rotundifolia
·	·	·	·	·	2	·	·	·	·	·	Epilobium alsinifolium
·	3	·	·	·	·	·	·	·	·	·	E. anagallidifolium
·	·	·	·	·	·	·	·	·	·	·	E. palustre
3	2	·	1	3	3	·	3	·	·	·	Euphrasia officinalis agg.
·	·	2	·	·	·	·	·	·	·	·	Galium hercynicum
1	2	·	·	3	3	3	·	·	·	·	Leontodon autumnalis
·	·	·	·	·	·	·	·	·	·	·	L. hispidus
·	·	·	·	·	1	·	2	·	2	·	Linum catharticum
·	·	·	·	·	2	·	·	·	·	·	Lysimachia nemorum
·	·	·	·	·	·	·	·	·	·	·	Parnassia palustris
·	·	·	·	·	·	·	·	·	·	·	Pedicularis palustris

Table 58

	1	2	3	4	5	6	7	8	9	10	11
Pedicularis sylvatica	·	+	·	·	·	·	·	·	·	·	+
Pinguicula lusitanica	·	·	·	·	·	·	·	·	·	·	1
P. vulgaris	·	1	1	2	3	2	1	1	1	·	3
Plantago lanceolata	·	·	·	·	2	·	·	·	·	·	2
P. maritima	·	·	·	·	2	·	·	·	·	·	2
Polygonum viviparum	·	·	2	·	·	·	·	·	·	+	·
Potentilla erecta	2	2	3	1	·	2	1	3	1	2	3
Prunella vulgaris	·	1	4	·	3	·	·	·	·	·	4
Ranunculus acris	·	·	·	·	2	·	·	·	·	·	3
R. flammula	·	2	·	·	·	·	·	·	·	·	3
Rhinanthus minor agg.	·	·	·	·	·	·	·	·	+	·	·
Sagina nodosa	·	·	·	·	·	·	·	·	·	·	·
S. procumbens	·	·	·	·	·	·	·	·	·	·	·
Saxifraga aizoides	3	1	+	2	·	·	·	·	3	2	·
S. stellaris	·	·	·	·	·	·	·	·	·	·	·
Succisa pratensis	3	1	·	2	·	2	·	2	·	2	5
Taraxacum officinalis agg.	·	1	·	·	2	·	1	·	·	·	·
Thalictrum alpinum	·	·	·	·	·	·	5	3	·	3	·
Thymus drucei	·	·	·	·	·	·	1	·	·	·	·
Trifolium repens	·	·	·	·	·	·	·	·	·	+	2
Utricularia minor	·	·	·	·	·	·	·	·	·	·	·
Viola riviniana	·	·	·	·	·	·	·	·	·	·	·
V. palustris	·	·	·	1	·	·	·	·	·	·	·
Acrocladium cuspidatum	·	·	3	·	·	2	·	3	·	·	2
A. giganteum	·	·	·	·	·	·	·	·	·	·	·
A. trifarium	·	·	·	·	·	·	·	·	·	·	·
Aulacomnium palustre	·	·	·	·	·	·	1	·	·	·	·
Brachythecium rutabulum	·	·	·	·	1	·	·	·	·	·	·
Bryum pseudotriquetrum	2	·	2	·	2	2	4	·	·	·	·
Campylium stellatum	4	3	4	3	2	4	3	3	2	·	8
Cinclidium stygium	·	·	·	·	·	·	·	·	·	·	·
Cratoneuron commutatum	·	3	2	1	3	·	4	·	3	·	3
C. filicinum	·	·	·	·	3	·	·	·	·	·	·
Ctenidium molluscum	4	·	4	4	·	3	·	5	4	5	2
Dicranum bonjeani	·	·	·	·	·	·	·	·	3	·	·
Ditrichum flexicaule	2	·	·	·	·	·	·	·	·	·	·
Drepanocladus fluitans	·	·	·	·	·	·	·	·	·	·	·
D. revolvens	3	1	2	3	3	3	1	2	8	·	·
Fissidens adianthoides	2	·	3	1	·	·	·	2	·	·	·
F. osmundoides	·	·	·	·	·	·	·	·	2	·	·
Hylocomium splendens	·	·	·	·	·	2	·	3	1	·	2
Hypnum cupressiforme	1	·	·	·	·	·	·	·	·	·	·
Meesia uliginosa	·	·	·	·	·	·	·	·	·	·	·
Mnium pseudopunctatum	2	·	·	·	·	·	·	·	·	·	·
M. punctatum	·	·	·	·	·	·	·	·	·	·	·
M. seligeri	·	·	·	·	·	·	·	·	·	·	2
Philonotis calcarea	·	·	·	·	·	·	·	·	+	·	·
P. fontana	·	·	·	·	·	·	·	·	·	·	2
Polytrichum alpinum	·	·	·	·	·	·	·	·	·	·	·
Pseudoscleropodium purum	·	·	·	·	·	·	·	2	·	·	·
Rhacomitrium lanuginosum	·	·	·	·	·	·	·	·	·	1	·
Rhytidiadelphus squarrosus	·	·	2	·	·	·	·	2	·	·	·
Scorpidium scorpioides	4	3	·	2	·	·	·	·	2	·	3
Sphagnum contortum	·	·	·	·	·	·	·	·	·	·	·
S. inundatum	·	·	·	·	·	2	·	·	·	·	·
Thuidium delicatulum	·	·	·	·	·	2	·	·	·	·	·
T. tamariscinum	·	·	·	·	·	2	·	·	·	·	1
Aneura multifida	·	·	·	·	·	2	·	·	·	·	·
A. pinguis	·	1	·	·	1	1	·	·	1	·	·
Calypogeia trichomanis	1	·	·	·	·	·	·	·	·	·	·
Chiloscyphus polyanthus	·	·	·	·	·	·	·	1	·	·	·
Lophocolea bidentata	1	·	·	·	·	·	·	2	·	·	·
Pellia fabbroniana	·	·	·	·	1	·	·	·	·	·	·
Plagiochila asplenioides	·	·	·	·	·	·	·	·	·	·	·
Preissia quadrata	·	·	·	·	1	·	·	·	·	·	·
Scapania aequiloba	·	·	·	·	·	·	2	·	·	·	·
S. irrigua	·	·	·	·	·	·	1	·	·	·	·
S. nemorosa	3	·	1	1	·	·	·	·	·	·	·
S. undulata	·	·	·	·	·	·	·	·	·	·	·
Number of species (129) (50)	37	29	35	30	29	32	28	30	32	26	51

(Average 31)

Constancy class V   5
   „   „   IV   10

LOCALITIES

1. Ardtulichan, Killiecrankie, Perthshire; 2. Glen Loch, nr. Pitlochry, Perthshire; 3. Glen Girnaig, Blair Atholl, Perthshire; 4. Creag Odhar, Blair Atholl, Perthshire; 5. Monadh Dubh, Isle of Rhum, Inverness-shire; 6. White Haugh, Glen Clova, Angus; 7. Meall Odhar, Devil's Elbow, Aberdeenshire; 8–10,15. Kinlochlaggan, Inverness-shire; 9. Meall Breac, Blair Atholl, Perthshire; 11. Abhainn Bruachaig, Kinlochewe,

(continued)

12	13	14	15	16	17	18	19	20	21	22	
.	.	.	.	.	.	.	.	.	.	.	Pedicularis sylvatica
.	.	.	.	.	.	.	.	.	.	.	Pinguicula lusitanica
.	2	3	3	1	1	1	2	.	2	2	**P. vulgaris**
.	.	.	.	.	.	.	.	.	.	.	Plantago lanceolata
.	.	.	.	.	.	.	.	.	.	.	P. maritima
3	.	.	.	.	.	3	.	.	.	.	Polygonum viviparum
3	.	1	2	1	.	.	.	.	.	.	Potentilla erecta
3	.	.	3	.	.	.	.	.	.	.	Prunella vulgaris
1	.	.	.	2	.	3	.	.	.	.	Ranunculus acris
.	1	.	.	3	2	.	.	.	.	.	R. flammula
.	.	.	.	.	.	.	.	.	.	.	Rhinanthus minor agg.
.	.	.	.	.	.	1	.	.	.	.	Sagina nodosa
.	1	.	.	.	.	2	.	.	.	.	S. procumbens
4	.	.	.	.	.	.	.	.	.	.	Saxifraga aizoides
.	.	.	.	.	.	.	.	.	.	2	S. stellaris
.	.	.	.	2	2	.	.	.	.	.	Succisa pratensis
1	.	.	.	1	1	.	.	.	.	.	Taraxacum officinalis agg.
.	3	.	2	.	.	.	.	.	.	.	Thalictrum alpinum
.	.	.	.	.	.	.	.	.	.	.	Thymus drucei
+	.	.	.	.	.	2	.	.	.	.	Trifolium repens
.	.	.	.	.	.	.	.	.	.	3	Utricularia minor
2	.	.	.	.	.	.	.	.	.	.	Viola riviniana
.	.	.	.	.	.	.	.	.	.	2	V. palustris
2	1	.	.	1	.	.	.	2	.	2	Acrocladium cuspidatum
.	.	.	.	.	.	.	.	3	.	.	A. giganteum
.	.	.	.	.	.	.	.	.	.	+	A. trifarium
.	.	.	.	.	.	.	.	.	.	.	Aulacomnium palustre
.	.	.	.	.	.	.	.	.	.	.	Brachythecium rutabulum
2	3	2	.	1	.	3	2	3	.	4	Bryum pseudotriquetrum
2	1	.	3	4	3	.	2	4	7	+	**Campylium stellatum**
1	.	.	.	.	.	.	.	.	.	.	Cinclidium stygium
6	9	8	4	.	.	8	8	3	.	.	Cratoneuron commutatum
.	.	.	.	.	1	.	.	2	.	.	C. filicinum
+	.	.	5	2	.	1	.	.	.	.	Ctenidium molluscum
.	2	.	.	.	.	.	.	.	.	.	Dicranum bonjeani
.	.	.	.	.	.	.	.	.	.	.	Ditrichum flexicaule
.	.	.	.	.	.	.	.	.	.	3	Drepanocladus fluitans
2	.	.	3	7	4	.	3	8	3	3	**D. revolvens**
3	1	2	2	+	.	.	2	+	3	.	Fissidens adianthoides
.	2	.	.	.	.	.	.	.	.	.	F. osmundoides
1	.	.	2	.	.	.	.	.	.	1	Hylocomium splendens
.	.	.	.	.	.	.	.	.	.	.	Hypnum cupressiforme
.	.	.	.	.	.	.	.	.	2	.	Meesia uliginosa
.	1	.	.	.	.	.	.	.	2	.	Mnium pseudopunctatum
.	.	.	.	.	.	.	.	.	.	1	M. punctatum
1	.	.	.	.	.	2	.	.	.	.	M. seligeri
4	5	3	.	.	.	.	4	+	1	.	Philonotis calcarea
.	.	.	.	1	.	2	.	.	.	2	P. fontana
.	.	.	.	.	.	.	.	.	.	1	Polytrichum alpinum
.	.	.	.	.	.	.	.	.	.	.	Pseudoscleropodium purum
.	.	.	.	.	.	.	.	.	.	.	Rhacomitrium lanuginosum
.	.	.	.	.	.	.	.	.	.	.	Rhytidiadelphus squarrosus
.	.	.	5	.	8	.	.	3	4	7	Scorpidium scorpioides
.	.	.	.	.	.	.	.	.	.	2	Sphagnum contortum
.	.	.	.	3	.	.	.	.	.	.	S. inundatum
.	.	.	.	+	.	.	.	.	.	.	Thuidium delicatulum
.	.	.	.	.	.	.	.	.	.	.	T. tamariscinum
.	.	.	.	2	.	.	.	.	.	.	Aneura multifida
.	2	2	2	.	.	.	2	.	.	2	A. pinguis
.	.	.	.	.	.	.	.	.	.	.	Calypogeia trichomanis
.	.	.	.	.	.	.	.	.	.	.	Chiloscyphus polyanthus
.	.	.	.	.	.	.	.	.	.	.	Lophocolea bidentata
.	.	.	.	.	.	1	.	.	.	3	Pellia fabbroniana
.	2	.	.	.	.	.	.	.	.	.	Plagiochila asplenioides
1	.	.	.	.	.	2	.	.	.	.	Preissia quadrata
.	.	.	.	.	.	.	.	.	.	.	Scapania aequiloba
.	.	.	.	.	.	.	.	.	.	.	S. irrigua
.	.	.	.	.	.	.	.	.	.	.	S. nemorosa
.	.	.	.	.	.	.	.	.	.	2	S. undulata
39	30	16	23	36	29	32	19	18	22	33	Number of species (129) (50)

(Average 23)

Ross-shire; 12,21. Ben Vrackie, Pitlochry, Perthshire; 13,14,19. Glen Markie, Monadhliath, Inverness-shire; 16. Cairn Derg, Glen Clova, Angus; 17. Corrie Burn, Glen Clova, Angus; 18. Caenlochan Glen, Angus; 20. Tulach Hill, Blair Atholl, Perthshire; 22. Beinn nan Eachan, Killin, Perthshire.

Table 59: Caricetum saxatilis

	1	2	3	4	5	6	7	8	9	10	11	12	13	14	15
Reference number	P52 204	P52 203	P52 201	P52 200	P52 077	P52 206	P52 208	P52 209	P52 213	R56 110	R57 085	R57 122	R57 120	R57 124	R58 015
Map reference	7409 2632	7409 2632	7409 2632	7409 2632	7409 2635	7421 2642	7421 2642	7421 2642	7418 2640	8194 2010	7866 2433	7746 2465	7746 2464	7856 2386	7386 2330
Altitude (feet)	3050	3050	3000	3000	2950	2600	2600	2650	2650	2800	2900	2750	2900	3200	3100
Aspect (degrees)	210	120	150	150	220	220	0	0	350	315	45	45	360	90	45
Slope (degrees)	1	1	3	3	4	3	5	5	2	25	28	15	10	38	20
Cover (per cent)	90	100	80	90	—	90	80	80	80	80	100	100	100	50	100
Height (centimetres)	15	15	15	15	—	10	15	20	20	—	20	16	—	—	—
Plot area (square metres)	5	5	6	4	4	4	4	2	1	8	4	4	4	4	4
Salix herbacea	·	·	·	·	·	·	·	·	1	·	·	·	·	·	·
Equisetum palustre	·	·	3	3	3	·	·	·	·	·	·	·	·	·	·
Lycopodium selago	·	1	·	·	·	2	1	·	·	·	·	1	·	1	1
Selaginella selaginoides	·	1	2	·	3	3	2	·	·	·	2	·	·	·	·
Agrostis canina	3	4	·	·	2	·	3	·	1	3	1	·	·	·	3
A. tenuis	·	·	·	·	·	·	·	2	·	·	3	·	3	3	·
Alopecurus alpinus	·	·	·	·	·	·	·	·	·	·	+	·	·	·	·
Deschampsia caespitosa	4	·	·	·	·	·	·	·	·	3	3	·	5	·	·
Festuca ovina agg.	2	3	·	1	·	·	2	1	1	·	2	·	3	·	2
F. rubra	2	·	·	·	·	·	1	·	·	·	4	·	·	·	2
Nardus stricta	·	·	·	·	·	·	·	·	·	4	2	3	3	4	2
Carex bigelowii	·	·	·	·	·	·	·	·	·	4	5	3	1	3	3
C. curta	·	·	·	·	·	·	·	·	·	·	2	·	·	·	·
C. demissa	·	·	3	3	4	3	2	1	1	·	·	2	2	·	·
C. dioica	·	·	3	2	1	3	·	4	3	·	·	·	·	·	·
C. echinata	·	·	4	4	2	1	3	2	·	2	6	·	·	·	·
C. nigra	3	3	5	4	4	·	·	4	1	·	·	·	·	·	·
C. pulicaris	·	·	·	·	·	·	2	·	·	·	·	·	·	·	3
C. saxatilis	6	8	7	7	6	5	6	5	8	7	6	9	8	7	8
C. vaginata	3	·	·	·	·	·	·	·	·	·	·	·	·	·	·
Eriophorum angustifolium	·	3	4	3	3	5	3	4	3	·	4	3	·	·	4
Juncus articulatus	·	·	·	·	·	1	·	·	·	·	·	·	·	·	·
J. biglumis	·	·	·	·	1	·	·	·	·	·	·	·	·	·	·
J. castaneus	·	·	1	·	·	·	·	·	3	+	2	2	·	·	·
J. triglumis	2	·	2	·	3	·	3	3	3	2	·	3	·	·	·
Luzula multiflora	·	·	·	·	·	·	·	·	·	·	1	·	·	·	·
L. spicata	·	·	·	·	·	·	·	·	·	3	·	·	·	·	·
Narthecium ossifragum	·	·	·	·	·	·	·	·	·	·	·	·	·	2	·
Tofieldia pusilla	·	·	·	·	1	·	·	·	·	·	·	·	·	·	·
Triglochin palustre	·	·	·	·	1	·	·	·	·	·	·	·	·	·	·
Alchemilla alpina	·	·	·	·	·	·	·	1	·	·	·	·	·	·	·
A. filicaulis	·	·	·	·	·	·	·	·	·	1	·	·	·	2	·
A. glabra	·	·	·	·	1	·	·	·	·	·	+	·	·	·	·
A. wichurae	·	·	·	3	·	·	·	·	·	·	·	·	·	·	·
Armeria maritima	·	·	·	·	·	·	·	·	·	·	·	2	2	·	+
Caltha palustris	2	1	·	1	·	·	·	2	·	3	4	·	·	3	+
Cardamine pratensis	·	·	·	·	3	·	·	·	·	·	·	·	·	·	·
Cerastium vulgatum	·	·	·	·	·	1	·	·	·	·	·	·	·	·	·
Cochlearia alpina	·	·	·	·	·	·	·	·	·	1	·	·	·	·	·
Epilobium anagallidifolium	·	·	·	·	·	1	·	·	·	·	·	2	1	·	·
Euphrasia scotica	·	·	3	3	·	·	2	·	·	·	·	·	·	·	·
Euphrasia sp.	·	·	·	·	·	·	·	·	·	1	·	·	·	·	·
Geum rivale	·	·	·	·	·	·	·	·	·	·	2	·	·	·	·
Leontodon autumnalis	1	·	·	·	1	·	·	·	·	·	·	·	·	3	+
Pinguicula vulgaris	·	·	·	·	2	2	2	3	·	·	1	2	·	·	1
Polygonum viviparum	1	·	3	3	2	·	3	3	3	·	3	3	2	·	3
Ranunculus acris	·	·	·	·	·	·	·	·	·	·	·	·	·	3	+
Rumex acetosa	·	·	1	·	·	·	·	·	·	3	·	·	·	·	·
Saxifraga aizoides	·	·	3	·	3	·	·	·	·	3	·	2	·	·	+
S. stellaris	·	·	·	·	2	·	·	·	·	2	2	·	·	·	·
Taraxacum officinalis agg.	·	·	·	·	·	·	·	·	·	+	·	·	·	·	·
Thalictrum alpinum	·	·	·	1	4	·	3	3	·	·	3	3	3	2	3
Viola palustris	·	2	2	1	2	·	1	·	·	·	·	·	·	·	+
Acrocladium cuspidatum	·	·	·	·	1	·	·	·	·	·	·	·	·	·	·
A. giganteum	·	·	1	3	·	·	·	·	·	·	·	·	·	·	·
A. sarmentosum	7	·	·	·	·	4	·	1	·	·	4	2	3	·	4
A. stramineum	·	·	1	1	·	·	·	·	·	·	·	·	·	·	·
A. trifarium	·	·	2	·	·	·	3	5	3	+	·	3	2	·	3
Blindia acuta	·	·	·	·	1	·	1	1	1	3	·	·	·	2	2
Bryum pseudotriquetrum	·	·	2	5	4	·	2	·	1	·	5	·	2	·	·
Campylium stellatum	·	·	·	·	·	·	·	·	1	+	·	3	1	·	·
Cinclidium stygium	·	1	·	·	·	·	·	1	·	·	·	·	·	·	·
Cratoneuron commutatum	·	·	6	5	3	·	·	·	·	·	·	·	·	·	·
Dicranella squarrosa	·	·	·	1	3	·	·	·	·	·	2	·	·	1	·
Dicranum scoparium	1	·	·	1	1	·	1	·	·	·	·	·	·	·	·
Drepanocladus exannulatus	2	·	·	·	·	3	·	·	·	·	2	·	·	·	·
D. revolvens	5	5	6	5	3	6	2	5	4	6	4	5	6	3	5
Fissidens adianthoides	·	·	·	·	·	·	·	·	·	·	1	·	·	·	·
F. osmundoides	·	·	2	·	3	·	2	·	1	·	·	·	·	2	·
Hylocomium splendens	2	2	1	2	1	3	2	3	2	2	2	·	·	2	2
Mnium hornum	·	·	·	·	·	·	·	·	·	·	·	·	·	·	3
M. pseudopunctatum	·	·	·	·	·	·	·	·	·	·	+	·	·	·	·

344

Table 59 (*continued*)

	1	2	3	4	5	6	7	8	9	10	11	12	13	14	15
Philonotis fontana	·	·	·	·	2	·	1	·	·	1	2	·	·	·	·
Polytrichum alpinum	·	·	·	·	·	·	·	·	·	·	1	·	·	·	·
P. commune	2	1	1	1	1	3	·	2	·	·	·	·	·	·	·
P. juniperinum	·	·	·	·	·	·	·	·	1	·	·	·	·	·	·
Rhacomitrium lanuginosum	1	2	·	·	·	·	·	·	·	1	·	·	·	·	2
Rhytidiadelphus loreus	·	·	·	·	·	1	·	1	2	·	1	·	·	·	·
R. squarrosus	·	1	·	1	·	·	·	·	·	·	2	·	·	·	·
R. triquetrus	·	·	·	·	·	·	1	·	·	·	·	·	·	·	1
Scorpidium scorpioides	·	·	·	2	·	·	·	1	3	·	·	+	·	·	·
Sphagnum cuspidatum	·	4	·	·	·	·	·	·	·	·	·	·	·	·	·
S. nemoreum	·	·	·	·	·	·	·	·	·	·	1	·	·	·	·
S. subsecundum	2	4	·	·	·	6	·	·	·	·	·	·	·	·	2
Tayloria lingulata	·	·	·	·	1	·	·	·	·	·	·	·	·	·	·
Anthelia julacea	·	·	·	·	·	·	·	·	·	·	·	·	·	2	·
Aneura multifida	·	·	·	·	·	·	1	·	·	·	·	·	·	·	·
A. pinguis	1	1	3	2	3	2	3	3	3	·	3	2	·	2	2
A. sinuata	·	·	·	·	·	·	·	·	·	·	·	·	·	·	3
Eucalyx obovatus	·	·	·	·	·	·	·	·	·	·	2	·	·	·	·
Lophozia lycopodioides	·	·	·	·	·	·	·	·	·	·	2	·	·	·	·
L. quinquedentata	·	·	·	·	·	·	·	·	·	·	·	·	·	·	3
Odontoschisma elongatum	·	·	·	·	·	·	1	·	·	·	·	·	·	·	·
Pellia cf. fabbroniana	·	·	·	·	·	·	·	·	·	·	2	·	·	·	·
Scapania irrigua	·	·	·	·	·	·	·	·	·	·	2	·	·	·	·
S. uliginosa	·	·	·	·	·	·	1	1	·	·	2	·	·	·	·
S. undulata	2	2	1	1	2	2	·	3	3	4	3	·	2	4	2
Sphenolobus politus	·	·	·	·	·	·	·	·	·	·	1	·	·	·	·
Stereocaulon evolutoides	1	·	·	·	·	·	·	·	·	·	·	·	·	·	·
Number of species (99)	22	20	26	25	38	19	29	24	24	27	41	20	17	18	30

(Average 24)

Constancy class V 5
    ,,   ,, IV 5

LOCALITIES

1–9. Ben Lawers, Perthshire; 10. Beinn Fhada, Kintail; 11. Creag Meagaidh, Inverness-shire; 12,13. Coire na Coichille, Ardverikie Forest, Inverness-shire; 14. Beinn a' Chaoruinn, Laggan, Inverness-shire; 15. Ben Dorain, Argyll.

Table 60 : Philonoto-Saxifragetum stellaris (1–23);

	1	2	3	4	5	6	7	8	9	10	11	12	13	14	15	16
Reference number	R57 125	M56 054	M56 041	M56 044	P52 143	M56 044	R57 027	P52 125	P52 144	R58 080	P52 142	M56 093	P52 127	P52 129	P52 141	P52 146
Map reference	7856 2386	8507 2102	8605 1975	8602 1973	7549 2721	8602 1973	9511 2308	7403 2650	7543 2720	8326 2162	7549 2721	8000 3008	7403 2650	7403 2650	7549 2721	7549 2720
Altitude (feet)	3200	2800	2150	2200	2700	2200	1700	2050	2700	2500	2700	3200	2050	2050	2700	2500
Aspect (degrees)	–	–	–	–	–	–	–	–	–	–	–	–	–	–	–	–
Slope (degrees)	–	–	–	–	–	–	–	–	–	–	–	–	–	–	–	–
Cover (per cent)	–	–	–	–	–	–	–	–	–	–	–	–	–	–	–	–
Height (centimetres)	–	–	–	–	–	–	–	–	–	–	–	–	–	–	–	–
Plot area (square metres)	4	2	3	2	0·5	4	4	0·5	1	4	0·5	4	0·5	0·3	0·5	1·5
Equisetum arvense	.	.	.	.	.	.	.	.	.	.	.	.	.	.	.	.
E. cf. palustre	.	.	.	.	.	.	.	.	.	.	.	.	.	.	.	.
Agrostis canina	.	.	.	.	.	.	4	.	.	.	.	.	.	.	.	1
A. stolonifera	.	.	.	.	.	3	.	3	3	5	.	.	2	2	2	2
A. tenuis	3	.	.	.	.	.	.	.	.	2	.	.	.	.	.	.
Anthoxanthum odoratum	.	.	1	.	.	.	3	1	.	.	.	.	2	3	.	.
Deschampsia alpina	.	.	.	.	.	.	.	.	.	.	.	.	.	.	.	.
D. caespitosa	5	3	+	3	5	4	3	2	4	4	5	2	.	.	3	.
Festuca ovina agg.	.	.	.	.	.	.	3	.	.	.	.	.	.	.	.	.
F. rubra	4	.	.	.	5	.	.	.	4	3	3	.	.	.	3	3
Nardus stricta	.	.	.	.	.	.	.	.	.	.	.	.	.	.	.	.
Poa annua	.	.	.	.	.	.	.	.	.	.	.	.	.	.	.	.
P. pratensis	.	.	.	.	.	.	.	.	.	.	.	.	.	.	.	2
P. trivialis	.	.	.	.	.	.	.	.	.	2	.	.	.	.	.	.
Carex bigelowii	3	.	.	.	.	.	2	1	.	.	.	.	.	.	.	.
C. curta	.	.	.	.	.	.	.	.	.	.	.	.	.	.	.	.
C. demissa	.	.	.	.	.	.	.	.	3	.	.	.	.	.	.	.
C. echinata	.	.	.	.	.	.	3	.	.	.	.	.	.	.	.	.
C. panicea	.	.	.	.	.	.	.	.	.	.	.	.	.	.	.	.
C. saxatilis	3	.	.	.	.	.	.	.	.	.	.	.	.	.	.	.
Eriophorum angustifolium	.	.	.	.	.	.	2	.	.	.	.	.	.	.	.	.
Juncus kochii	.	.	.	.	.	.	.	1	.	3	.	.	.	.	.	.
J. squarrosus	.	.	.	.	.	.	.	.	.	.	.	.	.	.	.	.
Alchemilla alpina	1	.	.	.	.	.	.	.	.	.	.	.	.	.	.	.
A. filicaulis	3	.	.	.	.	.	.	.	.	.	.	.	.	.	.	.
Caltha palustris	3	.	.	.	.	.	1	.	.	3	.	.	.	.	.	2
Cardamine pratensis	.	.	.	.	.	.	.	.	.	1	.	.	.	.	.	.
Cerastium cerastoides	.	.	.	.	.	.	.	.	.	.	.	.	.	.	.	.
C. vulgatum	3	.	.	.	.	.	.	.	.	.	.	.	1	.	.	.
Chrysosplenium oppositifolium	5	.	.	.	.	.	4	.	.	2	1	.	.	.	.	.
Epilobium alsinifolium	.	.	.	.	.	.	.	.	.	3	.	.	.	.	.	2
E. anagallidifolium	3	3	.	.	.	.	.	.	.	4	.	.	.	.	.	2
E. palustre	.	.	.	.	.	.	.	.	.	.	.	.	1	.	.	.
Geum rivale	3	.	.	.	.	.	.	.	.	.	.	.	.	.	.	.
Montia lamprosperma	2	.	.	.	.	.	.	.	.	.	.	.	.	.	.	.
Ranunculus acris	2	.	+	.	.	.	.	.	.	3	.	.	.	.	.	.
Rumex acetosa	.	.	.	.	.	.	2	.	.	3	.	.	.	.	.	.
Sagina procumbens	.	.	.	.	.	.	.	.	.	3	.	.	.	.	.	1
Saxifraga stellaris	3	2	5	4	3	.	4	3	3	3	2	3	3	2	3	3
Stellaria alsine	.	3	.	.	.	.	.	.	.	3	1	.	.	.	3	3
Thalictrum alpinum	3	.	.	.	.	.	.	.	.	.	.	.	.	.	3	3
Veronica humifusa	.	.	.	.	.	.	.	.	.	2	.	.	.	.	.	.
Viola palustris	3	.	.	.	.	.	.	.	.	3	.	.	.	.	.	.
Acrocladium sarmentosum	.	.	.	.	.	4	2	.	.	.	.	.	.	.	.	.
A. stramineum	.	.	.	.	.	.	.	.	.	.	.	.	.	.	.	.
Blindia acuta	.	.	1	.	.	.	.	.	.	.	.	.	.	.	.	.
Brachythecium rivulare	7	.	.	.	.	.	.	.	.	.	.	.	.	.	.	.
Bryum alpinum	.	.	1	.	.	.	.	.	.	.	.	.	.	.	.	.
B. pseudotriquetrum	4	.	.	.	.	.	2	.	.	.	.	.	.	.	.	1
B. weigelii	.	.	.	.	.	.	.	.	.	.	.	.	.	.	.	.
Dicranella squarrosa	2	.	.	.	1	.	3	1	1	3	1	6	10	10	10	9
Drepanocladus exannulatus	.	1	.	.	.	.	4	.	.	.	.	.	.	.	.	.
Hygrohypnum luridum	.	.	.	.	.	.	.	.	.	.	.	.	.	.	.	.
Oligotrichum hercynicum	.	.	1	.	.	.	.	.	.	.	.	.	.	.	.	.
Philonotis fontana	8	10	5	5	1	2	5	2	.	5	3	6	1	2	.	1
Pohlia glacialis	.	.	.	.	.	.	.	.	.	2	.	.	.	.	.	.
P. ludwigii	.	.	.	.	.	.	.	.	.	.	.	.	.	.	.	.
Polytrichum commune	.	.	2	1	.	.	.	.	2	.	.	.	.	3	1	.
Rhacomitrium aquaticum	.	.	2	.	.	.	.	.	.	.	.	.	.	.	.	.
Rhytidiadelphus squarrosus	.	.	.	.	.	.	.	.	.	.	.	.	.	.	.	.
Sphagnum auriculatum	.	1	.	.	.	.	.	2	2	.	.	.	.	.	.	.
S. girgensohnii	.	.	.	.	3	4	.	.	.	.	.	5	3	1	.	.
S. squarrosum	.	.	1	.	.	.	.	.	.	.	.	.	.	.	.	.
S. teres	.	.	.	.	1	.	.	.	.	.	.	.	.	1	.	.
Splachnum vasculosum	.	.	.	.	.	.	.	.	.	5	.	.	.	.	.	.
Alicularia scalaris	.	.	2	.	.	.	.	.	.	.	.	.	.	.	.	.
Aneura pinguis	.	.	.	.	.	.	2	.	.	.	.	.	.	.	.	.
Aplozia cordifolia	.	.	.	.	.	.	.	.	.	6	.	.	.	.	.	1

Pohlietum glacialis (24–31)

17	18	19	20	21	22	23	24	25	26	27	28	29	30	31	
M56	P52	R57	R56	M56	P52	R59	M58	R57	M57	R57	R57	R57	R58	R58	Reference number
061	126	042	076	042	145	004	047	093	120	181	092	104	043	056	
8568	7403	9335	8604	8605	7549	9213	8349	7876	7983	7917	7782	7721	8261	8816	Map reference
2243	2650	2422	1971	1975	2720	2298	2163	2432	2943	2492	2657	2492	2128	2257	
2400	2050	2250	1950	2150	2450	2500	3200	3350	3500	2850	2850	3600	3500	3250	Altitude (feet)
–	–	–	–	–	–	–	–	–	360	–	360	360	180	360	Aspect (degrees)
–	–	–	–	–	–	–	–	–	–	–	15	–	35	35	Slope (degrees)
–	–	–	–	–	–	–	75	100	100	100	100	100	100	100	Cover (per cent)
–	–	–	–	–	–	–	–	–	–	–	–	–	–	–	Height (centimetres)
4	1	4	4	1	0·5	4	4	4	4	4	4	4	4	4	Plot area (square metres)
1															Equisetum arvense
										1					E. cf. palustre
		4	1												Agrostis canina
3	2			3	2										A. stolonifera
		1		3	4					3					A. tenuis
	3														Anthoxanthum odoratum
			1												Deschampsia alpina
3		3	2	1	1	4	3	4	1	3	1	4	1	2	**D. caespitosa**
	2		2												Festuca ovina agg.
				3				2							F. rubra
			2												Nardus stricta
							2			2	3				Poa annua
															P. pratensis
													2		P. trivialis
			3									2			Carex bigelowii
												2			C. curta
		+													C. demissa
		3	4												C. echinata
			3												C. panicea
			2												C. saxatilis
												3			Eriophorum angustifolium
	2	3	2		3										Juncus kochii
			2												J. squarrosus
															Alchemilla alpina
															A. filicaulis
		3										3			Caltha palustris
															Cardamine pratensis
							2	3		2		1		1	Cerastium cerastoides
															C. vulgatum
		4					4			3	2				Chrysosplenium oppositifolium
															Epilobium alsinifolium
2					3		3			3		3	3		E. anagallidifolium
	3		2												E. palustre
+															Geum rivale
	3	3				4				4					Montia lamprosperma
							1								Ranunculus acris
															Rumex acetosa
															Sagina procumbens
2	4	3	4	2	3	4	3	2	2	3		3	3		**Saxifraga stellaris**
3	2			3	3	3	3			3	3				Stellaria alsine
															Thalictrum alpinum
					2								2		Veronica humifusa
															Viola palustris
	1	2	5									6			Acrocladium sarmentosum
								4		4					A. stramineum
															Blindia acuta
							1								Brachythecium rivulare
															Bryum alpinum
															B. pseudotriquetrum
							3				+		+		B. weigelii
1	2		4				2					6			Dicranella squarrosa
10	9	7	8			4		4				2			Drepanocladus exannulatus
							3							2	Hygrohypnum luridum
															Oligotrichum hercynicum
2	2	3	2	4	2	4	2	4		7		3	+		**Philonotis fontana**
							9	8	10	7	9	6	10	10	**Pohlia glacialis**
								4	+	2				2	P. ludwigii
															Polytrichum commune
															Rhacomitrium aquaticum
												2			Rhytidiadelphus squarrosus
	3	4	3	9	9	5									Sphagnum auriculatum
												3			S. girgensohnii
						3		3							S. squarrosum
					1										S. teres
										3					Splachnum vasculosum
															Alicularia scalaris
		2													Aneura pinguis
		3					1								Aplozia cordifolia

Table 60

	1	2	3	4	5	6	7	8	9	10	11	12	13	14	15	16
Aplozia riparia	·	·	·	·	·	·	1	·	·	·	·	·	·	·	·	·
A. sphaerocarpa	·	1	·	·	·	·	·	·	·	·	·	·	·	·	·	·
Chiloscyphus polyanthus	·	·	·	·	·	·	·	·	·	·	·	·	·	·	·	·
Eucalyx obovatus	·	·	·	·	·	·	·	·	·	·	·	·	·	·	·	·
Marchantia polymorpha	·	·	·	·	·	·	·	·	·	·	·	·	·	·	·	·
Pellia cf. epiphylla	·	·	·	·	·	·	·	·	·	4	·	4	·	·	·	·
Scapania dentata	·	1	8	8	4	8	5	·	·	·	·	4	·	·	·	·
S. nemorosa	·	·	·	·	·	·	·	·	·	·	·	·	·	·	·	·
S. uliginosa	·	·	·	·	10	·	5	10	10	10	10	·	·	·	4	·
S. undulata	·	·	·	·	·	·	7	·	·	·	·	·	·	·	·	·
Number of species (66) (40)	21	10	12	6	9	6	21	12	7	24	9	6	10	7	7	14

(Average 12)

Constancy class   V   3
,,   ,,   IV   2

LOCALITIES

1. Beinn a' Chaoruinn, Laggan, Inverness-shire; 2. Moruisg, Strath Carron, Ross-shire; 3, 4, 6. Toll Ban, Beinn Eighe, Ross-shire; 5, 9, 11, 15, 16, 22. Carn Mairg, Glen Lyon, Perthshire; 7. Foinaven, Reay Forest, Sutherland; 8, 13, 14, 18. Ben Lawers, Perthshire; 10, 24. Sgurr na Lapaich, Glen Cannich, Ross-shire; 12. Loch Etchachan, Cairngorms, Aberdeenshire; 17. Sgurr a' Ghlas Leathaid, Strath Bran, Ross-shire; 19. Ben Hee, Reay Forest, Sutherland; 20, 21. Ruadh Stac Beag, Beinn Eighe, Ross-shire; 23. Conival, Inchnadamph,

(continued)

17	18	19	20	21	22	23	24	25	26	27	28	29	30	31	
·	·	2	·	·	·	·	·	·	·	·	·	·	·	·	Aplozia riparia
1	·	·	·	·	·	·	·	·	·	·	·	·	·	·	A. sphaerocarpa
·	·	3	·	·	·	2	·	·	·	·	·	·	·	·	Chiloscyphus polyanthus
·	·	·	·	·	·	·	·	·	·	·	·	2	·	·	Eucalyx obovatus
·	·	·	·	·	·	·	·	·	·	4	2	·	·	·	Marchantia polymorpha
·	·	2	·	·	·	5	·	·	·	·	·	·	·	·	Pellia cf. epiphylla
1	·	3	4	3	·	·	·	+	·	·	·	3	·	·	Scapania dentata
·	·	·	·	·	·	·	·	4	·	·	·	·	·	·	S. nemorosa
·	2	·	2	·	2	·	1	4	·	3	·	·	·	·	S. uliginosa
·	·	7	2	·	·	3	·	·	·	·	·	2	·	·	S. undulata
12	15	17	25	6	10	17	15	13	4	17	7	19	8	5	Number of species (66) (40)

(Average 11)

Constancy class V 2
    „   „ IV 3

Sutherland; 25. Creag Meagaidh, Laggan, Inverness-shire; 26. Garbh Choire, Braeriach, Aberdeenshire; 27. A'Bhuidheanach, Laggan, Inverness-shire; 28. Coire Chuirn, Drumochter, Inverness-shire; 29. Ben Alder, Inverness-shire; 30. Carn Eige, Glen Affric, Inverness-shire; 31. Beinn Dearg, Inverlael, Ross-shire.

Table 61: Anthelia-Deschampsia caespitosa provisional nodum

	1	2	3	4		1	2	3	4
Reference number	R57	R58	R58	R57	Philonotis fontana	1	3	.	.
	100	045	014	101	Pohlia ludwigii	3	3	.	.
Map reference	7724	8344	7385	7723	P. nutans	2	.	.	.
	2498	2162	2329	2495	Polytrichum alpinum	.	.	2	.
Altitude (feet)	3450	3400	3200	3450	P. norvegicum	3	2	.	.
Aspect (degrees)	360	90	90	360	Rhacomitrium fasciculare	.	.	3	.
Slope (degrees)	5	3	15	20	R. heterostichum	2	.	.	.
Cover (per cent)	90	100	95	100	R. lanuginosum	.	.	2	.
Height (centimetres)	–	–	–	–	Sphagnum auriculatum	.	.	3	.
Plot area (square metres)	4	4	4	4	S. tenellum	.	.	1	.
Agrostis tenuis	.	.	3	.	Alicularia scalaris	4	.	.	.
Deschampsia caespitosa	3	2	5	3	**Anthelia julacea**	9	9	9	7
Nardus stricta	+	.	2	2	Gymnomitrium concinnatum	2	.	.	.
					Lophozia floerkii	3	.	.	.
Carex bigelowii	2	.	.	3	Marsupella emarginata	.	4	3	7
C. saxatilis	.	.	.	8	Moerckia blyttii	2	.	.	.
					Scapania dentata	3	4	3	2
Saxifraga stellaris	.	1	2	.	S. uliginosa	2	.	.	.
Taraxacum officinalis agg.	.	.	.	2					
Viola palustris	2	.	.	2	Number of species (28)	17	9	11	9
Dicranum starkei	3	.	.	.	(Average 11·5)				
Drepanocladus exannulatus	.	3	.	.					

1, 4. Ben Alder, Inverness-shire; 2. Sgurr na Lapaich, Glen Cannich, Inverness-shire; 3. Ben **Dorain,** Bridge of Orchy, Argyll.

Table 62: Narthecium-Sphagnum provisional nodum

	1	2	3		1	2	3
Reference number	M57	R58	R57	Juncus squarrosus	.	2	4
	102	042	273	**Narthecium ossifragum**	7	7	8
Map reference	7716	7960	7778	**Trichophorum caespitosum**	5	4	3
	2583	2971	3229				
Altitude (feet)	2500	2700	2450	Rhacomitrium lanuginosum	3	3	.
Aspect (degrees)	315	90	45	Sphagnum auriculatum	.	.	6
Slope (degrees)	5	10	15	**S. compactum**	4	2	4
Cover (per cent)	90	100	90	S. cuspidatum	.	.	2
Height (centimetres)	–	–	–	S. papillosum	.	.	4
Plot area (square metres)	4	4	4	S. russowii	.	.	3
				S. tenellum	2	8	4
Erica tetralix	.	2	.				
				Diplophyllum albicans	1	.	.
Lycopodium alpinum	+	.	.	Leptoscyphus taylori	1	.	.
L. selago	2	2	1				
				Cetraria islandica	2	.	.
Agrostis canina	.	.	1	Cladonia bellidiflora	2	.	.
Festuca ovina agg.	1	.	.	C. uncialis	2	2	.
Molinia caerulea	1	3	.				
Nardus stricta	3	3	3	Number of species (24)	17	11	14
Carex echinata	2	.	2	(Average 14)			
Eriophorum angustifolium	3	.	3				

1. Nr. Ben Udlamain, Drumochter, Perthshire; 2. Coire Odhar, Cairn Toul, Aberdeenshire; 3. Meikle Kilrannoch, Clova, Angus.

Table 63: Cratoneuron-Saxifraga aizoides nodum

	1	2	3	4	5	6	7	8	9	10	11
Reference number	P52 135	P52 136	P52 137	P52 139	P52 220	P52 150	P52 152	P52 202	R59 028	R56 097	R57 121
Map reference	7557 2724	7557 2724	7557 2724	7557 2724	7562 2744	7556 2623	7556 2723	7409 2635	7752 3143	8814 2213	7746 2465
Altitude (feet)	1600	1600	1650	1650	1075	1650	1650	3000	1750	1600	2900
Plot area (square metres)	–	–	–	–	6	–	1·5	1·5	4	4	4
Equisetum palustre	1	·	·	·	2	3	2	2	·	·	·
E. variegatum	·	·	·	·	·	·	·	·	2	·	·
Selaginella selaginoides	·	·	·	·	·	·	·	·	2	·	·
Agrostis canina	·	·	·	·	·	2	2	·	·	·	·
A. stolonifera	3	2	·	·	3	·	·	·	3	·	·
A. tenuis	·	·	·	·	·	2	2	·	·	4	3
Deschampsia caespitosa	1	·	3	·	·	·	2	2	2	2	2
Festuca ovina agg.	·	·	·	·	·	·	·	·	4	2	·
F. rubra	3	3	2	2	3	1	3	·	4	·	3
Poa alpina	·	·	·	·	·	·	·	·	·	·	1
P. pratensis	1	3	4	4	·	2	·	·	·	·	·
Carex demissa	·	·	·	·	·	·	·	·	·	1	·
C. dioica	·	·	·	·	·	3	·	3	·	3	·
C. nigra	·	·	·	·	·	2	·	3	·	1	·
C. panicea	·	·	2	·	·	3	·	·	3	2	·
C. pulicaris	·	·	·	·	·	·	·	·	·	2	·
C. saxatilis	·	·	·	·	·	·	·	1	·	·	·
Juncus articulatus	·	·	·	·	·	·	·	·	2	2	·
J. kochii	·	·	·	·	·	·	·	·	·	3	·
J. squarrosus	·	·	·	·	·	·	·	·	·	1	·
J. triglumis	·	·	·	·	·	·	·	·	1	·	·
Alchemilla glabra	·	·	·	·	·	·	·	2	2	·	·
Caltha palustris	3	·	·	·	·	·	·	·	·	·	2
Cardamine pratensis	2	3	3	2	2	3	3	·	1	·	·
Chrysosplenium oppositifolium	2	·	·	4	·	·	·	·	·	·	3
Cochlearia alpina	·	·	3	·	·	·	·	·	·	·	·
Epilobium alsinifolium	3	5	5	3	·	·	·	4	2	·	·
E. palustre	·	·	·	·	·	2	·	·	·	2	·
Geum rivale	·	·	·	·	·	·	·	·	·	2	·
Montia lamprosperma	·	·	3	·	·	·	·	·	·	3	·
Pinguicula vulgaris	·	·	·	·	·	2	·	·	1	·	·
Polygonum viviparum	·	1	·	1	2	·	·	·	4	·	·
Ranunculus acris	·	·	·	·	·	·	·	·	2	·	·
Rumex acetosa	2	·	·	1	·	·	·	·	·	·	·
Sagina procumbens	·	·	1	·	·	·	·	·	·	·	·
Saxifraga aizoides	2	1	1	2	3	1	·	·	7	+	+
S. stellaris	·	·	·	·	·	·	·	·	·	3	·
Taraxacum officinalis agg.	·	·	1	1	·	·	3	·	·	·	·
Thalictrum alpinum	·	·	·	·	·	·	·	3	·	1	·
Tussilago farfara	·	·	·	·	2	·	·	·	2	·	·
Acrocladium cuspidatum	·	1	·	·	·	·	·	·	·	·	·
Brachythecium rivulare	·	·	·	·	·	·	·	·	·	·	·
Bryum pseudotriquetrum	·	·	·	·	·	2	2	·	·	1	·
Cratoneuron commutatum	10	9	10	9	10	9	9	10	8	9	9
Dicranella squarrosa	·	·	·	1	·	·	·	·	·	3	·
Philonotis fontana	·	2	·	1	2	2	4	2	·	1	·
Aneura pinguis	·	·	·	·	·	·	·	·	2	1	·
Aplozia cordifolia	·	·	1	·	·	·	·	·	·	·	2
Pellia fabbroniana	·	·	1	·	·	·	·	·	·	·	·
Number of species (49)	12	10	14	12	10	15	10	16	19	21	10

Constancy class V 3 (Average 13)

„ „ IV 3

LOCALITIES

1–7. Schiehallion, Perthshire; 8. Ben Lawers, Perthshire; 9. Glen Shee, Perthshire; 10. Beinn Enaiglair, Inverlael, Ross-shire; 11. Ardverikie Forest, Inverness-shire.

Table 64: Cariceto-Saxifragetum aizoidis (1–18) [low-level

	1	2	3	4	5	6	7	8	9	10	11	12	13	14	15
Reference number	R57 274	R56 091	R56 066	R56 117	R57 153	R57 287	M56 098	M56 090	M56 060	M57 038	R57 123	R57 310	M56 049	M56 051	R56 102
Map reference	7778 3228	8802 2292	8717 2063	8183 1920	7962 2597	7625 2894	7905 3142	8795 2242	8574 2247	7563 2108	77– 24–	7690 2964	8723 1985	8508 2104	8133 1942
Altitude (feet)	2600	1900	1750	1300	2200	1100	1300	1900	1900	2100	2900	2000	2100	2100	2400
Aspect (degrees)	45	270	180	360	225	45	360	45	360	360	360	315	225	45	45
Slope (degrees)	20	27	7	25	18	12	3	0	0	2	10	10	0	0	30
Cover (per cent)	60	50	50	40	70	75	75	75	80	100	90	70	50	75	50
Height (centimetres)	–	–	–	–	–	–	–	–	5	–	–	–	–	–	–
Plot area (square metres)	4	16	16	16	4	4	4	4	4	4	4	4	4	4	16
Calluna vulgaris	·	·	·	2	·	·	·	1	1	·	·	·	·	·	·
Empetrum hermaphroditum	·	·	·	·	·	·	·	·	·	·	2	·	·	·	·
Erica tetralix	·	·	·	·	·	·	·	+	·	·	·	·	·	·	·
Myrica gale	·	·	·	·	·	·	·	·	·	·	·	·	·	·	·
Equisetum hyemale	·	·	·	·	·	+	·	·	·	·	+	·	·	·	·
E. palustre	·	·	·	·	·	·	3	·	·	·	·	·	·	·	·
E. variegatum	3	·	·	·	·	·	·	·	·	·	·	·	·	·	·
Lycopodium selago	·	·	·	·	·	·	·	1	·	·	·	·	·	1	·
Selaginella selaginoides	+	3	2	3	1	2	1	2	3	4	·	·	·	·	2
Agrostis canina	2	1	+	·	·	·	·	·	3	·	·	2	·	·	3
A. stolonifera	·	·	·	·	·	·	·	·	·	·	·	·	·	·	·
A. tenuis	·	·	·	·	·	·	·	·	·	·	1	·	·	·	·
Anthoxanthum odoratum	·	·	·	2	·	·	·	·	·	·	·	·	1	·	+
Briza media	·	·	·	·	·	·	1	·	·	·	·	·	·	·	·
Deschampsia caespitosa	·	3	·	2	·	·	·	·	+	1	3	1	·	+	3
D. flexuosa	·	·	·	·	·	·	·	1	·	·	·	·	·	·	·
Festuca ovina agg.	2	4	3	3	1	·	2	3	3	3	1	3	·	2	3
F. rubra	·	·	·	3	·	·	·	·	·	·	3	·	2	·	·
Molinia caerulea	·	2	2	1	·	4	·	1	·	·	·	·	·	·	·
Nardus stricta	·	2	2	·	·	·	·	1	1	1	·	·	·	1	4
Sieglingia decumbens	·	·	·	+	·	·	·	·	·	·	·	·	·	·	·
Carex atrofusca	·	·	·	·	·	·	·	·	·	·	3	·	·	·	·
C. bigelowii	·	·	·	·	·	·	·	·	·	·	1	·	·	·	·
C. demissa	4	3	3	3	3	5	3	4	2	4	6	4	4	4	4
C. dioica	·	·	2	3	·	·	4	3	·	+	·	3	1	3	·
C. echinata	·	·	·	·	·	·	·	·	·	·	·	·	·	·	2
C. flacca	·	·	·	·	5	3	·	·	·	·	·	·	·	·	·
C. hostiana	·	·	5	·	5	·	·	·	+	·	·	·	·	·	·
C. nigra	1	·	·	·	·	·	·	·	·	·	·	·	·	·	·
C. panicea	3	4	3	4	5	3	3	3	5	4	·	3	3	3	·
C. pulicaris	1	3	2	3	1	·	1	4	2	4	·	·	·	2	3
C. rostrata	·	·	·	·	·	·	·	·	·	·	·	·	·	·	·
C. saxatilis	·	·	·	·	·	·	·	·	·	·	3	·	·	·	2
Eleocharis multicaulis	·	·	·	·	·	·	·	·	·	·	·	·	·	·	·
E. pauciflora	·	·	·	·	5	3	·	·	·	·	·	3	·	·	·
Eriophorum angustifolium	2	·	1	·	1	·	·	2	·	·	·	·	·	1	·
E. latifolium	·	·	·	·	·	·	·	·	·	·	·	·	·	·	·
Juncus alpinus	·	·	·	·	·	2	2	·	·	·	3	2	·	·	·
J. articulatus	3	·	3	3	3	1	3	·	·	3	·	2	·	2	·
J. kochii	2	·	1	·	·	·	2	2	·	·	·	·	·	3	·
J. squarrosus	·	·	·	·	·	·	·	+	1	·	·	·	·	·	·
J. triglumis	3	2	3	3	+	·	+	2	·	1	2	2	+	3	3
Luzula multiflora	·	·	·	1	·	·	·	·	·	1	·	·	·	·	·
L. spicata	+	·	·	·	·	·	·	·	·	·	·	·	·	·	1
L. sylvatica	·	·	·	·	·	·	·	·	·	·	·	·	·	·	1
Narthecium ossifragum	·	·	·	·	·	·	·	·	·	·	·	·	2	·	1
Orchis ericetorum	·	·	·	·	·	·	·	·	·	·	·	·	·	·	·
Platanthera bifolia	·	·	·	·	·	·	·	·	·	·	·	·	·	·	·
Potamogeton polygonifolius	·	·	·	·	·	·	·	·	·	·	·	·	·	·	·
Schoenus nigricans	·	·	·	·	·	·	·	·	·	·	·	·	·	·	·
Tofieldia pusilla	2	+	·	·	1	+	·	2	4	3	+	2	1	·	·
Trichophorum caespitosum	·	·	2	·	·	2	·	1	1	·	·	·	1	1	·
Triglochin palustre	1	·	·	·	·	·	·	·	·	·	·	·	·	·	·
Alchemilla alpina	·	·	·	1	·	·	·	·	+	·	·	·	·	·	2
A. filicaulis	·	·	·	·	·	·	·	·	2	2	·	·	·	·	3
A. glabra	·	·	·	·	·	·	·	·	·	·	·	·	2	·	·
A. vestita	·	·	·	1	·	·	·	·	·	·	·	·	·	·	·
Armeria maritima	·	·	+	·	·	·	·	·	·	·	3	3	·	·	·
Campanula rotundifolia	·	·	·	·	·	·	·	·	1	·	·	·	·	·	·
Cerastium edmonstonii	·	·	·	·	·	·	·	·	·	·	·	·	·	·	·
Cherleria sedoides	·	·	·	·	·	·	·	·	·	·	·	·	·	·	·
Drosera anglica	·	·	·	·	·	·	·	·	·	·	·	·	·	·	·
D. intermedia	·	·	·	·	·	·	·	·	·	·	·	·	·	·	·
D. rotundifolia	·	·	·	·	·	·	·	·	·	·	·	·	·	·	·
Epilobium anagallidifolium	·	·	·	·	·	·	·	·	·	·	·	·	·	·	1
Euphrasia sp.	·	2	1	1	3	2	2	·	·	3	·	2	·	2	1
Galium boreale	·	·	·	·	·	·	·	·	1	·	·	·	·	·	·
G. hercynicum	·	·	·	·	·	·	·	·	1	·	·	·	·	·	·
Geum rivale	·	2	·	1	·	·	·	·	·	·	·	·	·	+	3
Hypericum pulchrum	·	·	·	1	·	·	·	·	·	·	·	·	·	·	·
Leontodon autumnalis	1	·	2	2	1	·	·	·	·	2	·	·	·	·	·
Linum catharticum	·	1	·	2	1	2	·	·	·	·	·	2	·	·	·
Lotus corniculatus	·	·	·	1	·	·	·	·	·	·	·	·	·	·	·
Menyanthes trifoliata	·	·	·	·	·	·	·	·	·	·	·	·	·	·	·
Oxyria digyna	·	·	·	·	·	·	·	·	·	·	·	·	·	·	·
Pedicularis palustris	·	·	·	·	·	·	1	·	·	·	·	·	·	·	·
P. sylvatica	·	·	·	·	·	·	·	·	·	·	·	·	·	·	·
Pinguicula lusitanica	·	·	·	·	·	·	·	·	·	·	·	·	·	·	·

facies (19–25)]; Schoenus nigricans provisional nodum (26–29)

16	17	18	19	20	21	22	23	24	25	26	27	28	29	
R56	R56	P52	R56	R56	R57	R58	R57	R57	P55	M58	P55	R58	R58	Reference number
065	086	198	088	058	243	140	031	030	014	051	020	141	002	
8729	8807	7405	8815	8626	7776	8004	9425	9422	9346	7647	9151	7949	9613	Map reference
2069	2203	2635	2118	2038	3289	1392	2223	2235	2237	1737	2092	1348	2689	
2100	1100	2650	1000	1400	200	500	600	–	100	600	450	150	100	Altitude (feet)
360	270	210	90	225	270	180	180	–	225	45	315	270	270	Aspect (degrees)
5	25	0	10	15	25	10	8	2	17	5	2	0	5	Slope (degrees)
20	60	80	50	80	95	30	70	80	80	80	80	100	100	Cover (per cent)
–	–	–	–	–	–	–	–	–	15	15	30	–	32	Height (centimetres)
16	16	1	16	16	4	4	4	4	4	4	4	4	4	Plot area (square metres)
·	·	·	2	·	·	2	·	·	·	·	·	·	·	Calluna vulgaris
·	·	·	·	·	·	·	·	·	·	·	·	·	·	Empetrum hermaphroditum
·	·	·	3	3	3	·	3	1	·	2	3	·	·	Erica tetralix
·	·	·	·	·	·	·	·	·	·	·	2	·	·	Myrica gale
·	·	·	·	·	·	·	·	·	·	·	·	·	·	Equisetum hyemale
·	·	·	·	·	·	·	·	·	·	·	·	·	·	E. palustre
·	·	·	·	·	·	·	·	·	·	·	·	·	·	E. variegatum
·	·	·	·	·	·	·	·	·	·	·	·	·	·	Lycopodium selago
2	2	·	·	2	1	·	3	·	3	2	·	·	·	Selaginella selaginoides
2	·	·	·	·	·	·	·	·	·	·	·	·	·	Agrostis canina
·	·	2	·	·	·	·	·	·	·	·	·	·	3	A. stolonifera
2	·	·	·	·	·	·	·	·	·	·	·	·	·	A. tenuis
·	·	·	·	·	·	·	·	·	·	·	·	·	·	Anthoxanthum odoratum
·	·	·	·	·	·	·	·	·	·	·	·	·	·	Briza media
3	·	·	·	·	·	·	·	·	·	·	·	·	·	Deschampsia caespitosa
·	·	·	·	·	·	·	·	·	·	·	·	·	·	D. flexuosa
3	4	·	·	2	·	·	·	·	·	·	·	·	·	Festuca ovina agg.
3	·	·	·	·	·	·	·	·	·	·	·	·	·	F. rubra
·	4	·	2	3	3	2	2	3	·	2	4	4	·	Molinia caerulea
·	·	·	·	·	·	·	·	·	·	·	·	·	·	Nardus stricta
·	·	·	·	·	·	·	·	·	·	·	·	·	·	Sieglingia decumbens
·	·	·	·	·	·	·	·	·	·	·	·	·	·	Carex atrofusca
·	·	·	·	·	·	·	·	·	·	·	·	·	·	C. bigelowii
3	5	4	2	·	·	·	3	·	2	·	2	·	·	C. demissa
3	4	2	3	·	·	3	·	·	·	2	·	·	·	C. dioica
·	1	·	2	·	·	·	·	·	2	·	3	·	·	C. echinata
·	·	·	·	·	·	·	·	·	·	·	·	·	·	C. flacca
·	5	·	4	4	6	+	4	·	3	·	·	·	·	C. hostiana
·	·	·	·	·	·	2	·	·	1	·	·	4	1	C. nigra
3	4	3	3	3	4	2	1	·	·	1	·	4	3	C. panicea
2	2	·	2	·	·	·	·	·	·	·	·	·	·	C. pulicaris
·	·	·	·	·	·	·	·	·	·	·	2	·	·	C. rostrata
·	·	·	·	·	·	·	·	·	·	·	·	·	·	C. saxatilis
·	·	·	2	·	·	·	·	·	·	·	·	·	·	Eleocharis multicaulis
·	3	3	·	4	3	4	·	·	4	·	·	3	·	E. pauciflora
2	1	·	·	1	3	·	2	3	1	1	2	3	3	Eriophorum angustifolium
·	3	·	3	+	3	3	+	·	·	·	·	·	·	E. latifolium
·	·	·	·	·	·	·	·	·	·	·	·	·	·	Juncus alpinus
·	5	·	4	3	3	3	·	·	·	2	·	4	·	J. articulatus
2	·	3	2	3	2	2	·	1	·	·	·	3	·	J. kochii
·	·	·	1	·	·	·	·	·	·	·	·	·	·	J. squarrosus
3	·	2	·	·	·	·	·	·	·	·	·	·	·	J. triglumis
2	·	·	·	·	·	·	·	·	·	·	·	·	·	Luzula multiflora
·	·	·	·	·	·	·	·	·	·	·	·	·	·	L. spicata
·	+	1	2	4	2	·	·	3	1	·	2	·	·	L. sylvatica
·	·	·	·	·	·	·	·	·	·	·	·	·	·	Narthecium ossifragum
·	+	1	2	4	2	·	3	1	·	·	2	·	·	Orchis ericetorum
·	·	·	·	·	·	·	·	·	·	·	2	·	·	Platanthera bifolia
·	·	·	·	·	1	·	·	1	2	4	·	·	·	Potamogeton polygonifolius
·	·	·	·	·	5	6	6	6	7	8	8	9		Schoenus nigricans
·	2	·	·	·	2	1	·	·	·	·	·	·	·	Tofieldia pusilla
+	·	·	4	3	·	2	6	4	2	4	·	·	·	Trichophorum caespitosum
·	·	·	+	·	1	·	·	·	·	·	·	·	·	Triglochin palustre
2	·	·	·	·	·	·	·	·	·	·	·	·	·	Alchemilla alpina
1	·	·	·	·	·	·	·	·	·	·	·	·	·	A. filicaulis
·	·	·	·	·	·	·	·	·	·	·	·	·	·	A. glabra
3	·	·	·	·	·	·	·	·	·	·	·	·	·	A. vestita
·	·	·	·	·	·	·	·	·	·	·	·	·	·	Armeria maritima
2	·	·	·	·	·	·	·	·	·	·	·	·	·	Campanula rotundifolia
·	·	·	·	·	·	·	·	·	·	·	·	·	·	Cerastium edmonstonii
3	·	·	·	·	·	·	·	·	·	·	·	·	·	Cherleria sedoides
·	·	·	3	4	·	2	+	2	1	·	3	·	·	Drosera anglica
·	·	·	·	·	·	·	·	·	·	3	·	·	·	D. intermedia
·	2	·	2	·	1	·	·	1	·	·	2	·	·	D. rotundifolia
·	·	·	·	·	·	·	·	·	·	·	·	·	·	Epilobium anagallidifolium
·	2	·	3	3	·	·	·	·	·	·	·	·	·	Euphrasia sp.
·	·	·	·	·	·	·	·	·	·	·	·	·	·	Galium boreale
·	·	·	·	·	·	·	·	·	·	·	·	·	·	G. hercynicum
·	·	·	·	·	·	·	·	·	·	·	·	·	·	Geum rivale
·	·	+	1	·	·	·	·	·	·	·	·	·	·	Hypericum pulchrum
·	·	·	·	·	·	·	·	·	·	·	·	·	2	Leontodon autumnalis
·	·	·	·	·	·	·	·	·	·	·	·	·	·	Linum catharticum
·	·	·	·	·	·	·	·	·	·	·	·	·	·	Lotus corniculatus
·	·	·	·	·	·	·	·	·	·	·	2	·	·	Menyanthes trifoliata
+	·	·	·	·	·	·	·	·	·	·	·	·	·	Oxyria digyna
·	·	·	·	·	·	+	·	·	·	·	·	·	·	Pedicularis palustris
·	3	+	·	·	1	·	·	·	·	·	·	·	·	P. sylvatica
·	·	·	1	·	1	·	2	·	1	3	·	·	·	Pinguicula lusitanica

Table 64

	1	2	3	4	5	6	7	8	9	10	11	12	13	14	15
Pinguicula vulgaris	2	2	.	.	2	2	.	2	+	2	2	2	2	2	2
Plantago maritima	.	3	2	3	.	.	.	.	.	3	.	.	1	1	.
Polygonum viviparum	.	+	.	.	.	.	.	.	1	.	1	.	.	.	.
Potentilla erecta	.	1	.	1	.	.	.	.	2	.	.	.	.	.	+
Prunella vulgaris	.	.	.	.	.	.	.	.	.	.	.	.	.	.	.
Ranunculus acris	.	2	.	.	.	.	.	.	.	.	.	.	.	+	2
R. flammula	.	.	2	2	.	.	.	3	.	.	.	.	.	3	.
Rhinanthus minor agg.	.	.	+	.	.	.	.	.	.	.	.	.	.	.	.
Rumex acetosa	.	.	.	.	.	.	.	.	.	.	.	.	.	.	2
Sagina nodosa	2	.	.	.	.	.	+	.	.	.	.	.	.	.	.
Saussurea alpina	.	.	.	.	.	.	.	.	.	1	.	.	.	.	.
Saxifraga aizoides	4	4	4	5	5	4	4	5	2	5	4	4	6	1	3
S. oppositifolia	3	3	.	.	.	.	.	.	5	.	2	.	.	4	3
S. stellaris	.	.	.	.	.	.	.	1	.	.	.	.	.	2	2
Silene acaulis	.	2	.	.	.	.	.	.	.	.	.	.	.	.	.
Succisa pratensis	.	.	.	1	.	.	.	1	.	+	.	.	.	.	.
Taraxacum sp.	.	2	.	1	.	.	.	2	2	2	.	.	.	.	2
Thalictrum alpinum	3	4	2	2	1	1	.	5	5	4	+	.	3	1	2
Thymus drucei	.	3	+	+	.	.	.	2	1	.	.	.	.	.	+
Tussilago farfara	.	.	.	.	.	.	1	.	.	.	.	2	.	.	.
Utricularia intermedia	.	.	.	.	.	.	.	.	.	.	.	.	.	.	.
U. minor	.	.	.	.	.	.	.	.	.	.	.	.	.	.	.
Viola palustris	.	2	.	1	.	.	.	1	.	.	.	.	.	+	+
V. riviniana	.	.	.	.	.	.	.	.	2	.	.	.	.	.	.
Acrocladium sarmentosum	.	.	.	.	.	.	.	.	.	.	.	.	.	1	3
A. stramineum	.	.	.	.	.	.	1	.	.	.	.	.	.	.	.
A. trifarium	.	.	.	.	.	.	.	.	.	.	3	.	.	.	.
Anomobryum filiforme	.	.	.	.	.	.	.	.	.	.	.	.	.	.	3
Blindia acuta	5	3	4	4	2	2	.	4	3	2	3	.	2	7	3
Brachythecium rutabulum	.	.	.	.	.	.	.	.	.	1	.	.	.	.	.
Breutelia chrysocoma	.	.	.	.	.	.	1	.	.	2	.	.	.	.	.
Bryum pseudotriquetrum	.	1	.	2	.	.	1	.	.	.	.	2	.	.	.
Camptothecium lutescens	.	.	.	.	.	.	.	.	.	2	.	.	.	.	.
Campylium stellatum	4	3	2	3	.	3	.	.	2	.	.	2	2	.	1
Campylopus atrovirens	.	.	.	.	.	.	.	.	.	.	.	.	.	.	.
Catoscopium nigritum	.	.	.	.	.	2	.	.	.	.	.	.	.	.	.
Cratoneuron commutatum	4	.	.	.	4	4	2	.	.	5	+	4	+	.	.
Ctenidium molluscum	.	2	.	2	.	2	.	.	3	2	.	2	.	.	1
Dicranella squarrosa	2	.	.	.	.	.	.	.	.	.	.	.	1	.	3
Ditrichum flexicaule	.	.	.	.	.	2	.	.	.	.	.	.	.	.	.
Drepanocladus revolvens	5	+	.	3	1	2	.	4	5	4	6	.	1	1	4
Fissidens adianthoides	3	.	.	.	.	2	.	.	.	.	.	.	.	.	.
F. osmundoides	.	.	.	2	.	.	.	.	1	4	.	.	.	.	.
Gymnostomum recurvirostrum	.	.	.	.	.	.	.	.	.	.	.	3	.	.	.
Hylocomium splendens	.	.	.	1	.	.	.	.	1	2	.	.	.	.	1
Meesia uliginosa	.	.	.	.	.	.	.	.	.	.	.	+	.	.	.
Mnium seligeri	.	.	.	.	.	.	.	.	.	1	.	.	.	.	.
Orthothecium rufescens	.	.	.	.	.	3	.	.	.	.	.	3	.	.	.
Philonotis calcarea	.	.	.	.	.	.	.	.	.	.	.	1	.	.	.
P. fontana	1	.	.	.	.	.	.	.	.	.	.	.	.	.	.
P. seriata	.	.	.	.	.	.	.	.	.	.	1	.	.	.	.
Pohlia sp.	.	.	.	.	.	.	.	.	.	.	1	.	.	.	.
Pseudoscleropodium purum	.	1	.	.	.	.	.	.	.	.	.	.	.	.	.
Rhacomitrium lanuginosum	.	.	.	.	.	.	.	.	.	.	.	.	.	.	.
Rhytidiadelphus loreus	.	.	.	.	.	.	.	.	.	.	.	.	.	.	1
R. triquetrus	.	1	.	.	.	.	.	.	1	.	.	.	.	.	.
Scorpidium scorpioides	.	.	5	.	5	5	5	.	.	.	6	3	.	.	.
Sphagnum inundatum	.	.	.	.	.	.	.	.	.	.	.	.	.	.	.
Tortella tortuosa	.	.	.	.	.	+	.	.	.	.	.	.	.	.	.
Alicularia scalaris	.	.	.	.	.	.	.	.	.	.	.	.	.	1	.
Anastrepta orcadensis	.	.	.	.	.	.	.	.	.	1	.	.	.	.	.
Aneura pinguis	2	2	1	2	1	.	1	.	.	1	.	2	.	.	2
Anthelia julacea	.	.	.	.	.	.	.	+	.	.	.	.	.	1	.
Blepharostoma trichophyllum	.	.	.	.	.	.	.	.	.	1	.	.	.	.	.
Calypogeia fissa	.	.	.	.	.	.	.	.	.	.	.	.	.	.	.
Eucalyx paroicus	.	.	.	.	.	.	.	.	.	.	.	.	.	.	2
Lophozia bantriensis	.	.	.	.	.	.	.	.	.	.	.	+	.	.	.
L. quadriloba	.	.	.	.	.	.	.	.	.	1	.	.	.	.	.
Marsupella emarginata	.	.	.	.	.	.	.	.	1	1	.	.	.	.	4
Pellia fabbroniana	.	.	.	.	.	.	.	.	.	.	.	.	.	.	1
Plagiochila asplenioides	.	.	.	.	.	.	.	.	.	2	.	.	.	.	.
P. spinulosa	.	.	.	.	.	.	.	.	.	2	.	.	.	.	.
Pleurozia purpurea	.	.	.	.	.	.	.	.	.	.	.	.	.	.	.
Scapania undulata	.	.	.	.	.	.	.	.	.	+	.	.	.	1	.	4
Number of species (133) (56) (49)	29	34	28	40	23	27	22	30	35	43	23	28	21	28	43

(Average 30)

Constancy class V 8
,, ,, IV 5

LOCALITIES

1. Glen Doll, Clova, Angus; 2. Am Faochagach, Strath Vaich, Ross-shire; 3, 16. Mullach Coire Mhic Fhearchair, Ross-shire; 4. Sgurr Mhic Bharraich, Loch Duich, Ross-shire; 5. Glen Markie, Monadhliath, Inverness-shire; 6. Ardtulichan, Killiecrankie, Perthshire; 7. Braemar, Aberdeenshire; 8, 17. Beinn Enaiglair, Inverlael, Ross-shire; 9. Sgurr a' Ghlas Leathaid, Strath Bran, Ross-shire; 10. Meall Mor, Glencoe, Argyll; 11. Ben Alder range, Inverness-shire; 12. Meall Breac, Blair Atholl, Perthshire; 13. Beinn Lair, Letterewe Forest, Ross-shire; 14.

(continued)

16	17	18	19	20	21	22	23	24	25	26	27	28	29	
1	2	3	2	1	1	2	1	2	1	2	1	·	2	**Pinguicula vulgaris**
4	2	·	·	2	·	·	·	·	·	·	·	·	·	Plantago maritima
1	·	·	·	·	·	·	·	·	·	·	·	·	·	Polygonum viviparum
·	·	·	·	·	2	·	·	·	1	2	·	2	·	Potentilla erecta
·	·	·	·	·	·	·	·	·	·	·	·	·	3	Prunella vulgaris
1	·	·	·	·	·	·	·	·	·	·	·	·	·	Ranunculus acris
·	·	·	·	2	·	·	·	·	·	·	·	·	·	R. flammula
·	·	·	·	·	·	·	·	·	·	·	·	·	·	Rhinanthus minor agg.
·	·	·	·	·	·	·	·	·	·	·	·	·	·	Rumex acetosa
·	·	·	·	·	·	·	·	·	·	·	·	·	·	Sagina nodosa
+	·	·	·	·	·	·	·	·	·	·	·	·	·	Saussurea alpina
3	4	3	4	+	4	·	3	·	·	·	·	·	+	**Saxifraga aizoides**
+	·	·	·	·	·	·	·	·	·	·	·	·	·	S. oppositifolia
1	·	·	·	·	·	·	·	·	·	·	·	·	·	S. stellaris
3	·	·	·	·	·	·	·	·	·	·	·	·	·	Silene acaulis
2	·	·	2	1	·	1	·	1	·	2	·	·	·	Succisa pratensis
·	·	·	·	1	·	·	·	·	·	·	·	·	·	Taraxacum sp.
3	2	·	·	·	·	·	·	·	·	·	·	·	·	**Thalictrum alpinum**
2	·	·	·	·	·	·	·	·	·	·	·	·	·	Thymus drucei
·	·	·	·	·	·	·	·	·	·	·	·	·	·	Tussilago farfara
·	·	·	·	·	·	·	·	·	·	·	3	·	·	Utricularia intermedia
·	·	·	·	·	·	·	·	·	·	3	·	·	·	U. minor
1	·	·	·	·	·	·	·	·	·	·	·	·	·	Viola palustris
·	·	·	·	·	·	·	·	·	·	·	·	·	·	V. riviniana
·	·	·	·	·	·	·	·	·	·	·	·	·	·	Acrocladium sarmentosum
·	·	·	·	·	·	·	·	·	·	·	·	·	·	A. stramineum
·	·	4	·	·	·	·	·	·	·	·	·	·	·	A. trifarium
·	·	·	2	·	·	·	·	·	·	·	·	·	·	Anomobryum filiforme
3	4	·	3	3	1	·	3	·	·	2	·	·	·	**Blindia acuta**
·	·	·	·	·	·	·	·	·	·	·	·	·	·	Brachythecium rutabulum
·	·	·	·	·	·	2	·	·	·	3	·	·	·	Breutelia chrysocoma
·	·	·	1	2	·	·	·	·	·	·	·	·	3	Bryum pseudotriquetrum
·	·	·	·	·	·	·	·	·	·	·	·	·	·	Camptothecium lutescens
·	4	·	4	5	3	3	4	3	4	3	5	1	5	**Campylium stellatum**
·	·	·	1	·	·	·	2	·	·	·	1	·	·	Campylopus atrovirens
·	·	·	·	·	·	·	·	·	·	·	·	·	·	Catoscopium nigritum
·	2	1	+	·	4	1	·	·	·	·	·	·	5	Cratoneuron commutatum
·	3	·	2	·	1	·	4	3	·	·	·	·	·	Ctenidium molluscum
·	·	·	·	1	·	·	·	·	·	·	·	·	·	Dicranella squarrosa
·	·	·	·	·	·	·	·	·	·	·	·	·	·	Ditrichum flexicaule
·	3	·	3	2	3	·	3	·	·	5	·	·	3	Drepanocladus revolvens
·	1	·	1	·	·	·	·	·	·	·	·	·	·	Fissidens adianthoides
·	·	·	·	·	·	·	·	·	·	·	·	·	·	F. osmundoides
·	·	·	·	·	·	·	·	·	·	·	·	·	·	Gymnostomum recurvirostrum
·	·	1	·	1	·	·	·	·	·	·	1	·	·	Hylocomium splendens
·	·	·	·	·	·	·	·	·	·	·	·	·	·	Meesia uliginosa
·	·	·	·	·	·	·	·	·	·	·	·	·	·	Mnium seligeri
·	·	·	·	·	·	·	·	·	·	·	·	·	·	Orthothecium rufescens
·	·	·	·	·	·	·	·	·	·	·	·	·	3	Philonotis calcarea
·	·	·	·	·	·	·	·	·	·	·	·	·	·	P. fontana
·	·	·	·	·	·	·	·	·	·	·	·	·	·	P. seriata
·	·	·	·	·	·	·	·	·	·	·	·	·	·	Pohlia sp.
·	·	·	·	·	·	·	·	·	·	·	·	·	·	Pseudoscleropodium purum
·	2	·	3	·	·	·	2	·	·	2	2	·	·	Rhacomitrium lanuginosum
·	·	·	·	·	·	·	·	·	·	·	·	·	·	Rhytidiadelphus loreus
·	·	·	·	·	·	·	·	·	·	·	·	·	·	R. triquetrus
·	5	6	3	6	8	2	6	5	3	·	3	·	·	**Scorpidium scorpioides**
·	·	1	·	·	·	·	·	·	·	·	3	·	·	Sphagnum inundatum
·	·	·	·	·	·	·	·	·	·	·	·	·	·	Tortella tortuosa
·	·	·	·	·	·	·	·	·	·	·	·	·	·	Alicularia scalaris
·	·	·	·	·	·	·	·	·	·	·	·	·	·	Anastrepta orcadensis
2	2	·	2	2	2	·	·	1	·	2	2	·	·	Aneura pinguis
·	·	·	·	·	·	·	·	·	·	·	·	·	·	Anthelia julacea
·	2	·	·	·	·	·	·	·	·	·	·	·	·	Blepharostoma trichophyllum
·	·	·	·	·	·	·	·	·	·	·	·	·	·	Calypogeia fissa
·	·	·	·	·	·	·	·	·	·	·	·	·	·	Eucalyx paroicus
·	·	·	·	·	·	·	·	·	·	·	·	·	·	Lophozia bantriensis
·	·	·	·	·	·	·	·	·	·	·	·	·	·	L. quadriloba
·	·	·	·	·	·	·	·	·	·	·	·	·	·	Marsupella emarginata
·	·	·	·	·	·	·	·	·	·	·	·	1	1	Pellia fabbroniana
·	·	·	·	·	·	·	·	·	·	·	·	·	2	Plagiochila asplenioides
·	·	·	·	·	·	·	·	·	·	·	·	·	·	P. spinulosa
·	·	·	·	·	·	·	·	2	·	2	1	·	·	Pleurozia purpurea
·	·	·	·	·	·	·	·	·	·	·	·	·	·	Scapania undulata
36	32	13	30	32	28	20	19	19	20	24	23	14	16	Number of species (133) (56) (49)

(Average 24)   (Average 19)

Moruisg, Strath Carron, Ross-shire; 15. The Saddle, Glen Shiel, Ross-shire; 18. Ben Lawers, Perthshire; 19. Nr. Dundonnell, Ross-shire; 20. Culaneilan, Kinlochewe, Ross-shire; 21. Moulzie, Glen Clova, Angus; 22. Kinloch Glen, Isle of Rhum, Inverness-shire; 23. Ben Stack, Sutherland; 24. Loch Eilanach, Ben Stack, Sutherland; 25. Glendhu, Kylesku, Sutherland; 26. Ben Resipol, Sunart, Argyll; 27. Loch Buine Moire, Inverpolly, Ross-shire; 28. Harris Glen, Isle of Rhum, Inverness-shire; 29. Druim Chuibhe, Bettyhill, Sutherland.

VEGETATION DISTRIBUTION MAPS

The system of mapping follows that used by the Botanical Society of the British Isles in constructing maps for the distribution of individual species of vascular plants (see Walters, 1954). Symbols are here used to show vegetational distribution; each 10 km. grid square containing a well-developed stand of the particular nodum is marked by a dot, circle or square. Fragmentary stands are shown by a smaller symbol, but this method of representation does not otherwise indicate the relative extent of the nodum within each square. The same map is often used for two different noda, the occurrence of both in the same square being shown by a hybrid symbol.

In mapping distribution we have identified stands of a nodum in the field largely from previous experience, once the nodum has been defined by the required number of lists. This means that only some of the distribution records are based on floristic lists. In no case do we claim to have established the complete distribution of a nodum and many localities remain to be added to some maps. We have tried, however, to establish the *range* of noda and believe that the maps show the main patterns of distribution.

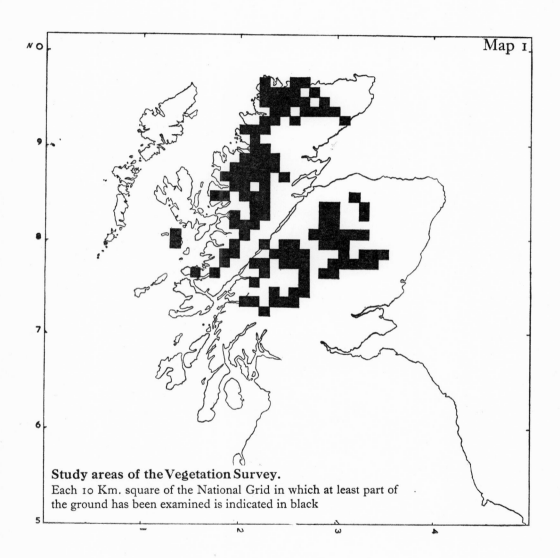

Map I

Study areas of the Vegetation Survey.
Each 10 Km. square of the National Grid in which at least part of
the ground has been examined is indicated in black

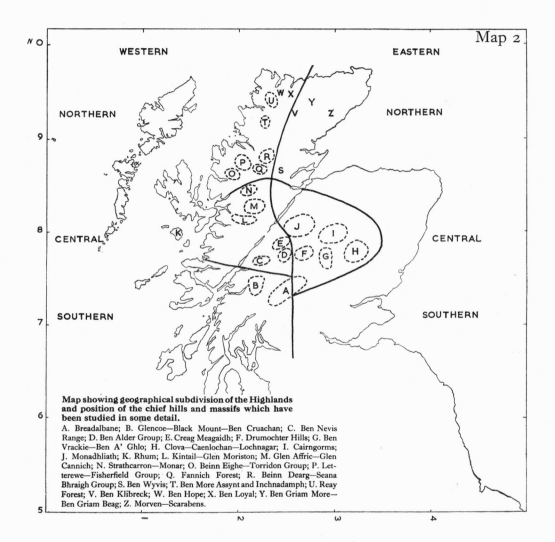

Map showing geographical subdivision of the Highlands and position of the chief hills and massifs which have been studied in some detail.

A. Breadalbane; B. Glencoe—Black Mount—Ben Cruachan; C. Ben Nevis Range; D. Ben Alder Group; E. Creag Meagaidh; F. Drumochter Hills; G. Ben Vrackie—Ben A' Ghlo; H. Clova—Caenlochan—Lochnagar; I. Cairngorms; J. Monadhliath; K. Rhum; L. Kintail—Glen Moriston; M. Glen Affric—Glen Cannich; N. Strathcarron—Monar; O. Beinn Eighe—Torridon Group; P. Letterewe—Fisherfield Group; Q. Fannich Forest; R. Beinn Dearg—Seana Bhraigh Group; S. Ben Wyvis; T. Ben More Assynt and Inchnadamph; U. Reay Forest; V. Ben Klibreck; W. Ben Hope; X. Ben Loyal; Y. Ben Griam More—Ben Griam Beag; Z. Morven—Scarabens.

Map 3

The main tendencies of woodland distribution

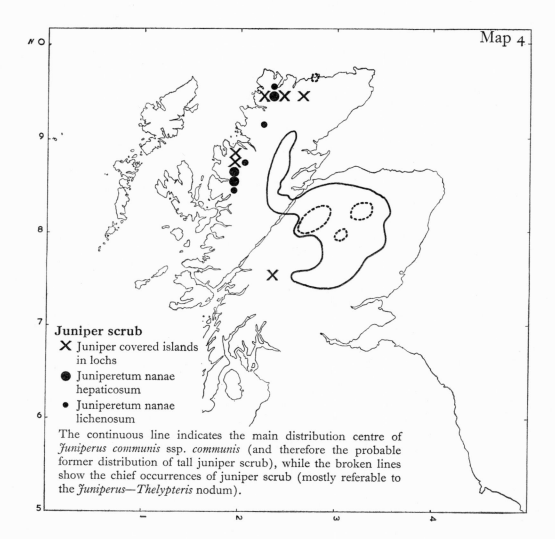

Map 4

Juniper scrub

✗ Juniper covered islands
    in lochs

⬤ Juniperetum nanae
    hepaticosum

• Juniperetum nanae
    lichenosum

The continuous line indicates the main distribution centre of
Juniperus communis ssp. *communis* (and therefore the probable
former distribution of tall juniper scrub), while the broken lines
show the chief occurrences of juniper scrub (mostly referable to
the *Juniperus—Thelypteris* nodum).

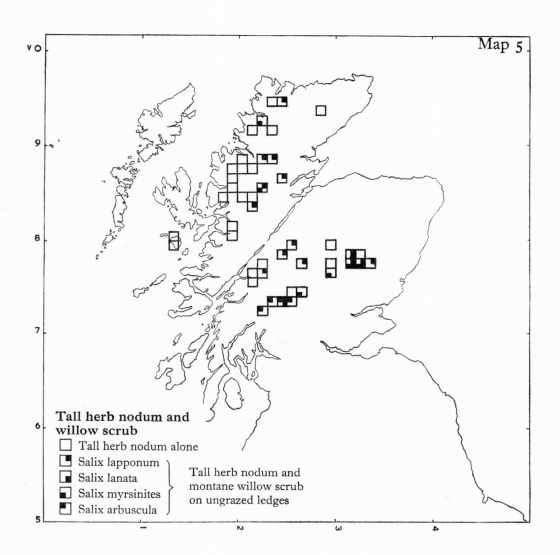

Map 5

Tall herb nodum and willow scrub

☐ Tall herb nodum alone

Salix lapponum

Salix lanata

Salix myrsinites

Salix arbuscula

Tall herb nodum and montane willow scrub on ungrazed ledges

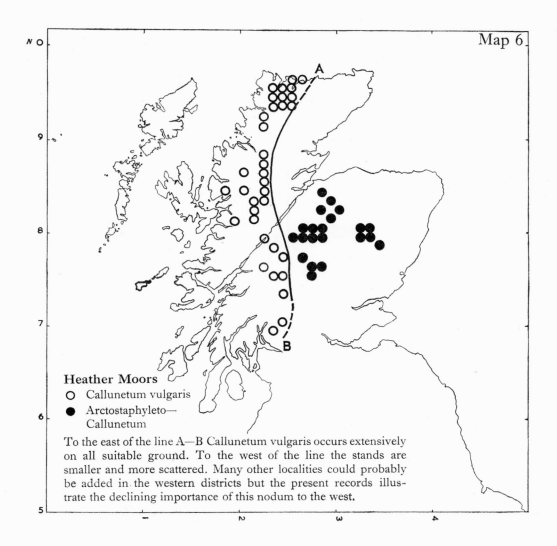

Map 6

Heather Moors

○ Callunetum vulgaris

● Arctostaphyleto—
  Callunetum

To the east of the line A—B Callunetum vulgaris occurs extensively on all suitable ground. To the west of the line the stands are smaller and more scattered. Many other localities could probably be added in the western districts but the present records illustrate the declining importance of this nodum to the west.

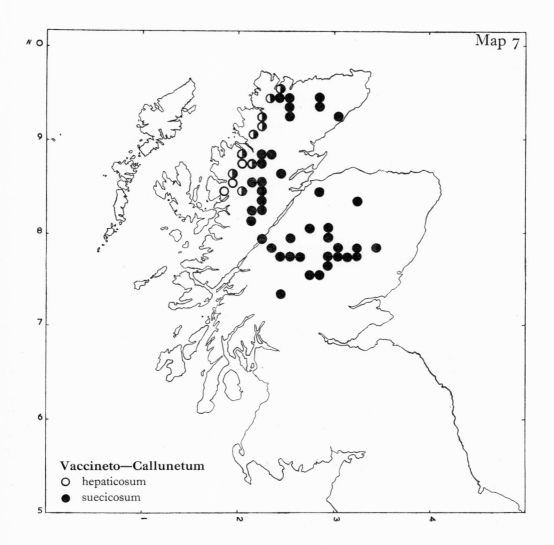

Map 7

Vaccineto—Callunetum
○ hepaticosum
● suecicosum

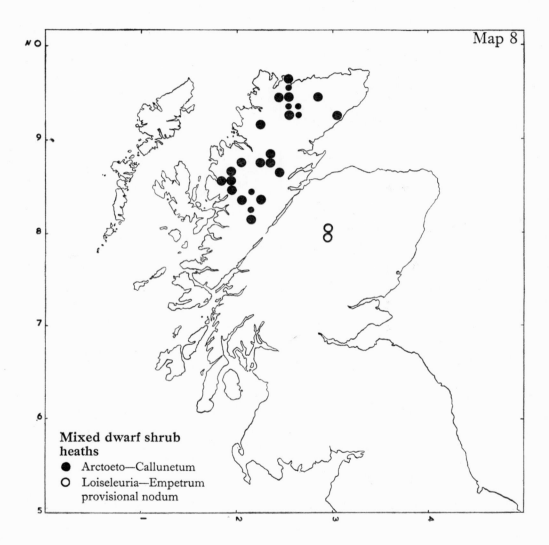

Map 8

Mixed dwarf shrub heaths
● Arctoeto—Callunetum
○ Loiseleuria—Empetrum provisional nodum

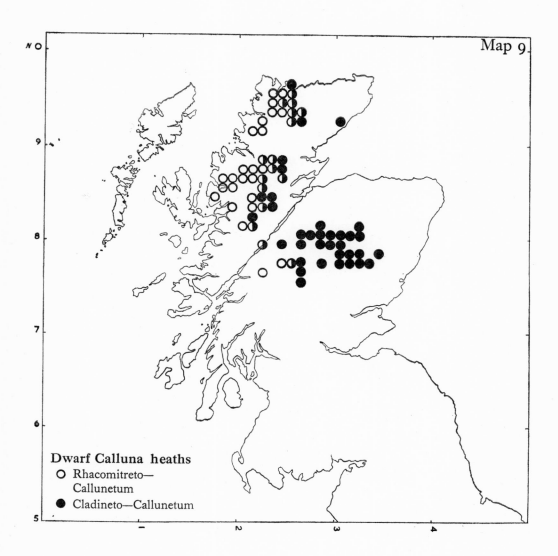

Map 9

Dwarf Calluna heaths
○ Rhacomitreto—
    Callunetum
● Cladineto—Callunetum

368

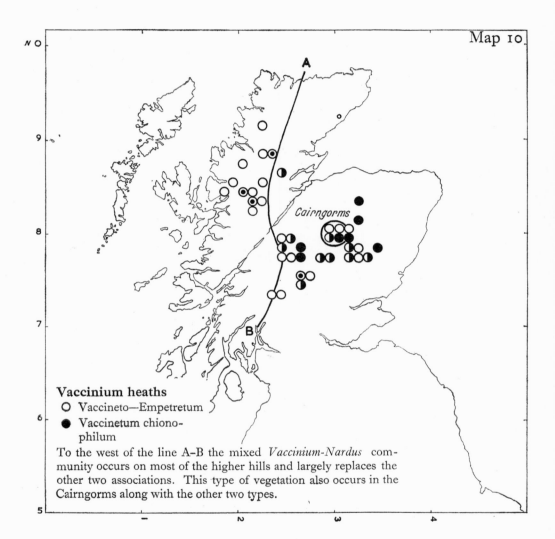

Vaccinium heaths
○ Vaccineto—Empetretum
● Vaccinetum chiono-
ph**il**um

To the west of the line A–B the mixed *Vaccinium-Nardus* community occurs on most of the higher hills and largely replaces the
other two associations. This type of vegetation also occurs in the
Cairngorms along with the other two types.

Map 10

Cairngorms

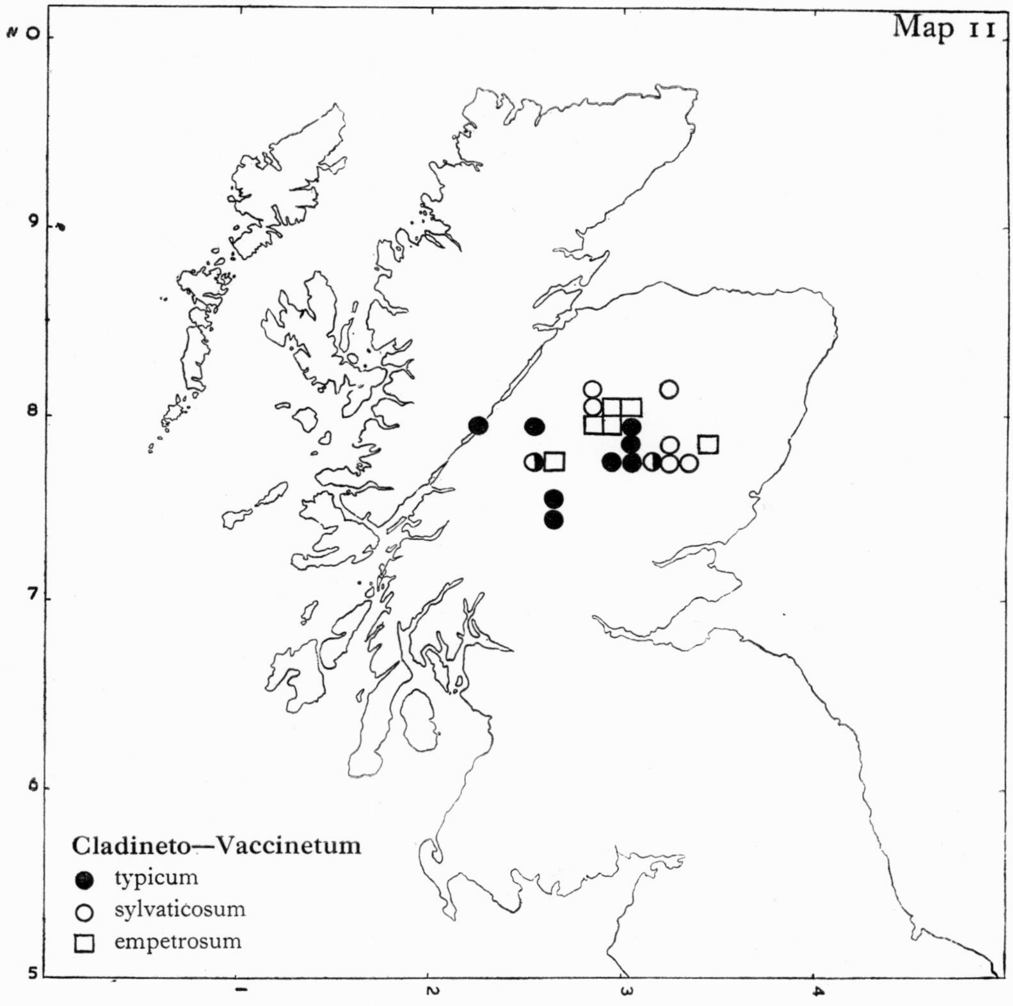
Map 11
NO
9
8
7
6
5
1
2
3
4
Cladineto—Vaccinetum
typicum
sylvaticosum
empetrosum

370

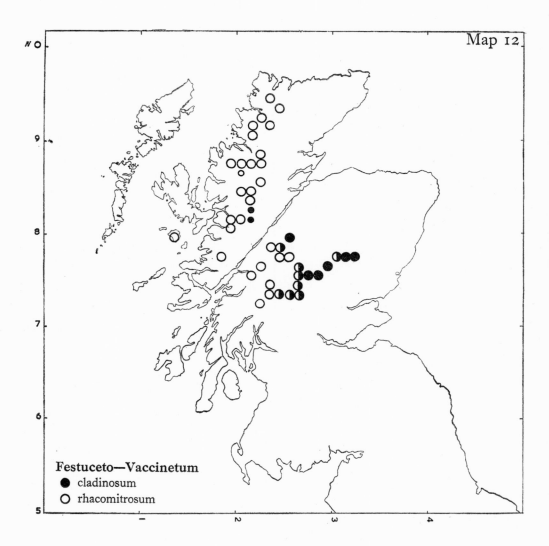

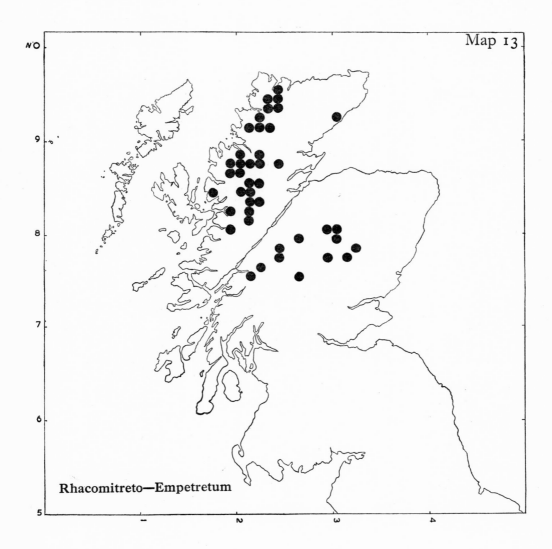

Map 13

Rhacomitreto—Empetretum

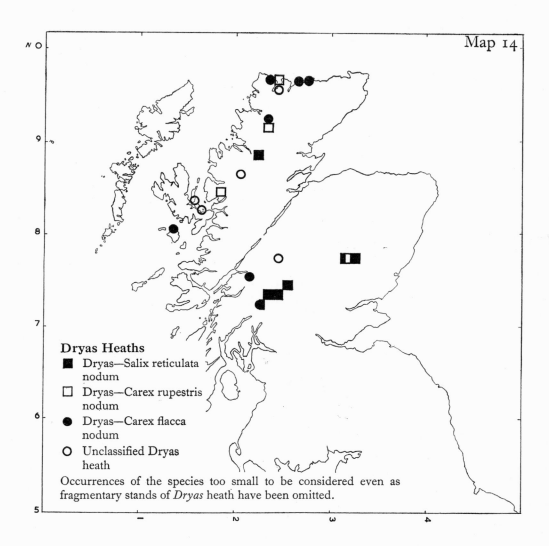

Map 14

Dryas Heaths

■ Dryas—Salix reticulata nodum

□ Dryas—Carex rupestris nodum

● Dryas—Carex flacca nodum

○ Unclassified Dryas heath

Occurrences of the species too small to be considered even as fragmentary stands of *Dryas* heath have been omitted.

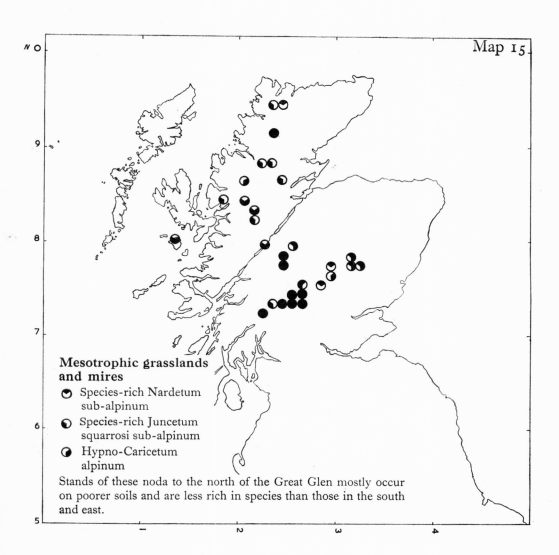

Map 15

Mesotrophic grasslands and mires

- Species-rich Nardetum sub-alpinum
- Species-rich Juncetum squarrosi sub-alpinum
- Hypno-Caricetum alpinum

Stands of these noda to the north of the Great Glen mostly occur on poorer soils and are less rich in species than those in the south and east.

374

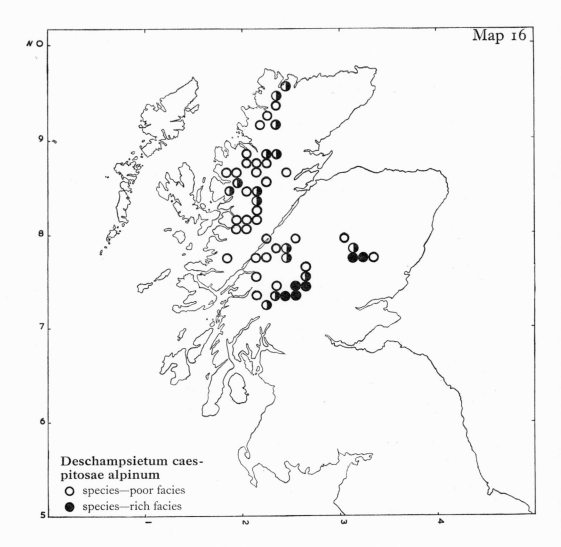

Map 16

**Deschampsietum caes-
pitosae alpinum**

○ species—poor facies

● species—rich facies

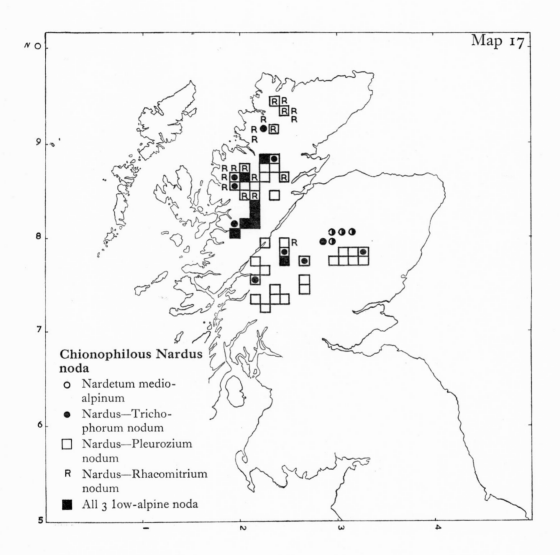

Map 17

Chionophilous Nardus noda

○ Nardetum medio-
alpinum

● Nardus—Tricho-
phorum nodum

□ Nardus—Pleurozium
nodum

R Nardus—Rhacomitrium
nodum

■ All 3 low-alpine noda

376

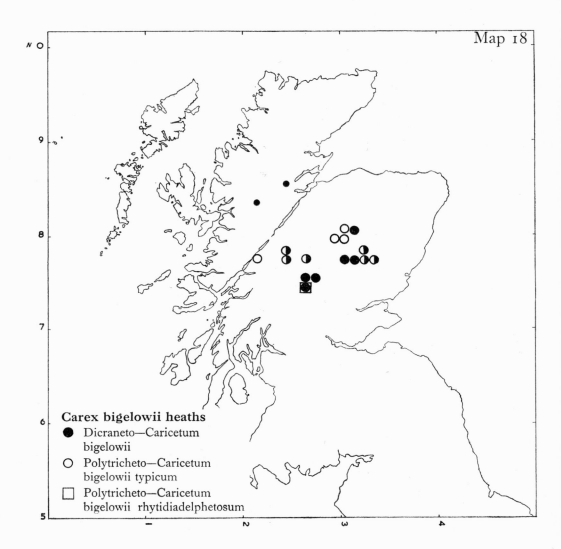

Map 18

Carex bigelowii heaths

● Dicraneto—Caricetum
   bigelowii

○ Polytricheto—Caricetum
   bigelowii typicum

☐ Polytricheto—Caricetum
   bigelowii rhytidiadelphetosum

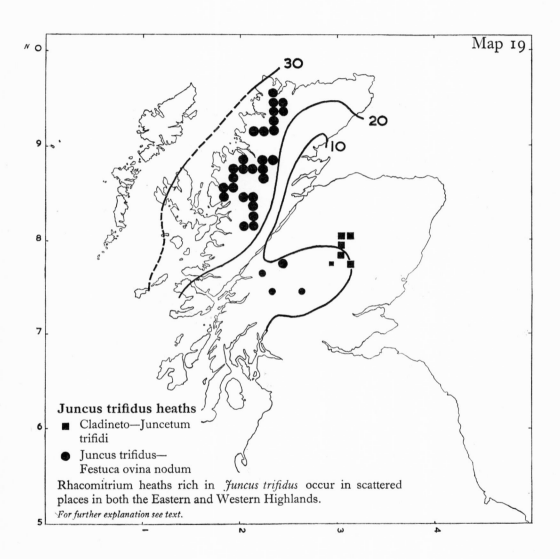

Map 19

Juncus trifidus heaths
■ Cladineto—Juncetum
trifidi
● Juncus trifidus—
Festuca ovina nodum

Rhacomitrium heaths rich in *Juncus trifidus* occur in scattered places in both the Eastern and Western Highlands.

For further explanation see text.

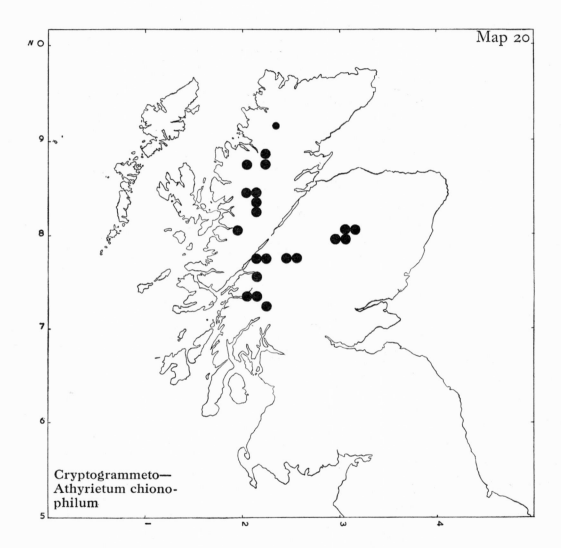

Map 20

Cryptogrammeto—
Athyrietum chiono-
philum

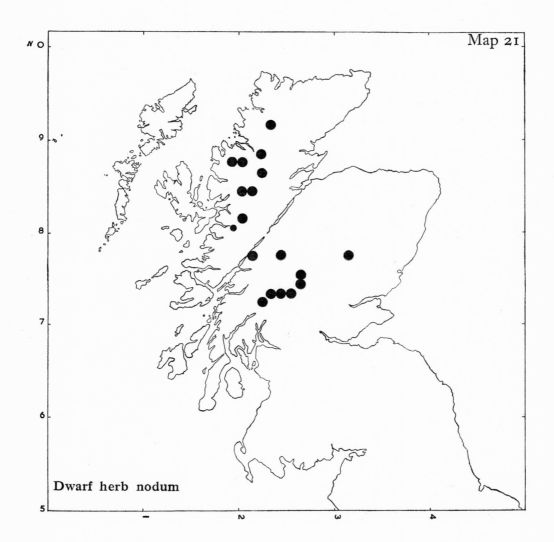

Map 21

Dwarf herb nodum

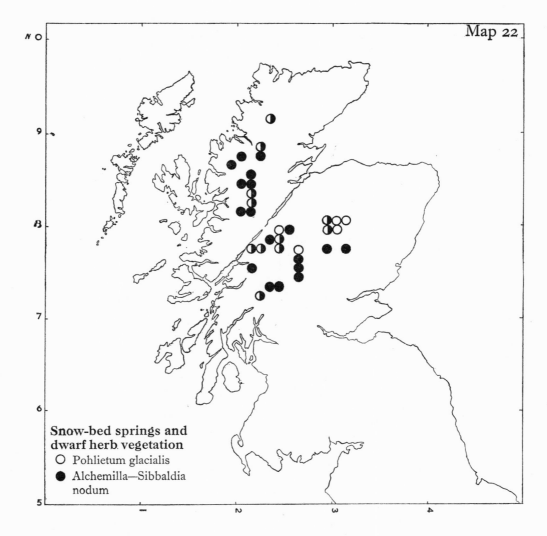

Map 22

Snow-bed springs and
dwarf herb vegetation
○ Pohlietum glacialis
● Alchemilla—Sibbaldia
nodum

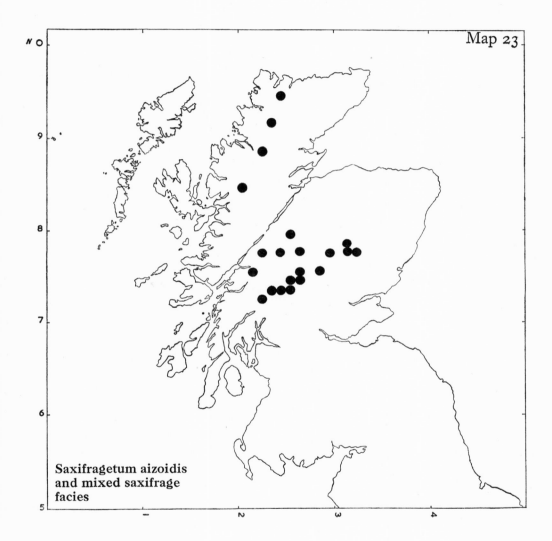

Map 23

Saxifragetum aizoidis
and mixed saxifrage
facies

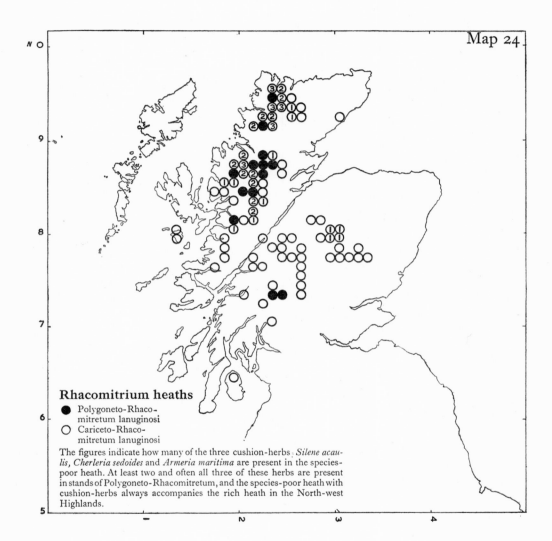

Map 24

Rhacomitrium heaths

● Polygoneto-Rhaco-
    mitretum lanuginosi
○ Cariceto-Rhaco-
    mitretum lanuginosi

The figures indicate how many of the three cushion-herbs *Silene acau-lis, Cherleria sedoides* and *Armeria maritima* are present in the species-poor heath. At least two and often all three of these herbs are present in stands of Polygoneto-Rhacomitretum, and the species-poor heath with cushion-herbs always accompanies the rich heath in the North-west Highlands.

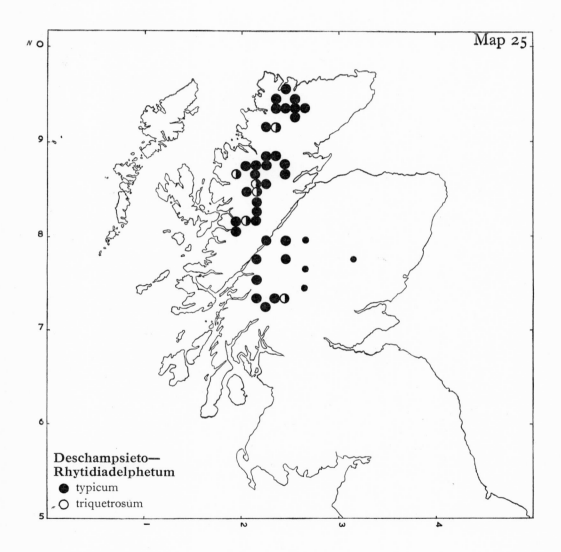

Map 25

**Deschampsieto—
Rhytidiadelphetum**
- ● typicum
- ○ triquetrosum

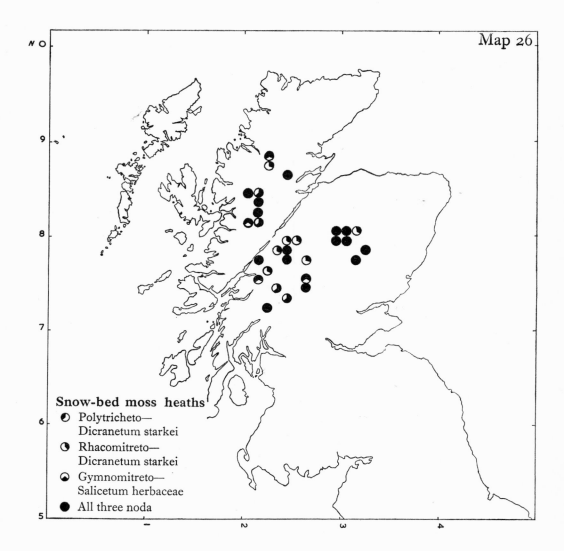

Map 26

Snow-bed moss heaths

- Polytricheto—
  Dicranetum starkei
- Rhacomitreto—
  Dicranetum starkei
- Gymnomitreto—
  Salicetum herbaceae
- All three noda

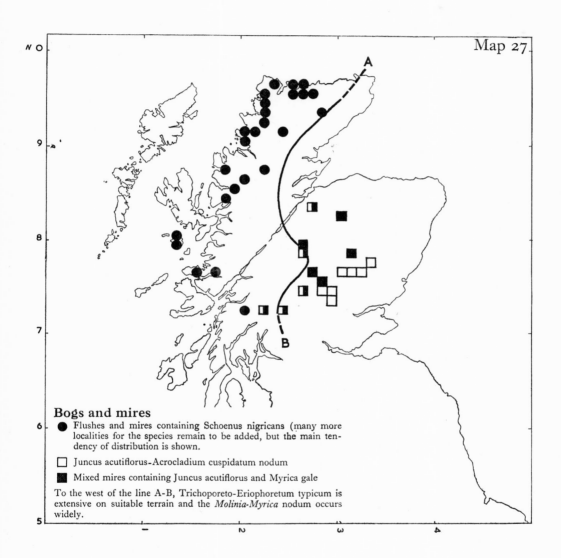

Bogs and mires

● Flushes and mires containing Schoenus nigricans (many more localities for the species remain to be added, but the main tendency of distribution is shown.

□ Juncus acutiflorus-Acrocladium cuspidatum nodum

■ Mixed mires containing Juncus acutiflorus and Myrica gale

To the west of the line A-B, Trichoporeto-Eriophoretum typicum is extensive on suitable terrain and the *Molinia-Myrica* nodum occurs widely.

Map 27

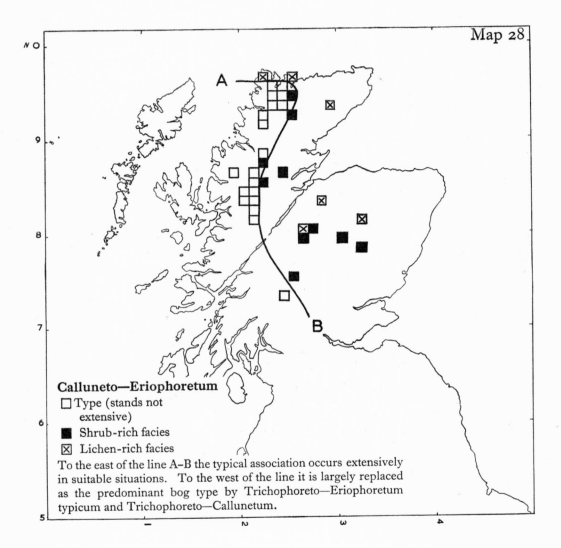

Map 28

Calluneto—Eriophoretum

☐ Type (stands not
   extensive)

■ Shrub-rich facies

☒ Lichen-rich facies

To the east of the line A–B the typical association occurs extensively
in suitable situations.   To the west of the line it is largely replaced
as the predominant bog type by Trichophoreto—Eriophoretum
typicum and Trichophoreto—Callunetum.

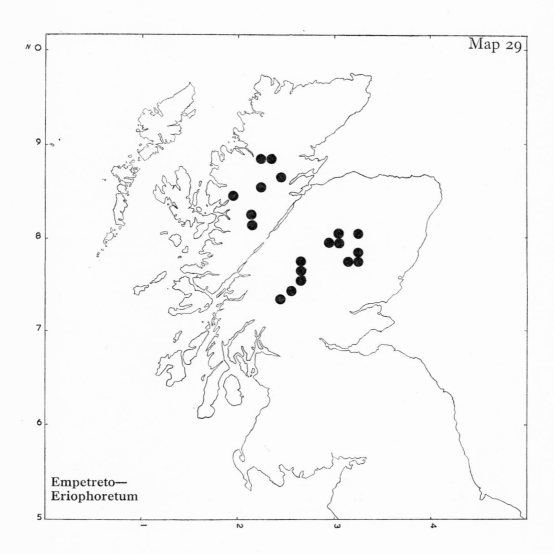

Map 29

Empetreto—
Eriophoretum

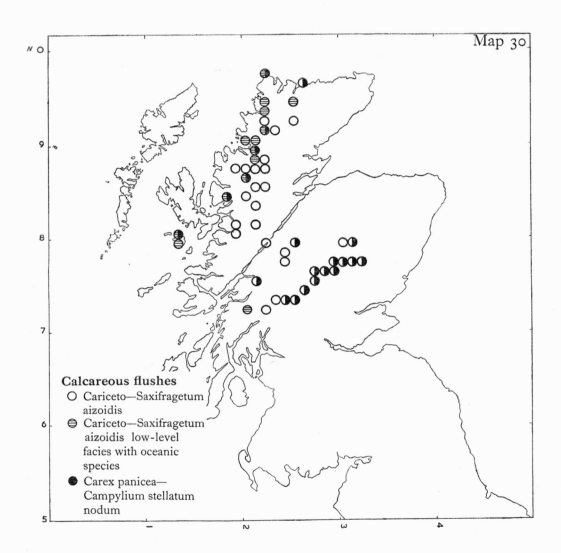

Map 30

Calcareous flushes

○ Cariceto—Saxifragetum aizoidis

⊖ Cariceto—Saxifragetum aizoidis low-level facies with oceanic species

● Carex panicea— Campylium stellatum nodum

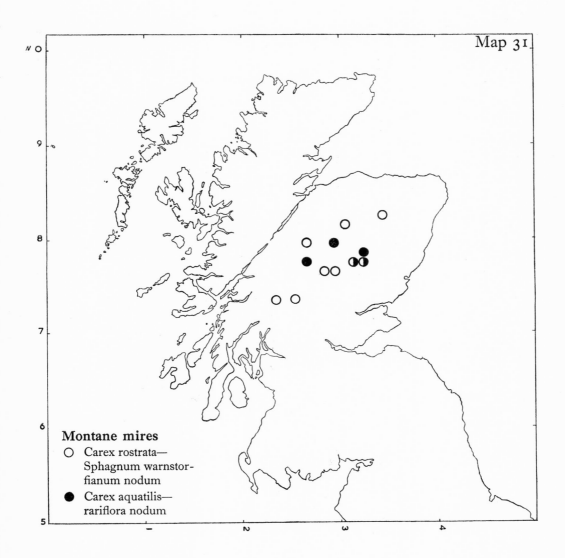

Map 31

Montane mires
○ Carex rostrata—
Sphagnum warnstor-
fianum nodum
● Carex aquatilis—
rariflora nodum

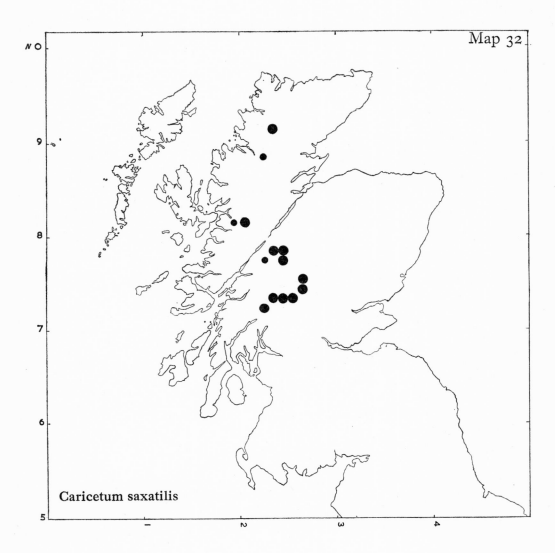

Map 32

Caricetum saxatilis

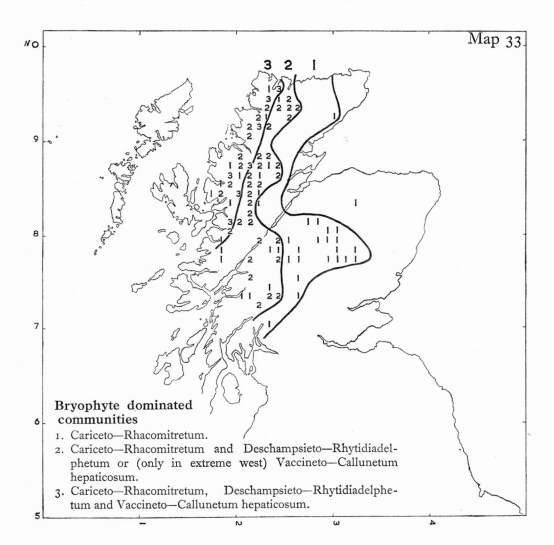

Map 33

Bryophyte dominated communities

1. Cariceto—Rhacomitretum.
2. Cariceto—Rhacomitretum and Deschampsieto—Rhytidiadel-phetum or (only in extreme west) Vaccineto—Callunetum hepaticosum.
3. Cariceto—Rhacomitretum, Deschampsieto—Rhytidiadelphe-tum and Vaccineto—Callunetum hepaticosum.

392

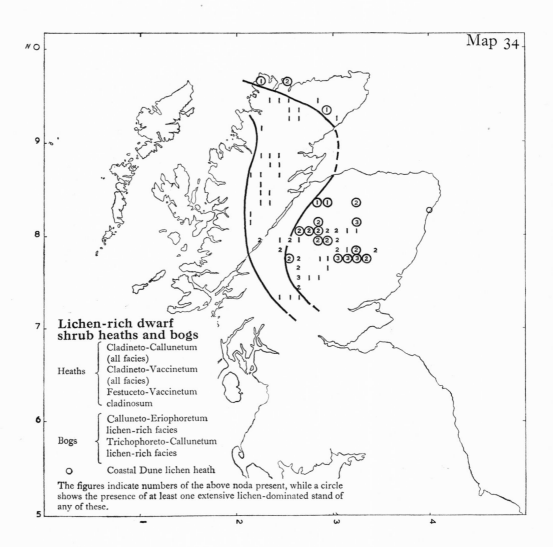

Map 34

Lichen-rich dwarf
shrub heaths and bogs

Heaths
⎰ Cladineto-Callunetum
⎱ (all facies)
   Cladineto-Vaccinetum
   (all facies)
   Festuceto-Vaccinetum
   cladinosum

Bogs
⎰ Calluneto-Eriophoretum
⎱ lichen-rich facies
   Trichophoreto-Callunetum
   lichen-rich facies

○   Coastal Dune lichen heath

The figures indicate numbers of the above noda present, while a circle
shows the presence of at least one extensive lichen-dominated stand of
any of these.

VEGETATION CHARTS

To give some idea of the range of vegetation likely to be found on a particular hill, areas of approximately 12–15 miles (19–24 km.) in diameter have been selected for each of the main regions of the Highlands and their noda arranged systematically (Figs. 31–36). Areas showing the greatest range of habitat and therefore of vegetation were chosen to represent the various regions: each includes at least one main massif and the adjoining low ground. Other lesser massifs and lower hills in the same region may have a narrower range of habitat and would then lack some of the noda of the 'type' area.

Vegetation types have been indicated in the charts in much the same order as they are dealt with in the text, but with a separation between the oligotrophic group on non-calcareous substrata and the mesotrophic-eutrophic group on calcareous substrata. Although classed as oligotrophic in Table 65, the *Alchemilla-Sibbaldia nodum* is often best developed on meso-trophic soils in the type areas and so has usually been placed under calcareous substrata. Conversely, while both facies of Festuceto-Vaccinetum are associated with the richer rocks in some districts, their soils seem invariably to be oligotrophic and the association is indicated under non-calcareous substrata. Each has been assigned as accurately as possible to its alti-tudinal range, but in many cases our observations are too few and the limits shown should be regarded only as approximate. Noda which are either extensively developed or are otherwise especially characteristic of the particular region are given in capitals, while those which are poorly represented and often fragmentary are in small italic type. These indications of extent are only relative, showing the status of each nodum from region to region, and not the pro-portional area of one nodum to another. For instance, types such as the *Salix lapponum-Luzula sylvatica nodum*, Polytricheto-Dicranetum starkei and Philonoto-Saxifragetum stellaris are never extensive, and the size of their largest stands would be fragmentary for an important type such as Callunetum vulgaris. A few unclassified vegetation types have been added to make the picture more complete.

North-west Region

The Ben More Assynt and Foinaven massifs are taken to represent the region, the first having a greater range and extent of meso- and eutrophic noda on the Inchnadamph limestone and calcareous Lewisian tracts and the second a richer development of dwarf shrub communi-ties, due to its less intensive exploitation. The hills surrounding Loch Maree and Lochan Fada could be taken as another type area: they lack certain noda associated with calcareous rocks but show two woodland types, pine and oakwood, which do not extend to the other area in North-west Sutherland. The Beinn Dearg–Seana Bhraigh area has a good range of vegetation, especi-ally of high level calcicolous types, but lacks two of the most characteristic noda, namely Juniperetum nanae and Vaccineto-Callunetum hepaticosum, and has eastern affinities in the presence of Cladineto-Callunetum, Vaccinetum chionophilum and shrub-rich Calluneto-Eriophoretum.

North-east Region

This region offers a very limited choice of areas, for Ben Wyvis and Ben Klibreck are the only high hills, and most of the country is rather low moorland and 'flowe'. Ben Wyvis has been preferred since it has a greater variety of late snow vegetation. Both these high hills have little calcareous rock and few meso- and eutrophic noda occur in the region. The only markedly calcicolous vegetation found on the hills is on the Old Red Sandstone of Ben Griam More and Ben Griam Beg.

West-central Region

The hills on either side of Glens Affric and Cannich have been chosen as the type area. The main alternatives are the Ben Nevis range or the area containing Creag Meagaidh and Ben Alder, both of which have a rather better range of calcicolous noda than the Affric-Cannich hills. Ben Nevis and its neighbours are, however, rather poor in shrub communities. The Creag Meagaidh-Ben Alder area has marked affinities with the East-central region, having well-developed Vaccinetum chionophilum and the two *Carex bigelowii* associations, and less extensive occurrences of widespread western noda such as Deschampsieto-Rhytidiadelphetum and the *Juncus trifidus-Festuca ovina nodum*. The Affric-Cannich area is rather similar to the type area of the North-west Region and differs mainly in its greater number of snow-influenced noda.

East-central Region

It was found necessary to include two areas to represent this region. The Cairngorms have the best selection of calcifuge vegetation, but they are not truly typical of the region, partly because the rock is almost entirely granite and partly because there are some 'western' features. The Dalradian hills of the Clova and Caenlochan district with their extensive exposures of calcareous rock have thus been chosen as a second area. The Lochnagar part of this massif is rather similar to the Cairngorms and is not included in the chart: likewise, the limited areas of calcareous rocks around the edge of the Cairngorms show nothing which is not present in Clova-Caenlochan and so are omitted. Elsewhere in the region, the Monadhliath, the Drumochter Hills and the Forest of Atholl all resemble each other, but are mainly non-calcareous hills, and have a more restricted range of vegetation than Clova-Caenlochan.

The calcareous hills at the eastern end of Breadalbane and around Blair Atholl show a more extensive development of calcicolous noda than any other part of the East-central region, but for other resaons they are not regarded as representative of this region. The Ben Lawers area, moreover, shows affinities with the South-west Region.

South-west Region

The western end of Breadalbane, from Ben Lui to Ben Heasgarnich, is regarded as the type area for this region. It contains a particularly good selection of calcicolous noda, and many of the other vegetation types of the region are represented as well. Calcifuge noda are better developed in the Glencoe and Black Mount areas, but over the region as a whole dwarf shrub communities are much less prominent than grasslands, evidently due to the long period of management for grazing stock. Extensive communities dominated by *Trichophorum caespitosum* and *Molinia caerulea* represent fire climax derivatives of Trichophoreto-Callunetum and Molinieto-Callunetum respectively, and have been referred to these noda on the chart.

NON-CALCAREOUS ROCKS

Mainly quartzose mica-schist and other siliceous rocks of the Dalradian Series

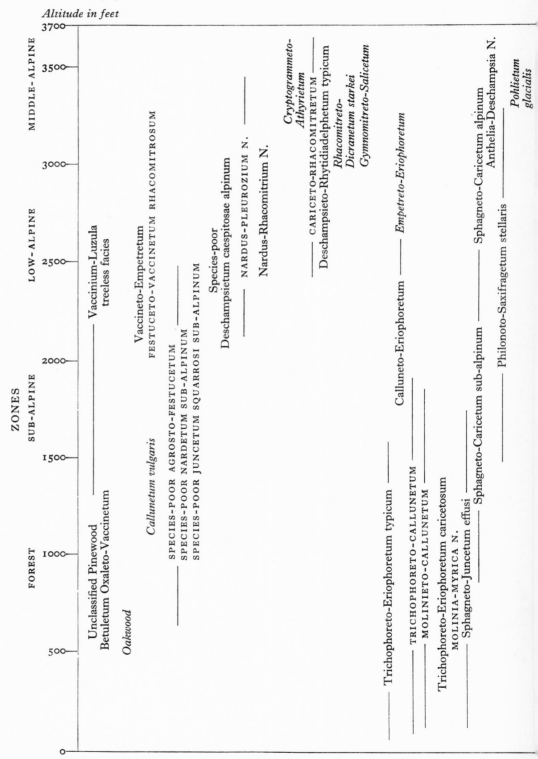

FIG. 31. VEGETATION TYPES OF TH

CALCAREOUS ROCKS

Sericite schist and associated limestones of the Dalradian Series

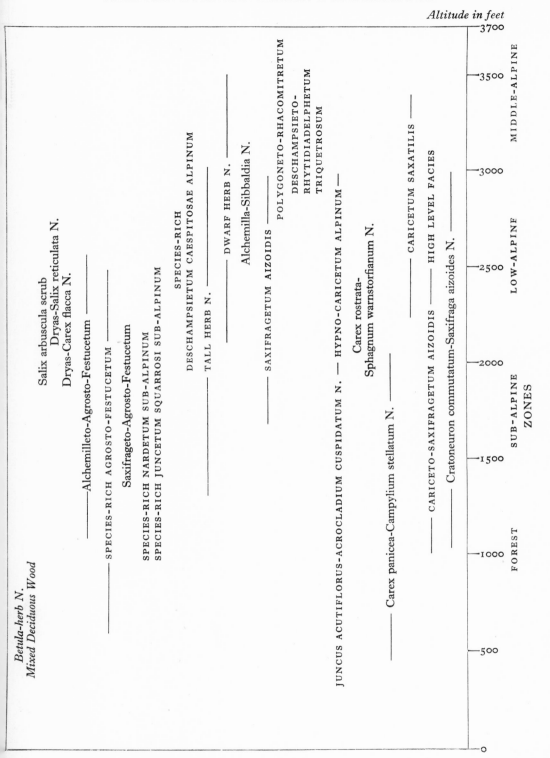

BEN LUI–BEN HEASGARNICH DISTRICT

NON-CALCAREOUS ROCKS

Granite, quartzose mica-schist and other siliceous rocks of the Dalradian Series

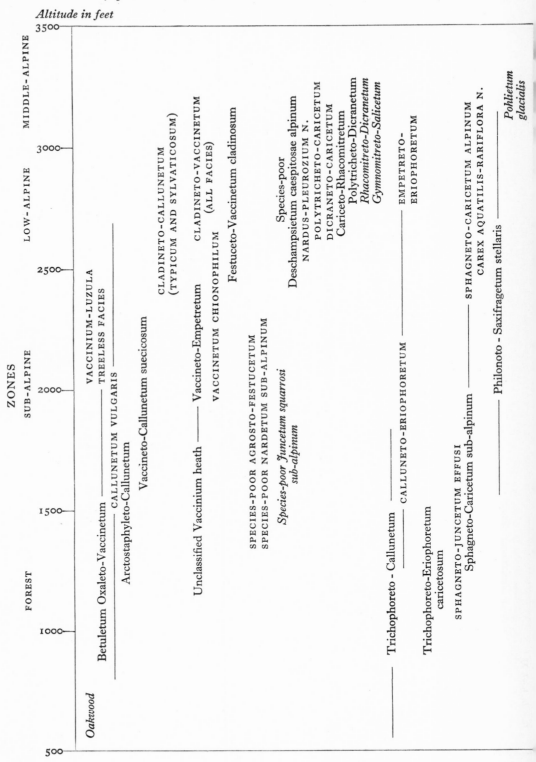

FIG. 32. VEGETATION TYPES OF TH

CALCAREOUS ROCKS

Sericite schist, hornblende schist and associated limestone, all of the Dalradian Series

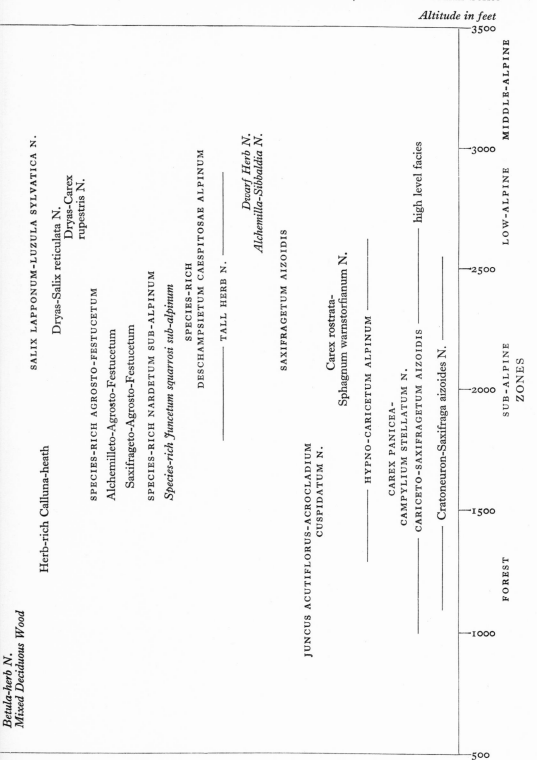

CLOVA-CAENLOCHAN DISTRICT

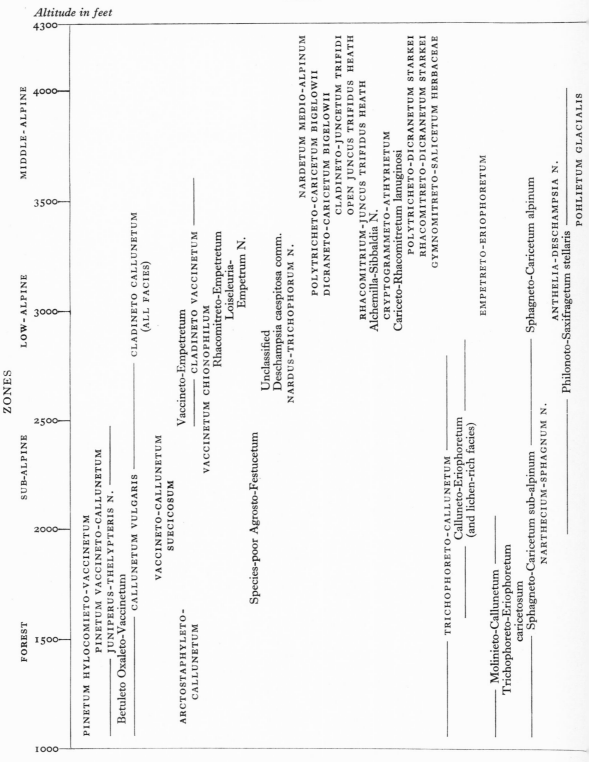

FIG. 33. VEGETATION TYPES OF THE CAIRNGORMS

NON-CALCAREOUS ROCKS

Granulite and acidic schists of the Moine Series

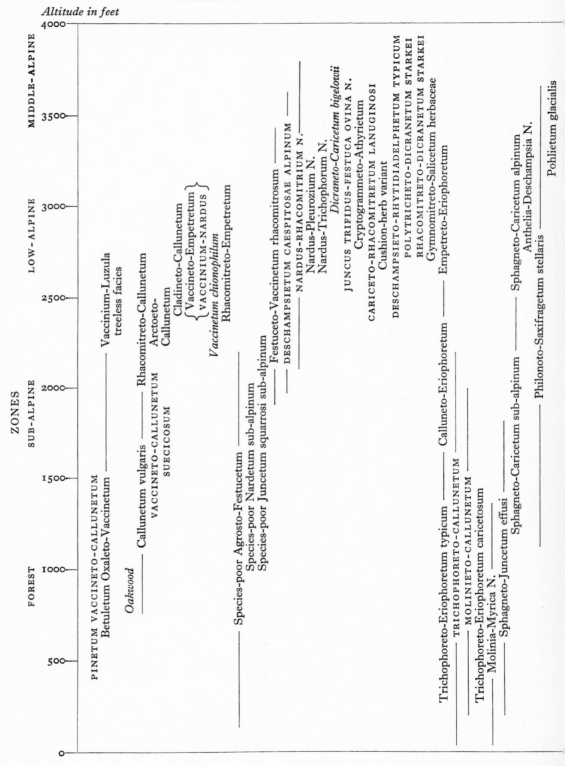

FIG. 34. VEGETATION TYPES OF TH

CALCAREOUS ROCKS

Calcareous schists of the Moine Series

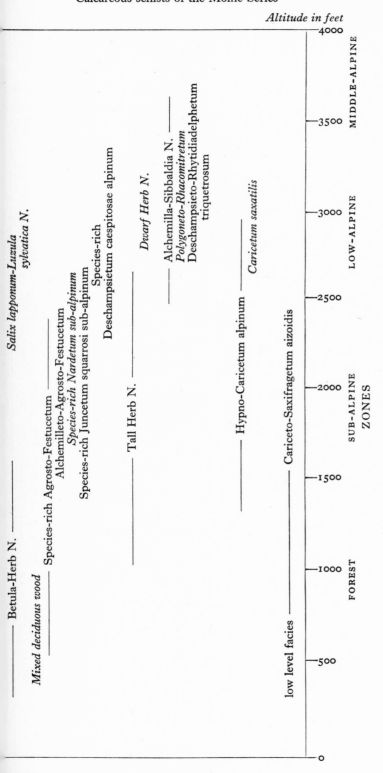

Altitude in feet

— 4000

MIDDLE-ALPINE

— 3500

LOW-ALPINE

— 3000

— 2500

SUB-ALPINE ZONES

— 2000

— 1500

FOREST

— 1000

— 500

— 0

Betula-Herb N. ————
Salix lapponum-Luzula sylvatica N.
Mixed deciduous wood
Species-rich Agrosto-Festucetum ————
Alchemilleto-Agrosto-Festucetum
Species-rich Nardetum sub-alpinum
Species-rich Juncetum squarrosi sub-alpinum
Species-rich Deschampsietum caespitosae alpinum
Dwarf Herb N.
———— Tall Herb N. ————
Alchemilla-Sibbaldia N.
Polygoneto-Rhacomitretum
Deschampsieto-Rhytidiadelphetum triquetrosum
———— Hypno-Caricetum alpinum
Caricetum saxatilis
Cariceto-Saxifragetum aizoidis
low level facies

INTAIL-GLEN AFFRIC DISTRICT

404

NON-CALCAREOUS ROCKS

Pelitic Moine schist

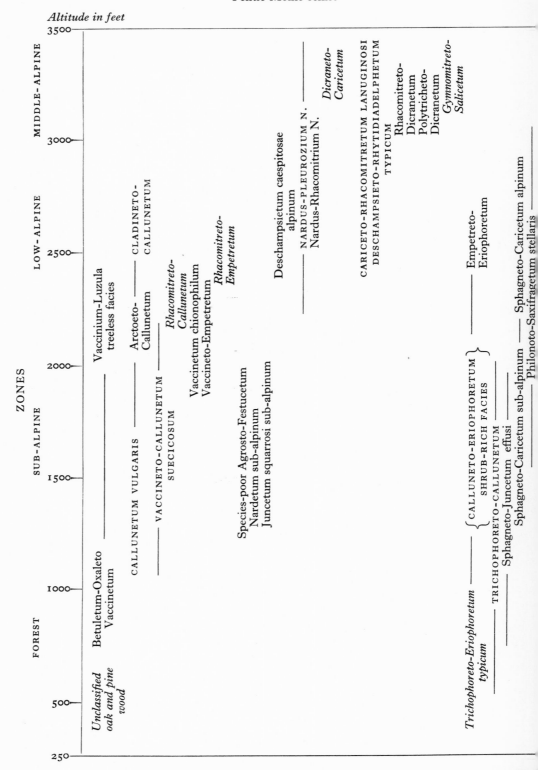

FIG. 35. VEGETATION TYPES OF THE BEN WYVIS ARE

CALCAREOUS ROCKS

Lime-bearing beds of Moine schist

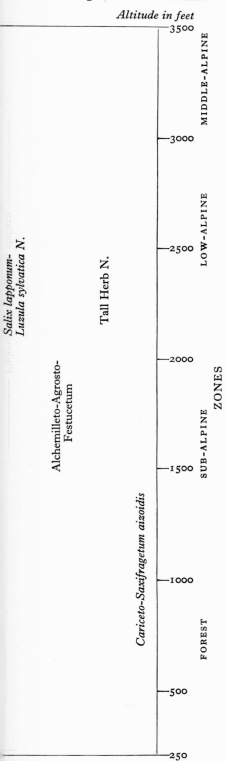

Altitude in feet

NON-CALCAREOUS ROCKS

Cambrian quartzite, acidic Lewisian gneiss and Moine granulite

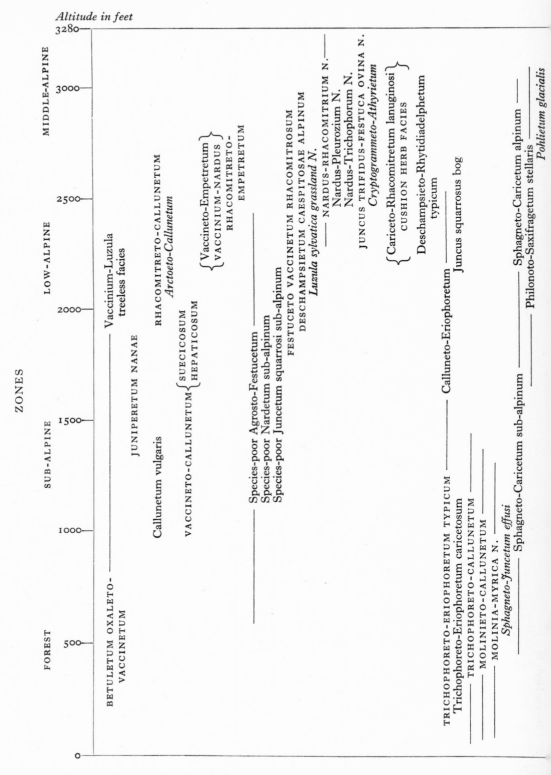

FIG. 36. VEGETATION TYPES OF THE BEN MORE ASSYNT–FOINAVEN DISTRIC

CALCAREOUS ROCKS

Durness limestone, serpulite grits and fucoid beds, calcareous Lewisian gneiss and calcareous Moine schist

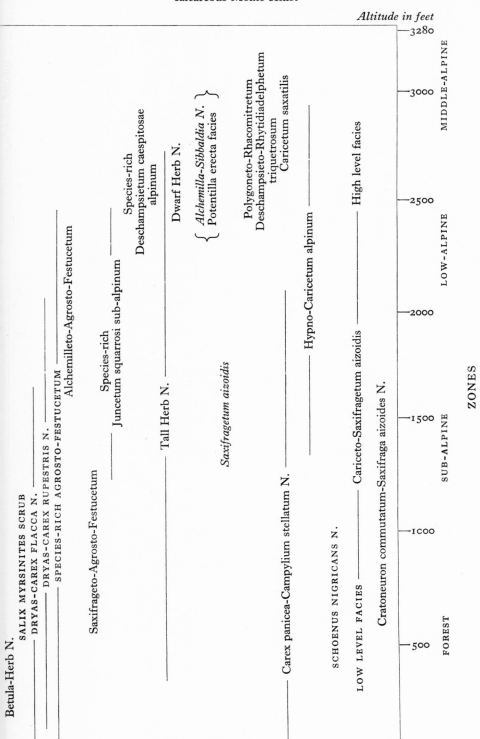

Altitude in feet

SOIL ANALYSES

1. Locality and habitat data may be obtained by looking up the reference number in the appropriate floristic table for the particular nodum. When soil samples do not refer to lists in the floristic tables (indicated by prefix X to reference no.), these data are given in supplementary lists appended to Tables 65–67.

2. Noda have been assigned to the three soil groups, oligotrophic to eutrophic, according to *average* values for exchangeable calcium. Some stands of a nodum may belong to a higher or lower trophic level. In a few noda the one or two samples so far analysed probably do not give a good measure of average soil conditions.

3. Peats giving more than 60 per cent loss on ignition are marked with an asterisk: they show disproportionately high values for certain ions, especially calcium, due to the volume/weight distortion on drying, and cannot fairly be compared with largely inorganic soils.

Table 65: Soil analyses of oligotrophic noda

Nodum	Reference No.	Soil type	pH	Loss on ignition %	Na (mg./100 gm.)	K (mg./100 gm.)	Ca (mg./100 mg.)	P₂O₅ (mg./100 gm.)
Pinetum Vaccineto-Callunetum	XM56C	Peaty podsol	3·6	80·0*	15·1	20·2	106·3	13·33
Betuletum Oxaleto-Vaccinetum	M56031	Slightly podsolised brown loam	5·2	14·6	4·9	19·8	12·7	0·6
Callunetum vulgaris	XR57073	Alpine podsol	4·6	17·6	7·3	14·7	10·5	0·52
Arctostaphyleto-Callunetum	M58018	Slightly podsolised brown loam	4·8	11·9	4·5	10·4	15·1	0·17
,,	XM58B		4·9	14·4	13·7	10·6	19·2	0·49
Vaccineto-Callunetum	XM56A	Ranker	3·6	75·4*	72·3	52·6	102·2	13·53
Arctoeto-Callunetum	M56001	Shallow alpine podsol with variable amount of humus	4·5	8·2	4·3	12·6	10·2	2·8
,,	M56002		4·9	23·1	5·9	20·4	19·5	0·80
,,	M55002		4·3	4·5	3·2	4·4	9·9	2·91
,,	M55008		4·6	18·2	17·5	12·7	31·4	0·88
Loiseleuria-Empetrum nodum	M56023	Alpine ranker	4·4	11·4	3·9	14·8	21·5	3·9
Cladineto-Callunetum	M56125	Shallow alpine podsol	4·3	14·5	3·9	10·3	7·6	0·43
,,	R56036		4·4	12·2	4·1	8·5	8·9	0·21
,,	M56024	Alpine ranker	4·3	19·1	6·2	15·4	24·0	4·82
Rhacomitreto-Callunetum	R56038	Alpine podsol	4·5	16·5	5·9	20·0	23·6	3·87
Vaccinetum chionophilum	M57073	Podsolic brown loam	3·8	17·4	8·1	20·3	48·9	2·11
,,	M56123	Shallow alpine podsol	4·1	40·6	5·4	17·9	4·2	0·53
Vaccineto-Empetretum	M56071	Podsolic brown loam with mor humus	4·7	9·9	3·6	11·0	6·6	0·6
,,	M56137		4·4	17·5	5·1	12·9	5·7	0·46
Cladineto-Vaccinetum	M57078	Shallow alpine podsol	3·7	17·4*	2·5	10·3	40·3	3·25
,,	M56032	Alpine ranker	3·9	87·8*	10·5	73·8	28·3	7·03
Festuceto-Vaccinetum	M57077	Brown loam with mor or moder humus, skeletal or slightly podsolised	4·7	17·8	2·6	8·7	12·5	0·45
,,	P52178		4·1	12·7	2·9	5·0	15·6	0·76
,,	P52179		4·3	12·3	2·8	10·9	5·6	0·37

Community	Sample no.	Soil type						
Festuceto-Vaccinetum	R57155	Brown loam with mor or moder humus, skeletal or slightly podsolised	4·5	27·3	4·8	20·9	28·4	0·63
" "	XR57327		4·9	58·9*	24·6	34·2	22·5	2·45
Alchemilleto-Agrosto-Festucetum (Rhacomitrium facies)	M56006	Skeletal or slightly podsolised shallow alpine loam	4·9	8·2	3·8	10·7	11·3	1·0
" " "	M56046		4·7	3·2	9·0	24·9	13·1	1·01
" " "	M57028		4·5	9·8	2·5	8·8	15·9	1·72
Nardetum sub-alpinum (species-poor facies)	P52158	Podsol	4·1	39·2	5·1	7·7	12·7	0·42
" " "	R57076	Gley podsol	4·7	60·4*	10·1	39·9	34·4	3·64
" " "	XR57061	Podsolised alluvium	4·8	48·3	10·0	23·0	48·3	0·82
Juncetum squarrosi sub-alpinum (species-poor facies)	P52177	Gley podsol	3·8	14·6	3·8	7·1	8·2	3·4
" " "	M56019	Shallow blanket peat	4·1	92·3*	39·0	48·0	59·2	18·1
Nardus-Pleurozium nodum	R56023	Alpine sod podsol	4·4	20·2	8·5	23·3	13·6	1·80
Nardus-Trichophorum nodum	M56027	Alpine sod podsol	5·0	6·3	3·5	4·4	6·1	1·08
Nardetum medio-alpinum	M56108	Alpine podsol	5·2	12·2	6·5	15·9	10·2	6·23
Polytricheto-Caricetum bigelowii rhytidiadelphetosum	P52214	Alpine podsol with variable amounts of humus and gleying	4·9	7·1	2·6	3·7	18·5	0·87
"	P52224		4·4	8·8	2·1	3·4	10·3	0·16
"	P52225		4·6	12·4	2·2	4·9	14·9	0·16
typicum	M56105		4·5	6·1	1·9	4·2	5·1	0·95
"	M57044		4·5	8·4	1·6	7·7	5·2	1·43
Dicraneto-Caricetum bigelowii	P52164	Alpine sod podsol with variable amount of gleying	3·7	83·3*	6·1	20·6	14·8	0·20
" "	P52175		4·2	6·1	2·0	2·1	15·3	1·74
" "	P52183		4·0	50·3	5·0	6·1	41·0	0·20
" "	P52191		4·1	28·1	4·6	11·2	7·6	3·04
" "	M56003		4·2	61·4*	11·3	38·6	25·5	19·67
" "	M57064	Alpine ranker	3·9	14·9	1·5	11·3	10·4	1·5
Cladineto-Juncetum trifidi	M56116	Shallow alpine podsol	4·3	3·5	1·2	4·0	2·0	0·64
Juncus trifidus-Festuca ovina nodum	R56041	Brown loam, evidently formed by truncation of alpine podsol, now subject to solifluction	4·7	3·9	5·8	4·5	3·9	1·12
" " "	R56052		4·9	4·8	3·1	2·0	6·6	0·43

Table 65: Soil analyses of oligotrophic noda—*(continued)*

Nodum	Reference No.	Soil type	pH	Loss on ignition %	Na (mg./100 gm.)	K (mg./100 gm.)	Ca (mg./100 gm.)	P_2O_5 (mg./100 gm.)
Juncus trifidus-Festuca ovina nodum	R56024	Brown loam, evidently formed by truncation of alpine podsol, now subject to solifluction	4·8	6·4	3·3	6·1	4·8	0·79
,, ,,	R57065		4·8	6·5	2·2	3·4	4·7	3·12
Cryptogrammeto-Athyrietum	M56135	Alpine ranker	4·1	82·6*	16·7	36·2	64·2	7·9
Alchemilla-Sibbaldia nodum	M56055	Periodically irrigated loam with moder humus horizon : sometimes podsolic	4·8	26·2	5·8	14·8	5·9	0·94
,, ,,	M56018		5·4	66·4*	13·5	28·4	8·2	3·6
,, ,,	R56033		4·6	12·8	20·8	11·4	27·2	0·91
,, ,, Potentilla erecta facies	M57034	Periodically irrigated loam with moder humus horizon : sometimes podsolic	4·8	63·7*	11·3	27·8	30·4	2·0
Cariceto-Rhacomitretum lanuginosi	M57032	Well developed but shallow alpine podsol	4·5	10·2	1·5	7·3	3·7	2·5
,, ,,	R56039		4·4	10·6	7·8	9·6	2·1	0·43
,, ,,	XR56032		4·2	5·3	7·0	4·0	10·3	0·13
,, ,, cushion herb facies	R56028	Well developed but shallow alpine podsol	4·8	8·9	4·4	6·0	17·8	0·78
Deschampsieto-Rhytidiadelphetum typicum	M57041	Alpine podsol	4·9	12·9	2·9	13·0	5·0	0·7
,, ,,	R56070	Alpine podsol	4·6	6·4	3·3	11·1	53·9	0·8
,, ,,	M56062	Redistributed blanket peat	4·1	88·2*	16·6	45·1	25·5	12·9
,, ,,	R57015	Alpine podsol	4·3	8·4	3·1	6·7	16·6	0·54
Polytricheto-Dicranetum starkei	M56113	Shallow alpine podsol, humus-rich and slightly gleyed	4·3	22·2	5·8	21·5	5·4	4·81
,, ,,	M56087		5·4	4·3	1·5	2·8	2·0	0·55
,, ,,	M56081		5·0	5·4	1·4	6·5	2·5	0·11
Rhacomitreto-Dicranetum starkei	R57080	Shallow alpine podsol	4·8	5·9	1·6	4·9	2·7	1·1
,, ,,	M57040	Skeletal solifluction soil	5·1	5·0	0·5	1·8	1·8	0·7
Gymnomitreto-Salicetum herbaceae	P52169	Amorphous solifluction soil	4·4	7·6	1·8	2·3	1·6	0·2
,, ,,	R58018	Shallow alpine podsol	6·5	6·3	14·2	11·1	74·6	1·31
,, ,,	M56097	Amorphous solifluction soil	4·9	3·6	1·9	1·9	12·4	0·12
Trichophoreto-Callunetum	XM56B	Shallow blanket peat	4·4	95·7*	39·8	27·5	82·4	1·56

Molinieto-Callunetum	XR58E	Shallow blanket peat	4·6	96·1*	48·8	49·1	204·0	14·6
Sphagneto-Juncetum effusi	XR5946A	Unhumified Sphagnum peat over gley	5·7	81·5*	14·7	39·1	54·3	0·61
Molinia-Myrica nodum	XR5931A	}Deep peaty gley	4·8	10·4	2·1	4·9	20·1	0·83
„ „	XR5955A		6·1	83·7*	—	—	48·1	—

Pinetum Vaccineto-Callunetum, Vaccineto-Callunetum, Cryptogrammeto-Athyrietum, Trichophoreto-Callunetum, Molinieto-Callunetum, Sphagneto-Juncetum, and the Molinia-Myrica nodum are regarded as oligotrophic, the high values for calcium being exaggerated by the high humus content. Some stands of the Alchemilla-Sibbaldia nodum are probably mesotrophic.

REFERENCE NUMBERS NOT IN FLORISTIC TABLES

		Map. ref.	Alt. (ft.)	Aspect	Slope
XM56C	Coille na Glas Leitire, Loch Maree, W. Ross	8652 1995	250	45	15
XR57073	Creag Meagaidh, Laggan, Inverness-shire	7858 2445	1800	115	35
XM58B	Edintian, Blair Atholl, Perthshire	7620 2842	1300	—	0
XM56A	Beinn Eighe, W. Ross	8644 1998	800	10	30
XR57327	Ard Nev, Isle of Rhum, Inverness-shire	7989 1349	1400	45	30
XR57061	Sgurr Mor Fannich, W. Ross	8730 2209	2000	360	25
XR56032	Am Faochagach, E. Ross	8777 2302	2750	120	7
XM56B	Beinn Eighe, W. Ross	8660 1983	500	45	10
XR58E	Isle of Rhum, Inverness-shire	8008 1372	400	360	10
XR5946A	Glen Lyon, Perthshire	7463 2648	1750	45	10
XR5931A	„ „ „	7482 2655	750	180	10
XR5955A	Bridge of Orchy, Argyll	7350 2317	1000	55	15

* High values for loss on ignition are marked by an asterisk, and the probability of soil volume/weight distortion (see p. 165) should be borne in mind when comparing the figures for exchangeable ions with those for less humus-rich soils.

Table 66: Soil analyses of mesotrophic noda

Nodum	Reference No.	Soil type	pH	Loss on ignition %	Na (mg./100 gm.)	K (mg./100 gm.)	Ca (mg./100 gm.)	P_2O_5 (mg./100 gm.)
Betula-herb nodum	R58004	Skeletal, slightly podsolised brown loam	5·3	8·6	6·2	9·7	34·9	0·27
,,	R57024		5·7	12·8	12·6	9·1	227·1	2·84
Vaccinium-Luzula treeless facies of birchwood	R58013	Alpine sod podsol	6·0	3·6	4·9	5·3	40·5	1·05
,, ,,	R57213		4·8	17·6	3·8	17·1	48·9	0·65
Herb-rich Callunetum	R56059	Periodically irrigated brown loam with mull humus	6·2	23·3	13·3	16·5	341·8	0·26
,, ,,	XR57339		5·3	9·4	20·4	12·9	63·8	1·48
,, ,,	XR58L		5·9	14·2	14·2	6·8	46·2	0·18
Juniperetum nanae	R57044	Ranker with moder humus	6·1	30·0	16·7	7·4	551·2	1·98
,,	M55011		4·1	84·9*	90·5	70·3	—	31·94
,,	XM56E		4·7	82·0*	47·4	55·6	264·6	15·79
,,	R57053		4·4	90·3*	67·8	48·6	344·7	15·7
Species-poor Agrosto-Festucetum	R56060	Skeletal podsolic brown loam	4·9	4·9	3·3	6·6	48·3	0·86
,,	R57059	Humus-rich alluvium	4·7	26·3	10·4	13·1	106·6	0·74
,,	M57012	Skeletal podsolic brown loam	5·0	35·4	55·7	25·4	38·1	0·88
,,	M56074	Skeletal podsolic brown loam	5·1	12·0	4·2	10·5	49·3	3·63
Alchemilleto-Agrosto-Festucetum	R56067	Skeletal brown loam subject to soil creep and/or irrigation	5·3	24·1	8·7	18·9	24·2	0·56
,,	R57196		6·0	17·7	6·8	14·0	323·6	0·13
,,	XR57128		5·2	11·8	4·1	11·4	61·7	1·42
,,	XR57326		5·5	6·5	9·6	8·8	19·6	0·87
Species-rich Agrosto-Festucetum	XR57233		5·2	10·9	3·2	16·0	135·5	2·42
,,	R57072		5·4	22·1	11·7	21·9	204·8	0·45
,,	R57166		6·0	11·9	5·2	7·3	226·2	0·08
,,	R57004	Periodically irrigated brown loam with good crumb-structure and mull humus, and containing earthworms	4·6	10·4	5·0	18·4	24·2	0·97
,,	R57252		5·3	12·8	5·7	13·4	75·8	1·01
,,	R56044		5·7	7·1	6·1	6·9	57·0	0·64
,,	XR58A		6·2	27·8	44·0	13·9	102·7	0·29

Vegetation type	Sample	Soil description						
Species-rich Agrosto-Festucetum	XR57337	Periodically irrigated brown loam with good crumb-structure and mull humus, and containing earthworms	7·2	7·4	17·5	19·6	198·5	1·23
" "	XR57333		5·2	22·5	63·3	37·6	226·0	1·19
Thalictrum-Ctenidium nodum	M55009	Irrigated peat	6·2	83·6*	35·2	22·3	91·6	5·45
" "	M56011	Irrigated brown loam	6·4	26·8	16·5	24·1	315·8	3·20
Species-rich Nardetum sub-alpinum	XR5927A	Irrigated brown loam or gley with mull humus	5·8	12·3	3·6	9·6	139·2	1·25
" "	XR5924A		6·0	9·1	—	—	222·7	—
Species-rich Juncetum squarrosi sub-alpinum	R58137	Mull humus or peat over wet gley	5·6	71·4*	18·6	36·2	69·4	3·55
" "	XR5940A		6·0	18·7	—	—	300·3	—
Species-poor Deschampsietum caespitosae alpinum	XR5957	Alpine sod podsol	5·2	17·5*	4·7	11·2	39·5	0·85
" "	XM5901		5·3	80·5*	—	—	27·2	—
Species-rich Deschampsietum caespitosae alpinum	XR59252B	Periodically irrigated brown loam with mull humus	5·4	13·0	5·6	13·4	76·0	1·0
Luzula-grassland nodum	M58029	Moist brown fibrous peat	4·5	93·2*	85·2	38·5	127·5	25·7
Tall Herb nodum	R57267	Periodically irrigated skeletal brown loam with mull humus	5·4	17·3	5·2	11·8	357·3	0·3
" "	R57086		5·1	13·7	12·2	16·0	136·0	0·7
" "	R57219		5·1	11·0	3·6	7·8	96·2	1·4
" "	R56061		5·3	6·8	6·5	6·3	67·5	2·2
" "	R56063	Periodically irrigated skeletal brown loam with mull humus. Slight podsolisation	4·8	11·3	6·9	15·8	29·1	1·6
" "	R57062	Periodically irrigated skeletal brown loam with mull humus	5·3	15·5	9·5	16·8	145·6	0·6
" "	XR57342		5·5	32·9	48·4	20·9	335·1	1·07
Dwarf Herb nodum	M56078	Periodically irrigated skeletal brown loam with mull humus: often stony	5·3	7·2	5·5	8·7	61·1	1·83
" "	M57048		5·4	5·5	10·3	7·3	367·1	15·12
" "	R56040		4·8	16·4	9·1	17·2	45·2	3·18
" "	R56051		4·9	16·6	9·2	15·6	42·8	1·12
" "	R56030		4·9	14·6	6·9	14·6	20·9	1·01
" "	P52195		5·7	7·2	3·2	4·9	44·3	3·72

Table 66: Soil analyses of mesotrophic noda—(continued)

Nodum	Reference No.	Soil type	pH	Loss on ignition %	Na (mg./100 gm.)	K (mg./100 gm.)	Ca (mg./100 gm.)	P_2O_5 (mg./100 gm.)
Dwarf Herb nodum	R57068	Periodically irrigated skeletal brown loam with mull humus: often stony	5·1	10·4	5·8	11·1	111·4	1·98
Polygoneto-Rhacomitretum lanuginosi	R56031	Shallow alpine podsol	4·9	14·8	4·2	10·3	15·6	0·2
,,	R56042		4·6	10·7	3·9	12·8	5·1	0·5
,,	M56020	Solifluction brown loam	5·2	29·6	8·0	20·4	20·5	1·7
,,	R57046		5·9	20·2	16·9	12·1	232·2	0·20
,,	R56046		4·6	6·4	4·4	7·2	8·0	0·39
,,	R57013	Shallow alpine podsol	5·1	13·9	9·9	14·4	61·4	2·13
Deschampsieto-Rhytidiadelphetum triquetrosum	M57003		4·8	12·0	1·5	11·1	18·9	0·45
,,	M58014	Skeletal brown loams, sometimes irrigated and with	5·4	14·9	41·7	20·9	303·0	0·66
,,	M55017	shallow mull humus layer	5·0	13·7	12·5	7·4	51·1	0·2
,,	M56053		4·8	9·2	3·3	12·8	14·0	1·28
Juncus acutiflorus-Acrocladium cuspidatum nodum	R58126	Gley with mull humus or peat	5·2	38·3	12·4	21·5	217·2	0·22
,,	R58096		5·5	20·1	—	—	161·2	—
Hypno-Caricetum alpinum	R58019	Gley with mull humus	5·4	29·2	7·7	8·8	77·8	0·3
,,	XR5913A		5·6	62·5*	—	—	280·8	—
Carex rostrata-Sphagnum warnstorfianum nodum	R57307	Unhumified Sphagnum peat	5·7	78·2*	16·6	34·9	690·2	0·66

Juniperetum nanae and the Carex rostrata-Sphagnum warnstorfianum nodum are regarded as mesotrophic, the high values for calcium being exaggerated by the high humus content. Some stands of Alchemilleto-Agrosto-Festucetum, Herb-rich Callunetum, the Thalictrum-Ctenidium nodum, the Tall Herb nodum, the Dwarf Herb nodum, Deschampsieto-Rhytidiadelphetum triquetrosum and probably species-rich Agrosto-Festucetum, are eutrophic. Some stands of species-poor Agrosto-Festucetum, species-poor Deschampsietum caespitosae, Polygoneto-Rhacomitretum, the Dwarf Herb nodum, and Deschampsieto-Rhytidiadelphetum typicum, are only oligotrophic. Most stands of species-rich Deschampsietum caespitosae probably have soils richer in calcium than the sample analysed.

REFERENCE NUMBERS NOT IN FLORISTIC TABLES

		Map. ref.	Alt. (ft.)	Aspect	Slope
XR57339	Monadh Dubh, Isle of Rhum, Inverness-shire	8028 1331	100	315	30
XR58L	Kilmory Glen, Isle of Rhum, Inverness-shire	8009 1364	100	–	0
XM56E	Beinn Eighe, W. Ross	8622 1993	1400	45	15
XR57128	Glen Markie, Monadhliadh, Inverness-shire	7995 2597	1700	250	35
XR57326	Askival, Isle of Rhum, Inverness-shire	7955 1387	1400	315	35
XR57233	Corrie Fee, Clova, Angus	7756 3253	1500	180	22
XR58A	Harris, Isle of Rhum, Inverness-shire	7958 1336	200	100	25
XR57337	Monadh Dubh, Isle of Rhum, Inverness-shire	8028 1332	250	270	10
XR57333	Fionchra, Isle of Rhum, Inverness-shire	8007 1339	1000	45	33
XR5927A	Carn Gorm, Glen Lyon, Perthshire	7497 2643	2500	80	25
XR5924A	Carn Gorm, Glen Lyon, Perthshire	7499 2642	2500	90	30
XR5940A	Meall Garbh, Glen Lyon, Perthshire	7449 2643	2500	45	20
XR5957	Ben Wyvis, E. Ross	8690 2473	2500	360	35
XM5901	Beinn Eighe, W. Ross	8640 1980	2300	45	35
XR50252B	Glen Doll, Clova, Angus	7764 3244	2000	45	35
XR57342	Fionchra, Isle of Rhum, Inverness-shire	8006 1339	1150	45	40
XR5913A	Ben Vrackie, Perthshire	7639 2963	2100	90	5

* High values for loss on ignition are marked by an asterisk, and the probability of soil volume/weight distortion (see p. 165) should be borne in mind when comparing the figures for exchangeable ions with those for less humus-rich soils.

Table 67: Soil analyses of eutrophic noda

Nodum	Reference No.	Soil type	pH	Loss on ignition %	Na (mg./100 gm.)	K (mg./100 gm.)	Ca (mg./100 gm.)	P_2O_5 (mg./100 gm.)
Dryas-Salix reticulata nodum	R57228	Skeletal brown loam	6·8	7·4	7·1	7·3	389·0	2·78
„ „ „	M58012	„	6·2	14·2	11·4	7·0	504·2	0·40
„ „ „	R57066	Skeletal brown loam with mull humus	6·3	18·7	20·1	13·9	416·2	3·04
Dryas-Carex rupestris nodum	M57076	Limestone rendzina	7·5	23·2	6·2	4·1	325·7	0·20
„ „ „	M56073	Skeletal red-brown loam	7·9	37·3	24·6	8·9	364·7	0·43
„ „ „	M56010	Skeletal red-brown loam	7·8	8·2	10·4	13·3	377·7	0·04
Arctostaphylos grass heath	XM58A	Limestone rendzina	7·8	12·7	183·8	6·7	448·9	1·37
Saxifrageto-Agrosto-Festucetum	XR5920A	Periodically irrigated brown loam with mull humus	6·3	18·6	—	—	461·9	—
„ „ „	XR5915A		6·5	38·7	—	—	1115·7	—
„ „ „	R57298		7·1	13·3	56·1	6·1	494·2	0·69
Saxifragetum aizoidis	R57201	Strongly irrigated skeletal brown soil with mull humus	6·8	7·5	9·2	15·3	720·1	0·48
	R57249		7·4	10·3	7·9	13·0	671·6	0·20
Mixed Saxifrage facies	R59039	Strongly irrigated skeletal brown soil with mull humus	6·3	14·2	—	—	258·8	—
Carex panicea-Campylium stellatum nodum	R57288	Strongly irrigated brown peat or mud of silt and mull humus	6·0	16·1	5·6	5·2	372·2	3·06
„ „ „	R57293		5·9	59·1*	—	—	992·0	—
Carex rostrata-brown moss nodum	R57297	Fen peat (Hypnum peat moor)	5·9	85·3*	25·0	8·2	2044·0	2·34
„ „ „	R57306		5·8	76·5**	—	—	933·5	—
Schoenus nigricans nodum	R58002	Calcareous marl	8·0	3·4	180·3	5·1	505·4	0·67
Caricetum saxatilis	P52204	Strongly irrigated peat or mud with variable proportions of silt, sand, gravel and humus	5·3	58·2	15·0	6·0	691·3	2·61
„ „	P52203		4·7	50·1	10·2	7·2	234·8	1·1
„ „	P52200		5·2	24·1	7·0	3·0	209·9	0·26
„ „	P52206		4·6	19·7	3·7	2·4	39·3	0·40

28+

	Ref. no.	Soil type						
Caricetum saxatilis	P52208	} Strongly irrigated peat or mud with variable proportions of silt, sand, gravel and humus	4·9	20·3	5·8	8·7	143·1	1·83
„ „	R57085		5·6	34·0	14·2	29·6	337·1	2·04
Cariceto-Saxifragetum aizoidis	P52149	} Strongly irrigated mud of silt, sand, gravel and humus	6·0	7·8	6·3	5·7	573·0	12·25
„ „	R57287		6·0	3·8	4·4	1·8	147·2	4·9
„ „	XR5937A		6·3	11·2	—	—	178·4	—
Salix lapponum-Luzula sylvatica nodum								
S. myrsinites facies	R58099	} Moist brown loam with mull humus	6·9	27·4	—	—	1071·0	—
S. lanata facies	R57238		5·7	12·8	9·4	8·7	494·8	0·65

Some stands of Caricetum saxatilis, Cariceto-Saxifragetum aizoidis and probably most willow scrubs dominated only by *Salix lapponum* are only mesotrophic.

REFERENCE NUMBERS NOT IN FLORISTIC TABLES

		Map. ref.	Alt. (ft.)	Aspect	Slope
XM58A	Edintian, Blair Atholl, Perthshire	7620 2842	1300	—	0
XR5920A	Ben Vrackie, Perthshire	7631 2942	1600	220	15
XR5915A	Ben Vrackie, Perthshire	7638 2962	2200	45	15
XR5937A	Meall Garbh, Glen Lyon, Perthshire . . .	7445 2647	2800	360	25

* High values for loss on ignition are marked by an asterisk, and the probability of soil volume/weight distortion (see p. 165) should be borne in mind when comparing the figures for exchangeable ions with those for less humus-rich soils.

Table 68: Analysis of Bog and Mire Waters

	pH	Ca++ (mg./litre)
OLIGOTROPHIC (Ca++ < 4 mg./litre)		
Trichophoreto-Eriophoretum typicum		
All samples from Rannoch Moor, Argyll		
*1. Sphagnum flats	4·3	—
*2. ,, ,,	4·4	0·33
*3. ,, ,,	4·3	0·29
*4. ,, pool	4·4	0·41
*5. ,, ,,	4·7	0·50
Calluneto-Eriophoretum		
1. Ben Vrackie, Perthshire; Sphagnum pool	4·1	0·57
Trichophoreto-Eriophoretum caricetosum		
*1. Rannoch Moor, Argyll	4·5	0·39
*2. ,, ,, ,,	4·3	0·31
*3. Bridge of Orchy, Argyll	4·8	—
*4. ,, ,, ,,	4·8	1·15
Molinia-Myrica nodum		
1. Glen Lyon, Perthshire	5·9	2·26
Sphagneto-Juncetum effusi		
*1. Ben Lawers, Perthshire	4·9	0·66
*2. ,, ,, ,,	5·0	0·78
*3. ,, ,, ,,	4·4	0·49
Carex rostrata-Sphagnum recurvum mire		
1. Ben Vrackie, Perthshire	4·2	1·44
2. ,, ,, ,,	4·9	1·50
Sphagneto-Caricetum sub-alpinum		
1. Ben Vrackie, Perthshire	4·5	1·27
2. ,, ,, ,,	6·3	4·00
3. Carn Gorm, Glen Lyon, Perthshire	5·7	1·44
*4. Ben Lawers, Perthshire	4·5	0·88
*5. ,, ,, ,,	4·9	0·84
*6. ,, ,, ,,	4·8	0·92
Sphagneto-Caricetum alpinum		
1. Glen Esk, Angus	5·3	2·20
Philonoto-Saxifragetum stellaris		
1. Ben Vrackie, Perthshire	6·1	3·85
2. Beinn Eighe, W. Ross	5·7	—
MESOTROPHIC (Ca++ > 4 mg./litre)	pH	Ca++ (mg./litre)
Juncus acutiflorus nodum		
1. Glen Lyon, Perthshire	6·3	4·72
*2. ,, ,, ,,	5·7	1·74
Hypno-Caricetum alpinum		
*1. Ben Lawers, Perthshire	6·3	5·54
Carex rostrata-Sphagnum warnstorfianum nodum		
1. Ben Vrackie, Perthshire	5·8	4·28
2. ,, ,, ,,	5·9	4·87
3. ,, ,, ,,	6·0	4·00
EUTROPHIC (Ca++ > 10 mg./litre)		
Carex rostrata-brown moss nodum		
1. Tulach Hill, Blair Atholl, Perthshire	6·8	12·46
2. ,, ,, ,, ,, ,,	6·7	12·56
3. ,, ,, ,, ,, ,,	6·5	—
4. ,, ,, ,, ,, ,,	6·8	16·72
5. ,, ,, ,, ,, ,,	6·8	19·80
6. Ben Vrackie, Perthshire	6·6	8·31

Table 68 (*continued*)

	pH	Ca++ (mg./litre)
Caricetum saxatilis		
*1. Ben Lawers, Perthshire	6·5	2·77
*2. ,, ,, ,,	5·9	1·49
Cariceto-Saxifragetum aizoidis		
1. Ardtulichan, Killiecrankie, Perthshire	6·8	13·03
2. ,, ,, ,,	6·9	12·82
3. Carn Gorm, Glen Lyon, Perthshire	6·8	5·28
*4. Ben Lawers, Perthshire	6·5	2·15
5. Rannoch Moor, Perthshire	7·2	—
Cratoneuron commutatum-Saxifraga aizoides nodum		
1. Tulach Hill, Blair Atholl, Perthshire	7·4	38·87
2. ,, ,, ,, ,, ,,	7·3	49·03
3. Ben Vrackie, Perthshire	7·3	22·77

* Samples collected after a day of heavy rain, giving an apparent dilution effect, especially in the meso-trophic and eutrophic mires. Caricetum saxatilis has, from the soil analyses, therefore been classed as mesotrophic.

422

Table 69: Plant Indicators of Soil
Exacting Calcicoles

Species found mainly or exclusively in eutrophic vegetation, i.e. a marked preference for soils containing > 300 mg. Ca/100 gm. and pH usually > 6·0.

Arabis hirsuta
Asplenium viride *
Carex atrata
C. capillaris
C. lepidocarpa
C. rupestris
Cystopteris fragilis
C. montana
Draba incana
Dryas octopetala
Equisetum hyemale
E. variegatum
Helictotrichon pratense *
Juncus alpinus
J. castaneus
Polystichum lonchitis
Potentilla crantzii
Salix arbuscula
S. lanata
S. myrsinites
S. reticulata
Saxifraga oppositifolia
S. nivalis
Sesleria caerulea

Bartramia halleriana
Camptothecium lutescens
Campylium protensum
Catoscopium nigritum
Cinclidium stygium

Cratoneuron commutatum (when dominant)
Distichium capillaceum
Ditrichum flexicaule
Encalypta (all British species)
Entodon orthocarpus
Fissidens cristatus
Grimmia funalis
G. torquata
Gymnostomum recurvirostrum
Mnium orthorrhynchum
Meesia uliginosa
Neckera crispa
Oncophorus virens
Orthothecium rufescens
O. intricatum
Philonotis calcarea
Plagiobryum zierii
Plagiopus oederi
Rhytidium rugosum
Thuidium abietinum
Tortella tortuosa

Lophozia quadriloba
Metzgeria pubescens
Scapania aspera
S. aequiloba

Peltigera venosa
Solorina saccata

* Species thus indicated are regarded as basiphiles by Ferreira (pers. comm.) since they grow as successfully on magnesium-rich as on calcium-rich substrata.

Table 70: Plant Indicators of Soil
Calcicoles

Species found only in mesotrophic to eutrophic vegetation, i.e. a marked preference for soils containing > 30 mg. Ca/100 gm. and pH usually > 4·8.

Alchemilla vulgaris agg. (all segregates)
Angelica sylvestris
Anthyllis vulneraria *
Asperula odorata
Asplenium adiantum-nigrum *
Bellis perennis
Botrychium lunaria*
Brachypodium sylvaticum
Briza media
Cardamine flexuosa
Carex caryophyllea
C. dioica
C. flacca *
C. hostiana
C. pulicaris
Cerastium alpinum *
Circaea lutetiana
Cirsium heterophyllum
C. vulgare
Coeloglossum viride
Crepis paludosa
Dactylis glomerata
Eleocharis pauciflora
Epilobium montanum
Eriophorum latifolium
Filipendula ulmaria
Fragaria vesca
Fraxinus excelsior
Galium boreale
Geranium robertianum
G. sylvaticum
Geum rivale
Heracleum sphondylium
Juncus articulatus
J. triglumis *
Koeleria gracilis *
Linum catharticum
Listera ovata
Lysimachia nemorum
Melica nutans
Mercurialis perennis
Orchis mascula
Oxyria digyna
Plantago lanceolata
Polystichum lobatum
Polygonum viviparum (except above 2500 ft. in W. Highlands)
Primula vulgaris
Prunella vulgaris
Ranunculus acris
R. ficaria
Rhinanthus minor agg. (all segregates)
Rubus saxatilis
Sagina nodosa *
Sanicula europaea

Saussurea alpina
Saxifraga aizoides
S. hypnoides *
Sedum rosea
Selaginella selaginoides
Senecio jacobaea
Thalictrum alpinum
Tofieldia pusilla
Trifolium repens
Trollius europaeus
Tussilago farfara
Valeriana officinalis
Veronica chamaedrys
Vicia sepium
V. sylvatica

Acrocladium giganteum
A. trifarium
Amphidium lapponicum
Anoectangium compactum
Barbula fallax
Camptothecium nitens
Campylium stellatum
Cratoneuron commutatum
C. filicinum
Ctenidium molluscum
Drepanocladus revolvens var. intermedius
D. vernicosus
Eurhynchium striatum
Fissidens adianthoides
F. osmundoides
Grimmia apocarpa
Gymnostomum aeruginosum
Hylocomium brevirostre
H. pyrenaicum
Hypnum hamulosum (except above 2500 ft. in W. Highlands)
Leptodontium recurvifolium
Mnium pseudopunctatum
M. seligeri
Pohlia cruda
Sphagnum contortum
S. subsecundum sens. strict.
S. teres
S. warnstorfianum

Aneura pinguis
Blepharostoma trichophyllum
Herberta adunca
Lophozia bantriensis
L. muelleri
Plagiochila asplenioides
Preissia quadrata

Peltidea leucophlebia

* Species thus indicated are regarded as basiphiles by Ferreira (pers. comm.) since they grow as successfully on magnesium-rich as on calcium-rich substrata.

Table 71: Plant Indicators of Soil
Calcifuges

Species found mainly or exclusively in oligotrophic vegetation (i.e. a marked preference for soils containing < 30 mg. Ca/100 gm. and pH usually < 4·5 and complete absence from soils containing > 300 mg. Ca/100 gm. and pH > 6·0.

Arctous alpina
Athyrium alpestre
Betula nana
Blechnum spicant
Carex binervis
C. curta
C. pauciflora
C. paupercula
C. pilulifera
C. rariflora
Chamaepericlymenum suecicum
Cryptogramma crispa
Digitalis purpurea
Drosera rotundifolia
Dryopteris filix-mas agg.
D. austriaca
Eriophorum vaginatum
Hymenophyllum wilsoni
Listera cordata
Loiseleuria procumbens
Lycopodium annotinum
L. clavatum
Melampyrum pratense
Orchis ericetorum
Pedicularis sylvatica
Rhynchospora alba
Rubus chamaemorus
Thelypteris oreopteris

Andreaea rothii
A. rupestris
Conostomum tetragonum
Campylopus atrovirens
C. flexuosus
Dicranella heteromalla
Dicranodontium uncinatum
D. denudatum var. alpinum
Dicranum fuscescens
D. starkei

Heterocladium heteropterum
Hypnum cupressiforme var. ericetorum
Leucobryum glaucum
Oligotrichum hercynicum
Plagiothecium undulatum
Pleurozium schreberi
Polytrichum alpestre
P. juniperinum
P. norvegicum
P. piliferum
Rhacomitrium heterostichum
Rhytidiadelphus loreus
Sphagnum auriculatum
S. compactum
S. cuspidatum
S. fuscum
S. imbricatum
S. inundatum
S. magellanicum
S. molle
S. nemoreum
S. papillosum
S. quinquefarium
S. rubellum
S. russowii
S. strictum
S. tenellum

Alicularia compressa
Bazzania trilobata
Diplophyllum albicans
Gymnomitrium concinnatum
G. crenulatum
Leptoscyphus anomalus
L. taylori
Lepidozia (all British species)
Marsupella emarginata
Odontoschisma sphagni
Pellia epiphylla

Table 72: Plant Indicators of Soil
Species which avoid the poorest soils

All these species are able to grow on oligotrophic soils but they avoid the most lime-deficient (< 15 mg. Ca/100 gm.) and highly acidic (pH < 4·5) substrata, especially mor peats.

Achillea millefolium
Alchemilla alpina (in E. Highlands)
Anemone nemorosa
Carex demissa
C. panicea (when abundant)
Cerastium vulgatum
Cirsium palustre
Cochlearia alpina
Corylus avellana
Epilobium alsinifolium
E. palustre
Equisetum sylvaticum
Festuca rubra
Galium verum
Helianthemum chamaecistus
Hieracium pilosella
Holcus lanatus
Lathyrus montanus
Leontodon autumnalis
Lotus corniculatus
Melica uniflora
Melandrium rubrum
Poa pratensis
Pyrola media
Rubus idaeus
Rumex acetosa
Sagina procumbens
Salix lapponum

Schoenus nigricans (when abundant)
Sibbaldia procumbens (outside late snow-beds)
Succisa pratensis (when abundant)
Taraxacum officinalis agg.
Thymus drucei
Viola lutea
V. riviniana (when abundant)

Acrocladium cuspidatum
Blindia acuta
Brachythecium rutabulum
B. plumosum
Breutelia chrysocoma
Bryum pseudotriquetrum
Climacium dendroides
Dicranum bonjeani
Drepanocladus uncinatus
Eurhynchium praelongum
Hylocomium splendens (when dominant)
Mnium undulatum
Rhytidiadelphus squarrosus (when dominant)
R. triquetrus (when dominant)
Thuidium tamariscinum (when dominant)

Chiloscyphus polyanthus
Lophozia quinquedentata
Pellia fabbroniana

Both subspecies of *Juniperus communis* might be included, for though most often growing on acidic rocks, they appear to be soil improvers, building up a mesotrophic layer of moder humus. The same is probably true of certain calcifuge ferns and *Luzula sylvatica*.

When present in abundance the following species of *Sphagnum* indicate water movement, and in tolerance of base-status they appear to lie between the completely oligotrophic species of Table 71 and the mesotrophic species of Table 70.

Sphagnum girgensohnii
S. lindbergii
S. palustre
S. recurvum

S. russowii (when dominant)
S. riparium
S. squarrosum

Table 73: Plant Indicators of Soil
Indifferents

Species which occur over an extremely wide range of soil calcium-status and pH, ranging from markedly oligotrophic to eutrophic noda.

Agrostis tenuis   M
Alchemilla alpina
Antennaria dioica
Armeria maritima
Arctostaphylos uva-ursi
Calluna vulgaris   O–M
Campanula rotundifolia (not on mor humus)
Cardaminopsis petraea
Carex bigelowii   O
C. echinata   O
C. nigra
C. panicea   M
C. rostrata
C. saxatilis   E
Cerastium edmonstonii
Cherleria sedoides
Deschampsia alpina
D. caespitosa   M
Drosera anglica   O
Empetrum hermaphroditum   O
Erica tetralix   O
Eriophorum angustifolium   O
Festuca ovina agg.
Galium hercynicum   O
Hypericum pulchrum
Juniperus communis (both subspecies)   O–M
Juncus acutiflorus
J. squarrosus
J. trifidus   O
Luzula multiflora
L. spicata
Lycopodium selago   O
Molinia caerulea   M
Myrica gale (probably not on eutrophic soils)   O
Nardus stricta

Phragmites communis   M–E
Pinguicula vulgaris   M
Potentilla erecta   O
Ramischia secunda
Salix herbacea   O
Schoenus nigricans   E
Silene acaulis
Sibbaldia procumbens
Solidago virgaurea
Succisa pratensis   M
Trichophorum caespitosum   O
Vaccinium myrtillus   O
V. uliginosum
V. vitis-idaea   O

Dicranum scoparium
D. majus   O
Hylocomium splendens
Philonotis fontana   O–M
Pseudoscleropodium purum
Ptilium crista-castrensis
Rhacomitrium canescens   O
R. lanuginosum   O
Rhytidiadelphus squarrosus   M
Sphagnum plumulosum (not on eutrophic peats)   O
Thuidium tamariscinum   M

Frullania tamarisci
Ptilidium ciliare   O

Cetraria aculeata   O
C. islandica   O
Cladonia gracilis   O

Many markedly oceanic species of bryophytes show a fairly wide range of tolerance for calcium status. Some of the above species only occur sparingly on soils at one or other end of the trophic series, and their optimum soil conditions are denoted by the letters O (oligotrophic), M (mesotrophic) and E (eutrophic).

Table 74: List of described vegetation types of the Highlands, with indications of their geographical distribution and soil preferences

Soil classes:
O = Oligotrophic
M = Mesotrophic
E = Eutrophic

Nodum	Table No.	Geographical Distribution	Soil Class
Pinetum Hylocomieto–Vaccinetum myrtillosum triquetrosum	4	Mainly E.C.	O
Pinetum Vaccineto–Callunetum	5	Widespread, but especially in W.	O
Betuletum Oxaleto–Vaccinetum Vaccinium–Luzula treeless facies	6	Widespread	O–M
Betula–herb nodum fern-dominated treeless facies	6	Widespread	M
Moss communities of birch and oakwoods	7	Mainly W.	O
Fraxinus–Brachypodium provisional nodum	8	Rare and scattered	E
Mixed deciduous woodland	A	Widespread but local	E–M
Alderwood	B	Widespread but local	M
Juniperus–Thelypteris nodum	9	Mainly E.C.	M
Low-level willow scrub		Local, mainly N.	O–M ·
Salix lapponum–Luzula sylvatica nodum	10	Mainly E.	M–E
Callunetum vulgaris	11	Widespread, but only extensive in E.	O
herb-rich facies	11A	Rare and scattered	M–E
Arctostaphyleto–Callunetum	12	Exclusively E.C.	O–M
Vaccineto–Callunetum	13		
hepaticosum		Exclusively W. and mainly N.W.	O
suecicosum		Widespread	O
Juniperetum nanae hepaticosum lichenosum	14	Mainly or exclusively (?) N.W.	M
Arctoeto–Callunetum	15	Mainly N.	O
Loiseleuria–Empetrum provisional nodum	15	Cairngorms only	O
Cladineto–Callunetum	16	Mainly E.	
typicum		Widespread in E.	O
arctostaphyletosum		Cairngorms only	O
sylvaticosum		Exclusively E.	O
Rhacomitreto–Callunetum empetrosum arctostaphyletosum	17	Mainly W.	O
Vaccinetum chionophilum	18	Mainly E.C.	O
Vaccineto–Empetretum	19	Widespread	O
hepatic-rich facies		Exclusively N.W.	O
Empetrum–hypnaceous moss provisional nodum	19	Rare and scattered	O
Vaccinium–Nardus provisional nodum	19	Mainly W. and Cairngorms	O
Cladineto–Vaccinetum typicum sylvaticosum empetrosum	20	Exclusively E.C.	O
Festuceto–Vaccinetum	21		
cladinosum		Mainly E.	O–M (?)
rhacomitrosum		Mainly W.	O
Rhacomitreto–Empetretum	22	Widespread, but especially in W.	O
Dryas–Salix reticulata nodum	23	Mainly Breadalbane–Clova	E
Dryas–Carex rupestris nodum	23	Mainly N.W.	E
Dryas–Carex flacca nodum	23	Rare and scattered	E
Arctostaphylos grass heath		One locality in E.C.	E
Species poor Agrosto–Festucetum	24	Widespread	O–M

Table 74 (*continued*)

Nodum	Table No.	Geographical Distribution	Soil Class
Alchemilleto Agrosto–Festucetum	25	Widespread	M
Rhacomitrium-rich facies		Mainly W.	O–M
Species-rich Agrosto–Festucetum	26	Widespread	M–E
Saxifrageto-Agrosto–Festucetum	26	Local, mainly Breadalbane–Clova	E
Thalictrum–Ctenidium provisional nodum	27	Rare and scattered	M–E
Nardetum sub-alpinum			
species-poor facies	28	Widespread, but especially in S.	O
species-rich facies	29	Local, mainly Breadalbane–Clova	M–E
Juncetum squarrosi sub-alpinum			
species-poor facies	28	Widespread, especially in W.	O
species-rich facies	29	Local, mainly in W.	M–E
Deschampsietum caespitosae alpinum			
species-poor facies	30	Widespread	O–M
species-rich facies		Widespread but local	M–E
Luzula sylvatica grassland nodum	31	Local	M
Molinia grasslands		Mainly in W.	O–M
Nardus–Pleurozium nodum	32	Mainly E.C.	O
Nardus–Trichophorum nodum	32	Mainly W. and Cairngorms	O
Nardus–Rhacomitrium nodum	32	Mainly W.	O
Nardetum medio-alpinum	33	Cairngorms only	O
Polytricheto–Caricetum bigelowii	34	Exclusively C. and mainly E.C.	O
typicum			
rhytidiadelphetosum			
Dicraneto–Caricetum bigelowii	35	Mainly E.C.	O
Cladineto–Juncetum trifidi	36	Cairngorms and adjoining hills	O
Juncus trifidus–Festuca ovina nodum	37	Mainly W.	O
Tall Herb nodum	38	Widespread	M–E
Cryptogrammeto–Athyrietum chionophilum	39	Widespread, but local and mainly in W.	O
Dwarf Herb nodum	40	Mainly W., but widespread in Breadalbane	M–E
Alchemilla–Sibbaldia nodum	41	Widespread, especially in W.	O–M
Potentilla erecta facies			
Saxifragetum aizoidis	42	Local, mainly in Breadalbane–Clova	E
mixed saxifrage facies			
Cariceto–Rhacomitretum lanuginosi	43	Widespread	O
Juncus trifidus facies	22	Widespread but local	O
cushion herb facies	44	Mainly W. and especially N.W.	O
Polygoneto–Rhacomitretum lanuginosi	44	Local and mainly W.	O–M
Deschampsieto–Rhytidiadelphetum	45		
typicum		Mainly W.	O
triquetrosum			M–E
Polytricheto–Dicranetum starkei	46	Widespread but local	O
Rhacomitreto–Dicranetum starkei	47	Widespread but local	O
Gymnomitreto–Salicetum herbaceae	48	Mainly C.	O
Gymnomitrium varians facies			
Trichophoreto–Eriophoretum typicum	49	Mainly W.	O
Rhacomitrium-rich facies			
Calluneto–Eriophoretum	50	Widespread, but especially in E.	O
shrub-rich facies		Mainly in E.	O
lichen-rich facies		Mainly in E.	O
Empetreto–Eriophoretum	51	Mainly C.	O
Trichophoreto–Callunetum	52	Widespread	O
Sphagnum-rich facies			
crustaceous lichen facies			
Cladonia sylvatica facies		Exclusively E.C.	

Table 74 (*continued*)

Nodum	Table No.	Geographical Distribution	Soil Class
Molinieto–Callunetum	52	Widespread, but especially in W.	O
Trichophoreto–Eriophoretum caricetosum	49	Widespread	O
Molinia–Myrica nodum . . .	53	Widespread, but especially in W.	O–M
Sphagneto–Juncetum effusi . . .	54	Widespread	O
Sphagneto–Caricetum sub-alpinum .	55	Widespread	O
Sphagneto–Caricetum alpinum . .	55	Widespread, but especially in C.	O
Carex aquatilis–rariflora nodum . .	55	Exclusively in E.C.	O
Juncus acutiflorus–Acrocladium cuspidatum nodum	56	Mainly in S.W. and E.C.	M
Hypno–Caricetum alpinum . . .	29	Widespread but local, mainly in Breadalbane–Clova	M
Carex rostrata–Sphagnum warnstorfianum nodum	57	C. and mainly E.C.	M
Carex panicea–Campylium stellatum nodum	58	Widespread but local, mainly in Breadalbane–Clova	M–E
Carex rostrata–brown moss provisional nodum	58	Rare and scattered	E
Schoenus nigricans provisional nodum	64	Rare, only in N.W. (?)	E
Caricetum saxatilis	59	Local in W., mainly Breadalbane	M–E
Philonoto–Saxifragetum stellaris . .	60	Widespread	O–M
Pohlietum glacialis	60	Local, mainly C.	O
Anthelia–Deschampsia caespitosa provisional nodum	61	Widespread but local	O
Narthecium–Sphagnum provisional nodum	62	Widespread but local	O
Cratoneuron commutatum–Saxifraga aizoides nodum	63	Widespread but local, mainly Breadalbane–Clova	E
Cariceto–Saxifragetum aizoidis . .	64	Widespread	M–E
high level facies		Widespread but local	M–E
low level facies		Mainly W.	M–E

Plate 1. Pinetum Hylocomieto–Vaccinetum

Abernethy Forest, Inverness-shire, at 750 ft.

A mature, even-aged stand of Scots Pine on a well-drained sandy soil. *Vaccinium myrtillus* and *V. vitis-idaea* are dominant, but in places with an even denser shade their growth becomes sparser and hypnaceous mosses assume dominance.

Plate 2. Pine Forest

Abernethy Forest, Inverness-shire, at 750 ft.

Perhaps the nearest approach to completely natural pine forest now to be found in Scotland. The photograph shows a clearing in the mature forest, with natural regeneration and trees of all ages, and there is a patchy understorey of juniper. The field layer of Hylocomieto–Vaccinetum beneath the dense forest shows an approach to Vaccineto–Callunetum in the clearing. The adjoining forest consists of pine stands of different ages, with similar clearings of all sizes. Although each patch of dense timber is fairly even-aged within itself there is thus a good deal of age diversity in the forest as a whole.

Plate 3. Birchwood–pinewood transition

Coille na Glas Leitire, Loch Maree, West Ross, at 200 ft.

Betuletum Oxaleto–Vaccinetum on seasonally irrigated brown-earths beside a small stream pass into Pinetum Vaccineto–Callunetum on peaty podsols of the damp slopes behind. The change in the field layer is shown by the replacement of *Vaccinium myrtillus* by *Calluna vulgaris* as the dominant.

Plate 4. Juniper-rich birchwood

Morrone, Braemar, Aberdeenshire, at 1500 ft.

The best example of this woodland-scrub combination yet found in Scotland. It lies on a limestone drift soil, and the field layer is species-rich in places.

Plate 5. Betuletum Oxaleto–Vaccinetum

Near Carrbridge, Inverness-shire, at 1500 ft.

This fern-rich stand is associated with junipers and so is referable also to the *Juniperus–Thelypteris nodum*. The vegetation contains *Blechnum spicant, Thelypteris dryopteris, T. phegopteris* and *Polystichum aculeatum*, grading into *Vaccinium myrtillus* dominated ground.

Plate 6. Sub-alpine scrub

Creag Fhiaclach, North-west Cairngorms, at 1900 ft.

This is one of the most elevated examples of natural forest in Britain and one of the few which show a natural altitudinal limit. The pines become increasingly stunted and scattered, and finally give way to an upper zone of juniper scrub with heather. This kind of vegetation is destroyed permanently by fire.

Plate 7. Juniperus–Thelypteris nodum

Nr. Tomintoul, Banffshire, at 1600 ft.

A dense growth of juniper, with *Thelypteris oreopteris, Blechnum spicant, Vaccinium myrtillus* and *Luzula sylvatica*, passing to *Calluna* heath in open places away from the shelter of the bushes.

Plate 8. Arctostaphyleto–Callunetum

Boat of Garten, Inverness-shire, at 900 ft.

The trailing mats of *Arctostaphylos uva-ursi* are intimately mixed with *Calluna vulgaris* and there is an abundance of *Genista anglica*.

Plate 9. Juniperetum nanae

Beinn Eighe Nature Reserve, West Ross, at 1700 ft.

A mixed dwarf shrub heath dominated by *Calluna vulgaris* and *Juniperus nana* and forming a discontinuous patchwork on quartzite moraine debris. Other dwarf shrubs such as *Arctostaphylos uva-ursi*, *Arctous alpina* and *Vaccinium* spp. are typically present and the bryophyte layer is dominated by mats of an unnamed species of *Herberta*.

Plate 10. Arctoeto–Callunetum

Glen Cannich, Inverness-shire at 2400 ft.

A close view of the prostrate dwarf shrub mat of a windswept spur. The completely flattened branches of *Calluna vulgaris* are over-grown with the pale coloured lichen *Ochrolechia frigida*. The reticulate leaves of *Arctous alpina* are mixed with *Calluna*, *Vaccinium uliginosum* and the distinctive foliose lichen *Platysma lacunosum*.

Plate 11. Transition from Rhacomitreto–Callunetum to Cariceto–Rhacomitretum

Spur of Am Faochagach, East Ross, at 2450 ft.

The prostrate heather mat shows increasing abundance of *Rhacomitrium* and passes rather rapidly into pure moss-heath, there being only a narrow mosaic ecotone. The broad ridges and plateaux behind, rising to 3150 ft., are covered mainly with *Rhacomitrium* heath rich in cushion herbs and by *Juncus trifidus–Festuca ovina* erosion surface.

Plate 12. Dryas octopetala–Salix reticulata nodum

Ben Lui, Argyll, at 2300 ft.

A steep bank of broken cliffs, with this community covering several square metres but grading into other rock-face vegetation. Also present are *Saxifraga oppositifolia, Carex flacca, Festuca ovina* agg., *Pinguicula vulgaris, Vaccinium uliginosum* and *Rhacomitrium lanuginosum*. The stand is that recorded in list 5 of Table 23.

Plate 13. Alchemilleto–Agrosto–Festucetum

Coire Chuirn, Drumochter, Inverness-shire, at 1500 ft.

A grazed grassland community on well-drained stream alluvium. This stand shows dominance of *Alchemilla alpina*, and associated species include *Thymus drucei, Vaccinium vitis-idaea, Viola riviniana, Agrostis* spp., *Festuca ovina* agg. and *Euphrasia officinalis* agg.

Plate 14. Deschampsietum caespitosae alpinum

Head of Caenlochan Glen, Angus, at 2700 ft.

This example lies at the foot of the cliffs with the tall herb ledge of Plate 17, and is clearly the grazed derivative of that community. It is the species-rich facies, although the characteristic herbs are not visible amongst the luxuriant growth of *Deschampsia caespitosa*. The stand passes into block scree lower down the slope and into tall herb ledges on the broken cliffs above.

Plate 15. Juncus trifidus–Festuca ovina community on windswept erosion surface

Am Faochagach, East Ross, at 3000 ft.

The finer soil material accumulates on the stable *Rhacomitrium* heath to the leeward, but the erosion face shows that the original vegetation and soil cover is still losing ground. Large patches of erosion surface are visible on the gently inclined top of the spur behind, and as the slope increases they form strips along the outer edge of solifluction terraces. These terraces, with their sinuous edges marked out by the shadowed banks below, are unusual in running obliquely down the slope instead of across it.

In the distance is the massive ridge of Ben Wyvis, covered along the whole length of its summit by a continuous carpet of *Rhacomitrium* heath.

Plate 16. Solifluction terraces and associated vegetation patterns

Am Faochagach, East Ross, at 3000 ft., with Fannich Forest beyond

An extensive and regular system of these terraces covers the gentle south and east slopes of the summit. The banks are usually steep and often slightly undercut—their appearance suggests that solifluction is active here. Above the bank is a zone of the *Juncus trifidus–Festuca ovina erosion surface*, passing into closed Cariceto–Rhacomitretum rich in cushion herbs (clumps of *Silene acaulis* are visible on the erosion surface). At the foot of the bank the moss heath often contains abundant *Nardus stricta*, *Deschampsia caespitosa* and *Empetrum hermaphroditum*—the beginnings of snow-bed vegetation.

Plate 17. Tall Herb Nodum

Ungrazed cliff ledge at 2800 ft., Caenlochan Glen, Angus

(List 1 of Table 38.) The luxuriant vegetation contains *Angelica sylvestris*, *Cirsium heterophyllum*, *Trollius europaeus*, *Sedum rosea*, *Valeriana officinalis*, *Luzula sylvatica*, *Filipendula ulmaria*, *Rubus saxatilis*, *Geranium sylvaticum* and *Polystichum lonchitis*, and contrasts with the herb-rich Deschampsietum caespitosae on the grazed slopes below. Some ledges on the same cliffs have montane willow scrub.

Plates 18–19. Tall herb and fern communities

Beinn Bhan, Applecross, West Ross, at 2400 ft.

A huge ungrazed 'ledge' of the Torridon sandstone cliffs (about 300 m. × 50 m.) is covered mainly by dense fern and *Vaccinium–Luzula* communities where the soil is un-irrigated, and by broad strips of tall herb vegetation where seepage lines appear (one is visible in the middle of the fern-bed). The dominant fern is *Athyrium alpestre*, but several other species, notably *Dryopteris abbreviata* and *D. austriaca*, are abundant. The tall herbs are mainly *Angelica sylvestris, Caltha palustris, Crepis paludosa, Ranunculus acris, Geum rivale, Filipendula ulmaria, Trollius europaeus* and *Valeriana officinalis*. This is a rather wetter type than the tall herb community of Plate 17.

Plate 20. Soil hummocks in Rhacomitrium heath

An Sgulan, Dalnaspidal Forest, Perthshire, at 2850 ft.

The ground is covered with a continuous carpet of *Rhacomitrium lanuginosum* (the typical Cariceto–Rhacomitretum) but it is locally thrown into series of solifluction hummocks, each averaging about 3–4 ft. in diameter. The foreground slopes slightly and shows a tendency to ridges rather than hummocks. The intervening depressions have a greater abundance of *Carex bigelowii* and grasses than the hummocks. These forms are widespread on elevated plateaux in the Highlands and sometimes show striking differences in vegetation between hummock and hollow, giving a mosaic pattern; in many places they probably represent fossil stone polygons and stripes.

Plate 21. Late snow-beds and associated vegetation

Carn Mairg, above Loch Rannoch, Perthshire, at 3000 ft.

The remaining snow patches are surrounded by dark areas of Polytricheto–Dicranetum starkei, passing below to snow-melt spring communities, and mixtures of *Nardus stricta* and *Vaccinium myrtillus* snow-bed vegetation. The more exposed summit areas are covered with Cariceto–Rhacomitretum.

Plate 22. Rhacomitreto–Dicranetum starkei

Sgurr na Lapaich, Glen Cannich, East Ross, at 3300 ft.

Well developed late snow-bed vegetation in the east corrie includes extensive stands of this type, grading into Polytricheto–Dicranetum starkei. The ground is moss dominated, mainly by *Rhacomitrium* spp. (especially *R. canescens*) and the sparse growth of vascular plants includes *Gnaphalium supinum*, *Saxifraga stellaris*, *Alchemilla alpina*, *Viola palustris*, *Deschampsia caespitosa* and *Carex bigelowii*.

Plate 23. Gymnomitreto–Salicetum herbaceae

Ben Heasgarnich, Forest of Mamlorn, Perthshire, at 3400 ft.

A late snow community of ground subject to amorphous solifluction. The picture shows a stand with particularly dense *Salix herbacea*, but the dark hepatic crust of *Gymnomitrium concinnatum* is visible in places.

Plate 24. Western blanket-bog with associated communities

Beinn Eighe from near Loch Bharranich, West Ross, at about 500 ft.

The level 'flowe' in the centre is covered with Trichophoreto–Eriophoretum typicum, fed by a runnel (foreground) which is bordered by a strip of the *Molinia–Myrica nodum*. The *Sphagnum*-rich flowe passes into Molinieto–Callunetum at the foot of the moraines and this gives way to Trichophoreto–Callunetum on the moraine sides and tops. The slopes of Beinn Eighe beyond are covered largely with the last two associations, although the crests of the moraines at low levels have the western *Calluna–Arctostaphylos* community recorded in lists 14, 15 of Table 17. Above 1000 ft. comparable sites often have Rhacomitreto–Callunetum.

Plate 25. Lichen-rich Calluneto–Eriophoretum

Ladder Hills, Banffshire, at 2600 ft.

Undisturbed blanket-bog with *Calluna vulgaris*, *Eriophorum vaginatum*, *Rubus chamaemorus*, *Sphagnum nemoreum* and patchy dominance of *Cladonia sylvatica–C. rangiferina* (light-coloured patches).

Plate 26. Complex of calcareous flush and mire vegetation

Devil's Elbow, Glen Shee, Perthshire, at 1600 ft.

Open, stony patches of Cariceto–Saxifragetum aizoidis passing to closed sedge sward of the *Carex panicea–Campylium stellatum nodum*. A large stand of the second type to the left has an abundance of *Eriophorum latifolium* and passes in wetter places into Hypno–Caricetum. Numerous mounds of heathy, oligotrophic vegetation are dotted about the area, and on badly drained ground away from the flushes there is Calluneto–Eriophoretum. Better drained ground has Nardetum sub-alpinum and Callunetum vulgaris, including the herb-rich facies of both where the soil is calcareous.

INDEX

Aberdeenshire, 32, 168
Abernethy Forest, 14, 128, 129
Abundance (species), 6
Achillea ptarmica, 117
Achnasheen, 95
Aconitetalia, 140
Acrobolbus wilsoni, 148
Acrocladium cuspidatum, 117, 118, 127
    giganteum, 127
    sarmentosum, 126, 130
       -rich Carex saxatilis sociation, 126
    stramineum, 127
    trifarium, 121, 123, 134
Adelanthus decipiens, 19, 148
Adenostyletalia, 140
Advance growth (pine), 14
Aeration (soil), 169
Agriculture, 150, 169
Agropyron donianum, 150, 175
Agrostis canina, 22, 50, 52–54, 58, 60, 61
    -Festuca grassland, 41, **51–57**, 61, 65, 66, 92
    spp., 24
    stolonifera, 24, 126, 130
    tenuis, 16, 20, 52–54, 58, 60, 61, 64, 84, 85, 94
Ajuga reptans, 24
    pyramidalis, 174
Albrecht, W. A., 169
Alchemilla alpina, 45, 46, 53, 57, 61, 77, 82, 84, 85, 91, 92, 173, 174, 177
    conjuncta, 175
    filicaulis, 174
    glabra, 55, 87
    glomerulans, 174
    grassland, 53, **54**, 57
    -Sibbaldia nodum, **85–87**, 139, 156, 164, 393, Map 22
    vestita, 55
    vulgris agg., 80, 84, 85
    wichurae, 174
Alchemilleto-Agrosto-Festucetum, **53**, **54**, 138, 163, Plate 13
Alchemilletum alpinae, 87
Alectoria ochroleuca, 36–38
Alectorieto-Arctostaphyletum uvae-ursi, 35
Alder (*Alnus glutinosa*), 23, 111
Alicularia scalaris, 97
Alliance, 9, 137–141
Allium ursinum, 11, 21

Alluvium, 54, 59
Alopecurus alpinus, 131, 174
Alpine hamada rawmark, 77
Alpine Nardus association, 71
    stricta sociation, 71
Alpine rawmark, 76
    sod podsol, 69
Alps, 29, 152
Alston Moor, 105
Amann's Oceanicity Formula, 144
Amat Forest, 11
Amblyodon dealbatus, 134
Am Faochagach, 159
Anastrepta orcadensis, 31, 68
Anastrophyllum donianum, 31, 32
Anderson, M. L., 16
Andreaea nivalis, 155
Anemone nemorosa, 16, 18, 22
Aneura pinguis, 125
Angelica sylvestris, 22, 80
Angus, 26, 103, 116, 168
An Socach, 75
Antennaria dioica, 29
Anthelia-Deschampsia caespitosa provisional nodum, **132**, 139, 156
    spp., 99, 125, 131, 132
    -Cesia-rich Carex rufina sociation, 132
    juratzkana-Gymnomitrium varians sociation, 100
Anthelietum, 99, 100
Anthoxantho-Deschampsietum flexuosae, 74, 87
Anthoxanthum odoratum, 16, 22, 24, 52, 54, 58, 60, 61, 72, 96
Anthropogenic vegetation, 46, 51, 58, 62, 64, 65–67, 137, 138, 143
Anthyllis vulneraria, 50
Aonach Beag, 62, 160
    Mor, 91, 155, 160
Applecross, 35, 63, 81, 82
Aplozia cordifolia, 130, 131
Arabis alpina, 175
Arctic-alpine grassland, 46, 54
    species, 152
Arctic regions, 152, 160
    climate, 158, 159
Arctoeto-Callunetum, **34**, **35**, 36–39, 104, 138, 148, 163, Plate 10, Map 8
Arctostaphyleto-Callunetum, 28, **30**, **31**, 39, 50, 137, 145, 162, 163, Plate 8, Map 6
    -Cetrarion nivalis, 138

30

Arctostaphylos-grass heath, **50**, 150, 163
    uva-ursi, 30, 33, 36, 50, 56, 104, 151,
      170, 174
Arctous alpina, 34, 103, 104, 148, 150, 174
    -Loiseleuria nodum, 34
Ardlair, 10
Ardnamurchan, 20
Ardtulichan, 135
Arenaria norvegica, 175, 177
Argyll, 11, 22, 102, 128, 152, 168, 176
Armeria maritima, 90–92, 148, 153, Map 24
Arran, 133
Arrhenatheretalia elatioris, 138
Arrhenatherum elatius, 22
Artemisia norvegica, 77
Ash (*Fraxinus excelsior*), **20**, **21**, 24
Asia, 138
Asperula odorata, 22
Asplenium viride, 174
Association, 7
    element, 9
Assynt, 149
Astragalus alpinus, 49, 175
Atholl, 41, 103, 394
Athyrium alpestre, 82, 166, 174
    filix-femina, 22, 24
Athyrietum alpestris, 82
Atlantic times, 104
Aulacomnium palustre, 13, 112, 119, 127
    turgidum, 92
Aulacomnieto-Sphagnetum warnstorfiani, 120
Authorities (Botanical nomenclature), 3

Banffshire, 159
Bartsia alpina, 49, 175
Basalt, 11, 20, 166
Basiphilous species, 16, 17, 111, 112, 118, 120,
    127, 166, 172, (*see also* calcicolous species)
Bazzania pearsoni, 31
    trilobata, 19
Beijerinck, W., 29
Beinn Bhan, 63, 81, 82
    Bhrotain, 69
    Damph, 32
    Dearg, 78, 90, 96, 176, Map 2
    Eighe, 14, 33, 34, 58, 89, 93, 94, 105,
      159, Map 2
    Enaiglair, 66
    a'Ghlo, 44, Map 2
Ben Alder, 38, 62, 73, 84, 95, 176, 394, Map 2
    a'Bhuird, 69
    Cruachan, 146, Map 2
    Griam Mor, 104, 394, Map 2
    Heasgarnich, 94, 134, 394
    Hope, 71, 77, 79, 87, 146, 170, 176, Map 2
    Hutig, 110
    Klibreck, 38, 110, 159, 393, Map 2
    Lawers, 45, 53, 54, 59, 71–73, 77, 81, 85,
      95, 99, 125, 150, 157, 166, 168, 175, 394
    Loyal, 64, 104, Map 2

Ben Lui, 1, 26, 81, 87, 88, 125, 134, 168,
    394
    MacDhui, 69, 159
    More Assynt, 48, 67, 68, 89, 90, 159,
      176, 393, Map 2
    Nevis, 72, 81, 84, 90, 91, 160, 176, 394,
      Map 2
    Rinnes, 32, 159
    Vrackie, 120, 123, 168, Map 2
    Wyvis, 36, 38, 39, 61, 74, 90, 94, 95,
      160, 168, 393, Map 2
Bettyhill, 34, 121, 122, 124, 134, 151, 170, 176
Betula-herb *nodum*, 12, **16–18**, 30, 31, 84, 138, 163
Betula nana, 25, 37, 103–105, 148, 150, 174
    bog, 103
    -rich Cetraria nivalis, Cladonia
      sylvatica association, 37
    odorata, 12
    pubescens, 11, 12, 16, 20, 24, 104
    spp. *see* birch
    verrucosa, 104
Betuleto-Vaccinietum lapponicum, 17
Betuletum Oxaleto-Vaccinetum, 12, **15–18**, 39,
    81, 137, 163, Plate 5
Birch (wood, scrub), 10, 11, 13, **15–20**, 21, 23,
    25, 31, 34, 37, 43, 44, 65, 66, 80, 99, 140, 149,
    151, 163, Plates 3, 4, Map 3
Bird Cherry, *see Prunus padus*
Black Mount, Map 2
Blair Atholl, 50, 56, 121, 122, 136, 163, 394
Blanket bog, 31, 52, 59, 60, 101, 103–107, 110,
    112–115, 123, 124, 128–131, 135, 143, 147,
    Plate 24
Blechnum spicant, 16, 25, 39, 40.
Blindia acuta, 134
Blizzards, 158
Block scree, 18, 32, 42, 47, 63, 82
Bonar Bridge, 11
Borgefjell Mountains, 73
Botanical Society of the British Isles, 6, 357
Brachypodium sylvaticum, 20, 22
Brachythecium rutabulum, 23
Bracken (*Pteridium aquilinum*), 16, 17, 21, 24,
    66, 83
Braemar, 75, 135
Braeriach, 69
Breabag, 67
Breadalbane, v, 1, 26, 46, 48, 53, 55, 60, 67, 73,
    74, 80, 84, 85, 87, 89, 118, 121, 125, 133, 134,
    136, 157, 162, 168, 170, 175, 176, 394, Map 2
Braun-Blanquet, J., 9, 12, 14, 17, 34, 137–141
British rainfall, 146
Briza media, 50, 120
Brockmann-Jerosch, H., 144, 147, 152
Brown earth (soil), 11, 17, 22, 29, 30, 49, 50,
    54, 81, 84, 91, 93, 162, 163, 169
'Brown mosses', 119, 120, 122, 127, 134
Bryales, 117
Bryonia dioica, 24
Bryum pseudotriquetrum, 120

Burges, A., 1, 42, 71
Burren, 50
Butterburn-North Tyne moors, 105

Caenlochan, 48, 66, 74, 81, 84, 110, 115, 119, 125, 168, 394, Map 2
Cairngorm Nature Reserve, 157
Cairngorms, 1, 11, 25, 28, 31, 32, 34, 35, 37, 44–46, 62, 68–74, 76, 79, 82, 83, 86, 90, 91, 98–100, 106,–108, 116, 131, 132, 145, 146, 148–150, 153, 155, 157, 158–160, 176, Maps 2, 10
Cairnwell, 44, 45, 49, 50, 91, 163
Caithness, 1, 146, 148
Calamagrostis lanceolata, 24
Calcicolous species, vegetation, 21, 58, 95, 136, 137, 140, 148, 151, 153, 166, **167**, 168, 170, 171, 174–176
Calcifuge species, vegetation, 111, 136, 137, 148, 170, 172, 173, 175, 176, 394
Calcite, 168, 170
Calcium, 49, 54, 55, 57, 62, 80, 87, 111, 121, 131, 133, 136, 153, 164, 166–174, 409
    determination, 165
Calluna-lichen heath, **36**, 150, Map 9
    -*Pleurozium nodum*, 29
    vulgaris, 12, 13, 15, 25, 28, 30, 31, 33–37, 52, 56, 60, 64, 65, 67, 91, 101, 103, 105, 108, 110, 112, 123, 128, 133, 149, 151, 158, 170
Calluneto-Eriophoretum, 31, 32, 35, 36, 40, 59, 61, **103–105**, 106, 107, 110, 114, 120, 123, 128, 136, 141, 145, 163, 174, 393, Plate 25, Maps 28, 34
Calluneto-Genistetum, 30
Calluneto-Ulicetalia, 29
Callunetum vulgaris, 15, **28–30**, 31, 32, 36, 40, 42, 49, 53, 59, 66, 104, 107–109, 122, 137, 145, 158, 163, 164, 393, Map 6
Caltha palustris, 24, 126
    ssp. *minor*, 130
Calypogeia trichomanis, 13
Cambrian rocks, 33, 35, 92, 105, 108
Cambridge (Cairngorm investigation), 155
Campanula rotundifolia, 50, 53, 173
Camptothecium nitens, 118, 119
Campylium stellatum, 120–122, 124, 127, 134, 153
Campylopus flexuosus, 12
    shawii, 33
Canker (ash), 21
Cape Wrath, 103
Card index, 6, 7
Cardamine hirsuta, 26
    pratensis, 127, 133
Cardaminopsis petraea, 174
Carex acutiformis, 24
    aquatilis, 115, 116
        -*rariflora nodum*, **115–117**, 141, Map 31
    atrata, 49, 174
    atrofusca, 134, 175, 177

Carex bigelowii, 32, 41, 43–46, 67–69, 72–75, 89, 92–94, 96, 106, 115, 150, 173, 177, 394, Map 18
    binervis, 24, 60
    capillaris, 49, 150, 174
    caryophyllea, 55
    curta, 115, 126, 129
    demissa, 119, 120, 125, 127, 134
        -panicea nodum, 120, 136
    dioica, 120, 123, 125, 127
    echinata, 58, 112, 114, 115, 118, 120, 125, 126, 128, 129
    flacca, 48, 50, 120
    flava-Campylium   stellatum-Drepanocladus intermedius sociation, 136
    -grahami, 175
    hostiana, 120, 134
        -demissa nodum, 136
    lachenalii, 116, 175, 177
    lasiocarpa, 120, 124, 126–129
    limosa, 102, 123, 126, 129
    microglochin, 134, 175
    nigra, 112–115, 118–120, 125, 126, 128, 129, 170
    norvegica, 175
    panicea, 54, 58, 112, 118, 120, 134, 170
        -Campylium stellatum nodum, 56, 57, 118, **120–122**, 124–126, 133–136, 141, 151, 162, 164, Map 30
    paniculata, 127
    pauciflora, 102, 128, 173
    paupercula, 129
    pilulifera, 52, 58, 60
    pulicaris, 54, 58, 112, 118, 120, 127
    rariflora, 115, 175, 177
    remota, 22, 24
    rostrata, 116, 119, 120, 122–126, 128, 129, 170
        -brown moss provisional nodum, 121, **122–124**, 128, 136, 141, 151, 164
        -Sphagnum recurvum mire, 119
            warnstorfianum nodum, 27, **119, 120**, 123, 141, 164, Map 31
    rupestris, 48, 49, 150, 174
    saxatilis, 86, 115, 125, 174
        -Drepanocladus intermedius sociation, 126
    sylvatica, 22
    vaginata, 174
Caricetalia curvulae, 138, 140
    fuscae, 141
Cariceto-Rhacomitretum lanuginosi, 9, 36, 46, 68, 78, **89–92**, 93–95, 116, 138, 145, 149, 150, 163, 164, 166, Plate 11, Maps 24, 33
        -Saxifragetum aizoidis, 56, 88, 121, 122, 124, 125, **133–136**, 141, 145, 153, Map 30
Caricetum bigelowii-lachenalii, 73, 74

Caricetum saxatilis, **125**, **126**, 133–135, 141, 156, 158, 162, 165, 172, 173, Map 32
Caricion atrofuscae-saxatilis, 141
　　bicoloris-atrofuscae, 141
　　canescentis-fuscae, 141
Carlisle, A., *see* Steven, H. M.
Carn a'Chlarsaich, 45
　　a'Gheoidh, 91
　　Ban Mor, 91
　　Eige, 131
　　Mairg, 45
　　nan Gobhar, 160
　　nan Sac, 91
Cassiopeto-Salicion herbaceae, 139
Catoscopium nigritum, 134
Cattle, 169
Cawdor, 104
Cerastium alpinum, 84, 174
　　cerastoides, 131, 155, 174
　　edmonstonii, 174
Cetraria aculeata, 34, 36
　　crispa-Cladonia sylvatica-Juncus trifidus association, 76
　　hiascens, 69, 72
　　islandica, 34, 36, 43, 44, 46, 48, 68, 69, 75, 92
　　nivalis, 36, 38
　　　　-Alectoria ochroleuca-rich Loiseleuria association, 35
Cetrarietum delisei, 37, 71
　　nivalis, 35
Chamaemoreto-Sphagnetum acutifolii, 106
Chamaenerietum angustifolii nudum, 81
Chamaenerion angustifolium, 80
Chamaepericlymenum suecicum, 31, 32, 39, 40, 43, 174
Chara spp., 123, 136
Characteristic species, 9
Charcoal, 12
Cherleria sedoides, 72, 77, 84, 90–92, 148, 153, 170, 174, Map 24
Cheviots, 2, 105, 114
Chionophilous species, vegetation, 39, 44, 58, 61, 63, 67, 69, 71, 74–76, 84, 86, 106, 116, 137, 139, 143, 155–157, 162, Map 17
Chionophobous species, vegetation, 33, 35, 77, 89, 95, 137, 138, 140
Chomophytic species, 48
Chrysosplenium oppositifolium, 22, 24, 130
Cicerbita alpina, 80, 81, 175, 177
Cinclidium stygium, 118
Circaea intermedia, 20
　　lutetiana, 22
Cirsium heterophyllum, 17, 20, 22, 80
　　palustre, 22, 24, 26, 117
Cladineto-Callunetum, 31, 34, **35–38**, 39, 40, 43, 44, 49, 70, 90, 91, 104, 110, 138, 145, 158, 163, 164, 393, Maps 9, 34
　　-Juncetum trifidi, **75–77**, 139, 145, 156, 158, 164, 168, Map 19

Cladineto—*cont.*
　　-Vaccinetum, 9, 42, **43–45**, 46, 138, 139, 145, 156, 163, 166, Maps 11, 34
Cladium mariscus, 127, 153
Cladonia alpestris, 37
　　alpicola, 73
　　bellidiflora, 69, 73, 75, 82
　　coccifera, 106
　　deformis, 13
　　delessertii, 69
　　gracilis, 43, 46, 75
　　impexa, 28, 33, 50
　　mitis, 37
　　pyxidata, 13, 75
　　rangiferina, 13, 36, 43
　　sylvatica, 13, 34, 36, 41, 43, 45, 46, 69, 75, 103, 106, 107
　　　　-rangiferina-rich Calluna association, 37
　　　　-rich Empetrum association, 44
　　　　　　Vaccinium myrtillus association, 44, 46
　　squamosa, 13
　　uncialis, 31, 33, 34, 36, 45, 46, 58, 68, 75, 89, 92, 106
Cladonietum alpestris, 37
Clapham, A. R., 3
Clare (County), 50
Climatic Optimum, 50, 176, 177
Climatological Atlas, 77, 144, 147, 155
Climax vegetation, 14, 19, 151
Cloud cover, 150
Clova, 26, 43, 48, 53, 55, 72, 74, 75, 84, 87, 104, 110, 115, 119, 121, 133, 149, 168, 175, 176, 394, Map 2
Cochlearia alpina, 174
　　micacea, 174
Coille Gaireallach, 21
　　na Glas Leitire, 14
Coire Chuirn, 53
　　Heasgarnich, 94
Cololejeunea minutissima, 148
Colluvium, 54, 55, 58
Conopodium majus, 16, 18, 22
Conostomum tetragonum, 97
Conservation, 1, 34
Constancy, 7
Continentality (climatic), 152, 157
Coppice, 20
Corrie Fee, 168
Corylus avellana, *see* hazel
Cover (vegetative), 6
Craig Fonvuick, 21
Crampton, C. B., 1
Crataegus monogyna, *see* hawthorn
Cratoneureto-Saxifragetum aizoidis, 133
Cratoneureto-Saxifragion aizoidis, 142

Cratoneuron commutatum, 23, 120–122, 127, 133, 134

    -Saxifraga aizoides nodum, 133, 142

    decipiens, 133

Crannach Wood, 11

Creag Meagaidh, 62, 90, 94, 394, Map 2

Crepis paludosa, 22, 23

Cromarty Firth, 35

Cronkley Fell, 50

Crompton, E., 66

Cross Fell, 44, 61

Cryptogramma crispa, 82, 140, 174

Cryptogrammeto-Athyrietum chionophilum, **82–84**, 140, 147, 156, 158, 163, Map 20

Cryptogrammetum crispi, 83

Ctenidium molluscum, 23, 54, 87, 120, 121

Curr Wood, 14

Cushion-herbs, 78, 90, 150, 153, Map 24

Cyclo-climax, 19

Cystopteris montana, 87, 175, 177

Dactylis glomerata, 20

Dahl, E., vi, 5, 7, 9, 25, 27, 35, 37, 42, 71, 73, 74, 76, 81, 87, 91, 92, 94, 99, 100, 106, 120, 123, 131–133, 137–140, 151, 155, 159, 165, 176, 177

Dalradian metamorphic series, 45, 75, 84, 121, 125, 133, 134, 161, 167–169, 171, 394

Dalwhinnie, 146

Damann, A. W. H., 29

Darling, F. F., 11

Deer, 20, 21, 23, 58, 63, 66, 111

Deeside, 15, 19

Denmark, 117

Deschampsia alpina, 131, 174

    caespitosa, 22, 24, 26, 51, 61–63, 73, 80, 82, 84, 85, 87, 94–96, 116, 126, 130–132

        -Geranium sylvaticum association, 64

        grassland, **61–64**, 73

    flexuosa, 12, 13, 16, 26, 30, 31, 33, 39, 43, 44, 60, 61, 64, 77, 81, 82, 89, 92, 100

        -Polytrichum alpinum sociation, 73

        -Dicranum fuscescens sociation, 74

Deschampsieto-Myrtilletalia, 138, 139

    -Rhytidiadelphetum, 61, 63, 74, 84, 85, 91, **94–96**, 139, 156, 158, 162–164, 394, Maps 25, 33

Deschampsietum caespitosae alpinum, 56, **61–64**, 85, 94, 139, 140, 156, 158, 163, 164, Plate 13, Map 16

Deschampsietum caespitosae alpicolum, 64

Deschampsieto-Anthoxanthion, 139

Diapensia lapponica, 77, 175

Dicranella squarrosa, 130, 131

Dicraneto-Caricetum bigelowii, 43, 46, 63, 72, **73**, **74**, 89, 91, 94, 95, 116, 139, 145, 156, 164–166, Map 18

Dicranetum starkei, 99

Dicranodontium uncinatum, 31

Dicranum bergeri, 135

    falcatum, 96, 155

    fuscescens, 69, 73, 74

        -Carex bigelowii sociation, 73

    glaciale, 155

    majus, 23

    scoparium, 23, 28, 29, 31, 39, 50, 69

    starkei, 96, 97, 99, 155

    undulatum, 30

Differential species, 9

Digitalis purpurea, 22

Diplophyllum taxifolium, 97

Ditrichum flexicaule, 50

Dollar Law, 37, 44, 105

Dolomite, 20, 48, 49, 58, 92, 93, 105, 133, 159, 161, 163, 168, 176

Domin scale, 6, 88

Dominance, 7, 9

Draba incana, 174

    rupestris, 175

Drainage impedance, 155, 158

Drepanocladus exannulatus, 130

    fluitans, 127

    intermedius-Campylium-stellatum-rich Carex panicea sociation, 136

    revolvens, 119, 120, 122, 125, 127, 134

Drosera anglica, 102, 123, 134

    rotundifolia, 101, 103, 112

Dryas octopetala, 47–50, 85, 88, 150–153, 170, 174

    -Empetrum hermaphroditum heath, 48

    heath, 55, 148, 149, 159, 163, 173, Map 14

Dryas octopetala noda, **47–50**, 88, 140, 163, 166, Plate 12, Map 14

Dryopteris aemula, 148

    austriaca, 22

    borreri, 26

    filix-mas, 22

    spinulosa, 26

    spp., 24, 83

Dryoptero-Calamagrostidion, 140

Drumochter, 53, 90, 160, 394, Map 2

Dubh lochan, 129

Dulnain Bridge, 14

Du Rietz, G. E., 51, 139

Durness, 20, 21, 48, 55, 58, 133, 163, 168, 176

Durno, S. E., 34, 104

Dwarf Herb *nodum*, 54, 55, 63, **84**, **85**, 88, 92, 125, 126, 139, 140, 153, 156, 158, 162, 163, Map 21

Earthworms, 55, 57, 84

Ecotype, 105, 153

Edderton, 25

Edintian, 50
Eididh nan Clach Geala, 86
Eleocharis multicaulis, 126
      pauciflora, 120, 127
Elm (*Ulmus* spp.), 21, 22
Elyno-Seslerietalia, 140
Empetreto-Eriophoretum, 106, 110, 115, 116,
    133, 141, 145, Map 29
Empetreto-Vaccinetum, 42
Empetrum heath, 44, 47
Empetrum hermaphroditum, 12, 28, 29, 31, 34–
    36, 39, 41–44, 46, 47, 49, 68, 89, 91, 103, 105,
    150, 151, 170, 173
      rubrum, 47
      -*Vaccinium* zone, 71
Endymion nonscriptus, 16, 20
England (North), 21, 22, 29, 37, 46, 52, 55, 64,
    65, 81, 82, 114, 117, 121, 124, 131, 133
Epilobium alsinifolium, 174
      anagallidifolium, 130–132, 150, 173
      hirsutum, 24
      hornemanni, 132
      montanum, 22, 26
      palustre, 117, 126
Equisetum fluviatile, 126
      hyemale, 134
      palustre, 126
      variegatum, 120, 134, 174
Erica cinerea, 30
      tetralix, 56, 101, 103, 106, 108, 112, 122,
      126, 128, 170
Erigeron borealis, 175
Eriophoretum vaginati, 104
Eriophorum angustifolium, 24, 102, 103, 112,
    114, 115, 118, 120, 123–126, 128, 129
      latifolium, 120, 134
      vaginatum, 31, 101, 103, 106, 107, 112,
      116, 128
Erosion surface, 72, 75, 77, 79, 89, 91, 93, 105,
    151, 160
Ettrick Hills, 64
Eupatorium cannabinum, 24
Eurhynchium myosuroides, 23
      myurum, 23
      praelongum, 23
      striatum, 23
Eutrophic species, vegetation, 49, 80, 92, 111,
    117, 118, 120–127, 135, 136, 138, 141, 151,
    167–172, 174
Evapo-transpiration, 147, 153
Exclusive species, 9
Exposure (wind), 75, 77, 142, 153, 154, 158,
    159, 169

Facies, 8
Faeroes, 39, 79, 92, 94
Fagetalia sylvaticae, 138
Fannich Forest, 90, 159, Map 2
Fell field, 79

Felspar, 77
Fen, 6, 101, 118, 120, 123, 124, 126, 127, 129,
    153
Fennoscandia, 64, 152, 176, 177
Ferreira, R. E. C., 77, 87, 166–168, 171, 172
Festuca ovina, 45, 50, 52–54, 58, 60, 77, 84, 87,
    91, 94, 118, 119, 134
          -*Cladonia sylvatica* sociation, 46
      rubra, 22, 54, 87, 133
Festuceto-Vaccinetum, 43, **45**, **46**, 49, 52, 53,
    74, 138, 163, 166, 393, Maps 12, 34
Filipendula ulmaria, 20, 22, 24, 25
Fionn Bheinn, 95
      Loch, 23
Fissidens adianthoides, 120
Flowe, 102, 107, 128
Flush vegetation, 101, 130–136, 143, 151, 153,
    163, 170, 174, Plate 26
Foinaven, 33, 93, 146, 393
Forest, **10–24**, 65, 138, 143, Map 3, Maps A,
    B (endpocket)
Forest zone, 2, 25, 31, 51, 121, 151, 163, 176
    limit, 17, 81, 142, 149, 150
Fragaria vesca, 22
France, 29
Fraser, G. K., 113
Fraxinus-Brachypodium sylvaticum nodum, **20**,
    21, 22, 138, 163
      excelsior, *see* ash
Frost, 27, 147, 155, 157, 158, 162

Galium aparine, 24
      boreale, 174
      hercynicum, 16, 24, 26, 39, 44, 52, 58, 60,
      61, 67, 82, 89, 94, 113, 141
      palustre, 24, 126
      verum, 50
Galloway, 102, 108, 113, 125
Galway (County), 34
Genista anglica, 29, 30
Gentiana verna, 55, 121
      nivalis, 175, 177
Geranietum sylvaticae alpicolum, 81
Geranium lucidum, 22
      robertianum, 22
      sylvaticum, 80, 173
Germany, 29
Geum rivale, 22, 80
      urbanum, 22
Gimingham, C. H., 31
Gjaerevoll, O., 68, 71, 73, 74, 82, 83, 87, 88,
    95, 99, 100, 132, 139, 140, 165
Glacial drift, 12, 17, 18, 21, 55, 167, 172
Glas Maol, 73, 74, 116
Glechoma hederacea, 24
Glen Affric, 61, 131, 159, 160, Map 2
      Banchor, 30
Glencoe, 32, 176, 394, Map 2

Glen Callater, 168
    Cannich, 74, Map 2
    Clova, 66, 107, 134
    Garry (Atholl), 102
    Loch, 168
    Lyon, 66, 113
    Moriston, 11, Map 2
    Muick, 110
    Shee, 41, 66
    Shiel, 107
    Tilt, 41, 84, 176
    Torridon, 107
Gley (gleying), 74, 93, 95, 101, 111, 112, 114, 119, 163, 164
Gnaphalium supinum, 96, 155, 173
        -Dicranum starkei sociation, 99, 100
    norvegicum, 175, 177
Gneiss, 161, 168, *see also* Lewisian and Moine Series
Godwin, H., 49, 176
Goodyera repens, 12, 16
Grampians, 146
Granite, 37, 45, 68, 75, 133, 145, 160, 161, 168, 394
Grantown-on-Spey, 107
Grassland, 2, 5, 27, 36, 48, **51–57**, 58, 59, 65–67, 104, 105, 110, 112, 114, 120, 121, 126, 131, 135, 143, 163, Map 15
" Gravestones" (solifluction), 78, 160
Great Glen, 35, 37, 39, 45, 80, 84, 94, 102, 117, 173, 174, Map 15
Green, F. H. W., 147
Greig-Smith, P., 144, 147, 148
Grenz horizon, 102
Grouse moor, 29, 66
Growing season, 151, 155
Gymnomitreto-Salicetum herbaceae, 77, 79, **97–100**, 139, 156, 160, 164, Plate 23, Map 26
Gymnomitrium alpinum, 97
    concinnatum, 96, 97
    varians, 96, 97, 155

Handley, W. R. C., 15
Hansen, H. M., 79
Hawthorn (*Crataegus monogyna*), 21
Hazel (*Corylus avellana*), 11, 16, 20, 21, 24, 151, 163
Heather, *see Calluna vulgaris*
    burning, *see* moor burning
    moor, 11, 13, 15, **28–30**, 31, Map 6
Hebrides, 1, 20, 150, 168, 176
Heddle, R. G., 57
Hedera helix, 22, 24
Helianthemum chamaecistus, 22, 50, 55, 170, 173
Helictotrichon pratense, 50
Hepatic crust, 160
Heracleum sphondylium, 80, 173
Herbaceon, 139, 140

Herberta adunca, 33
    hutchinsiae, 31
    sp. nov., 33
Herb-rich Callunetum, 29, 65, 163
High-Alpine zone, 100
High altitude Nardus stricta sociation, 67
High Force, 17
Highland Boundary Fault, 167
Hippuris vulgaris, 136
Hirkjølen (Norway), 12
Holcus lanatus, 16, 26
Holdgate, M. W., 123, 125, *see also* Wace, N. M.
Holly (*Ilex aquifolium*), 13, 22–24
Homogeneity, 7, 8
Homogyne alpina, 175
Hulten, E., 117, 147
Humidity (atmospheric), 143–146, 148–150
Humus (fern), 63, 82
    (mild), 14, 17
    (raw), 12, 14, 29, 37, 39, 41, 42, 47, 52, 54, 55, 59, 64, 74, 75, 86, 91, 93, 97, 161, 170
Hydrophilous species, 58, 60, 74, 87, 95, 101, 119, 120, 121, 137
Hydrophytes, 126
Hydroseres, 111, 128, 129
Hygro-Festucetum ovinae, 94
Hylocomieto-Betuletum nanae juniperetosum, 25
    -Callunetum, 30
Hylocomium brevirostre, 23
    splendens, 12, 13, 16, 23, 26, 28, 30, 31, 39, 41, 52, 54, 58, 60, 61, 67, 80, 95, 103, 106, 118, 119, 125
    umbratum, 23
Hymenophyllum tunbrigense, 148
Hypericum hirsutum, 22
    pulchrum, 22
Hypnaceous mosses, 18, 39, 42, 43, 45–47, 52, 67, 68, 71, 87, 92, 94, 103, 122, 160, 170
Hypno-Caricetum alpinum, 60, **118**, **119**, 120, 121, 141, 164, Map 15
Hypnum callichroum, 82
    cupressiforme, 28–30, 33, 50, 101, 108
    hamulosum, 92
    peat moor, 122

Iceland, 2, 35, 39, 47, 48, 79, 91, 92, 94, 95
Ilex aquifolium, *see* holly
Inch Lonaig (Loch Lomond), 23
Inchnadamph, 21, 26, 168, 176, 393, Map 2
Indices of floristic similarity, 9, 137
Ingram, M., 1, 71, 76
Insolation, 144, 153
Inverlael, 78
Inverness, 107
Inverness-shire, 24, 30, 102, 128, 146, 152
Inverpolly Forest, 23
Ireland, 3, 4, 50, 102, 124, 148, 152

Irrigation, 17, 26, 40, 49, 52–55, 57, 58, 63, 68, 72, 80, 81, 84–86, 92, 93, 98–100, 108, 112–114, 119–121, 124, 126, 130, 132, 133, 135, 139, 155, 158, 162, 163, 166, 170, 172
Isle of Wight, 148
Isolepis setacea, 120
Ivy, *see Hedera helix*

Jamesoniella carringtonii, 31
Jan Mayen, 91
Jefferies, T. A., 113
Jones, E. W., 1, 3, 71, 160
Jubula hutchinsiae, 148
Juncetum squarrosi sub-alpinum, 56, 58, **59–61**, 63, 104, 114, 119, 123, 138, 163, 164, 170, Map 15
Juncetum trifidi nudum, 76
             scoticum, 76
Juncus acutiflorus, 65, 109, 113, 117–119, 123, 148, 170, Map 27
      -Acrocladium cuspidatum nodum, **117, 118**, 141, 164, Map 27
    alpinus, 120, 134, 175
    articulatus, 109, 112, 118, 120
    biglumis, 134, 175, 177
    castaneus, 134, 175
    effusus, 26, 113, 114, 117, 126
    kochii, 112, 120, 123, 126, 129
    spp., 24
    squarrosus, 36, 39, 40, 51, 60, 61, 65, 91, 114, 119, 126, 141, 170
    trifidus, 38, 46, 70, 75–77, 79, 83, 89, 149, 150, 173
      -Festuca ovina nodum, 75, **77–79**, 89, 90, 93, 97, 138, 145, 151, 158, 160, 164, Plate 15
      Rhacomitrium heath, 89
    triglumis, 134, 150, 174
Junipereto-Arctostaphyletum, 34
Juniperetum nanae, 32, **33, 34**, 110, 138, 148, 149, 163, 168, 173, 393, Plate 9, Map 4
Juniperion nanae, 34, 138
Juniperus-Arctostaphylos sociation, 33
    communis, 11–13, 16, 25, 151, 170
      scrub, 11, **25, 26**, 138, Plate 4, Map 4
    nana, 33, 104, 150
      scrub, **33, 34**, 166
    -Thelypteris nodum, **25, 26**, 34, 137, 138, Plate 7, Map 4
Jutland, 29, 30

Keltneyburn, 21
Killarney, 18, 23
Killiecrankie, 22, 134–136
Kingussie, 126
Kintail, Map 2
Kishorn, 169, 176
Knaben, G., 37, 44, 83, 109, 115
Knockan, 159, 168, 176

Knock Fell (Pennines), 105
Kobresia simpliciuscula, 134, 175
Kobresio-Dryadion, 50, 140
Koeleria gracilis, 50
Koenigia islandica, 175
Kotilainen Index, 142, 144
Krajina, V., 138
Kubiena, W. L., 37, 49, 69, 76, 77, 92, 122, 163

Lactucion alpinae, 80, 81, 140
Ladder Hills, 104
Lakeland (Lake District), 2, 37, 42, 44, 54, 57, 59, 61, 81, 87, 102, 105, 113, 114, 117, 120, 121, 133, 136, 153, 155
Land use, 1, 142
Lappmark, 72, 73, 99
Late-glacial Period, 49, 176
Lathyrus montanus, 30
Latitude, 147, 152
Laxford Bridge, 123
Layer (vegetation), 6
Leach, W., 82
Leaching, 159, 161, 162, 168, 170
Lecidia alpestris, 97
Lemming, 71
Leontodon autumnalis, 118, 120
Lepidozia pinnata, 19
Leptodontium recurvifolium, 33, 80
Letterewe Forest, Map 2
Leuco-Scheuchzerion, 141
Lewisian Series, 67, 84, 108, 125, 134, 168, 393
Lichen bog, 103, 104, Map 34
    heath, 37, 38, 91, 142, Map 34
Lichen-rich Vaccinium-Festuca association, 45
Lichen-rich vegetation, 145
Life-form (of species), 2, 142, 149, 150
Ligustrum vulgare, 24
Limestone, 21, 45, 47–50, 55–57, 84, 121, 122, 124, 125, 133–135, 161, 163, 168, 169, 175, 176, 393
    (sugar), 50, 136, 170
    pavement, 21
Linum catharticum, 50, 54
Lismore, 21
Listera cordata, 41
Lobaria spp., 19
Loch Arkaig, 11
    Broom, 78, 86
    Coire, 24
    Garten, 14, 128
    Insh, 126
    Kishorn, 21
    Laggan, 68
    Lochy, 43
    Lomond, 23
    Maree, 10, 11, 34, 393
    Meadie, 110
    Rannoch, 11
    Shiel, 102

Loch Sionascaig, 23
     Syre, 34
     Tanna, 133
     Treig, 24
Lochnagar, 72, 73, 89, 106, 150, 394, Map 2
Loiseleuria procumbens, 34, 35, 68, 150, 173, Map 8
Loiseleurieto-Arctostaphylion, 138
Lonicera periclymenum, 16, 26
Lophocolea bidentata, 23, 127
Lophozia floerkii, 82, 96
Lophozieto-Salicetum herbaceae, 100
Lorne Plateau, 11
"Loss on Ignition", 165, 409
Lotus corniculatus, 30
Low-alpine *Nardus* noda, **67–69**, Map 17
     Zone, 28, 34, 38, 69, 73, 83, 89, 99, 140, 149, 163
Lowe, J., 23
Luzula arcuata, 97, 132, 150, 155, 175, 177
     campestris, 26, 52
     multiflora, 24, 52, 58
     pilosa, 22
     spicata, 150, 173
     sylvatica, 13, 16, 17, 22, 24, 26, 63, 64, 80, 81, 141
     -grassland *nodum*, **64**, 142
Luzuleto-Cesietum, 100
Lycopodium alpinum sociation, 74, 173
     annotinum, 174
     selago, 34, 132, 173
Lysimachia nemorum, 16, 20, 23–25
        -*Crepis paludosa nodum*, 23
     vulgaris, 24

Macaronesian-Tropical bryophytes, 148
MacGillivray, W., 175
Macgregor, M., *see* Crampton, C. B.
Machair, 1
MacVicar, S. M., 3
Magnesium, 164, 166, 167, 171, 172
Marchantia polymorpha var. *alpestris*, 131
Marchesinia mackaii, 148
Marl, 124, 164
Marram dunes, 151
Masfjord (Norway), 109
Mastigobryeto-Piceetum, 14
Mastigophora woodsii, 31
Matterdale Common, 120
Mayo (County), 34
McVean, D. N., v, 1, 16, 20, 23–26, 28, 33–35, 38, 41, 47, 50, 68, 71, 78, 81, 89, 91, 92, 94, 95, 103–105, 142, 144, 145, 150, 155
Meall Cumhan, 81
     a'Ghiubhais, 58
     nan Tarmachan, 26, 134
     Odhar, 43
Meesia uliginosa, 134

Melampyrum pratense, 12
Melandrium dioicum, 11
Melica uniflora, 22
Melt water, 40, 62, 72, 86, 98, 99, 132, 139, 155, 158, 159
Mentha aquatica, 24, 118
Menyanthes trifoliata, 102, 120, 123, 126–129
Mercurialis perennis, 11, 21, 22
Mesotrophic species, vegetation, 111, 117–123, 126–128, 141, 167–169, 171, 174, Map 15
Metcalfe, G., 1, 29, 35, 37, 71
Mica schist, *see* Dalradian metamorphic series and Schist
Middle-alpine Zone, 28, 38, 51, 73, 89, 149, 163
Migration (species), 148, 177
Minimal Area, 6
Minuartia verna, 55, 175
     rubella, 175
Mniobryo-Epilobietum hornemanni, 132
Mniobryo-Epilobion hornemanni, 141
Mnium hornum, 16
     pseudo-punctatum, 119
     seligeri, 120
     undulatum, 16, 23, 26
Moder humus, 35, 36, 52, 54, 56, 163, 172
Moerckia blyttii, 155
Moffat Hills, 61, 64, 119, 120, 155
Moidart, 148
Moine metamorphic series, 35, 84, 87, 108, 125, 133, 134, 153, 161, 167, 168
     Thrust, 167, 168
Moles, 55
Molinia caerulea, 14, 24, 33, 34, 56, 64, 67, 101, 103, 108, 109, 112, 113, 122, 394
     grassland, **64, 65**, 109
     -*Myrica nodum*, 64, 108, 109, **112, 113**, 118, 142, Map 27
Molinieto-Callunetum, 29, 64, 65, 107, **108, 109**, 129, 142, 145, 163, 394
Molinietum, 113
Monadhliath hills, 102–104, 394, Map 2
Monar Forest, Map 2
Montia lamprosperma, 130
Montio-Cardaminetalia, 141
Moor burning, 13, 15, 31, 32, 34, 37, 40, 65–67, 104, 105, 107–109, 135, 159
Mor humus, 12, 15, 18, 36, 56, 172
Morrone, 135
Morven, Map 2
Morvern, 11, 20
Mosaic (vegetation), 90
Moss heath, **89–100**, 132
Mount Keen, 110
Mudstone, 42, 93, 105, 110, 159, 168
Mull humus, 15, 17, 18, 22, 54–57, 60, 62, 84, 89, 163
Mull (Isle of), 11, 146, 148
Myosotis alpestris, 55, 84, 175
     scorpioides, 24

Myrica gale, 24, 101–103, 112, 113, 118, 126, Map 27

Nardeto-Agrostion tenuis, 138
　　　-Caricion bigelowii, 71, 138, 139
Nardetum chionophilum, 71
Nardetum medio-alpinum, **69–72**, 75, 76, 83, 98, 139, 145, 156, 158, 164, Map 17
　　　sub-alpinum, 52, 56, **58**, 59, 60, 61, 63, 65, 119, 123, 138, 163, 164, 170, Map 15
Nardus grassland, 41
　　　-Pleurozium nodum, 39, **67**, **68**, 71, 74, 91, 95, 106, 116, 139, 155, 156, 164, Map 17
　　　-Rhacomitrium provisional *nodum*, 35, **68**, **69**, 71, 89, 91, 106, 138, 139, 156, 158, 163, 164, Map 17
　　　stricta, 36, 39, 40, 42, 44, 45, 47, 51, 52, 58, 60, 61, 67–71, 73, 74, 110, 112, 115, 118, 123, 126, 132, 158, 170
　　　-Trichophorum nodum, 35, 37–40, 67, **68**, 70, 71, 83, 91, 95, 106, 139, 156, 158, 164, Map 17
Narthecium ossifragum, 24, 34, 101, 103, 112, 126, 128, 132, 142
　　　-Sphagnum provisional *nodum*, **132**, 133, 141
National grid, 1, 167, Map 1
Nature Conservancy, 147
　　　Reserves, 33, 147
Neolithic Period, 10
Nephromium arcticum, 13, 92
Netherlands, 29
Nicholson, I. A., 29
Nitrates, nitrification, nitrogen, 25, 81, 164, 169
Nivation hollows, 37
Nodum (definition), 5, 8
Nordhagen, Rolf, vi, 2, 17, 25, 27, 35, 37, 42–44, 46, 49–51, 64, 71, 76, 81–83, 85, 88, 91, 94, 99, 105, 120, 126, 131–133, 136, 138–141
Norway, 2, 25, 27, 29, 37, 42, 44, 47, 71, 77, 81, 82, 91, 94, 99, 106, 109, 115, 136, 137, 142, 143, 145
Nuphar pumila, 127, 129
Nymphaea occidentalis, 127, 129

Oak (*Quercus* spp.), 10, 11, **15–20**, 21, 23–25, 65, 151, Map 3
Oban, 11
Oceanicity, 142–145, 147, 148, 150–153, 157, 158
Oceanic species, 19, 31, 32, Map 30
Ochrolechia frigida, 34
　　　gemminipara, 97
Ogg, W. G., *see* Heddle, R. G.
Old Red Sandstone, 167, 394
Oligotrichum hercynicum, 96, 97

Oligotrophic species, vegetation, 49, 53, 56, 80, 81, 95, 111, 116, 119, 123, 126, 128, 131, 133, 135, 136, 138–141, 143, 151, 162, 168–170, 172
Oppositifolietum, 88
Order, 9, 137–139
Orkney, 1, 151
Orthothecium rufescens, 134
Orton (Westmorland), 125
Ostenfeld, C. H., 79
Osvald, H., 109
Oviksfjällen Mountains, 74
Oxalis acetosella, 14, 16, 22, 24, 26, 40, 45, 64
Oxycocco-Empetrion hermaphroditi, 105, 138, 140
　　　-Ledetalia palustris, 140
Oxycoccus microcarpus, 103
　　　palustris, 127, 129
Oxyria digyna, 150, 174, 177
Oxytropis campestris, 175
　　　halleri, 175
Oykell (River), 67

Parnassia palustris, 87, 118
Parphe, 149
Patton, D., 1
Pearsall, W. H., v, 1, 61, 102, 104, 105, 110, 153, 162
Peat, 10, 32, 33, 35, 37, 39, 44, 58, 60, 69, 73, 86, 102, 104–107, 111–114, 116, 118, 119, 123, 126, 128, 133, 135, 136, 143, 145, 161, 163, 165, 168, 169, 172, 409
　　　(calcareous), 124
　　　erosion, 59, 67, 102, 109, 110, 134
　　　(fen), 58, 122, 164
　　　gley, 60, 117, 164
　　　(redistributed), 59, 163
　　　(unhumified), 165, 409
　　　(vol./wt. distortion), 165, 409
Pedicularis palustris, 126
Pellia epiphylla, 127
Pennines, 2, 44, 57, 59, 103–105, 114, 136, 155
Per-glacial survival, 177
Perthshire, v, 1, 11, 21, 22, 49, 50, 56, 92, 102, 122, 123, 128, 135
Peucedanum palustre, 24
pH, 17, 35, 44, 46, 49, 50, 54, 55, 57, 59, 60, 69, 73, 74, 76–78, 81, 82, 84, 86, 92, 93, 95, 101, 102, 112–114, 117, 119–121, 123, 126, 134, 136, 161, 164, 166, 169, 172
　　　determination, 165
Philonotis calcarea, 120
　　　fontana, 118, 130, 131, 133
Philonoto-Saxifragetum stellaris, 116, **130**, **131**, 141, 393
Phleum commutatum, 61, 175
Phosphate, 164, 166, 169
　　　determination, 165
Photography, 6
　　　(aerial), 75

Phragmites communis, 24, 126, 129
Phyllodoce caerulea, 41, 175
Phyllodoco-Juncetum trifidi, 71
Phyllodoco-Vaccinion, 138, 139
Phyllodoco-Vaccinetum myrtilli, 42, 71
Pigott, C. D., 17, 50, 55, 81, 121, 122, 136
Pine (*Pinus sylvestris*), 10, 11–15, 19, 25, 28, 31, 34, 104, 128, 129, 138, 149, 151, 393, Plates 1, 2, 3, Map 3
Pineto-Vaccinietum myrtilli, 12
Pinetum Hylocomieto-Vaccinetum, 11–13, 14, 16, 17, 31, 137, 145, 163, Plate 1
        Vaccineto-Callunetum, 12, 13–15, 16, 17, 31, 32, 137, 145, 163
Pinguicula lusitanica, 134
      vulgaris, 24, 87, 120, 134
Place names (spelling), 3
Plagiochila asplenioides, 16, 23
Plagiothecium striatellum, 92
     undulatum, 13, 31
Plantago lanceolata, 50
     maritima, 173
Platysma glaucum, 34, 36
     lacunosum, 34, 36
Pleuroclada albescens, 155
Pleurozia purpurea, 32, 33, 102
Pleurozium schreberi, 12, 16, 28, 30, 31, 39, 41, 43, 44, 52, 53, 60, 67, 94, 103
Poa alpina, 175
      balfourii, **175**
      flexuosa, 175, 177
      glauca, 175
      x *jemtlandica*, 175, 177
      nemoralis, 22
      trivialis, 24
Podsol, podsolisation, 12, 29, 30, 37, 39, 42, 44, 46, 47, 49, 52–55, 57, 59, 62, 69, 72–74, 76, 77, 83, 86, 91, 93, 95, 97, 104, 108, 114, 161, 162–164, 169
     (Alpine sod podsol), 164
     (gley), 59, 60
     (Northern nano-podsol), 92, 163
     (truncated), 17, 52
Pohlia albicans var. *glacialis*, 130–132
     ludwigii, 96
Pohlietum glacialis, **131**, **132**, 141, 156, Map 22
Pollen analysis, 10
Polygoneto-Rhacomitretum lanuginosi, 84, 85, 90, **92–94**, 140, 153, 164, 166, Map 24
Polygonum viviparum, 17, 54, 87, 92, 93, 96, 118, 174
Polypodium vulgare, 22
Polystichum lobatum, 22
     lonchitis, 150, 174
Polytricheto-Caricetum bigelowii, 9, 37, 62, 70, **72**, **73**, 74, 95, 139, 145, 156, 160, 164, Map 18
      -Dicranetum starkei, 76, 82, 83, **95–100**, 132, 139, 156, 164, 166, 393, Map 26

Polytrichetum norvegici, 99
Polytrichion norvegici, 139, 140
Polytrichum alpinum, 32, 61, 72, 73, 82, 84, 92, 94, 96
           nodum, 72
     commune, 26, 113–115
     norvegicum, 96, 155
Pool and hummock complex, 102, 110, 128, 129
Poore, M. E. D., v, 1, 5, 7, 9, 21, 23, 25, 26, 28, 29, 33, 35, 38, 41, 45–47, 50, 53, 54, 67–69, 71–74, 78, 80, 84, 85, 89, 92, 93, 95, 99, 103, 105, 121, 125, 126, 134, 136, 137, 140, 142, 144, 145, 150, 155, 165
Post-glacial Period, 49, 143, 176
Potamogeton polygonifolius, 24, 123, 127, 128
Potassium, 164, 166, 169
     determination, 165
Potentilla crantzii, 175
         -*Polygonum viviparum sociation*, 85
     erecta, 16, 22, 26, 52, 53, 58, 60, 86, 87, 108, 112–114, 117
     palustris, 120, 126, 128, 129
     sterilis, 22
Potentilleto-Polygonion vivipari, 140
Praeger, R. L., 34, 50
Precipitation, 143, 144, 146, 147, 150, 153, 155, 158, 161, 162
     /Evaporation (N/S) ratio, 146
Preferential species, 9
Presence, 7
Primula farinosa, 121
     scotica, 121
     vulgaris, 16, 20, 22
Prunella vulgaris, 22, 24, 25, 54
Prunus padus, 11, 21, 25
     spinosa, 24
Ptilidium celiare, 41, 45, 67
Ptilium crista-castrensis, 12, 13
Pyrola media, 18, 30, 104

Quartz, 77
Quartzite, 21, 33, 35, 41, 45, 52, 67, 75, 93, 105, 108, 110, 153, 160, 168
Quaternary period, 173
Quercetalia roboris, 17, 138
Quercus spp., *see* oak

Radiation, 144
Radula carringtoni, 148
Rain days, 146, 147
Rainfall, *see* precipitation
Rain shadow, 153
Raised bog, 128
Ranker soil, 33, 35, 37, 39, 47, 91, 163
Rannoch Moor, 102, 128, 129
Ranunculeto-Oxyrion digynae, 80, 139, 140
Ranunculetum acris acidophilum, 95

Ranunculo-Anthoxanthion, 139
Ranunculus acris, 22, 26, 53, 54, 58, 61, 63, 87, 94, 96, 112
  -*Anthoxanthum odoratum sociation*, 96
  ficaria, 16
  flammula, 127
  glacialis, 132
  repens, 16
Ratcliffe, D. A., 29, 61, 65, 102, 114, 117
Reay Forest, 90, 149, Map 2
Recurrence surfaces, 102
Regeneration (alder), 24
  (birch), 19, 20
  (oak), 19, 20
  (pine), 14, 15
  complex, 102
Relict species, 173, 176, 177
Rendzina, 49, 163
Resipol Burn, 22
Rhacomitreto-Callunetum, 35–37, **38**, **39**, 86, 138, 145, 163, Plate 11, Map 9
Rhacomitreto-Caricetum bigelowii, 9, 92
Rhacomitreto-Dicranetum starkei, 86, **95–100**, 132, 139, 156, 164, Plate 22, Map 26
  -*Empetretum*, 39, 42, **46**, **47**, 74, 93, 138, 164, Map 13
Rhacomitrium aquaticum, 155
  canescens, 84, 91, 96
  -*Carex bigelowii nodum*, 47, 89, 95
  fasciculare, 96, 97, 99, 100
    sociation, 99
  heath, 38, 44, 46, 47, 68, 69, 71, 74, 75, 77–79, 85, 89–95, 106, 131, 137, 148, 150, 153, 154, 160, Plate 20, Map 24
  heterostichum, 96, 155
  lanuginosum, 29, 33, 34, 38, 41–43, 45–47, 50, 53, 54, 58, 68, 71, 73, 75, 77, 84, 89, 91–94, 97, 103, 110, 142, 145, 149, 170
Rhidorroch Lodge, 11
Rhinanthus borealis, 175
Rhododendron, 20
Rhum (Isle of), 29, 66, 102, 109, 118, 125, Map 2
Rhytidiadelphus-Deschampsia caespitosa nodum, 95
  loreus, 16, 23, 26, 31, 39, 41, 43, 61, 64, 67, 72, 82, 92, 94, 95
  squarrosus, 23, 52, 54, 58, 60, 61, 64, 67, 94, 117, 118, 127
  triquetrus, 12, 23, 94
Rhytidium rugosum, 48, 50, 154
Richards, P. W., 3, 18
Robertson, R. A., *see* Nicholson, I. A.
Robinson, G. W., 52
Rondane (Norway), 25, 27, 35, 37, 42, 72–74, 76, 81, 87, 92, 99, 100, 105, 106, 123, 124, 133

Rosa spp., 26
Ross-shire, 11, 23, 25, 32, 34, 36, 48, 66, 78, 93, 95, 96, 105, 106, 148, 159
Rothiemurchus, 17
Rowan (*Sorbus aucuparia*), 11–14, 16, 20, 21, 23–25
Rubus chamaemorus, 31, 103, 128, 174
  fruticosus agg., 26
  idaeus, 16, 22
  saxatilis, 174
Rumex acetosa, 22, 26, 55, 61, 63, 64
  acetosella, 25
Rumiceto-Salicetum lapponae, 27
Rupestral species, 48, 88, 172

Sagina saginoides, 84, 175
  intermedia, 175
Salicetalia herbaceae, 139, 140
Salicetum herbaceae, 99, 100
Salix arbuscula, 26, 175, Map 5
  atrocinerea, 24–27
  aurita, 24–27, 113, 120
  capraea, 25
  herbacea, 73, 77, 82, 92, 93, 96, 97, 150, 155, 173, 177
    -*Anthelia juratzkana-Gymnomitrium varians sociation*, 100
  lanata, 26, 175, Map 5
  lapponum, 26, 27, 175, Map 5
    -*Carex inflata-Sphagnum warnstorfii sociation*, 120
    -*Luzula sylvatica nodum*, **26**, **27**, 88, 140, 393
  myrsinites, 26, 120, 150, 175, Map 5
  repens, 151, 170
  reticulata, 48–50, 175
  spp., *see* willow
Salt marsh, 1
Sambucus nigra, 24
Sand-dunes, 1, Map 34
Sandstone, 161, 167, 394, *see also* Torridon sandstone
Sanicula europaea, 22
Saussurea alpina, 150, 174
Saxifraga aizoides, 54, 56, 57, 87, 88, 121, 133, 134, 136, 174, 177
  cespitosa, 175
  cernua, 175
  hirculus, 122, 175
  hypnoides, 87, 174, 177
  nivalis, 150, 175
  oppositifolia, 87, 88, 150, 153, 174, 177
  rivularis, 150, 155, 175, 177
  stellaris, 96, 115, 130, 131, 173, 177
Saxifrageto-Agrosto-Festucetum, 49, **54–57**, 85, 87, 88, 121, 138, 139, 162, 163
Saxifragetum aizoidis, 57, **87**, **88**, 139, 163, Map 23
Scandinavia, 1, 2, 15, 25, 35, 42, 59, 68, 76, 80, 92, 95, 99, 117, 120, 142, 143

Scapania dentata, 132
    nimbosa, 31, 32
    ornithopodioides, 31
    uliginosa, 130
    undulata, 125, 130
Scapanietum uliginosi, 131
Scarabens, Map 2
Scheuchzeria palustris, 102
Scheuchzerietalia palustris, 102, 141
Schist, 41, 45, 53, 55, 60, 67, 84, 92, 125, 133, 153, 160–162, 168, 169
"Schneetälchen", 89, 96, 97
Schoenetum nigricantis, 124
Schoenion ferruginei, 141
Schoenus nigricans, 109, 113, 118, 123–125, 127, 129, 134, 147, 151, 153, Map 27
    nodum, **124**, **125**, 135, 145, 164, 173, Map 27
Scorpideeto-Caricetum limosae, 123
Scorpidium scorpioides, 120–124; 127, 134, 153
Scrophularia nodosa, 22
Sea spray, 29, 124, 125, 153
Seana Bhraigh, 48, 81, 106, 176, Map 2
Sedum rosea, 80, 150, 174, 176, 177
    villosum, 175
Selaginella selaginoides, 53, 54, 84, 87, 112, 118–121
Selective species, 9
Senecio aquaticus, 118
    jacobaea, 22, 50
Sericite schist, *see* schist
Serpentine, 167
Sesleria caerulea, 55, 175
Sgurr na Feartaig, 93
    a'Ghlas Leathaid, 95
    na Lapaich, 74, 79
Sheep, 18–21, 23, 27, 41, 48, 59, 63, 65, 66, 83, 104, 111, 113, 169
Shell sand, 20, 47, 48, 121, 122, 124, 134, 151, 168, 170, 176
Shetland, 1, 26, 64, 79, 103, 150, 151, 167
Sibbaldia procumbens, 82, 84, 86, 87, 96, 173, 174
            nodum, 80, 85, 140
Sibbaldietum procumbentis, 87
Sieglingia decumbens, 29
Sikilsdalen (Norway), 27, 46, 133, 136
Silene acaulis, 55, 84–86, 90–92, 94, 148, 150, 153, 170, 174, 177, Map 24
Sissingh, G., *see* Braun-Blanquet, J.
Sjörs, H., 128
Skeletal soils, 62
Skiddaw, 37, 44
Skye, 11, 21
Sleat (Skye), 21
Slioch, 66
Smith, R., 1, 89
Smith, W. G., 29, 54, 59, 99
Snowdon, 155
Snowdonia, 42, 61

Snow cover, 27, 35, 37, 38, 42–44, 46, 47, 61–63, 67, 69, 70, 73, 74, 76, 77, 81–87, 89, 94, 99, 131, 132, 139, 143, 147, 148, 150, 154, **155–158**, 159, 162, 169, 174, 177, Plate 21
    Survey of Great Britain, 157
"Soak", 128, 129
Sodium, 164, 166, 169
    determination, 165
Sogn (Norway), 37, 44, 83, 109
Sognefjell (Norway), 99
Soil analysis, 165
    hummocks, 73, 159, 160, Plate 20
    sampling, 6, 164
Solanum dulcamara, 24
Solifluction, 44, 62, 78, 86, 93, 97, 98, 100, 139, 155, **158–160**, 164
    (amorphous), 159
    ostioles, 159
    (structured), 159, 160
    terraces, 78, 155, 159, 160, Plate 16
Solorina crocea, 77, 97, 155
    saccata, 49
Sorbus aucuparia, *see* rowan
Southern Uplands, 2, 37, 41, 42, 44, 52, 59, 65, 82, 105, 114, 117, 119, 121, 136, 155
Spain, 29
Sparagmite, 105
Sparganium minimum agg., 127
Species-poor Agrosto-Festucetum, **52**, 53, 57, 58, 66, 138, 163, 164
    -rich Agrosto-Festucetum, 29, 49, **54–57**, 66, 85, 121, 124, 138, 162, 163
Species-rich Dryas association, 49
    Saxifraga association, 88
Spence, D. N., 20, 26, 34, 64, 79, 81, 150, 151, 166
Speyside, 15, 30
Sphaerophorus globosus, 34, 92
Sphagneto-Caricetum alpinum, 110, **115**, 126, 133, 141, 145, 164
            sub-alpinum, 61, 110, **114**, 115, 119, 128, 129, 141, 164
    -Juncetum effusi, **113**, **114**, 117, 141, 164
Sphagnum auriculatum, 102, 114, 129, 130, 131
    compactum, 132
    contortum, 119, 120, 127
    cuspidatum, 102, 127, 129
    fuscum, 103, 105, 136
    girgensohnii, 113
    imbricatum, 102, 135
    lindbergii, 115
    magellanicum, 102, 103, 129
    nemoreum, 31, 103, 136
    palustre, 113, 114, 127
    papillosum, 101–103, 114–116, 123, 125–127, 129, 136
    recurvum, 26, 112–114, 127–129
    riparium, 115
    rubellum, 101, 103

Sphagnum russowii, 113, 115, 127
  spp., 13, 18, 24, 29, 39, 41, 45, 60,
    65, 73, 101, 103, 106, 107, 110, 111,
    113, 117, 123, 140
  squarrosum, 113, 119, 127
  subsecundum, 114, 119, 127
  tenellum, 132
  teres, 119, 127
  warnstorfianum, 119, 127
Splachnum vasculosum, 130
Springs, 6, 110, 111, 115, 130–136, 141, 143,
  174
Spruce (*Picea abies*), 25, 138
Stack Wood, 19
Stainmore, 105
Stand (vegetation), 6
Stereocaulon vesuvianum, 77
Stellaria alsine, 130
  graminea, 26
Steindorsson, S., 47, 48
Steven, H. M., 15
Sticta damaecornis, 148
  spp., 19
St. Kilda, 64
Stone, soil polygons, 78, 93, 100, 159, 160
  stripes, 159, 160
Strathcarron, 148, Map 2
Strath Suardal, 21
Strathy bog, 110
Strontian, 11
Sub-Alpine Nardus association, 71
Sub-Alpine scrub, **25–27**, 150, 151, Plate 6
  zone, 31, 51, 80, 83, 140, 149, 150,
    163
Sub-Atlantic times, 34
Succisa pratensis, 22, 80, 112, 126
Sunart, 22, 102, 148
Sunbiggin Tarn, 123
Sutherland, 1, 11, 19–21, 24, 32–35, 48, 64,
  102, 104, 106, 110, 121–124, 134, 148, 151,
  152, 158, 168, 170, 393
Sweden, 29, 74, 128
Sylene (Norway), 25, 27, 35, 37, 43, 44, 64,
  71, 76, 83, 85, 88, 136

Tall Herb *nodum*, 26, 27, 63, **80–82**, 88, 140,
  163, 165, 166, 173, Plates 17, 18, Map 5
Tamm, O., 15
Tansley, A. G., 1, 10, 22, 29, 42, 46, 54, 55,
  59, 99, 102, 104, 124, 147
Taraxacum officinalis agg., 22, 50
Tay (River), 81
Teesdale, 17, 55, 81, 121, 122, 133, 136
Temperature (air), 144, 147, 148, 151, 169
  gradient, 148–150, 155
  (limiting), 152, 176, 177
  (spring water), 131
Terraces, *see* solifluction
Teucrium scorodonia, 22

Thalictrum alpinum, 53, 57, 58, 118, 119, 134,
  150, 174
  -*Ctenidium* provisional *nodum*, **57**, **58**,
    139
Thamnium alopecurum, 23
Thelypteris dryopteris, 22, 64
  oreopteris, 16, 17, 22, 26, 82, 83, 142
  palustris, 24
  phegopteris, 22
Thermophilous species, 147, 148, 152
Thlaspi alpestre, 175
Thuidium tamariscinum, 16, 26, 52, 80
Thymus drucei, 50, 53, 54, 77, 84, 92
Timber, 169
Tofieldia pusilla, 120, 134, 150, 175
Tokavaig Wood, 21
Toll Creagach, 159
Torridon sandstone, 33, 35, 45, 54, 63, 78, 87,
  108
Tortella tortuosa, 50
Tree limit (alpine), 152
  (polar), 152
Trichomanes speciosum, 148
Trichophoreto-Callunetum, 29, 31, 32, 37, 38,
  65, 103, **106–108**, 109, 129, 133, 135, 141,
  163, 394, Maps 28, 34
    -Eriophoretum caricetosum, 103, 108,
      112, 114, 135, 164
        typicum, 38, 65, **101**, **102**, 103,
          104, 106–108, 110, 112, 113,
          124, 128, 129, 141, 145, 146,
          163, Maps 27, 28
Trichophoretum, 91
Trichophorum caespitosum, 33, 34, 39, 58, 60,
  67–70, 101, 103, 105–110, 112, 132, 394
Triglochin palustre, 127
Trientalis europaea, 13, 18, 26
Tristan da Cunha, 47
Trollius europaeus, 17, 55, 80
Tufa, 133
Tulach Hill, 56, 122, 134, 136
Tutin, T. G., *see* Clapham, A. R.
Tüxen, R., 29
Tveitnes, A., 109
Tweedsmuir, 119, 155

Uist, 26, 64
Unst, 150
Ulex gallii, 29
Ulmus glabra, 21
Urtica dioica, 24, 25
Utricularia intermedia, 127–129
  minor, 127, 129, 136
  vulgaris, 123, 127, 129, 136, 153
Ultra-basic rock, 108, 124, 125

Vaccineto-Callunetum, 28, 29, **31–33**, 39, 41,
  104, 123, 137, 138, 141, 142, 145, 148, 150,
  154, 163, 172, 393, Maps 7, 33

Vaccinetum chionophilum, 32, **39–41**, 42–45, 49, 53, 139, 145, 155, 156, 158, 163, 166, 393, Map 10

Vaccineto-Empetretum, 32, 40, **41–43**, 44, 45, 47, 69–71, 74, 106, 139, 156, 158, 163, 166, Map 10

Vaccinio-Piceetalia, 13, 17, 137
    -Piceion, 137, 138

Vaccinium-Alchemilla grassland nodum, 53
    -Chamaepericlymenum nodum, 41
    -Empetrum heath, 46, 48, Map 10
    -grass heath, 46
    heath, 28, 44, 114, Map 10
    -lichen heath, **43–45**, Map 11

Vaccinium myrtillus, 12, 13, 16, 17, 20, 25, 26, 31, 36, 39, 41–43, 45, 46, 52, 53, 62, 64, 65, 68, 69, 81, 89, 103, 128, 158, 170
    -Nardus provisional *nodum*, 156, Map 10
    uliginosum, 32, 39, 41, 170, 173
    vitis-idaea, 12, 13, 16, 25, 29–31, 45, 50, 170

Vågå (Norway), 72

Valeriana officinalis, 23

Valley bog, 101

Veronica alpina, 175
    chamaedrys, 23
    fruticans, 175
    humifusa, 131
    officinalis, 23

Vestergren, T., 155

Viburnum opulus, 24

Vicia sepium, 23

Viola palustris, 115, 119, 127, 129
    riviniana, 14, 16, 20, 23, 26, 30, 52, 54, 60, 61

Viscaria alpina, 175

Vlieger, J., *see* Braun-Blanquet, J.

Wace, N. M., 47

Wales (North), 2, 22, 29, 37, 46, 52, 59, 65, 81, 82, 102, 105, 113, 114, 117, 131, 133, 136, 148, 153, 155

Walker, D., *see* Ratcliffe, D. A.

Wallace, E. C., *see* Richards, P. W.

Walters, S. M., 5, 357

Warburg, E. F., *see* Clapham, A. R.

Warren Wilson, J., 91, 99, 159

Watson, W., 3

Watt, A. S., 1, 25, 29, 71, 160

Webb, D. A., 170

Weberetum commutatae acidophilum, 99

Westmorland, 123, 125

Wet days, 146, 147

White Coombe, 37
    Mounth, 43

Whiten Head, 35, 104

Willow (*Salix* spp.), 23, 24, 80, 111, 113, 120
    scrub, 25, 26, 80, 81, 140, Map 5

Wilson, A., 150

Wind damage, 142, 150
    speed, 77, 78, 144, 151, 152

Woodland, *see* forest

Woodsia alpina, 175
    ilvensis, 175

Xeromorphic species, 137

Yapp, W. B., 19

Yew (*Taxus baccata*) wood, 23

Yorkshire, 50

Zonation (altitudinal), 1, 2, 10, 11, 28, 51, 89, 142, 149, **150**